The Wilson Chronology of the Arts

Other Titles in the Wilson Chronology Series

The Wilson Chronology of Science and Technology

The Wilson Chronology of Ideas

The Wilson Chronology of Women's Achievements

The Wilson Calendar of World History

The Wilson Chronology of Asia and the Pacific

The Wilson Chronology of the Arts

George Ochoa and Melinda Corey

The H. W. Wilson Company

New York • Dublin

1998

Library of Congress Cataloging-in-Publication Data

Ochoa, George.
   The Wilson chronology of the arts / by George Ochoa and Melinda
   Corey.
     p.   cm.
   Includes bibliographical references and index.
   ISBN 0-8242-0934-6
   1. Art—Chronology. I. Corey, Melinda. II. H. W. Wilson
   Company. III. Title.
N5306.026 1997
701′ .02′ 02—dc21   97-23541
                                                        CIP

Printed in the United States of America

07 06 05 04 03 02 01 00 99 98 10 9 8 7 6 5 4 3 2 1

The H. W. Wilson Company
950 University Avenue
Bronx, NY 10452

http://www.hwwilson.com

To Martha

Contents

Acknowledgments

We are indebted to John Cameli, Andrea Orrill, and Timothy Wright, diligent researchers and contributors, and to Tom Brown, for keyboarding parts of the manuscript. We also thank Paul Fargis and Sheree Bykofsky of The Stonesong Press, Phebe Kirkham of Ballantine, and Michael Schulze, Hilary Claggett, Lynn Amos, Joseph Sora, and John O'Sullivan of H. W. Wilson. Finally, we thank Mary F. Tomaselli for indexing the book.

Introduction

Beginning with prehistoric rock engravings in Australia and ending with contemporary art installations, the 4,000 entries in *The Wilson Chronology of the Arts* answer a basic question: What do artists do? By tracing hundreds of artists' accomplishments over hundreds of centuries, it becomes clear that what an artist does is work, and in great variety. Often, as with Michelangelo or Joan Miró, it is in many different forms; with haiku poet Bashō or television talk-show host Jay Leno, it is almost exclusively in one artistic arena. Sometimes, as with poet Emily Dickinson or photographer Eugène Atget, it is with little or no outside acknowledgment; other artists, like filmmaker Akira Kurosawa or composer Richard Wagner, are recognized in their day. The amount of work can also vary: Shakespeare wrote dozens of plays and sonnets, Thoreau one book of lasting fame.

By placing artists' work in a timeline format, the book also offers a broad view of the artistic world of a given age. We include both popular and elite forms: Art objects in the 18th century include statuary as well as tableware; music in the 1970s spans everything from disco to punk rock to Philip Glass's *Einstein on the Beach*. Readers will also see what art forms were gaining favor at a particular time. For example, from the number of significant plays produced, the English Renaissance shows the rise of dramatic art. Similarly, the number of poetry collections published during the 19th century (by writers as varied as Tennyson, Whitman, and Baudelaire, to name a few) points to the strength of poetry as an art form. The breadth and quality of films made in one single year, 1939, suggests the strength of that art: *Gone with the Wind*, *The Wizard of Oz*, *The Rules of the Game*, and *Stagecoach*, among many others.

The sidebars distributed throughout *The Wilson Chronology of the Arts* further showcase or comment on the artistic process. A sidebar on photographer Walker Evans's technique for portraiture suggests the inherent voyeurism of the photographic art. Another, on the painter Goya and the composer Beethoven, spotlights how the two artists responded to their shared deafness.

The Wilson Chronology of the Arts is global in scope and comprehensive in coverage, emphasizing such well-established art forms as painting, sculpture, architecture, literature, and film without neglecting the oral traditions and decorative art forms of nonliterate societies or such emerging art forms as performance art and installations.

Because one of the functions of a chronology is to place events in context, we hope readers will find that larger truths about art emerge from this timeline. Art is work; it is created by people of all kinds; it is intended to reach others; and it changes in form and in public perception over time.

GEORGE OCHOA and MELINDA COREY
Dobbs Ferry, New York, December 1997

A Note to the Reader

The Wilson Chronology of the Arts is arranged by year and within each year by category. The categories are as follows:

ARCH	Architecture
DANCE	Dance
DECO	Decorative arts
DRAMA	Theatrical works, including drama, comedy, musicals, and performance art
FILM	Film
GRAPH	Graphic arts, including printmaking and illustration
LIT	Literature, including prose and poetry
MISC	Miscellaneous
MUSIC	Music
PAINT	Painting and drawing
PHOTO	Photography
SCULP	Sculpture
TV&R	Television and radio

In the timeline, B.C. dates are indicated by negative numbers, A.D. dates by positive numbers.

Throughout prehistory, antiquity, and the early Middle Ages, it is often difficult to place exact dates. Therefore, most of the dates in this book up to the year A.D. 1000 can be considered approximate. After A.D. 1000, dates can generally be considered exact unless marked with a *c.* for *circa*.

Birth and death dates have mostly been left out of the main text. However, the birth and death dates of many of the artists named in the chronology are included in the appendix.

B.C.

−43,000	At Panaramitee, Australia, humans make petroglyphs, rock engravings of circles, dots, arcs, and other nonrepresentational designs. **SCULP**
−33,000	In France and other sites in Europe, beads, pendants, and other body ornamentation are fashioned from bone fragments and animal teeth. **DECO**
−33,000– −23,000	At Patna, India, and other sites in South Asia, ostrich eggshells, perhaps used as containers, are engraved with decorative, nonrepresentational patterns. **DECO**
−30,000– −28,000	The world's earliest known wall paintings—images of bears, mammoths, and other animals—are painted with charcoal and iron pigments in a cave near Avignon, France. **PAINT**
−30,000– −20,000	In Germany and elsewhere in Europe, sculptures are made from stone, bone, ivory, antler, and horn. Some depict animals, and others, called "Venuses," are of exaggerated female shapes (e.g., the four-inch Venus of Willendorf). **SCULP**
−28,000	In Europe, flutes, the earliest known musical instruments, are made from bones. **MUSIC**
−27,000	In Tanzania ocher fragments and ocher-stained palettes appear, evidence of the art of painting. **PAINT**
−26,000	At the Apollo II cave in Namibia, Africa, artists paint stone slabs with black and red figurines of animals such as the zebra and black rhinoceros. **PAINT**
−25,000	In the area of Europe that will eventually become the Czech Republic, weaving and fired-clay ceramics have been invented. **DECO**
−25,000– −20,000	In the Pyrenees and Spain spears are decorated with grouped incisions and simplified animal carvings. **DECO**
−25,000– −18,000	Rock engravings are made in Arabia and India. **SCULP**
−24,000	In Europe humans make huts as long-term dwellings. One example from Moravia indicates use of a low outer wall of clay and limestone with a timber superstructure and a roof of animal skins and brushwood. **ARCH**

−20,000−−10,000	In France and Spain paintings are made on cave walls. Images include horses, bison, and cattle as well as nonrepresentational designs such as dots and lines, along with stenciled silhouettes of hands. PAINT
−20,000−−15,000	Animal sculpture becomes much more common in central and eastern Europe as artists carve ivory statuettes of felines, horses, and bison. SCULP
−20,000−−10,000	In France and Spain people decorate caves with realistic and abstract engravings and lifelike bas-relief animal sculptures. SCULP
−15,000	In Europe pierced staffs begin to feature finely engraved animal decorations. DECO
−15,000	Throwing sticks made of reindeer horn are frequently decorated with animal carvings or reliefs. DECO
−15,000	Artists in the Lascaux Cave in southern France paint lifelike animals on cave walls, using earth pigments such as ocher. Paint is applied with bundled grasses, reeds, or hands, or blown through hollow bones. PAINT
−15,000	Two bison are modeled in clay in the cave of Le Tuc d'Audoubert, France. SCULP
−13,000	In Mezhirich in eastern Europe huts are built from mammoth bones. ARCH
−13,000	At the Wargata Mina cave, Tasmania, stenciled silhouettes of hands are rendered on cave walls by blowing pigment over human hands. PAINT
−12,000	Crosshatching and shaded applications of color begin to enhance the modeling of cave engravings. SCULP
−11,000	At Bhimbetka, India, animals and abstract figures are painted on rocks. PAINT
−10,000	By now, across much of the inhabited world, including Europe, Asia, Africa, and the Americas, the art of building tents and huts from such materials as timber, animal bones, hides, and brushwood has become widespread. In some sites, notably in Australia, simple windbreaks made of branches are used as shelters. ARCH
−9000	In Japan *jomon* (cord-marked) pottery vessels are made, notable for their pointed bases and cord-marked patterns. DECO
−8000	The first cities appear in Mesopotamia (Iraq) and elsewhere in the Near East, notably Jericho in Palestine. ARCH
−8000	Africans weave matting from palm fronds and other fibrous materials for use in bedding and walls. DECO

| −8000 | In Australia rock paintings of animals are made. | PAINT |

| −7000 | In Jericho mortar is invented for use with sun-dried brick. | ARCH |

| −7000 | Clay pottery appears in Asia Minor (Turkey) and the Near East. | DECO |

| −7000 | In the Saharan plateaus, which will gradually turn to desert after 6000 B.C., animals are painted on rock walls, ushering in a long tradition of rock painting in the region. | PAINT |

| −7000 | The faces of human skulls from Jericho are individually reconstructed in tinted plaster with pieces of seashells for the eyes. These Neolithic "sculptured heads" point the way to Mesopotamian portrait sculpture. | SCULP |

| −6000 | Fertility goddesses made of baked clay appear in a number of religious shrines throughout Anatolia, or Asia Minor (Turkey). | SCULP |

| −5900 | In Mesopotamia (Iraq) the Ubaid culture begins to build temples consisting of a single mud-brick room with an altar and offering temple. | ARCH |

| −5400– −4300 | During the Late Ubaid period in Mesopotamia (Iraq), mud-brick houses are built on a tripartite plan, consisting of a large rectangular room in the center with rows of smaller rooms on either side. | ARCH |

| −5000 | In the Near East nuggets of gold, silver, copper, and other metals come into use as ornaments and trade goods. | DECO |

| −5000 | In China ritual jade objects are fashioned with abrasives. | DECO |

| −5000 | Near Eastern influences reach the Balkans with the creation of baked clay fertility goddesses in that region. | SCULP |

| −4300– −3100 | In Mesopotamia (Iraq) during the Uruk period, elaborately decorated temples, raised on platforms, are built following the tripartite plan of houses of the Late Ubaid period. *See also* 5400–4300 B.C., ARCH. | ARCH |

| −4000 | In Mesopotamia (Iraq) building bricks are fired in kilns. | ARCH |

| −4000– −3000 | Eastern Europe becomes a major center of the potter's art and the clay modeling of free-standing figures. | MISC |

| −4000 | In Egypt rattles and clappers are used in ritualistic music to exorcise evil spirits. | MUSIC |

−4000– −2000	Artists from the settlement of Vinca in Serbia create hundreds of triangular clay heads with pierced ears to which can be attached hair, headdresses, or earrings. SCULP
−3500	In the Near East the Sumerians develop cuneiform, the system of pictograms wedged into clay tablets that is the earliest known form of writing. LIT
−3500	Sumerian sculptors from Uruk in the Near East create marble cult statues with heads inlaid with colored materials and topped with either gold or copper. SCULP
−3300	The pottery wheel is invented in Sumeria. By 3000 B.C., it is also developed in China, probably independently. DECO
−3100	The Egyptians invent an early form of hieroglyphics. LIT
−3100	At the beginning of the Egyptian First Dynasty, artists start to use bronze tools for carving. SCULP
−3000	Clothing dyes are in use in China and Egypt. DECO
−3000	Pottery and stylized stone figurines of humans are made in Ecuador. Independent pottery styles will develop elsewhere in the Americas, notably Mexico and Georgia, by 2400 B.C. DECO
−3000	Egyptian goldsmiths make fine jewelry from gold and precious and semi-precious stones. DECO
−3000	Harps of several designs are played in Mesopotamia (Iraq). MUSIC
−3000– −2155	During the Old Kingdom in Egypt (First to Sixth Dynasties), wall paintings in tombs feature fractional representation, in which the shoulders and eyes are viewed frontally while the head and feet are in profile. Hierarchical scaling is also common, in which some figures are enlarged to illustrate their social prominence. PAINT
−3000	In Egypt, red earthenware statuettes of lions are produced, predecessors to the Great Sphinx. *See* 2500 B.C., SCULP. SCULP
−3000	Hieroglyphic reliefs celebrating King Narmer's victory over Lower Egypt appear on a ceremonial slate palette. The palette demonstrates a break from prehistoric traditions as a strictly Egyptian style emerges, marked by a strong sense of order and clarity. SCULP

−3000	With the political unification of Upper and Lower Egypt, artists aim to spread the image of a new society and the glory of the pharaoh. Bas-relief carvers use divided compositions and simplified human forms. SCULP
−2778– −2160	During the Third to Tenth Dynasties of the Old Kingdom, harps with small bow-shaped resonators, long vertical flutes, and double clarinets are played in Egypt. MUSIC
−2650	The pyramid of Zoser in Egypt, the world's first large stone structure, is designed by Imhotep, physician, architect, and counselor to Zoser. Also called the Step Pyramid, it is almost 200 feet high. ARCH
−2600	Sumerian sculptors create simplified and schematic groups of cylindrical marble figures representing gods and temple worshippers. SCULP
−2550	The Great Pyramid of Giza is built under the supervision of the Egyptian pharaoh Cheops, or Khufu. The pharaohs Chefren, or Khafra, and Menkure, or Mycerinus, will also build pyramids at Giza in, respectively, c. 2500 B.C. and c. 2470 B.C. ARCH
−2500	The cities of Mohenjo-Daro and Harappa arise in the Indus Valley. The houses are uniformly constructed of mud brick and laid out according to a plan. ARCH
−2500	Glass ornaments are in use in Egypt. DECO
−2500	Performances are given in temples in pharaonic Egypt. Coronation dramas are staged in which each scene is enacted at a different station along a given route. DRAMA
−2500	The oldest written story, the Sumerian *Epic of Gilgamesh*, is set into writing for the first time. It concerns the adventures of Gilgamesh and the "wild man" Enkidu. *See also* 3500 B.C., LIT. LIT
−2500– −2001	A five-tone scale is used in Chinese music. MUSIC
−2500	Egyptian sculptors create a more cubic and impersonal view of the human body for royal portrait statues to be placed in funerary temples and tombs. SCULP
−2500	Egyptian pharaoh Chefren, or Khafra, supervises the building of the Great Sphinx at Giza. SCULP
−2423	A marked differentiation becomes apparent among Egyptian funerary stelae of the Sixth Dynasty. Sculptors ignore the old rules of human proportions and begin to enlarge the head and elongate the eyes and hands. SCULP

−2400   Limestone portrait busts begin to appear in Old Kingdom Egypt, perhaps echoing the Neolithic custom of keeping the head of the deceased separate from the rest of the body.   SCULP

−2400   Egyptian sculptors focus more on observation rather than established conventions by creating painted limestone reliefs illustrating scenes of daily life for the tomb of Ti at Saqqara, Egypt.   SCULP

−2340   At the beginning of his rule, Sargon sets up an imperial workshop in northern Mesopotamia (Iraq) to mass-produce monuments of royal victory to be sent throughout the empire. For the next two centuries, sculptors will work without variety or spontaneity but will achieve a technical perfection in the rendering of the human anatomy.   SCULP

−2300   In Peru a monumental temple is built of stone and mud.   ARCH

−2300–   In India, Harappan civilization engages in copper and pottery production. It
−1700   also produces small steatite (soapstone) seals with pictographic representations of animals and humans that some consider the country's first art objects.   DECO

−2300   Near Eastern engravers of Akkad establish the iconography of classical Babylonia through detailed depictions of the gods and their attributes.   SCULP

−2200   Sumerian sculptors complete reliefs illustrating Naram-Sin's victorious army on a large stone stele. It is the earliest known monument to honor a conqueror.   SCULP

−2160–   In the Egyptian Middle Kingdom (11th to 17th Dynasties), barrel-shaped
−1580   drums, perhaps imported from sub-Saharan Africa, and asymmetrical lyres, imported from Asia, are played. Flute melodies probably move in large intervals. The long-neck lute appears toward the end of the period.   MUSIC

−2160–   During the Middle Kingdom in Egypt, wall paintings in rock-cut tombs or in
−1785   cliffsides feature more freely drawn figures and more foreshortening than in Old Kingdom images.   PAINT

−2160   A new type of capital, the uppermost member of a column or pilaster, featuring the sculpted head of the goddess Hathor on both sides appears at the beginning of Middle Kingdom Egypt and is used throughout this period (11th to 17th Dynasties).   SCULP

−2150   Sumerian ruler Gudea assembles a workshop of sculptors and has numerous diorite statues of himself placed in the shrines of the Sumerian city-state of Lagash.   SCULP

−2100	The Sumerians build the ziggurat at Ur. A pyramidal brick platform on top of which a temple is erected, the ziggurat is ascended by means of zigzag ramps. Some ziggurats reach nearly 300 feet in height. ARCH
−2000	The palace of Minos at Knossos, Crete, is constructed. It features light and air shafts and interior bathrooms with a water supply. ARCH
−2000	Minoan sculptors of Crete create terra-cotta statuettes. SCULP
−2000	Egyptian sculptors at the beginning of the 12th Dynasty develop a new type of pharaonic portrait, known as the "pessimistic king," that features deep-set eyes and sad faces. SCULP
−2000– −200	Popular art forms in Japan during the Jōmon period include small clay sculptures and cooking vessels. SCULP
−1900	As the Near Eastern kingdom of Ugarit prospers from its trade with Egypt, statuettes of gods and goddesses in the guise of warriors reveal an Egyptian influence which will grow steadily for several centuries. SCULP
−1830	In Babylonia temple service music evolves from simple chanted hymns to a complete liturgical service, with five to 27 selections interspersed with instrumental music. The practice of using a particular melody for a certain poem type develops. MUSIC
−1760	Hammurabi, the founder of the Babylonian dynasty, has his law code inscribed in a diorite stele on which Hammurabi is portrayed confronting the sun god Shamash. SCULP
−1600– −1100	Mycenaean citadels (fortified hilltop palaces) are constructed of stone blocks without mortar and are decorated with paintings and sculpture. ARCH
−1600	In the Near East, glass is used to form objects and vessels and is also used as a glaze for pottery. DECO
−1600	The world's first purely phonetic alphabet is invented by the Phoenicians. Based on symbols for sounds, not things or syllables, it is the ancestor of all modern Western alphabets. LIT
−1580– −1085	The New Kingdom in Egypt (18th to 20th Dynasties) is marked by a surge in temple construction, including funerary temples and public temples to the sun god Amun-Ra, associated with the pharaoh. The buildings employ stone post-and-lintel construction with closely spaced columns. Examples include the temples at Karnak (c. 1280 B.C.) and Luxor (c. 1390 B.C.). ARCH

–1580– –1085	During the New Kingdom in Egypt, the papyrus scrolls of the *Book of the Dead*, a collection of spells related to the afterlife, are illustrated with images of the deceased appearing before the gods. GRAPH
–1580– –1085	The New Kingdom sees a great flowering of Egyptian music. Older instruments appear in new forms, often splendidly decorated. New instruments include double oboes, trumpets, short lutes, and the sistrum. Melodies move in smaller intervals and there is evidence of antiphonal and responsorial singing, men's and women's choruses, strophic songs, and liturgical music. MUSIC
–1580	Egyptian sculptors of the New Kingdom create more slender and graceful human figures. This delicate rendering of the body and its features will continue to the end of the 18th Dynasty, across the reigns of Tutankhamen and Haremhab. SCULP
–1550	Artists from central Crete produce bronze votive figurines with a strong concave bend of the back to correspond to the customary Minoan ideal of prayer. SCULP
–1550	Sculptors in the Tehuacán Valley of the southern Puebla region of central Mexico begin to make little clay figures. The figurine cult will soon spread throughout Mesoamerica, with distinct styles developing in different regions. SCULP
–1523– –1027	Artisans of the Shang dynasty in China produce ritual bronze vessels, many decorated with stylized animal heads. DECO
–1523– –1027	During China's Shang dynasty, three types of pottery are produced: red earthenware, burnished black or dark brown ware, and gray ware. DECO
–1523– –1027	During the Shang dynasty, the Chinese develop a system of writing. LIT
–1500	The Shang palace complex at Anyang, China, consists of a south-facing rectangular hall within a courtyard rimmed by galleries. That pattern will be adapted for palaces and temples throughout the Shang dynasty (1523–1027 B.C.). ARCH
–1500	The rebuilt Minoan palace at Knossos, Crete, is three stories tall with post-and-lintel construction, using stone lintels and pointed wooden columns tapering downward. The palace walls are painted with fresco decorations, depicting dolphins and scenes in which youths leap over bulls. *See* 2000 B.C., ARCH. ARCH
–1500	Terra-cotta vessels in animal form become common in Cretan art and are central to Minoan religious cults. DECO
–1500– –486	Indian art forms include stone sculptures, cave paintings, and embellished palaces. MISC

-1480	The funerary temple of Queen Hatshepsut in Egypt is a rock-cut cliff sanctuary fronted by three terraced courtyards faced with colonnades. Long ramps lead from the valley to the temple. ARCH
-1450	An upright harp as tall as a man, along with a kithara, are painted on the walls of the tomb of Paser in Egypt. MUSIC
-1400– -1200	The Mycenaeans of mainland Greece adapt many architectural elements of Minoan Crete, including decoration with frescoes. ARCH
-1400– -1200	The Mycenaeans produce Minoan-influenced terra-cotta figurines. SCULP
-1400	Sculptors in central Mexico make an important technical innovation by creating effigies that are partly or entirely hollow. This construction will allow greater size. SCULP
-1379– -1361	A temple to Aton, the sun-disk god, is erected by Egyptian pharaoh Akhenaton, who briefly introduces monotheistic worship to Egypt in his capital at Tell al-'Amarna. His reign, known as the Amarna period, also introduces short-lived innovations in art, including greater realism and emotion in depictions of people, along with curvilinear contouring of bodies. MISC
-1350	Silver and gold trumpets are buried in the tomb of Tutankhamen in Egypt. MUSIC
-1250	Mycenaean architects build the Lion Gate, which uses post-and-lintel construction with corbeled arches. A great stone relief of two lions is carved over the doorway of the hilltop fortress. This new manner of integrating architecture with sculpture will be seen throughout ancient Greek temple construction. ARCH
-1200	The Olmec civilization of Mesoamerica (Mexico and Central America) constructs pyramids and stone monuments. ARCH
-1200	The dye known as Tyrian purple is invented by the Phoenicians. Obtained from a Mediterranean snail, it will be a favorite of the rich and powerful throughout antiquity. DECO
-1200	The Egyptians weave linen from flax stalks. DECO
-1200	Artists introduce the jaguar, the constrictor snake, the condor, and the eagle as the main iconographic sources of pre-Columbian temple art throughout the sculptures and reliefs at the temple of Chavín de Huantar in the northern highlands of Peru. SCULP

–1100s	The oldest material in the Christian Bible begins to be compiled. Written in Hebrew, these sacred scriptures, known to Christians as the Old Testament, will continue to be compiled until the second century B.C. The New Testament will be written (probably in Greek) during the first century A.D. LIT
–1150	Sculptors of the Olmec culture in central Mexico create figures that combine realistic human and animal elements. This style will proliferate for centuries throughout Mesoamerica in the form of hollow ceramic figures, carved axes, and stone relief sculptures. SCULP
–1100– –1000	In central China, high quality bronzeware is created, showing technical decoration unsurpassed in Bronze Age civilization. Items include cookware, tools, weapons, and personal pieces. DECO
–1085– –945	In the 21st Dynasty in Egypt, the ankh, a sacred hieroglyph symbolizing life, adorns many royal bracelets and ornaments. DECO
–1027– –256	The Chou dynasty introduces a classic period in Chinese civilization, exemplified in the philosophical writings of Confucius, Lao-tzu, Chuang-tzu, and Meng-tzu (Mencius). The oldest collection of Chinese poetry, the *Shih Ching* (*The Book of Odes*), which mentions the existence of drums (ku) and bells (chung), and the use of music during agricultural festivals, is composed, as is the oldest Chinese historical work, *Shu Ching* (*The Book of Documents*), and the work of divination, *I Ching* (*The Book of Changes*). These are part of the *Wu Ching* (*Five Classics*), which will inform Confucianism, among other Eastern philosophies. LIT
–1000– –612	Assyrian palace architecture employs brick arch-and-vault construction and ziggurats similar in design to those of the Sumerians, but smaller. *See also* 2100 B.C., ARCH. ARCH
–1000	The Adena culture of the Ohio River valley in North America produces stone pipes depicting standing male figures. DECO
–1000	Lightweight woven mats of reeds, willows, and cattails are made in North America. They are used to sit on, to sleep on, and to cover huts. DECO
–1000	Bronze lures (horns) are made in Denmark using lost-wax (circe perdue) techniques. MUSIC
–1000	Rock gongs are used in Nigeria to make ceremonial music. MUSIC
–1000	The Olmec civilization of central Mexico creates colossal stone portrait heads at ceremonial precincts near the isthmus of Tehuantepec. SCULP

–900– –700	Abstract geometric patterns predominate in Greek pottery painting. Some vases, such as the Dipylon amphora, are more than five feet high. DECO
–900	The music performed in Solomon's temple in Jerusalem probably includes trumpets and choral singing accompanied by stringed instruments. MUSIC
–900	The Nok culture of Nigeria produces a series of sculpted, triangular terra-cotta heads. These heads represent the earliest Nigerian attempt at portraiture and will continue to appear through A.D. 200. SCULP
–900	Artists of the Paracas culture from the south coast of Peru begin to model clay for use as mummy masks and figurative spouted bottles with deeply incised sculptural decoration. This tradition will continue for six centuries. SCULP
–883	At the beginning of his reign, Assyrian king Ashurnasirpal II is the first to introduce thematic wall decoration to the Near East, with sculpted depictions of court ceremonies at home and battles abroad. SCULP
–870	Assyrian sculptors erect the "White Obelisk," which features a narrative relief that wraps around the monument from the bottom to the top. This feature will be seen again a thousand years later in Rome with the scenes on Emperor Trajan's column. SCULP
–858	Assyrian king Shalmaneser II dedicates monuments at Balawat featuring bronze friezes ornamented in relief with scenes of his conquests. SCULP
–800	The Adena culture of the Ohio River valley builds circular, conical-roofed houses 13 to 32 feet in diameter. ARCH
–800	Egyptian coffins are painted on the outside with scenes of the deceased making offerings to the dead, and on the inside with extracts from the *Book of the Dead*. DECO
–800– –700	Babylonian music makes use of five-tone and seven-tone scales. MUSIC
–800– –700	In Greece music is part of everyday life for all social classes. Professional bards (Rhapsodes) intone epics of war and adventure; choral and dramatic music also develop. MUSIC
–700s	In Italy, the Etruscans invent the true arch, as opposed to the corbeled arch used by the Greeks. ARCH
–700s	Greek poet Homer composes the epics the *Iliad* and the *Odyssey*, both based on legendary material concerning the Trojan War. Homer's influence will reverberate throughout the history of Western literature; literary descendants

will include Virgil's *Aeneid* (19 B.C.), Dante's *Divine Comedy* (A.D. 1307–1321), John Milton's *Paradise Lost* (A.D. 1667), and James Joyce's *Ulysses* (A.D. 1922).
                                                                                              LIT

–700s   Greek poet Hesiod writes the *Theogony*, the oldest surviving account of the origin of the Greek gods, and *Works and Days*, advice on farming and moral life.   LIT

–750   The Nubians build a temple to Amun-Ra at Jebel Barkal, influenced by Egyptian designs.   ARCH

–750   Greek artists begin to look for what they consider to be the essential forms of objects to create simple bronze sculptures.   SCULP

–750   Greek sculptors produce an ivory statuette of a nude goddess that incorporates an Eastern sculptural form and an orderly construction of the human figure. This figure will serve as a precursor to later sculptural creations.   SCULP

–725   The incorporation of ivory carvings and metalwork from Phoenicia, which reflects Mesopotamian as well as Egyptian styles, influences new motifs for Greek art.   SCULP

–722–   These years are the subject of the *Ch'un ch'iu* (*Spring and Autumn Annals*), a
–481   chronicle of the feudal state of Lu, where Confucius is born in the sixth century B.C.   LIT

–722   A long series of reliefs from the Assyrian palace of Sargon II at Dur Sharrukin, illustrating the conquests of the royal armies, is the first large-scale visual narrative to describe the progress of specific events in time.   SCULP

–700–   Etruscan architects in Italy design tombs with interiors resembling domestic
–500   settings, decorated with low reliefs and containing sarcophagi ornamented with terra-cotta figures.   ARCH

–700–   The basic building material for much Greek architecture is marble, a smooth
–500   limestone, or dolomite that can be cut to fit the definite lines of the building design.   ARCH

–700–   During the archaic period, the Greeks develop their basic temple structure: a
–500   rectangular stone post-and-lintel edifice with a pitched roof and fluted columns on all four sides. The Greek architectural orders are developed, systematizing temple proportions and ornamentation. The oldest order, the Doric, employs heavy baseless columns topped by plain capitals; the Ionic order uses slender columns with bases and carved spiral scrolls on the capitals; the Corinthian order is characterized by slender columns, bases, and capitals ornamented with carved acanthus leaves. The Doric order is named for the

mainland Greeks, the Dorians; the Ionic for the Ionian tribes of the Greek islands and Asia Minor; and the Corinthian for the Greek city-state of Corinth. ARCH

–700–
–500

During the archaic period of Greek art, pottery painting incorporates both Mesopotamian motifs, such as hybrid animals, and Greek geometric designs. Narrative art concentrating on figures becomes increasingly common. DECO

–700

Low relief carving dominates the pre-Columbian sculptural repertory at Chavín de Huantar in the northern highlands of Peru. Chavín carvers begin to reduce anatomical details to straight lines and curves and execute details through engraving. SCULP

–700

Olmec artists in central Mexico shape votive axes out of light green jadeite, detailed with flaring eyebrows and cats' eyes in relief. These features will become more common in Chavín art of Peru than in Mesoamerica. SCULP

–600s

Archaic pottery painting in Greece employs the black-figured style, with black figures or designs painted on clay that becomes orange-red after firing. *See also* 500s B.C., DECO. DECO

–600s

In Mesoamerica the Zapotec invent a system of hieroglyphics that is the earliest known writing system in the western hemisphere. LIT

–600s

Sparta becomes a great center of music, drawing poet-musicians such as Alcman, Tyrtaeus, and the semilegendary Terpander. Religious festivals frequently include musical competitions. MUSIC

–675

Human-shaped pottery urns appear in Etruscan tombs. DECO

–669

Assyrian king Ashurbanipal begins to decorate his palace at Ninevah with a series of elaborate reliefs depicting his defeat of the Elamites in the battle at the Ulai. He will also adorn his palace with sculptures illustrating his lion-hunting expeditions. SCULP

–650

Artists in Crete make statues by nailing hammered sheets of bronze over a wood core. This technique, termed sphyrelaton, allows for the creation of larger-sized bronze statues before the development of hollow bronze casting. SCULP

–650

The first truly free-standing stone images of the human form are created as votive offerings in Greece. These figures, known as kouros for male youths and korai for maidens, are produced in large numbers and reveal an Egyptian influence, typified in the cubic character or three-dimensionality of the anatomy and by the stance that shows a rigid, left leg set forward. SCULP

-600– -500	Greek philosopher and mathematician Pythagoras is credited with developing the octave, a first step in the creation of musical scales. MUSIC
-600– -500	The Greeks create groups of tones called modes, the forerunners of modern major and minor scales. MUSIC
-600– -500	The vina, the main instrument of melody in India, develops. It is made of two hollow gourds connected by strings and bamboo reeds. MUSIC
-600	Greek artists begin to decorate stone temples with architectural sculpture in the pediment, free-standing terra-cotta figures above the pediment, and carved reliefs in the frieze below the pediment. SCULP
-600	High relief carvings decorate the pediment of the temple of Artemis at Corfu. The symmetrical arrangement of the composition within a confined zone recalls the Lion Gate at Mycenae as well as Sumerian ornamentation. *See also* 1250 B.C., ARCH. SCULP
-500s	The audience hall of Darius and Xerxes and the palace at Persepolis are grand examples of Persian architecture. The columns of the audience hall draw on Egyptian and Ionian Greek sources; the palace's double bull capital and column reflect Assyrian and Persian ornamental tradition. ARCH
-500s	In Greece the red-figured style of pottery painting emerges, in which backgrounds are painted black and the figures are the orange-red of fired clay. *See also* 600s B.C., DECO. DECO
-500s	Chinese philosopher Lao-tzu founds the system of thought known as Taoism, expounded (probably in the fourth or third century B.C.) in the verse and prose work the *Tao-te ching*. LIT
-500s	Early this century Greek lyric poet Sappho, born in Lesbos, leads a group of women devoted to music and poetry. Her work will survive only in fragments. LIT
-580	The marble kouros figures of Kleobis and Biton from Delphi feature what will become known as the "archaic smile" which serves not as a display of emotion but as a symbol for a higher state of being. The "archaic smile" will fall out of use after 500 B.C. SCULP
-575	The François vase by Greek potter Ergotimos and potter and painter Cleitias is a two-foot-high krater decorated with five tiers of mythological scenes. Exekias is another skilled Greek potter and painter of the sixth century B.C., as seen in the Dionysus kylix, a wine cup from about 540 B.C. DECO

−570	A marble kore figure from the temple of Hera on the island of Samos depicts the human body in drapery utilizing a smooth, close-fitting, continuous flow of lines. SCULP
−551– −479	Chinese philospher Confucius considers music an ordering force in the universe and a mirror of character. Knowledge of music is considered essential to the ability to govern. MUSIC
−550	Relief carving of elongated human figures and glyphs becomes the predominant form of sculpture among the post-Olmec cultures of central Mexico for the next four centuries. SCULP
−530	Artists from the Ionian island Siphnos produce marble sculpture for the facade of the treasury at Delphi. SCULP
−525	Greek vase painter Psiax paints the forceful, compact scene *Herakles Strangling the Nemean Lion* on a black-figured amphora. DECO
−525	Archaic Greek sculptors create kouros figures in the manner of the black-figure vase painter Psiax by rendering anatomical details and emphasizing the swelling curves of the human body. SCULP
−522	Greek lyric poet Pindar, also known as the Dircaean Swan, is born (*d.* 438 B.C.). His works include *Epinicia* (*Odes of Victory*), *Encomia* (*Laudatory Odes*), *Scolia* (festive songs), *Hymns*, and *Choral Dithyrambs to Dionysus*. LIT
−518	Darius I begins to decorate the double stairway leading up to the academic hall at his palace in Persepolis with low reliefs of marching figures. The repetitive and solemn nature of the subject matter will be typical of all Persian sculpture as sculptors ignore the tradition of Assyrian visual narrative. SCULP
−500	Artists of the Alexander culture in the middle Tennessee River valley fashion pottery by separating the base, body, and rim into different decorative fields. This concept of pottery will influence ceramic development throughout the Gulf coast. DECO
−500– −300	Actors in Greece perform plays in open-air theaters before a stage wall. The theaters are lit by natural light, there is no scenery, and the actors wear masks and long, decorated robes. DRAMA
−500– −300	The sayings of the Chinese philosopher Confucius (551–479 B.C.) and anecdotes about him and his disciples are collected in the *Lun-yu* (*Analects*). LIT
−500– −450	The primary Greek musical instruments are the aulos (the most important wind instrument in ancient Greece), kithara, and lyre. MUSIC

–500–   Classical music proper is perfected by Greek lyric poet Pindar, who begins to
–450   write his orchestral odes, and by the new Athenian tragic and comic drama-
             tists. Choral music is at its height.   MUSIC

–500   The Daima, an iron-using culture from the Nigeria-Cameroon border region,
             begin to make clay figurines of cows, goats, sheep, and human beings.   SCULP

–500   Etruscan artists cast a large bronze statue of a she-wolf. Romans will place the
             statue in the temple of Jupiter on the Capitoline Hill as the wolf becomes the
             totemic animal of Rome. Bronze images of Romulus and Remus, the mytho-
             logical cofounders of the Roman city-state, will be added in the Renaissance.
                                                                                     SCULP

–490   The Greek pottery painter known as the Foundry Master paints *Lapith and Centaur*
             on the interior of a red-figured kylix (wine cup).   DECO

–490   The Persian limestone relief carving of Darius and Xerxes from the treasury at
             Persepolis reveals Ionian Greek influences in the rendering of overlapping
             details. Persian carvings during the Achaemenid dynasty will be a synthesis of
             many diverse styles and will show a preoccupation with decorative effects.
                                                                                     SCULP

–490   Relief carving is abandoned in favor of placing statues specifically designed to
             fit the triangular frame of the pediment at the temple of Aphaia in Aegina. For
             the first time, Greek sculptors soften the lines to create individual details of the
             musculature.   SCULP

–480   Greek historian Herodotus is born (*d.* c. 425 B.C.). Known as the father of his-
             tory, he will write the anecdotal and charming, if unreliable, *History of the
             Persian Wars.*   LIT

–480   Greek sculptors begin to create statues that explore emotions and states of
             mind. This early classical, or severe, style will feature little ornamentation and
             focus on expressive, moody facial types.   SCULP

–480   In Athens a marble statue of a standing youth, attributed to Critius, breaks the
             150-year-old kouros stance by featuring contrapposto (positioning of the
             body to achieve a symmetrical balance). Contrapposto will allow sculptors to
             animate the human body in a more relaxed natural manner. *See also* 650 B.C.,
             SCULP.   SCULP

–472   Greek playwright Aeschylus's tragedy *The Persians* is produced. His *Seven
             Against Thebes* will be produced in 469 B.C., his *Suppliant Women* in 466–459
             B.C., and his *Prometheus Bound* at a date that will be lost to history. The first
             great playwright of ancient Athens, Aeschylus writes perhaps 90 plays, but only

seven will survive. Over the course of his career, he moves from writing chorus- and dance-centered drama to actor/character-centered drama, helping to change the direction of Greek theater.   DRAMA

–461–
–429

Pericles serves as leader of the Athenian democracy during the period of its greatest flourishing. A patron of the arts, he encourages the development of architecture, sculpture, painting, music, and drama. *See also* 423–404 B.C., LIT.   MISC

–460

Greek sculptors produce marble pedimental sculpture for the temple of Zeus at Olympia, depicting the victory of the Lapiths over the Centaurs under the aegis of Apollo. This compact group of interlocking figures is typically severe as the narrative struggle is expressed through facial emotions as well as gesture.
                                                                              SCULP

–460

A large, free-standing nude bronze statue of either Poseidon or Zeus in motion is the most important achievement of early classical Greek sculpture in the severe style. The statue will be recovered from the sea near the coast of Greece in 1956.   SCULP

–458

Greek playwright Aeschylus's trilogy *Oresteia* is produced. It includes the tragedies *Agamemnon, Choëphoroi* (*The Libation Bearers*) and *Eumenides*.   DRAMA

–450–
–400

Greek red-figured vase painting incorporates several characteristics of Greek sculpture of the period, including implied movement and classical contrapposto. The figures also become more naturalistic.   DECO

–450–
–400

During the classical period of Greek art, mural painting develops. It will be documented by later Roman copies, though no original examples will survive. The Erechtheum in Athens is built to contain a picture gallery, the first known example of a room especially designed for displaying paintings.   PAINT

–450

Greek sculptor Myron from Argos, working in Athens, creates his bronze statue of the *Discobolus* (*Discus Thrower*). Only a Roman marble copy will survive. SCULP

–450

Greek sculptor Polyclitus executes the *Doryphorus* (*Spearbearer*) and the *Diadumenus* (*Youth Binding a Fillet on His Hair*). His views on mathematical proportions in sculpture will be highly influential.   SCULP

–450–
–432

Greek sculptor Phidias, one of the most famous sculptors of antiquity, produces many of his greatest works, including the colossal statues of Zeus in the temple at Olympia and of Athena in the Parthenon. Both statues will be lost to history; the former will be considered one of the Seven Wonders of the (Ancient) World. His other works include the Lemnian Athena. *See also* 447 B.C., SCULP.   SCULP

–448   Aristophanes, who will become a great writer of Greek Old Comedy, is born
           (*d.* c. 388 B.C.). He will write about 40 plays, 11 of which will survive. Most of
           his comedies will be parodies and satires focused on public figures and social
           issues of his day. *See also* 425 B.C. and 411 B.C., DRAMA.   DRAMA

–447–   Greek architects Ictinus and Callicrates design the Parthenon, the temple to
–432   Athena on the Acropolis in Athens. A signal masterpiece of Greek architecture,
           it stands on a three-step stylobate and is surrounded by 46 Doric columns. It
           contains numerous impressive sculptures. *See* 447 B.C., SCULP.   ARCH

–447   Numerous artists, assembled from different parts of Greece and having differ-
           ent technical backgrounds, begin work on the Parthenon sculptures under the
           supervision of Phidias. The entire program of pedimental sculpture, metopes,
           and frieze will be completed c. 432 B.C. The Parthenon sculptors' concentra-
           tion on graceful rhythms and the optical effects of light and shade will be
           known as the Phidian, or high classical, style and will dominate Athenian
           sculpture to the end of the fifth century. This style will become a standard for
           Western art in antiquity and modern times.   SCULP

–441   Greek playwright Sophocles writes the tragedy *Antigone*. By now, he has also
           written the tragedies *Ajax* and *Trachiniae*. Of more than 100 plays written by
           Sophocles, only seven will survive. His well-plotted tragedies feature incisive
           language and richly drawn characters facing moral dilemmas in the midst of
           crisis.   DRAMA

The Multipurpose Temple

Regarded as one of the greatest achievements of classical Greek architecture, the
Parthenon was originally erected as a place of worship. It remained a place of worship
for thousands of years—but not to the same gods. Built between 447 and 432 B.C. on
the Acropolis, the fortified sacred hill above Athens, the Doric temple was originally
dedicated to the goddess Athena Parthenos—the virginal Athena, daughter of Zeus and
namesake and patron of Athens. About 1,000 years later, in the sixth century A.D., long
after Greece had been absorbed into the Roman Empire and the Roman Empire had
become Christian, the temple became a church, with the Virgin Mary taking the place
of the virginal Athena. After another millenium, following the conquest of Greece by
the Ottoman Turks in the 15th century, the Parthenon became a mosque, with a
minaret added for good measure.

Despite its service to three great religions, the ageless temple was nearly destroyed
by being put to the service of the god of war. Used for storing gunpowder, the central
section was demolished by an explosion during a siege in 1687.

−440   A marble statue of a dying Niobid carved for the pediment of a Doric temple
           is the earliest known large female nude in Greek art. The sculptor positions the
           body in action commonly reserved for the male nude and displays a typically
           high classical feeling of pathos in the facial expression.   SCULP

−438   The tragedy *Alcestis* by the Greek playwright Euripides is produced. Only 19 of
           his 92 plays will survive. Most of his highly dramatic tragedies focus on indi-
           vidual passions and present a largely fatalistic view of life. His writing is
           unusually realistic for the day, employing colloquial language.   DRAMA

−437−   The Propylaea, designed by Mnesicles, is constructed on the Acropolis in Athens.
−432   Serving as the western entry gate to the Acropolis, it includes both Doric and
           Ionic columns.   ARCH

−431   Greek playwright Euripides's tragedy *Medea*, in which Medea revenges her hus-
           band Jason's infidelity by killing their two children and Jason's lover, is pro-
           duced.   DRAMA

−431   Greek historian Xenophon is born (*d.* 355 B.C.). He will write such works as
           Anabasis, Memorabilia, and *Cyropaedia.*   LIT

Ancient Prequels

In Hollywood parlance, a prequel is a sequel depicting events that happened before the
previous film. Thus, *Butch Cassidy and the Sundance Kid* (1969) was followed by *Butch
and Sundance: The Early Days* (1979). Far from being a modern marketing ploy, this
dramatist's technique is as old as ancient Athens.

Sophocles's tragedy *Antigone,* set in legendary Thebes and first staged in 441 B.C.,
concerned the courage of the title character in defying a royal order against burying her
rebel brother, despite the penalty of death. The Theban material clearly interested the
playwright, because the play was followed around 429 B.C. by *Oedipus Tyrannus*
(*Oedipus Rex*). This tragedy, set many years earlier, concerned Antigone's father
Oedipus, who blinds himself in horror after unwittingly killing his father and sleeping
with his mother. It ends with Antigone still a young girl, leading her father away.

The playwright's last tragedy, *Oedipus at Colonus,* produced after the author's death
in 406 B.C., takes place after the second play but before the first. In it, Antigone leads
her blinded father Oedipus to the vicinity of Athens, where he is exalted at his death
by the gods. Thus, the first play in the cycle was followed by a prequel, which in turn
was followed by a sequel, which was nevertheless another prequel relative to the first
play. For clarity, Hollywood would most likely now label the cycle Antigone I, II, and III.

-430–
-428
The tragedy *Heraclidae* (*Children of Heracles*) by the Greek playwright Euripides is produced.   DRAMA

-430
Greek sculptors begin to explore the decorative aspects of the "wind-blown" style of rendering drapery developed by the sculptors of the Parthenon. The resulting sculpture will stress grace, softness, and elegant flourishes.   SCULP

-429
Greek playwright Sophocles writes the tragedy *Oedipus Tyrannus* (*Oedipus Rex*), his most famous and perhaps his greatest play. The Greek philosopher Aristotle will view *Oedipus Tyrannus* as the ideal tragedy.   DRAMA

-428
The tragedy *Hippolytus* by Greek playwright Euripides is produced.   DRAMA

-427
Greek philosopher Plato is born (*d.* 348 B.C.). He will couch his philosophy in dialogues such as the *Crito, Euthyphro, Phaedrus, Republic,* and *Symposium,* known for their literary quality as well as for their philosophical content. He will also write the *Apology,* an account of the defense made by Socrates at his trial for impiety and corruption of youth.   LIT

-426
The tragedy *Hecuba* by Greek playwright Euripides is produced.   DRAMA

-425
The Acharnians, a comedy by the Greek playwright Aristophanes, is produced. It will be followed by his comedies *The Knights* (424 B.C.), *The Clouds* (423 B.C.), *The Wasps* (422 B.C.), *The Peace* (421 B.C.) and *The Birds* (414 B.C.).   DRAMA

-423–
-404
Greek historian Thucydides (c. 460–c. 401 B.C.) writes the well-researched *History of the Peloponnesian War,* which reports and analyzes contemporary events more objectively and critically than previous historical narratives. Primarily a military history (up to 411 B.C.) of the war between Athens and Sparta (431–404 B.C.), it includes Athenian general Pericles' eloquent funeral oration and a clinical description of the plague that wiped out an estimated quarter of the Athenian population (including Pericles) between 430 and 428 B.C.   LIT

-421–
-405
The Erechtheum on the Acropolis in Athens, possibly designed by Mnesicles, has three Ionic porticoes, including the Porch of the Caryatids, and the sanctuaries dedicated to Athena, Poseidon, and the Athenian king Erechtheus. ARCH

-420
Greek sculptor Polyclitus executes a colossal gold and ivory statue of Hera for a new temple at the Argive Heraion.   SCULP

-415
The tragedy *Trojan Women* by Greek playwright Euripides is produced. It will be followed by his tragicomedy *Iphigenia in Tauris* (414 B.C.), his tragicomedy *Ion* and his tragedy *Electra* (both 413 B.C.), his high comedy *Helen* (412 B.C.), his pageant play *Phoenician Women* (411–409 B.C.), his tragedy *Orestes* (408 B.C.), and his tragedy *Bacchae* (production date unknown).   DRAMA

−411   Aristophanes's *Lysistrata*, a comedy in which Greek women withhold sex to force the men to end a war, is produced. It will be followed by *Thesmaphoriazusae* (*Women at the Festival*) (410 B.C.), *The Frogs* (405 B.C.), *Ecclesiazusae* (*Women in Parliament*) (392 B.C.) and *Plutus* (*Wealth*) (388 B.C.).   DRAMA

−410   Athenian sculptors create large numbers of marble grave stelae decorated with reliefs and exported throughout the Greek world.   SCULP

−409   Greek playwright Sophocles writes the tragedy *Philoctetes*. The date he wrote the tragedy *Electra* will be forgotten, but historians will speculate that he wrote it prior to this year. His tragedy *Oedipus at Colonus*, probably written near the end of his life, will be produced posthumously in 401 B.C.

    DRAMA

−407   The marble figure of Nike from the balustrade of the Temple of Athena Nike shows the emergence of the carving of "wetlike" drapery that clings to the human body.   SCULP

−400   The Moche people succeed the Chavín culture in the northern highlands of Peru and begin to produce modeled pottery and small objects of bone and shell.   DECO

−400   The people of the Recuay-Vicus, a satellite of the Moche culture from the northern highlands of Peru, create large hollow vessels in a variety of figurative shapes.   DECO

−400– −100   In China, Chou dynasty art is characterized by the emergence of naturalistic human representation and smooth, gentle shapes.   SCULP

−400   The late Adena culture of the Ohio River valley engrave designs composed of broad lines into simple, rectangular stone tablets. The tablets are not distributed but the iconography will spread throughout the eastern woodlands. SCULP

−300s   The earliest known written collection of Aesop's fables appears. The Greek fabulist is said to have lived around 600 B.C.   LIT

−390   Greek sculptors create marble images for the temple of Asclepius at Epidaurus depicting human suffering and experiences of pain. These sculptures will act as a precursor to a tradition of agonized faces in fourth century and Hellenistic art.

    SCULP

−384   Greek philosopher Aristotle is born (*d.* 322 B.C.). His *Poetics* will be regarded as a cornerstone of Western literary criticism.   LIT

-372   Chinese philosopher Meng-tzu (Mencius) is born (*d.* 289 B.C.). His collection of teachings, *The Book of Mencius*, is a prime example of classical Chinese prose.   LIT

-369   Chinese philosopher Chuang-tzu is born (*d.* 286 B.C.). The work attributed to him, the *Chuang-tzu* (*Master Chuang*), is a classic of Taoist thought and Chinese literature.   LIT

-351   Demosthenes, the vaunted Greek orator, writes his first *Philippic*, directed against Philip II of Macedon, military foe of Greece. Other *Philippics* will follow in 344 and 341 B.C.   LIT

-351   At the Mausoleum at Halicarnassus, Asia Minor (Turkey), Greek sculptor Scopas completes his marble frieze illustrating the battle of the Greeks and Amazons. He also finishes his colossal portrait statue of Mausolus, the earliest Greek portrait to show a specific personal character. Individual likeness will soon play an important part in Hellenistic sculptural works.   SCULP

-330   The figurative innovations of Greek sculptor Lysippus are evident in his bronze statue *Apoxymenos* (*Youth Scraping Himself with a Strigil*). Highly influential among Hellenistic sculptors, Lysippus develops a slenderer set of proportions than those of Polyclitus (*see* 450 B.C., SCULP) and, as court sculptor to Alexander the Great, develops the "personality portrait" genre.   SCULP

-325–
-100   During the Hellenistic period, Greek artistic styles spread throughout the Mediterranean world. The styles tend to be more sensual, emotional, and naturalistic than the classical ideal.   PAINT

-320   Greek philosopher Aristoxenus, pupil of Aristotle, writes on the musical theory of scales.   MUSIC

-316   *Dyscolus* (*The Bad-Tempered Man*), a comedy by Greek playwright Menander, is produced. Out of more than 100 plays written by him, it is the only one that will survive in complete form. The greatest writer of Greek New Comedy, he discards the topicality of Old Comedy to create comedies of manners. Their plots and stock characters will serve as models for Roman playwrights such as Plautus. Other plays of Menander include *Samia* (*The Girl from Samos*), *Perikeiromene* (*The Rape of the Locks*), and *Aspis* (*The Shield*). *See also* 448 B.C. and 254 B.C., DRAMA.   DRAMA

-300–
-250   The hydraulos, the organ of ancient Greece, is invented by Ctesibius of Alexandria. Its wind supply is provided with water instead of bellows and its keyboard mechanism will be rediscovered in the tenth century A.D.   MUSIC

−300	Athenian sculptor Praxiteles creates the first completely nude cult image of the goddess Aphrodite. Female nudes will become a common form of statuary in Hellenistic and Roman times. SCULP
−300	A marble statue of Apollo exhibits extreme Praxitelean qualities of soft modeling. This statue, known as the Apollo Belvedere, will become popular during the 18th and 19th centuries A.D. when Johann Winckelmann and Goethe find it to be the perfect embodiment of classical beauty. Numerous plaster casts of the Apollo will appear in museums, art academies, and colleges throughout the Greek revival of the 18th century A.D. SCULP
−300	Under the influence of Greek portraiture, individual likenesses begin to appear in the sculptured heads on Etruscan bronze statues. SCULP
−300–−200	The Yayoi period in Japanese art is marked by Chinese influences, fine workmanship, and familiarity with bronze and iron. SCULP
−200s–−100	In India, the Great Stupa is built, a Buddhist monument of great national importance. ARCH
−200s	Lucius Afranius writes *Togata*, a comedy based on daily life in ancient Rome. Several hundred fragments from 44 of his plays will survive. It will be said that he introduced the subject of homosexuality into the theater. DRAMA
−200s	Apollonius of Rhodes, librarian at Alexandria, Egypt, composes the *Argonautica*, an epic account of the voyage of Jason and the crew of the *Argo* in search of the Golden Fleece. LIT
−200s	In India the Sanskrit verse epic, the *Ramayana*, is composed, though some parts date from as early as 500 B.C. Ascribed to the poet Valmiki, it tells of exiled Prince Rama's efforts to rescue his wife and regain his kingdom. LIT
−200s	Early this century Greek poet Theocritus, considered the inventor of the pastoral, writes his *Idylls*, of which 32 will survive. LIT
−280	Sostratus of Cnidus constructs the lighthouse on Pharos near Alexandria, Egypt. Projecting light from concave mirrors, the 300-foot structure will be one of the Seven Wonders of the (Ancient) World. ARCH
−280	The Colossus of Rhodes, a 105-foot high statue of the sun god, Helios, is constructed on the harbor at Rhodes; it will be one of the Seven Wonders of the (Ancient) World. SCULP
−273–−232	In India, the reign of Ashoka brings the country's first examples of imperial art, such as the caves inscribed with the virtues of Dharma and the Ashokan edict

columns. During this time, sculpture emerges as a prime artistic medium in India.   SCULP

−254   Roman playwright Titus Maccius Plautus is born (*d.* 184 B.C.). He will write and produce about 130 verse comedies that Romanize the plots and characters of the Greek New Comedy and will long serve as a source of inspiration to comic playwrights in the West. His plays include *Menaechmi* (*The Twins*), *Aulularia* (*The Pot of Gold*), *Mercator* (*The Merchant*), *Asinaria* (*The Comedy of Asses*), *Cistellaria* (*The Casket*), *Mostellaria* (*The Haunted House*), *Pseudolus*, *Amphitruo* (*Amphitryon*), and *Casina. See* 316 B.C., DRAMA.   DRAMA

−239   Roman poet Quintus Ennius, known as the father of Latin literature, is born (*d.* 169 B.C.). His works will include the Roman historical epic *Annales*.   LIT

−234   Roman politician Marcus Portius Cato (Cato the Elder) is born (*d.* 149 B.C.). Known for espousing the values of moral rectitude and military vigilance, he will be admired for his prose style, though only his treatise *De re rustica* (or *De agri cultura*) will survive.   LIT

−230   A Hellenistic bronze statue of a dying Gaul is dedicated to Attalus I of Pergamum in Asia Minor (Turkey) to celebrate his victories over the Gauls.   SCULP

−214   Emperor Shih Huang Ti (Cheng), founder of the Ch'in dynasty (221–207 B.C.), begins construction on portions of what will become the Great Wall of China, most of which will be constructed during the Ming dynasty (A.D. 1368–1644). Eventually it will stretch 1,500 miles from the Pacific Ocean to central Asia.   ARCH

−206–   During the Han dynasty in China, popular decorative art forms include
A.D. 220   bronzeware, earthenware, lacquerware, and the highly prized stoneware with brown or olive glaze called Yüehware, a forerunner to porcelain.   DECO

−206–   Performances mixing story dramatization, singing, and dancing are presented
A.D. 220   during the Han dynasty in China.   DRAMA

−206–   During the Han dynasty in China, literature and the arts flourish, Confucian
A.D. 220   thought is systematized and becomes dominant, and the first historical annal, the *Shih chi*, is written.   MISC

−200–   In India most of the encyclopedic Sanskrit epic the *Mahabharata* is composed,
A.D. 200   though some additions will be made as late as A.D. 600. The longest poem in world literature, the digressive work tells primarily of a royal dynastic struggle and includes the religious classic, the *Bhagavad-Gita* (*The Song of God*), which takes the form of a dialogue between Lord Krishna and Prince Arjuna.   LIT

−200	The Chinese found an imperial bureau to establish an absolute system of pitch. MUSIC
−200	A marble statue of a winged Nike from Samothrace is carved as a victory monument. The figure displays a High Hellenistic style of animated and wind-blown drapery to create an active relationship with the surrounding space. SCULP
−100s– A.D. 100s	In southeast China, light gray and brown pottery is produced, some with geometric impressions approximating basketweave. DECO
−100s	Rome conquers Greece and assimilates Greek artistic and intellectual traditions. Roman painting, sculpture, drama, and poetry will be strongly influenced by the Greeks. Roman copies of Greek sculptures will survive to modern times, transmitting the image of originals long since destroyed. MISC
−100s	In India, the Bharat is created, a significant monument of Buddhist mythology. SCULP
−100s	During India's Shunga period, the Buddhist worship hall (chaitya) at Bhaja is created. It has over 1200 rock-cut chambers. SCULP
−180	Hellenistic Greek sculptors carve a great marble frieze representing the Battle of the Gods and the Titans, to symbolize the victories of Attalus I, for the Altar of Zeus at Pergamum. SCULP
−177	The death of Chinese general Ho Ch'ü-ping generates an early example of large sculpture in China, with two large horses made of boulders at the general's tomb. SCULP
−170	Lucius Accius, who will become a renowned playwright of ancient Rome, is born (d. 85 B.C.). Only the titles and some lines from about 40 of his tragedies will survive. Some of his plays will be modeled on Greek dramas, and others will be wholly original. His work will often feature the melodramatic plots, exaggerated characters, and overblown rhetoric typical of Roman tragedy. DRAMA
−170	Scholars in the court of Eumenes II of Pergamum in Asia Minor (Turkey) invent parchment, a writing surface made from hides. It eventually replaces papyrus. GRAPH
−106	Marcus Tullius Cicero, considered the greatest Roman orator, is born (d. 43 B.C.). His orations will include the treatises against Catiline (63 B.C.), the *Philippics* (directed against Marc Antony, 44 B.C.), and orations in defense of Sestus, Plancius, and Milo (50s B.C.). He will also write works of philosophy and rhetoric. He will be murdered by his political opponents, including fol-

lowers of Marc Antony and Octavius (later the first Roman emperor, Augustus). *See also* 55 B.C., 54–51 B.C., and 47–44 B.C., LIT.   LIT

–100–
1 B.C.   In India, Andhran art matures, its graceful and lively elements affecting the country's artistic development.   SCULP

–100   The Hopewell culture in southern Ohio creates stone platform pipes in the form of animals, sculpted with the same degree of realism found in Adena figures (*see* 1000 B.C., DECO).   SCULP

–100   In Mesoamerica, Mayan stelae are decorated with hieroglyphic characters and low reliefs of costumed figures.   SCULP

–98   Roman poet Lucretius is born (*d.* 55 B.C.). He will be best known for *De rerum natura* (*On the Nature of Things*), a didactic poem on the nature of the universe based on the philosophies of Democritus and Epicurus.   LIT

–90   The bronze statue of Aulus Metellus, also known as *L'Arringatore*, introduces the Roman gesture of address and salutation, which will reappear in hundreds of Roman statues.   SCULP

–84   Roman poet Catullus is born (*d.* c. 54 B.C.). Of his works, 116 poems will survive, including his love lyrics to Lesbia (pseudonym for Clodia), which will influence later love poetry.   LIT

–75   Marble portraiture appears in Rome during the rule of Lucius Sulla. Roman portraits will depart from the expressive, psychological Hellenistic renderings by utilizing the custom of preserving the face of the dead in wax; this enables sculptors to create detailed records of an individual's face.   SCULP

–59–
A.D. 17   Roman historian Livy (Titus Livius) lives. Thirty-five volumes of his 142-volume history of Rome, *Ab urbe condita libri*, will survive.   LIT

–58–
–44   Roman general and statesman Julius Caesar writes *Commentaries on the Gallic War*, a historical work famed for its clear, strong style. He also writes *Commentaries on the Civil War* in 45 B.C.   LIT

–55   Master of the Roman art of public speaking, Cicero writes his treatise on oratory, *De oratore*.   LIT

–54–
–51   Roman orator Cicero writes *De re publica*, a six-volume work on political philosophy.   LIT

–50   In Mesoamerica the Mayan civilization develops a more refined system of writing than that used by the Zapotec. *See* 600s B.C., LIT.   LIT

−47−
−44
Cicero writes several philosophical works, including *Tusculanae disputationes,* *De natura deorum, De divinatione, De senectute, De amicitia,* and his guide to Stoic morality, *De officiis.*　　　　　　　　　　LIT

−40
In China *Li chi (The Book of Rites)* is composed, incorporating older material dealing with proper behavior and ritual.　　　　　　　　　　LIT

−38
In China the octave is subdivided into 60 notes.　　　　　　　　　　MUSIC

−37
Roman poet Virgil completes the *Eclogues,* or *Bucolics.* This collection of ten pastoral poems establishes his literary reputation.　　　　　　　　　　LIT

−37−
−30
Roman poet Virgil composes the agricultural poem, the *Georgics.* Written in four volumes, the poem celebrates farming and is patterned after Hesiod's *Works and Days.*　　　　　　　　　　LIT

−23
Roman poet Horace composes his first notable collection of poems, *Odes,* or *Carmina.* In this year the first three of this four-volume set of odes appear.　LIT

−22
Roman poet Horace composes *Epistulae (Epistles).*　　　　　　　　　　LIT

−20−
1 B.C.
Roman poet Ovid is established as an important writer with his collections *Amores* and *Heroides.* The former is a book of love poems, the latter takes the form of epistles from legendary women abandoned by men.　　　　　　　　　　LIT

−20
Roman sculptors erect a marble statue of the emperor Augustus at the villa of his wife, Livia. The statue, called Augustus of Primaporta, combines aspects of the divine ruler seen in Egyptian and ancient Near Eastern sculpture with an idealized head similar to Hellenistic portraits of Alexander the Great.　　SCULP

−19
The *Aeneid,* Roman poet Virgil's epic poem on the founding of Rome by Trojan refugee Aeneas, is left unfinished upon his death. Drawing on Homer's *Iliad* and *Odyssey* (eighth century B.C.), the poem will influence Western writers through the ages, notably Dante in *The Divine Comedy* (A.D. 1307–1321).　　LIT

−13
Roman poet Horace composes *Ars poetica (The Art of Poetry),* in which he details the process of writing poetry.　　　　　　　　　　LIT

−13
The Roman senate votes to have a monument known as the Altar of Peace (or Ara Pacis) constructed and set up on the Campus Martius in Rome. Roman sculptors decorate the wall screening the altar with a frieze depicting allegorical and legendary scenes as well as a procession led by Augustus. The entire sculptural program will be completed in 9 B.C.　　　　　　　　　　SCULP

–4   Lucius Annaeus Seneca, who will become a philosopher, orator, statesman, and playwright in Rome, is born at Corduba (*d.* A.D. 65). Seneca's plays, the only dramas surviving in complete form from ancient Rome, will all be adaptations of Greek plays. The dramas may have been meant to be read aloud rather than staged. The tragedies of Seneca, for which dates are unknown, will include *Hercules Furens, Medea, Phaedra, Troades* (*Trojan Women*), *Agamemnon, Oedipus, Phoenissae* (*Phoenician Women*), and *Thyestes*. He will perhaps also be the author of *Hercules Oetaeus*. His work will have an influence on Shakespeare, evident in *Richard III* (*see* c. A.D. 1591–1594, DRAMA) and *Titus Andronicus* (*see* c. A.D. 1590–1592, DRAMA), and on Ben Jonson.   DRAMA

–3   Roman poet Ovid composes *Ars amatoria* (*Art of Love*).   LIT

A.D.

1   The Recuay culture in the valleys of northern Peru model thin-walled ceramics from a fine-textured white kaolin clay. Typical creations include large hollow vessels in a variety of shapes with a unique double spout arrangement.   DECO

1   The marble group that will become known as the *Laocoön* is created by the sculptors Agesander, Polydorus, and Athenodorus of Rhodes. Admired in classical times as one of the greatest sculptures ever made, it will be rediscovered in Rome in 1506 and will exert a profound influence on such Renaissance sculptors as Michelangelo. The group depicts the Trojan priest Laocoön and his two sons being crushed to death by snakes, as described in Book II of Virgil's *Aeneid*. *See* 19 B.C., LIT.   SCULP

1   The spread of Greek aesthetics throughout the Roman Empire produces a market for copies as sculptors begin to introduce the mechanical process of pointing. This method, originating in Athens, involves making plaster casts of originals and then preparing stone or bronze copies. In Rome, the demand will be for mass-produced marble versions of classical sculpture, which will need the addition of a support to make them stable.   SCULP

1   Roman sculptors in Tivoli erect a portrait statue of a general from the Late Republic. The pose and gestures are derived from statues of Hellenistic rulers. SCULP

8	Roman poet Ovid composes the multibook collection of mythological tales, *Metamorphoses*. He is exiled this year by Roman emperor Augustus Caesar. LIT
23	Roman scholar Pliny the Elder is born (*d.* 79). His 37-volume *Historia naturalis* (*Natural History*) will become an important scientific work during the Middle Ages. LIT
50–100	The books of the Bible's New Testament are written in Greek by members of early Christian communities in the Mediterranean region. LIT
55	Roman historian Tacitus is born (*d.* 120). He will write *Germania*, a social history of Germany; *Annales*, a study of the Julian dynasty; and *Historiae*, a history of the years 69–96. LIT
60	Roman satirist Juvenal is born (*d.* 140). He will write 16 satires, primarily about the vices of the age. LIT
65	Roman poet Lucan writes the *Pharsalia*, an epic on the civil war between the opposing forces of Julius Caesar and Pompey. LIT

The Banished Poet

How best to punish a sophisticated literary figure? Banish the person to the provinces. That was what Roman emperor Augustus Caesar did to the poet Ovid in A.D. 8. Known for his witty, sensuous, amorous verse, he was the most illustrious living poet among Rome's literati when he slighted Augustus in ways that were never clearly defined. Perhaps Augustus, who was pursuing a campaign of moral reform, was offended by Ovid's *Ars amatoria* (*Art of Love*), a satiric manual in verse teaching readers of both sexes how to gain lovers. There were also unnamed charges of personal immorality. In any case, the 50-year-old Ovid's "error" led to his exile to the Black Sea port of Tomis, now Constantsa, Romania. There, separated from his wife, his works banned from public libraries, he lived out the remaining ten years of his life.

For one accustomed to urban comforts and high culture, it was a dreadful punishment. At the far edge of the Roman Empire, the windswept outpost was only semi-Hellenized, severe in climate, and periodically attacked by barbarians. Ovid made the best of it, serving in Tomis's home guard, taking an interest in local politics, writing poetry in the local language, and warmly accepting the honors given him by the townspeople. Still, Rome was never far from his thoughts, as was attested to in *Tristia* and *Letters from the Black Sea*, both books of elegiacs lamenting his exile.

Even in his darkest moments, Ovid claimed that the emperor had no power over poetry. Indeed, despite Augustus's ban, Ovid's works have survived and influenced writers to the present day.

69   Roman biographer and historian Suetonius is born (*d.* 140). He will write *De vita Caesarum* (*Lives of the Caesars*), a series of biographies of the Roman emperors from Caesar to Domitian.   LIT

79   Mount Vesuvius erupts near Naples, burying the towns of Pompeii and Herculaneum. The art and architecture of the buried towns, excavated in 1738, will spur the neoclassical movement of the 18th century.   MISC

79   Preserved at Pompeii are illusionistic frescoes by Roman artists that employ shading or modeling, foreshortening, overlapping, and atmospheric perspective. PAINT

80   The Roman Colosseum is built. Seating 50,000 people, it is the largest public structure up to its time. Supported by an arch-and-vault system, it features three levels of arched openings decorated with Doric, Ionic, and Corinthian columns.   ARCH

81   Roman sculptors decorate a triumphal arch with marble relief panels commemorating the victories of the Emperor Titus. The sculptors successfully illustrate a crowd of figures in depth through different layers of relief.   SCULP

96   Spanish-born Roman rhetorician Quintilian writes the influential educational treatise *Institutio oratoria* (*On the Training of an Orator*).   LIT

100s   Early this century, the Pantheon in Rome is built; a domed, cylindrical temple 144 feet in diameter, it has an attached portico featuring Corinthian columns. ARCH

100s   Sanskrit drama, encompassing both religious and secular themes, begins in India. It will flourish for the next millennium.   DRAMA

100s   *Ch'u tz'u* (*The Elegies of Ch'u*), a Chinese poetry anthology, is composed, though attributed to the fourth century B.C. Chinese poet Ch'ü Yüan.   LIT

100s   During the Kushan dynasty, Indian coins are struck for the first time for use on caravan routes.   MISC

100s   Roman artistic style and imagery strongly affect sculpture and other art forms in northern India.   SCULP

100   Greek biographer Plutarch writes *Parallel Lives,* a series of paired biographies of famous Greeks and Romans. The book will provide background for such Shakespeare plays as *Julius Caesar* (c. 1599).   LIT

100   The Vicus culture along Peru's north coast creates a unique style of figurative clay sculpture. Artists shape compact bodies with shoulders that blend into an abstract form comprising both arms and legs.   SCULP

105	In China Ts'ai Lun invents paper, a writing and drawing surface that can be made more cheaply than papyrus or parchment. It will reach Europe in 1320. GRAPH
113	Roman sculptors complete a continuous spiral band of relief, begun in 106, that covers a column celebrating Emperor Trajan's victories against the Dacians. The scenes recount the history of the Dacian wars and are carved in a shallow relief that breaks the tradition of foreshortening and perspective. These stylistic aspects will dominate medieval art. *See also* 870 B.C., SCULP. SCULP
121	Roman emperor Marcus Aurelius is born (*d.* 180). He will write the classic work of Stoic philosophy *Meditations*. LIT
122	Hadrian's Wall, 72 miles long, is built by the Romans in Britain to defend against the Picts and other northern tribesmen. ARCH
125	Lucian of Samosata, Greek satirist, is born (*d.* 200). His satires will include *The True History*, which describes a trip to the moon, *Dialogues of the Dead*, and the novel *Lucius; or, The Ass*. His biting, wide-ranging wit will influence later writers such as Jonathan Swift and Voltaire. He will be considered the inventor of satirical dialogue. LIT
150	The peoples of the Hopewell culture in southern Ohio begin to direct their trade of flint, effigy platform pipes, and pottery toward the south and east. DECO
161	Roman sculptors begin work on a bronze equestrian statue of Marcus Aurelius in the tradition of equestrian images established by Julius Caesar. The statue will be completed in 180. SCULP
180	Roman sculptors begin to use the drill to create exaggerated details in the modeling of hair on marble portrait busts. SCULP
200s	Indian dramatist Bhāsa writes verse dramas that include *Svapnavasavadatta* (*The Dream of Vasavadatta*). LIT
200s	Late this century, in the purge of Confucianism, the emperor of China orders all musical instruments destroyed. MUSIC
200s–700s	Plaster is used as an inexpensive substitute for marble in Indian sculpture. SCULP
200s	Over the course of the century, representations of Bodhisattva Maitreya fertility spirits in Indian statuary are supplanted by visions of the Buddhist savior. SCULP

250   Stone masks become the predominant form of sculpture in the urban Mexican
           complex of Teotihuacán. Artists create simple, uniform masks inlaid with
           shells or small gems.   SCULP

260   A relief depicting the triumph of Shapur I over the Emperors Philippus the
           Arab and Valeria is carved in rock at Naksh-i-Rustam, the burial place of the
           Persian Achaemenid kings, near Persepolis. The blending of Roman and Near
           Eastern elements, evident in this relief, will also be seen in Shapur's palace at
           Ctesiphon, near Babylon.   SCULP

300s   The art of Chinese scroll painting develops, typically depicting courtly life and
           landscapes.   PAINT

300s–400s In India, the red sandstone sculpture known as Standing Buddha is created, an
           example of the era's finely hewn style.   SCULP

300   The Nazca culture from the Peruvian Rio Grande Valley decorate vessel sur-
           faces with two-dimensional polychrome scenes rather than with the type of
           modeling prefered in northern Peru.   DECO

300   At the beginning of India's Gupta period, when the arts start to flourish under
           imperial patronage, sculpture takes on a new naturalism through a more refined
           system of aesthetics. The holy cities of Mathura and Sarnath will be the centers of
           sculptural production.   SCULP

306   In Rome construction begins on the Basilica of Constantine or Maxentius,
           which employs concrete vaulting to reach vast dimensions—328 by 249 feet,
           with a central aisle 114 feet high. Basilicas, long civic halls with low side aisles
           and high central aisles or naves, were first developed in Hellenistic Greece and
           widely adopted by the Romans.   ARCH

306   A colossal statue of Constantine will be built for the Basilica of Constantine or
           Maxentius, which is begun this year. The eight-and-a-half-foot-high head has
           enormous eyes in proportion to the face.   SCULP

315   The Arch of Constantine near the Colosseum in Rome is decorated with sculp-
           ture copied from earlier Imperial monuments. Sculptors carve a frieze in a new
           Constantinian style that ignores all the devices developed since the fifth cen-
           tury B.C. to create spatial depth. The depiction of the emperor in a frontal pose
           surrounded by other figures is derived from Near Eastern art and will appear
           throughout Christian art compositions.   SCULP

320   Sculpture begins to play a secondary role in Early Christian art. The biblical
           prohibition of graven images is interpreted to apply to large cult statues wor-

shiped in pagan temples. As a consequence, sculpture develops in an anti-monumental direction toward small-scale forms.   SCULP

333   The construction of what will become known as Old St. Peter's Church begins in Rome. Though it will not survive to modern times, it will be remembered as a prominent example of early Christian basilicas (*see* 306, ARCH), the design of which is based on Roman civic basilicas. The altar is located in an apse, or semicircular niche, at the eastern end, with the main entrance at the western end. An atrium, or courtyard, and a narthex, or entrance hall, precede access to the nave, or central aisle. The design will provide the model for Christian church architecture in the West for centuries to come.   ARCH

344–405   The most eminent painter of the Han period in China is Ku K'ai-chih. Known for their vitality, his works include the scroll *Admonitions of the Imperial Instructress.*   PAINT

350   The Schola Cantorum, a school for church song, is founded in Rome.   MUSIC

350   Limestone stelae carved with scenes of Buddha leaving his family and his palace home become a standard part of Indian Buddhist imagery.   SCULP

Buddhism Goes East

Buddhism was introduced to China in the first century A.D., but it was not until the fourth century that it became a major influence, beginning in northern China. The religion originated in India in the sixth and fifth centuries B.C. Merchants and monks then transported it along the Silk Road that ran from northern India to central Asia to northern China. The spread of Buddhism to China led to a burgeoning of creativity in the arts—sculpture, painting, and architecture—as fourth- and fifth-century artists sought to embody the new religious beliefs in concrete form. Among the most stunning works, adapted from central Asian models, were cave temples containing colossal statues of Buddha carved from the rock. Sitting or standing, sculptures at sites such as Yunkang and Lungmen towered more than 40 or 50 feet in height.

The first great Chinese Buddhist shrine complex was Dunhuang, located in Kansu on the trade routes from India and central Asia. It contains more than 300 rock-cut shrines decorated with fresco murals and painted clay sculptures. Details such as elongated halos, columnar bodies, and exaggerated ripples in the hems of garments already began to add a distinctly Chinese identity to the borrowed images, an identity that would be fully realized by the sixth century.

354	Christian philosopher St. Augustine of Hippo is born (*d.* 430). He will trace his conversion to Christianity in *Confessions* and present a defense of the Christian religion in the multivolume *De civitate Dei* (*The City of God*). LIT
359	The Roman sarcophagus of Junius Bassus displays a mixture of Old and New Testament scenes carved in relief. Early Christian relief images move away from a narrative purpose toward the reflection of symbolic meaning. SCULP
370–800	During the migration period, invading Teutonic tribes such as the Visigoths, Ostrogoths, Vandals, Lombards, and Franks introduce new decorative art styles to Europe, particularly in gold objects such as fibulae and buckles. DECO
370	Roman poet Claudian is born (*d.* 404). He will write *Claudianus Major* and *Claudianus Minor*. LIT
375–415	In India during the reign of Chandra Gupta II, early examples of wall paintings are created in caves at Ajanta. PAINT
375	Christ giving the law to Peter, or the Traditio Legis, becomes a very popular image in Early Christian tomb reliefs. Roman sculptors create a Theodosian style showing Eastern influence in the carving of strong, well-rounded bodies. SCULP
380	Roman emperors, consuls, and high officials demonstrate a renewed interest in individual characterization by continuing the custom of erecting portrait statues of themselves in public places. SCULP
386	Hymn singing is introduced to the West by St. Ambrose, bishop of Milan, though Hilary, bishop of Poitiers (c. 315–366), has also been credited. Among the best-known early hymns from this period is *"Te Deum laudamus"* ("We Praise Thee, O God"). MUSIC
390	The first "Alleluia" hymns are introduced in Christian churches. MUSIC
390	Ivory panels, designed for private ownership, display a more conservative style than those found among the large official monuments sponsored by the church or state. SCULP
400s	A mosaic on the theme of the Good Shepherd is constructed at the mausoleum of Galla Placidia in Ravenna, depicting Christ as a young, beardless man surrounded by a flock of lambs. DECO
400s	In the Middle East, stamps are cut on wood for printing fabrics. GRAPH

400	Ceramics originating among the Lake Woodland populations of western Florida feature elaborate ceremonial decoration consisting of incised geometric and floral motifs and modeled forms of birds and animals. DECO
400–700	Japanese music begins to flourish as it gradually adopts styles and instruments from an eclectic variety of sources—Chinese ceremonial music (fifth century), Korean Buddhist song (sixth century), and Indian ceremonial dance (seventh century). New instruments, such as the zitherlike koto, will be introduced from China in the ninth and tenth centuries. MUSIC
400	Indian sculptors create an elegantly proportioned statue of Buddha standing with his right hand posed in a protective gesture. This image of Buddha will become the type most often represented in South Asian art. SCULP
425–500	Early examples of Hindu temples are built in India at Aihole. Among them are the Ladkham and Gaudar Temples. ARCH
450	Germanic tribes, including the Angles, Saxons, and Jutes, now overrunning Britain, introduce the new decorative styles of the migration period in such portable objects as brooches and cloisonné ware. DECO
450	Following Jewish and Byzantine tradition, Roman Catholic church services employ alternative singing between soloist and congregation. MUSIC
460–480	To mark the rise of Buddhism in China, the cave temples of Yün-kang at Ta-T'ung are carved. The temples are carved from limestone by thousands of artisans and represent an important example of religious art. SCULP
477	Chinese sculptors of the northern Wei dynasty create a gilt bronze statue of Maitreya, the Buddha of the Future. It will be the largest and most important bronze statue made during the period. SCULP
500s	The church of San Vitale is constructed in Ravenna, Italy. The domed, octagonal church has the central plan characteristic of Eastern (Byzantine) churches, as opposed to the longitudinal plan of Western churches (*see* 333, ARCH). The church is decorated with mosaics, including *Emperor Justinian and His Attendants*. ARCH
500s	Over the next three centuries, Korean pottery incorporates Chinese standards but also shows its own humor and perception of the world. DECO
500s	By now, the Chinese have invented block books, a form of printing in which a woodcut block of text and illustrations is used to print an entire page. *See also* 1450, GRAPH. GRAPH
500s	Chinese sculpture and pottery reflect Western influences. SCULP

500   Woodland population centers along the entire coast of the Gulf of Mexico employ a variety of decorative techniques to produce an assortment of pottery styles. These styles feature both abstract designs and naturalistic animal forms.
DECO

500   Roman philosopher Boethius writes on musical theory in *De institutione musica*. His views that music is a corollary of mathematics and that it has a strong influence on character development will be widely held throughout the Middle Ages.
MUSIC

500   Sculptors from the ancient Gandhara region of northwest India and northern Pakistan produce small portable bronze images of Buddha standing on a

---

Outlaw Writers

The association of the literary life with legal trouble spans eras and continents. In addition to Roman poet Ovid (*see* 8, LIT), here are a few other famous writers who have had difficulties staying on the right side of the law:

- Boethius—Roman philosopher, author of *The Consolation of Philosophy*, was imprisoned for treason by Theodoric the Great, Ostrogoth ruler of Rome, and was executed in 525.
- Miguel de Cervantes—Spanish novelist, author of *Don Quixote*, which he began writing in 1605 while serving a prison term for fraud committed when he was a government tax inspector.
- John Milton—English poet, author of *Paradise Lost*, was arrested in 1660 for advocating republican government just as King Charles II was being restored to power.
- Oliver Goldsmith—English poet, playwright, and novelist narrowly escaped arrest for debt when his novel *The Vicar of Wakefield* (1766) was sold on his behalf by his friend Samuel Johnson.
- Fyodor Dostoyevsky—Russian novelist, author of *Crime and Punishment*, was arrested in 1849 and served four years in a labor camp in Siberia for political crimes.
- O. Henry (William Sydney Porter)—American short-story writer, author of the short-story collection *The Four Million* (1906), began writing stories while serving a three-year sentence for having embezzled funds when he was a bank teller.
- Aleksandr Solzhenitsyn—Russian novelist, author of *The Gulag Archipelago*, served time in Soviet labor camps for political crimes and was deported in 1974, only to return to Russia in 1994 after the fall of the Soviet Union.
- Salman Rushdie—British writer, was condemned to death in 1989 by the Iranian government, which accused him of blasphemy for writing the novel *The Satanic Verses*. He has been forced to live in hiding since.

pedestal. These Gandharan-style Buddhas will serve as prototypes for early Buddhist images and iconography throughout the Far East and South Asia. SCULP

500   An ivory diptych from the eastern Roman Empire depicts the archangel Michael in a classical style that recalls the winged Victories of Graeco-Roman art. SCULP

524   While in prison awaiting execution for treason against the Ostrogoth ruler of Rome, Theodoric the Great, Roman philosopher Boethius writes the meditative treatise *The Consolation of Philosophy*. LIT

526   The Ostrogoth ruler of Rome, Theodoric the Great, is laid to rest in what will become known as Theodoric's tomb in Ravenna. The tomb will be considered an important example of migration-period architecture. ARCH

532–535 The church of Santa Sophia (Hagia Sophia) is constructed in Constantinople. Designed by Anthemius of Tralles and Isidorus of Miletus, it will be considered the greatest masterpiece of Byzantine architecture. Its dome, 184 feet from the floor and 112 feet in diameter, appears to float on a cushion of sunlight entering through a ring of arched windows at the dome's base. ARCH

532–535 Sculptors carve new ornamental motifs, derived from classical architecture, for the moldings and capitals at the church of Santa Sophia in Constantinople. SCULP

537   In Canton, China, the Pagoda of the Temple of the Six Banyon Trees is built; it will be rebuilt in 1098. It is a prominent example of the pagoda, a type of Buddhist tower found in Nepal, China, and Japan. Pagodas will reach up to 15 stories in height and assume square, hexagonal, or octagonal shapes. ARCH

538–600 In Japan, Chinese-inspired Buddhist art is popular. SCULP

Ancient Tie-Dyeing

The craft of tie-dyeing originated in sixth-century India. Indian artisans developed the technique of producing patterns on cloth by tying portions of fabric with waxed thread or rags before dipping the cloth into a vat of dye. Skill in tying and folding the cloth resulted in a limitless number of patterns in a variety of colors, consisting of spots, small circles, transverse bands, or zigzags. This traditional craft, which was originally associated with muslin turbans, was known as bandhnu. From that Hindi word, by way of Portuguese traders, comes the modern term bandanna for a large, figured, brightly colored handkerchief.

550	Veracruz artists along the Gulf Coast of Mexico fashion the sides of stone heads to resemble the thin blade of an axe or hacha. SCULP
590–604	Developed under Pope Gregory, antiphonal Gregorian chant (plainsong) comes into use in the Roman Catholic Church,. MUSIC
600s–700s	The Bodh Gaya, Mahabodhi Temple, is constructed in Bihar, India, and becomes an important pilgrimage destination. ARCH
600s	Islamic civilization begins to develop strong craft traditions in the production of carpets, ceramics, enamel, and metalwork. DECO
600s	Because the Arabic language in which the Koran (*see* 651, LIT) is written is considered sacred, and because Islamic law forbids most kinds of representational images, great attention is paid in Islamic art to calligraphy, or handwriting as expression of beauty. GRAPH
600s	Indian poet Bhartrhari writes some of the greatest Sanskrit lyric poetry. His works include *Renunciation, Passion of Love,* and *Good Conduct.* LIT
600s	The 18-foot sculpture of Shiva, the three-headed Mahesamurti, is carved in sandstone at the Shiva Temple in India. SCULP
600	Pope Gregory reorganizes the Schola Cantorum (*see* 350, MUSIC), an important center in Rome for the training of singers and teachers throughout Europe. MUSIC
600	The crwth (also called crowd or chrotta), a Celtic stringed instrument reminiscent of the Greek kithara, is developed. MUSIC
618–907	Rod puppets appear during the T'ang dynasty in China. Originating in Bengal, the puppets have also become popular in Bali, Java, and Thailand. DRAMA
618–907	The T'ang dynasty is the golden age of Chinese poetry, notable for such poets as Wang Wei, Li Po, Po Chü-i, and Tu Fu. This is also the period during which fiction becomes established in China. LIT
618–907	Painting in China during the T'ang dynasty is marked by its refined representation of the world and a naturalistic use of color. PAINT
618–907	During China's T'ang dynasty, statues of seated Buddhas are made using a dry-lacquer technique. Numerous layers of lacquer-soaked cloth are first molded over a wooden base, then the figure is painted in gesso, polychrome, and gilt. SCULP

618–907	China's T'ang dynasty strongly informs Japanese sculpture, particularly during Japan's Nara period (710–784). Works include large bronze statues of Bodhisattva, which indicate a marriage of Chinese thinking and Japanese craftsmanship. SCULP
630–668	The seaport Mamallapuram (near what will become known as Madras) becomes an artistic center in India during the reign of Narasimha Varman I. SCULP
651	The teachings of Islam's founder, Muhammad, are collected into a volume of 114 chapters known as the Koran (Qur'an). LIT
670	Old English poet and monk Caedmon writes hymns, of which only the first, which will become known as "Caedmon's Hymn," will survive. LIT
690	Artists begin to create sandstone statues of Ganesha, the elephant-headed Hindu god of auspiciousness, during the pre-Angkor period in Southeast Asia. SCULP
691	The mosque of Omar at Jerusalem, known as the Dome of the Rock, is built, following a domed, octagonal Byzantine plan. ARCH
699–759	Chinese poet and artist Wang Wei is a leading force in the refinement of ink landscape painting, which will become a major art form in the country over the next centuries. PAINT
700s	Celtic and Germanic artists render ill-proportioned human figures as they attempt to reproduce Early Christian compositions on bronze plaques which will be used to adorn book covers. DECO
700s	*The Lindisfarne Gospels* and *The Book of Kells* are examples of the Hiberno-Saxon style of illuminating manuscripts. The pages are illustrated with interlacing patterns of hybrid animals, people, and birds, as well as jewel-like crosses. GRAPH
700s	The Old English narrative epic poem *Beowulf* is composed anonymously. Based on Norse legends fused with accounts of sixth-century Danish history (told to the English by Danish invaders), *Beowulf* recounts the adventures of the warrior Beowulf, who confronts Grendel and other monsters. LIT
700s	In the Arab world, the tradition of *adab*, or "literature," begins. These secular writings draw on Persian and Arab sources in a clear, polished Arabic prose style. LIT
700s	The xylophone is invented in Southeast Asia or Oceania. It will be introduced to Europe in the 1500s and to China in the 1700s. MUSIC

700	The Chinese invent porcelain, a form of pottery that will eventually spread to Europe under the popular name "china." DECO
700	Mayan sculptors in Mesoamerica create stelae bearing a single figure in low relief and carvings full of symbolic motifs and hieroglyphic elements. SCULP
700–1200	In northern India, the medieval age sees the creation of accomplished works of Brahmanic and Buddhist art. SCULP
701	Chinese poet Li Po (or Li T'ai-po) is born (*d.* 762). He will write some of the best known and most beautiful Chinese lyric poetry. LIT
725	In China during the T'ang dynasty, the court orchestra of Emperor Ming Huang (Li Lung-chi) employs a five-note scale without semitones, harmony, or polyphony. Gongs, drums, bells, and flutes are among the instruments used. MUSIC
726–843	An imperial Byzantine ban on religious images forces artists to use only abstract symbols, such as floral patterns and crosses, in Byzantine church decor. DECO
731	English scholar and historian the Venerable Bede publishes *Ecclesiastical History of the English People*. LIT
750	The Old English poem *The Dream of the Rood* is composed. LIT
750	Gregorian chant (plainsong) is practiced in Germany, France, and England. MUSIC
750	In western Europe, water organs are replaced by wind organs, developed in Constantinople. MUSIC
750	A new style of stone sculpture is introduced in Mesoamerica as artists from Copán, Honduras, carve human and animal figures to heroic scale from three-dimensional models rather than from drawings. SCULP
757	Arab writer Ibn al-Muqaffa' dies. A *kâtib*, or government official, he translated several works from Persian into Arabic, including *Kalîfah wa-Dimnah*. LIT
757–790	The Kailasanatha Temple is carved from the hills at Elura in India, an important site for Indian sculpture. The work offers a complex representation of the temple of Shiva. SCULP
786–987	The mosque at Cordoba, Spain, is built. It is notable for its many interior columns and its system of round, horseshoe-shaped arches. ARCH

792–805	The Palatine (or Palace) Chapel of Charlemagne is built in Aachen, Germany, following a more monumental, massive design than the domed Byzantine churches on which it is based. ARCH
800s	The Great Mosque at Samarra, Mesopotamia (Iraq), is constructed. One of the largest mosques ever built, it is notable for its spiral minaret probably modeled on Mesopotamian ziggurats. ARCH
800s	Gregorian music is recorded with neumes, notes similar to the accent marks in Greek poetry from which they are believed to derive. MUSIC
800s	As Islamic civilization spreads, it contributes musical instruments to Europe, Southeast Asia, and Africa. In Africa, new varieties of drums, lutes, reed pipes, and long trumpets are introduced. In Europe, the Arabs introduce lutes, kettledrums, and trumpets. MUSIC
800–810	Frankish king Charlemagne's gospel book, the *Coronation Gospels*, employs classical elements in its illustrations, including foreshortening and modeling (shading). GRAPH
800	Charlemagne, bearing the papal designation Emperor of the West, enacts Pope Gregory's plan for unifying the church through a common music by ordering all Gallican songbooks destroyed. MUSIC
800	Islamic law bans large-scale human or animal figures for public display. Images of living things are approved solely for small-scale or everyday objects. SCULP
800	A statue of a standing Maitreya from Nepal exhibits the influences of Indian art by depicting the tribhanga pose. This statue will be one of the country's largest bronzes. SCULP
800	For the first time in Nigeria, copper alloys are used artistically, in bronze funerary objects and figurines created by the Igbo Ukwu culture east of the Niger River. SCULP
816–835	The *Gospel Book of Archbishop Ebbo of Reims* depicts the evangelists in energetic, emotional renderings. GRAPH
820s	Wooden animal heads carved with geometric patterns are created for posts on Scandinavian Viking ships. DECO
825	Carolingian artists of Frankish king Charlemagne's court school begin to carve deeply layered ivory plaques of the four Evangelists. SCULP

850   Church modes, a system that will lead in the 17th century to major and minor
           scales, emerges.   MUSIC

855   Polyphony, music that combines several simultaneous voice parts, begins with
           "vertical" broadening of Gregorian chant.   MUSIC

855   Toltec rulers establish the city of Tollan and dominate Mesoamerican art with
           warrior motifs and images of death on columns and relief slabs.   SCULP

860   Toltec motifs influence Maya carving styles in the Yucatán Peninsula.
           Sculptural detail will be either reduced or eliminated.   SCULP

863   The Cyrillic alphabet is invented by Macedonian missionary Cyril and his
           brother Methodius. It will become the alphabet of Russians and other eastern
           peoples.   LIT

868   The earliest known dated woodcut appears in China in the Buddhist scripture
           Diamond Sutra, the first printed book.   GRAPH

869   Arab writer al-Jâhiz dies. He is known for his scholarly and witty works on
           many subjects, including philosophy, politics, and zoology.   LIT

870   *Musica enchiriadis* (*Handbook of Music*), a musical manuscript using Latin letters
           for musical notation, is the earliest treatise dealing with polyphony (therein
           termed organum).   MUSIC

897–1185   During the Fujiwara period in Japan, art reflects emphasis on worldly beauty
           and artistic finesse. One representative artist is Jōcho, creator of such works as
           the Amida Buddha, which is built of several separate pieces that are assembled
           later.   SCULP

900s   Liturgical dramas are performed in European churches. Chanted in Latin, the
           plays are characterized by biblical themes and are usually matched to the sea-
           son of the year. There is no scenery other than that provided by the interior of
           the church, and the actors—priests and choirboys and, later, possibly nuns—
           wear liturgical robes, sometimes with small additions to indicate gender and
           status. These dramas will continue to be performed for several hundred years.
                                                                                       DRAMA

900s   *Jongleurs* or *menestrels* (minstrels) perform from town to town in France, play-
           ing and singing *chansons de geste* and other secular songs.   MUSIC

900   Part song in fourths, fifths, and octaves begins to develop.   MUSIC

900	Artists of the Chola dynasty in South India cast bronze statues of Parvati, the consort of Siva, using the lost-wax process. SCULP
918–1392	In Korea during the Koryō period, pottery and porcelain are unsurpassed throughout the Far East. DECO
960–1271	During the Sung dynasty in China, porcelain and other pottery surpass others worldwide in technical and artistic excellence, with new glazes and treatments developed. Landscape painting also reaches artistic heights. MISC
962–1024	During the Ottonian period (so called for Saxon king Otto I, crowned Holy Roman Emperor in 962), Germany leads Europe in sculpture, architecture, and manuscript illumination. MISC
975	The Exeter Book is compiled, preserving such Old English poems as "The Wanderer," "The Seafarer," "The Phoenix," "Widsith," "The Whale," "Christ," "Deor," "Juliana," "Wulf and Eadwacer," "The Husband's Message," and "The Wife's Complaint." LIT
975	An Ottonian sculptor rejects Byzantine tradition by carving a more monumental, expressive image of Christ for a wooden crucifix. The powerful realism displayed in the crucifix will become a strong element in German art. SCULP
980	Graeco-Roman iconography influences Byzantine styles as sculptors carve scenes of Greek mythology on ivory caskets intended for wedding gifts. DECO
980	A 400-pipe organ is in use at Winchester Monastery, England. MUSIC
991	Viking invaders and Saxon defenders clash near Maldon in Essex, England. The incident is recounted in the Old English poem "The Battle of Maldon," written shortly afterward. LIT
1000s	The Kandariya Mahadeva temple at Khajuraho in north central India is constructed. Its many stone towers contribute to the effect of a single monumental tower. ARCH
1000s	Africans construct the great wall and highly decorated buildings of the city of Zimbabwe, the ruins of which will be found by Europeans in 1870. ARCH
1000s	A mosaic in the dome of the monastery church at Daphne, Greece, depicts Christ as Pantocrator, or stern judge of humankind. This is an image frequently found in Byzantine churches of this period. DECO

1000s	The oldest surviving books in India are illuminated palm-leaf manuscripts of Pala Buddhist and Jain scripture from this period. Such manuscripts had been produced since before the first century A.D. GRAPH
1000s	Anglo-Norman prelate Theobald writes the first medieval bestiary, the Latin *Physiologus*. The form, which presents allegorical and descriptive verses about animals real and imaginary, will be popular in the 12th and 13th centuries. LIT
1000s	In European church music, Gregorian chant (plainsong) gives way to polyphonic singing. MUSIC
1000s	The jongleurs, or minstrels, of France organize into brotherhoods, which will evolve into guilds. MUSIC
1000s	In China Fan K'uan is the northern Sung dynasty's greatest landscape painter. PAINT
1000s	The work of Chinese artist and monk Chü-jan epitomizes Chinese landscape painting style and influences Chinese painters for centuries afterward. His works, which include "Seeking the Tao in the Autumn Mountains," reflect the more pleasant landscapes of southern China and project a natural unity, without a single element dominating the scene. PAINT
1000s	By now, Buddhist icons in Indian art often combine much decoration with a remote countenance. SCULP
1000	In Germany, the illuminations of the *Gospel Book of Otto III* blend Carolingian and Byzantine elements. The book is made at the Reichenau Monastery, one of the greatest centers of manuscript illumination during this period. GRAPH
1000	Japanese court lady and writer Murasaki Shikibu writes the novel *Tale of Genji*. Translated into English by Arthur Waley in 1925–1933, it will be considered by many the world's first novel. LIT
1000	Italian music theorist and monk Guido d'Arezzo invents the musical staff, the arrangement of horizontal lines on which music is written. MUSIC
1000	Neumes, early music notations, show more specific musical intervals, manner of performance, and pitch. MUSIC
1000	In the Islamic world, arabesque, a style that employs scrolling or interlacing plant ornamentation, becomes an important motif. PAINT
1000	The West African Djenne civilization in Mali creates ceramic statuettes of kneeling figures with crossed arms and hands placed on shoulders. Most Djenne figurative terra-cottas will feature this pose. SCULP

1000	Artists of the Late Heian period in Japan produce a bronze statue of Zao Gongen, the tutelary deity of Mount Kimpu in the Yoshino Mountains. The statue's active pose will become a conventional mode for the representation of Buddhist guardian figures. SCULP
1001–1033	In Germany the Hildesheim cathedral (St. Michael's), commissioned by Bernward, bishop of Hildesheim, is a prominent example of Ottonian architecture. ARCH
1015	Bishop Bernward of Hildesheim commissions a pair of bronze doors for the two entrances leading to the ambulatory in St. Michael's Church at Hildesheim. The doors will differ from Roman and Byzantine doors by featuring biblical scenes in high relief carved into individual, horizontal fields. SCULP
1023	Construction begins on Durham cathedral in England. Its solidity of design makes it a prime example of Romanesque architecture. ARCH
1026	Italian music theorist and monk Guido d'Arezzo introduces solmization, a system of syllables used for designating degrees of the scale (do, re, mi, fa, sol, la, ti). MUSIC
1041	In China movable type made from clay blocks is used by printer Pi Sheng. GRAPH
1063	Construction begins on St. Mark's in Venice, a lavishly decorated Byzantine church that follows the plan of the Greek cross (a central dome with four projecting arms of equal length). ARCH
1082–1135	In China, the patronage of Emperor Hui-tsung sets a standard for Eastern rulers, generating decades of fine work, notably in bird and flower paintings. PAINT
c. 1090	Sculptors decorate the pilgrimage church of St. Sernin at Toulouse in southern France with massive, Roman-style figures of the Apostles. SCULP
1100s–1300s	Hoysala forces take power in India and build ornate temples that contrast with the sleek, geometric Pallava temples of the recent past. ARCH
1100s	The anonymous French epic *Chanson de Roland* (*The Song of Roland*) is composed, telling of Frankish king Charlemagne's paladin Roland and his heroic death at the Battle of Roncesvalles. LIT
1100s	The Middle English lyric "The Cuckoo Song" is written, which begins "Sumer is ycomen in, /Loude sing cuckou!" LIT
1100s	German monk Theophilus writes *De diversis artibus*, the most important extant treatise on medieval European arts and crafts. It makes mention of techniques

for producing oil paint centuries before it will become the dominant medium for Western painting. *See* 1500s, PAINT.   PAINT

1100s   The Yoruba from the eastern part of Benin and southwestern Nigeria cast portrait heads in the lost-wax technique. This method will become common to many West African metalwork traditions.   SCULP

1100s   Sculptors in Tuscany revive an interest in Late Antique and Early Christian art in the execution of New Testament scenes carved on marble sarcophagi. SCULP

c. 1100–1200   The music school of the Abbey of St. Martial in Limoges applies the polyphonic style in sequences and sacred music.   MUSIC

c. 1100–1400   During the southern Sung dynasty in China, landscape painting becomes less monumental than in the past and more intimate and poetic.   PAINT

c. 1100   A more animated style of carving becomes characteristic of numerous Spanish Romanesque ivory plaques.   SCULP

c. 1100   The portal sculpture of the abbey at Moissac, north of Toulouse, rejects earlier Romanesque stiffness. Sculptors decorate the trumeau and jamb with fluid, Moorish-influenced human and animal forms.   SCULP

c. 1100   A wood and gold leaf guardian statue of Fudo Myo-O becomes the central icon of the Kuhonji Gomado during the Late Heian period in Funasaka, Japan, northwest of Kyoto.   SCULP

c. 1100   The Chancay people from Peru's central coast produce ceramic scenes illustrating the daily activities of village houses. They also produce wooden human figures and mummy masks.   SCULP

1113–1150   Khmer emperor Suryavarman II supervises the building of the temple complex Angkor Wat in Cambodia. Notable for its sculptural ornamentation, it will be sacked and abandoned in 1177.   ARCH

1118   French philosopher and theologian Peter Abelard consummates his affair with his student Héloïse. After he is later castrated by her irate uncle, he will become a monk and she a nun. Their exchange of letters will enter the literature of star-crossed love.   LIT

1125   In southern France poet-musicians called troubadours establish a tradition of songs in the vernacular. In the mid-12th century, the movement spreads to northern France (trouvères) and Germany (minnesingers).   MUSIC

c. 1125	Classical monuments influence the development of Romanesque style throughout Provence, France. Statues for church portals will be carved almost entirely in the round with rich details. SCULP

| 1127 | St. Bernard of Clairvaux denounces the sculptured decoration of churches as diversions that tempt churchgoers to read in marble rather than in books. SCULP |

| c. 1135 | English ecclesiastic and chronicler Geoffrey of Monmouth publishes the chronicle *History of the Kings of Britain* in Latin, one of the main sources of Arthurian legend drawn upon by later writers. LIT |

| c. 1135 | Northern Romanesque artists in Cologne choose walrus ivory over elephant ivory to carve scenes depicting the Infancy and Passion of Christ. The pricked drapery will become a hallmark of the Cologne style. SCULP |

| 1137 | The abbey of St. Denis near Paris, designed by Abbé Suger, is one of the first major examples of Gothic architecture. Distinctive features include flying buttresses, pointed ribbed vaults, light upright supports, and stained-glass windows, all of which contribute to an impression of interior openness and light. ARCH |

| 1145 | Sculptors begin to carve the portals of Chartres cathedral in France in an Early Gothic style that emphasizes order and clarity. The cathedral will be rebuilt after a fire in 1195. The new transept façades will receive three large and lavishly sculpted portals by 1220. SCULP |

| c. 1150–1250 | The period later called "ars antiqua" is represented by the musical forms organum, clausula, conductus, and most significantly, the motet. Its greatest advances are the use of three and four voice parts and the establishment of strict rhythm based on rules called the rhythm modes. MUSIC |

| c. 1150 | Formal and symmetrical polychromed-oak statues of the Virgin and Child enthroned become popular in the Auvergne region of France. SCULP |

| 1151 | Léonin (Leoninus), French composer and master of the school of Notre Dame, composes for two-part organ in what will be called the "ars antiqua" style. MUSIC |

| c. 1160–1190 | The Arthurian romances of French poet Chrétien de Troyes include *Yvain, or the Knight of the Lion; Eric and Enide; Launcelot, or the Knight of the Cart;* and *Percival, or the Story of the Grail.* LIT |

| c. 1160 | A vigorously carved statue of the Annunciation to the Virgin is completed for the apse of the Romanesque church of San Martin in the village of Fuentidueña, north of Madrid. SCULP |

1163	Construction begins on the cathedral of Notre Dame de Paris, a major achievement of early Gothic architecture. Famous for its sculptures, portals, and rose window, it will be mostly completed by 1250, although additions will be made into the 14th century. ARCH

c. 1170   German poet Wolfram von Eschenbach is born (*d. c. 1220*). His works include *Willehalm, Parzival,* and *Titurel.* LIT

c. 1180   Italian sculptor and architect Benedetto Antelami attempts to recapture the classical contrapposto for his statue of David which will be placed on the facade of the Fidenza cathedral in Lombardy. SCULP

1182   Artists from Khurasan, Persia (Iran), create a bronze incense burner in the shape of a stylized, smoke-breathing animal. DECO

1184   The cathedral at Sens, France, designed by William of Sens, will be considered an important example of early Gothic architecture. ARCH

1185–1568   In the Kamakura and Muromachi periods in Japan, narratives known as *Gunki monogatari,* or "medieval war tales," are written. Emphasizing martial virtues such as courage and loyalty, they depict the Japanese civil wars of 1156–1221. LIT

1185–1333   In Japan, the Kamakura dictatorship shows itself in a more vigorous, virile artistic style. Two central sculptors of the era are Kōkei and Unkei; the painting style developed during the time is known as Yamato-e, or Japanese, painting. PAINT

1190–c. 1240   In China, the Ma-Hsia school dominates painting styles. Created by artists Ma Yüan and Hsia Kuei, the school is characterized by its lyricism. PAINT

1193   Beginning with the victory of Islam over Hindus in India, many temples are destroyed and mosques built. Among them is the Quwwat ul-Islam, or "Might of Islam." ARCH

1193   Indigo is imported from India to Europe for use in dying fabrics. DECO

1194   A fire destroys most of Chartres cathedral in France (*see* 1145, SCULP), leading to a reconstruction that will be completed early in the 13th century. Its graceful interior nave, masterful stained glass, and strong vertical orientation mark it as the first major example of High Gothic architecture. ARCH

1200s   Caddoan workshops from the Mississippi River valley craft massive figurative pipes to be smoked on ritual occasions. DECO

1200s	The Mississippian culture of North America produces carved sandstone masks and stone ceremonial axes engraved with figurative and facial designs. This Mississippian effigy tradition will be continued by the Cherokee Indians in the making of stone pipes until the 18th century. DECO
1200s	Karagoz, shadow puppet shows, are presented throughout the Middle East. They will remain popular for centuries to come, especially in the Ottoman Empire. DRAMA
1200s	Mystery plays, depicting biblical events or the lives of saints, and morality plays, instructing through entertainment, are performed in Europe. Mystery plays derive from liturgical drama (see 900s, DRAMA) but differ in several ways: words are spoken rather than chanted, the vernacular is used, and the plays are presented outdoors on portable wagons; in addition, the actors are often lay people and props are used. Morality plays, staged by preaching friars, will be popular for several centuries. DRAMA
1200s	The portative organ, a small portable organ, is used in Europe. It is played only with the right hand while a small bellows is operated with the left. A related instrument, the positive organ, is placed on a table and requires an assistant for the bellows. MUSIC
1200s	In the Far East, Zen Buddhism infuses artistic styles with economy and spiritual sensibility. PAINT
1200s	The Etowah culture from the Mississippi River valley sculpt images of their founding ancestors in stone and wood. These cult figures will be placed in shrine houses and will appear for nearly two centuries. SCULP
1200	In Germany, Latin monastic songs are preserved in a collection called the *Carmina Burana*. In 1937 they will be set to new music for voices and orchestra by German composer Carl Orff. MUSIC
1200	Neumes take on a square shape and will continue to maintain this form in the book of Roman Catholic Church chants. MUSIC
1200–1400	Gothic painting in northern Europe is best represented by illuminations on manuscript pages, while in Italy painters turn to large-scale panels and frescoes. Italian painters of the period include Cimabue, Giotto, and Duccio. PAINT
c. 1200	Ateliers of Limoges in the Limousin region of France produce six plaques consisting of gilded figures attached to an enamel ground for the altar of the abbey of Grandmont. SCULP

c. 1210   German poet Gottfried von Strassburg writes the unfinished epic *Tristan und Isolde*.   LIT

1212   In Japan Kamo Chōmei writes *Hojo-ki* (*An Account of My Hut*), a personal narrative infused with Buddhist attitudes.   LIT

1220s   German masters trained in the sculptural workshops of the great French cathedrals transplant a new Gothic style throughout Germany. Most sculptural work in Germany will be done for church interiors rather than exteriors.   SCULP

1220–1260   Salisbury cathedral is constructed, a prominent example of early Gothic architecture in England.   ARCH

1220–1270   In France, Amiens cathedral is constructed, an example of the refinement of Gothic architecture.   ARCH

c. 1225   Masters and workshops from various other building sites begin work on the vast sculptural program for Reims cathedral in France. The work will be completed by 1245 in a High Gothic style that will echo the monumental classicism of large-scale Roman sculpture.   SCULP

1231   The Mongol invasion nearly decimates fine arts in Korea over the next decades. MISC

c. 1240   Parisian masters working for the royal court create the "S-curve" design for figurative sculpture. This pattern will become standard in High Gothic sculpture. SCULP

c. 1250   An anonymous English writer composes the only surviving Middle English bestiary. *See also* 1000s, LIT.   LIT

1250   Franco of Cologne, who will be regarded as the inventor of time signatures, writes about the notation of time values for musical notes. His system will remain in use until 1600.   MUSIC

1250   Pérotin (Perotinus), master of the school of Notre Dame and the foremost representative of French *ars antiqua*, composes organa in three and four parts. Some of the short two-part compositions (clausulae) by Pérotin and his collaborator will be transformed into motets. *See also* c. 1150–1250 and 1265, MUSIC.   MUSIC

c. 1250   The Naumburg Master completes his statues and reliefs for the choir screen at Naumburg cathedral in Germany.   SCULP

1257–1289   French sculptors carve the doorway decorations for the monastery church of Moutiers-St.-Jean in Burgundy in a typically High Gothic style.   SCULP

1260	Italian sculptor Nicola Pisano finishes the carving of his Roman-influenced narrative scenes for a marble pulpit in the baptistery of Pisa cathedral. Beginning in 1302, his son Giovanni will also furnish a marble pulpit for the cathedral but in the elegant, Gothic style of the French royal court. SCULP
1265	Franco of Cologne and Pierre de la Croix develop the motet, a central form of early polyphonic music. Frequently a three-part composition, it flourishes throughout the century. MUSIC
1270	Chinese painter Mu-ch'i Fa-ch'ang paints *Six Persimmons*. PAINT
c. 1280–1290	Italian painter Bencivieni di Pepo, known as Cimabue, executes the panel painting *Madonna Enthroned with St. Francis*. His formal approach, incorporating both abstract Byzantine and some naturalistic elements, will become known as neo-Byzantine style or the Greek manner. PAINT
1285	French musician and playwright Adam de la Halle creates *Le Jeu de Robin et Marion*. Written for the Anjou court in Naples, it will be regarded as the first comic opera. MUSIC
1285	Italian painter Duccio (Duccio di Buoninsegna) paints the *Rucellai Madonna* in Florence. PAINT
1290s	The unidentified Master of the St. Francis Cycle paints the frescoes, depicting the life of St. Francis, on the nave walls of the Upper Church of San Francesco in Assisi, Italy. The frescos will sometimes be attributed to Florentine painter Giotto and dated as late as the 1320s, though these claims will be contested. PAINT
1290s	French sculptors, working from oak, carve groups of angels carrying either candlesticks or the instruments of Christ's passion. These sculptures are placed on the tops of columns around church altars. SCULP
c. 1290	Italian poet Dante Alighieri composes *La vita nuova* (*The New Life*), a collection of poems and prose inspired by his love for Beatrice. Later important works will include *De vulgari eloquentia* (*On the Vernacular Tongue*, 1304–1306) and *De monarchia* (*On World Government* or *On Monarchy*, c. 1313). *See also* 1307–1321, LIT. LIT
1296	Construction begins on Florence cathedral in Italy, which combines the pointed ribbed vaults of French Gothic architecture with a classical exterior. A dome will be added in the 15th century. ARCH

1300s   Chinese pottery is revolutionized by the development of underglazing of
               pieces with blue cobalt. The underglaze produces unsurpassed resonance and
               color.   DECO

1300s   Major cycles of English mystery (or miracle) plays, which flourish this centu-
               ry, include the York Cycle, the Wakefield (or Towneley) Cycle, and the Chester
               Cycle. In the 1400s, the Coventry (or N Town) Cycle will be added. *See also*
               1200s, DRAMA.   DRAMA

1300s   Passion plays, dramas depicting the last days of Christ's life on earth, are staged
               in Europe. They will remain popular through the next century. An elaborate
               passion play will continue to be staged every ten years in Oberammergau,
               Germany.   DRAMA

1300s   Lauda, religious performances involving choral singing, dialogue, and narra-
               tion, become popular in Italy.   DRAMA

1300s   The tradition of Nō, carefully structured performances including the recitation
               of stories from classical literature and rhythmic dancing, begins in Japan. A
               complete Nō performance consists of five plays, each with a different theme.
                                                                                   DRAMA

1300s   Chinese novelist Lo Kuan-chung writes the sprawling historical novel *San Kuo
               chih yen-i* (*The Romance of the Three Kingdoms*).   LIT

1300s   In India, the illustration of books becomes popular. Commonly illustrated
               titles include the *Gita Govinda*, the *Baramasas*, and *Bhagavata Purana*.   PAINT

1300s   The Virgin with Child becomes a frequent subject for votive statues in parish
               churches, cathedrals, oratories, and monastic chapels throughout France,
               Germany, and the Netherlands.   SCULP

c. 1300   Artists from the Late Mississippian period create stone, terra-cotta, and wood-
               en images depicting the deceased. These figures will guard the remains of the
               dead in temples.   SCULP

1301   Italian sculptor Giovanni Pisano carves a marble lectern in the shape of an
               eagle for the pulpit of the church of Sant' Andrea in Pistoia. He will produce
               other such eagles in Siena and Perugia.   DECO

1304–1374   Italian poet Petrarch lives. He composes the influential poetry of *Rime* or
               Rime sparse (*Scattered Lyrics*) and the prose works *De viris illustribus* (*On
               Illustrious Men*) and *De vita solitaria* (*On the Solitary Life*).   LIT

c. 1305–
1306
Florentine painter Giotto (Giotto di Bondone) paints the fresco cycle of the Arena Chapel at Padua, a work that displays his skill at conveying narrative and emotion. Regarded as the father of modern Western painting, he introduces new naturalistic ideals and powerful, solid figures in marked contrast to earlier Byzantine conventions.   PAINT

c. 1305–
1310
Florentine painter Giotto is probably the creator of the unsigned panel painting *Ognissanti Madonna*.   PAINT

1307–1321
Italian poet Dante Alighieri writes the epic that will come to be known as *The Divine Comedy*. Consisting of *Inferno*, *Purgatorio*, and *Paradiso*, the 100-canto work tells of the poet's journey through the worlds of the afterlife, guided by the spirit of the Roman poet Virgil. The epic begins, "In the middle of the journey of our life I came to myself within a dark wood where the straight way was lost."   LIT

1308–1311
Italian artist Duccio paints the altarpiece *Maesta* (*Majesty*) for Siena cathedral in Italy. Duccio is an important innovator, reworking neo-Byzantine conventions.   PAINT

c. 1310–
1430
Ars nova, "new style art," is the term coined by French prelate Philippe de Vitry for the new, strongly contrapuntal style of music.   MUSIC

1315
Italian painter Simone Martini, a follower of Duccio and a major innovator in the international Gothic style, paints the large fresco of the *Maesta* in the Siena town hall, combining Byzantine and Gothic conventions. He will rework it in 1321.
                                                                                    PAINT

1317
In Naples, Italian painter Simone Martini paints an altarpiece of St. Louis of Toulouse, with predella (subsidiary) scenes presenting the most innovative use of perspective to date.   PAINT

1322
Pope John XXII issues a decree at Avignon, banning the use of counterpoint in church music.   MUSIC

1332–1357
Gloucester cathedral is constructed. The cathedral is an example of High Gothic architecture in England, characterized by the Perpendicular style, which employs ceiling vaults with complex decorative networks of ribs. ARCH

1333
Italian painters (and brothers-in-law) Simone Martini and Lippo Memmi paint the *Annunciation*.   PAINT

1334
Florentine painter Giotto is appointed architect to Florence cathedral, although the design will be altered after his death in 1337.   ARCH

1340	French poet and composer Guillaume de Machaut, among the first to use music as a form of artistic expression, is a leading composer of this century and will be considered the bridge between ars antiqua (*see* c.1150–1250, MUSIC) and ars nova (*see* c.1310–1430, MUSIC). His sacred and secular music will include 23 motets. MUSIC
1342	In Avignon, while serving the papal court, Italian painter Simone Martini paints *Christ Reproved by His Parents*. PAINT
c. 1350	Chinese influence is exhibited in the painted images of Persian illuminated manuscripts, such as the *Summer Landscape* in *Album of the Conqueror* (Sultan Mohammed II). GRAPH
c. 1350–1400	The Middle English poetic romance *Sir Gawain and the Green Knight* is composed, as are the poems "Pearl," "Patience," and "Cleanness." LIT
1350–1352	Italian writer and poet Giovanni Boccaccio writes the *Decameron*, a collection of tales whose framing story is set in 1348, the year of the Black Death. LIT
1350–1400	English poet William Langland composes the allegorical poem *Piers Plowman*. LIT
1350–1400	The anonymous mystical treatise *The Cloud of Unknowing* is written in England. LIT
c. 1350–1550	The mastersinger movement in Germany is a popular development upon the tradition of minnesingers (*see* 1125, MUSIC). MUSIC
1350–1400	Jain traders bring paper, which by the mid-16th century replaces palm-leaf as a painting surface, to India. Paper expands vertical possibilities for the form and entertains Persian influences. PAINT
1360s	The Yoruban civilization of Ita Yemoo in Nigeria creates a series of small terracotta figures wearing crowns before casting them in bronze. SCULP
1360	The stringed keyboard instruments, the clavichord and cembalo (harpsichord), begin to develop. MUSIC
1364	French poet and composer Guillaume de Machaut's Mass for Four Voices, the first to be written in four parts, is composed for the coronation of Charles V at Reims. MUSIC
1368–1644	In China during the Ming era, porcelain is decorated in blue and white, with growing refinements in body and glaze. DECO
1368–1644	During the Ming dynasty, Chinese art reaches its greatest artistic flowering, inspiring the modern Chinese aesthetic. MISC

1368–1644	During the Ming dynasty in China, painting becomes largely the practice of the cultured and literate, the Confucian scholar-administrator class. Their art becomes known as Wen-jên-hua, or "literary men's painting." Painters of the era include Shên Chou, Hsing Shêng-mo, and Tai Chin. **PAINT**
1369	English poet Geoffrey Chaucer writes the poem *The Book of the Duchess*. **LIT**
1372–1380	During this period, English poet Geoffrey Chaucer writes *House of Fame* and some lyric poems. **LIT**
1375–1425	The international Gothic style, marked by fine naturalistic detail and aristocratic elegance, becomes common in painting, sculpture, and the decorative arts in northern Europe and Italy. **MISC**
1378	As the papacy returns from the "Babylonian captivity" in Avignon, bringing its court musicians with it, Rome starts to become the center of European music. **MUSIC**
1380–1386	During these years, English poet Geoffrey Chaucer writes the poems *Parlement of Foules*, *Troilus and Criseyde*, *Legend of Good Women*, some short poems, and the prose work *Boece*. **LIT**
c. 1385	*The Second Shepherds' Play*, written by the unnamed Wakefield Master, is the finest English example of a mystery play. It is the second of two plays in the Wakefield (or Towneley) cycle depicting the shepherds' adoration of the infant Jesus. *See also* 1300s, DRAMA. **DRAMA**
1385–1393	Dutch sculptor Claus Sluter executes his elaborate sculptural program for the Chartreuse of Champmol while working for the Duke of Burgundy at Dijon. The project includes his powerful figures for the Well of Moses. Sluter's rendering of character type and expressive handling of drapery will earn him the title of founder of the Burgundian school. **SCULP**
c. 1387–1400	English poet Geoffrey Chaucer composes his unfinished Middle English masterpiece, *The Canterbury Tales*, a collection of poetic tales told by pilgrims who are journeying to Canterbury. It begins, "Whan that Aprill with his shoures soote." **LIT**
c. 1387	English writer Thomas Usk writes *The Testament of Love*, an allegorical prose work. **LIT**
1391–1392	English poet Geoffrey Chaucer writes the prose work *A Treatise on the Astrolabe*. **LIT**
1391–1465	French poet Charles, duc d'Orléans, lives. "Oft in My Thought" and "My Ghostly Father" are among his poems. **LIT**

1394–1427	Japanese architects build the Kinkaku, or Golden Pavilion, in Kyoto. Like the Ginkaku, or Silver Pavilion (c. 1500), also in Kyoto, the edifice is built as a Zen center for meditation and recreation. ARCH
1400s	Chinese enamelwork is now done in cloisonné and Chinese lacquer is developed for decorative arts. DECO
1400s	In Japan, the Tosa family of painters, who emphasize playfulness, counter the Kanō School and become important to the development of Japanese arts and crafts. DECO
1400s	Masque, a type of theatrical show involving music, poetry reading, and elaborate costumes and scenery, becomes popular in Italy and France. It will come into vogue in England in the 16th century. DRAMA
1400s	Early this century, English mystic Margery Kempe writes the autobiographical work *The Book of Margery Kempe*. LIT
1400s	The Early Renaissance period takes shape in Florence, with painters, sculptors, architects, and writers taking inspiration from Classical models to express a humanistic spirit. Prominent Florentine patrons of the arts include most notably the Medici, the ruling family of Florence and Tuscany for most of this period. Their most famous son is Lorenzo the Magnificent (1449–1492), himself a humanist poet. The century becomes known as the *quattrocento* ("four hundred"). MISC
1400s	The simple three-part harmony known as *faux bourdon* (false bars) is used in English and continental music composition. MUSIC
1400s	Early this century, Florentine architect Filippo Brunelleschi invents scientific perspective, a systematic, mathematically based method of representing depth on a flat surface. Put into practice by the Florentine painter Masaccio, the technique will be essential to Western painting until the late 19th century. *See* 1425–1428, PAINT. PAINT
1400s	Early Renaissance painters in Italy use fresco and tempera as their major media. Fresco, in which pigment is applied to a fresh lime-plaster ground, dates from Classical antiquity. Tempera, in which pigment is mixed with a gum or glue, especially egg, has been used in Europe since the early 13th century. Both media are water-based. *See also* 1500s, PAINT. PAINT
1400s	The palette, a flat board with a hole for the thumb, used for arranging paints, first appears in Europe. Until now, individual containers have been used for mixing paints. PAINT

1400s	In Japan, the Kanō School of painting establishes itself through the works of professional court painters Kanō Masanobu (c. 1434-1530) and Kanō Motonobu (1475–1550). A powerful force in Japanese art, the Chinese-influenced Kanō School will continue into the 19th century. PAINT
1400s	Early this century, humanists and artists in Italy begin to collect ancient sculpture, especially small bronzes. Contemporary artists will produce portrait busts and bronzes of their own patterned after antique models. SCULP
1400s	The Death of the Virgin becomes a popular subject in 15th-century art. Sculptural compositions will be based on the iconography of many Netherlandish (Flemish) paintings. SCULP
1400s	At the height of the Benin empire in Nigeria, bronze and ivory sculpture flourishes. SCULP
c. 1400–1425	The first extant European woodcuts (in which a wodcut block is used to print a page) are religious images, probably distributed at pilgrimage sites. Woodcut playing-cards appear by 1450. GRAPH
c. 1400	English mystic Julian of Norwich writes the prose work *A Revelation of Divine Love*. LIT
1402	Florentine sculptor Lorenzo Ghiberti wins a competition to decorate the doors for the Baptistery in Florence. He will complete a total of 28 bronze panels for the doors in 1424. SCULP
c. 1410	The anonymous Franco-Flemish manuscript illuminator known as the Boucicaut Master completes a "book of hours" that is a prime example of the international Gothic style. GRAPH
1411–1413	Florentine sculptor Donatello, one of the greatest European sculptors of this century, executes the *St. Mark*, the first in a series of standing figures in niches for Orsanmichele and Florence cathedral. The series will include the *St. George* (c. 1415–1417) and end with the *Zuccone* (probably 1436). Donatello's fresh conception of the human figure, drawing on classical models, helps to define Renaissance style. SCULP
1414	Florentine sculptor Nanni di Banco completes four marble statues of saints, the *Quattro Coronati*, for one of the niches on the exterior of Orsanmichele in Florence. SCULP
1416	Flemish manuscript illuminators the Limburg (Limbourg) brothers, Herman, Jean (Jannequin), and Paul (Pol), die, probably from plague. Their most

famous work, characteristic of international Gothic style, is the book of hours entitled *Très Riches Heures du Duc de Berry*.   GRAPH

1417   Florentine sculptor Donatello creates the bronze plaque of *St. George Slaying the Dragon*, illustrating a scene in depth with the illusion of perspective for the first time in carved relief.   SCULP

1420s   In northern Europe, especially Flanders, Flemish artists such as Robert Campin (the Master of Flémalle) and Jan and Hubert van Eyck begin to experiment with oil as a medium for panel painting. Campin paints the *Mérode Altarpiece*, with the Annunciation as his subject (c. 1425–1430); the van Eycks paint the *Ghent Altarpiece* (c. 1425–1432), which uses atmospheric perspective. Its depictions of Adam and Eve are the first large-scale nudes in northern European panel painting.   PAINT

1420–1436   Florentine architect Brunelleschi gains fame as an architect for the enormous, double-shell dome he constructs for the Florence cathedral. He originates Renaissance architectural style through his creative elaboration on Roman models.   ARCH

1421   Florentine architect Brunelleschi begins the San Lorenzo church, one of his several churches epitomizing the Early Renaissance architectural values of serene harmony and rational order.   ARCH

c. 1425   *The Castle of Perseverance* is a prime example of medieval English morality plays. It is the earliest in the collection known as the Macro Plays, which also include *Mankind* (c. 1473) and *Wisdom, Who Is Christ* (c. 1460). Morality plays depict human dilemmas through the use of allegorical figures such as Covetousness, Flesh, World, and Good Deeds. *See also* c. 1495, DRAMA.   DRAMA

1425–1428   Florentine painter Tommaso di Giovanni di Simone Guidi, known as Masaccio, paints the polyptych for the Carmelite church in Pisa. In Florence, he paints the fresco of St. Peter in the Brancacci Chapel, Santa Maria del Carmine, and the fresco entitled *Trinity* in Santa Maria Novella. In his short life (1401–1428), he becomes highly influential by employing scientific perspective, using a single consistent light source, and applying to painting characteristics of Donatello's sculpture, particularly the clothed nude and contrapposto. Masaccio is also noted for drawing inspiration from Giotto in depicting grand, weighty figures.   PAINT

1425   Florentine sculptor Donatello makes a gilt bronze panel depicting the Feast of Herod for the baptismal font of San Giovanni in Siena, using Brunelleschi's system of linear perspective.   SCULP

1430   Florentine architect Brunelleschi begins work on the Pazzi Chapel.   ARCH

1430   The Burgundian school of music (centered in the duchy of Burgundy, includ-
              ing what will become the Netherlands, Belgium, and eastern France), is the
              center of European music. Its composers include Guillaume Dufay and Gilles
              Binchois.   MUSIC

c. 1430   Sienese sculptor Jacopo della Quercia rediscovers the ancient beauty of the
              nude in his marble relief *The Creation of Adam*. His nude figures will later influ-
              ence Michelangelo's compositions.   SCULP

1430   Florentine sculptor Donatello completes his bronze statue *David*, the first life-
              size nude statue since antiquity to be completely free-standing.   SCULP

1433–1434   Flemish painter Jan van Eyck paints *Man in a Red Turban* (1433) and *Giovanni
              Arnolfini and His Bride* (1434), also known as *The Arnolfini Wedding*.   PAINT

c. 1435   Florentine painter Tommaso di Cristoforo Fini, known as Masolino, paints the
              fresco *Baptism of Christ*.   PAINT

c. 1435   Flemish painter Rogier van der Weyden paints *Descent from the Cross*.   PAINT

c. 1435   Italian sculptor Luca Della Robbia carves the Cantoria, a variety of marble
              reliefs for the Florence cathedral. He will later concentrate on sculpture in
              terra-cotta and run a workshop to produce small Madonna panels and altar-
              pieces for village churches.   SCULP

1436   Italian artist, architect, and art theorist Leon Battista Alberti writes a treatise on
              painting in *Della pittura*, which contains the first explanation of scientific per-
              spective (credited to Brunelleschi). The most important art theorist of the
              Renaissance, Alberti will also write on architecture and sculpture.   PAINT

1437   Counterpoint in musical composition is developed by English composer John
              Dunstable.   MUSIC

1437   Florentine painter Fra Filippo Lippi begins painting the *Barbadori Altarpiece*,
              one of the first examples of the *sacra conversazione*, a depiction of the Virgin
              and Child with saints in a single scene. Fra Angelico, Domenico Veneziano,
              and others will also paint in this genre.   PAINT

1440s   Florentine painter Fra Filippo Lippi helps to popularize tondi, paintings cir-
              cular in shape.   PAINT

1440s   Italian painter Domenico Veneziano paints the altarpiece for Santa Lucia dei
              Magnoli and the fresco cycle *Scenes from the Life of the Virgin*; the latter will not
              survive.   PAINT

1440s	During the reign of Aztec king Montezuma I in Tenochtitlán, Mexico, a new style of sculpture emerges. Sculptors translate Aztec myths pictorially in relief. SCULP
1443–1453	Florentine sculptor Donatello works in Padua, where he produces the bronze monument of Gattamelata, the first life-size equestrian statue since antiquity. He also executes the sculptural decoration for the High Altar of the church of San Antonio. SCULP
1445–1460	The *Lochamer Liederbuch*, one of the earliest collections of German polyphonic songs, is compiled. It contains both monophonic melodies and three-part settings with tenor melody. MUSIC
1446–1451	Italian painter and writer Leon Battista Alberti builds the Palazzo Rucellai, which makes use of superimposed orders (classical orders placed one on top of another on the surface of a multistoried wall, as in the Roman Colosseum). He will also become known for his churches, including San Andrea and San Sebastiano in Mantua. ARCH
1450s	Florentine sculptors revive the ancient Roman tradition of realistic portrait sculpture. SCULP
1450	In Europe block books are introduced, in which a woodcut block combining text and illustrations is used to print an entire page. By 1480, the time-consuming process will have been made obsolete by Gutenberg's invention of movable metal type. *See* 1454, GRAPH. GRAPH
1450	The Chinese print pages using movable wooden type. GRAPH
c. 1450–1600	The Flemish school of composers (living in what will become Holland, Belgium, and northern France), gains dominance in Western music. Its members include Jean d'Okeghem, Josquin Desprez, Jacob Obrecht, Adriaan Willaert, and Orlando di Lasso. MUSIC
c. 1450	Florentine sculptor and architect Bernardo Rossellino erects his marble tomb of Leonardo Bruno in the church of Santa Croce in Florence. His composition of a figure lying over a sarcophagus flanked by ornamented pilasters will become the prototype of the Renaissance monument. SCULP
c. 1452–1465	Italian painter Piero della Francesca paints the fresco cycle *Legend of the True Cross* in San Francesco in Arezzo. His style combines weighty grandeur in the tradition of Masaccio with an even more pronounced attention to geometric structure. PAINT

1452–1466	Florentine painter Fra Filippo Lippi paints the fresco cycle on Saint Stephen and Saint John the Baptist in Prato cathedral. Lippi will be remembered for his linear, decorative style. **PAINT**
1454	Using movable metal type in a printing press of his own invention, Johannes Gutenberg of Germany prints his first 300 copies of the Bible in Latin. The Gutenberg Bible is the first book in Europe to be printed with movable type. **GRAPH**
c. 1455	Florentine painter Paolo Uccello demonstrates his passion for scientific perspective in the panel series *Battle of San Romano*. **PAINT**
c. 1455	Italian painter Andrea Mantegna paints *Agony in the Garden* and the fresco *St. James Led to His Execution*. Working in Padua, Mantegna helps to bring Masaccio's use of perspective and clothed nudes from Florence to northern Italy. **PAINT**
c. 1455	Flemish painter Rogier van der Weyden paints *Francesco d'Este*. **PAINT**
c. 1460s	Italian painter Piero della Francesca paints the *Flagellation*. **PAINT**
c. 1460s	Florentine painter Paolo Uccello paints *The Hunt in the Forest*. **PAINT**
1460s	The Bellini family of painters, Jacopo Bellini and his sons Gentile and Giovanni, is active in Venice. Jacopo is best known for his experiments in perspective and composition, as recorded in the hundreds of drawings in his sketchbooks. **PAINT**
c. 1460	Venetian painter Giovanni Bellini paints *Agony in the Garden*. **PAINT**
c. 1466	Italian painter Andrea Mantegna paints *Dead Christ*, notable for its extreme foreshortening, the shortening of lines to produce the illusion of depth. **PAINT**
1470s	Large wooden altar shrines, carved in intricate detail characteristic of the Late Gothic, become popular in Germanic countries. **SCULP**
c. 1470	Florentine painter and sculptor Andrea del Verrocchio reintroduces the putto, a chubby, often winged, nude child popular in classical art, to Early Renaissance sculpture as the center of his design for a bronze fountain for one of the Medici villas near Florence. **SCULP**
1472	Italian artist and scientist Leonardo da Vinci is enrolled as a painter in the fraternity of St. Luke, Florence. It will be speculated that he is responsible for one of the angels depicted in *Baptism of Christ*, a painting by his master Verrocchio.

Other paintings from Leonardo's Florentine period (until c. 1481) will include the *Annunciation* and the unfinished altarpiece *The Adoration of the Magi.* PAINT

1473–1519   St. George's Chapel in Windsor is constructed. ARCH

1474   After 425 years of construction, Winchester cathedral in England is completed. ARCH

1474   The first book printed in English is *The Recuyell of the Historyes of Troye,* a prose romance by Raoul Lefèvre, translated from the French and printed by English printer William Caxton in Bruges, Belgium. Caxton will return to England to set up England's first printing press (1476–1477) and embark on an extensive publishing program. LIT

1474   Italian painter Andrea Mantegna completes the fresco decoration of the Camera degli Sposi (Bridal Chamber) in the palace of the Gonzaga family in Mantua. The work resurrects classical Roman illusionistic painting of architecture, which appears to extend the space of the room, a motif soon adopted by other artists. PAINT

Passé Sculpture

At any given time, the great classics of art seem eternal in their greatness. But in fact, all works of art are subject to decay—not only in their material composition, but even more fatally in critical estimation. Here are a few works of antiquity that were once considered essential to the canon of great sculpture but have since faded in importance:

Apollo Belvedere—Roman marble copy of a Greek bronze of the god Apollo, discovered in the 15th century. Celebrated by neoclassical artists and critics as a pinnacle of ancient art, it dropped in reputation in the 19th century. In the 20th century, art historian Kenneth Clark described it this way: "in no other famous work of art are idea and execution more distressingly divorced."

Laocoön Group—Hellenistic or Roman marble group executed probably in the first century and discovered in the 16th century. Praised by Michelangelo and having profoundly influenced baroque and neoclassical sculpture, it too fell in estimation in the 19th century. Twentieth-century art historian H. W. Janson commented that "its dynamism has become uncomfortably self-conscious."

Medici Venus—Roman copy of a Greek statue of Venus, discovered in the 17th century. Considered an enduring model of feminine beauty until the 19th century, it was described by 20th-century art historian Martin Robertson as "among the most charmless remnants of antiquity."

c. 1475   Florentine painter, goldsmith, and sculptor Antonio del Pollaiuolo looks to action scenes on ancient painted vases to create a bronze, free-standing statue of Hercules and Antaeus posed in a violent struggle.   SCULP

c. 1476   Flemish painter Hugo van der Goes paints the *Portinari Altarpiece.*   PAINT

c. 1478   Italian painter Alessandro di Mariano Filipepi, known as Sandro Botticelli, paints the poetic allegory *Primavera*, which shows the influence of Fra Filippo Lippi in its linear, graceful style.   PAINT

c. 1480s   Italian artist Leonardo da Vinci paints *The Lady with an Ermine.*   PAINT

c. 1480–1495   Italian painter Andrea Mantegna paints the series *Triumph of Caesar.*   PAINT

c. 1480   Italian painter Sandro Botticelli paints the mythological work *The Birth of Venus*, reflecting Neoplatonic views of pagan myth as allegories of divine truth.   PAINT

c. 1480   Florentine painter Filippino Lippi, son of Fra Filippo Lippi, paints *The Vision of St. Bernard.*   PAINT

c. 1481   Italian architect Donato Bramante begins his first building, Santa Maria presso San Satiro in Milan.   ARCH

c. 1481   Italian artist Leonardo da Vinci leaves Florence for Milan, where he stays until 1499. Among his works from this period are many drawings, including artistic sketches, scientific observations of nature, and technical plans for proposed machines.   GRAPH

1481–1482   Italian painters decorating the Sistine Chapel in the Vatican in Rome include Sandro Botticelli, Pietro Perugino, Domenico Ghirlandaio, and Cosimo Rosselli. *See also* 1508–1512, ARCH.   PAINT

1482   Portuguese explorers and missionaries come in contact with the Kongo tribes living along the lower Congo River. African sculptors will create brass crucifixes derived from early Portuguese prototypes to be used as power tokens by village chiefs.   SCULP

1484   Belgian music theorist and composer Johannes Tinctoris writes the treatise *De inventione et usu musicae.*   MUSIC

1484   Florentine painter Filippino Lippi completes Florentine painter Masaccio's fresco cycle in the Brancacci Chapel, Santa Maria del Carmine. *See* 1425–1428, PAINT.   PAINT

1485   English prose writer Sir Thomas Malory's *Le Morte d'Arthur* is published posthumously. This collection of Arthurian romances will be the principal vehicle through which the legends of King Arthur and his knights will be perpetuated to future generations of readers.   LIT

c. 1485   Italian artist Leonardo da Vinci paints the *Madonna of the Rocks*, which employs a subtle form of chiaroscuro (strongly contrasting light and dark) known as *sfumato* ("up in smoke"). Leonardo is considered a pioneer in the use of chiaroscuro, which will reach its height in the paintings of Rembrandt in the 17th century. The painting exists in two versions.   PAINT

1485   Venetian painter Giovanni Bellini paints the large oil *San Giobbe Altarpiece*, depicting the Madonna and saints. The teacher of Venetian painters Giorgione and Titian, Giovanni Bellini is the leader of Renaissance painting in Venice.
                                                                      PAINT

1486   Isabel of Castile commissions Spanish sculptor Gil de Siloé to create an elaborate alabaster tomb for her parents, Juan II of Castile and Isabella of Portugal. Gil de Siloé will employ other artists to help carve many of the figures and complete the tomb in 1493.   SCULP

1487   Italian poet Matteo Maria Boiardo publishes the first two books of his unfinished romantic epic *Orlando Innamorato* (*Roland in Love*), which draws on the Carolingian legends shared by *The Song of Roland* (*see* 1100s, LIT). *See also* 1532, LIT.
                                                                      LIT

1488–1493   Florentine painter Filippino Lippi paints a fresco cycle, depicting St. Thomas Aquinas, in the Carafa Chapel, Santa Maria sopra Minerva, Rome.   PAINT

1489–1507   The Palazzo Strozzi in Florence is built.   ARCH

1490   Dance performances, the origins of ballet, are introduced at French, Burgundian, and Italian courts for weddings, receptions for foreign sovereigns, and other festive occasions. The loose sequences of dances, based on steps of the conventional courtly repertory, are performed in sumptuous costume and reflect the theme of the occasion.   DANCE

c. 1490   Dutch painter Geertgen tot Sint Jans paints *Nativity*, notable for its striking use of light and shadow on the round heads of its figures.   PAINT

c. 1491–   Florentine sculptor, painter, and architect Michelangelo (Michelangelo
1492   Buonarroti) executes the marble relief of *The Battle of the Lapiths and Centaurs*, while under the patronage of Lorenzo de' Medici, who dies in 1492.   SCULP

1493	Holy Roman emperor Maximilian I appoints Flemish composer Heinrich Isaac court composer and Paul von Hofhaimer court organist. MUSIC
c. 1495	The English morality play *Everyman* is first performed. The allegorical drama tells the story of Everyman's anxious search for companions to stand by him as he faces Death. In the end, only Good Deeds will accompany him. *See also* c. 1425, DRAMA. DRAMA
1495	Leading French composer Josquin Desprez is appointed organist and choirmaster at Cambrai cathedral in France. MUSIC
c. 1495	Italian artist Leonardo da Vinci paints the mural *Last Supper*, which soon begins to deteriorate due to the experimental medium the painter employed (a mixture of tempera and oil paint). PAINT
c. 1495	Italian sculptor Tullio Lombardo carves a marble statue of Adam for the funerary monument of Doge Andrea Vendramin in the church of Santi Giovanni e Paolo. It will be the first large-scale classical nude since antiquity. SCULP
1496	Venetian painter Gentile Bellini paints the large canvas *Procession of the Relic of the True Cross*. PAINT

Military Etchings

The art of etching, used for making prints and book illustrations since the 16th century, began not as a printmaking technique but as a way of decorating armor. The first such example, dating from the late 15th century, is an Italian breastplate decorated using the basic principle of etching: biting a design into metal with acid.

The technique of etching requires the artist to cover the metal with a substance, such as beeswax, bitumen, or resin, that will resist the action of acid. The artist uses a steel needle to draw the design by cutting through the covering substance, or ground, and exposing the metal underneath. The metal is then immersed in a bath of dilute acid, such as nitric, which bites into the metal wherever it has been exposed. The image can be "stopped out," or shaded, by applying acid-resisting varnish to selected parts of the design before immersing, then reimmersing the plate as often as needed so that some parts of the design are bitten deeper than others.

As applied to armor, the result was a handsome chest engraving to impress foes in battle and courtiers at home. But by the early 16th century, graphic artists, such as the Germans Albrecht Dürer and Albrecht Altdorfer and the Swiss Urs Graf, were already applying the military technology to peaceful uses. By applying ink to the etched plate, any number of paper images could be produced, and a new graphic art technique was created.

1496–1497	Italian sculptor, painter, and architect Michelangelo sculpts the *Bacchus*. SCULP
1498	German painter and engraver Albrecht Dürer, the leading artist of the Renaissance in northern Europe, publishes the woodcut series *Apocalypse*, which raises the art of woodcut to a new height. He will also be famed for his engravings, drawings, watercolors, and oil paintings. GRAPH
c. 1498–1499	While in his 20s in Rome, Italian sculptor, painter, and architect Michelangelo sculpts the *Pietà*, the greatest work of his early period. SCULP
1499	Italian printer Aldo Mannucci (Aldus Manutius) publishes the illustrated book *Hypnerotomachia Poliphili*, which includes some of the most esteemed woodcuts from the period. GRAPH
1499	English poet John Skelton publishes *The Bowge of Court*, a satirical dream-allegory on contemporary court life. LIT
1500s	Benin artists in Nigeria produce art for the king, who is considered divine, and his court. Ivory pendant masks combining Benin symbolism with Portuguese figures are created to be worn by the king on his hip during funerary ceremonies. DECO
1500s	Late this century, in England, theaters such as the Globe Theatre flourish. Most are open air and probably decorated, though there is no real scenery. The actors use props and, most likely, wear contemporary costumes whether or not they are appropriate to the play's setting. *See also* 1599, DRAMA. DRAMA
1500s	Line engraving begins to supersede the woodcut as the preferred mode for printing illustrations. However, woodcuts will survive into the 18th century for popular items such as broadsheets and printers' decorations. GRAPH
1500s	Emblem books, printed collections of symbolic images, become popular in Europe from now into the 17th century. GRAPH
1500s	Chinese novelist Wu Ch'eng-en writes the comic fantasy novel *Hsi-yü chi* (*Monkey*), describing the magical adventures of a Buddhist priest in search of sacred scriptures in India. LIT
1500s	Aztec conquests assure a supply of skilled artists and craftsmen to be brought to the capital to work and train Aztec apprentices. Aztec carvers will begin to create realistic sculpture in the round. MISC
1500s	Late this century, art academies begin to appear in Italy as private associations of artists. These academies will become formal institutions that will take over the functions of the guilds. MISC

1500s	Italian architects Giulio Romano and Michelangelo adapt the prevailing classical architectural style into the freer, more individualistic style known as mannerism. MISC
c. 1500s	German religious reformer Martin Luther, founder of Protestantism, influences ecclesiastical music. He encourages simple melodies and a return to the early Christian custom of communal singing. The chorale, or Lutheran hymn, develops, and scales as they will become known to posterity come into use. MUSIC
1500s	Madrigals in new forms become popular in small Italian courts, composed for weddings and other ceremonies. Instrumental preludes and interludes (ritornellos, also found in motets), mark the beginnings of chamber music. MUSIC
1500s	In Italy oil paint becomes the dominant medium for painting. Preferred in northern Europe since the 15th century, it will become (and endure as) probably the most important medium used by Western painters. *See also* 1400s, PAINT. PAINT
1500s	Within the Islamic sultanates in India, Deccani art develops, emphasizing opulence and intricate compositions. PAINT
1500s	Japanese artists are greatly influenced by Chinese artistic styles, excepting a few, like Japanese ink painter Sesshū (1420–1506), who eschews Chinese imagery for Japanese landscapes. PAINT
1500s	The Lamar culture of the Mississippian southeast reduce the diversity of sculptural imagery and concentrate on rendering rattlesnakes, panthers, thunderbirds, and death mask motifs. SCULP
1500s	Late this century, the Counter-Reformation in Italy sees an increase in the literal sculptural depictions of the martyrdoms of saints. SCULP
1500	Antwerp cathedral, begun nearly 150 years earlier in 1352, is completed. ARCH
1500	After his sojourn in Italy, French composer Josquin Desprez resides at the French court of Louis XII. MUSIC
1500	Mastersingers' songs are reformed by German composer Hans Folz of Nuremberg, and worldly subjects are now admitted. MUSIC
c. 1500–1520	This period in Italy will become known as the High Renaissance, a time of great achievement in painting and sculpture, dominated by such artists as Leonardo da Vinci, Michelangelo, and Raphael. PAINT

| 1500 | Italian painter Sandro Botticelli paints *Mystic Nativity*. Like many of his later paintings, it is more grave and intense than his earlier works. **PAINT** |

1500   Italian painter Sandro Botticelli paints *Mystic Nativity*. Like many of his later paintings, it is more grave and intense than his earlier works. **PAINT**

1500   Venetian painter Gentile Bellini paints the large canvas *Miracle at Ponte di Lorenzo*. **PAINT**

1501   Italian printer Aldo Mannucci (Aldus Manutius) designs the typeface that will become known as italic. Previous European volumes have used roman and gothic letters. Aldus also designs a Greek type. **GRAPH**

1501   Ottaviano dei Petrucci of Venice uses movable type to print music, including *Harmonice Musices Odhecaton A*, a collection of 96 Franco-Flemish polyphonic chansons (popular songs). **MUSIC**

c. 1501   Venetian painter Giovanni Bellini paints his best-known portrait, *Doge Leonardo Loredan*. **PAINT**

1501–1504   In Florence, Italian painter Michelangelo completes the monumental 13-foot nude marble sculpture *David*. Influenced by Hellenistic sculpture, it is notable for its sense of action in repose and of youthful defiance and restlessness. **SCULP**

1502–1509   Italian architect Donato Bramante builds the classically inspired Tempietto in the cloister of the church of San Pietro in Montorio in Rome. **ARCH**

1502–1516   French composer Josquin Desprez composes his three books of Masses. **MUSIC**

1502–1507   Dutch painter Gerard David completes the triptych *St. John the Baptist*. **PAINT**

1503   England's Canterbury cathedral, begun in 1070, is completed. **ARCH**

1503   Italian artist Leonardo da Vinci paints the *Mona Lisa*, perhaps the world's most famous painting. The half-length portrait is noted for its enigmatic smile and deep, atmospheric tonalities. **PAINT**

1503   German painter Matthias Grünewald (Matthias Gothardt) paints *The Mockery of Christ*. **PAINT**

1504   German painter and engraver Albrecht Dürer engraves the *Fall of Man*. **GRAPH**

1504   German painter and engraver Lucas Cranach the Elder paints *Rest on the Flight into Egypt*, an example of the attention to landscape characteristic of the Danube School, which also comprises Albrecht Altdorfer and Wolf Huber. **PAINT**

1504   Italian painter Giorgione completes his *Madonna* in Castelfranco cathedral. **PAINT**

1504	At the age of 21, Italian painter Raphael paints *Marriage of the Virgin*, a stronger and more graceful work than that done by his master Perugino on the same subject. Raphael is soon recognized as one of the greatest painters of his day. PAINT
1504–1589	Japanese artist Sesson follows in the footsteps of Japanese ink painter Sesshū. PAINT
1505–1506	Italian painter Raphael paints *Madonna with the Goldfinch*. The artist will become known for his many images of the Madonna. PAINT
1505	Venetian painter Giovanni Bellini paints the *San Zaccaria Altarpiece*, a remarkable example of *sacra conversazione*. PAINT
1505–1506	German painter and engraver Albrecht Dürer paints a series of landscape watercolors. PAINT
1505	Italian painter Giorgione paints *The Tempest*, a mysterious landscape with figures. PAINT
1506	The reconstruction of St. Peter's Church, Rome, begins under the direction of Italian architect Donato Bramante, commissioned by Pope Julius II. Replacing the basilica erected 11 centuries earlier, the new church will take over 150 years to complete. Other architects working on the project will include Raphael, Antonio da Sangallo the Younger, Michelangelo, Giacomo della Porta, Carlo Maderna, and Giovanni Bellini. *See also* 333, ARCH. ARCH
1506	German painter and engraver Lucas Cranach the Elder completes the altarpiece entitled *St. Catherine*. PAINT
1506	The first-century sculpture *Laocoön* is rediscovered in a vineyard in Rome. Its classical grandeur and expression of emotions will influence artists in the Renaissance, baroque, and neoclassical periods. Among those influenced by the work is the Italian artist Michelangelo, who visits it at once upon its discovery. SCULP
1506	German sculptor Tilman Riemenschneider completes the altar at St. Jakob's in Rothenburg. SCULP
1507	Venetian painters Giorgione and Titian (Tiziano Vecellio) paint frescoes for the exterior of the Fondaco dei Tedeschi. PAINT
1508–1511	Italian architect Baldassare Peruzzi builds the Villa Farnesina in Rome. ARCH
1508–1512	Italian sculptor, painter, and architect Michelangelo completes the painting of the Sistine Chapel in the Vatican. The ceiling features scenes of the Creation,

Adam and Eve, Noah, and images of prophets and sibyls foretelling Christ's birth. *See also* 1481–1482, PAINT.
ARCH

1508   The first chiaroscuro woodcut, a woodcut with tonal effects produced by printing on one sheet from several blocks of different tone, is *The Emperor Maximilian on Horseback,* by German painter and wood engraver Hans Burgkmair the Elder.
GRAPH

1508–1512   Venetian painter Lorenzo Lotto, known for his idiosyncratic style, works in Rome, painting works of *sacra conversazione.*
PAINT

1508   At the age of 25, Italian artist Raphael is summoned to Rome by Pope Julius II, where he will work until his death in 1520. In 1508–1511, he executes *The School of Athens* and the *Disputà,* frescoes in the Stanza della Segnatura, a papal room in the Vatican.
PAINT

1509   Dutch humanist and scholar Desiderius Erasmus composes the humanist satire *The Praise of Folly.*
LIT

1509   Florentine painter Andrea d'Agnolo, known as Andrea del Sarto, paints *Miracles of St. Philip.*
PAINT

1510   German painter and engraver Albrecht Dürer completes the print series *Great Passion* and *Life of the Virgin.*
GRAPH

c. 1510–1515   Dutch painter Hieronymus Bosch paints the triptych *The Garden of Earthly Delights,* so called for its sensuous center panel. The left panel represents Eden, the right Hell. Bosch will be known for his fantastic, grotesque, richly symbolic style, as seen in paintings such as *The Temptation of St. Anthony* and *Ship of Fools.*
PAINT

1510   Venetian painter Sebastiano Luciani, known as Sebastiano del Piombo, paints *Salome.*
PAINT

c. 1512   Italian artist Raphael designs the Chigi Chapel in Santa Maria del Popolo. His combination of architecture with sculpture, painting, mosaic, stucco work, and other forms of interior decoration exert a powerful influence in the baroque period.
DECO

1512–1517   German painter and engraver Hans Baldung Grien executes the altarpiece for Freiburg cathedral, including the center panel *Coronation of the Virgin.*
PAINT

1512   Florentine painter Andrea del Sarto paints *The Annunciation.*
PAINT

1512–1514	Italian artist Raphael, renowned as a portrait artist, paints the portrait of Pope Julius II. During this period he also paints *The Sistine Madonna*, his most famous version of the Madonna and Child, and the fresco *Galatea*. PAINT
1513–1520	Italian political philosopher Niccolò Machiavelli writes *La mandragola* (*The Mandrake*), perhaps the best comedy of the Italian Renaissance. DRAMA
1513–1514	German painter and engraver Albrecht Dürer engraves his master prints: *Knight, Death and the Devil*; *St. Jerome in His Study*; and *Melencolia I*. GRAPH
1513	English poet John Skelton publishes *A Ballad of the Scottish King*. LIT
1513	Renaissance patron of the arts Pope Julius II dies. His successor, Pope Leo X, begins the Vatican sculpture gallery. SCULP
c. 1513	Italian artist Michelangelo sculpts the *Slaves* for the tomb of Pope Julius II, though the two figures are not included in the final monument when it is erected in 1545. The *Slaves* will be preserved in the Louvre, Paris. SCULP
1513	German sculptor Tilman Riemenschneider completes the tomb of Emperor Henry II at Bamberg cathedral. SCULP
1514	German painter and engraver Lucas Cranach the Elder, well known as a portraitist, paints the full-length portraits of the duke and duchess of Saxony. PAINT
1514	Italian painter Antonio Allegri, known as Correggio, paints his *St. Francis* altarpiece. PAINT
1514	Venetian painter Giovanni Bellini paints the mythological *Feast of the Gods*, which, after his death in 1516, will be altered by his pupil Titian. PAINT
1515	Italian artist Raphael is named architect in chief of St. Peter's Church in Rome. ARCH
1515	German painter and engraver Albrecht Dürer uses the new technique of etching to produce the *Agony in the Garden*. GRAPH
c. 1515–1516	Italian artist Michelangelo sculpts *Moses* for the tomb of Pope Julius II. Of the 40 large figures the artist at first envisioned for the tomb, it is ultimately the only sculpture of his that decorates the tomb. *See also* c. 1513, SCULP. SCULP
1515	German painter Matthias Grünewald paints the *Isenheim Altarpiece*, noted for its emotional intensity, brilliant color, and gruesome depiction of Christ's crucifixion. SCULP

1516 English statesman and author Thomas More publishes *Utopia*. Written in Latin, it is a narrative about a visit to the fictitious ideal land of the title, which is taken from the Greek words for "no place" and "good place." The book will generate a tradition of utopian narratives in such works as Jonathan Swift's *Gulliver's Travels* (1726) and Samuel Butler's *Erewhon* (1872). LIT

c. 1516 Italian painter Tiziano Vecellio, known as Titian, paints the allegory *Sacred and Profane Love* and his first great altarpiece, *The Assumption*. PAINT

1516 King Francis I invites Italian artist Leonardo da Vinci to France. PAINT

1516 Flemish painter Quentin Massys paints his portraits of Erasmus and Petrus Egidius as a gift for English humanist Sir Thomas More. The portraits establish the pictorial motif of the scholar in his study. PAINT

1517 Italian political philosopher Niccolò Machiavelli composes *Il principe* (*The Prince*), which will become an infuential work of political philosophy. Among his other works are *Discoursi* (*Discourses*, 1513–1517). LIT

Moses Analyzed

Michelangelo's statue *Moses* (c. 1515–1516), admired as one of the world's great sculptures, represented only failure to the artist himself. He had planned to complete 40 large figures for the tomb of Pope Julius II, which he was commissioned to construct in 1505; 40 years later, when the much-scaled-down monument was finally unveiled, he had contributed only one finished sculpture, *Moses*. Despite this, the statue has had many admirers through the centuries, not least of them the Viennese founder of psychiatry, Sigmund Freud.

On his periodic visits to Rome, beginning in 1901, Freud made a point each time of scrutinizing *Moses* in the church of San Pietro in Vincoli. "In 1913," he wrote, "through three lonely September weeks, I stood daily in the church in front of the statue, studied it, measured it, drew it, until that understanding came to me that I only dared to express anonymously in the paper." The paper to which he referred, "The Moses of Michelangelo," published in 1914, laid out his theory that the statue represented a supreme moment of self-control, in which the subject held himself back from anger against the Israelites who had sinned in worshipping the golden calf. This he connected to Michelangelo's own desire to control his temper, to raise "himself with this self-criticism above his own nature." Freud also alluded to his own struggle to control his anger against foes and estranged followers of his theory of psychoanalysis.

1517	After Flemish composer Heinrich Isaac's death, Swiss composer Ludwig Senfl becomes court composer to Emperor Maximilian I. MUSIC
1517	Florentine painter Andrea del Sarto paints the altarpiece *Madonna of the Harpies*. PAINT
1517	Italian artist Raphael paints the large composition the *Transfiguration*, which will stand above his bier at his funeral when he dies at age 37 in 1520 (*b.* 1483). PAINT
1518	German painter Albrecht Altdorfer paints the altarpiece for St. Florian near Linz. PAINT
1518	Italian artist Raphael paints the portrait of Pope Leo X, depicted with cardinals in attendance. PAINT
1518–1523	Italian painter Titian paints three mythological works for Alfonso d'Este: *Bacchus and Ariadne*, the *Worship of Venus*, and the *Bacchanal*. PAINT
1518–1520	Italian painter Correggio undertakes his first large-scale commissions, the decoration of the abbess's room in the convent of San Paolo (c. 1518) and the dome for the church of San Giovanni Evangelista (1520). PAINT
1519–1526	Italian painter Titian paints the Pesaro altarpiece (*Madonna of the Pesaro Family*), remarkable for its innovative diagonal composition. PAINT
1520–1521	German painter and engraver Albrecht Dürer travels in the Netherlands, keeping a diary with drawings that is the first of its kind in art history. GRAPH
1520	In Italy the period known as the High Renaissance (begun 1500) comes to an end as the mannerist period (ending 1600) begins. It will be marked by a reaction against the classical tendencies of the High Renaissance and by elaboration and innovation that will long be condemned by critics as artificial and decadent, though some in the 20th century will come to view it more positively. MISC
1521	Italian painter Jacopo Palma, known as Palma Vecchio, or Il Vecchio, paints *Adoration*. PAINT
1522	German painter and engraver Lucas Cranach the Elder creates woodcuts for the first German edition of the New Testament. GRAPH
1522	Beginning this year with the poem *Colyn Cloute*, English poet John Skelton makes attacks on prelate-statesman Cardinal Wolsey that will also include *Speke, Parrot* (1521) and *Why come ye nat to Courte?* (1522–1523). LIT

1522-1523   Italian painter Girolamo Francesco Mazzola, known as Parmigianino, paints
                 frescoes in the cathedral in Parma.   PAINT

1524   Italian artist Michelangelo designs the Laurentian Library to house the Medici
                 family's collection of books and manuscripts.   ARCH

1524   Italian artist Parmigianino paints *Self-Portrait in a Convex Mirror*.   PAINT

1525   The printing of English humanist William Tyndale's English translation of the
                 New Testament begins at Cologne. His translation of this and other sections of
                 the Bible will be banned and Tyndale will be executed for heresy in 1536, but
                 his work will form the basis for the King James version of the Bible, authorized
                 in 1604 and published in 1611.   LIT

1525   German painter and engraver Albrecht Dürer publishes the *Treatise on Measurement*,
                 a theoretical study on proportion.   PAINT

1525   Italian painter Palma Vecchio paints *Three Sisters*.   PAINT

1526   German painter and engraver Albrecht Dürer paints the two panels of the *Four Apostles*.
                                                                                         PAINT

1526-1527   In Rome since leaving his native Parma in 1524, Italian artist Parmigianino
                 paints *The Vision of St. Jerome*. He leaves Rome for Bologna in 1527 after Rome
                 is sacked by German troops.   PAINT

1526-1530   Italian painter Correggio paints the dome of Parma cathedral, which develops
                 the illusionist motif of portraying a celestial scene as if it were taking place in
                 the sky overhead.   PAINT

1527   Flemish composer Adriaan Willaert becomes maestro di capella at St. Mark's,
                 inaugurating the Venetian school of progressive, innovative Flemish and
                 Italian composers.   MUSIC

1527   German painter Hans Holbein the Younger, visiting in England (1526-1528),
                 paints *Thomas More and His Family*, the first group portrait of full-length figures
                 at home.   PAINT

1528   Italian diplomat and writer Baldasarre Castiglione publishes *Il cortegiano* (*The
                 Courtier*), a work in dialogue form concerning courtly manners and education.
                 The book will be popular and influential across Europe. *See also* 1561, LIT.   LIT

1528   *Four Books on Human Proportion*, by German painter and engraver Albrecht
                 Dürer, is published posthumously.   PAINT

1529	Italian sculptor and architect Jacopo Sansovino is appointed state architect of Venice. ARCH
1529	German church musician and composer Martin Sohr, known as Martin Agricola, publishes *Musica instrumentalis deudsch,* an excellent account of contemporary instruments. MUSIC
1529	German painter Albrecht Altdorfer paints the *Battle of Issus,* part of a series of battlepieces from antiquity. PAINT
1529	Venetian painter Lorenzo Lotto paints *Christ and the Woman Taken in Adultery.* PAINT
c. 1530	In Germany painter Hans Holbein the Younger makes numerous designs for stained glass. DECO
1530	Flemish composer Philippe Jacques Verdelot and Italian singer and composer Costanzo Festa, choirmaster at the Papal Chapel in Rome, are the first to have madrigals in the new form published in Italy. MUSIC
c. 1530	German painter and engraver Lucas Cranach the Elder paints the highly stylized *Judgment of Paris,* one of many of his works on mythological subjects. PAINT
c. 1530	Italian painter Correggio paints *Adoration of the Shepherds* and *The Loves of Jupiter.* PAINT
1530	Italian painter Titian paints the portrait of Cardinal Ippolito de' Medici. PAINT
1532	Italian poet Ludovico Ariosto publishes the final version of his masterpiece, the comic romantic epic *Orlando Furioso (Roland Mad)* (published in shorter form in 1516), which continues the story of Boiardo's *Orlando Innamorato. See also* 1487, LIT. LIT
1532–1564	French writer François Rabelais composes the multivolume satire about the search for the Oracle of the Holy Bottle, *Gargantua and Pantagruel.* LIT
1533	German painter Hans Holbein the Younger paints the double portrait *The Ambassadors.* PAINT
1534	Regensburg cathedral in Germany, begun nearly three centuries earlier in 1275, is completed. ARCH
1534	St. Basil's Basilica in Moscow is begun (completed 1561). ARCH

1534	Italian artist Michelangelo completes the tomb of the Medici and moves from Florence to Rome, where he works for the papacy for the remainder of his life. ARCH
1535	In Zurich, the first complete English translation of the Bible, translated by Miles Coverdale, is published. LIT
c. 1535	Italian painter Parmigianino paints *Madonna of the Long Neck*, a refined, elegant work that will become one of the standard examples of mannerism. He also paints the erotic *Cupid Carving His Bow*. PAINT
1536	German composer and master of the polyphonic Heinrich Finck's collection of songs, *Schöne Auserlesene Lieder*, is published posthumously. MUSIC
1536–1541	Italian artist Michelangelo paints the *Last Judgment* in the Sistine Chapel. PAINT
1537	Italian sculptor and architect Jacopo Sansovino begins the Library of San Marco and the facade of the Doge's palace loggietta in Venice. ARCH
1537–1551	Italian architect Sebastiano Serlio (1475–1554) publishes the six volumes of the influential architectural treatise *Tutte l'opere d'architettura*. Two more volumes will be published after his death, one in 1575 and the other not until 1967. Used by craftsmen as a pattern-book, the work will spread Renaissance style across Europe. ARCH
1537	The first conservatories of music are founded in Naples and Venice. MUSIC
1537	Having settled permanently in England in 1532, German painter Hans Holbein the Younger executes the wall painting in Whitehall Palace of Henry VIII with his parents and third wife, Jane Seymour. PAINT
1538–1540	During these years, Italian painter Titian paints the *Venus of Urbino* (1538), *A Young Englishman* (1540), and *Ecce Homo* (1543). PAINT
1539	Flemish-born French painter Jean Clouet, court painter to French king Francis I, is praised as the "equal of Michelangelo" by French poet Clément Marot. PAINT
c. 1540s	German painter and designer Hans Holbein the Younger executes numerous designs for decoration and produces miniature paintings. DECO
1540	Italian architect Andrea Palladio builds the Villa Godi in Lonedo. ARCH
c. 1540	Spanish sculptor Alonso Berruguete completes his wood reliefs in an "anti-classical" mannerist style for the choir stalls of Toledo cathedral. SCULP

1541	François Clouet, son of Flemish-born painter Jean Clouet, succeeds his father as court painter to French king Francis I. PAINT
1542–1550	Italian artist Michelangelo's last paintings, created years before his death in 1564 (b. 1475), include the frescoes *Conversion of St. Paul* and *Crucifixion of St. Peter* in the Cappella Paolina in the Vatican. PAINT
1543	Florentine goldsmith and sculptor Benvenuto Cellini creates a gold boat-shaped saltcellar for King Francis I of France. SCULP
1544	Italian painter and architect Francesco Primaticcio works with Florentine painter Giovanni Battista Rosso (Il Rosso Fiorentino) on the decoration of the royal palace at Fontainebleau, France. Their work will help establish the style of French mannerism associated with the school of Fontainebleau, a sensual, elegant style often combining mural painting with stucco ornament. DECO
1544	German painter and engraver Hans Baldung Grien completes *The Bewitched Stable Boy*, which presents erotic themes in allegorical fashion. GRAPH
1545–1550	Italian architect Andrea Palladio builds the Palazzo Thiene in Vicenza. His symmetrical, classically inspired palaces and villas in or near Vicenza will greatly influence English architecture and decoration, leading to the movement called Palladianism in the 18th century. ARCH
c. 1545	The performance of commedia dell'arte, a form of improvised comedy that will remain popular in Italy through the early 18th century, is first recorded. DRAMA
1546	Italian artist Michelangelo becomes architect of St. Peter's Church. The drum of the dome he designs will be nearly complete at the time of his death, in 1564; the dome will be completed afterward and a long nave will be added in the 17th century. *See also* 1506, ARCH. ARCH
1546	King Francis I of France commissions French architect Pierre Lescot to begin building the new Louvre palace in Paris. The Louvre will not be completed for more than a century. ARCH
1546	German painter and engraver Lucas Cranach the Elder paints the portrait of German religious reformer Martin Luther. PAINT
1546–1548	Portraits by Italian painter Titian during this period include that of Pope Paul III and his nephews (1546) and that of King Charles V of Germany on horseback (1548). PAINT

1547   Swiss humanist Heinrich Loris (Henricus Glareanus) publishes *Dodecachordon*
            a treatise on the expansion of church modal scales to 12 tones.   MUSIC

1548   Italian painter Jacopo Robusti, known as Tintoretto, paints *Miracle of the Slave*,
            which will be considered a masterpiece of foreshortening technique.   PAINT

1549   English poet Sir Thomas Wyatt's first published collection is the posthumous
            Certayne Psalmes, a version of the penitential psalms.   LIT

1549   Flemish composer Adriaan Willaert, founder of the Venetian school of com-
            posers, combines Dutch and Italian musical styles in *Fantasie e Ricercari*.   MUSIC

1549   French sculptor Jean Goujon completes his reliefs for the Fontaine des
            Innocents in Paris. His figurative carving, combining classical details with a
            delicate slenderness, is the antithesis of contemporary Italian styles and will
            become the archetype for French Renaissance sculpture.   SCULP

1550–1556   Suleiman's Mosque in Constantinople is built.   ARCH

1550–1570   Italian architect Palladio builds the Palazzo Chiericati, Villa Rotunda, and
            Villa Barbaro in Vicenza.   ARCH

1550   Italian painter and art historian Giorgio Vasari publishes *Lives of the Artists*,
            which will long influence critical opinion and provide information on the
            lives of Italian Renaissance painters, sculptors, and architects.   MISC

1550   English composer and writer John Marbeck's *The Boke of Common Praier Noted*
            is the first musical setting of English liturgy.   MUSIC

1551   Italian composer Giovanni da Palestrina becomes director of music at St.
            Peter's in Rome.   MUSIC

1551   Italian painter Titian paints the portrait *Philip II*.   PAINT

1551–1553   Flemish painter Pieter Brueghel travels to Italy through France, making land-
            scape drawings of the Alps on his journey.   PAINT

1552   Italian natural philosopher Giambattista della Porta invents the convex lens
            and uses it to refine the camera obscura, an artist's tool for tracing, invented
            by Roger Bacon 300 years earlier.   GRAPH

1553   Italian painter Paolo Caliari, known as Veronese, paints the ceiling of the
            Doge's palace, Venice.   PAINT

1554–1557	English poet Henry Howard, earl of Surrey, is the first to use blank verse (unrhymed iambic pentameter) in a published English work. He introduces what other publishers call "this strange meter" in his posthumously published translation of part of Virgil's *Aeneid* (Book IV, 1554; Book II, 1557). Blank verse will become a widely used verse form in English poetry, for example, in the plays of Shakespeare. LIT
1554	Italian composer Giovanni da Palestrina's *First Book of Masses* is dedicated to Pope Julius III, who honors him by making him a member of the Vatican's Sistine Choir. MUSIC
1554	In England Dutch portrait painter Anthonis Mor paints the portrait of Mary Tudor. In England, he is known as Sir Anthony More; in Spain, as Antonio Moro. He will influence the development of royal and aristocratic portraits, especially in Spain. PAINT
1554	Italian painter Titian paints *Danaë, Venus and Adonis,* and *Perseus and Andromeda.* PAINT
1555–1560	Gray's Inn hall in London is built. ARCH
1555	Flemish composer Orlando di Lasso publishes his first collections of madrigals on poems by Italian writer Petrarch, and madrigals and motets on Italian, French, and Latin texts. MUSIC
1555	Italian painter Tintoretto paints *St. George and the Dragon.* PAINT
1556–1605	Under the Akbar empire in India, the Mughal School of painting, which unites Persian and Indian influences, is established. PAINT
1557	A reproduction of Flemish painter Pieter Brueghel's parable drawing *The Big Fish Eat Little Fish* is published by engraver Hieronymous (Jerome) Cock, who will execute many printed versions of Brueghel's drawings. GRAPH
1557	In England printer Richard Tottel publishes an influential collection of poems known as *Songs and Sonnettes* or *Tottel's Miscellany.* It includes poems by Sir Thomas Wyatt, Henry Howard, earl of Surrey, Nicholas Griswold, and others. LIT
1558	Italian composer Gioseffo Zarlino's *Institutioni harmoniche* defines modern major and minor scales. MUSIC
1558	Flemish painter Pieter Brueghel paints *Children's Games.* PAINT
c. 1559–1575	Italian poet Torquato Tasso writes the romance *Gerusalemme liberata* (*Jerusalem Delivered*). LIT

1559   The first edition of *A Mirror for Magistrates*, a collection of didactic poetry on
             fortune, wickedness, and the lives of great men, is published in English. Later
             editions and supplements will appear in 1563, 1574, 1578, 1587, and 1610.   LIT

c. 1560s   The first modern violins begin to be developed by Gasparo Bertolotti da Salò
             and Giovanni Paolo Maggini in Brescia, and the Amati brothers in Cremona,
             Italy.   MUSIC

1560   A new English translation of the Bible, written by Protestant English exiles in
             Geneva, is published. The Geneva Bible becomes the most popular and influ-
             ential English Bible until the King James version (1611).   LIT

1560   Flemish composer Orlando di Lasso becomes court Kapellmeister in Munich,
             where he is encouraged to produce a prodigious amount of music. His famous
             Seven Penitential Psalms (c. 1565) are included in the manuscripts at the Royal
             Library of Music, founded by Duke Albert.   MUSIC

1560   Italian painter Tintoretto paints *Susannah and the Elders*.   PAINT

1560   Italian painter and art historian Giorgio Vasari begins building the Uffizi in
             Florence for Duke Cosimo de' Medici. The principal public gallery of Florence,
             it will contain the world's greatest collection of Italian paintings.   PAINT

1561–1565   Flemish architect Cornelis Floris builds Antwerp town hall, considered the
             most influential building in Flanders of the 16th century.   ARCH

1561   Sir Thomas Hoby's English translation of Castiglione's *The Courtier* (1528) is
             published. Its content will influence courtly manners and political life in
             England; its literary style will influence Sir Philip Sidney, Edmund Spenser,
             and William Shakespeare.   LIT

1562   The hall of the Middle Temple in London is built.   ARCH

1562   In Venice Italian painter Tintoretto paints *Christ at the Sea of Galilee*. PAINT

1562   Italian painter Veronese paints *The Marriage at Cana*.   PAINT

1563   The first true art academy, the Accademia del Disegno in Florence, is founded by
             Duke Cosimo de' Medici at the urging of painter and art historian Giorgio
             Vasari. It is headed by Cosimo and Michelangelo.   MISC

1563   English composer and organist William Byrd, age 20, becomes organist at
             Lincoln cathedral.   MUSIC

1563   French sculptor Germain Pilon develops his own style by taking elements from antiquity, the works of Italian artist Michelangelo, and the Gothic tradition for the carving of the tomb of French king Henry II in the abbey church of St. Denis in Paris. He will collaborate with Italian architect Francesco Primaticcio and complete the monument in 1570.   SCULP

1564   Italian composer Giovanni da Palestrina presents *Missa Papae Marcelli*, a mass named for Pope Marcellus II.   MUSIC

1564   Italian artist Michelangelo's last work, the last of his several sculptural renderings of the *Pietà*, is left unfinished at the time of his death.   SCULP

1565   Italian architect Andrea Palladio builds the Church of San Giorgio Maggiore in Venice, combining traditional basilican church form and classical detail.   ARCH

1565   The lead pencil is in use in Europe.   GRAPH

1565   Residing in Brussels since 1563, Flemish painter Pieter Brueghel paints the series *The Months*, of which five will survive to the 20th century, including *Hunters in the Snow*.   PAINT

1565   Italian painter Tintoretto paints *Flight into Egypt*.   PAINT

1567   Flemish painter Pieter Brueghel paints *Adoration of the Magi*.   PAINT

1567   Italian painter Titian paints *Jacopo de Strada*.   PAINT

1568–1574   English architect Robert Smythson builds Longleat House in Wiltshire.   ARCH

1568   Flemish painter Pieter Brueghel paints *The Faithlessness of the World* and *The Blind Leading the Blind* in his series of works based on proverbs.   PAINT

1568   Spanish painter Juan Fernández de Navarrete, known as El Mudo because he is deaf and mute, is appointed court painter to Spanish king Philip II. By his death in 1579, de Navarrete will have completed eight of the 32 altarpieces he was commissioned to execute. His eclectic style will help to disseminate Italian influence throughout Spain.   PAINT

c. 1570   Vocal polyphonic a cappella style reaches its zenith with the Italian composer Giovanni da Palestrina and the Flemish composer Orlando di Lasso.   MUSIC

1570   English goldsmith and painter Nicholas Hilliard is appointed court miniaturist and goldsmith by English queen Elizabeth I. Though best known for his miniature paintings, he will also paint full-size portraits of Elizabeth and others.
                                    PAINT

c. 1570   Florentine sculptor Battista Lorenzi erects a marble statue of Alpheus and Arethusa, illustrating a tale from Ovid, in a grotto at Alamanno Bandini's villa Il Paradiso. The liveliness with which the figures are represented anticipates the baroque style.   SCULP

1571   Italian architect Andrea Palladio builds the Loggia del Capitanio in Vicenza.   ARCH

1572   English composer and organist William Byrd joins his compatriot Thomas Tallis, an important composer of anthems and services with English texts, as organist at the Chapel Royal in London.   MUSIC

1573   Having conquered Mexico, the Spanish begin to build the Mexico City cathedral, which will be completed in 1813.   ARCH

1573   Italian painter Veronese is summoned before the Inquisition for including irreverent figures such as dwarfs and buffoons in a painting of the Last Supper. To pacify the authorities, the painting's name is changed to *The Feast in the House of Levi*.   PAINT

1575   English composers and organists William Byrd and Thomas Tallis compose *Cantiones sacrae*, 34 motets dedicated to Queen Elizabeth I.   MUSIC

1576   The Theatre, England's first permanent structure for the performance of plays, is constructed at Shoreditch. *See also* 1599, DRAMA.   DRAMA

1576   Spanish composer Tomás Luis de Victoria publishes *Liber primus*, a volume of masses and canticles.   MUSIC

1576   Italian painter Titian dies (*b.* 1488 or 1490), leaving his last work, *Pietà*, unfinished; it is completed by his pupil, Palma Giovane.   PAINT

1577   English author Raphael Holinshed publishes *Chronicles of England, Scotlande, and Irelande*, which will provide source material for many plays by English dramatist William Shakespeare, including *King Lear*, *Macbeth*, and *Cymbeline*.
                                                                              LIT

1577   The art academy Accademia di San Luca is founded in Rome.   MISC

1577   Spanish painter Doménikos Theotokópoulos, known as El Greco, paints the *Assumption of the Virgin*, an altarpiece in San Domingo el Antiguo, Toledo.   PAINT

1578   English writer John Lyly publishes the prose fiction work *Euphues, the Anatomy of Wit*, which introduces the ornate, exaggeratedly refined style that will become known as euphuism. Tremendously popular, the book will generate a sequel by Lyly, *Euphues and His England*, in 1580.   LIT

1578–1615   The Monoyama period in Japan yields original works that break from Chinese influence and continue to inspire Japanese art for centuries.   PAINT

1579   English poet Edmund Spenser publishes the first edition of his first major work, *The Shepheardes Calendar*, pseudonymously written under the name Immerito (unworthy). The popular collection consists of 12 pastoral poems, one for each month of the year.   LIT

1580   French essayist Michel de Montaigne publishes his first two books of *Essays*, which introduce the literary form that will become known as the personal essay.   LIT

1581   *Le Ballet comique de la reine* is organized by an Italian resident of France, Balthasar de Beaujoyeulx. Combining the features of French dances and masquerades with those of the pastorales and Italian interludes, it is often considered the starting point of ballet.   DANCE

1583   In Japan Toyotomi Hideyoshi begins construction of Osaka castle.   ARCH

The First Ballet

The first ballet was the brainchild of a mother-in-law who was not above getting involved in her daughter-in-law's sister's wedding. The mother-in-law was Italian-born Catherine de Médicis (1519–1589), queen consort of French king Henry II, mother of three kings, generous patroness of the arts, and powerful political figure in France for much of the 16th century. In 1581, her son King Henry III was on the throne, and his wife, Queen Louise, had a sister who was getting married. Catherine, ever the matriarch, wanted to stage a lavish entertainment for the occasion. She commissioned court musician and dance master Baldassare di Belgioioso, known to the French as Balthasar de Beaujoyeulx, to design an appropriate spectacle. On October 15, 1581, at the Louvre, Beaujoyeulx staged *Le Ballet comique de la reine*, often regarded as the first ballet.

Six hours in length, combining song, dance, pantomime, and poetry, the spectacle's narrative concerned the escape of Odysseus from the sorceress Circe. But more important was its original use of extended choreographed steps rather than free motion. Drawing on French and Italian court dance traditions, Beaujoyeulx sought to achieve the "geometrical arrangement of many persons dancing together under a diverse harmony of instruments."

Though it lacked many of the formal elements of classical ballet that would be codified by the 19th century, a new art form had been born. Catherine herself helped to spread the word about it, distributing reports of her spectacle throughout the continent.

1583 Flemish sculptor Giambologna (also known as Jean Bologne or Giovanni da Bologna) working in Florence, creates a larger-than-life marble group depicting the Rape of the Sabine Women. His sculpture is the first large marble composition intended to be seen from all sides. SCULP

c. 1585– 1589 *The Spanish Tragedy*, an extremely popular play by English dramatist Thomas Kyd, is produced. Some authorities will later contend that Kyd helped write *Titus Andronicus*, a play by English dramatist William Shakespeare. DRAMA

1585 Italian painter Veronese paints the *Triumph of Venice* on the ceiling of the Hall of the Great Council in the Doge's palace, Venice. PAINT

1586 St. John Lateran in Rome is rebuilt. ARCH

c. 1587– 1588 *Tamburlaine the Great, Parts I and II*, dramas by English dramatist Christopher Marlowe, are produced. DRAMA

1587–1588 Italian composer Claudio Monteverdi publishes eight books of madrigals. MUSIC

1588 "My Mind to Me a Kingdom Is," a poem by English poet Sir Edward Dyer, is published. LIT

1588 English composer and organist William Byrd's *Psalms, Sonets & songs of sadnes & pietie* attests to his mastery of expressive polyphony. MUSIC

1588 *Musica Transalpina*, a collection of 57 Italian madrigals provided with English texts, is published by Nicholas Yonge in London; it will foster greater interest in England in the Italian style. MUSIC

1589 Thoinot Arbeau (anagram for Jehan Tabourot), a French church dignitary from Langres, publishes *Orchésographie*, an important treatise on dancing. DANCE

c. 1589– 1590 English dramatist Christopher Marlowe writes the play *The Jew of Malta*. It will survive only in a version revised by an unknown other. DRAMA

1589 English composer and organist William Byrd writes *Songs of sundrie natures*. MUSIC

1590s English poet John Donne (*b*. 1572) writes most of his great love poetry and his five *Satires*, though little of his poetry will be published until after his death in 1631. The first and most influential of the metaphysical poets, he will be known for his energetic, vigorous style and his use of conceits—ingenious, paradoxical, concentrated comparisons, often with a philosophical bent. *See* 1633, LIT.

LIT

c. 1590–
1592
The plays of English dramatist William Shakespeare begin to be produced. His earliest plays include the history plays *Henry VI Parts 1, 2,* and *3,* the tragedy *Titus Andronicus,* and *The Comedy of Errors,* based principally on the *Menaechmi* of Plautus (*see* 254 B.C., DRAMA).   DRAMA

c. 1590
Richard Burbage (1567?–1619) is one of the principal actors of his day, playing every major role in the plays of English dramatist William Shakespeare, including Richard III, Hamlet, Othello, and King Lear. He also performs in the plays of Ben Jonson and Beaumont and Fletcher.   DRAMA

c. 1590
English dramatist Christopher Marlowe writes the drama *The Tragical History of Dr. Faustus.* Though it will survive only in a version adapted by others, it will be Marlowe's most frequently revived play.   DRAMA

c. 1590
The Old Wives' Tale, a comedy by English dramatist George Peele, is written and produced. Peele's earlier comedy *The Arraignment of Paris* was probably produced in 1581.   DRAMA

1590
A portion of English poet Sir Philip Sidney's prose romance *Arcadia* is published posthumously. Known as New Arcadia, it represents Sidney's revised version of the first three books of an earlier unpublished romance that is known as Old Arcadia. In 1593, the countess of Pembroke will publish a hybrid of New Arcadia and the lost books of the unrevised Old Arcadia.   LIT

1590
English poet Edmund Spenser publishes the first three books of *The Faerie Queene,* a monumental romantic verse epic originally intended to span 12 books. Though the work is never completed, three more books (IV-VI) will be added in the edition of 1596. The posthumous edition of 1609 will add the "Mutability Cantos."   LIT

1590
Spanish painter El Greco paints *St. Jerome.*   PAINT

c. 1591–
1594
English dramatist William Shakespeare writes the history play *Richard III.*   DRAMA

1591
English poet and playwright Robert Greene publishes *The Art of Conny-Catching,* a humorous, journalistic account of confidence games in London.   LIT

1591
English poet Sir Philip Sidney's sonnet sequence *Astrophel and Stella* is published posthumously. It is the first great Elizabethan sonnet cycle.   LIT

1592–1597
Korean potters are brought to Japan to enhance ceramic production.   DECO

c. 1592
English dramatist William Shakespeare writes the comedy *Two Gentlemen of Verona.*   DRAMA

c. 1592	English dramatist Christopher Marlowe writes the tragedy *Edward II*, chronicling the personal and political adversities faced by a homosexual king. DRAMA
1592	English poet Samuel Daniel publishes the sonnet cycle *Delia*. LIT
1592	English poet and playwright Robert Greene excoriates English dramatist William Shakespeare in his pamphlet *Groatsworth of witte bought with a million of Repentance*. He calls Shakespeare "an upstart crow, beautified with our feathers." LIT
1592	Ludovico Zacconi publishes *Prattica di musica*, with extensive descriptions of instruments and directions for executing ornaments. MUSIC
1592	Italian painter Tintoretto paints *The Last Supper*. PAINT
c. 1593–1594	English dramatist William Shakespeare writes the comedies *The Taming of the Shrew* and *Love's Labour's Lost*. DRAMA
1593	English dramatist William Shakespeare publishes a mythological narrative poem, *Venus and Adonis*. LIT
1593	*The Phoenix Nest*, a poetic miscellany, is published in England, containing poems by Thomas Lodge, George Peele, Nicholas Breton, and possibly Sir Walter Raleigh. LIT
1593	Italian writer Cesare Ripa's *Iconologia*, published this year, will become a standard reference on iconography for artists. MISC
1593	Spanish painter El Greco paints *The Crucifixion* and *The Resurrection*. PAINT
c. 1594–1596	English dramatist William Shakespeare writes the tragedy *Romeo and Juliet*. The archetypal story of starcrossed young lovers will be the basis for works in many media, including a Berlioz symphony (1839), a Gounod opera (1867), an orchestral piece by Tchaikovsky (1869, revised 1880), a ballet by Prokofiev (1938), the Broadway musical *West Side Story* with music by Leonard Bernstein and lyrics by Stephen Sondheim (1957), and film versions by George Cukor (1936) and Franco Zeffirelli (1968), among others. DRAMA
c. 1594–1595	English dramatist William Shakespeare writes the history play *King John*. DRAMA
c. 1594–1598	English dramatist William Shakespeare writes the comedy *The Merchant of Venice*, in which the vengeful moneylender Shylock demands a pound of flesh in payment of Antonio's debt. DRAMA

1594   The Lord Chamberlain's Men (known after 1603 as King's Men), an acting company, is started by English dramatist William Shakespeare and several other performers. Shakespeare will write most of his plays for the group, and he will remain a member for about 20 years. In 1623, two members of the King's Men will publish all of Shakespeare's plays in folio form.   DRAMA

1594   English dramatist William Shakespeare publishes the narrative poem *The Rape of Lucrece*.   LIT

1594   English pamphleteer and dramatist Thomas Nashe publishes *The unfortunate traveller, or the life of Jack Wilton*, perhaps the first picaresque novel in English.   LIT

1594–1597   English theologian Richard Hooker publishes the first five books of his work *Of the Lawes of ecclesiasticall politie* (Books I-IV, 1594; Book V, 1597). Books VI and VIII (1648) and VII (1661), published posthumously, are of dubious authenticity. The apology for the organization of the English church is a masterpiece of theology and literary style.   LIT

1594   Italian painter Michelangelo Merisi, known as Caravaggio, paints *The Musical Party*.   PAINT

c. 1595–   English dramatist William Shakespeare writes the comedy *A Midsummer Night's Dream* and the historical play *Richard II*.   DRAMA
1596

1595   English poet Edmund Spenser publishes the sonnet sequence *Amoretti* and the marriage hymn *Epithalamion*.   LIT

1595   English poet Michael Drayton publishes *Endimion and Phoebe*, an erotic mythological poem later revised as *The Man in the Moon* (1606, 1619).   LIT

1595   English poet Sir Philip Sidney's critical treatise *An Apologie for Poetrie* is published posthumously in two editions, one under the title of *The Defence of Poesie*.   LIT

1595   English poet Edmund Spenser publishes *Colin Clouts come home againe*, a pastoral poem based on a character in *The Shepheardes Calendar* (*see* 1579, LIT). LIT

c. 1596–   English dramatist William Shakespeare's history plays *Henry IV, Part 1* and *Part 2* introduce the rotund, high-living scoundrel Falstaff, companion of Prince Hal, who will become Henry V in the play of that title (c. 1599). Falstaff will also appear in *The Merry Wives of Windsor* (c. 1597–1601).   DRAMA
1598

1596   English poet Edmund Spenser publishes *Four Hymns* and *Prothalamion*, a marriage poem.   LIT

c. 1597–   English dramatist William Shakespeare writes the comedy *The Merry Wives of*
1601   *Windsor.*   DRAMA

1597   English poet Michael Drayton publishes *Englands Heroicall Epistles.* Modeled
              on Ovid's *Heroides*, it earns him the title of "our English Ovid."   LIT

1597   The first edition of English philosopher Francis Bacon's *Essays* is published.
              The first English essayist, he will become known for writing in a style that is
              more formal and aphoristic than that of French essayist Michel de Montaigne,
              who will become recognized as the founder of the genre. This edition contains
              ten essays; a second edition will contain 38 (1612); a third 58 (1625).   LIT

1597   *Dafne*, perhaps the first opera ever, is performed in Florence. Written by Italian
              composers Jacopo Peri and Jacopo Corsi, it will be lost to history.   MUSIC

1597   English composer Thomas Morley publishes *A Plaine and Easie Introduction to*
              Practicall Musick, describing forms and compositional techniques.   MUSIC

1597   Italian composer Orazio Vecchi presents the madrigal-comedy *L'Amfiparnaso.* MUSIC

1597   Spanish painter El Greco paints *St. Martin and the Beggar.*   PAINT

c. 1598–   English dramatist William Shakespeare writes the comedies *Much Ado About Nothing*
1599   and *As You Like It.*   DRAMA

1598   *Every Man in His Humour*, the first popular comedy by English playwright Ben
              Jonson, is produced. William Shakespeare plays the part of Kno'well.   DRAMA

1598   *Hero and Leander*, a narrative poem by English dramatist Christopher Marlowe,
              is published posthumously.   LIT

1598   Flemish painter Jan Brueghel paints *Adoration of the Kings.*   PAINT

c. 1599   English dramatist William Shakespeare writes the history play *Henry V.* DRAMA

c. 1599   English dramatist William Shakespeare writes *Julius Caesar*, a drama about the
              assassination of the Roman dictator that begins the period of the playwright's
              great tragedies.   DRAMA

c. 1599–   English dramatist William Shakespeare writes the tragedy *Hamlet*, which will
1601   be considered by many his greatest work and by some the greatest play ever
              written. The drama of the prince of Denmark's quest to avenge the murder of
              his father by his uncle Claudius includes the soliloquy "To be or not to be"
              (act 3, scene 1, lines 55–87), in which Hamlet contemplates suicide. The play's
              sources include *Historica Danica* (1514).   DRAMA

1599	The original Globe Theatre opens in London. Constructed by English actor Richard Burbage and his brother Cuthbert, it is actually the reassembled Theatre (*see* 1576, DRAMA), which has been moved from Shoreditch to the Bankside south of the Thames. The largest Elizabethan playhouse, it will accommodate the first productions of most of Shakespeare's best plays. Destroyed by fire in 1613 and rebuilt immediately, it will be closed by Puritans in 1642 and torn down two years later. In 1997 it will be reopened 200 yards from the original site after an eight-year reconstruction project. DRAMA
1599	"The Passionate Shepherd to His Love," a lyric poem by English dramatist Christopher Marlowe, is published posthumously. It begins with the famous lines "Come live with me and be my love, / And we will all the pleasures prove." LIT
1599	A long-running pamphlet war between English pamphleteers Thomas Nashe and Gabriel Harvey comes to an end this year when church authorities order confiscation of their works. LIT
1600s	Meddahs, storytellers expert in parody and satire, entertain in sultan's courts and coffeehouses in the Ottoman Empire. DRAMA
1600s	Elaborate mourning ceremonies, in which dasteh (groups of mourners) flagellate and cut themselves while chanting, are performed in the streets of Persia (Iran). By the 19th century, these ceremonies will have grown larger and will have been performed with increasing frequency. DRAMA
1600s	Italian marionette shows are performed in London, and the character Punch is created. Punch will become the buffoon of nearly every British puppet show, and in the early 1700s, he will be joined by a wife, first named Joan, then Judy. By the 1800s, the two will have taken the form of hand puppets. Punch and Judy shows in England and abroad continue to be performed in subsequent centuries. DRAMA
1600s	Kabuki theater develops into a stylized—and highly commercialized—art form. Wearing beautiful costumes and accompanied by music and clappers, actors perform historical and contemporary plays and dances. Crowd-pleasing material is eventually favored heavily in order to compete effectively with *Jōruri* (*see* 1700s, DRAMA). Kabuki endures for centuries in Japan and abroad. DRAMA
1600s	French artist and engraver Jean Berain creates elaborate, sometimes bejeweled costumes for actors performing the works of Molière and other playwrights at the court of Louis XIV. DRAMA
1600s	Rome, Milan, and Turin each have theaters for puppet shows. Marionettes are popular in Italy and throughout Europe, as they will be through the 19th century. DRAMA

c. 1600s   Late this century, the overture emerges in two types: French, established by Jean-Baptiste Lully, and Italian, established by Alessandro Scarlatti.   MUSIC

1600s–1700s   Harps are used occasionally in operas (e.g., Monteverdi's *L'Orfeo*). Their regular use in orchestras will not become established until the 19th century.   MUSIC

1600s–1700s   During these years, Chinese painting styles fall roughly into two categories: traditionalists, like the Six Great Masters of the Ch'ing dynasty, and individualists, who explore different avenues from traditional gentlemanly work.   PAINT

c. 1600s   Huge ancestral figures carved from volcanic rock are lined up on raised platforms on Easter Island in the Pacific.   SCULP

1600s   Akan cultures of southern Ghana and the Ivory Coast begin to modify traditional forms of wooden sculpture to produce commemorative terra-cotta heads and figures of the royal family.   SCULP

c. 1600   Shamba Bolongongo, king of the BaKuba people of what will become known as Zaire, Africa, is a patron of the arts who welcomes representatives from craft guilds and introduces such innovations as embroidery and the weaving of raffia cloth.   DECO

c. 1600–   English dramatist William Shakespeare writes the comedy *Twelfth Night.*   DRAMA
1602

1600   As mannerism comes to an end, baroque, originating in Rome, will become the dominant visual style in Europe until about 1750. It is characterized by vigorous movement, emotional intensity, and a concern for balance and wholeness.   MISC

1600   Italian composers Giulio Caccini's and Jacopo Peri's opera *Euridice* premieres in Florence. It will survive as the earliest opera still extant nearly four centuries later.   MUSIC

1600   Italian composer Emilio de' Cavalieri's *La rappresentazione di anima e di corpo* is produced in Rome. Considered the first oratorio, its music consists almost exclusively of recitative and short choruses.   MUSIC

1600   The solo song with lute and viol accompaniment is popular in England, due in large part to the airs of John Dowland.   MUSIC

1600–1608   Flemish painter Peter Paul Rubens resides in Italy, where his personal style is formed and where he produces such works as *Marchesa Brigida Spinola-Doria.*   PAINT

1600–1868	During the Tokugawa period in Japan, the color-print movement thrives, chiefly the *ukiyo-e,* or painting of the passing world. This art, which includes painting of actors and celebrities, generates government censorship. PAINT
c. 1601– 1604	English dramatist William Shakespeare writes the satiric tragedy *Troilus and Cressida,* based on the same legendary love affair that inspired English poet Geoffrey Chaucer's poetic version (c. 1386). In the same period he writes the comedy *All's Well That Ends Well.* DRAMA
1601	Lute songs by English poet and composer Thomas Campion are published in *A Book of Airs,* composed with Philip Rossiter. More books of airs will follow in about 1613 and 1617. MUSIC
1601	English composer Thomas Morley publishes *Triumphs of Oriana,* a collection of madrigals in praise of Queen Elizabeth by 25 different composers. MUSIC
1601	Italian painter Caravaggio paints *The Conversion of St. Paul.* PAINT
1602	The poem *The Burning Babe* by English poet Robert Southwell is published posthumously with several other of his works. Southwell (*b.* 1561), a Jesuit priest, died a Catholic martyr's death in England in 1595. LIT
1602	English poet and composer Thomas Campion argues against rhyme and for classical meters in the treatise *Observations in the Art of English Poesy.* His arguments will be countered by Samuel Daniel's *Defence of Rime* in 1603. LIT
1602	A new vocal style is introduced in the song collection *Nuove Musiche* by Italian composer Giulio Caccini, a major step in the development of the opera, oratorio, cantata, and baroque music in general. Caccini's work serves to counteract the Flemish emphasis on counterpoint and artful elaboration. The prevailing polyphonic a cappella style is replaced with accompanied solo song (aria, monody, recitative). MUSIC
1602	German composer Hans Leo Hassler publishes a collection of lieder, *Lustgarten.* MUSIC
c. 1603– 1604	English dramatist William Shakespeare writes the comedy *Measure for Measure* and the tragedy *Othello.* DRAMA
1603	Queen Elizabeth's death brings to an end the Elizabethan period of literature in England. It is followed by the Jacobean period under James II (1603–1625). LIT
1604	The sons of Flemish composer Orlando di Lasso publish 516 of his motets in the six volumes, *Magnum opus musicum.* MUSIC

1604	Italian painter Caravaggio paints *The Deposition*. PAINT

c. 1605   English dramatist William Shakespeare's tragedy *King Lear*, the drama of the legendary king of Britain whose decline begins when he divides his kingdom between his untrustworthy daughters Goneril and Regan while banishing his faithful daughter Cordelia.   DRAMA

c. 1605–
1608   English dramatist William Shakespeare writes the tragedy *Timon of Athens*.
                                                                                              DRAMA

1605   English philosopher Francis Bacon publishes the treatise *The Advancement of Learning*, which begins the project he refers to as *Instauratio Magna*, a proposal for educational and scientific reform based on a new vision of human knowledge, one that depends on experiment and observation. Bacon's ideas, expressed in a concise, masterful prose style, will contribute to the development of the scientific method. *See also* 1620, LIT.   LIT

1605   The first of two parts of *Don Quixote de la Mancha*, a novel by Spanish novelist and playwright Miguel de Cervantes, is published. The second part of the comic saga of a man who feels called to set right the world's imperfections will be published in 1615.   LIT

1605   Spanish composer Tomás Luis de Victoria's masterpiece, a Requiem Mass for Empress Maria, is his last published work.   MUSIC

1605   English composer John Dowland composes *Lachrymae*, or *Seaven Teares in Seaven Passionate Pavans . . . set forth for the Lute, Viols, or Violins in five parts*.   MUSIC

1605   Italian artist Annibale Carraci paints the frescoes in the Palazzo Farnese, Rome. PAINT

1606   The Grande Galerie of the Louvre in Paris is completed. *See* 1546, ARCH.   ARCH

c. 1606–
1608   English dramatist William Shakespeare writes the tragedy *Macbeth*, the drama of the Scottish nobleman who, with his wife Lady Macbeth, murders King Duncan in order to gain the throne. During this period he also writes the tragedy *Antony and Cleopatra* and the romance play *Pericles*.   DRAMA

1606   *Volpone, or the Fox*, which will be considered one of the best of English playwright Ben Jonson's comedies, is produced.   DRAMA

1606   English poet Michael Drayton publishes *Poems Lyric and Pastoral*, containing imitations of the Roman poet Horace's *Odes*.   LIT

1607–1614	Italian architect Carlo Maderna adds a nave and facade to St. Peter's Church, Rome, thus determining that the church will take the form of a Latin rather than a Greek cross. ARCH
1607	Italian composer Claudio Monteverdi's opera *L'Orfeo* is produced in Mantua. It combines the archaic style of the earliest operas with greater expressiveness and dramatic impact. MUSIC
c. 1608	English dramatist William Shakespeare writes the tragedy *Coriolanus* and the romance play *Cymbeline*. DRAMA
1608	English writer Joseph Hall publishes *Characters of Vertues and Vices*, a collection of character sketches. This genre of writing, popular at this time, originated with the *Charakteres* of Greek philosopher Theophrastus in the third century B.C. LIT
1608	Italian composer Claudio Monteverdi composes his opera *L'Arianna*, a work which will become lost except for "Lamento d'Arianna." MUSIC
1608	Italian composer Girolamo Frescobaldi, who advances the organ and its technique, is made organist at St. Peter's, Rome. MUSIC
1608	Notable paintings include Italian painter Domenichino's *The Scourging of St. Andrew* and Spanish painter El Greco's *Golgotha* and *Cardinal Taverna*. PAINT
c. 1609	English dramatists Francis Beaumont and John Fletcher's play *Phylaster, or Love Lies Bleeding* is produced, and their famous collaboration begins. They will write six or seven plays together, including *The Maides Tragedy* (c. 1610) and *A King and No King* (1611), and their work will be popular with sophisticated audiences of the day. Each had written plays alone in the past, and Fletcher will do so again in the future. DRAMA
1609	*Epicoene, or the Silent Woman*, a comedy by English dramatist Ben Jonson, is produced. DRAMA
1609	English dramatist William Shakespeare's sonnets are published. The 154 sonnets, most of which were probably written before 1600, are dedicated to Mr. W.H., who may be either the earl of Southampton or the earl of Pembroke. Sonnets 1–126 are mainly about the poet's relationship with a youth, Sonnets 127–154 about his relationship with a mistress known as the Dark Lady. Among the sonnets that will be best remembered is Sonnet 18, "Shall I compare thee to a summer's day." LIT

1609   English philosopher Francis Bacon publishes the Latin work on classical mythology *De Sapientia Veterum*, which will later be translated as *The Wisdom of the Ancients* (1619). LIT

1609   Flemish painter Peter Paul Rubens paints his self-portrait with his wife, Isabella Brant. PAINT

1610–1643   The Louis XIII style of interior decoration and architecture prevails in France. It marks a transition from Italian-influenced baroque style to French classicism. *See also* 1661–1715, DECO. DECO

c. 1610–1611 English dramatist William Shakespeare writes the romance plays *The Winter's Tale* and his last great work, *The Tempest*. The latter introduces the sorceror Prospero, the sprite Ariel, the monster Caliban, and Prospero's daughter Miranda, all of whom dwell in isolation on an island until they are visited by a crew shipwrecked in a tempest raised through Prospero's magic. Among the works inspired by *The Tempest* are British poet Robert Browning's poem "Caliban upon Setebos," Russian composer Pyotr Ilich Tchaikovsky's symphonic fantasy (1873), British novelist Aldous Huxley's novel *Brave New World* (1932), and the science fiction film *Forbidden Planet* (1956). DRAMA

1610   English dramatist Ben Jonson's *The Alchemist* premieres. English poet and critic Samuel Taylor Coleridge will later call it one of the "three most perfect plots ever planned." *See* 1749, LIT. DRAMA

1610   English poet John Donne publishes his most important prose work, *Pseudo-Martyr*, which encourages English Roman Catholics to become Anglicans. LIT

1610   German composer Michael Praetorius publishes a collection of church hymns, *Musae sioniae*. MUSIC

1610–1614   With the triptychs *Raising of the Cross* and *Descent from the Cross*, Flemish painter Peter Paul Rubens establishes himself as one of the most significant painters in northern Europe. PAINT

1611   A new English translation of the Bible, authorized by King James I, is published. The King James Bible, also known as the Authorized Version, will have an enduring influence on English literary style. It is heavily dependent on previous English translations, including those of English humanist William Tyndale (1525), Miles Coverdale (1535), and the Geneva Bible (1560). LIT

1611–1612   English poet John Donne writes two long poems, *The Anniversaries*, on the death of Sir Robert Drury's daughter Elizabeth. LIT

1612	English dramatist John Webster's *The White Devil* is produced. His *The Duchess of Malfi* will be produced in 1614. Both are plays set in Renaissance Italy, and both will be seen as masterpieces of 17th-century English drama. DRAMA
1612	The poem "What Is Our Life?" by English poet and explorer Sir Walter Raleigh is printed in a madrigal setting. Raleigh is also known for "The Nymph's Reply to the Shepherd," a response to English dramatist Christopher Marlowe's "Passionate Shepherd" (1599). LIT
1612	English poet Michael Drayton publishes the first part of *Poly-Olbion*, a 30,000-line historical-geographical poem about the English countryside. The second part of this, his masterpiece, will appear in 1622. LIT
c. 1613	English dramatist William Shakespeare's last play, which some authorities will consider to have been coauthored by John Fletcher, is the historical drama *Henry VIII*. DRAMA
1613	Italian composer Claudio Monteverdi is made maestro di cappella at St. Mark's, Venice, where he will remain until his death in 1643. MUSIC
1613	*Parthenia*, a collection of music for virginals (a type of harpsichord) by English composers William Byrd, John Bull, and Orlando Gibbons, is presented to Princess Elizabeth and Prince Frederick on their wedding. MUSIC
1614	*Bartholomew Fair*, the last successful comedy by English dramatist Ben Jonson, is produced. DRAMA
1615	Once a notorious rake and writer of love lyrics, English poet John Donne becomes an Anglican minister, reflecting his shift in recent years toward religious writing. He will compose religious verse and prose works, and more than 160 of his sermons will survive. His *Holy Sonnets* date from this decade. LIT
1615	Adriano Banchieri founds Accademia de' Floridi in Bologna for the promotion of literature, science and the arts, including the cultivation of music. MUSIC
1615–1619	German composer Michael Praetorius writes his three-volume encyclopedia of music *Syntagma musicum*. MUSIC
1616–1635	English architect Inigo Jones builds the Queen's House at Greenwich (1616–1635) and the Banqueting House in Whitehall (1619–1622). The latter includes a painted ceiling by Flemish painter Peter Paul Rubens. Jones's classical style is highly influential in England. ARCH
1616	*Epigrams* and *The Forest*, verse collections by English dramatist Ben Jonson, are published. LIT

1616   The musical society Collegium Musicum is founded in Prague.   MUSIC

1616   Dutch painter Frans Hals paints *Banquet of the Officers of the St. George Militia*, which sets a new standard for energetic, informal group portraits. In the 1620s and 1630s, Hals's group portraits will be in high demand by prosperous, ambitious members of the Dutch mercantile class.   PAINT

1617   Biagio Marini, one of the first great composers for violin, publishes *Musical Events*, sonata for solo violin, in Italy.   MUSIC

1617   German composer Johann Hermann Schein writes his dance suite, *Banchetto musicale* in Leipzig. The suite, as a composition in several movements and not merely a succession of pieces each in a particular mood and rhythm, is a German phenomenon.   MUSIC

1617   German composer Heinrich Schütz becomes Kapellmeister of the electoral chapel at Dresden, a position he will hold until 1672.   MUSIC

1617   Flemish painter Peter Paul Rubens paints the dynamic and colorful mythological painting *The Rape of the Daughters of Leucippus*.   PAINT

c. 1618   The Chinese novel *Chin p'ing mei* (*The Plum in the Golden Vase*, also known as *The Golden Lotus*), which will become known for its naturalism and erotic content, is published. The anonymous author describes the fall of the Sung dyanasty (960–1279).   LIT

1618–1625   Italian sculptor, architect, and painter Gian Lorenzo Bernini, one of the greatest artists of the Italian baroque era, executes four life-size sculptures: *Aeneas, Anchises, and Ascanius; The Rape of Proserpine; David*; and *Apollo and Daphne*. The dynamic vigor and emotion of the works represent a decisive break with late mannerism.   SCULP

1619   The most extensive and important collection of music for virginals, the *Fitzwilliam Virginal Book*, containing 297 compositions by nearly every composer of the virginalist school, is compiled in England by Francis Tregian.   MUSIC

1619   German composer Heinrich Schütz's *Psalms of David* reflects the opulent texture and coloration of the Venetian tradition.   MUSIC

1620s   While running a very prolific painting studio in high demand in Flanders, Flemish painter Peter Paul Rubens also designs tapestries, festival decorations, architectural decorations, and book illustrations.   DECO

1620s   Pedro Calderón de la Barca, one of the greatest playwrights of Spain's Golden
             Age and, from middle age on, a Roman Catholic priest, begins to have his
             work produced. He will write comedies, tragedies, histories, and *autos sacra-
             mentales* (religious allegories)—some 200 plays in all by the time of his death
             in 1681.   DRAMA

1620   English philosopher Francis Bacon writes the Latin work *Novum Organum*
             (*New Instrument*), which forms the second part of the *Instauratio Magna*, the
             program of educational and scientific reform begun in *The Advancement of
             Learning* (*see* 1605, LIT). The work seeks to add inductive reasoning to the tools
             of deductive inquiry that had been outlined in Greek philosopher Aristotle's
             treatises of logic known as the *Organum*, or instrument.   LIT

1621   English writer Robert Burton publishes his only book, *The Anatomy of Melancholy*,
             a strange, seriocomic, paramedical study of melancholy, with many learned quo-
             tations and frequent digressions on religion, politics, and a host of other subjects.
                                                                                         LIT

1621   Flemish painter Anthony Van Dyck travels to Italy, where he develops his ele-
             gant baroque style. His works there in the 1620s include portraits of Genoese
             nobility.   PAINT

1622–1625   Flemish painter Peter Paul Rubens paints a series of 25 paintings on the life of
             Marie de Médicis of France.   PAINT

1623   The first folio edition of English dramatist William Shakespeare's plays is pub-
             lished seven years after his death.   DRAMA

1624   English philosopher Francis Bacon publishes *Apophthegms New and Old*.   LIT

1624   Italian composer Claudio Monteverdi produces his madrigal opera in one act,
             Il Combattimato di Tancredi e Clorinda, in Venice.   MUSIC

1624   Dutch painter Frans Hals paints *The Laughing Cavalier*.   PAINT

1624–1638   For St. Peter's Church in Rome, Italian sculptor Bernini executes the bal-
             dacchino (canopy) over the High Altar and the statue of St. Longinus.   SCULP

1625   Italian sculptor, architect, and painter Bernini begins working at the Barberini
             palace, where he produces a series of technically superior portrait busts of
             Cardinal Scipione Borghese and others.   SCULP

1626	St. Peter's Church in Rome, the largest church in the Christian world, is dedicated by Pope Urban VIII. Construction of the church began in 1506. Bernini will make additions between 1629 and 1662 that include interior details and a forecourt with a piazza. ARCH
1627	English playwright John Ford's drama *'Tis Pity She's a Whore*, considered provocative because of its depiction of incest, is produced. DRAMA
1627	*The New Atlantis*, an unfinished Utopian fiction in Latin by English philosopher Francis Bacon, is published posthumously. LIT
1627	German composer Heinrich Schütz presents *Dafne* (libretto by Martin Opitz), the first German opera, at Torgau. The music will be later lost in a fire. MUSIC
1627	French painter Simon Vouet is named court painter to King Louis XIII. The leading French artist of the first half of the 17th century, he has an eclectic style that combines classical and baroque tendencies. PAINT
c. 1628	Dutch painter Frans Hals paints *The Jolly Toper*. PAINT
c. 1628	In Rome French painter Nicolas Poussin paints the altarpiece *The Martyrdom of St. Erasmus* and the more personal work *Inspiration of the Poet*. PAINT
1628	Dutch painter Rembrandt takes his first pupil, Gerrit Dou. Other painters taught by Rembrandt will include Carel Fabritius, Philips de Koninck, Nicolaes Maes, and Aert de Gelder. PAINT
1629	English poet John Milton writes his first great English lyric, "Ode Upon the Morning of Christ's Nativity." LIT
1630s	Pupils of Dutch painter Frans Hals now working in Holland include genre painters Adriaen Brouwer and Adriaen van Ostade. Two other pupils and genre painters, Judith Leyster (*see* 1630, PAINT) and Jan Miense Molenaer, are married in 1636 and share a studio. Genre painting, scenes of everyday life that often suggest a story, are a popular form in Dutch art of the 17th century. PAINT
1630–1648	The Taj Mahal is constructed in Agra, India, by Shah Jahan as a mausoleum in memory of his wife. ARCH
c. 1630	Spanish painter José de Ribera paints *Martyrdom of St. Bartholomew*. PAINT
1630	Dutch painter Judith Leyster paints *The Jolly Companion*, considered more complex than that which influenced it, *The Jolly Toper* (c. 1628), a work by her teacher, Dutch painter Frans Hals. PAINT

1630–1714	Chinese individualist painter and theorist Tao Chi (also known as Shih-tao) breaks from past Chinese artistic rigidity to imbue works with emotion. His influence will carry into future centuries in the East. PAINT
1632–1633	English sculptor and architect Nicholas Stone designs the three classical gateways in the Botanic Garden, Oxford. ARCH
1632–1634	Flemish painter Peter Paul Rubens paints the *Garden of Love*, noted for its lush color and brushwork. PAINT
1632	Dutch painter Rembrandt paints *The Anatomy Lesson of Dr. Tulp*, a radically dramatic group portrait. The artist will paint nearly 50 portraits in 1632 and 1633. PAINT
1632	Flemish painter Anthony Van Dyck (*b.* 1599) becomes court painter to King Charles I of England, a position he holds until his death in 1641. His portrait style will strongly influence English painters, including Thomas Gainsborough. PAINT
1633	English poet John Donne's *Collected Poems* is published, including *Songs and Sonnets* and *Divine Poems*. LIT
1633	Shortly after the death this year of English poet and divine George Herbert (*b.* 1593), his collection *The Temple* is published, containing about 160 poems. Centered on religious themes, they employ the technique of metaphysical conceits developed by English poet John Donne. Among the poems that will become best known are "Easter Wings" and "The Altar." LIT
1633	English poet Thomas Carew publishes *An Elegy Upon the Death of the Dean of Paul's, Dr. John Donne*. LIT
1634	The masque *Comus,* by English poet John Milton, is first performed. DRAMA
1634	English poet Thomas Carew's masque *Coelum Britannicum* is performed before English king Charles I. He is one of a group of writers, also including Sir John Suckling and Richard Lovelace, known as the Cavalier poets because they flourish at Charles's court (1625–1649) before civil war brings about the king's dethroning and execution. DRAMA
1635	French architect François Mansart completes the Hôtel de la Vrillière, an example of Renaissance classical architecture. Mansart's grand-nephew Jules Hardouin-Mansart will become the chief architect of the royal buildings for Louis XIV in 1699. ARCH
1635	Italian composer Girolamo Frescobaldi writes *Fiori musicali di toccate*, which later influences German composer Johann Sebastian Bach. MUSIC

1635	Flemish painter Peter Paul Rubens completes a series of paintings on the reign of King James I of England. **PAINT**
1635	Dutch painter Frans Hals paints *Lucas de Clercq* and *Feyntje van Steenkiste*, notable for their monochromatic effects. **PAINT**
1635–1636	French painter Claude Gellée, known as Claude Lorrain, after his birthplace, begins to compile his *Liber Veritatis* (*Book of Truth*), using drawings to document his many paintings from this time on. He will be considered one of the greatest landscape painters of all time, and his work will inspire the picturesque tradition in England. **PAINT**
1635	Spanish sculptor Juan Martinez Montañes completes a gilt and polychromed wood statue of St. John the Baptist for the convent of Nuestra Señora de la Concepción in Seville. **SCULP**
1636	French mathematician Marin Mersenne publishes his most important work, *Harmonie Universelle*, covering experiments on the physical properties of sound and detailing contemporary musical instruments. **MUSIC**
c. 1636	French painter Nicolas Poussin paints *Rape of the Sabine Women*, which exemplifies the artist's rational, linear style and his devotion to classical design and themes. Poussin, the most influential French painter of the 17th century, is the leading exponent of French classical style (sometimes called baroque classicism). Sources of his paintings during the 1630s include Roman mythology and the Old Testament. **PAINT**
1636	Dutch painter Rembrandt paints *The Blinding of Samson*, notable for its turbulence and dramatic lighting, influenced by Italian painter Caravaggio. **PAINT**
1637	*Le Cid*, a tragicomedy by the French playwright Pierre Corneille, is produced in Paris. **DRAMA**
1637	Teatro San Cassiano, the first public opera house, opens in Venice, with a paying clientele including all social classes. This transformation of opera from courtly entertainment to a public spectacle leads to changes in both music and libretto that will include more lavish staging, more characters, bolder musical effects, and more plot complications and burlesque comic episodes. Virtuoso soloists are featured and aria and recitative become two distinct forms. **MUSIC**
1638	English poet John Milton publishes the elegy *Lycidas* in a volume of verses memorializing his deceased Cambridge classmate Edward King. **LIT**
1639	*Chi soffre speri* by Marco Marazzoli and Virgilio Mazzocchi, the first comic opera, is presented in Rome. **MUSIC**

1639	The opera *Adone* by Italian composer Claudio Monteverdi is produced at Teatro San Cassiano, Venice. MUSIC
1639	French painter Nicolas Poussin paints *The Gathering of the Manna*. PAINT
1640s	In the last decade of his life, Flemish painter Peter Paul Rubens paints *Hélène Fourment with Two of Her Children, The Judgment of Paris, Three Graces,* and *Venus and Adonis*. PAINT
1640	*Horace*, a tragedy by French playwright Pierre Corneille, opens in Paris. *Cinna* and *Polyeucte*, also tragedies, will open in 1641 and 1642, respectively. DRAMA
1640	Dutch painter Philips Wouwerman establishes his career by joining a painters' guild. A student of Dutch painter Frans Hals, he becomes known for his hilly landscapes, usually with horses. PAINT
1640	French painter Nicolas Poussin, resident in Rome since the 1620s, returns to Paris briefly to oversee the decoration of the Grande Galerie of the Louvre and to paint altarpieces. After unpleasant intrigues, he will return to Rome in 1642. PAINT
1641	English poet John Milton publishes three anti-episcopal pamphlets, *Of Reformation in England, Of Prelatical Episcopacy,* and *Animadversions Upon the Remonstrant's Defence Against Smectymnuus*. LIT
1641	Italian composer Claudio Monteverdi's first public opera *Il Ritorno d'Ulisse in patria* is produced in Venice. MUSIC
1641	Dutch painter Frans Hals paints *Regents of the St. Elizabeth Hospital*, marking a shift to darker, more sober group portraits than his earlier work. PAINT
1641	Italian sculptor, architect, and painter Bernini, skilled in creating portrait busts, executes the bust of Cardinal Richelieu, which earns him an invitation to work at the court of Louis XIV in Paris. He will sculpt the bust of Louis XIV in 1655. SCULP
1642–1652	Italian sculptor, architect, and painter Bernini builds the Cornaro Chapel. With his marble group *Ecstasy of St. Theresa*, it exemplifies his ideal of joining sculpture, architecture, and painting in a harmonious whole. ARCH
1642	German painter and engraver Ludwig von Siegen of Utrecht invents the mezzotint, a method of engraving in tone. GRAPH
1642	English physician and writer Sir Thomas Browne publishes *Religio Medici (A Doctor's Faith)*, a masterpiece of 17th-century prose in which the author examines his own religious beliefs. LIT

1642	Italian composer Claudio Monteverdi's opera *L'Incoronazione di Poppea* (the first on a historical rather than mythological subject), is performed at Teatro di Santi Giovanni e Paolo in Venice, Europe's second public opera house. MUSIC
1642	Dutch painter Rembrandt paints *The Shooting Company of Captain Frans Banning Cocq*, also known as *The Night Watch*, which will become his most famous group portrait. PAINT
1642	Spanish painter José de Ribera paints *The Clubfooted Boy*. PAINT
1643–1645	English poet John Milton publishes a series of tracts advocating the legality of divorce on grounds of incompatibility. He writes these shortly after being abandoned by his wife Mary Powell; she will later return to him and bear him three daughters. During the same period he publishes *Areopagitica*, a classical oration in favor of freedom of the press, and the treatise *Of Education*. LIT
1643	Francesco Cavalli, the first popular opera composer in Venice, presents *Egisto*. MUSIC
1644–1911	During the Ch'ing (Manchu) dynasty in China, many encyclopedias, compendia, and works of literary and philological scholarship are composed. LIT
1645	English poet John Milton publishes a volume of his early poems, including *L'Allegro*, *Il Penseroso*, and *At a Solemn Music*. LIT
1645	French composer Jean-Baptiste Lully becomes violinist at the French court. MUSIC
1645	Cardinal Mazarin, adviser to Anne of Austria, who is regent for her son, French king Louis XIV (1638–1715; reigned 1643–1715), encourages the production of Italian operas in France. *La Finta Pazza* by Francesco Paolo Sacrati may be the first opera produced in Paris. MUSIC
1646	English poet Richard Crashaw publishes *Steps to the Temple*, a collection of his devotional verses, influenced by contemporary Italian models and infused with the spiritual concerns that led him to convert to Catholicism. LIT
1646	English physician and writer Sir Thomas Browne publishes *Pseudodoxia Epidemica* (*Vulgar Errors*), a compendium of delusive beliefs with Browne's refutations of them. LIT
1647	English poet Abraham Cowley's *The Mistress*, a collection of witty metaphysical love lyrics, is published. LIT
1648–1651	Italian sculptor, architect, and painter Bernini designs the *Fountain of the Four Rivers* in Rome. ARCH

1648	English poet Robert Herrick publishes the collection *Hesperides*, which contains 1,200 poems heavily influenced by classical models and his association with English poet Ben Jonson. A section called *Noble Numbers* includes poems on sacred themes. Among what will become Herrick's best-known works is "To the Virgins, to Make Much of Time," which begins, "Gather ye rosebuds while ye may." LIT
1648	In France King Louis XIV establishes the Royal Academy of Painting and Sculpture, later reorganized by French politician Jean-Baptiste Colbert (*see* 1663, MISC). SCULP
1649	English poet John Milton publishes *The Tenure of Kings and Magistrates* and *Eikonoklastes*, pamphlets attacking monarchy and justifying the execution this year of English king Charles I. Milton is made secretary of foreign tongues to English leader Oliver Cromwell's Council of State. LIT
1649	English poet Richard Lovelace publishes the verse collection *Lucasta*, which includes "To Althea, from Prison" and "To Lucasta, Going to the Wars." A second *Lucasta* volume will be published posthumously in 1657. LIT
1649	Italian composer Francesco Cavalli's opera *Giasone* is performed in Venice. MUSIC
1650	English metaphysical poet Henry Vaughan publishes *Silex Scintillans* (*The Fiery Flint*), a collection of devotional verses on the theme of the hard heart producing a spiritual flame when struck by divinely ordained afflictions. Influenced by George Herbert, the poems include "Peace," which begins, "My soul, there is a country / Far beyond the stars." LIT
1650	Spanish painter José de Ribera paints *The Adoration of the Shepherds*. PAINT
c. 1650	The practice of miniature painting is established in India, with early examples created in the states of Basohli, Kahlur (Bilaspur), and Mankot. PAINT
1651	English metaphysical poet Henry Vaughan publishes *Olor Iscanus* (*The Swan of Usk*), a collection of poems on his native Wales. LIT
1651	By now, English poet John Milton is effectively blind, though he continues to write, producing such pamphlets as *Defensio Pro Populo Anglicano* (*Defence of the English People*), to be followed in 1654 by *Defensio Secunda* (*Second Defence*). LIT
1651	English philosopher Thomas Hobbes publishes *Leviathan*, a treatise on political philosophy arguing that absolute obedience to supreme state authority when it is successful in maintaining the peace is needed to prevent people from destroying each other. LIT

1651	English poet and dramatist Sir William Davenant publishes the verse epic *Gondibert.* LIT
1652	The minuet, a French country dance, becomes fashionable at court when King Louis XIV is said to dance the first minuet composed by Jean-Baptiste Lully. It quickly spreads throughout Europe, superseding older types of dance, and establishing a new period of dance music. DANCE
1652–1653	Dutch painter Rembrandt creates such etchings as *Christ Preaching* (1652) and *The Three Crosses* (1653). He will rework the latter in the 1660s. Rembrandt's etchings will be regarded as among the best exemplars of that art; he will also become known for his drawings done with reed pen. GRAPH
1652	*Carmen Deo Nostro* (*A Song to Our Lord*), a final collection of English poet Richard Crashaw's work, is published posthumously. LIT
1652–1654	Englishwoman Dorothy Osborne writes letters to her fiancé, essayist and diplomat Sir William Temple. These will be published in 1888 and admired by such writers as Virginia Woolf. LIT
1652	John Hilton publishes his collection of English catches, rounds, and canons, *Catch As Catch Can.* MUSIC
1652	Dutch painter Carel Fabritius paints *The Goldfinch.* PAINT
1653	English writer Izaak Walton publishes *The Compleat Angler*, the classic treatise on fishes and fishing. LIT
1653	English dramatist James Shirley's elaborate masque, *Cupid and Death*, with music by Matthew Locke and Christopher Gibbons, is produced. MUSIC
1653	Jean-Baptiste Lully becomes court composer for instrumental music for Louis XIV in France. MUSIC
1653	Dutch painter Rembrandt paints *Aristotle Contemplating the Bust of Homer.* PAINT
1653	Dutch painter Jacob van Ruisdael paints *Bentheim Castle.* PAINT
1655	Now completely blind, English poet John Milton writes the sonnet "When I consider how my light is spent," which ends, "They also serve who only stand and wait." He also publishes the pamphlet *Pro Se Defensio/Defence of Himself.* LIT
1655	Dutch painter Rembrandt paints *The Polish Rider* and *The Slaughtered Ox.* PAINT

1656	The first English opera, *The Siege of Rhodes*, with libretto by Sir William Davenant and music by Matthew Locke and others, is produced at Rutland House in London. MUSIC

1656   Spanish painter Diego Velázquez paints *The Maids of Honor*, remarkable for its fluid brushwork and rich color. **PAINT**

1657   English poet Abraham Cowley's *Miscellanies*, published this year, includes his uncompleted epic poem, *Davideis*, and irregular odes in imitation of Greek poet Pindar. **LIT**

1657   Adam Krieger, master of German baroque lieder, presents *Deutsche Lieder*. **MUSIC**

1658–1670   Italian sculptor, architect, and painter Bernini designs San Andrea al Quirinale church. **ARCH**

1658   On October 24 French playwright Jean-Baptiste Molière and his troupe so impress King Louis XIV with performances of Corneille's *Nicomède* and Molière's own comedy *Le Docteur amoureux* (*The Doctor in Love*) that he grants them use of a Paris theater, launching Molière's career as a writer. **DRAMA**

1658   English physician and writer Sir Thomas Browne publishes *Hydriotaphia: Urne-Buriall*, a discussion of funeral practices that branches into a meditation on life and death, and *The Garden of Cyrus*, a treatise on the quincunx, a particular kind of five-spot pattern. **LIT**

1659   Italian sculptor, architect, and painter Bernini begins the Palazzo Chigi-Odescalchi, which strongly influences baroque palace architecture. **ARCH**

1659   French playwright Molière's comedy *Les Précieuses ridicules* (*The Affect Ladies*) is produced. It will be followed by Molière comedies *Sganarelle, ou Le Cocu imaginaire* (*Sganarelle, or the Imaginary Cuckold*, 1660), *L'École des maris* (*The School for Husbands*, 1661) and *Les Fâcheux* (*The Bores*, 1661). **DRAMA**

c. 1660s   Dutch painter Jan Vermeer paints several genre paintings famed for their serenity, harmony, and exquisite lighting. Usually involving everyday activities in domestic settings, they include *Young Woman with Water Jug* and *Lady Reading a Letter*. His landscape *View of Delft* also dates from this period. **PAINT**

1660   Women begin to act in plays in London. Previously, men had almost always performed both male and female roles. Women had begun to appear on stage in Italy and France somewhat earlier. **DRAMA**

1660   In protest of the impending restoration of the English monarchy, John Milton
            publishes the pamphlet *The Ready and Easy Way to Establish a Free
            Commonwealth*. With the monarchy restored later this year, Milton's works are
            publicly burned and Milton himself is fined and briefly imprisoned.   LIT

1660   English poet John Dryden celebrates the Restoration of King Charles II with
            the poem *Astrae Redux*.   LIT

1660–1669   English politician Samuel Pepys keeps his *Diary*. Active in the politics of the
            day, Pepys recreates a lively social tableau in his writings. Parts of the work will
            be first published in 1825.   LIT

1660   Italian composer Francesco Cavalli's opera *Serse* is performed for the marriage
            of Louis XIV in France.   MUSIC

c. 1660   Dutch landscape painter Jacob van Ruisdael paints *The Jewish Cemetery*.   PAINT

1661   French painter Charles Le Brun designs the Galerie d'Apollon at the Louvre. ARCH

1661–1715   The *Louis Quatorze* style of interior decoration and architecture, with its classi-
            cal rationality and formality, prevails in France during the reign of Louis XIV,
            who takes control of his government in 1661 upon the death of Cardinal
            Mazarin (*see* 1645, MUSIC). The *Louis Quatorze* style is especially evident in tex-
            tiles, furniture, and ornaments of the period. *See also* 1723–1774 and
            1774–1793, DECO.   DECO

1661   In France Louis XIV founds the Académie Royale de Danse.   MUSIC

1661   English composer Matthew Locke becomes court composer to King Charles II.
                                                                                   MUSIC

1661   French painter Charles Le Brun, known for his decorative classicism influenced by
            Poussin, paints *The Family of Darius Before Alexander*.   PAINT

1661   Dutch-born painter Sir Peter Lely, acclaimed as the "best artist in England," is
            named principal painter to the Restoration court of King Charles II. His works
            include *The Windsor Beauties*, *Flagmen*, and *The Family of the Earl of Carnarvon*. PAINT

1662   King Louis XIV of France takes control of the Gobelins tapestry works. Under
            Jean-Baptiste Colbert and director of the works Charles Le Brun, Gobelins will
            produce lavish furnishings of all kinds for the royal palaces. Because of the
            king's financial troubles, it will return to making only tapestries after 1699.   DECO

1662	French playwright Molière's *L'École des femmes* (*The School for Wives*) is produced. *La Critique de l'École des femmes* and *L'Impromptu de Versailles*, both of which will be produced in 1663, will be Molière's humorous counterattacks on his critics. DRAMA
1662	Rembrandt paints *The Syndics of the Cloth Guild*, often considered the apex of Dutch portait painting. PAINT
1662	French painter Charles Le Brun becomes painter to the court of King Louis XIV. Le Brun will dominate French painting, design, and artistic theory for decades. PAINT
1663	Drury Lane, which will become perhaps London's most famous theater, opens. There will be a second and third Drury Lane, and the fourth, which will open in 1812, will continue operating indefinitely. DRAMA
1663	English satirist Samuel Butler publishes the first part of *Hudibras*, a mock-heroic poem satirizing the Puritan regime recently unseated by the Restoration of King Charles II. Part two will follow in 1664, part three in 1678. LIT
1663	French politician Jean-Baptiste Colbert changes the focus of the Royal Academy of Painting and Sculpture to exercise central control over artistic theory, teaching, and exhibition. Painter Charles Le Brun serves as director of the academy, under Colbert's supervision. Colbert's program of patronage and strict domination of the arts helps to make France more important than Italy as Europe's artistic center. *See also* 1648, SCULP, and 1662, DECO. MISC
1664	Flemish painter Adam Frans van der Meulen moves to Paris, where he becomes an assistant to Charles Le Brun, making paintings and designs for tapestries, often depicting contemporary battles. DECO
1664	*Le Mariage forcé* (*The Forced Marriage*) and *La Princesse d'Elide*, two comedies by French playwright Molière, are produced. Molière also produces the first three acts of *Tartuffe*, his controversial attack on religious hypocrisy. A revised version of *Tartuffe* will be performed once in 1667, but the play will be denounced and banned until 1669. DRAMA
1664	*La Thébaïde, ou Les Frères ennemis* (*The Thebaid, or the Enemy Brothers*), the first play by French playwright Jean Racine, is staged by French playwright Molière. Racine's tragedy *Alexandre le Grand* (*Alexander the Great*) will be produced in 1665. DRAMA
1664	German composer Heinrich Schütz's *Christmas Oratorio*, performed in Dresden, strikes a balance between Italianate style and solid contrapuntal Lutheran tradition. MUSIC

1664   Dutch painter Frans Hals, now 84, paints *The Governors of the Almshouse* and *Lady Regents of the Almshouse*, two moving group portraits that mark the climax of his career. Hals dies two years later.   PAINT

1665–1667   Italian architect Francesco Borromini designs San Carlo alle Quattro Fontane in Rome, the walls of which have a powerful sense of dynamic movement.   ARCH

1665   French playwright Molière's comedy *L'Amour Médecin* (*Love's the Best Doctor*) is produced. His comedies *Le Misanthrope* and *Le Médecin malgré lui* (*The Doctor in Spite of Himself*) will be produced in 1666, and *L'Avare* (*The Miser*) and *Amphitryon* will be produced in 1668. *The Miser* is derived from Roman playwright Plautus's *Aulularia* (*The Pot of Gold*).   DRAMA

1665   Dutch painter Rembrandt paints *The Jewish Bride*, notable for its psychological depth and flamelike color.   PAINT

1666   The great London fire this year forces rebuilding of many edifices. English architect Sir Christopher Wren redesigns many formerly Gothic churches in baroque style. *See* 1675–1710, ARCH.   ARCH

1666   English preacher and writer John Bunyan publishes his spiritual autobiography, *Grace Abounding to the Chief of Sinners*.   LIT

1666   Italian composer Antonio Cesti becomes Kapellmeister at the court in Vienna.   MUSIC

1666–1737   Italian violin maker Antonio Stradivari begins making violins. He will make more than 1000 instruments, including violins, violas, and cellos.   MUSIC

1667   English poet John Dryden's comedy *Secret Love* is performed.   DRAMA

1667   English poet John Milton publishes his masterpiece, *Paradise Lost*, a blank verse epic on the Fall of Man and the expulsion of Adam and Eve from Eden. Proposing to "justify the ways of God to men," the epic's form is modeled on the works of Homer and Virgil. A second edition in 1674, the year of Milton's death (*b.* 1608), will expand the poem from 10 books to 12. A companion work, *Paradise Regained*, will appear in 1671.   LIT

1667   English poet John Dryden publishes the poem *Annus Mirabilis* (*The Year of Wonders*).   LIT

1667   The French Royal Academy of Painting and Sculpture holds its first official annual exhibition, known as the Salon because of its location in the Salon d'Apollon in the Louvre.   MISC

1667	Italian composer Antonio Cesti's opera *Il Pomo d'oro* (*The Golden Apple*) is a hit in Vienna. **MUSIC**
c. 1668	Mexican poet and nun Juana Inés de la Cruz's play *Amor es Mas Laberinto* (*Love Is a Greater Labryinth*) is produced. She will write other plays on both religious and secular themes, as well as poetry and essays. **DRAMA**
1668	English poet John Dryden's heroic tragedy *The Conquest of Granada* is performed. **DRAMA**
1668	*Les Plaideurs* (*The Litigants*), the only comedy by French playwright Jean Racine, is produced. **DRAMA**
1668	English poet Abraham Cowley's *Several Discourses by way of Essays, in Verse and Prose* is published posthumously. **LIT**
1668	John Dryden becomes poet laureate of England and publishes *Essay of Dramatic Poesy*, a critical prose work. **LIT**
1668	Danish composer Dietrich Buxtehude becomes organist at St. Mary's Church in Lübeck. **MUSIC**
1669–1710	The palace of Versailles is constructed for King Louis XIV of France. The Garden Front, with its formal classical approach, is designed by French architects Louis Le Vau and Jules Hardouin-Mansart. The interior rooms feature lavish baroque decoration. The gardens, extending for miles, are designed in formal style by André Lenôtre. Charles Le Brun designs the Galerie des Glaces and the Great Staircase. **ARCH**
1669	Pierre Perrini is granted a Royal patent for founding the Académie Royale des Operas in France, to produce operas in the French language similar to those given in Italy. **MUSIC**
1669	In his final year Dutch painter Rembrandt (b. 1606) paints his last two self-portraits, along with *The Return of the Prodigal Son* and the unfinished *Simeon with the Christ Child in the Temple*. **PAINT**
1670s–1690s	Ninsei, the best-known Japanese artist-potter of the Tokugawa period, works in his area of specialty, enameled pottery. **DECO**
1670	The colonnade of the Louvre, designed by Louis Le Vau and Claude Perrault, is completed in Paris. **ARCH**

1670   *Le Bourgeois gentilhomme* (*The Bourgeois Gentleman*), one of French playwright Molière's finest and best-known comedies, is produced. His *Les Amants magnifiques* (*The Magnificent Lovers*) is also produced.   DRAMA

1670   *Bérénice*, a tragedy by French playwright Jean Racine, is produced. *Bajazet*, *Mithridate* and *Iphigénie*, all Racine tragedies, will be produced in 1672, 1673, and 1674, respectively.   DRAMA

1670   English composer John Blow is organist at Westminster Abbey until 1680.   MUSIC

1671   English poet John Milton publishes *Paradise Regained*, a four-book poem on the temptation of Jesus in the wilderness that serves as a companion to *Paradise Lost* (*see* 1667, LIT), and *Samson Agonistes*, a closet verse tragedy (not meant for performance) on Samson and Delilah.   LIT

1671   The opera *Pomone* by Robert Cambert is performed at the opening festivities for the Académie Royale de Musique in Paris and is a great success.   MUSIC

1671–1674   Italian sculptor, architect, and painter Bernini sculpts *The Blessed Lodovica Albertoni*.   SCULP

1672   French playwright Molière's satire *Les Femmes savantes* (*The Learned Ladies*) is produced. *Le Malade imaginaire* (*The Imaginary Invalid*), Molière's final play, will be produced in 1673, and he will act in it on the night of his death. DRAMA

1673   English poet John Milton publishes *Of True Religion, Heresy, Schism, and Toleration*.   LIT

1673   The opera *Cadmus et Hermione*, by French composer Jean-Baptiste Lully, is produced.   MUSIC

1674   English poet John Milton (*b.* 1608) dies the same year that the second, expanded edition of his epic poem *Paradise Lost* is published. *See* 1667, LIT.   LIT

1675–1710   English architect Sir Christopher Wren rebuilds St. Paul's cathedral in London, combining classical style and baroque influences.   ARCH

1675   English dramatist William Wycherley's comedy *The Country Wife* is produced. It will be viewed as one of the masterpieces of Restoration drama, and it will be revived frequently. Wycherley's comedy *The Plain Dealer* will be produced in 1676.   DRAMA

1675   English composer Matthew Locke composes incidental music to Thomas Shadwell's *Psyche*.   MUSIC

1677   The tragedy *Phèdre*, which will generally be regarded as the greatest play by French playwright Jean Racine, is produced.   DRAMA

1677   English poet John Dryden completes *All for Love; or, the World Well Lost*, a Restoration tragedy that takes its plot from English dramatist William Shakespeare's *Antony and Cleopatra*. It will be considered by many Dryden's greatest play.   DRAMA

1678   English dramatist and novelist Aphra Behn's comedy *The Rover; or, the Banish't Cavaliers* is produced. The story of women who insist on sowing their wild oats the way men do, it will be seen as her best play. Behn will be the first woman in England to earn a living by writing.   DRAMA

1678   English preacher and writer John Bunyan publishes *The Pilgrim's Progress*, a masterpiece of Christian allegory written largely during his imprisonment for refusing to cease his Noncomformist preaching.   LIT

1678   In Hamburg the first German opera house is opened; two years later French ballets will be performed for the first time in Germany.   MUSIC

1679   Italian composer Alessandro Scarlatti's first opera, *Gli equivoci nel sembiante*, opens in Rome.   MUSIC

1680   La Comédie-Française is founded by King Louis XIV. Run by its *sociétaires* (member actors), it will ultimately become France's foremost theater, continuing to operate indefinitely.   DRAMA

1681   The collection *Miscellaneous Poems* by English poet Andrew Marvell is published posthumously. Few of his poems have been published before this date, but his reputation will grow with the centuries. Among his best-known works are "The Garden," "The Mower's Song," and "To His Coy Mistress," which begins, "Had we but world enough, and time."   LIT

1681   English poet John Dryden publishes *Absalom and Achitophel*, a narrative poem in heroic couplets, using an Old Testament story to satirize contemporary politics.   LIT

1682   English poet John Dryden publishes his satirical attack on poet and playwright Thomas Shadwell, *Mac Flecknoe*. Shadwell had attacked Dryden in *The Medal of John Bayes* (also 1682). Dryden also publishes *Religio Laici*, a poem on his religious faith.   LIT

1682   Following a nearly two-month long captivity during King Philip's War (1675–1676; King Philip is the name given by settlers to Wampanoag chief Metacomet), an uprising of Wampanoag, Narragansett, and Nipmuck warriors against English settlers in New England, pioneer Mary Rowlandson writes of her ordeal in *The Sovereignty and Goodness of God . . . Being a Narrative of the Captivity and Restauration of Mrs. Mary Rowlandson*. Immensely popular, it is likely the first Indian-captivity narrative in print.   LIT

1682   French painter Claude Lorrain paints *Ascanius and the Stag*.   PAINT

1683   English composer Henry Purcell becomes court composer to King Charles II.   MUSIC

1683   French sculptor Pierre Puget completes his emotionally charged marble statue of Milo of Crotona. Puget's baroque style of expressive drama will not be accepted at the French court until after the death of French politician Jean-Baptiste Colbert (*see* 1663, MISC).   SCULP

1687   English poet John Dryden's *A Song for St. Cecilia's Day* is performed at a public concert. Dryden's second ode for St. Cecilia's Day, *Alexander's Feast*, will be performed in 1697.   LIT

1687   French sculptor François Girardon finishes a wax model derived from the equestrian *Marcus Aurelius* on the Capitoline Hill for an equestrian statue of Louis XIV. The final statue will be destroyed in the French Revolution.   SCULP

1688   English dramatist and novelist Aphra Behn publishes the prose romance *Oroonoko*.   LIT

1688   English composer Henry Purcell becomes organist at Westminster Abbey, following his teacher John Blow.   MUSIC

1689   English poet Andrew Marvell's political satire *The Last Instructions to a Painter*, written in 1667, is published posthumously. Marvell's other satires include *Clarindon's House-Warming* and *The Loyal Scot*.   LIT

1689   Japanese poet Matsuo Bashō writes *The Narrow Road to the Deep North*, a work interweaving travel sketches and haiku. He is the most important developer and practitioner of the three-line haiku verse form.   LIT

1689   English composer Henry Purcell's dramatic opera *Dido and Aeneas*, written for a fashionable girls' school, is performed.   MUSIC

1689   German-born painter Sir Godfrey Kneller and English painter John Riley are
            jointly named principal painters to William III and Mary II of England. The
            leading portraitist of his day, Kneller will be known for his mass production of
            high society portraits, employing a large team of artists. Riley will become bet-
            ter known for his portraits of ordinary people, including *The Scullion* and
            Bridget Holmes.   PAINT

c. 1690   Artists of China's Ch'ing dynasty (1644–1912; established by the Manchus)
            decorate porcelain figures in the *famille verte* palette of enamels that are applied
            directly onto the unglazed porcelain body.   DECO

1690   English composer Henry Purcell's stage music for *Dioclesian* premieres. He will
            write music for several productions that contain spoken dialogue, including
            King Arthur (1691), *The Fairy Queen* (1692), and *The Tempest* (1695).   MUSIC

1691   German organist and theorist Andreas Werckmeister's treatise *Musikalische
            Temperatur* suggests the octave be divided into 12 equal half-steps.   MUSIC

1693   *Teodora*, an opera by Italian composer Alessandro Scarlatti, opens.   MUSIC

1695   *Love for Love*, a Restoration comedy of manners by the English dramatist
            William Congreve, opens in London.   DRAMA

1696   German composer Johann Kuhnau's *Fresh Fruit for the Clavier*, with the sonata as
            a piece in several contrasting movements, is a harbinger of the classical sonata.
                                                                                   MUSIC

1697   English poet John Dryden's translation of Roman poet Virgil's *Aeneid* is published.
                                                                                   LIT

1700s   The rich architectural styles of baroque and rococo become popular through-
            out Europe and reach a peak of expression in Germany and Austria, exempli-
            fied in designs such as the German Wurzburg Residenz.   ARCH

1700s   During the early to middle Ch'ing period (1644–1912), China is unsurpassed
            in its porcelain production, with Europe importing large quantities of porce-
            lain wares. Chinese jadework is similarly prized.   DECO

1700s   Two dyeing techniques for fabrics are developed in Japan at the beginning of
            the century: stencils for block printing and rice-paste resist dyeing. The process
            of wood block printing streamlines the manufacture of fabric.   DECO

1700s	Much of Asante (or Ashanti) art in Ghana consists of wood objects covered with gold leaf, ornaments, and charms. An example is the *sika gwa*, or "golden stool," which, according to legend, comes down from heaven this century and is given to Asante king Osai Tutu. It will survive to modern times as a sacred relic used during the installation of kings. DECO
1700s	*Jōruri* puppet theater, which has existed for at least a century, reaches the height of its popularity in Japan. By now, the puppets are large, with movable eyes, fingers, and feet, and three performers manipulate each one to enact stories written by playwrights. DRAMA
1700s	European actors wear powder makeup, usually mixed with some sort of liquid or grease before application, to help indicate the age and general appearance of the characters they are portraying. In the early 1800s, many will switch to wearing powder-based paint applied over a grease foundation. DRAMA
1700s	The palette knife becomes popular for mixing and scraping paint. PAINT
1700s	Early this century the European art of modeling wax is introduced to America. Colonial artists begin to create small wax portraits. SCULP
1700s	Early this century the bourgeoisie begins to build private collections of art. As a result, a market for drawing room figurines and statuettes emerges. SCULP
1700	English dramatist William Congreve's *The Way of the World*, which will be regarded by some as the greatest Restoration comedy, is presented. DRAMA
1700	Published in the last year of his life, English poet John Dryden's last major work is *Fables, Ancient and Modern*, which is prefaced by a fine critical essay. LIT
1700	German-born painter Sir Godfrey Kneller paints *Matthew Prior*, one of his first portraits. PAINT
1701	Music publisher Henry Playford establishes a weekly series of concerts at Oxford. MUSIC
1701	French painter Hyacinthe Rigaud paints the majestic state portrait *Louis XIV*. PAINT
1702	British novelist and journalist Daniel Defoe, a religious dissenter, publishes the satirical pamphlet *The Shortest Way with the Dissenters*, for which he is fined, imprisoned, and pilloried. Defoe will write more than 250 pamphlets. LIT
1702	American clergyman Cotton Mather writes *Magnalia Christi Americana*, a wide-ranging ecclesiastical history of New England that sounds a clarion call for the renaissance of religious spirit in the colonies. LIT

1702   Japanese painter Ogata Kōrin unites the Kano and Yamato imperial schools of
              painting.   PAINT

1703   French sculptor Pierre Le Gros breaks17th-century tradition by placing his poly-
              chrome marble statue of St. Stanislas Kostka under the altar at the Convent of
              Sant'Andrea al Quirinale in Rome.   SCULP

1704   Writer and clergyman Jonathan Swift publishes *The Battle of the Books* and *A
              Tale of a Tub*, two powerful satires on intellectual corruption. Born in Dublin
              of English parents, he was educated in Ireland and worked in both England
              and Ireland; he is traditionally identified as English but became an Irish patri-
              ot in his later years.   LIT

1704–1708   French painter Jean-Antoine Watteau begins his career studying under Claude
              Gillot, whose preference for theatrical subjects will be shared by Watteau in such
              paintings as *Love in the French Theater*.   PAINT

1705   German-born British composer George Frideric Handel's first opera *Almira*,
              composed at age 19, premieres at the Hamburg opera house.   MUSIC

1706–1710   German-born British composer George Frideric Handel is in Italy, where his
              music becomes influenced by the leading musicians of Rome, Florence,
              Naples, and Venice.   MUSIC

The Secret of Porcelain

Until the 18th century one of the best-kept secrets of the trade between China and the
West was porcelain. Europeans loved the white, thin, strong pottery, miraculous for its
translucent, shimmering quality. But because no European could figure out how to
make it, porcelain in the West remained a rare and costly commodity from its introduction in the 13th century. In time, French, Italian, and English potters learned to
make a handsome facsimile out of a mixture of clay and ground glass with a modified
lead glaze. But this soft paste or artificial porcelain was still far from the real thing.

The secret of porcelain was finally cracked in 1708–1709 at Meissen, Saxony, by
German chemist Johann Friedrich Böttger, who combined a clay base with ground
feldspar. This mixture, it turned out, duplicated the Chinese formula which combined
kaolin (china clay) and a ground feldspathic rock called petuntse. The Chinese monop-
oly was broken, and porcelain became increasingly available in Europe.

1707   Irish playwright George Farquhar's comedy *The Beaux' Strategem* premieres.
             Farquhar's *The Constant Couple* and *The Recruiting Officer*, both comedies, had
             been produced in 1700 and 1706, respectively. *The Recruiting Officer* will be
             revived frequently.   DRAMA

1708–1709   The method of manufacturing porcelain, already known in China, is rediscov-
             ered in Europe at Meissen, Germany, near Dresden.   DECO

1708   German composer Johann Sebastian Bach becomes court organist, chamber
             musician, and concertmaster to the Duke of Weimar.   MUSIC

1708   Bavarian sculptor Andreas Schlüter erects his bronze equestrian statue of
             Frederick William I in front of the royal palace.   SCULP

1709–1711   Under the pseudonym Isaac Bickerstaff (first used by Jonathan Swift; *see* 1704,
             LIT), English essayists Sir Richard Steele and Joseph Addison publish the peri-
             odical *The Tatler*. Appearing three times a week, the paper presents urbane, rea-
             soned views on entertainment, poetry, and society.   LIT

1709   English poet Alexander Pope's first published work is *The Pastorals*.   LIT

1709   The first pianoforte (later shortened to piano) is made by Bartolomeo
             Christofori of Florence. Unlike the earlier harpsichord, its strings are struck by
             hammers activated by keys, allowing the loudness of its sound to be varied by
             the touch of the fingers. By the end of the 18th century it becomes the princi-
             pal keyboard instrument in Europe and America.   MUSIC

1709   The oldest known portrait effigy from New England is a carved gravestone for
             Reverend Jonathan Pierpont in Wakefield, Massachusetts.   SCULP

1710   German-born British composer George Frideric Handel becomes music direc-
             tor at the electoral court at Hanover, Germany.   MUSIC

1710   French sculptor Antoine Coysevox creates a marble statue of Marie-Adelaide of
             Savoy, the Duchess of Burgundy, portrayed as the goddess Diana.   SCULP

1711   Irish-born English clergyman and writer Jonathan Swift publishes the ironic
             Argument Against Abolishing Christianity.   LIT

1711–1712   English essayists Joseph Addison and Sir Richard Steele publish the daily peri-
             odical *The Spectator*, the successor to *The Tatler* (1709–1711). Addison will
             revive it briefly in 1714.   LIT

1711   English poet Alexander Pope publishes *Essay on Criticism*, a didactic poem in
             the manner of Roman poet Horace.   LIT

1711	The clarinet is used for the first time in an orchestra. MUSIC
1711	The oratorio *Rinaldo,* by German-born British composer George Frideric Handel, is a sensation when it premieres at London's Haymarket Theater. Handel will stay in England permanently as of 1712 and will become naturalized in 1726. MUSIC
1711	English trumpeter John Shore invents the tuning fork, an instrument used to indicate absolute pitch. MUSIC
1712	English poet Alexander Pope publishes the first version of his mock-epic poem *The Rape of the Lock;* an expanded edition will appear in 1714. LIT
1713	In England the Scriblerus Club is formed, an association of Tory writers and intellectuals, including Jonathan Swift, Alexander Pope, John Gay, Thomas Parnell, and John Arbuthnot. LIT
1714	German sculptor Balthasar Permoser collaborates with architect Mathäus Pöppelmann to decorate the Zwinger at Dresden. SCULP
1715–1723	Fine curved lines and bronze reliefs are characteristic of Régence style in France, named for the regency of Philippe II, duc d'Orléans. DECO
c. 1715	Chinese novelist Ts'ao Hsueh-ch'in is born (*d.* 1763). His most famous work will be the psychologically subtle autobiographical work *Hung lou meng* (*The Dream of the Red Chamber*), about the fall of an aristocratic family. LIT
1715–1720	English poet Alexander Pope publishes his translation of Greek poet Homer's *Iliad* in heroic couplets. It is a great commercial success, as is his translation of *The Odyssey,* making him one of the first nondramatic poets to earn enough from writing to enable him to live independently. LIT
c. 1715	In France the rococo style of painting, decoration, and architecture emerges, marked by grace, lightness, and refinement. Rococo decoration incorporates such motifs as flowers, shells, and scrolls. Great French rococo painters include Watteau, Boucher, and Fragonard. In architecture, Gabriel, and in sculpture, Falconet, embody rococo principles. Associated with Louis XV style, rococo will spread throughout 18th-century Europe. *See* 1723–1774, DECO. MISC
1715	Vaudeville, popular musical comedies, appear in Paris. MUSIC
1715	English painter and writer Jonathan Richardson writes *An Essay on the Theory of Painting,* a treatise on the seriousness of painting that influences painter Joshua Reynolds, among others. PAINT

1717   David Garrick, who will become one of the greatest English actors, is born in
            Hereford, England (*d*. 1779). An extraordinarily versatile and creative per-
            former, Garrick will do some of his best work playing Abel Drugger in English
            dramatist Ben Jonson's *The Alchemist*, Archer in Irish playwright George
            Farquhar's *The Beaux' Strategem*, and the title character in English dramatist
            William Shakespeare's *Hamlet*.   DRAMA

1717   English poet Alexander Pope's *Collected Poems* is published, including "Ode for
            Music on St. Cecilia's Day," "Eloisa to Abelard," and "Elegy to the Memory of
            an Unfortunate Lady."   LIT

1717   The orchestral suite *Water Music* by German-born British composer George
            Frideric Handel is performed.   MUSIC

1717   German composer Johann Sebastian Bach becomes concert master to Prince
            Leopold of Anhalt-Coethan, where he will write many instrumental composi-
            tions for solo and group performance.   MUSIC

1717–1718   Italian opera is fashionable in England. The Royal Academy of Music organizes
            to present operas to the London public.   MUSIC

1717   French painter Jean-Antoine Watteau paints *Embarkation for Cythera*, a work of
            sensuous brushwork and pastel tones that wins him admission to the Royal
            Academy. Watteau's style influences not only painting but fashion and garden
            design.   PAINT

1718–1721   The six Brandenburg Concertos, dedicated to Duke Christian Ludwig of
            Brandenburg, are composed by German composer Johann Sebastian Bach.
            They represent the artistic peak of the baroque concerto.   MUSIC

1719   English novelist and journalist Daniel Defoe publishes the novel *Robinson
            Crusoe*, based on the true story of shipwrecked sailor Alexander Selkirk. LIT

1719   German-born British composer George Frideric Handel becomes director of
            the Royal Academy of Music, where he will write some of his most accom-
            plished operas.   MUSIC

1720   Haymarket Theatre opens in London. It will be rebuilt in 1820 and will be
            London's leading theater in the mid-19th century.   DRAMA

1720   English painter and engraver William Hogarth begins working in London as
            an engraver of billheads and book illustrations.   GRAPH

1721   German composer Georg Philipp Telemann arrives in Hamburg as director of
            music.   MUSIC

1721   The Bishop of Toledo hires Spanish sculptor Narciso Tomé to execute a monu-
        ment to the Blessed Sacrament for the Toledo cathedral. Tomé's Transparente
        Altar, which will combine polychrome marbles, gilt stucco work, and frescoes,
        will be completed in 1732.   SCULP

1722   *La Surprise de l'amour* (*The Surprise of Love*), a romantic drama by French play-
        wright and novelist Pierre Carlet de Marivaux, is produced. The unusual sensitiv-
        ity and subtlety of his dialogue can be seen here and will be evident in most of
        his many other plays, including *La Double Inconstance* (*The Double Inconstancy*,
        1723).   DRAMA

1722   Novels published this year by prolific English novelist and journalist Daniel
        Defoe include *Moll Flanders, A Journal of the Plague Year,* and *Colonel Jack.*   LIT

1722   German composer Johann Sebastian Bach completes Book I of *The Well-
        Tempered Clavier* as teaching materials for his children. Book II will be com-
        pleted in 1744.   MUSIC

1722   *Treatise of Harmony* by French composer Jean-Philippe Rameau is published in
        Paris. This landmark development in the theories of harmony shifts the
        emphasis away from counterpoint to a symphonic style using chords.   MUSIC

1722   Austrian sculptor Johann Lukas von Hildebrandt creates marble figures to be
        used as pillars in the Hall of Atlantes at the Upper Belvedere Palace in Vienna.
        The sequence will influence 18th-century architects through its interaction of
        decorative and spatial volumes.   SCULP

1723–1774   The *Louis Quinze* style of interior decoration and architecture prevails in France
        during the reign of Louis XV, whose regent, Philippe II, duc d'Orléans, guided
        the young king for eight years until Philippe's death in 1723. (The transition-
        al *régence* style, lasting from 1715 to 1723, was characterized by the curved,
        delicate lines and intricate ornamentation of early rococo). The *Louis Quinze*
        style further develops rococo ornamentation, frequently employing shell and
        scroll motifs, and introduces chinoiserie—decoration influenced by Chinese
        art, with exotic and scenic motifs—to Europe. The manifestations of chinois-
        erie in interiors, furniture, and textiles will influence the English cabinetmak-
        er Thomas Chippendale and become a popular feature of American colonial
        style. *See also* 1661–1715 and 1774–1793, DECO.   DECO

1723   German composer Johann Sebastian Bach becomes cantor at St. Thomas's
        school in Leipzig, Germany, where he will write many of his cantatas and
        choral masterpieces.   MUSIC

1724–1725   Irish-born English clergyman and writer Jonathan Swift earns fame as an Irish patriot when he publishes the *Drapier Letters*. Written under the pseudonym M. B. Drapier, the public letters urge the populace not to accept debased coinage from England.   LIT

1724   The Three Choirs Festival, combining the choral forces of Gloucester, Hartford, and Worcester, is founded in England.   MUSIC

1725–1775   Rococo, an artistic style characterized by frivolous elegance and luxury that began in France early in the 18th century, spreads to Germany and Italy. Its musical counterpart, gallante style, emphasizing pleasantnesses and prettiness, replaces the impressive grandeur of the baroque style.   MUSIC

1725   The Prague opera house (Standetheater) is founded.   MUSIC

1725   Four violin concertos by Italian composer Antonio Vivaldi, collectively known as *The Four Seasons*, are published.   MUSIC

1726   The Belgian ballerina Marie de Camargo debuts at the Paris Opera.   DANCE

1726   Irish-born English clergyman and writer Jonathan Swift publishes his greatest work, *Gulliver's Travels*, a satirical account of Dr. Lemuel Gulliver's adventures in Lilliput, Brobdingnag, Laputa, and Houyhnhnmland.   LIT

1727   His Majesty's Admiralty Office in New England announces that carved motifs other than the lion may be used for ships' figureheads. Human figures will begin to appear after 1750.   DECO

c. 1727–   Giovanni Battista Tiepolo, considered one of the greatest Italian painters of the
1728   18th century, paints the fresco cycle in the Archbishop's Palace in Udine. His work is rich, grand, and colorful in the tradition of Italian decorative painting.
                                                                                              PAINT

1728   English playwright John Gay's *The Beggar's Opera* is produced. The first ballad opera (a genre satirizing Italian opera that was to become popular at this time), it includes songs arranged by John Christopher Pepusch. Its tale of the highwayman Macheath will be the basis for German dramatist and poet Bertolt Brecht and German-born American composer Kurt Weill's *The Threepenny Opera* (1928).   DRAMA

1728   English poet Alexander Pope publishes the mock epic satire *The Dunciad*, in which he wittily and mercilessly attacks his literary enemies, especially critic Lewis Theobald and playwright Colley Cibber. An expanded edition will be published in 1743.   LIT

1728	French painter Jean-Baptiste-Siméon Chardin is received into the Royal Academy for his still life *The Rayfish*. Chardin is known for his naturalistic still lifes and simple, serious genre paintings, often set in kitchen interiors. His works also include *Benediction, Return from Market, Blowing Bubbles, Madame Chardin, Pipe and Jug,* and *The Young Governess*. **PAINT**
1729	Irish-born English clergyman and writer Jonathan Swift publishes the satirical pamphlet *A Modest Proposal*, which ironically advocates the eating of the Irish by the English. **LIT**
1729–1766	American statesman and writer Benjamin Franklin purchases the weekly periodical *The Pennsylvania Gazette* from publisher Samuel Keimer and brings it to success, using it as a forum for his views. The weekly will remain in print until 1815. **LIT**
1729	The choral work *Passion According to St. Matthew* by German composer Johann Sebastian Bach premieres at St. Thomas's church in Leipzig on Good Friday. **MUSIC**
1729	Spanish sculptor Pedro de Ribera mixes French, Italian, and native Spanish motifs in his stone decoration of the portal of the Hospicio de San Fernando in Madrid. **SCULP**
1730s	Colonial American cabinetmakers and artisan carvers begin to copy the more elaborate models illustrated in European design books. **DECO**
1730s	Lavish stucco decorations appear on the facades of private houses throughout Bavaria. **DECO**
1730	Scottish poet James Thomson publishes the collected edition of *The Seasons*, consisting of *Winter, Summer, Spring,* and *Autumn*. The work will remain popular throughout the 18th century. **LIT**
1731	Irish-born English clergyman and writer Jonathan Swift, still very much alive, publishes the ironic poem *Verses on the Death of Dr. Swift*. **LIT**
1731–1735	English poet Alexander Pope's book of poems *Moral Essays* (or *Ethics*) is published. **LIT**
1731	The first public concert on record in America is held in Boston, Massachusetts. **MUSIC**
c. 1731	English painter and engraver William Hogarth paints the six scenes of *The Harlot's Progress*, a "morality play" in which a sequence of anecdotal pictures is used to make moral and satirical points. Having invented this form, Hogarth popularizes it with engravings of this sequence and later ones. **PAINT**

1732   French writer François-Marie Arouet, known as Voltaire, writes *Zaïre*. Based on
                English dramatist William Shakespeare's *Othello*, it will generally be considered
                his dramatic masterpiece. However, most of his plays will not prove enduring,
                and he will be remembered for his writing in other genres.   DRAMA

1732–1757   American statesman and writer Benjamin Franklin publishes *Poor Richard's
                Almanack*, an annual compendium of practical information and plain philo-
                sophical thinking.   LIT

1732   *Sonate da Cimbalo di piano e forte*, probably the first compositions for modern
                piano, are published by Italian composer Lodovico Giustini.   MUSIC

1732   The Academy of Ancient Music is founded in London.   MUSIC

1732   The Covent Garden Opera House opens in London.   MUSIC

1733–1734   English poet Alexander Pope publishes the four poetic epistles of his *Essay on
                Man*, establishing him as a philosophical and ethical poet.   LIT

1733   English poet Alexander Pope publishes *Imitations of Horace*.   LIT

1735   The Imperial ballet school is founded at St. Petersburg, Russia.   DANCE

1735   English poet Alexander Pope publishes a complete version of *An Epistle to Dr.
                Arbuthnot* (an early version appeared in 1727). The poem will be regarded as
                Pope's most masterful rhetorical performance in the mode of Roman poet
                Horace.   LIT

1735   The ballad opera *Flora* at Charleston, South Carolina, is the first musical the-
                ater presentation in the English colonies.   MUSIC

1735   English painter and engraver William Hogarth paints *The Rake's Progress* (eight
                scenes), his best-known "morality play." *See also* c. 1731, PAINT.   PAINT

1735   English painter and engraver William Hogarth opens an academy in London,
                forerunner of the Royal Academy. Hogarth helps to establish a British style dis-
                tinct from that of the continent.   PAINT

1737   Bavarian sculptor Johann Baptist Zimmerman completes his French-influ-
                enced stuccoes throughout the shooting lodge of Amalienburg in the park of
                Schloss Nymphenburg.   SCULP

1738   English critic and writer Samuel Johnson publishes the poem *London*, an imi-
                tation of Roman poet Juvenal's tenth satire.   LIT

1738   Planned excavation begins at Pompeii and Herculaneum in Italy. The archae-
            ological discoveries prompt a revival of interest in classical antiquity that spurs
            the neoclassical movement in art and architecture. *See* 79, MISC, and 1760s, DECO. MISC

1738   German composer Johann Sebastian Bach completes his *Mass in B minor*.   MUSIC

1738   French sculptor Nicolas-Sébastien Adam begins work on a minutely detailed
            marble figurine of Prometheus. It will be completed in 1762 and submitted to
            the Royal Academy.   SCULP

1739   The dramatic oratorio *Saul*, by German-born British composer George Frideric
            Handel, is well received in London. It signals the start of his commitment to
            the English oratorio, which appeals to a bourgeois audience uncomfortable
            with aristocratic Italian opera.   MUSIC

1740s   Stone portrait busts appear as grave markers from Massachusetts to South
            Carolina.   SCULP

1740   German architect Johann Balthasar Neumann decorates the grand staircase at
            the Schloss Augustusburg in Brühl with polychrome stuccoes and wrought-
            iron railings.   DECO

1740   American wood-carver Simeon Skillin opens his shop to create work for the fur-
            niture shops and shipyards of Boston. His sons, John and Simeon Jr., will work
            in the shop until 1778 and become New England's leading carvers.   DECO

1740   English novelist Samuel Richardson publishes the novel *Pamela: or Virtue
            Rewarded*, which will be parodied by English novelist Henry Fielding in *Shamela*
            (1741) and *Joseph Andrews* (1742).   LIT

1740–1780   Under the reign of Maria Theresa, the queen of Bohemia and Hungary who
            exercises power over the Holy Roman Empire, Vienna develops into an impor-
            tant center for music and the arts.   MISC

c. 1740   English painter and engraver William Hogarth paints *The Shrimp Girl* and
            Captain Coram.   PAINT

1740   French sculptor Robert Le Lorrain completes his stone decorative reliefs on the
            Hôtel de Rohan, Paris. Le Lorrain will play a leading role in the emergence of
            rococo sculpture.   SCULP

1740   The lead Basin of Neptune, by French sculptors and brothers Lambert-Sigisbert
            and Nicolas-Sébastien Adam, is added to Louis XIV's 17th-century ensemble in
            the gardens of Versailles.   SCULP

1741   American theologian Jonathan Edwards publishes his sermon, *Sinners in the Hands of an Angry God,* which details his seminal ideas about the inadequacies of humans and the need for salvation from God. The work vividly describes the horrors of Hell for the unrepentant.   LIT

1742   German-born British composer George Frideric Handel's oratorio *Messiah* premieres at the New Music Hall in Dublin.   MUSIC

1742   English painter and engraver William Hogarth paints *Taste in High Life.*   PAINT

1743   English painter and engraver William Hogarth paints the six-scene work *Marriage à la Mode.*   PAINT

1743   At age 87, esteemed French painter Nicolas de Largillière is named director of the French Royal Academy. The artist has painted about 1,500 portraits, many of wealthy middle-class individuals.   PAINT

1744   English critic and writer Samuel Johnson publishes *Life of Savage,* a biography of his late friend, poet Richard Savage. In later biographies he will portray Sir Thomas Browne (1758) and Richard Ascham (1761).   LIT

1744   The Madrigal Society is founded in London.   MUSIC

1744   Spanish sculptor Ignacio de Vergara completes his marble decoration of the entrance to the palace of the Marqués de Dos Aguas in Valencia.   SCULP

1745   Bohemian composer Johann Stamitz becomes conductor of the Mannheim School, a highly trained group of musicians who form the orchestra at the court of Mannheim, Germany. Stamitz's style of orchestral music and performance lays the foundation for the formal development of the sonata.   MUSIC

1745   Italian painter Giovanni Battista Tiepolo paints the decorations in the Palazzo Labia in Venice, assisted by Gerolamo Mengozzi-Colonna.   PAINT

1745   French sculptor Edme Bouchardon combines classical modeling with contemporary rococo details throughout his marble composition for the Fountain of the Seasons, to be placed along the Rue de Grenelle, Paris.   SCULP

1745   Italian sculptor Nicola Salvi begins work on both the marble facade and statue of Neptune for the Trevi Fountain. It will be completed in 1762 and installed in the Piazza di Trevi, Rome.   SCULP

1746   English poet William Collins, who will be a favorite of later romantic poets, publishes *Odes on Several Descriptive and Allegorical Subjects.*   LIT

1747–1748   English novelist Samuel Richardson publishes his masterpiece, the epistolary novel *Clarissa: or The History of a Young Lady*. The longest novel written in English, running to over one million words, it tells the tale of the seduction and rape of the unfortunate Clarissa Howe by the notorious libertine Robert Lovelace.   LIT

1747   German-born British composer George Frideric Handel composes the biblical oratorio *Judas Maccabaeus*.   MUSIC

1748   The Royal Danish Ballet is founded in Copenhagen. It will be known for the delicacy of its productions.   DANCE

1748   French writer Voltaire writes the philosophical tale *Zadig, or la Destinée*. Later tales will include *Micromégas*.   LIT

1748   A jury system of selection is introduced to the Salon, the French Royal Academy's regular official exhibition of painting and sculpture. *See also* 1667, MISC.   MISC

1749   *Irene*, the only play by English critic and writer Samuel Johnson, is produced by the actor David Garrick in London. It will run for only nine performances, but Johnson will earn more money from it than he will from any of his other works.   DRAMA

1749   English novelist Henry Fielding publishes the novel *The History of Tom Jones*, a comic novel about a foundling who grows up to be a high-spirited young man. Condemned by many for immorality, the novel has an intricate plot that will be called by English poet and critic Samuel Taylor Coleridge one of "the three most perfect plots ever planned" (along with Greek playwright Sophocles's *Oedipus Tyrannus*, 429 B.C., and English dramatist Ben Jonson's *The Alchemist*, 1610).   LIT

1749   English critic and writer Samuel Johnson publishes *The Vanity of Human Wishes*, his longest and best-known poem.   LIT

1749   Italian sculptor Antonio Corradini displays virtuoso carving in the rendering of drapery for his marble statue of Modesty in the Sansevero Chapel, Naples.   SCULP

c. 1750s   French painter François Boucher paints several portraits of Madame de Pompadour, mistress and confidante of King Louis XV.   PAINT

1750s   In England conversation pieces by such painters as Arthur Devis and Thomas Gainsborough are a popular form. In these group portraits, two or more subjects converse or otherwise mix politely in a domestic or landscape setting.   PAINT

c.1750–1800   In Africa, Gèlèdé masquerades begin among the Yoruba people. Involving wooden headpieces, costumes, drums, dances, and songs, the ceremonies pay homage to women and to the cosmic forces they represent. Both religious ritual and theatrical performance, Gèlèdé will continue to be practiced thereafter in Nigeria and Benin.   DRAMA

1750–1752   British critic and writer Samuel Johnson writes more than 200 moral essays and commentaries for the twice-weekly periodical *The Rambler*.   LIT

1750   French sculptor Jean-Baptiste Pigalle allows the Sèvres manufactory to publish an altered version of his marble statuette *Child with Birdcage* in biscuit, an uncolored, ersatz marble.   SCULP

c. 1750   The Baule people, led by Queen Awura Pokou, emigrate from Ghana to the Ivory Coast, where they will remain. Their religious beliefs are symbolized by wooden sculptures and masks, such as the red or black *kple-kple* mask, representing Guli, spirit of the dead, and the black mask, representing Gu, god of the wind.   SCULP

1751   The minuet becomes a fashionable dance in Europe.   DANCE

1751   *La locandiera* (*The Mistress of the Inn*), the masterpiece of Italian comic playwright Carlo Goldoni, is produced. In this and other plays, Goldoni challenges the traditions of commedia dell'arte.   DRAMA

1751   English poet Thomas Gray publishes "Elegy Written in a Country Churchyard."   LIT

1751   Scottish novelist Tobias George Smollett publishes *The Adventures of Peregrine Pickle*. Like his other comic adventure novels, including *The Adventures of Roderick Random* (1748) and *The Expedition of Humphrey Clinker* (1771), it is rich with characterization and satire.   LIT

1751–1780   French encyclopedist and philosopher Denis Diderot and others compile the multivolume *Encyclopédie, ou Dictionnaire Raisonné des Sciences, des Arts et des Métiers*.   LIT

1751   French painter François Boucher paints *Reclining Girl*, one of his many playfully sensual paintings.   PAINT

1752   The invasion of Italian opera buffs in Paris divides the city into pro-Italian and pro-French music lovers, marking the end of French baroque opera and stimulating the development of the opéra comique. From 1750 to 1850 French music will be largely restricted to efforts to build up a new "grand opera."   MUSIC

1752   German-born British composer George Frideric Handel composes the biblical
              oratorio *Jephitha*.   MUSIC

1752   Spanish artists Felipe de Castro and Luis Salvador Carmona establish the
              Academy of San Fernando to banish the substitution of extravagant French
              styles for native Spanish traditions. As a result, late 18th-century sculpture in
              Spain will reveal a mixture of Spanish naturalism with a closer study of the
              antique.   SCULP

1753   English painter and engraver William Hogarth publishes the aesthetic treatise
              The Analysis of Beauty.   PAINT

1753–1754   English painter Joshua Reynolds, who will be credited with raising the artist to
              a new position of respect in England, gains notice for his portrait *Commodore
              Keppel*, based on the *Apollo Belvedere*, a classical statue discovered in the late
              15th century and greatly admired into the late 18th century.   PAINT

1753   French painter Claude-Joseph Vernet is commissioned by King Louis XV to
              paint a series of seaports. He is the founder of a painting dynasty that will
              include his son Antoine-Charles-Horace (Carle) Vernet and grandson Émile-
              Jean-Horace (Horace) Vernet.   PAINT

1755   European design books assist colonial wood-carvers in the decoration of the
              chancel of St. Michael's Church in Charleston, South Carolina. For the first
              time, American carvers employ classical motifs such as dentils, pilasters, and
              Corinthian capitals.   ARCH

1755   English critic and writer Samuel Johnson publishes *A Dictionary of the English
              Language*, a landmark of lexicography that he has compiled by himself over the
              course of eight years.   LIT

Commercial Art

Sir Joshua Reynolds, 18th-century England's most important portrait painter and art
theorist, was a businessman as much as a fine artist. By the late 1750s he was seeing
150 sitters a day and employing a large team of assistants and drapery painters. By the
1760s he was earning the handsome annual income of £6,000. This was in addition to
his duties as first president of the Royal Academy (from 1768) and his delivery of the
classic lectures known as Discourses on Art. So busy was his schedule that on the day
he was knighted, April 21, 1769, he had to sandwich in his visit to the king between
two sittings with paying subjects.

1756   Irish-born British statesman and writer Edmund Burke publishes *A Philosophical Enquiry into the Origin of Our Ideas of the Sublime and Beautiful*. This work of aesthetics, with its emphasis on the sublime, will have a powerful influence on romantic artists and writers.   MISC

1757   Italian painter Giovanni Battista Tiepolo decorates rooms in the Villa Valmarana near Vicenza.   PAINT

1757–1770   The Kishangarh painting style gains popularity in India. It is noted for its large-size miniature paintings of 18 inches or more.   PAINT

1757   Genoese sculptor Francesco Queirolo captures the 18th century's obsession with allegory and its elaborate system of symbols in his marble sculpture of Count Antonio Sangro for the Sansevero Chapel in Naples.   SCULP

1757   French sculptor Jean-Baptiste Lemoyne epitomizes the style of Louis XV with a long series of portrait busts designed to feature the king at every age.   SCULP

1758–1760   English critic and writer Samuel Johnson publishes *The Idler*, a series of essays.   LIT

1758   The first English manual on guitar playing is published.   MUSIC

1759   English critic and writer Samuel Johnson publishes the philosophical romance *Rasselas*.   LIT

1759   Irish-born English poet, playwright, and novelist Oliver Goldsmith publishes *An Enquiry into the Present State of Polite Learning in Europe*.   LIT

1759   French writer Voltaire composes the satirical novel *Candide, ou L'Optimisme*, an attack on Leibnitzian optimism built around the adventures of the naive title character and his tutor Dr. Pangloss.   LIT

1759–1768   English novelist Laurence Sterne writes the comic novel *Tristram Shandy*. His later works include the unfinished *A Sentimental Journey Through France and Italy*.   LIT

1760s   Scottish architect Robert Adam, working with his brother James Adam, designs and decorates Osterly Park (1761–1780) and Syon House (1762–1769) near London. Highly prolific, Robert Adam achieves an elegant, distinctive, influential blend of styles that encompasses architecture, furniture, and interior decoration.   ARCH

1760s	The Greek taste, a fashion for ornamentation superficially inspired by classical Greek models, begins to hold sway in France and England. It will remain popular into the early 19th century, leaving its mark on furniture, decoration, and costume. DECO
1760s	Neoclassicism takes shape in Germany in the writings of art historian Johann Winckelmann (*see* 1764, MISC) and the paintings of Anton Mengs. Inspired by the excavations of Pompeii and Herculaneum (*see* 1738, MISC), the movement in art and architecture will spread across Europe and, by the early 19th century, into the United States. It seeks to recapture the heroic grandeur and civic ideals of ancient Greek and Roman art, as well as classical content and forms, marked by linearity and rationality. PAINT
1760s	Swiss sculptor Franz Anton Bustelli produces immensely popular porcelain figures drawn from Italian comedy while working at the Nymphenburg manufactory near Munich. SCULP
c. 1760	American painter John Singleton Copley paints such portraits as *Colonel Epes Sargent*. PAINT
c. 1760	Italian painter Giovanni Battista Tiepolo paints *A Young Woman with a Macaw*. PAINT
1760	While working in England French sculptor Louis-François Roubillac creates the French rococo marble tomb for Lady Elizabeth Nightingale to be placed in London's Westminster Abbey. SCULP
1762–1763	Scottish biographer James Boswell keeps the private diary that will be published nearly two centuries later as *Boswell's London Journal* (1950). LIT
1762	Irish-born English poet, playwright, and novelist Oliver Goldsmith's *Letters from a Citizen of the World* is published, a collection of satirical essays on Britain from the point of view of a fictitious Chinese visitor. LIT
1762	French philosopher Jean-Jacques Rousseau writes the philosophical treatise on government and the populace, *Du contrat social* (*The Social Contract*), and the philosophical romance *Émile, ou Traité de l'éducation*, about nature and child development. LIT
1762	French encyclopedist and philosopher Denis Diderot composes the satiric novel *Le Neveu de Rameau* (*Rameau's Nephew*). Among his later novels is *Jacques le fataliste* (1796). LIT
1762	Austrian composer Wolfgang Amadeus Mozart, age six, tours Europe as a musical prodigy. MUSIC

1763	On May 16 English critic and writer Samuel Johnson meets the young Scotsman James Boswell, who will become his biographer. *See* 1791, LIT. LIT
c. 1763	English painter Thomas Gainsborough paints *Mary, Countess Howe*, one of many elegant portraits that will make him a founding member of the Royal Academy in 1768. PAINT
1763	French painter Joseph-Marie Vien paints *The Cupid Seller*. PAINT
1764	French engraver Pierre-Simon Fournier develops the first system for measuring and naming sizes of type. GRAPH
1764	English novelist Horace Walpole publishes the Gothic novel *The Castle of Otranto*. LIT
1764	German archaeologist and critic Johann Winckelmann publishes his *History of Ancient Art Among the Greeks*, the first book to include the phrase "history of art" in the title. His theoretical treatises, which also include *Reflections on the Painting and Sculpture of the Greeks* (1755), analyze and praise Greek art, and are extremely influential in the development of both neoclassicism and the discipline of art history. *See* 1760s, PAINT. MISC
1764	Austrian composer Wolfgang Amadeus Mozart, age eight, writes his first symphony. Four years later, he will have composed his first operas, *Bastien und Bastienne* and *La finta semplice*. MUSIC
1765	English critic and writer Samuel Johnson publishes his eight-volume edition of English dramatist William Shakespeare's plays, noted for its critical preface. LIT
c. 1765	Welsh painter Richard Wilson, one of the first British artists to concentrate on landscapes, paints *Snowdon from Llyn Nantlle*. PAINT
1765	French painter Jean-Honoré Fragonard, influenced by François Boucher, is admitted to the Royal Academy for his painting *Coresus Sacrifices Himself to Save Callirrhoe*. His work is noted for its fluid brushwork, gaiety, whimsy, and charm. His specialty will be aristocratic love scenes. His works will include *Love's Vow*, *The Swing*, and *The Music Lesson*. PAINT
1765	French painter François Boucher, famed for his frivolous, artificially elegant style, becomes director of the Royal Academy and painter to King Louis XV. His body of work includes portraits, mythological allegories, decorations for such royal abodes as Versailles and Fontainebleau, and designs for stage settings and everyday objects. PAINT

1765   American painter John Singleton Copley paints *The Boy with a Squirrel,* a por-
            trait highly praised when exhibited in London.   PAINT

1766   Irish-born English clergyman and writer Jonathan Swift's *Journal to Stella* is
            published posthumously. The letters to his beloved Esther Johnson (whom he
            called "Stella") were composed in the 1710s.   LIT

1766   Irish-born English poet, playwright, and novelist Oliver Goldsmith publishes
            his only novel, *The Vicar of Wakefield.*   LIT

1766   Swiss painter Angelica Kauffmann moves to London, where she becomes a
            founding member of the Royal Academy in 1768. She will adorn many interi-
            ors by Scottish architect and designer Robert Adam. *See* 1760s, ARCH.   PAINT

1766   English sculptor Joseph Wilton is commissioned by Americans to create a mar-
            ble statue of English statesman William Pitt out of gratitude for his vehement
            opposition to the Stamp Act, which was imposed by Britain on the colonies in
            1765 and is repealed this year. The statue will be erected on September 7,
            1770, at the intersection of Wall and William Streets in New York City.   SCULP

1767   In a forerunner to minstrel shows, a white actor named "Tea," his face black-
            ened with cork, performs an early "Negro Dance" with the American Company
            in Philadelphia.   DANCE

1767   John Street Theater, the first permanent theater for the production of plays in
            New York City, opens on December 7. It will operate until 1798.   DRAMA

1769–1790   As first president of the Royal Academy, founded in 1768, English painter Joshua
            Reynolds delivers the lectures published as *Discourses on Art.* His exposition of
            neoclassical style, favoring idealized generalization over observed particulars, is
            highly influential.   MISC

1769   English painter Joshua Reynolds is knighted. Throughout his career, he will
            paint more than 2,000 portraits and history paintings, depicting such eminent
            Britons as the writers Samuel Johnson and Edmund Burke.   PAINT

1770s   Austrian composer Wolfgang Amadeus Mozart's symphonies are influenced by
            Italian symphonists, especially his K. 81, 95, 112, 132, 162, and 182, while a
            new influence, the music of Franz Joseph Haydn, is apparent in symphonies
            like Mozart's K. 133. After Mozart's first tour of Italy, he composes his first
            symphonies that show something approaching a mastery of the symphonic
            form: two symphonies in A (K. 114 and 134) in 1771–1772 and one in F (K.
            130) in 1772.   MUSIC

| 1770s | French sculptor Claude Michel, known as Clodion, exemplifies the erotic side of rococo sculpture with his small terra-cotta statuettes of satyrs.   SCULP |

1770s   French sculptor Claude Michel, known as Clodion, exemplifies the erotic side of rococo sculpture with his small terra-cotta statuettes of satyrs.   SCULP

1770   American statesman and architect Thomas Jefferson, who will write the Declaration of Independence in 1776, begins designing Monticello, the Virginia mansion in which he will live for 56 years. Built by his artisan slaves in Palladian style, Monticello will be occupied by Jefferson in 1772. He will continue making improvements on it for decades.   ARCH

1770   Irish-born English poet, playwright, and novelist Oliver Goldsmith's best-known poem, *The Deserted Village*, is published.   LIT

1770   English painter Thomas Gainsborough paints one of his most famous portraits, *The Blue Boy*.   PAINT

1770–1771   In his third and fourth *Discourses*, English painter Joshua Reynolds propounds the grand manner of history and portrait painting, in which the subjects are elevated and idealized. The tradition is rooted in the work of such 17th-century artists as Poussin.   PAINT

1770   American painter Benjamin West paints *The Death of Wolfe*, which takes the radical step in history painting of portraying figures in contemporary dress.   PAINT

1770   English sculptor Joseph Wilton erects his lead equestrian image of English king George III in New York City. Patriots will dismantle the statue in 1776.   SCULP

1771–1790   American statesman and writer Benjamin Franklin writes but does not complete *The Autobiography of Benjamin Franklin*, taking it to the end of the 1750s. Its optimism and unadorned writing style mark it as a distinctly American work.   LIT

1772   The first barrel organs are produced by Flight and Kelly, a London firm of organ builders. Barrel organs will enjoy great popularity in rural English churches into the 19th century.   MUSIC

1772   American painter Benjamin West, in England since 1763, becomes historical painter to King George III. He is the first American painter to win a reputation in Europe.   PAINT

1772   American sculptor Patience Lovell Wright leaves for England to create numerous portraits of the high bourgeoisie and aristocracy. In 1781 she will model American inventor, writer, and statesman Benjamin Franklin's likeness in wax while in Paris.   SCULP

| 1773 | The waltz becomes fashionable in Vienna. | DANCE |

1773   The Bolshoi ballet school opens in Russia and will become one of the foremost purveyors of classical, realistic ballet in the world.   DANCE

1773   Irish-born English poet, playwright, and novelist Oliver Goldsmith's comedy *She Stoops to Conquer* is produced.   DRAMA

1773   American inventor, writer, and statesman Benjamin Franklin publishes the *Edict by the King of Prussia*, a satire about England and Germany that reflects Franklin's stand against the Townshend Act. The piece was published in the *Philadelphia Public Advertiser.*   LIT

1773   In London American slave Phillis Wheatley publishes the collection *Poems on Various Subjects, Religious and Moral.* The book establishes her as the first female African-American poet.   LIT

1773–1774   The more than 20 symphonies Austrian composer Wolfgang Amadeus Mozart composes at Salzburg include his first two "masterwork" symphonies, no. 25 in G Minor (K. 183) and no. 29 in A (K. 201).   MUSIC

1774–1793   Classical revival, with its straight lines and symmetry, characterizes the *Louis Seize* style of interior decoration and architecture, which prevails during the reign of Fench king Louis XVI. *See also* 1661–1715 and 1723–1774, DECO.   DECO

1774   German poet Johann Wolfgang von Goethe writes the short novel *The Sorrows of Young Werther.* Later works include the play *Iphigenia in Tauris* and the novel *Die Wahlverwandtschaften* (1809).   LIT

1774–1789   French painter Élisabeth Vigée-Lebrun paints many portraits of her friend, Queen Marie Antoinette, before the French Revolution sends the artist into exile (1789) and the queen to the guillotine (1793).   PAINT

1774   French painter Jacques-Louis David, who, beginning in the 1780s, will become the dominant figure of French neoclassical painting, wins the Prix de Rome with *Antiochus and Stratonice.*   PAINT

1775   *The Rivals*, the enormously popular first play of Irish playwright Richard Brinsley Sheridan, is produced. It will be revived frequently. Sheridan's *St. Patrick's Day; or the Scheming Lieutenant*, a farce, and *The Duenna*, a comic opera, are also produced this year.   DRAMA

1775   English critic and writer Samuel Johnson publishes *A Journey to the Western Islands of Scotland.*   LIT

1775–1823	Under the rule of Raja Sansar Chaud in Kangra, India, miniature painting reaches its height, with the evocation of Krishna and feminine beauty its central concerns. **PAINT**
1776–1788	English historian Edward Gibbon publishes the six volumes of *The History of the Decline and Fall of the Roman Empire*. **LIT**
1776	American statesman and architect Thomas Jefferson writes the Declaration of Independence., which is adopted on July 4 by the 13 American colonies. Inspired by the theories of English philosopher John Locke and French philospher Jean-Jacques Rousseau, among others, it states in part, "We hold these truths to be self-evident, that all men are created equal, that they are endowed by their Creator with certain unalienable Rights, that among these are Life, Liberty, and pursuit of Happiness." **LIT**
1776	American writer Thomas Paine publishes the pamphlet *Common Sense*, in which he exhorts the need for American independence from England. **LIT**
1776–1783	American writer Thomas Paine publishes *The American Crisis*, a series of 16 pamphlets written during and after the war for independence; the first *Crisis* paper begins with the words, "These are the times that try men's souls." **LIT**
1777	Irish-born English dramatist and statesman Richard Brinsley Sheridan's *The School for Scandal*, considered one of the greatest English comedies of manners, is produced. Sheridan's *A Trip to Scarborough* is also produced this year. Last year he became manager of the Drury Lane Theatre (*see* 1663, DRAMA). **DRAMA**
1777	English painter Thomas Gainsborough, one of the first great English landscape artists, paints the landscape *The Watering Place*. **PAINT**
1777	American painter Benjamin West paints *Saul and the Witch of Endor*. **PAINT**
1777	French sculptor Jean-Jacques Caffiéri exhibits his neoclassical design for the monument to Major-General Richard Montgomery at the Paris Salon. The statue will not be erected until 1789 under the east portico of St. Paul's Chapel in New York City. **SCULP**
1778	German composer Ludwig van Beethoven, age eight, is presented by his father as a six-year-old music prodigy. **MUSIC**
1778	La Scala opera house opens in Milan, Italy. **MUSIC**
1778	Austrian composer Wolfgang Amadeus Mozart composes piano sonatas K. 310 in A minor, and 330–333, which will be among his best known in the genre. **MUSIC**

1778	Austrian composer Wolfgang Amadeus Mozart composes Symphony in D (*Paris*, K. 297), which will be among his most critically acclaimed works. MUSIC
1778	Settled in England since the American Revolution began, American painter John Singleton Copley turns to history painting, producing such works as *Brook Watson and the Shark*. PAINT
1779	At the time of his death, English cabinetmaker Thomas Chippendale (*b.* 1718) has had a broad and lasting influence in his designs of chairs, cabinets, bookcases, mirror frames, and tables. His work has combined Queen Anne and Georgian styles with chinoiserie, rococo, and Gothic. *See also* 1723–1774, DECO. DECO
1779	English novelist Fanny Burney (also known as Madame d'Arblay) writes the young woman's coming-of-age novel *Evelina, or The History of a Young Lady's Entrance into the World.* Later novels include *Cecilia, or Memoirs of an Heiress* (1782) and *Camilla* (1796). LIT
1779	The opera *Iphigenia in Tauris*, by German composer Christoph Willibald Gluck, premieres in Paris. MUSIC
1780s	Austrian composer Wolfgang Amadeus Mozart composes many great piano concertos, among them K. 450 in B-flat, K. 451 in D, and K. 453 in G (all 1784). Three important concertos in 1784–1785 include K. 459 in F, K. 466 in D minor, and K. 467 in C. MUSIC
1780	The Spanish dance bolero is invented by dancer Sebastiano Cerezo. DANCE
1780	The first modern pianoforte is made in Paris by Sébastien Érard. MUSIC
1781	English critic and writer Samuel Johnson publishes *The Lives of the Poets*, a collection of 52 essays on individual poets, combining biography and criticism. LIT
1781	Swiss-born British painter Henry Fuseli paints the grotesque work *The Nightmare*. PAINT
1782	French-born American farmer Michel-Guillaume-Jean de Crèvecoeur publishes *Letters from an American Farmer*, which addresses the life of the land and the American character. LIT
1782	French sculptor Étienne Falconet, working with portraitist Marie-Anne Collot, completes his bronze equestrian statue of Peter the Great to be placed in the Square of the Decembrists, St. Petersburg, Russia. SCULP

1783   English actor John Philip Kemble successfully debuts in London in a distinctive portrayal of Hamlet. He will make his mark in classical tragic roles. His sister Sarah Siddons's stage career will flourish around the same time, and she will also excel in tragedy, giving her greatest performance as Lady Macbeth. John and Sarah's younger brother Charles will be a less accomplished actor, though ultimately he will do well in romantic and comic parts. Stephen, a fourth sibling, will be best known for putting his great circumference to use as Falstaff. Fanny Kemble, Charles's daughter, will give outstanding performances in a number of tragic and romantic roles, including Juliet.   DRAMA

1783   English poet George Crabbe publishes *The Village*, a realistic poem about rural life.   LIT

1783   English artist and poet William Blake publishes *Poetical Sketches*, his first book of poems.   LIT

1783   English painter Thomas Gainsborough paints *The Mall*, an example of the genre of fancy pictures, in which idealized peasants are depicted in rural settings.   PAINT

1783   American painter John Singleton Copley paints *The Death of Major Peirson*.   PAINT

1784   The first American woman who is a professional writer, historian Hannah Adams publishes *Alphabetical Compendium of the Various Sects . . . from the Beginning of the Christian Era*.   LIT

1784   The Paris Conservatoire National de Musique opens.   MUSIC

1784   American artist Joseph Wright, son of Patience Lovell Wright, completes his wax bas-relief profile portrait of George Washington. Wright will be commissioned by the government to make designs for coins it will soon print.   SCULP

1785   American statesman and architect Thomas Jefferson designs the Virginia state capitol, notable for its neoclassical approach based on Roman models.   ARCH

1785   English poet William Cowper publishes *The Task*, a meditative poem evoking English country life.   LIT

1785   A year after the death of his friend English critic and writer Samuel Johnson, Scottish biographer James Boswell publishes an account of a voyage they took together in 1773, *The Journal of a Tour to the Hebrides*.   LIT

1785–1786	While working on *Le Nozze di Figaro* (*The Marriage of Figaro*, K. 492), Austrian composer Wolfgang Amadeus Mozart composes three piano concertos. The first two are in a comparatively light mood, while the third (K. 491) in C minor is one of his great tragic creations. The C-major concerto of December 1786 (K. 503) is considered its triumphal counterpart. MUSIC
1785	French sculptor Jean-Antoine Houdon arrives in Philadelphia on September 14 to study George Washington's features for a monumental sculpture commissioned by the Virginia assembly. The marble statue will be placed in the rotunda of the Virginia state capitol in 1796. SCULP
1786	Scottish poet Robert Burns publishes *Poems, Chiefly in the Scottish Dialect.* LIT
1786	Austrian composer Wolfgang Amadeus Mozart's opera *The Marriage of Figaro* premieres in Vienna. MUSIC
1786–1797	American painter John Trumbull paints the much-reproduced *The Declaration of Independence.* PAINT
1787	Scottish poet Robert Burns begins collecting and writing hundreds of songs, traditional and new, for *Scots Musical Museum*, including "Auld Lang Syne" and "A Red, Red Rose." MUSIC
1787	Austrian composer Wolfgang Amadeus Mozart's opera *Don Giovanni* premieres in Prague. MUSIC
1787	French painter Jacques-Louis David paints *The Death of Socrates*. Like his other neoclassical paintings of the decade, including *The Oath of the Horatii* (1784) and *Brutus and His Dead Sons* (1789), it embodies a stern republican idealism and a commitment to classical aesthetic principles, against rococo frivolity and lightness. PAINT
1788	Among the last seven symphonies Wolfgang Amadeus Mozart composed while living in Vienna are three "great symphonies": E-flat (no. 39, K. 543), G Minor (no. 40, K. 550), and C Major *Jupiter* (K. 551). In this year he also composes the orchestral serenade *Eine Kleine Nachtmusik* (K. 525). MUSIC
1789	Edmund Kean, who will become one of the greatest English stage actors, is born in London (*d.* 1833). He will give his best performances in Shakespearean roles, particularly Shylock, Macbeth, Richard III, and Iago. DRAMA
1789	*The Power of Sympathy*, believed to be the first novel written in the United States, is completed. The book's author was originally thought to be Sarah Wentworth Morton; William Hill Brown will come to be considered the probable writer. LIT

1789	French painter Jacques-Louis David is active in the French Revolution, both through political activity and through his paintings, which embody republican principles. PAINT
c. 1790–1840	Greek revival is an important movement in European and American architecture, drawing on models taken from ancient Greece. ARCH
1790	English wood engraver Thomas Bewick publishes fine wood engravings in *A General History of Quadrupeds*. His other illustrated works of natural history will include *A History of British Birds* (1797, 1804). Bewick's finely detailed work will make wood engraving popular for book illustrations until the end of the 19th century. GRAPH
1790	English artist and poet William Blake publishes his most important prose work, *The Marriage of Heaven and Hell*. LIT
1790	Irish-born British statesman and writer Edmund Burke publishes the conservative treatise *Reflections on the Revolution in France*. American writer Thomas Paine will reply to it in support of revolution in *The Rights of Man* (1791–1792). LIT
1791	The waltz becomes fashionable in England. DANCE
1791	Scottish biographer James Boswell completes *The Life of Samuel Johnson LL.D.*, considered by many the best biography in the English language. LIT
1791	Scottish poet Robert Burns publishes the narrative poem *Tam O'Shanter*. LIT
1791	French writer Donatien-Alphonse-François de Sade, known as the Marquis de Sade, writes *Justine, ou les Malheurs de la vertu*. Later works include *Juliette* (1797). LIT
1791–1795	Austrian composer Franz Joseph Haydn composes his 12 London Symphonies, including the famous *Surprise Symphony* (no. 94), for the Salomon Concerts in London. MUSIC
1791	Austrian composer Wolfgang Amadeus Mozart's last opera, *The Magic Flute* (K. 620), premieres in Vienna in the year of Mozart's death (*b.* 1756). MUSIC
1792	*The Farmer's Almanac* is published for the first time by American printer Robert Bailey Thomas, who also founded and edited it. Later renamed *The Old Farmer's Almanac*, it will be published annually hereafter. LIT
1792	American painter Ralph Earl paints *Oliver Ellsworth and His Wife*. PAINT

1793	English poet William Wordsworth publishes the poem "An Evening Walk" and the collection *Descriptive Sketches*. **LIT**
1793	Italian violin virtuoso Niccolò Paganini, age 11, makes his debut in Genoa. **MUSIC**
1793	French painter Jacques-Louis David paints *The Death of Marat*. **PAINT**
1794	English artist and poet William Blake publishes *Songs of Innocence and of Experience*, which includes the poems "The Lamb," "The Chimney Sweeper," "The Tyger," "The Garden of Love," "A Poison Tree," and "The Sick Rose." Like Blake's subsequent illuminated books, the volume is lavishly illustrated with etchings by the author. **LIT**
1794	English novelist Ann Radcliffe publishes the Gothic novel *The Mysteries of Udolpho*. **LIT**
1794	*Tammany, or The Indian Chief* by James Hewitt, an early American opera, is performed. **MUSIC**
1794–1796	French painter Jacques-Louis David paints *Intervention of the Sabine Women*. **PAINT**
1795–1796	American painter Gilbert Stuart paints a definitive series of portraits of America's first president, George Washington. Of his three different types of Washington portraits, the most famous, the Athenaeum type, will be used on the U.S. one-dollar bill. **PAINT**
1796	American wood-carver Samuel McIntire collaborates with furniture maker William Lemon to decorate a chest with European-influenced classical detail for Mrs. Elizabeth Derby. **DECO**
1796	English novelist Matthew Lewis publishes the Gothic novel *The Monk*. **LIT**
1796	English painter J. M. W. (Joseph Mallord William) Turner, who will be considered one of the greatest landscape artists of the 19th century, completes *Fishermen at Sea*, his first oil painting to be exhibited at the Royal Academy. **PAINT**
1797	German writer Ludwig Tieck writes the play *Der gestiefelte Kater* (*Puss in Boots*). His later works will include the realistic short novel *Des Lebens Uberflub* (*Life's Overflow*, 1837). **DRAMA**
1797	French painter Pierre-Narcisse Guérin wins the Prix de Rome, marking the beginning of a career that will include serving as teacher to romantic painters Eugène Delacroix and Théodore Géricault. **PAINT**

1798   German printer Aloys Senefelder invents lithography, a process for printing images based on the incompatibility of oil and water. It becomes a popular medium for fine and commercial artists.   GRAPH

1798   English poets William Wordsworth and Samuel Taylor Coleridge publish the collection *Lyrical Ballads*, often regarded as the founding work of English romanticism. It includes Coleridge's "The Rime of the Ancient Mariner" and "The Nightingale" and Wordsworth's "The Idiot Boy," "The Thorn," "The Mad Mother," "Lines Written in Early Spring," and "Lines Composed a Few Miles Above Tintern Abbey." A second edition will appear in 1800 (with a famous preface by Wordsworth), a third in 1802.   LIT

1798–1799   English poet William Wordsworth composes the "Lucy" poems and the first, two-part version of the autobiographical poem *The Prelude*. Revised throughout his life, *The Prelude* will not be published until 1850, after his death.   LIT

1798   American novelist Charles Brockden Brown publishes the Gothic novel *Wieland*.   LIT

1799   In Philadelphia English-born Benjamin Henry Latrobe, regarded as the first professional American architect, designs the Greek revivalist Bank of Pennsylvania, based on an Ionic temple.   ARCH

1799   Spanish painter Francisco de Goya issues the series of engravings *Los Caprichos*. They display the grotesque, satirical, nightmarish elements that will become associated with his name. He will complete hundreds of etchings, lithographs, and drawings in addition to his hundreds of paintings.   GRAPH

1799   American historian Hannah Adams publishes *A Summary History of New-England*.   LIT

1799   The oratorio *The Creation*, by Austrian composer Franz Joseph Haydn, premieres in Vienna.   MUSIC

1799   German composer Ludwig van Beethoven composes Symphony no. 1 in C Major and Piano Sonata Op. 13 (*Pathétique*).   MUSIC

1799   Swiss-born British painter Henry Fuseli opens Milton Gallery in London, exhibiting dozens of his own paintings on literary subjects. He had previously contributed to John Boydell's Shakespeare gallery.   PAINT

1800s   Decorative artists in Japan experiment in a number of forms, such as lacquer goods, metal work, and small carvings in ivory and wood.   DECO

1800s   Costumes and scenery become increasingly realistic on stages in England and throughout Europe. More and more, historical research is undertaken to ensure accuracy in design. By the end of the century, actors are dressed largely as their characters would have been in real life, and plays are usually performed with sets that include appropriate furniture and accessories.   DRAMA

1800s   In China popular plays combine spoken dialogue with singing, dancing, and acrobatics. Most are histories or adaptations of legends or novels. There is usually no scenery other than a decorated backcloth, and the few props are mostly symbolic (for instance, a horsehair duster represents spirituality). Costumes and makeup can be elaborate, and the acting is highly stylized. This form of theater will endure indefinitely.   DRAMA

1800s   Historical dramas and pageant plays, many of them about Indians and frontiersmen, become popular in the United States. There are enough theaters that a number of American playwrights are able to support themselves through writing, though none produce works of lasting fame. Gas lighting is installed in theaters, improving illumination.   DRAMA

1800s   Western-style theater begins in Egypt, Syria, and Turkey. Translations of European plays and plays written by Middle Easterners are performed throughout the region.   DRAMA

1800s   Professional Parsi theater companies, presenting both South Asian plays and adaptations of work by Western playwrights, flourish in India. They will continue to be popular through the early 20th century.   DRAMA

1800s   Increasingly in Europe and America responsibility for all aspects of the production of a play is shouldered by an individual specifically hired for that purpose, and the profession of directing comes into being. Previously, playwrights, chief actors, and stage managers had supervised—sometimes in only a minimal way—the staging of plays. (Until 1956 directors will be called producers in England.)   DRAMA

1800s   As British forces dominate India, the Indian art of miniature painting declines and eventually dies. Other types of Indian folk art become commercialized and by the 20th century eradicated by the tools of Western industrialism, such as lithography.   MISC

1800s   Throughout India, Western painting influences neutralize regional art styles.   PAINT

1800s   By the beginning of the century, Japanese artists establish themselves as the leading force in painting throughout the East.   PAINT

1800s	The Maori of New Zealand carve representations of Mother Heaven and Father Earth on the fences of their fortified villages, meeting places, and storehouses. The sexual organs illustrating the union of the divinities will be removed during the Victorian period. **SCULP**
1800s	Artists from the Tonga Islands create goddess figures of walrus ivory, bored with a hole so they can be suspended. Most Polynesian figure sculpture will be destroyed under early Western influence. **SCULP**
1800s	White traders introduce metal carving tools to Northwest Coast settlements. Native Americans carve an abundance of monumental poles, grave markers, and doorposts to commemorate important tribal events. **SCULP**
c. 1800–1850	Japanese printmakers such as Andō Hiroshige, Katsushika Hokusai, and Kitagawa Utamaro create representative prints of the Ukiyo-e movement, portraying scenes from evanescent everyday life, with settings including theaters, brothels, and bathhouses. Japanese prints brought to Europe this century exercise a strong influence on avant-garde French artists. **GRAPH**
1800–1900	Romanticism is the prevailing movement in modern music, characterized in music by subjective, emotional qualities and freedom of form, in reaction to the formalistic classical tradition. The movement's contributions will include the character piece for piano, the art song for voice, and the symphonic poem for orchestra. **MUSIC**
c. 1800	Spanish painter Francisco de Goya paints the group portrait *Family of Charles IV* along with the erotic pair of portraits the *Clothed Maja* and *Naked Maja*. **PAINT**
c. 1800	In Britain picturesque scenes, those with varied and irregular detail, are the favorite of landscape artists such as Thomas Girtin. **PAINT**
1801	French novelist François-Auguste-René de Chateaubriand writes the novel *Atala*. His later works will include the romance *René* (1802) and *Le Génie du christianisme* (1802). **LIT**
1801	Swiss-born British painter Henry Fuseli publishes *Lectures on Painting*. **PAINT**
1801	French painter Jean-Auguste-Dominique Ingres wins the Prix de Rome with the history painting *Envoys from Agamemnon*. **PAINT**
1801	English sculptor John Flaxman sculpts the monument to Lord Mansfield. Flaxman is known not only for his neoclassical monumental style but for his designs for potter Josiah Wedgwood (1775–1787) and his illustrations for works such as the *Iliad* and the *Odyssey* (1793). **SCULP**

1802	*A Tale of Mystery*, a play by English playwright Thomas Holcroft that will be generally considered the first melodrama produced in England, opens in London. **DRAMA**
1802	English poet and critic Samuel Taylor Coleridge publishes "Dejection: An Ode," to which his friend William Wordsworth will reply in "Intimations of Immortality" (1807). **LIT**
1802	French writer Anne-Louise-Germaine de Staël writes the early feminist novel *Delphine*. She will later write the novel *Corinne* (1807). **LIT**
1802	German composer Ludwig van Beethoven composes Symphony no. 2 in D Major, Op. 36, and Piano Sonata in C-sharp Minor, no. 2 (*Moonlight*). **MUSIC**
1802	American painter Benjamin West paints *Death on a Pale Horse*. **PAINT**
1803–1820	English artist and poet William Blake writes and engraves the illustrated poem *Milton*, which seeks to correct the moral and religious "errors" of John Milton's *Paradise Lost* (1667). **LIT**
1803	German composer Ludwig van Beethoven composes Sonata for Violin and Piano, Op. 47 (*Kreutzer*). **MUSIC**
1804–1820	English artist and poet William Blake's *Jerusalem: The Emanation of the Great Albion* is the last of his prophetic books, incorporating his personal mythology. **LIT**
1804	German composer Ludwig van Beethoven composes Symphony no. 3 in E-flat Major (*Eroica*). The "heroic symphony" is written in homage to Napoleon, but Beethoven withdraws the planned dedication when Napoleon takes the title of emperor. **MUSIC**
1805–1818	American architect Benjamin Henry Latrobe designs the Roman Catholic cathedral in Baltimore, the first cathedral in the United States. **ARCH**
1805	British poet and essayist Leigh Hunt, who will be considered a pioneer in dramatic criticism, begins writing about the theater. His work will continue to appear until at least 1821. **DRAMA**
1805	Italian composer Niccolò Paganini begins touring Europe as a violin virtuoso. **MUSIC**
1805–1807	As Napoleon's official painter, French artist Jacques-Louis David paints *Coronation of Napoleon*. **PAINT**
1805	English painter J. M. W. Turner paints *Shipwreck*. **PAINT**

1805   Italian sculptor Antonio Canova completes his neoclassical tomb for the Archduchess Maria Christina in Vienna's Church of the Augustinians. He will later produce a colossal nude statue of Napoleon and carve a marble portrait of Napoleon's sister, Pauline Borghese, as a reclining Venus in 1808.   SCULP

1806   German composer Ludwig van Beethoven composes Symphony no. 4 in B-flat Major, Op. 60, and Violin Concerto, Op. 61.   MUSIC

1807   *Tears and Smiles*, a comedy of manners by American playwright James Nelson Barker, is produced in Philadelphia. Barker's *The Indian Princess; or La Belle Sauvage*, the first play about Native Americans to be staged in America, will be produced in 1808.   DRAMA

1807   English poet William Wordsworth publishes *Poems in Two Volumes*, which includes "Intimations of Immortality from Recollections of Early Childhood" and "I Wandered Lonely as a Cloud."   LIT

1807   The Accademia di Belle Arti, the municipal picture gallery of Venice and one of Italy's major collections, is founded by order of Napoleon.   PAINT

1808   English poet and critic Samuel Taylor Coleridge delivers 18 lectures titled "On Poetry and the Principles of Taste" at the Royal Institute, the first of many lecture series he will deliver in the coming years.   LIT

1808   British poet and essayist Leigh Hunt begins editing the radical weekly the *Examiner*, which will introduce poets John Keats and Percy Bysshe Shelley to the public.   LIT

1808   German composer Ludwig van Beethoven composes Symphony no. 5 and Symphony no. 6, (*Pastoral*). The descriptive title of the movements of the latter, each suggesting a different scene from life in the country, marks the beginning of 19th-century program music.   MUSIC

1808   French painter Antoine-Jean Gros, Napoleon's official painter of battles, completes *Napoleon at Eylau*.   PAINT

1808   French painter Jean-Auguste-Dominique Ingres paints *The Valpinçon Bather*, one of his many pictures of bathers.   PAINT

1809   American writer Washington Irving publishes the satiric overview of New York in *A History of New York, from the Beginning of the World to the End of the Dutch Dynasty, by Diedrich Knickerbocker*. The book establishes Irving as a writer; his character Knickerbocker will also appear in *The Sketch Book* (1819).   LIT

1809	Dutch painter Wouter Johannes van Troostwijck paints *The Rampoortje*, a landscape featuring a gate in winter.	PAINT

1810–1814	Spanish painter Francisco de Goya paints *The Disasters of War* series of etchings depicting atrocities committed during Napoleon's invasion of Spain.	GRAPH

1810	Scottish writer Walter Scott publishes the poem *The Lady of the Lake*.	LIT

1811	English novelist Jane Austen publishes *Sense and Sensibility*.	LIT

1811	With Thomas Jefferson Hogg, English poet Percy Bysshe Shelley publishes the pamphlet *On the Necessity of Atheism*, resulting in his expulsion from Oxford.	LIT

1812	English chemist and physicist William Hyde Wollaston invents the camera lucida, a device that projects the image of an object onto a flat surface where a drawing can be traced.	GRAPH

1812	The brothers Jacob and Wilhelm Grimm, the founders of German philology, publish what will become known as *Grimm's Fairy-Tales*, compiled from interviews with peasants.	LIT

1812	English poet George Gordon, Lord Byron, publishes the first two cantos of *Childe Harold's Pilgrimage*, which introduces the idea of the moody, rebellious,

The Other Deaf Artist

German composer Ludwig van Beethoven's battle with deafness is well known. He began to lose his hearing around 1800, while entering his 30s, and was completely deaf by 1819. Though the incurable condition led him at one point to contemplate suicide, Beethoven went on to produce some of his greatest music, informed by his inner struggles and victories, culminating in the Ninth or Choral Symphony in 1824.

During the same years, another deaf artist was creating works of equal stature in a different medium. Spanish painter Francisco de Goya had been deaf since 1793, when he contracted a mysterious illness, possibly labyrinthitis or lead poisoning. Previously known for light rococo works, his period of convalescence led him to paint darker, more macabre pictures, in his words, "to occupy an imagination mortified by the contemplation of my suffering." For the rest of his career, his greatest works were predominantly grotesque, nightmarish scenes, including those in the etching series *The Disasters of War* (1810–1814) and the "Black Paintings" (1820s). The latter were painted in a country residence near Madrid he called the Quinta del Sordo—House of the Deaf Man.

tempestuous Byronic hero. The third canto will appear in 1816, the fourth in 1818.   LIT

1812   The Gesellschaft der Musikfreunde is founded in Vienna. It will become the oldest and most important music society of Austria.   MUSIC

1812   German composer Ludwig van Beethoven composes Symphony no. 7, Op. 92 and Symphony no. 8 Op. 93.   MUSIC

1813–1818   English writer William Hazlitt reviews plays for the *Champion*, the *Examiner*, the *Morning Chronicle*, and *The Times*.   DRAMA

1813   English novelist Jane Austen publishes the elegantly comic novel *Pride and Prejudice*, on the romance between Elizabeth Bennet and FitzWilliam Darcy.   LIT

1813–1814   English poet Lord Byron publishes the oriental tales, which include *The Giaour*, *The Corsair*, and *Lara*.   LIT

1813   English poet Percy Bysshe Shelley publishes his first major poem, *Queen Mab*.   LIT

Lord Elgin's Marbles

Few art collectors have won as much fame—and notoriety—as British diplomat Thomas Bruce, seventh Lord Elgin, who obtained for Great Britain the group of sculptures known as the Elgin Marbles. Comprising most of the sculptures from the Parthenon in Athens, along with other classical Greek works, Elgin persuaded the Ottoman Turks to part with them in 1801–1803; they were sold to Great Britain in 1816, and are now in the British Museum. Given that the Turks were an occupying power who had no moral right to sell part of Greece's heritage, Elgin's deal sparked controversy then and now. But artists and critics in England were only too happy to get the chance to study the sculptures up close. Previously, art aficionados had been restricted for the most part to later Hellenistic and Roman copies, which lacked the classical purity of the originals. Painter Benjamin Robert Haydon, viewing the Elgin Marbles in 1808, was astonished by the combination of faithfulness to nature and idealized grandeur. He wrote:

> That combination of nature and idea which I had felt was so much wanting for high art was here displayed to midday conviction. My heart beat! If I had seen nothing else I had beheld sufficient to keep me to nature for the rest of my life. But when I turned to the [sculpture of] Theseus . . . the Ilyssus . . . and . . . the figure of the fighting metope . . . when I saw, in fact, the most heroic style of art combined with all the essential detail of actual life, the thing was done at once and for ever.

1813	Swedish poet Esaias Tegnér publishes the collection *Hjälten*. His later collections will include *Frithiof's Saga* (1825), and *Nattvardsbarnen* (1820, translated into English by American poet Henry Wadsworth Longfellow). LIT
1813	The London Philharmonic Society is founded. MUSIC
1814	English poet William Wordsworth publishes *The Excursion*, a philosophical poem in nine books. LIT
1814	Scottish poet and novelist Walter Scott publishes the romance *Waverley*, his first in a series of "Waverley novels" set in Scotland that also include *Guy Mannering* (1815) and *Rob Roy* (1818). LIT
1814–1815	German composer and writer E. T. A. (Ernst Theodor Amadeus) Hoffmann composes the collection of fantastic tales *Fantastiestücke* (*Fantasy-pieces*). He will also write the collection *Nachtstücke* (*Night-pieces*, 1817). LIT
1814	German poet Friedrich Rückert publishes the collection of political poems *Geharnischte Sonette* (*Harnessed Sonnets*). Among his later works are *Kindertotenlieder* (*Songs on Children's Deaths*, 1872), set to music by Gustav Mahler. LIT
1814	Austrian composer Franz Schubert begins his most prolific period of musical composition. By 1828 he will have written more than 600 German songs. MUSIC
1814	German composer Ludwig van Beethoven presents the final version of his opera *Fidelio*. MUSIC
1814	French painter Jean-Auguste-Dominique Ingres paints the *Grande Odalisque*, a picture of a harem slave done in neoclassical style. PAINT
1814	Spanish painter Francisco de Goya paints *The Third of May, 1808*, an emotionally wrenching picture of Spanish citizens executed by Napoleon's troops in Madrid. PAINT
1815	English poet Lord Byron publishes *Hebrew Melodies*, which includes the poem "She Walks in Beauty." LIT
1816	English novelist Jane Austen publishes *Emma*. LIT
1816	English poet and critic Samuel Taylor Coleridge publishes *Christabel and Other Poems*, which includes the fragment "Kubla Khan." LIT

1816   While spending the summer at Lake Geneva, Switzerland, English poet Percy Bysshe Shelley, his wife, English novelist Mary Wollstonecraft Shelley, and their friend English poet Lord Byron, engage in a ghost-story competition that results in Mary Wollstonecraft Shelley's writing the novel *Frankenstein, or The Modern Prometheus*, which will be published in 1818. In the same summer, Percy Bysshe Shelley writes the philosophical poems "Hymn to Intellectual Beauty" and "Mont Blanc."   LIT

1816   English poet Percy Bysshe Shelley publishes *Alastor, or The Spirit of Solitude*. LIT

1816   American lawyer and linguist John Pickering writes an early study of the American language, *A Vocabulary, or, Collection of Words and Phrases Which Have Supposed to Be Peculiar to the U.S. of America*.   LIT

1816   English painter John Martin paints *Joshua Commanding the Sun to Stand Still*, typical of his spectacular, melodramatic scenes.   PAINT

1817   English poet and critic Samuel Taylor Coleridge publishes *Biographia Literaria*, an idiosyncratic compendium of critical theory, philosophy, and autobiography. LIT

1817   English poet Lord Byron publishes the closet tragedy *Manfred*.   LIT

1817   English poet John Keats publishes *Poems*, his first collection.   LIT

1817   American poet William Cullen Bryant publishes the poem "Thanatopsis" in the *North American Review*.   LIT

1818   English novelist Jane Austen's *Northanger Abbey*, a satire of Gothic fiction, is published posthumously.   LIT

1818   English novelist Mary Wollstonecraft Shelley publishes the Gothic horror novel *Frankenstein, or The Modern Prometheus*. The story of the man who is ultimately destroyed by the monster he has created will become a fixture of popular literature and scholarly study and will be adapted for the stage and screen many times. Especially notable will be James Whale's film *Frankenstein* (1931), starring Boris Karloff and Colin Clive. *See also* 1816, LIT.   LIT

1818   English poet Percy Bysshe Shelley publishes the political pamphlet *The Revolt of Islam* and the poem "Ozymandias," while fellow-poet John Keats publishes *Endymion: A Poetic Romance*.   LIT

1818–1819   French painter Théodore Géricault paints his most famous work, *The Raft of the Medusa*, renowned for its epic, grisly treatment of a controversial contemporary event, a shipwreck considered by some to be due to government incompetence.   PAINT

| 1819 | Architecture courses are conducted for the first time at the École des Beaux Arts in Paris. Up until this time, the practice of being an architect did not require formal training and accreditation. ARCH |

1819   Architecture courses are conducted for the first time at the École des Beaux Arts in Paris. Up until this time, the practice of being an architect did not require formal training and accreditation.   ARCH

1819–1824   English poet Lord Byron publishes 16 cantos of his unfinished satirical epic *Don Juan*, written in ottava rima.   LIT

1819   English poet Percy Bysshe Shelley publishes the poetic drama *The Cenci* and the poem "Ode to the West Wind."   LIT

1819   English poet John Keats writes most of his greatest poems, including the ballad "La Belle Dame Sans Merci," the sonnet "Fame," and the odes "On a Grecian Urn," "To a Nightingale," "On Melancholy," "On Indolence," "To Psyche," and "Ode to Autumn." He also writes the poems "The Eve of St. Agnes" and "Lamia." Many of these works will be published in his collection of 1820, one year before his death.   LIT

1819   Scottish poet and novelist Walter Scott publishes his most popular novel, *Ivanhoe*, set in medieval England during the reign of Richard I.   LIT

1819   German composer Ludwig van Beethoven's Piano Sonata in B-flat, Op. 106 (*Hammerklavier*), is published the year he becomes completely deaf.   MUSIC

1820s   Spanish painter Francisco de Goya paints the "Black Paintings," a series of macabre images done principally in black, gray, and brown.   PAINT

1820s   Artists in the Haida settlement in the Queen Charlotte Islands, British Columbia, create totem poles of argillite stone featuring prehistoric tribal motifs. Artists will begin to depict subjects favored by Western visitors to supply an active tourist market.   SCULP

1820   English poet Percy Bysshe Shelley publishes his masterpiece, the poetic drama *Prometheus Unbound*. Among his other works this year are the political odes "To Liberty" and "To Naples," the political essay "A Philosophical View of Reform," and the lyric poems "The Cloud" and "To a Skylark."   LIT

1820   Cuban poet José María Heredia publishes "En el teocalli de Cholula." Among his later poems will be "Niagara" (1824).   LIT

1820–1825   British essayist Charles Lamb, writing under the name Elia, contributes a series of essays to *London Magazine*, collected in 1823 as *Essays of Elia* and 1833 as *The Last Essays of Elia*. They include "A Dissertation on Roast Pig" and "Blakesmoor in H—shire."   LIT

1820   American writer Washington Irving publishes his best-known work, *The Sketch Book of Geoffrey Crayon, Gent.*, which contains the tales of Rip Van Winkle and the Legend of Sleepy Hollow.   LIT

1820   French poet Alphonse-Marie-Louis de Lamartine publishes the collection *Les Premières méditations*. His later collections will include *Nouvelles méditations poétiques* (1823) and *Harmonies poétiques et religieuses* (1830).   LIT

1820   Russian poet Aleksandr Pushkin publishes the poem *Ruslan i Lyudmila* (*Ruslan and Ludmilla*). Among his later works will be the verse novel *Eugene Onegin* (1833) and the Gothic-influenced story "The Queen of Spades" (1834).   LIT

1821   English poet Percy Bysshe Shelley writes his best-known prose work, the essay "The Defence of Poetry," though it will not be published until 1840, after his death. He also publishes *Adonais*, his elegy on the death of John Keats.   LIT

1821   British poet Thomas Lovell Beddoes publishes the collection *The Improvisatore*.   LIT

1821   British essayist Thomas De Quincey publishes *Confessions of an English Opium Eater*, along with numerous other pieces that will appear in *London Magazine* from 1821 to 1824.   LIT

1821   The romantic opera *Der Freischütz* by German composer Carl Maria von Weber premieres in Berlin.   MUSIC

1821   French painter Théodore Géricault paints *Derby at Epsom*, one of several pictures with horse racing as the subject.   PAINT

1821   Bristish painter John Constable paints the landscape *The Hay Wain*. His romantic approach to landscapes, with its broken color and careful observation of clouds and light, will influence such painters as Delacroix.   PAINT

1822   English poet Lord Byron publishes the poem *The Vision of Judgement*, a satirical response to Robert Southey's poem *A Vision of Judgement* (1821), in the preface of which Southey had attacked the immoral attitudes represented in Byron's poem *Don Juan*.   LIT

1822   English poet Percy Bysshe Shelley drowns in a boating accident, leaving his last poem, *The Triumph of Life*, unfinished.   LIT

1822   French writer Comte Alfred-Victor de Vigny publishes the volume *Poèmes*. Among his later volumes will be *Poèmes antiques et modernes* (1826) and *Les Destinées* (1862).   LIT

1822	Polish poet Adam Mickiewicz publishes the volume of ballads and romances, *Ballady i romanse*. Among his later volumes will be *Pan Tadeusz* (1834), a historical poem about his native country. LIT
1822	Hungarian composer and pianist Franz Liszt, age 11, debuts as a child prodigy at the piano in Vienna. MUSIC
1822	German composer Ludwig van Beethoven's Missa Solemnis in D, Op. 123 and Austrian composer Franz Schubert's Unfinished Symphony are composed. MUSIC
c. 1822	French painter Théodore Géricault paints *A Kleptomaniac*, one of several portraits of mental patients. PAINT
1822	French painter Eugène Delacroix, who will be considered one of the greatest French romantic painters, first comes to public attention with *The Barque of Dante*. Two years later he paints *The Massacre at Chios*. His works will be noted for their color, brushwork, emotional intensity, and dramatic approach. PAINT
1822	French physicist Joseph Nicéphore Niepce creates the first permanent photographic representation. He will come to work with French inventor Louis-Jacques-Mandé Daguerre to make the first daguerreotype in 1839. PHOTO
1823–1841	American novelist James Fenimore Cooper writes the novels known as the Leatherstocking tales. Featuring the character Natty Bumppo, they include *The Pioneers* (1823), *The Last of the Mohicans* (1826), *The Prairie* (1827), *The Pathfinder* (1840), and *The Deerslayer* (1841). LIT
1824	The Shakers in Hancock, New York, design the first round barn. Characterized by divisions that form feeding stations, it will be popular with dairy farmers. ARCH
1824	Italian poet Count Giacomo Leopardi publishes the volume *Canzoni*. Among his later volumes will be *Versi* (1826) and *Canti* (1836). LIT
1824	The National Gallery is founded in London. It will move to its new site in Trafalgar Square in 1838. PAINT
1824	French painter Jean-Auguste-Dominique Ingres completes the *Vow of Louis XIII* for the cathedral of Montauban. The work gains him a reputation as the leader of French neoclassicists. Other works by Ingres in this decade and the next include *The Apotheosis of Homer* (1827), *The Martyrdom of St. Symphorian* (1834), and *Antiochus and Stratonice* (1834–1840). PAINT

1825   Russian poet Aleksandr Pushkin writes the tragedy *Boris Godunov*, an explo-
        ration of the nature of power and resistance to tyranny modeled after English
        dramatist William Shakespeare's historical plays.   DRAMA

1825   English writer William Hazlitt publishes *The Spirit of the Age*, a collection of his
        essays.   LIT

1825   Symphony No. 9, *Choral*, by German composer Ludwig van Beethoven pre-
        mieres. Perhaps his greatest achievement, it is the first choral symphony to
        achieve popularity and establishes the genre. It concludes with a magnificent
        setting of German poet Johann Friedrich von Schiller's "Ode to Joy."   MUSIC

c. 1825–   In the United States, the Hudson River school of landscape painting flourish-
1875   es, combining naturalism and grandeur in depicting wilderness areas such as
            the Hudson River valley and the Catskill Mountains. Leaders of the school
            include Thomas Cole, Thomas Doughty, and Asher B. Durand. Other mem-
            bers include Albert Bierstadt, John F. Kensett, Samuel F. B. Morse, and Frederick
            E. Church.   PAINT

1826   Landscape drawings by English painter J. M. W. Turner are published in
        Picturesque Views of the Southern Coast of England.   GRAPH

1826   Danish poet and novelist Bernhard Severin Ingemann publishes the historical
        novel *Valdemar Seier* (*Waldemar, Surnamed Seir, or the Victorious*). Other novels
        will include *Erik Menveds Barndom* (*The Childhood of King Eric Menved*, 1828)
        and *Kong Erik og de Fredløse* (*King Erik and the Outlaws*, 1833).   LIT

1826   German composer Felix Mendelssohn composes the orchestral overture *A
        Midsummer Night's Dream*, setting the standard for concert overtures of the
        period. It will be another 17 years before he adds the incidental music, includ-
        ing the familiar "Wedding March."   MUSIC

1827   American poet and short-story writer Edgar Allan Poe anonymously publishes
        his first collection, *Tamerlane and Other Poems*.   LIT

1827   Italian novelist and poet Alessandro Manzoni publishes the historical novel *I
        promessi sposi*. Among his many Christian works are the essay *Osservazioni sulla
        morale cattolica* (1819) and the poetry collection *Inni sacri* (*Sacred Hymns*,
        1822).   LIT

1827   German poet and journalist Heinrich Heine publishes the volume of poetry
        Buch der Lieder (*Book of Songs*). Among his later works will be *Französische
        Zustand* (*The Situation in France*, 1832) and *Zur Geschichte der Religion und
        Philosophie in Deutschland* (*On the History of Religion and Philosophy in Germany*,
        1834).   LIT

1827   French painter Eugène Delacroix paints *Death of Sardanapalus*, based on a
            poem by Lord Byron.   PAINT

c. 1828   In what may be the first example of actual minstrel dancing, white American
            actor Thomas Dartmouth Rice adapts for the stage a jig danced by a black man
            named Daddy Jim Crow. Using the stage name Daddy "Jim Crow" Rice, he
            becomes an immediate success and spawns a new form of entertainment,
            which will reach its zenith of popularity from 1850 to 1870. Jim Crow laws, a
            series of statutes legalizing racial segregation in the South, which will be enact-
            ed from the 1880s onward and which will not be formally dismantled until the
            civil rights legislation of the 1950s and 1960s, will be believed to have been
            named for this minstrel character. The name Jim Crow will become associated
            with a segment of minstrel shows called the "walk around," in which white
            actors in blackface caricature black Americans.   DANCE

1829   French writer Prosper Mérimée publishes the novel *La Chronique du temps de
            Charles IX*. Among his later novels will be *Colomba* (1841) and *La Double
            Méprise* (1833).   LIT

1829   Polish pianist and composer Frédéric Chopin debuts in Vienna and is hailed
            as a "Young Mozart."   MUSIC

1829   The opera *William Tell*, by Italian composer Gioacchino Rossini, premieres in
            Paris.   MUSIC

1829   German composer Felix Mendelssohn revives interest in the works of German
            composer Johann Sebastian Bach when he conducts a performance of *Passion
            According to St. Matthew* in Berlin, 100 years after it was first performed in Leipzig.
                                                                                   MUSIC

1830   *Hernani*, a drama by the French writer and playwright Victor Hugo, opens at
            the Théâtre-Français, leading to a riot over the play's political content.   DRAMA

1830   British poet Alfred Tennyson (who will be made a lord in 1883) publishes
            Poems Chiefly Lyrical.   LIT

1830   British novelist Edward Bulwer-Lytton publishes the crime novel *Paul Clifford*,
            which begins memorably, "It was a dark and stormy night." Bulwer-Lytton,
            along with novelists such as William Harrison Ainsworth, specializes in
            Newgate novels, works of crime fiction often based on true cases and so called
            in reference to Newgate Prison.   LIT

1830   French novelist Marie Henri Beyle, known as Stendhal, publishes *Le Rouge et le noir* (*The Red and the Black*). It and his future novel *La Chartreuse de Parme* (*The Charterhouse of Parma*, 1839) will be considered important milestones in the development of the modern realistic and psychological novel.   LIT

1830   French poet and novelist Théophile Gautier publishes the volume of poetry *Poésies*. Later examples of his finely wrought poetic works include *La Comédie de la mort* (1838) and *Émaux et camées* (1852).   LIT

1831   French writer Victor Hugo publishes the novel *The Hunchback of Notre Dame*, about the doomed love of Quasimodo for the beautiful Esmerelda. It will be the basis of memorable films in 1923 and 1939.   LIT

1832   *Le Roi s'amuse* (*The King Enjoys Himself*), a play by French writer Victor Hugo, is produced. It will be used as the libretto for Verdi's opera *Rigoletto*.   DRAMA

1832   French graphic artist Honoré Daumier, who will be considered one of the greatest caricaturist of the 19th century, is imprisoned for his political cartoons lampooning the government of Louis-Philippe.   GRAPH

1832   American poet and editor William Cullen Bryant publishes the poem "A Forest Hymn."   LIT

1832   French novelist Amandine Dudevant, known as George Sand, publishes the controversial novel *Indiana*. Among her later works will be the novels *Consuelo* (1842) and *François le champi* (1847).   LIT

1832   Finnish poet and novelist Johan Ludvig Runeberg publishes the novel *The Elk Hunters*. Among his later prose works will be *Tales of Ensign Stal* (1848, 1860), about his country's soldiers during the Russo-Finnish War.   LIT

1832   French composer Hector Berlioz's prototypical program symphony *Symphonie fantastique* premieres in Paris. It exhibits his idée fixe, a recurring theme in each movement, forerunner of the leitmotiv.   MUSIC

1832   American sculptor Horatio Greenough begins to carve a marble statue of American president George Washington derived from the classical Greek statue of Zeus. It will be completed in 1841 and stand outside the Capitol.   SCULP

1833   American builder Augustus Deodat Taylor invents the balloon frame house, which becomes popular for its sturdiness and ease of construction.   ARCH

1833   Scottish historian and essayist Thomas Carlyle publishes *Sartor Resartus*, a satirical, spiritual, wide-ranging philosophical work heavily influenced by German romanticism.   LIT

1833	American poet and short-story writer Edgar Allan Poe publishes the story "MS Found in a Bottle." A prize-winning entry in a Baltimore newspaper contest, it brings him fame as a writer of short stories. LIT
1833	French novelist Honoré de Balzac publishes the novel *Eugénie Grandet*. Among his later novels will be *Le Père Goriot*; he will refer to his complete span of works as *La Comédie humaine* (*The Human Comedy*). LIT
1833	The literary sketch "A Dinner at Poplar Walk" (later retitled "Mr. Minns and His Cousin") appears in the *Monthly Magazine* in December of this year, the first published writing of British novelist Charles Dickens. *See* 1836, LIT. LIT
1833	German composer Robert Schumann helps found the leading music journal, *Die Neue Zeitschrift für Musik*. His articles establish the early reputations of German composer Johannes Brahms, French composer Louis-Hector Berlioz, and Polish composer Frédéric Chopin, among others. MUSIC
1833	German composer Felix Mendelssohn's *Italian Symphony* premieres in London. MUSIC
1833	French sculptor François Rude combines neoclassical and romantic elements in his sculpture of *La Marseillaise* for the Arc de Triomphe in Paris. SCULP
1834	Austrian ballerina Fanny Elssler makes her debut at the Paris Opera. DANCE

Before the Phonograph

Early in the 19th century, Swiss watchmakers developed the music box, a cabinet containing a mechanical device that could reproduce music automatically when activated by clockwork; the precisely arranged pins of its rotating cylinder would play musical tones when struck by the teeth of a metal comb. By 1835–1845 cylinder music boxes had reached such high quality that they could reproduce a variety of instrumental effects, including bells, drums, and chimes. Six or seven tunes could be set on one cylinder; some boxes had interchangeable cylinders, each with different tunes, so that listeners could load whatever cylinder suited their mood that evening. In the 1880s and 1890s, cylinders gave way to less cumbersome disks operating on the same mechanical principle.

At their peak, music boxes were handsome pieces of furniture, ranging in size from tabletop to free-standing, often made of fine wood lined with chromolithographic prints and inlaid with materials such as brass or mother of pearl. However, Edison's invention of the phonograph in 1877, and its commercial development in the early 20th century, spelled the end of the music box era.

1834   French poet and playwright Alfred de Musset writes *Lorenzaccio,* a historical drama which is probably his greatest work for the stage. Most of de Musset's other plays will be comedies such as *Le Chandelier* (*The Decoy,* produced in 1848) and *On ne Bandine pas avec l'amour* (*There's No Trifling with Love,* 1861). He was the lover of French writer George Sand and will become the lover of French actress Rachel. *See* 1838, DRAMA.   DRAMA

1834   French sculptor Antoine-Auguste Préault exemplifies the physical and emotional violence of the romantic spirit in his bronze relief, *Slaughter.*   SCULP

1835   French graphic artist Honoré Daumier begins drawing caricatures for the magazine *Charivari.*   GRAPH

1835   Russian writer Nikolai Gogol publishes the short novel *Taras Bulba.*   LIT

1835–1872   Danish writer Hans Christian Andersen publishes more than 150 fairy tales, including "The Little Match Girl," "The Red Shoes," "The Ugly Duckling," and "The Emperor's New Clothes."   LIT

Emerson and Thoreau

When American transcendentalist Ralph Waldo Emerson gave his landmark 1837 Harvard commencement address "The American Scholar," the audience included one student who would come to embody his views in ways that made him a "more real" transcendentalist than Emerson himself: Henry David Thoreau.

Thoreau first became acquainted with Emerson's belief in the unity of nature and action earlier at Harvard, through the essay "Nature" (1836). During his adult years, his life became intertwined with Emerson's. He submitted writings to Emerson's periodical *The Dial,* tutored one of his relatives, and eventually was employed as a handyman at his estate. More important were the ways Emerson's views informed Thoreau's decisions throughout his life. As a young adult, Thoreau rejected the business world by not becoming part of the family manufacturing business (though he later became part of it). Later in his life he attempted his experimental existence at Walden Pond, refused to pay a poll tax that would support the Mexican War, and aided in helping fugitive slaves gain passage to Canada.

Through all these actions, Thoreau embodied Emerson's belief in the divinity of the commonplace, the need to "embrace the common . . . and sit at the feet of the familiar." His lifework also embraced Emerson's belief in the unity of human action and nature. Thoreau's life showed that "[a] right action seems to fill the eye, and to be related to all nature."

| 1836 | French-born architect Augustus Pugin publishes *Contrasts*, which argues for the superiority of medieval over contemporary architecture. Pugin is a central figure in the Gothic Revival, which brings Gothic styles back into vogue in Europe and the United States, particularly in the building of churches. **ARCH** |

| 1836 | Russian writer Nikolai Gogol's satire *Revizor*, later widely known as *The Inspector General*, is produced. This send-up of bureaucracy—and the response of citizens to bureaucracy—will be seen by many, despite its comic exaggerations, as the best early example of Russian social realism. **DRAMA** |

| 1836–1837 | British novelist Charles Dickens publishes *Sketches by Boz*, a collection of descriptive essays, short stories, and character sketches originally published in magazines, often under the pseudonym "Boz." In the same period he publishes *The Posthumous Papers of the Pickwick Club*, his first novel. Like his later novels, it is issued in monthly numbers and subsequently published in complete form. **LIT** |

| 1836 | American essayist and poet Ralph Waldo Emerson publishes his first book, *Nature*. Its call for spiritual transformation arouses controversy among more conservative critics and thinkers. **LIT** |

| 1836 | German composer Robert Schumann premieres his piano composition *Fantasia in C major*. **MUSIC** |

| 1836 | Russian composer Mikhail Glinka's opera *A Life for the Tsar* premieres in St. Petersburg. It is the first popular opera in the Russian language and inaugurates the nationalist movement. **MUSIC** |

| 1836 | American painter Thomas Cole, a founder of the Hudson River school, paints the landscape *The Oxbow* and the historical series *The Course of Empire*. See c.1825–1875, PAINT. **PAINT** |

| 1837–1839 | British novelist Charles Dickens publishes *The Adventures of Oliver Twist or, The Parish Boy's Progress*, his second novel. **LIT** |

| 1837 | Scottish historian and essayist Thomas Carlyle publishes the history *The French Revolution*. **LIT** |

| 1837 | American writer Nathaniel Hawthorne publishes the story collection *Twice-Told Tales*. Containing such stories as "The Minister's Black Veil," it establishes him as a noteworthy figure in American writing. **LIT** |

| 1837 | American essayist and poet Ralph Waldo Emerson publishes his address to the Phi Beta Kappa Society at Harvard University, "The American Scholar." In it, he issues a clarion call for independence in American thought. **LIT** |

1837–1839   French inventor Hippolyte Bayard develops a method for making photographs and presents them publicly one month before French inventor Louis-Jacques-Mandé Daguerre displays his work in 1839. With support from the French government, Daguerre and his method will become the more successful.   PHOTO

1838   *Ruy Blas*, probably the best play of Victor Hugo, a French writer better known for his poetry and fiction, is produced.   DRAMA

1838   Rachel (Élisa Félix), who will be considered one of the greatest actresses of 19th-century France, makes her debut at the Comédie-Française, playing Camille in Corneille's *Horace*. During the next 20 years she will appear in many classical tragedies, attracting a huge following in France and abroad.   DRAMA

1838–1839   British novelist Charles Dickens publishes *The Life and Adventures of Nicholas Nickleby*, his third novel.   LIT

1838   American poet and short-story writer Edgar Allan Poe publishes the short novel *The Narrative of Arthur Gordon Pym*. The New England whaling tale had been serialized in the *Southern Literary Messenger* in 1837. Over the next decade Poe will publish several stories, including "The Fall of the House of Usher" (1839), "Murders in the Rue Morgue" (1841), "The Masque of the Red Death" (1842), and "The Tell-Tale Heart" (1843).   LIT

1838   American essayist and poet Ralph Waldo Emerson presents "The Divinity School Address" to the Harvard Divinity School. His comments on the divinity of Christ lead to great debate.   LIT

1838   Johanna Maria (Jenny) Lind, the "Swedish Nightingale," debuts in Carl von Weber's *Der Freischütz* in Stockholm.   MUSIC

1839–1842   Austrian ballerina Fanny Elssler tours the United States.   DANCE

1839   Austrian composer Franz Schubert's Symphony in C Major, conducted by German composer Felix Mendelssohn, premieres posthumously in Leipzig.

    MUSIC

1839   The first commercially viable photographic process, the daguerreotype, is developed by French inventor Louis-Jacques-Mandé Daguerre. In this technique, a direct positive image is made on a silver-coated plate. The same year British astronomer Sir John Herschel first uses the word *photography*, basing the term on the Greek words for light and writing. He will also apply the terms "positive" and "negative" to the photographic process. *See also* 1837–1839, PHOTO.   PHOTO

1840s   American settlers expanding into what will become the western United States after the Mexican War (1846–1848) encounter the arts of Native Americans of

1840s	the region. Native Americans of the western plains weave baskets with complex geometric designs, make elaborately beaded costumes, and design ceremonial masks. The Hopi and Zuni (Pueblo) tribes of the Southwest are known for their ceremonial costumes, masks, and kachina (spirit) dolls, while the Navajo are known for sandpainting, the creation of temporary artworks made of colored sand, used as part of religious ritual. DECO
1840s	In France the Barbizon School of landscape painting flourishes, led by painter Théodore Rousseau and also including Charles-François Daubigny, Narcisse-Virgile Diaz de La Peña, and others. PAINT
1840s	The possibilities of portrait photography are explored in the early studies of artists turned photographers such as D. O. Hill and Robert Adamson. PHOTO
1840s	American photographers Albert Sands Southworth and Josiah Johnson Hawes become known for their distinctive daguerreotype portraits. They photograph important American figures of the day, including American essayist and poet Ralph Waldo Emerson, American lawyer and statesman Daniel Webster, and American jurist Oliver Wendell Holmes. PHOTO
1840–1860	In London the Houses of Parliament are designed by Sir Charles Barry, with exterior and interior ornamentation by French-born architect Augustus Pugin. ARCH
1840–1841	British novelist Charles Dickens publishes *The Old Curiosity Shop*, his fourth novel. LIT
1840–1844	American essayists and transcendentalists Ralph Waldo Emerson and Margaret Fuller establish the transcendentalist periodical *The Dial*. LIT
1840	American poet and short-story writer Edgar Allan Poe publishes the collection *Tales of the Grotesque and Arabesque*, which contains the short story "The Fall of the House of Usher." LIT
1840	Russian poet and novelist Mikhail Lermontov publishes the novel *A Hero of Our Time*. During his life he will publish several influential poems, including "Angel," "The Testament," and "Demon." LIT
1840	Robert Schumann, a leading composer of the romantic German lieder (art song), writes more than 100 songs during this year, in which he also marries pianist Clara Wieck. MUSIC
1840	American painter Thomas Cole paints the allegorical series *The Voyage of Life*. PAINT

1841	British novelist Charles Dickens publishes *Barnaby Rudge, A Tale of the Riots of Eighty,* his fifth novel. His first historical novel, it focuses on the anti-Catholic riots instigated by Lord George Gordon in 1780. LIT
1841	Scottish historian and essayist Thomas Carlyle publishes *On Heroes, Hero-Worship and the Heroic in History.* LIT
1841–1846	British poet Robert Browning publishes the series of poetic pamphlets entitled *Bells and Pomegranates.* The works include *Pippa Passes* (1841), *Dramatic Lyrics* (1842), *Dramatic Romances and Lyrics* (1845), and *Luria and A Soul's Tragedy* (1846). Poems from this series include "My Last Duchess," "Soliloquy of the Spanish Cloister," "The Pied Piper of Hamelin," and "The Bishop Orders His Tomb in St. Praxed's Church." LIT
1841	American essayist and poet Ralph Waldo Emerson publishes the collection *Essays: First Series,* which includes his philosophical works "The Over-Soul" and "Self-Reliance." LIT
1841	British physicist William Henry Fox Talbot invents a new photographic process, in which paper positives are printed from a paper negative (the calotype). The forerunner of modern photographic processes, the calotype process will displace that of French inventor Louis-Jacques-Mandé Daguerre. *See also* 1839, PHOTO. PHOTO
1842	*Marriage,* a comedy by Russian writer Nikolai Gogol, is produced. DRAMA
1842	British poet Alfred Tennyson publishes *Poems,* a highly acclaimed work that includes "Locksley Hall" and "Ulysses." An earlier *Poems* (1832) included "The Lady of Shalott," and "The Lotus-Eaters." LIT
1842	American poet Henry Wadsworth Longfellow publishes the mythic poem *Evangeline: A Tale of Acadie.* Among his other poems based on the early years of American life are "The Village Blacksmith" (1842), "The Wreck of the Hesperus" (1841), and "Paul Revere's Ride" (1863). LIT
1842	Russian writer Nikolai Gogol publishes the short story "The Overcoat," which will be an influential work of realism for generations of writers. This year he also publishes the novel *Dead Souls.* LIT
1842	English politician, historian, and poet Thomas Babington Macaulay publishes the poetry volume *Lays of Ancient Rome.* His later works will include the essay collection *Critical and Historical Essays* (1843) and *History of England from the Accession of James the Second* (1848–1861). LIT

| 1842 | The New York Philharmonic Society is founded by violinist Ureli C. Hill and other American musicians. MUSIC |

1842   The New York Philharmonic Society is founded by violinist Ureli C. Hill and other American musicians. MUSIC

1842   Hungarian pianist and composer Franz Liszt becomes court music conductor at Weimar, making it the new European center for music. MUSIC

1843   Scottish historian and essayist Thomas Carlyle publishes *Past and Present.* LIT

1843   American poet and short-story writer Edgar Allan Poe publishes the short story "The Gold Bug," about a search for buried treasure. Originally published in *The Dollar Newspaper*, it will appear in the collection *Tales* in 1845. LIT

1843   British art critic John Ruskin publishes the first volume of *Modern Painters;* later volumes will follow in 1846, 1856, and 1860. PAINT

1844   Spanish playwright José Zorrilla y Moral's drama *Don Juan Tenorio* is produced. Other works about the legend of Don Juan—who may never have existed—include Austrian composer Wolfgang Amadeus Mozart's opera *Don Giovanni* (1787), English poet Lord Byron's poem *Don Juan* (1819–1824), Irish-born British playwright George Bernard Shaw's *Don Juan in Hell* (1907), and French playwright Edmond Rostand's *La Dernière nuit de Don Juan* (*The Last Night of Don Juan*, c. 1910). DRAMA

1844   British novelist Charles Dickens publishes the long story *A Christmas Carol*, which introduces archetypal miser Ebenezer Scrooge, who is haunted on Christmas Eve by his deceased partner Jacob Marley and the Spirits of Christmas Past, Christmas Present, and Christmas Yet to Come. LIT

1844   British novelist William Makepeace Thackeray publishes *Barry Lyndon*, recounting the adventures of an Irish scoundrel. LIT

1844–1845   German poet Johann Ludwig Uhland publishes the collection *Alte hoch- und niederdeutsche Volkslieder* (*Old South and North German Folk-Songs*). Earlier works include *Ernst, Herzog von Schwaben* (*Duke Ernst of Swabia*, 1818). LIT

1844   French novelist and playwright Alexandre Dumas père publishes the swashbuckling novels *The Count of Monte Cristo* and *The Three Musketeers*. Among his later novels will be *The Black Tulip* (1895, published posthumously). LIT

c. 1844   English landscape painter J. M. W. Turner paints *Rain, Steam, and Speed*. Like many of his later paintings, it portrays light, space, and elemental forces in increasingly abstract form. PAINT

1844–1848   French painter Théodore Chassériau paints allegorical scenes of Peace and War for the Cour des Comptes in the Palais d'Orsay in Paris. PAINT

1845–1846   American writer Margaret Fuller publishes two feminist works: *Woman in the 19th Century* (1845) and *Papers on Literature and Art* (1846).   LIT

1845   American poet and short-story writer Edgar Allan Poe publishes the poem "The Raven" in the periodicals *The American Review* and the *Evening Mirror* to immediate success.   LIT

1845   German composer Robert Schumann writes Concerto in A Minor.   MUSIC

1845   The first American grand opera, *Leonora*, by American composer William Henry Fry, premieres in Philadelphia.   MUSIC

1846   In Britain *Poems by Currer, Ellis and Acton Bell* is published. The names are pseudonyms for British novelists Charlotte, Emily, and Anne Brontë.   LIT

1846   British painter and poet Edward Lear publishes his first *Book of Nonsense*, a collection of limericks for children. Many books of nonsense will follow, and he will become famous for such poems as "The Owl and the Pussycat" and "The Jumblies."   LIT

1846   American novelist Herman Melville publishes his first novel, *Typee: A Peep at Polynesian Life*. Partly autobiographical, the book concerns two whalemen who abandon their ship to live with a South Seas tribe. The novel is a commercial success.   LIT

1846   American writer Nathaniel Hawthorne publishes the collection *Mosses from an Old Manse*, which includes the stories "Young Goodman Brown," "The Birthmark," and "Rappaccini's Daughter."   LIT

1846   American poet and short-story writer Edgar Allan Poe publishes "The Cask of Amontillado" in the periodical *Godey's Lady's Book*.   LIT

1846   The oratorio *Elijah*, by German composer Felix Mendelssohn, premieres in Birmingham, England.   MUSIC

1847   British novelist Charlotte Brontë publishes *Jane Eyre*, her sister Emily Brontë *Wuthering Heights*, and their sister Anne Brontë *Agnes Grey*.   LIT

1847–1848   British novelist William Makepeace Thackeray publishes his masterpiece, *Vanity Fair*, the novel that introduces the scheming Becky Sharp.   LIT

1847   American novelist Herman Melville publishes the novel *Omoo: A Narrative of Adventures in the South Seas*, a popular sequel to *Typee*.   LIT

1848–1850	British novelist William Makepeace Thackeray publishes *The History of Pendennis*, a semiautobiographical portrait of one of the "gentlemen of our age." LIT
1848	British poet Arthur Hugh Clough publishes the verse-novel *The Bothie of Tober-na-Vuolich*. LIT
1848–1858	Hungarian pianist and composer Franz Liszt composes 12 symphonic poems (orchestral music based on an extramusical idea). MUSIC
1848	The Pre-Raphaelite Brotherhood is formed by British painters Holman Hunt, John Everett Millais, Dante Gabriel Rossetti, William Michael Rossetti, F. G. Stephens, James Collinson, and Thomas Woolner. The artists advocate a return to the artistic standards that prevailed before Italian Renaissance painter Raphael. They will influence other 19th-century artists and writers, including British artists William Morris and Edward Burne-Jones. PAINT
1849	In New York City American inventor James Bogardus builds the first prefabricated homes. ARCH
1849	British poet Matthew Arnold publishes *The Strayed Reveller and Other Poems*. LIT
1849–1850	*The Personal History of David Copperfield*, the eighth novel by British writer Charles Dickens, is published. LIT
1849	American writer Henry David Thoreau publishes the essay that will become known as "Civil Disobedience" in the periodical *Aesthetic Papers*. Titled in the magazine "Resistance to Civil Government," it is spurred by Thoreau's opposition to American involvement in the Mexican War. In the same year Thoreau publishes *A Week on the Concord and Merrimack Rivers*. LIT
1849–1850	British painter Dante Gabriel Rossetti paints *The Annunciation*. PAINT
1849	Stereophotography, which uses a double-lens camera to produce two views that together produce a three-dimensional view, is developed. It will remain popular over the next three decades. PHOTO
1849–1851	Traveling to the Near East with French novelist Gustave Flaubert, French photographer and writer Maxime Du Camp takes a series of photographs of the land that establish him in the new practice of topographical photography. PHOTO
1850s	Minstrel shows, featuring white actors performing in blackface, become common in the United States. The shows will remain popular for two decades; the practice of performing in blackface will continue into the 20th century. DRAMA

1850s   Limelights—blocks of lime heated so that they give off a glow—come into general use as stage illuminators. By the 1890s most theaters will have electric lights but not necessarily electric stage lighting systems.   DRAMA

1850s   Music-hall entertainment becomes popular in England. At first, mostly singers are featured, but over time, dancers, magicians, comedians, and acrobats will be added. These variety shows, similar to American vaudeville (*see* 1881, DRAMA), will flourish through the early 20th century. English headliners will include Joseph Grimaldi and Gracie Fields, while French music-hall stars will include Maurice Chevalier and Edith Piaf   DRAMA

1850s   Inexpensive, tawdry paperbound novels called penny dreadfuls in Britain and dime novels in the United States become popular.   LIT

1850s   American novelists Nathaniel Hawthorne and Herman Melville meet in the Berkshires of New England. They come to affect each other's work significantly, notably in the cases of Melville's *Moby-Dick* and Hawthorne's *The House of Seven Gables* (both 1851). Their meeting is recalled in Melville's "Hawthorne and His Mosses."   LIT

1850s   Inexpensive photographic portraits become available to all social classes, produced by large-scale photographic operations like that built by French photographer André Adolphe Eugène Disderi. The portraits measure four by two and a half inches; the process for making them is patented in 1854.   PHOTO

1850s   In France the possibilities for artistic expression are explored by members of the Société Française de Photographie, such as photographers Charles Marville, Charles Negre, and Gustave Le Gray.   PHOTO

1850   German playwright Friedrich Hebbel completes *Herodes and Marianne*.   DRAMA

1850   British philosopher and critic George Henry Lewes begins writing theater criticism. His work will appear for four years in *The Leader*, a publication he founded, and later in other venues. He will become the companion of British novelist George Eliot.   DRAMA

1850   Shortly after his death this year, William Wordsworth's autobiographical blank-verse poem, *The Prelude*, begun in 1798 and worked on throughout his life, is published for the first time. The 14-book poem will later be found to exist in a two-part version (1799) and a 13-book version (1805).   LIT

1850   British poet Alfred Tennyson publishes *In Memoriam*, an elegy on the death of his friend Arthur Hallam, and succeeds William Wordsworth as Poet Laureate.   LIT

1850   British poet Elizabeth Barrett Browning publishes *Sonnets from the Portuguese*, love
            poems written to Robert Browning before their secret marriage in 1846. It
            includes Sonnet 43, which begins, "How do I love thee? Let me count the ways."
                                                                                          LIT

1850   British painter Dante Gabriel Rossetti's best-known poem, "The Blessed Damozel,"
            is published.   LIT

1850   American essayist and poet Ralph Waldo Emerson publishes *Representative Men*,
            a book of essays.   LIT

1850   *Catiline*, a tragedy in verse by Norwegian playwright Henrik Ibsen, premieres.
                                                                                          LIT

1850   American writer Nathaniel Hawthorne publishes *The Scarlet Letter*, the story of
            Puritan sin and redemption as seen through the illicit love affair between
            Hester Prynne and the Reverend Dimmesdale, and the jealous actions of Roger
            Chillingsworth. It will become his best-known work.   LIT

1850   American composer Stephen Foster's "De Camptown Races (Gwine to Run All
            Night)" becomes popular in the United States.   MUSIC

1850   The Swedish soprano Jenny Lind begins a highly successful two-year tour of
            America, under the direction of American entrepreneur Phineas T. Barnum.   MUSIC

1850   The opera *Lohengrin*, by German composer Richard Wagner, is premiered in
            Weimar, Germany, with Franz Liszt conducting.   MUSIC

1850   German composer Robert Schumann completes his Symphony no. 3 (*Rhenish*).
                                                                                        MUSIC

1850   At the Salon, French painter Gustave Courbet exhibits *The Stonebreakers*, *The
            Burial at Ornans*, and *The Peasants at Flagey*, three works that establish him as
            the leader of the realist school of painting. *The Stonebreakers* will be lost in the
            American and British firebombing of Dresden in February 1945 during World
            War II.   PAINT

1850   American painter George Caleb Bingham completes *Raftsmen Playing Cards*.   PAINT

1850   English Pre-Raphaelite painter Sir John Everett Millais completes *Christ in the
            Carpenter's Shop*.   PAINT

1850   French realist painter Jean-François Millet completes *The Gleaners* and *The
            Sower*.   PAINT

1850	Pioneering American photographer Mathew Brady publishes a collection, *Gallery of Illustrious Americans*, to wide notice. PHOTO
1851	The Crystal Palace, an 18-acre iron, glass, and wood building that will affect skyscraper design, is designed by British architect Sir Joseph Paxton. ARCH
1851	British engineer William Cubitt builds King's Cross Station, in London. ARCH
1851	American designer Thomas Walter is named the architect of the U.S. Capitol. He is responsible for building the dome of the U.S. House of Representatives building and wings in the U.S. Senate building. ARCH
1851	Danish choreographer and dancer Auguste Bournonville presents the ballet *Kermesse in Bruges*, which, like his earlier ballets, combines romanticism with a feeling for everyday life. DANCE
1851	Austrian ballerina Fanny Elssler, definitive ballerina of the romantic era, retires from the stage after performing worldwide for more than 25 years. DANCE
1851	The cartoons of John Tenniel appear in the British periodical *Punch*. GRAPH
1851	The *New York Times* is first published, under the editorship of American newspaperman Henry Raymond. LIT
1851	American writer Nathaniel Hawthorne publishes *The House of Seven Gables*. LIT
1851–1853	British art critic John Ruskin writes *The Stones of Venice*. LIT
1851	German poet and critic Heinrich Heine publishes *Romanzero*. LIT
1851	American novelist Herman Melville publishes his tragic tale of whaling, obsession, and redemption, *Moby-Dick; or, The Whale*. The daring novel earns little in royalties and elicits only limited critical appreciation. LIT
1851	The opera *Rigoletto*, by Italian composer Giuseppi Verdi, premieres in Venice. Together with the operas *Il Trovatore* (1853) and *La Traviata* (1853), it represents a high point in Italian opera. MUSIC
1851	The opera *Sappho*, by French composer Charles Gounod, is premiered in Paris. MUSIC
1851	German composer Robert Schumann completes the rewriting of his 1849 *Manfred* Overture. MUSIC
1851	German-born painter Emanuel Leutze, who spent many years in the United States, paints *Washington Crossing the Delaware*. PAINT

1851   American painter George Caleb Bingham completes *The Trappers' Return*. PAINT

1851   French painter Jean-Baptiste-Camille Corot completes *La Danse des Nymphes* (*The Dance of the Nymphs*). PAINT

1851   The wet collodion process for developing photographs, which creates a negative image with the fine detail of a daguerreotype, is developed by British photographer Frederick Scott Archer. PHOTO

1851   High-speed flash is used to capture movement in photographs. PHOTO

1852   American mechanic Elisha Graves Otis patents the safety elevator. Operating by a system of rope, grips, and ratchets, the cagelike device will permit the development of skyscrapers. ARCH

1852   Paddington Station in London is designed by Brunel and Wyatt. ARCH

1852   The *Hungarian Dances*, a collection of 21 dances for piano by German composer Johannes Brahms, is published in four volumes. DANCE

1852   *Masks and Faces*, by British playwrights Charles Read and Tom Taylor, premieres at the Haymarket Theatre in London. DRAMA

1852   *La Dame aux camélias*, by French playwright Alexandre Dumas fils, premieres at the Théâtre du Vaudeville in Paris. DRAMA

1852   The American comic periodical *Diogenes, Hys Lantern* publishes the first cartoon rendition of Uncle Sam, a character representing the United States. GRAPH

1852   Five of British novelist Charles Dickens's long stories with a Christmas theme are collected in *Christmas Books*, containing *A Christmas Carol*, "The Chimes," "The Cricket on the Hearth," "The Battle of Life," and "The Haunted Man." *See also* 1844, LIT. LIT

1852   British novelist William Makepeace Thackeray publishes his most elaborately planned novel, *The History of Henry Esmond*. LIT

1852   British critic and poet Matthew Arnold publishes *Empedocles and Other Poems*. LIT

1852   American novelist Harriet Beecher Stowe publishes the antislavery novel *Uncle Tom's Cabin*, which becomes one of the best-selling books of the century. Traveling drama troupes that perform parts of the book will become popular in parts of the United States. LIT

1852	British doctor and scholar Peter Mark Roget publishes the *Thesaurus of English Words and Phrases*. LIT
1852–1853	British novelist Charles Dickens publishes his ninth novel, *Bleak House*, the story of the interminable lawsuit of Jarndyce and Jarndyce. LIT
1852	French writer Prosper Mérimée publishes *Carmen*. LIT
1852	American writer Nathaniel Hawthorne publishes *The Blithedale Romance*, based on his 1841 experience living in the utopian community Brook Farm. LIT
1852	Russian writer Ivan Turgenev publishes the story collection *Sportsman's Sketches*, which establishes him as an important writer. LIT
1852	The opera *Dmitry Donskoy*, with music by Russian court musician Anton Grigoryevich Rubinstein, premieres in St. Petersburg, Russia. MUSIC
1852	British painter Ford Madox Brown paints *The Last of England*, an example of English realism. PAINT
1852	French painter Gustave Courbet completes *Les Demoiselles de Village*. PAINT
1852	British painter Holman Hunt completes *The Light of the World*. PAINT
1853	British designer P. C. Albert oversees the rebuilding of Balmoral Castle, in Scotland. ARCH
1853	French designer Georges Haussmann oversees the rebuilding of the Paris boulevards and Bois de Boulogne. ARCH
1853	The comedy *Die Journalisten*, by German playwright Gustav Freytag, is premiered in Breslau, Germany. DRAMA
1853–1855	British novelist William Makepeace Thackeray publishes the panoramic social novel *The Newcomes*, subtitled *Memoirs of a Most Respectable Family*. LIT
1853	British critic and poet Matthew Arnold publishes *The Scholar-Gipsy*, an elegy based on a legend about an Oxford student who becomes part of a group of gypsies. LIT
1853	American writer Nathaniel Hawthorne publishes *Tanglewood Tales*. LIT
1853	American novelist Herman Melville publishes "Bartleby the Scrivener," a short story about a clerk who "would prefer not to." The story will later appear in

the collection *Piazza Tales* (1856) along with other well-known works including "Benito Cereno."   LIT

1853   British novelist Elizabeth Gaskell publishes *Cranford*. The domestic novel was first serialized in the magazine *Household Words* from 1851 to 1853.   LIT

1853   British novelist Charlotte Brontë publishes *Villette*.   LIT

1853   German-born Henry Steinway (born Heinrich Steinweg) begins to manufacture pianos with his three sons in New York. Over the years, the Steinway name will become known for high-quality piano manufacture; the firm will continue to retain facilities in New York.   MUSIC

1853   Italian composer Giuseppe Verdi completes the opera *La Traviata*. It and another of his operas, *Il Trovatore*, premiere this year.   MUSIC

1853   "My Old Kentucky Home, Good Night," which will become one of Stephen Foster's most beloved compositions, debuts in the United States in June. It is one of his several "plantation melodies."   MUSIC

1853   German composer Richard Wagner begins more than two decades of work on the four operas that comprise *Der Ring des Nibelungen* (*The Ring of the Nibelung*). The four works, with their dates of completion, consist of *Das Rheinold* (1854), *Die Walküre* (1856), *Siegfried* (1871), and *Götterdammerüng* (1874). *See also* 1876, MUSIC.   MUSIC

1853–1861   In the last decade of his life, French painter Eugène Delacroix (*d.* 1863) paints *Jacob and the Angel* and *Heliodorus Expelled from the Temple*.   PAINT

1853   French painter Rosa Bonheur completes *The Horse Fair*.   PAINT

1853–1854   London's Photographic Society and France's Société Française de Photographie are founded to promote the new scientific art internationally.   PHOTO

1854   *Bednost ne porok* (*Poverty Is No Crime*) by Russian playwright Aleksandr Nikolayevich Ostrovsky, premieres in Moscow.   DRAMA

1854   British novelist Charles Dickens publishes his tenth novel, *Hard Times*.   LIT

1854–1855   British novelist Elizabeth Gaskell publishes *North and South*, which centers on labor turmoil in the industrial north of England.   LIT

1854   American poet John Greenleaf Whittier publishes "Maud Muller," a narrative poem of unrequited love between a maid and a judge that ends with the rueful observation, "For all of the sad words of tongue or pen / The saddest of these: 'It might have been.'"   LIT

1854   British poet Alfred Tennyson publishes *Charge of the Light Brigade*, honoring Lord Cardigan and the Crimean War Battle of Balaclava.   LIT

1854   British novelist Charlotte Mary Yonge publishes *The Heir of Redclyffe*. It will establish her as a novelist of Victorian middle-class life.   LIT

1854   The antiliquor novel *Ten Nights in a Barroom and What I Saw There*, by American novelist Timothy Shay Arthur, is published, and serves as the source for a long-lived play adaptation by William Pratt (1858).   LIT

1854   The Astor Library, a precursor to the New York Public Library system, begins operation. At its opening, the library has 80,000 volumes.   LIT

1854   American writer Henry David Thoreau publishes the work *Walden*, a chronicle of his attempt to "live deliberately," based on his months at Walden Pond in Concord, Massachusetts. It contains his observation that "the mass of men lead lives of quiet desperation."   LIT

1854   The Christmas Oratorio, *The Infant Christ*, by French composer Hector Berlioz, is premiered in Paris. His 1849 work, *Te Deum*, will be premiered in Paris the next year.   MUSIC

1854   American songwriter Stephen Foster's "Jeanie with the Light Brown Hair" debuts.   MUSIC

1854–1857   Hungarian pianist and composer Franz Liszt completes the tone poem *Préludes* and the composition *A Faust Symphony*.   MUSIC

1854   British painter Dante Gabriel Rossetti completes *Found*.   PAINT

1854   French romantic painter Eugène Delacroix produces *Christ on the Sea of Galilee*.   PAINT

1854   American painter James Abbott McNeill Whistler travels to Paris to study painting for four years. He will remain in Europe for the rest of his life.   PAINT

1854   French painter Gustave Courbet paints *The Winnowers* and *Bonjour, Monsieur Courbet*.   PAINT

1854   In Mali, Africa, Islamic conqueror el-Hajj Umar encounters resistance from a people he calls the Bambara, meaning "infidel." Their distinctive masks and carvings embody their religious beliefs, including acknowledgment of a creator-god and veneration of the antelope for teaching people to grow crops.   SCULP

1855   *Le Demi-Monde* by French playwright Alexandre Dumas fils, is staged.   DRAMA

1855   British poet Robert Browning publishes the poem *Childe Roland to the Dark Tower Came*. Its title comes from a piece of a song in English dramatist William Shakespeare's *King Lear*, Act 3, Scene 4.   LIT

1855   In the same year, the *Daily News* is founded in New York, the *Daily Telegraph* begins publication in Britain, and *Leslie's Illustrated Newspaper*, founded by American publisher Frank Leslie, is started. *Leslie's* will be known for its liberal use of illustrations and its titillating stories, and within two decades the *Daily Telegraph* will become the world's best-selling newspaper.   LIT

1855   British poet Robert Browning publishes the collection *Men and Women*, which contains, among other poems, "Fra Lippo Lippi" and "Andrea del Sarto."   LIT

1855   British critic and poet Matthew Arnold publishes the elegy "Stanzas from the Grande Chartreuse."   LIT

1855   American poet John Greenleaf Whittier publishes "The Barefoot Boy," a poem about growing up in the countryside.   LIT

1855   American poet Henry Wadsworth Longfellow publishes *Hiawatha*, about the life and heroic works of the title character, a member of the Ojibway tribe.   LIT

1855–1857   British novelist Charles Dickens publishes his 11th novel, *Little Dorrit*, about the effects of debtor's prison on the Dorrit family, particularly on the eponymous Amy Dorrit.   LIT

1855   *The Age of Fable* is published by American scholar Thomas Bulfinch. It provides an overview of the mythology of several countries and regions, and will remain a standard in the field.   LIT

1855   American poet Walt Whitman publishes in limited edition his collection of poems, *Leaves of Grass*, which includes those that will become known as "Song of Myself" and "I Sing the Body Electric."   LIT

1855   *Rip Van Winkle*, by George Frederick Bristow, the first American grand opera on an American subject, premieres in New York City.   MUSIC

1855   "Listen to the Mockingbird" by American composer Richard Millburn and lyricist Alice Hawthorne (Septimus Winner), becomes popular.   MUSIC

1855   Russian composer Mikhail Glinka completes *Festival Polonaise*.   MUSIC

1855   The opera *Les Vêpres Sicilennes*, by Italian composer Giuseppe Verdi, premieres
            in Paris.   MUSIC

1855·   Trio in B Major by German composer Johannes Brahms premieres in New
            York.   MUSIC

1855   French painter Gustave Courbet organizes the *Pavillion du Réalisme* for the Paris
            World Fair. Among the realist works exhibited are his *The Painter's Studio*.   PAINT

1855   American painter George Caleb Bingham completes *Verdict of the People*.   PAINT

1855   The Crimean War is captured in 360 photographs by British photographer
            Roger Fenton, who uses a wet collodion process to develop his work. A few of
            his photographs depict combat, representing one of the earliest instances of
            battlefield photography.   PHOTO

1856   Mauve, the first chemical dye, is discovered by British chemist William Henry
            Perkin.   DECO

1856   British actress Ellen Terry, nine years old, makes her stage debut as Mamillius
            in English dramatist William Shakespeare's *The Winter's Tale*. Over the next 50
            years, she will garner praise playing most of Shakespeare's major female roles
            and a variety of other parts. She will carry on a long correspondence with Irish-
            born British dramatist George Bernard Shaw and, late in life, deliver highly
            regarded lectures on Shakespeare.   DRAMA

1856   British poet Elizabeth Barrett Browning publishes *Aurora Leigh*.   LIT

1856   French novelist Gustave Flaubert publishes the novel *Madame Bovary*, the story
            of the provincial Emma Bovary, whose dissatisfaction with her bourgeois life
            leads her to commit adultery and rack up debts; these acts fuel her desperation
            and she ultimately commits suicide. In rendering the life of an ordinary
            woman with unprecedented detail, Flaubert achieves a benchmark in the his-
            tory of the novel as a literary genre.   LIT

1856   The National Portrait Gallery, the national collection of portraits of famous
            Britons, is founded in London.   PAINT

1857–1887   Urban park planner Frederick Law Olmsted designs Central Park in New York
            City, one of the earliest attempts to design a natural-looking public park in the
            United States.   ARCH

1857   American lithographers Nathaniel Currier and James M. Ives enter into part-
            nership in New York and begin a prolific career as the depictors of popular
            scenes of everyday urban and rural American life. Their business will run until
            1907.   **GRAPH**

1857   British novelist Anthony Trollope publishes *Barchester Towers*, one of his six
            novels set in the fictional county of Barsetshire.   **LIT**

1857   Norwegian novelist, poet, and playwright Bjørnstjerne Bjørnson publishes the
            peasant novel *Synnøve Solbakken* (*Trust and Trial*). Among his later works will
            be the realist plays *Redaktøren* (*The Editor*, 1874) and *Over Aevne I* (*Beyond Our
            Power*, 1883, 1895).   **LIT**

1857   French poet Charles Baudelaire publishes the collection *Les Fleurs du mal* (*The
            Flowers of Evil*). It will become one of the best-known works of the symbolist
            poets.   **LIT**

1857   Pre-Raphaelite British artists William Morris, Dante Gabriel Rossetti, and
            Edward Burne-Jones work together on frescoes at the Oxford Union Society.   **PAINT**

1857   In Britain photographer Oscar Rejlander enjoys huge success with the allegor-
            ical multiphoto composition *The Two Paths of Life*. Influenced by *The Rake's
            Progress* by 18th-century English painter and engraver William Hogarth, it
            illustrates the good and ill paths a young man may choose.   **PHOTO**

1858   British artist William Morris publishes the poetry collection *The Defence of
            Guenevere and Other Poems*.   **LIT**

1858   Using the name Artemus Ward, American journalist Charles Farrar Browne
            publishes the first of his comic letters in the Cleveland *Plain Dealer*. The letters
            of the fictitious uneducated businessman spark a career in writing and lectur-
            ing that will continue until Browne's death in 1867.   **LIT**

1858   American jurist Oliver Wendell Holmes publishes *The Autocrat of the Breakfast
            Table*, a book collecting his *Atlantic Monthly* pieces on American society and
            topics of the day. Poems are also included. Several "Breakfast Table" sequels
            will follow until 1890.   **LIT**

1858   American poet Henry Wadsworth Longfellow publishes the poem "The Courtship
            of Miles Standish," which sells widely.   **LIT**

1858   The New York Symphony Orchestra gives its first public concert.   **MUSIC**

1858   Photographer Henry Peach Robinson establishes himself as a chronicler of the
            Victorian scene with his multiple-negative composition of a life near its end,
            Fading Away.   PHOTO

1859   British novelist Charles Dickens publishes his 12th novel, *A Tale of Two Cities*.
            His second and last historical novel, it is set during the French Revolution and
            introduces the self-sacrificing Sydney Carton.   LIT

1859   British poet Alfred Tennyson publishes the first four books of *Idylls of the King*.   LIT

1859   British novelist and poet George Meredith publishes his first novel, *The Ordeal
            of Richard Feverel*.   LIT

1859   British poet and translator Edward FitzGerald publishes his free translation of *The
            Rubáiyát of Omar Khayyám*, based on the work of the 12th-century Persian poet.
                                                                                       LIT

1859   French poet Frédéric Mistral publishes the work *Mirèio*. Among his later works
            will be *Lou Pouème Jóu Rose*. He will share the 1904 Nobel Prize for literature
            with Spanish dramatist José Echegaray.   LIT

1859   French photographer Gaspard-Félix Tournachon (also known as Nadar) creates
            the romantic and pleasing *Sarah Bernhardt*, a portrait of the French actress.
                                                                                       PHOTO

1859   American sculptor Erastus Dow Palmer works directly from live models to cre-
            ate *White Captive*, his first attempt at an undraped neoclassical nude.   SCULP

1860s   Melodrama becomes popular on the American stage—and, with it, a melodra-
            matic style of acting. Plays featuring adventure and romance, a number of them
            imports from France, are staged with histrionic performers. Melodrama will
            remain popular throughout the rest of the century, though, over time, it will be
            increasingly replaced by theater presenting serious subjects in realistic ways.   DRAMA

1860s   American photographer Alexander Gardner chronicles the U.S. Civil War in
            removed, unheroic compositions that become widely seen in mass periodicals
            of the day. The former assistant to American photographer Mathew Brady
            becomes important to the development of photojournalism.   PHOTO

1860s   Photographer Julia Margaret Cameron becomes known for her lyrical portraits
            of important men and women of the Victorian era.   PHOTO

1860s   In Europe stock photographs of city scenes, landscapes, and artworks become
            available through large stock houses. Among the more well known of such

firms are those run in England by Francis Firth and in Italy by the Alinari brothers.   PHOTO

1860s   American photographer William Henry Jackson becomes known for his photographs of Native Americans and the West. By the end of the next decade, after working with the Haden Geological Survey, he will begin his own photographic company.   PHOTO

1860   The golden era of wood carving begins in the Pacific Northwest. Artists will produce numerous examples of poles, masks, helmets, bowls, and rattles.   DECO

1860   British novelist Charles Dickens publishes the first edition of *The Uncommercial Traveller*, a collection of essays and sketches. Subsequent editions will appear in 1865 and posthumously in 1875.   LIT

1860–1861 British novelist Charles Dickens publishes his 13th novel, *Great Expectations*, which introduces the characters of Pip and Miss Havisham.   LIT

1860   British art critic John Ruskin publishes *Unto This Last*, a collection of essays on political economy that emphasizes the responsibilities of employers toward employees.   LIT

1860   American critic William Dean Howells writes one of his first books, *Lives and Speeches of Abraham Lincoln and Hannibal Hamlin*. The book about the presidential campaign yields Howells a political appointment as American consul to Venice.   LIT

1860   American writer Nathaniel Hawthorne publishes the novel *The Marble Faun*.   LIT

1860   Nationalism in music begins to gain strength as a reaction against the dominance of German music. The movement places strong emphasis on national elements and resources of music and is most popular in such "peripheral" European nations as Bohemia, Norway, Russia, Spain, and England.   MUSIC

1860   American sculptor John Quincy Adams Ward models his bronze *Indian Hunter* from sketches he made studying Native Americans in the Dakotas. He will enlarge the statue for another version to be placed in New York City's Central Park.   SCULP

1861   British artist William Morris cofounds a firm for the hand-manufacture of home decor, Morris, Marshall, Faulkner and Co. (reconstituted in 1875 as Morris and Co.). The firm sparks a revival in decorative arts, influenced by Morris's designs for wallpaper, embroideries, chintzes, tapestries, and carpets. The firm also becomes known for its stained glass, painted tiles, furniture, and stenciled mural decoration.   DECO

1861   British caricaturist Charles Samuel Keene begins a long association with the
           magazine *Punch*.   GRAPH

c. 1861   American poet Emily Dickinson writes poem 288, which begins, "I'm
           Nobody! Who are you? / Are you—Nobody—Too?" and 465, which begins, "I
           heard a Fly buzz—when I died—." They will become two of her best-known
           works.   LIT

1861–1862   British novelist William Makepeace Thackeray publishes his last completed
           novel, *The Adventures of Philip*.   LIT

1861–1865   American poet Walt Whitman serves as a volunteer nurse during the Civil War
           and visits many of the Army camp hospitals. The experience informs his 1865
           collection of poems, *Drum-Taps*.   LIT

1861   Employing a team of several photographers, American photographer Mathew
           Brady begins systematic photographic coverage of the American Civil War.
                                                                              PHOTO

1862   British poet Christina Rossetti publishes *Goblin Market and Other Poems*.   LIT

1862   British novelist and poet George Meredith publishes his most important col-
           lection of poetry, *Modern Love*.   LIT

1862   American poet Emily Dickinson makes her first batch of poems public by
           sending them to Massachusetts clergyman Thomas Wentworth Higginson. LIT

1862   French writer Victor Hugo publishes the novel *Les Misérables*, about the fate of
           peasant Jean Valjean after he steals a loaf of bread. The book will be the basis
           of a long-running Broadway musical that will premiere in 1987.   LIT

1862   A chronological catalogue of Austrian composer Wolfgang Amadeus Mozart's
           works, prepared by German music-lover Ludwig Köchel, is published. The
           Köchel or "K" numbers will be universally used to identify Mozart's com-
           positions.   MUSIC

1862   French graphic artist Honoré Daumier paints *The Third Class Carriage*.   PAINT

1863   On November 19, at the dedication of a national cemetery on the battlefield
           of Gettysburg, Pennsylvania, where the Union and Confederate armies suf-
           fered a combined total of about 48,000 casualties this summer, American pres-
           ident Abraham Lincoln delivers his one-paragraph Gettysburg Address, which
           begins, "Four score and seven years ago our fathers brought forth on this con-
           tinent a new nation, conceived in Liberty, and dedicated to the proposition
           that all men are created equal."   LIT

1863   At the Salon des Refusés, an exhibition held in Paris to display creations reject-
            ed by the official Salon, artists represented include Édouard Manet, Paul
            Cézanne, Camille Pissarro, and James Whistler. Despite ridicule from many
            quarters, the event undermines the power of the official Salon, encouraging
            other independent exhibitions.   PAINT

1863   French painter Jean-Auguste-Dominique Ingres paints the *Turkish Bath.*   PAINT

1863   French painter Édouard Manet paints *Luncheon on the Grass,* which creates a
            scandal for its depiction of a female nude picnicking with two clothed men.
            Rejected by the official Salon, it is presented at the Salon des Refusés. Manet's
            Olympia, depicting a nude prostitute in a pose drawn from Titian's *Venus of
            Urbino,* also creates controversy, in part because her straightforward gaze, nei-
            ther ashamed nor flirtatious, is considered disarming in its directness.   PAINT

1864   American actors Edwin Thomas Booth, John Wilkes Booth, and Junius Brutus
            Booth Jr., three brothers, appear together for the only time in *Julius Caesar.* Edwin
            Thomas Booth, particularly good in tragic roles, will be considered one of the
            greatest 19th-century American actors. John Wilkes Booth, a less distinguished
            but still good performer, will go down in history as the assassin of President
            Abraham Lincoln (*see* 1865, DRAMA). Junius Brutus Booth Jr. will do moderately
            well as an actor and a theater manager. Their father, Junius Brutus Booth Sr., was
            a popular actor in England and America earlier in the century.   DRAMA

1864–1865   British novelist Charles Dickens publishes *Our Mutual Friend,* his 14th novel
            and the last he will complete.   LIT

1864   British poet Alfred Tennyson publishes a volume of poems that includes
            "Enoch Arden" and "Tithonus."   LIT

1864   British poet Robert Browning publishes *Dramatic Personae,* which includes the
            poems "Caliban Upon Setebos" and "Abt Vogler."   LIT

1864   British theologian John Henry Newman publishes *Apologia pro Vita Sua*
            (revised 1865), a defense of his conversion from Anglicanism to Roman
            Catholicism. Newman will be made a cardinal in 1879. He will also publish
            The Grammar of Assent, an argument for religious belief, in 1870.   LIT

1864–1869   Russian novelist Leo Tolstoy composes *War and Peace,* his epic novel of Russia
            before (from 1805), during, and after (to 1820) the 1812 invasion of the coun-
            try by Napoleon. Featuring more than 500 characters in a plot that alternates
            between chapters exploring personal lives and those describing battles in great
            detail, *War and Peace* demonstrates Tolstoy's philosophy of history, which
            takes as its premise the idea that events are beyond the control of not only
            individuals but humanity itself.   LIT

1864   French writer Jules Verne publishes the novel *Journey to the Center of the Earth.* This and subsequent works mark him as one of the founders of science fiction.   LIT

1864   Russian novelist Fyodor Dostoyevsky writes the long story "Notes from Underground," which appears in the journal *Epoch,* published by his brother and edited by himself. A highly philosophical and psychological work, "Notes from Underground" illustrates the author's conviction that human nature is irrational.   LIT

c. 1865   Opera singer Ludwig Leichner invents grease paint. It will come into general use among actors over the next 25 years, after which actors will also use liquid and "pancake" makeup.   DRAMA

1865   On April 14 American actor John Wilkes Booth assassinates President Abraham Lincoln during a performance of the British play *Our American Cousin* at Ford's Theatre in Washington, D.C. *See also* 1864, DRAMA.   DRAMA

1865   British critic and poet Matthew Arnold publishes *Essays in Criticism*, First Series, with its famous introduction, "The Function of Criticism at the Present Time." The Second Series will be published posthumously in 1888.   LIT

1865   British mathematician and writer Charles Dodgson, known as Lewis Carroll, publishes *Alice's Adventures in Wonderland*, featuring a White Rabbit who fears he is late, a disappearing Cheshire Cat, a narcoleptic Dormouse, and a Mad Hatter, among other memorable characters. (The eponymous Alice is inspired by the real-life little girl Alice Liddell, for whom he writes the story.) Like its sequel, *Through the Looking-Glass*, it features illustrations by Sir John Tenniel. Popular among children and adults alike, both stories reflect the author's skillful manipulation of symbolism and inverted logic.   LIT

1865   American poet Walt Whitman publishes his elegy to the late president Abraham Lincoln, "When Lilacs Last in the Dooryard Bloom'd." It will come to be considered the finest poem written about the assassinated president.   LIT

1865   American writer Samuel Langhorne Clemens, known as Mark Twain, publishes the yarn "The Notorious Jumping Frog of Calaveras County," the title character of which he heard about in his travels to mining camps in the western United States. The tall tale is widely reprinted and gains Twain much notice.   LIT

1865   French art theorist Hippolyte Taine publishes *Philosophie de l'art*, in which he articulates a positivist view of aesthetics.   MISC

1865   German composer Richard Wagner's opera *Tristan and Isolde* (completed in 1859) premieres in Munich. Its intensely dramatic style increases the expressive use of melody and chord.   MUSIC

1866   *Brand*, a verse play by Norwegian playwright Henrik Ibsen, is produced. *Peer Gynt*, also a verse play, will be produced in 1867. The two will be early critical and commercial successes for Ibsen. He will not write any subsequent verse plays.   DRAMA

1866   British critic and poet Matthew Arnold publishes the poem "Thyrsis," commemorating his friend and fellow poet Arthur Hugh Clough, who died in 1861.   LIT

1866   British poet Algernon Charles Swinburne publishes *Poems and Ballads*, which includes "Garden of Proserpine" and "Hymn to Proserpine."   LIT

1866   French novelist Pierre Loti (pen name of Louis-Marie-Julien Viaud) publishes the novel *Pêcheur d'Islande* (*An Iceland Fisherman*). Among his later novels will be *Mon Frère Yves* (1883) and *Matelot* (1893).   LIT

1866   French poet Paul Verlaine publishes the volume *Poèmes saturniens*. Among his later volumes will be *Fêtes galantes* (1869) and *Sagesse* (1881).   LIT

1866   French writer Alphonse Daudet publishes the story collection *Lettres de mon moulin* (*Letters from My Window*). Among his later works will be the novels *Le Nabab* (1877) and *Numa Roumestan* (1881).   LIT

1866   Russian novelist Fyodor Dostoyevsky publishes *Crime and Punishment*, a novel of guilt and redemption that introduces the scholar and axe-murderer Raskolnikov.
                                                                                            LIT

1867   British critic and poet Matthew Arnold publishes the poem "Dover Beach," which uses the metaphor of the ebbing of the sea as a metaphor for the waning power of faith in the modern world.   LIT

1867   American writer and minister Horatio Alger Jr. publishes the *Ragged Dick Series* of books for boys.   LIT

1867–1868   French impressionist painter Frédéric Bazille paints *Family Reunion*.   PAINT

1868   American burlesque, a form of theatrical variety show including dancing by chorus girls, comes into being. Striptease acts will be added around 1920.   DRAMA

1868–1869   British poet Robert Browning publishes the poem *The Ring and the Book*.   LIT

1868–1870   British artist William Morris publishes the epic poem *The Earthly Paradise*. LIT

1868   In *Overland Monthly* magazine, American humorist writer Bret Harte publishes the short story "The Luck of Roaring Camp," about the California Gold Rush.
                                                                                            LIT

1868	Russian novelist Fyodor Dostoyevsky publishes the novel *The Idiot*, which he will consider his favorite work. LIT
1868	British novelist Wilkie Collins, whom some will consider to have been the first English author of detective fiction, writes the mystery novel *The Moonstone*. LIT
1868	American novelist Louisa May Alcott publishes *Little Women, or Meg, Jo, Beth, and Amy*, which becomes a best-seller on the strength of its popularity with young people. A sequel, *Little Men*, will follow in 1871. LIT
1868	Japanese painter Yokoyama Taikan is born. As an important artist of the conservative tradition, he will attempt to reestablish Japanese-style painting, or Nihon-ga. PAINT
1869	British critic and poet Matthew Arnold publishes *Culture and Anarchy*, a collection of essays that outlines his belief in the power of art, literature, and humanistic studies to improve individuals and society. The essays include "Sweetness and Light," "Barbarians, Philistines, Populace," and "Hebraism and Hellenism." LIT
1869	British novelist Anthony Trollope publishes *Phineas Finn*, one of his six Palliser novels, which will be noted for their depiction of Victorian politics. LIT
1869	American writer Mark Twain publishes *The Innocents Abroad*, a collection of accounts of his journey overseas in 1867. LIT
1869	French novelist Gustave Flaubert publishes the novel *L'Education sentimentale*, about life during the reign of Louis-Philippe. During the previous decade he also published the novel *Salammbô*. LIT
1869	Russian writer Ivan Turgenev publishes the novel *Fathers and Sons*, which will be considered one of his finest works. Earlier in the decade he published the novel *A Nest of Gentlefolk* (1862). LIT
1869	French sculptor Jean-Baptiste Carpeaux carves *The Dance*, derived from rococo compositions, for the façade of the Paris Opera. SCULP
1870s	In England the aesthetic movement begins to gain strength, advocating the doctrine of "art for art's sake." Spokespeople for aestheticism include British essayist and critic Walter Pater and Irish poet and dramatist Oscar Wilde. MISC
1870	British novelist Charles Dickens's *The Mystery of Edwin Drood* is published, his 15th and final novel, left incomplete at his death. LIT

1870	French writer Jules Verne publishes the science-fiction adventure novel *Twenty Thousand Leagues Under the Sea*. LIT
c. 1870	American artist Winslow Homer paints *The Morning Bell*. PAINT
1870	The Metropolitan Museum of Art, which will come to house one of the finest art collections in the world, is founded in New York City. It will move to its new site in Central Park in 1880. PAINT
1871	British novelist Thomas Hardy, now an architect, publishes his first novel, *Desperate Remedies*. LIT
1871	American poet Walt Whitman writes his critical prose work about American ideals, *Democratic Vistas*. Affected by the excesses of the Gilded Age, he attacks corruption in business and politics and challenges Americans to reestablish their democratic ideals. LIT
1871	French symbolist poet Arthur Rimbaud publishes the work *Le Bateau ivre* (*The Drunken Boat*). Among his later works will be the autobiographical *Une Saison en enfer* (*A Season in Hell*, 1873). LIT
1871–1893	French novelist Émile Zola publishes the multivolume series of novels *Les Rougon-Macquart*. The series includes the novels *Germinal*, *Nana*, and *L'Assommoir*. He will also become known for his open letter, "J'accuse," to the president of France concerning the Dreyfus affair. LIT
1871–1872	Russian novelist Fyodor Dostoyevsky completes the novel *The Possessed*. LIT
1871	Société Nationale de Musique is founded in Paris by composer Camille Saint-Saëns and Henri Bussine. The society encourages native composers by giving performances of their works, ushering in the French musical renaissance. MUSIC
1871	The Paris Commune, an insurrectionary government, appoints French painter Gustave Courbet as head of its arts commission. When the Commune falls later this year, Courbet is imprisoned and will later be forced to flee to Switzerland, where he will reside for the remainder of his life. PAINT
1871	American artist James Abbott McNeill Whistler paints the portrait that will become known as *Whistler's Mother*. PAINT
1872	Swedish playwright August Strindberg writes *Mäster Olof*, his first major play. It will be produced in 1881. DRAMA
1872	*A Month in the Country*, generally seen as the finest play by Russian writer Ivan Turgenev, is produced for the first time. It was written in 1850. DRAMA

1872	French actress Sarah Bernhardt wins acclaim playing Cordelia in *King Lear* and the Queen in Victor Hugo's *Ruy Blas*. She will soon give a superb performance in Racine's *Phèdre*, and many will regard her as the greatest actress of her day. DRAMA
1872	American novelist Ned Buntline (pen name of Edward Zane Carroll Judson) publishes *The Scouts of the Plains*, one of more than 400 dime novels he will be credited with writing. LIT
1872	British novelist Thomas Hardy publishes *Under the Greenwood Tree*. LIT
1872	British novelist Samuel Butler publishes the satirical dystopian novel *Erewhon*, which will be followed by *Erewhon Revisited* in 1901. LIT
1872	American writer Mark Twain publishes *Roughing It*, a highly popular account of his travels cross-country to the West. LIT
1873	British essayist and critic Walter Pater publishes *Studies in the History of the Renaissance*. LIT
1873	American writers Mark Twain and Charles Dudley Warner collaborate on the novel *The Gilded Age*. The novel captures the post–Civil War era and provides its moniker. LIT
1873	German novelist Paul Heyse publishes the novel *Kinder de Welt* (*Children of the World*). He will win the Nobel Prize for literature in 1910. LIT
1873–1876	Russian novelist Leo Tolstoy writes the tragic love story *Anna Karenina*. Among his later works are *The Death of Ivan Ilyich* (1886) and an essay on literary aesthetics, "What Is Art" (1897–1898). LIT
1873	French writer Jules Verne publishes the novel *Around the World in Eighty Days*, a romance about the winning of a bet by protagonist Phileas Fogg. It will be the basis of a film in 1956. LIT
1873	Russian composer Nikolay Rimsky-Korsakov's opera *Ivan the Terrible*, concerning the eponymous 16th-century tsar Ivan IV Vasilyevich, premieres in St. Petersburg. MUSIC
1873–1874	French painter Paul Cézanne paints *House of the Hanged Man*, characteristic of his impressionist period. PAINT
1873	American photographer Timothy O'Sullivan's photograph *Ancient Ruins in the Canyon de Chelle, N.M., in a Niche 50 Feet Above the Present* is an example of his pioneering landscape photography of the American West. Among other notable

landscape photographers of the era are Carleton Watkins and William Henry Jackson. **PHOTO**

1874   British novelist Thomas Hardy publishes *Far from the Madding Crowd*, his first major commercial success and the first of several novels to use the name "Wessex" for the fictional region of England based on rural Dorchester, where he spent much of his early life. **LIT**

1874   Spanish novelist Pedro Antonio de Alarcón publishes the humorous work *El sombrero de tres picos* (*The Three-Cornered Hat*). Among his later works will be the short novel *El capitán Veneno* (*Captain Venom*, 1881). **LIT**

1874   The bold and innovative Russian nationalist opera *Boris Godunov* by Russian composer Modest Mussorgsky premieres in St. Petersburg. Mussorgsky will be considered the greatest of "The Mighty Five," a group of Russian nationalist composers that also includes Mily Balakirev, Aleksandr Borodin, César Cui, and Nikolay Rimsky-Korsakov. **MUSIC**

1874   The operetta *Die Fledermaus* by Austrian composer Johann Strauss premieres. **MUSIC**

c. 1874   American artist James Abbott McNeill Whistler paints *Nocturne in Black and Gold: The Falling Rocket*. **PAINT**

1874   In France, the term "impressionist" is coined derisively for a group of artists independently exhibiting their work this year. Committed to recording fleeting observations of reality with vivid color to capture an immediate impression, the group includes, or soon comes to include, Claude Monet, Pierre-Auguste Renoir, Edgar Degas, Camille Pissarro, Paul Cézanne, Berthe Morisot, Mary Cassatt, Armand Guillaumin, Alfred Sisley, and Frédéric Bazille. Among the impressionist works first exhibited this year is *Impression—Sunrise* by Monet, the artist most dedicated to the movement. **PAINT**

1875   British poet Gerard Manley Hopkins writes the poem "The Wreck of the Deutschland," which, like the rest of his poems, will go unpublished during his lifetime. *See* 1918, LIT. **LIT**

1875   American poet Sidney Lanier establishes himself as a poet with the publication of "Corn" in *Lippincott's Magazine*. **LIT**

1875   French composer Georges Bizet's opera *Carmen* premieres in Paris. The violent love story is criticized as obscene and inappropriate for the stage, but will become one of the most popular operas ever written. **MUSIC**

1875   American realist painter Thomas Eakins completes *The Gross Clinic*, a quietly
            forceful portrayal of surgery. It and similar paintings, like the 1889 *The Agnew
            Clinic*, will generate conflict because of their honesty and lack of sentimentality.   PAINT

1875   French sculptor Frédéric Auguste Bartholdi completes his final model of *Liberty
            Enlightening the World* as a gift from the French people to the United States in
            memory of French assistance during the War of Independence. He will collab-
            orate in the execution of the project with French architect Gustave Eiffel to
            engineer an iron and steel framework to attach thin sheets of beaten copper.
            The Statue of Liberty will be inaugurated in the fall of 1886 in New York
            Harbor.   SCULP

1876   Russian composer Pyotr Ilich Tchaikovsky composes *Swan Lake*, one of the first
            ballets to make use of leitmotiv. It will become one of the most often pro-
            duced ballets in dance history.   DANCE

1876   American writer Mark Twain publishes what will become one of his best-
            known works, *The Adventures of Tom Sawyer*. The episodic tale of Tom, his

---

An Ugly Duckling Called *Swan Lake*

When Pyotr Ilich Tchaikovsky's ballet *Swan Lake* premiered in 1877 at the Moscow
Imperial Bolshoi Theatre it was far from the respected work it is today. The work that
the Russian composer hoped would broaden his range beyond symphonies was viewed
instead as a mediocre evening of dance. Although Tchaikovsky's music was touted by
critic Herman Laroche as the work of a master "at the height of his genius," the choreography and dancing were so uninspired that it led the critic to write, "I must say that
I had never seen a poorer presentation on the stage of the Bolshoi Theatre."

Not until a decade later did *Swan Lake* begin to resemble the ballet performed and
renowned today. Following an 1894 Tchaikovsky memorial in St. Petersburg that
included portions of *Swan Lake*, Russian choreographers Lev Ivanov and Marius Petipa
decided to restage the ballet. One of their changes was to elevate the quality of ballerina used for the ballet, hiring the respected Italian dancer Pierina Leganani for the part
of the Snow Queen. A more complex change came in the choreography itself. In two
of the ballet's acts the choreography was driven by the music rather than the strengths
of the lead ballerina, as was the common practice.

The new adaptation of *Swan Lake* premiered in January 1895 in St. Petersburg, to
great success. Over the years, this more organic approach to *Swan Lake* had profound
effects on the choreography of 20th-century ballet. Yet like the ugly duckling that
becomes a graceful swan, *Swan Lake* had to undergo an artistic transformation to establish it as a groundbreaking work of modern ballet.

friend Huck Finn, Becky Thatcher, and Aunt Polly will inspire three sequels, including *Huckleberry Finn* (1884).   LIT

1876   American novelist Henry James publishes the novel *Roderick Hudson.*   LIT

1876   *The Harvard Lampoon* magazine is founded by a group of Harvard students including Ralph Curtis and Samuel Sherwood.   LIT

1876   French symbolist poet Stéphane Mallarmé publishes the poem *L'Après-midi d'un faune* (*The Afternoon of a Faun*). The work will inspire French composer Claude Debussy to compose the musical work in its name (1894). Among Mallarmé's other works will be the poem "Le Cygne" ("The Swan," 1885).   LIT

1876   German archaeologist Heinrich Schliemann uncovers the Royal Shaft Graves at Mycenae. His discoveries will encourage the study of Bronze Age Greek art.   MISC

1876   The Bayreuth Festspeilhaus opens with the first complete performance of German composer Richard Wagner's *The Ring of the Nibelung,* a cycle of four operas. *See also* 1853, MUSIC.   MUSIC

1876   German composer Johannes Brahms completes his Symphony in C Minor.   MUSIC

1876   Norwegian composer Edvard Grieg completes his *Peer Gynt* suite of incidental music to the eponymous play by Henrik Ibsen (*see* 1866, DRAMA).   MUSIC

1876   French impressionist Pierre-Auguste Renoir paints *Le Moulin de la Galette.*   PAINT

1876   French painter Edgar Degas paints *The Glass of Absinthe* and *Prima Ballerina.*   PAINT

1877   Norwegian playwright Henrik Ibsen's *Pillars of Society,* a drama exploring hypocrisy, is produced.   DRAMA

1877   American novelist Henry James publishes the novel *The American.*   LIT

1877   French novelist Gustave Flaubert publishes the story collection *Trois Contes,* which includes the story "Un Coeur simple."   LIT

1877   German composer Johannes Brahms's Symphony in D Major premieres. MUSIC

1877   American inventor Thomas Alva Edison invents the phonograph.   MUSIC

1877   In a photo experiment, American photographer Eadweard Muybridge generates a series of 24 images of a horse in motion. The series of photos, taken as a horse travels along a track, becomes instrumental in the development of

motion pictures. His work is influenced by the motion studies of French physiologist Étienne-Jules Marey.   PHOTO

1878   British novelist Thomas Hardy publishes *The Return of the Native*, the story of
            the unfortunate marriage between idealistic schoolmaster Clym Yeobright and
            the passionate Eustacia Vye.   LIT

1878   American novelist Henry James publishes *Daisy Miller*, the short novel about a
            young American woman disrupting European precedent. An ongoing debate
            about the satirical nature of James's portrait of the character will ensue, gain-
            ing the work wide publicity.   LIT

1878   Danish writer Karl Gjellerup publishes the novel *En Idealist*. Among his later
            works will be *Germanernes laerling* (1882) and *Der Pilger Kamanoto* (1906). LIT

1878   Czech poet, novelist, and journalist Jan Neruda publishes the story collection
            Povídky malostranské (*Tales of the Little Quarter*) and the poetry collection *Pisně
            kosmické* (*Cosmic Songs*). His collection *Zpěvy pátční* (*Friday Songs*) will be pub-
            lished posthumously in 1896.   LIT

1878   German composer Johannes Brahms composes his Violin Concerto in D
            which takes its place alongside the works of German composers Ludwig van
            Beethoven and Felix Mendelssohn.   MUSIC

1878   French anthropologist and ethnographer Dr. Jules-Théodore-Ernest Hamy
            establishes the Musée de Trocadéro in Paris to house ritual objects and works
            of art brought in from the colonies of various scientific missions to America,
            Africa, and Oceania.   SCULP

1878   French sculptor Auguste Rodin, among the most important sculptors of the
            19th century, executes his first major work, *The Age of Bronze*, which is contro-
            versial for its naturalistic depiction of a nude warrior.   SCULP

1879   *A Doll's House*, a naturalistic drama by Norwegian playwright Henrik Ibsen, is
            produced. In the next century it will be championed by feminists as a tale of a
            quest for female independence.   DRAMA

1879   British novelist and poet George Meredith publishes *The Egoist*. LIT

1879–1882   American historian Henry Adams writes two biographies, *Life of Albert Gallatin*
            (1879) and *John Randolph* (1882).   LIT

1879–1880   Russian novelist Fyodor Dostoyevsky publishes the novel *The Brothers Karamazov*,
            the work of sin, religion, and psychology as seen through the lives of the four
            sons of Fyodor Pavlovich Karamazov.   LIT

1879–1882   French painter Paul Cézanne paints *Still Life with Apples*, one of his many still lifes.   PAINT

1880s   European visitors to what will become Zaire, Africa begin to note the region's artistic forms, including elaborate masks used in initiation rites and public entertainment. Made of wood or basketry, they vary in design from grotesque to playful to naturalistic. The groups making the masks include the BaPende, BaYaka, BaSuku, and BaJokwe.   DECO

1880s–1890s Artists such as Paul Gauguin, Edvard Munch, and Felix Vallotton produce original woodcut illustrations, reviving a technology little used for artistic purposes since it was superseded by line engraving in the 16th century. In the 20th

---

Critics vs. Artists

In the mid- to late 19th century, British art critic John Ruskin was the preeminent arbiter of artistic culture. His support of artistic movements, such as the Pre-Raphaelites, established forms of artistic expression in the public eye. Throughout his career, his critical stance was consistent. While he believed in beauty for its own sake, he was even more attached to the idea that art must be linked to public morality: It should be a "visible sign of national virtue," he said.

Following these principles, Ruskin, in 1877, dismissed American painter James McNeill Whistler's impressionistic *Nocturne in Black and Gold: The Falling Rocket*. Ruskin accused Whistler of "flinging a pot of paint in the public's face" and complained about the painting's 200-guinea cost. The contentious and wild Whistler, who was well established in the European artistic community, sued Ruskin for libel. What resulted was one of the art world's most celebrated trials.

The trial surrounding the 1,000-pound lawsuit was marked by two elements: the absence of Ruskin, due to mental breakdowns, and Whistler's spirited defense of his artworks, some of which had been exhibited to the audience upside down.

In the end, the court sided with Whistler, the man who believed that art "should be independent of all claptrap—should stand alone, and appeal to the artistic sense of eye or ear, without confounding [it] with emotions entirely foreign to it, as devotion, pity, love, patriotism, and the like." But the court awarded him only a farthing's damages and ordered him to pay half of the court costs.

Owing to the trial, Whistler, previously a respected, successful painter, faced a diminished reputation in the marketplace. He sold his house and was forced to declare bankruptcy in 1879. It would take several years and a different art form—etchings—before he would reestablish his place in the artistic community. Ruskin descended into the mental illness that first showed its signs during the trial. He spent the last years of his life in isolation and ceased writing.

century other artists, notably such German expressionists as Ernst Kirchner and Franz Marc, will also produce innovative woodcuts.   GRAPH

1880s   In France various post-impressionist styles arise that are informed by but in reaction against impressionism. The neo-impressionism of French painter Georges Seurat is one example; French painters Paul Cézanne and Paul Gauguin and Dutch painter Vincent van Gogh are also considered post-impressionist artists.   PAINT

1880s   French physiologist Étienne-Jules Marey experiments with the artistic and scientific boundaries of photography in works such as *Walking in Front of a Black Wall* (c. 1884).   PHOTO

1880   American writer Lewis Wallace publishes the novel *Ben Hur*.   LIT

1880   American historian Henry Adams's novel *Democracy*, about a U.S. senator who accepts a bribe of $100,000, captures the driving power of capitalistic pursuits during the Gilded Age.   LIT

1880   American writer Joel Chandler Harris publishes his first collection of Uncle Remus stories, *Uncle Remus: His Songs and Sayings*. Several sequels will follow, including *Uncle Remus and His Friends* (1892) and *Told by Uncle Remus* (1905).   LIT

1880   French sculptor Auguste Rodin is commissioned to make a bronze portal for the proposed Museum of Decorative Arts. His design, *The Gates of Hell*, will never be completed, though its nearly 200 figures, worked on over a 20-year period, will provide the basis for numerous independent sculptures, including *The Thinker* (1889).   SCULP

1881   American Louis Comfort Tiffany establishes an interior decorating firm in New York that becomes famous for its glass vases, lamps, stained glass, and mosaics. *See also* 1890s, DECO.   DECO

1881   British actress Lillie Langtry makes her debut in Irish-born British playwright Oliver Goldsmith's *She Stoops to Conquer*. Called "the Jersey Lily," she will be better known for her great beauty than for her acting ability.   DRAMA

1881   Vaudeville, an American form of theatrical entertainment combining song, dance, magic acts, and comedy sketches, moves from its origins in barrooms to its status as a major attraction when Tony Pastor presents a show in New York City. Popular until 1932, when it will have been eclipsed by the advent of radio and motion pictures, vaudeville will feature such performers as W. C. Fields, Harry Houdini, Eddie Cantor, and Jack Benny, among others.   DRAMA

1881   Chinese writer Chou Shu-jen, known as Lu Hsün, is born (d. 1936). He will be considered China's greatest 20th-century writer, known particularly for his short stories (which will be translated into English in 1960 as *Selected Stories of Lu Hsün*). LIT

1881   British painter Dante Gabriel Rossetti publishes the sonnet sequence *The House of Life*, which is severely criticized for its sensuality. LIT

1881   American novelist Henry James publishes the novel *The Portrait of a Lady*. The story of young American Isabel Archer will become one of his best-known studies of European and American culture. LIT

1881   French writer Anatole France (pen name of Jacques Thibault) publishes the novel *Le Crime de Sylvestre Bonnard* (*The Crime of Sylvester Bonnard*). Among his later works will be the novel *Le Lys Rouge* (*The Red Lily*, 1894) and *L'Île des pingouins* (*Penguin Island*, 1908). LIT

1881   The French government withdraws official sponsorship from the annual exhibition known as the Salon, which then becomes run by a group of artists called the Société des Artistes Français. MISC

1881   French painter Pierre-Auguste Renoir paints *Luncheon of the Boating Party*. PAINT

1881   Photographer Frederic Ives produces the first color photograph. It will not be until decades later, in 1907, that a more practical process is developed for color photography. PHOTO

1882   *The Silver King*, a very popular melodrama by British playwrights Henry Arthur and Henry Herman, opens. DRAMA

1882   Cuban poet José Martí publishes the work *Ismaelillo*. Among his later works will be *Versos libres* (pub. 1913) and *Versos sencillos* (1892). LIT

1882   Russian composer Pyotr Ilich Tchaikovsky composes the *1812 Overture*. MUSIC

1882   The Berlin Philharmonic Orchestra is founded. MUSIC

1882   A year before his death, French painter Édouard Manet paints one of his greatest works, *A Bar at the Folies-Bergère*. PAINT

1883   James O'Neill, an Irish-born American actor, begins playing Edmond Dantès in a stage adaptation of French dramatist Alexandre Dumas père's *The Count of Monte Cristo*, a role he will be seen in at least 6,000 times over the next 30 years. He will become the father of playwright Eugene O'Neill (*see* 1920, DRAMA). DRAMA

1883	Scottish novelist Robert Louis Stevenson publishes *Treasure Island*. LIT
1883	American writer Mark Twain publishes the autobiographical *Life on the Mississippi*. LIT
1883	Belgian poet Émile Verhaeren publishes the collection *Les Flamandes*. Among his later collections will be *Les Villes tentaculaires* (1895). LIT
1883	French writer Guy de Maupassant publishes the novel *Une Vie*. His short stories will include "The Necklace," "Le Rendezvous," and "The Umbrella." LIT
1883	The Metropolitan Opera House opens in New York. MUSIC
1883–1884	French painter Georges Seurat paints *Bathers, Asnières*. PAINT
1884	Norwegian playwright Henrik Ibsen's drama *The Wild Duck* is produced. Realism is coupled with symbolism in this and subsequent Ibsen works, including *The Lady from the Sea* (1888). DRAMA
1884	Irish-born British playwright George Bernard Shaw joins the Fabian Society, for which he will lecture on social and political reform. DRAMA
1884	The Lyceum Theatre School for Acting, which will become the American Academy of Dramatic Arts, is founded in New York City. Students will eventually include the actors Edward G. Robinson, Spencer Tracy, Lauren Bacall, Anne Bancroft, Ruth Gordon, Hume Cronyn, Jason Robards Jr., and Rosalind Russell. DRAMA
1884	American novelist Henry James publishes in *Longman's Magazine* his essay explaining his aesthetics of writing, "The Art of Fiction." The work will be collected in *Partial Portraits* in 1888. LIT
1884	In France the Salon des Indépendants is established as a rival annual exhibition opposed to the official Salon, held since 1667. MISC
1884	German composer Johannes Brahms completes his Symphony in F Major. MUSIC
1884	Italian-born American painter John Singer Sargent moves to London, where he becomes famous for painting flattering portraits of American and British celebrities and socialites, among them Isabella Stuart Gardner, the Wyndham sisters, Henry Marquand, and William Merritt Chase. PAINT
1885–1887	American architect Henry Hobson Richardson designs the seven-story Marshall Field Wholesale Store in Chicago. ARCH

1885   The first skyscraper, the Home Insurance Building, is built in Chicago. Designed by American architect William Jenney, it is a ten-story steel-framed marble building. Advances in iron technology and the invention of the elevator allow the skyscraper to become an important part of modern architecture. ARCH

1885   *The Magistrate,* a farce by British playwright Arthur Pinero, premieres in London. Pinero's *The Schoolmistress, Dandy Dick,* and *The Cabinet Minister*—all successful farces—will be produced in 1886, 1887, and 1890, respectively. DRAMA

1885   British novelist Henry Rider Haggard publishes the romance *King Solomon's Mines.* Other adventure novels by Haggard will include *She* (1887). LIT

1885   American writer Mark Twain sees the U.S. publication of his boyhood-inspired novel, *The Adventures of Huckleberry Finn.* Over the years the story of Huck Finn and escaped slave Jim will become a standard of American literature. LIT

1885   American writer William Dean Howells publishes the realistic novel of morality, *The Rise of Silas Lapham.* LIT

1885   German composer Johannes Brahms completes his Symphony in E Minor. MUSIC

1885   The operetta *The Mikado,* by William S. Gilbert and Sir Arthur Sullivan, premieres in London. MUSIC

1885   In England Czech composer Antonín Dvořák composes the D minor symphony (no. 7), initially referred to as no. 2. MUSIC

1885–1887   French painter Paul Cézanne paints the *Mont Sainte-Victoire* series. PAINT

1885   Dutch painter Vincent van Gogh paints *The Potato Eaters.* PAINT

1885–1895   French sculptor Auguste Rodin completes the monumental group *The Burghers of Calais.* SCULP

1886   Russian novelist Leo Tolstoy writes *The Power of Darkness,* a play about the Russian peasantry. He will complete two more plays, *The First Distiller* and *The Fruits of Enlightenment,* over the next five years. DRAMA

1886   British poet Alfred Tennyson publishes *Locksley Hall Sixty Years After.* LIT

1886   British novelist Thomas Hardy publishes *The Mayor of Casterbridge,* which recounts the rise and tragic fall of grain merchant Michael Henchard. LIT

1886	Scottish novelist Robert Louis Stevenson publishes the horror novel *The Strange Case of Dr. Jekyll and Mr. Hyde* and the sea romance *Kidnapped*. LIT
1886	American novelist Henry James publishes the novel *The Bostonians.* LIT
1886	American painter Thomas Eakins is forced to resign from the Pennsylvania Academy of Fine Arts because of his use of nude models in art classrooms. PAINT
1886	In France neo-impressionist paintings by Georges Seurat, Camille Pissarro, and Paul Signac are exhibited at the final impressionist exhibition. Neo-impressionism employs an approach to light and color inspired by the impressionists but built on a systematic theoretical basis. The theory behind the movement is known as divisionism; the technique employed is pointillism, in which small dots of pure color are combined to create vivid, formal color effects. Among the works exhibited is *Sunday Afternoon on the Island of La Grande Jatte* by Georges Seurat, the work most associated with the movement. PAINT
1886–1891	French painter Paul Gauguin is the center of the Pont-Aven school of artists. Gauguin and Émile Bernard jointly develop the style of painting called synthetism or symbolism, in which forms are simplified into flat areas of unnatural color. PAINT
1886	French painter Edgar Degas paints *The Tub*. PAINT
1886	A halftone photo-engraving process, using multisized dots on the page, is invented by American Frederic Ives. PHOTO
1887	British novelist Thomas Hardy publishes the novel *The Woodlanders*. LIT
1887	British physician and novelist Arthur Conan Doyle publishes his first Sherlock Holmes story, the novel *A Study in Scarlet*. From now until 1927, Doyle will write a total of four novels and 56 short stories featuring the master detective. The other Holmes novels will be *The Sign of Four* (1890), *The Hound of the Baskervilles* (1902), and *The Valley of Fear* (1915). LIT
1887	The tragic opera *Otello* by Italian composer Giuseppe Verdi premieres in Milan. MUSIC
1887	American inventor Thomas Alva Edison invents the first motorized phonograph. MUSIC
1888	Construction of the Washington Monument is completed. At a height of 553 feet, it is the tallest masonry building in the world. ARCH

1888	The Arts and Crafts Exhibition Society is founded in England. Drawing on the writings of British art critic John Ruskin and French-born architect Augustus Pugin, the arts and crafts movement seeks to restore craftsmanship to the manufacture of household and workplace items, in revolt against mass produced, low-quality goods. **DECO**
1888	Swedish playwright August Strindberg writes the drama *Fröken Julie* (*Miss Julie*). It will become his best-known and most frequently revived work. He also writes the drama *Creditörer* (*The Creditors*). He wrote *Fadren* (*The Father*) in 1887. **DRAMA**
1888	*Ubu-roi*, a parody by French poet and playwright Alfred Jarry, is produced as a marionette play. It will receive a live stage production in 1896, and it will be regarded by many as one of the earliest precursors to the theater of the absurd. **DRAMA**
1888	British writer Thomas Hardy publishes the novel *Tess of the d'Urbervilles*, the story of a sensitive young woman driven to murder, for which she is eventually hanged. The same year Hardy begins to publish short stories with *Wessex Tales*. Other story collections will include *A Group of Noble Dames* (1891) and *Life's Little Ironies* (1894). **LIT**
1888	American journalist and reformer Edward Bellamy publishes the novel *Looking Backward*, a look into how the future century may be corrupted by economic inequality. **LIT**
1888	American novelist Henry James publishes the short novel *The Aspern Papers*, about one man's attempt to gain possession of the writings of a fictional romantic poet named Jeffrey Aspern. **LIT**
1888–1891	French novelist and journalist Maurice Barrès publishes the novel trilogy *Le Culte du moi*. Among his later novels will be the series *Les Bastions de l'Est* (1905–1921). **LIT**
1888	Swedish novelist and poet Verner von Heidenstam publishes his first poetry collection, *Vallfart och Vandringsår*. Among his later works will be the collection *Dikter* (1895). **LIT**
1888	Under the pseudonym "Phin," writer Ernest Lawrence Thayer publishes the baseball poem "Casey at the Bat," about the hapless at-bat of the hero of the Mudville team. **LIT**
1888	Russian composer Pyotr Ilich Tchaikovsky's Symphony no. 5 in E Minor premieres in St. Petersburg. **MUSIC**

1888	Russian composer Nikolay Rimsky-Korsakov's symphonic suite *Scheherazade* premieres in St. Petersburg. **MUSIC**
1888	French painter Paul Gauguin paints *Vision After the Sermon* (*Jacob Wrestling with the Angel*), notable for its use of unnatural color and flat, curvilinear patterns. **PAINT**
1888–1890	French painter Paul Cézanne paints *The Kitchen Table*. **PAINT**
1888	French painter Berthe Morisot paints *La Lecture* (*Reading*). **PAINT**
1888	Dutch painter Vincent van Gogh paints *Night Cafe*. **PAINT**
1888	American inventor George Eastman develops the low-cost, hand-held camera. It will expand the possibilities for photographic expression over the next several decades. **PHOTO**
1889	French architect Gustav Eiffel designs what will become known as the Eiffel Tower. **ARCH**
1889	American architect Louis Henry Sullivan, whose basic principle is that "form follows function," designs his first skyscraper, the Wainwright Building. He is the leading figure in the Chicago School of architecture. **ARCH**
1889	Irish poet and dramatist William Butler Yeats publishes *The Wanderings of Oisin and Other Poems*; the title work is a mystical narrative poem based on Irish folklore. **LIT**
1889	Three years before his death, British poet Alfred Tennyson publishes a collection containing "Crossing the Bar," which at his request will appear as the final poem in all collections of his work. **LIT**
1889	American writer Mark Twain publishes the satiric time-travel novel *A Connecticut Yankee in King Arthur's Court*. **LIT**
1889–1891	American historian Henry Adams publishes the nine-volume *History of the United States of America During the Administrations of Thomas Jefferson and James Madison*. **LIT**
1889	The symphonic poem *Don Juan* by German composer Richard Strauss premieres at Weimar. **MUSIC**
1889	The gamelan orchestra, central to Balinese and Javanese music, is showcased at the Paris Exposition, where it influences French composer Claude Debussy. This type of orchestra includes metallophones and the violinlike *rebob*. **MUSIC**

1889	After cutting off a piece of his left ear, Dutch painter Vincent van Gogh has himself committed to an asylum at St. Rémy near Arles. During his year here he creates 150 paintings, including *Starry Night* and *Yellow Cornfield*. PAINT
1889	French sculptor Auguste Rodin completes his most famous work, *The Thinker.* SCULP
1890s	The decorative style known as art nouveau emerges, emphasizing curvilinear patterns, often of plant and flower forms. It influences illustration and the graphic arts as well as the design of furniture, jewelry, and architectural ornamentation. Practitioners include graphic artist Aubrey Beardsley in England; the Czech artist Alphonse Mucha in France; painter Gustav Klimt in Austria; and glassware designer Louis Comfort Tiffany in the United States. The style will flourish until the beginning of World War I. DECO
1890s	The theater marquees on New York City's Broadway are electrified, and the street becomes known as "the Great White Way." DRAMA
1890s	British illustrator Aubrey Beardsley becomes known for his sensuous black-and-white drawings, often on grotesque or erotic subjects. His illustrations include those for editions of Irish writer Oscar Wilde's *Salomé* (1894; *see 1896,* DRAMA), English poet Alexander Pope's *Rape of the Lock* (1896; *see 1712,* LIT), and Ben Jonson's *Volpone* (1898; *see 1606,* DRAMA). GRAPH
1890s	Through his photographs of landscapes and churches, British photographer Frederick Henry Evans becomes known as a leader in the practice of artistic photography. He is part of the group known as the Linked Ring. PHOTO
1890	*Sleeping Beauty,* by Russian composer Pyotr Ilich Tchaikovsky, is produced by the Kirov Ballet. The classical troupe will also become known for its production of Tchaikovsky's *Swan Lake.* Its original name was the Imperial Russian Ballet. DANCE
1890	*Hedda Gabler,* which will be considered one of the greatest dramas by Norwegian playwright Henrik Ibsen, premieres. DRAMA
1890	Irish writer Oscar Wilde publishes the novel *The Picture of Dorian Gray.* LIT
1890	The *Literary Digest,* a current events periodical, is founded in New York City by I. K. Funk. With circulation reaching 2 million at its height, it will continue in publication until 1938. Eventually it will be subsumed by the news magazine *Time.* LIT
1890	American writer William Dean Howells publishes *A Hazard of New Fortunes,* a novel of social conscience and realism set in New York. LIT

1890–1891	French painter Claude Monet paints the series *Haystacks*. PAINT

1890	French painter Georges Seurat paints *Le Chahut* and *Woman Powdering Herself*, a year before his death of meningitis at 31. PAINT

1890	Danish-born American photographer and police reporter Jacob Riis publishes the sociological and photographic study *How the Other Half Lives*. His realistic photographs of New York City living conditions prompt a revision of tenement housing laws. PHOTO

1890–1930	Photographer Peter Henry Emerson champions naturalistic photography in his rural and landscape photos, such as *Haymaking in the Norfolk Broads* (c. 1890). His work is meant to contrast with the more obviously manipulated photographs of the time. PHOTO

1891	British artist William Morris founds the Kelmscott Press, which seeks to produce books of lasting beauty. He invents the Golden and Troy typefaces for this purpose. Among the press's finest works will be the folio Chaucer of 1896, with borders by Morris and illustrations by British artist Edward Burne-Jones. DECO

1891	German actor and playwright Frank Wedekind's *Frühlings Erwachen* (*Spring Awakening*) is produced in Berlin. Given the subjects it explores—the sexual affair of two teenagers, abortion, homosexuality—and its antiauthoritarian stance, the play will prove extremely controversial. It will continue to be revived thereafter. DRAMA

1891	American inventors Thomas Alva Edison and W. K. L. Dickson patent the Kinetograph camera and Kinetoscope viewer, the world's first motion picture system. Edison's company will be an important force in the American film industry until 1917. FILM

1891	British novelist George Gissing publishes *New Grub Street*, an account of the struggles of writers in Victorian England. LIT

1891	British artist William Morris expounds his belief in a medieval-based socialism in the utopian novel *News from Nowhere*. LIT

1891	American writer William Dean Howells champions the new realism in *Criticism and Fiction*. He claims that realism will be more successful than romanticism in its shared aims "to widen the bounds of sympathy, to level every barrier against aesthetic freedom, [and] to escape the paralysis of tradition." LIT

1891	Swedish novelist and short-story writer Selma Lagerlöf publishes the novel *Gösta Berlings saga*. Among her later works will be the story collection *Jerusalem* (1901–1902). LIT
1891	Italian novelist Matilda Serao publishes the work *Il paese di cuccagna*. LIT
1891–1895	French painter Claude Monet paints the *Rouen Cathedral* series, notable for its depiction of variations in lighting and seasonal conditions. PAINT
1891	French artist Paul Gauguin leaves France for Tahiti, where his painting will be influenced by the "primitive art" of indigenous peoples. PAINT
1891	French naive artist Henri Rousseau paints *Surprised! (Tropical Storm with a Tiger)*. PAINT
1891	American painter Mary Cassatt paints *The Bath*. PAINT
1892	Norwegian playwright Henrik Ibsen's *The Master Builder*, which will be considered among his best works, premieres. It will be followed by Ibsen's *Lillie Eyolf* (produced in 1894), *John Gabriel Borkman* (1896), and *When We Dead Awaken* (1900). DRAMA
1892	*Lady Windermere's Fan*, a comedy by Irish writer Oscar Wilde, is produced at the St. James Theatre in London. His comedies *A Woman of No Importance* and *An Ideal Husband* will be produced in 1893 and 1895, respectively. DRAMA
1892	*Widowers' Houses*, the first play by Irish-born British playwright George Bernard Shaw, premieres on December 9. *The Devil's Disciple* will be staged in New York in 1897. DRAMA
1892	Irish poet and dramatist William Butler Yeats publishes *The Countess Kathleen and Various Legends and Lyrics*. Selected poems from this and his 1889 volume, *The Wanderings of Oisin and Other Poems*, will later be combined under the title *Crossways* and placed at the beginning of his collected *Poems*. Other poems from *Countess Kathleen* will be collected under the title *The Rose*, including "To the Rose Upon the Rood of Time," "Cuchulain's Fight with the Sea," and "The Lake Isle of Innisfree." LIT
1892	British writer Rudyard Kipling publishes the short-story collection *Soldiers Three* and the poetry collection *Barrack-Room Ballads and Other Verses*, both of which draw on his experiences in colonial British India. The poetry collection includes the ballad "Gunga Din," which includes the refrain, "You're a better man than I am, Gunga Din." LIT

1892   Norwegian novelist and poet Knut Hamsun (pen name of Knut Pedersen)
                publishes the novel *Mysterier* (*Mysteries*). Among his later works will be *Pan*
                (1894) and *Victoria* (1898).   LIT

1892   American writer Ambrose Bierce publishes the short-story collection *In the
                Midst of Life,* which includes "An Occurrence at Owl Creek Bridge."   LIT

1892   Czech composer Antonín Dvořák becomes director of the National Conservatory
                of Music in New York City.   MUSIC

1892   French painter Henri de Toulouse-Lautrec paints *At the Moulin Rouge,* which
                vividly captures the spirit of the Paris nightclubs he frequents.   PAINT

1892   The first Nabis painting exhibition is held in Paris. Influenced by French
                painter Paul Gauguin, the Nabis, who include Paul Sérusier, Maurice Denis,
                Pierre Bonnard, and Édouard Vuillard, use color and line expressively. PAINT

1892   German graphic artist and painter Max Liebermann founds the Sezession
                (Secession) in Berlin. Sezession groups, representing an attempt to break from
                artistic tradition, are also set up in Munich (1892) and in Vienna (1897). PAINT

1893   *The Second Mrs. Tanqueray,* a drama by British playwright Arthur Pinero, is pro-
                duced. Pinero's *The Notorious Mrs. Ebbsmith* will be produced in 1895. DRAMA

1893   Czech composer Antonín Dvořák composes his ninth and last symphony in E
                minor *From the New World* (referred to as no. 5).   MUSIC

1893   The symphony *Pathétique,* by Russian composer Pyotr Ilich Tchaikovsky,
                premieres.   MUSIC

1893   African-American painter Henry O. Tanner, a student of Thomas Eakins, paints
                The Banjo Lesson.   PAINT

1893–1894   American painter Mary Cassatt paints *The Boating Party,* which shows the influ-
                ence of Japanese prints.   PAINT

1893   Norwegian painter Edvard Munch initiates his *Frieze of Life* series of works on
                love and death by exhibiting six paintings of the *Love* series, including *The Kiss*
                (1892), whose subject will be reworked as a woodcut (1897–1902), and *The
                Scream* (1893), in which swirling forms and unnatural color contribute to a
                sense of anxiety and despair.   PAINT

1894   Russian choreographer Lev Ivanov and French choreographer Marius Petipa
                adapt the book and choreography of Tchiakovsky's *Swan Lake,* turning it into
                a pioneering work of modern ballet. They also choreographed Tchiakovsky's

The Nutcracker (1892), while Petipa choreographed *Sleeping Beauty* (1890).

DANCE

1894   *Les Romanesques*, a satire by French playwright Edmond Rostand, is produced. The American musical *The Fantasticks* (*see* 1960, DRAMA) will take its story from the play.

DRAMA

1894   British novelist George Du Maurier publishes *Trilby*, which introduces the sinister hypnotist Svengali.

LIT

1894   British writer Rudyard Kipling publishes *The Jungle Book*, a collection of stories and poems centering on the boy Mowgli, who is raised by animals in the jungle. A sequel, *The Second Jungle Book*, will follow in 1895.

LIT

1894   American writer Mark Twain publishes *The Tragedy of Pudd'nhead Wilson*, a novel of slavery and intolerance centering on a mulatto slave.

LIT

1894–1897   In Britain the literary and art periodical the *Yellow Book* becomes the standard-bearer of fin-de-siècle decadence.

MISC

1894   French composer Claude Debussy composes his symphonic poem *Prelude to the Afternoon of a Faun*. It is one of the first and most convincing realizations of musical impressionism.

MUSIC

1895   Russian composer Pyotr Ilyich Tchaikovsky's ballet *Swan Lake* has its first complete performance in St. Petersburg.

DANCE

1895   *The Importance of Being Earnest*, the comic play by Irish writer Oscar Wilde, is produced at the St. James Theatre in London. The play will close a few months later, following Wilde's arrest for "committing indecent acts" (engaging in homosexual activity). (He will be convicted and sentenced this year to two years of hard labor.)

DRAMA

1895   *Guy Domville*, the first of several unsuccessful plays by American novelist Henry James, is produced.

DRAMA

1895   Swedish playwright August Strindberg begins his "Inferno Crisis," a period of mental illness that will last two years and include several psychotic episodes.

DRAMA

1895   French inventors Louis and Auguste Lumière patent the Cinématographe, a combination camera-projector. Unlike Thomas Alva Edison's Kinetoscope, which exhibits movies peepshow-style, the Cinématographe is able to project movies onto a screen. *See also* 1891, FILM.

FILM

1895   Polish novelist Henryk Sienkiewicz publishes *Quo Vadis?*

LIT

1895   British novelist Joseph Conrad publishes his first novel, *Almayer's Folly*.   LIT

1895   British novelist Thomas Hardy publishes *Jude the Obscure*, the tragic story of
             the illicit passion between stonemason Jude Fawley and his cousin Sue
             Bridehead. Readers and reviewers are outraged by what they consider the
             novel's immorality, and Hardy decides to write no further novels, turning
             instead to poetry.   LIT

1895   British novelist H. G. Wells publishes *The Time Machine*, the first of a group of
             science-fiction novels that will also include *The Island of Dr. Moreau* (1896),
             The War of the Worlds (1898), and *The First Men in the Moon* (1901).   LIT

1895   Twenty-four-year-old American novelist Stephen Crane publishes what will be
             considered his masterwork, *The Red Badge of Courage*. The tale of coming of age
             during the Civil War was originally serialized in the *Philadelphia Press* in 1894.
             Crane had no war experience before writing the book.   LIT

1896   Irish writer Oscar Wilde's *Salomé* (1894) is produced in Paris by the French actress
             Sarah Bernhardt (*see* 1872, DRAMA). (It was shown privately the previous year in
             Britain, where it was publicly banned.) It will later be used as the libretto of an
             opera by the German composer Richard Strauss (*see* 1905, MUSIC).   DRAMA

1896   *The Seagull*, a tragic drama by Russian playwright Anton Chekhov, is produced.
             DRAMA

1896   British artist William Morris publishes the prose romance *The Well at the
             World's End*.   LIT

1896   British poet A. E. Housman publishes the collection *A Shropshire Lad*, which
             includes "To an Athlete Dying Young" and "Terence, This Is Stupid Stuff."   LIT

1896   American poet Paul Laurence Dunbar publishes the collection *Lyrics of Lowly
             Life*, which will become the best-known work of the pioneering African-
             American artist. It begins with an introduction by American writer William
             Dean Howells.   LIT

1896   American novelist Sarah Orne Jewett publishes her spare Maine–based novel,
             The Country of the Pointed Firs.   LIT

1896   The opera *La Bohème* by Italian composer Giacomo Puccini premieres in
             Turin.   MUSIC

1897–1898   German graphic artist Käthe Kollwitz creates the series of etchings *Weavers'
             Revolt*; with *Peasants' War* in 1902–1908, it will establish her reputation as an
             artist of social protest.   GRAPH

1897	British novelist Joseph Conrad publishes *The Nigger of the "Narcissus."*	LIT
1897	Irish writer Bram Stoker publishes the Gothic novel *Dracula.*	LIT
1897	British writer Rudyard Kipling publishes the novel *Captains Courageous*, the tale of a spoiled rich boy's education at sea.	LIT
1897	American novelist Henry James publishes the novels *The Spoils of Poynton* and *What Maisie Knew.*	LIT
1897	American poet Edwin Arlington Robinson publishes the poem "Richard Cory," about the "gentleman from sole to crown" who ". . . one calm summer night, / Went home and put a bullet through his head."	LIT
1897	German composer Gustav Mahler becomes conductor at the Vienna State Opera, a positon he will hold until 1907. During this period of his greatest activity, he composes Symphony no. 4 in G Major (1899–1900), no. 5 in C-sharp Minor (1901–1902), no. 6 in A Minor (1903–1905), no. 7 in E Minor (1904–1905), and no. 8 in E-flat Major (1907). He also composes the	

Count Irving

Vampire folklore and Gothic horror fiction played a part in inspiring Irish writer Bram Stoker's 1897 novel *Dracula*. But the personality of Count Dracula may owe as much to a real-life acquaintance of Stoker: British actor and theater manager Sir Henry Irving.

The first actor to be knighted (in 1895), Irving, born John Henry Brodribb, was well known for performing in Shakespearean roles and staging popular melodramas, often concerning the supernatural. The productions at his Lyceum Theatre in London were marked by spectacular costumes and sets. A commanding, egotistical, difficult figure, he was identified with roles such as Mephistopheles in *Faust* and was held to have a Svengali-like influence over his wife, British actress Ellen Terry. Among those who came into his circle of power was Stoker, who served as acting manager of the Lyceum during the time that he was writing *Dracula*.

It has been speculated that Stoker partly based his supernaturally dominating vampire on Irving, and that he perhaps hoped that Irving would play Count Dracula in a stage version. If so, his hopes were dashed; Irving showed no interest in the property. A staged reading was held at the Lyceum around the time of the book's publication, but Irving stayed out of the cast. Legend has it that the great actor caught a few moments of the show on his way to his dressing room. Asked what he thought as he parted, his one-word answer, loud enough for all to hear, was "Dreadful!"

Kindertotenlieder for voice and orchestra (1901–1904) and the five Rückert songs for voice and orchestra (1901–1902).   MUSIC

1897   French composer Vincent d'Indy presents the opera *Fervaal* in Brussels.   MUSIC

1897   American composer Scott Joplin writes the ragtime song "Maple Leaf Rag." Named for the social club above the saloon in Missouri where he played piano, it will usher in the age of ragtime and give Joplin the moniker "King of Ragtime writers."   MUSIC

1897   French painter Henri Rousseau paints *The Sleeping Gypsy*.   PAINT

1897–1917   French painter Edgar Degas, his eyesight failing, lives in nearly complete seclusion and devotes himself to his art.   PAINT

1897   French sculptor Auguste Rodin's plaster cast statue of French novelist Honoré de Balzac is completed but rejected as too radical by those who commissioned it, the Society of Men of Letters. It will not be cast in bronze and set up until 1939, 22 years after Rodin's death in 1917.   SCULP

1898   The Moscow Art Theater is founded by Russian actor and director Konstantin Stanislavsky and Russian playwright and director Vladimir Nemirovich-Danchenko. All of Russian dramatist Anton Chekhov's major plays will be produced there, as will plays by English dramatist William Shakespeare, Russian novelist Leo Tolstoy, and Russian novelist Nikolai Gogol, and many others. The theater will serve as a training center in which actors will learn Stanislavsky's new methods of acting. *See* 1936, DRAMA.   DRAMA

1898   *Cyrano de Bergerac*, a romantic comedy by French playwright Edmond Rostand, is produced. Rostand's most famous play, it will be revived frequently.
                                    DRAMA

1898   *Trelawny of the 'Wells,'* a comedy by British playwright Arthur Pinero, is produced. This tale of life in the mid-Victorian theater world will be Pinero's most enduring play.   DRAMA

1898   British novelist Thomas Hardy publishes *Wessex Poems and Other Verses*, which includes "Hap," a meditation on fate and chance.   LIT

1898   American novelist Stephen Crane writes the model short story "The Open Boat" based on his experiences covering a Cuban revolution in 1896 for a newspaper syndicate, during which he escapes a sinking ship by joining four other passengers in an open boat.   LIT

1898 | American novelist Henry James publishes the psychological ghost tale *The Turn of the Screw*, a novella about the relationship of two children to their governess, who is convinced that the children are under the spell of two ghosts, including that of their former governess.   LIT

1898 | American journalist Finley Peter Dunne publishes the first collections of his popular satiric columns for the Chicago *Post* featuring the fictional character Mr. Dooley. The books, *Mr. Dooley in Peace and War* and *Mr. Dooley in the Hearts of His Countrymen*, lead to several sequels.   LIT

1898 | Swedish poet Erik Karlfeldt publishes the collection *Fridolins visor*. His later works will include *Fridolins lustgård* (1901) and *Hösthorn* (1927). Offered the Nobel Prize for literature several times while serving as permanent secretary to the Nobel Committee for Literature (from 1912), he will become the first person to refuse the prize, on grounds of conflict of interest and out of a desire to give others a chance. Six months after his death, in 1931, he will be awarded the Nobel Prize for literature. (The rules prohibiting posthumous awards will not apply to Karlfeldt, because he will have been nominated prior to his death).   LIT

1898 | German poet Arno Holz publishes the collection *Phantasus*. The next year he will publish the collection *Revolution of Lyric Poetry*.   LIT

1898 | German painter Paula Modersohn-Becker joins the colony of landscape painters at Worpswede, which also includes her future husband, Otto Modersohn (mar-

Abbott and Atget

Frenchman Eugène Atget, now perhaps the most highly esteemed photographer of the 19th century, labored in relative obscurity during his lifetime. The master of the unadorned photograph remained little known until he was reintroduced to the world by a young 20th-century American photographer. When Berenice Abbott was apprenticing in France with American artist Man Ray, she came to know the works of Atget. Although Atget made his living as a documentary photographer who took photos of Paris, his work was purchased by leading modern artists, including Abbott's teacher Man Ray.

Over the years, as the direct style of photojournalism became the dominant photographic aesthetic, Abbott set herself to inform the artistic world of Atget's defining role in its development. Her efforts were collected in *The World of Atget* (1964). By the time of the book's reprinting in 1979, Atget had been established as the central photographer of his century.

ried 1901). She later comes under the influence of French painter Paul Gauguin.

PAINT

1898–1905   French painter Paul Cézanne paints *The Bathers*.   PAINT

1898   French symbolist painter Gustave Moreau dies (*b.* 1826), leaving his works to the newly established Musée Gustave Moreau in Paris; among them are *Oedipe et le Sphinx* (1864), *Orphée* (1865), and *Hésiode et la Muse* (c. 1891).   PAINT

1898–1927   French photographer Eugène Atget records simple, everyday elements and occurrences in Paris. His uncluttered, haunting work will be championed by Spanish artist Pablo Picasso and American artist Man Ray, among others.   PHOTO

1898   French sculptor Auguste Rodin completes *The Kiss*.   SCULP

1899   *Uncle Vanya*, a drama by Russian playwright Anton Chekhov, is produced.   DRAMA

1899   Irish poet and dramatist William Butler Yeats publishes *The Wind Among the Reeds*, which includes the poems "The Song of Wandering Aengus," "The Valley of the Black Pig," "The Secret Rose," and "He Wishes His Beloved Were Dead."   LIT

1899–1900   American writer Mark Twain completes "The Man That Corrupted Hadleyburg," a dark tale about the limits of a town's self-proclaimed honesty.   LIT

1899   Polish novelist Wladyslaw Reymont publishes *Ziemia obiecana* (*The Promised Land*), about the effects of the industrial age on modern society. Among his later novels are *Chlopi* (*The Peasants*, 1904–1909) and the trilogy *Rok 1794* (1913–1918). He will win the Nobel Prize for literature in 1924.   LIT

1899   American short-story writer and novelist Kate Chopin publishes her last novel, *The Awakening*, about a woman's self-discovery; it will be ignored for over 60 years because of its controversial treatment of extramarital love.   LIT

1899   Finnish composer Jean Sibelius presents the solidly romantic Symphony no. 1 in E Minor.   MUSIC

1899   German composer Richard Strauss presents the last of his successful symphonic poems, *Ein Heldenleben* (*A Hero's Life*), in Frankfurt.   MUSIC

1899   French painter Claude Monet begins the *Waterlilies* series, which he will continue until near the end of his life in 1926. The subject of the paintings is his water garden at Giverny.   PAINT

1899   French painter Henri Matisse begins experimenting with bright, strongly contrasting colors. *See also* 1905, PAINT.   PAINT

1899	African motifs decorate some of the pavilions at the opening of the Universal Exhibition in Paris. SCULP
1900s	The cakewalk, a dance of African origin, sweeps the United States. It is originally popularized by American black entertainers Egbert Williams and George Walker. DANCE
1900s	The syncopated dance style called buck and wing, brought to the American stage by dancer James McIntyre, is now being referred to as tap dancing. DANCE
1900s	The BaJokwe people of central Africa develop a chief's chair that shows European influence in its broad design but purely African characteristics in its ornamentation, which takes the form of human and animal figures. The BaJokwe people also become known internationally for stylized female masks used in ritual dances. The mask, called *mwana po*, is worn by a male dancer impersonating a female spirit. DECO
1900s	Comic troupes perform partly preplanned, partly improvised shows, which sometimes include music and dance, in Iran and Turkey. They often make fun of authority figures and use sexual themes in humorous skits. DRAMA
1900s	In the Western world plays are usually staged with realistic costumes and scenery, but increasingly, especially with avant-garde works, symbolic and abstract designs are introduced. With technological advances, stage lighting systems become more sophisticated, and lighting begins to play a greater role. DRAMA

The Birth of the Cakewalk

The influence of African-American dance forms on American popular dance saw its beginnings in the 19th century with entertainment known as minstrel shows and extended to the social dance with the craze for the cakewalk. A centuries-old slave dance, the cakewalk had originally become popular before the Civil War among Southern plantation owners. Afterward, it experienced minor success in jazz clubs. It was not until years later, when black entertainers Egbert Williams and George Walker introduced the dance in their stage performances, that it entered high society and took the country by storm. Savvy promoters Williams and Walker fueled public interest by challenging 19th-century millionaire William K. Vanderbilt to a cakewalk contest. This was the impetus the two entertainers needed to make the cakewalk the rich man's dance of choice for years to come.

1900s	Theater in Africa is used both to help mollify people unhappy with colonial rule and to propagate anticolonialism and marshal support for independence. **DRAMA**
1900s	Artists from Bamana villages near Bougouni and Dioica in southern Mali, Africa, create large wooden figures to appear in celebrations of the Jo society, a separate association of initiated men and women. **SCULP**
1900s	The Fang people of the rain forests of Gabon, Equatorial Guinea, and southern Cameroon carve wooden heads or figures to mount on top of reliquary boxes containing the skulls of ancestors. **SCULP**
1900s	The Asmat people from southern Irian Jaya (or New Guinea) carve mbis poles to display in front of the men's ceremonial house during funerary rituals. **SCULP**
c. 1900	In the mountainous Maprik district of New Guinea, the Abelam people build elaborate ceremonial houses, decorated with painting and sculpture. These cult houses are used to shelter artists and store ceremonial objects. **ARCH**
c. 1900	In the Micronesian islands Western explorers collect examples of highly developed crafts, including jewelry, ornaments, basketry, matting, decorated fabrics, and finely made tools and weapons. **DECO**
c. 1900	Artists in the Massim district of New Guinea decorate everyday objects such as blades and dugout canoes with elaborate spirals, scrolls, openwork, figures of people and animals, and other ornamentation. The style extends to the nearby Trobriand Islands. **DECO**
1900	British novelist Joseph Conrad publishes *Lord Jim*. **LIT**
1900	British novelist H. G. Wells publishes *Love and Mr. Lewisham*, one of several realistic novels drawn on his experiences growing up in the lower middle classes. Others of these novels will include *Kipps: The Story of a Simple Soul* (1905) and *Tono-Bungay* (1909). **LIT**
1900	American poet and scholar William Vaughan Moody publishes his well-received political poem, "An Ode in Time of Hesitation," about the tumultuous dedication of the Saint Gaudens monument to Col. Robert Gould Shaw, the head of the first enlisted African-American regiment, which was active during the Civil War. **LIT**
1900	American writer Booker T. Washington publishes *Up from Slavery*, an autobiography of his rise from Southern slave (*b.* 1856) to cofounder (1881) of the Tuskegee Institute in Alabama. **LIT**

1900   American writer L. Frank Baum publishes *The Wonderful Wizard of Oz*, a chil-
            dren's story about the journey of Dorothy and her dog, Toto, to the land of
            Oz. In 1939 the story will be adapted for the silver screen as Victor Fleming's
            popular musical film *The Wizard of Oz*, starring Judy Garland.   LIT

1900   French novelist Sidonie-Gabrielle Colette, known simply as Colette, publishes
            the first of the four Claudine novels, *Claudine à l'école*. The novels will be pub-
            lished under the pseudonym Willy. Among her later works will be the com-
            ing-of-age novel *Gigi* (1944).   LIT

1900   Italian writer Gabriele D'Annuzio publishes the novel *Il fuoco* (*The Flame of
            Life*). Among his works is the play *La gioconda* (1898). Both are based on his
            relation with actress Eleonora Duse.   LIT

1900   Brazilian novelist and poet Joachim Maria Machado de Assis publishes what
            will be his best-known work, the comic novel *Don Casmurro*.   LIT

c. 1900   Impressionism in music reaches its height in the late 19th and early 20th cen-
            turies, chiefly represented in the works of French composer Claude Debussy.
            Its vague, intangible style, a reaction against such "German" achievements as
            the sonata, symphony, thematic material, and developmental techniques,
            introduces various devices antithetical to the features of classical and roman-
            tic harmony.   MUSIC

Vacationing with Frank Lloyd Wright

As with the work of any artist, the best way to appreciate an architect's work is to view
it in person. American architect Frank Lloyd Wright worked in so many styles and parts
of the United States that a survey of his work would require a cross-country tour. With
that in mind, a Frank Lloyd Wright vacation itinerary might look like this:

New York City—Guggenheim Museum (designed 1942; completed 1959)
Bear Run, Pennsylvania—Fallingwater (1937–1939); an example of international
     modern house design
Chicago, Illinois—Robie house (1908); example of his prairie school houses
Oak Park, Illinois—Unity Temple (1906)
Racine, Wisconsin—Johnson Wax Company factory complex (1936–1950); an exam-
     ple of organic architecture
Spring Green, Wisconsin—Taliesin (1911; burned and rebuilt in 1915; burned and
     rebuilt in 1925); his home and studio
Bartlesville, Oklahoma—skyscraper (1955); an example of his later work
Paradise Valley, Phoenix, Arizona—Taliesin West (1938–1959); his winter home

1900   Italian composer Giacomo Puccini's opera *Tosca* opens in Rome.   MUSIC

1900–1910   A form of jazz music called ragtime becomes popular in the United States. In New Orleans a form of jazz that comes to be known simply as New Orleans jazz also develops.   MUSIC

1900   French painter Paul Gauguin publishes the book *Noa Noa*, a memoir of his experiences in Tahiti.   PAINT

1900–1904   In his blue period Spanish artist Pablo Picasso, who will become the best-known artist of the 20th century, produces such works as *La Vie* (1903) and the engraving *The Frugal Repast* (1904). His characteristic subjects in this period, painted in blue tones, are the socially downtrodden.   PAINT

c. 1900   The secession movement in photography, represented by artists such as Alfred Stieglitz and Edward Steichen, argues for recognition of photography as an art form on the level of painting.   PHOTO

1901   American architect Frank Lloyd Wright completes the lecture *The Art and Craft of the Machine*, detailing his ideas about modern architecture.   ARCH

1901   *Three Sisters*, a drama by Russian playwright Anton Chekhov, is produced. It tells the story of the Prozorov sisters and their desire to escape country provincialism for the worldliness of Moscow.   DRAMA

1901   Swedish playwright August Strindberg writes the dramas *Dödsdansen* (*The Dance of Death*) and *Kronbruden* (*The Crown Bridge*). Two years earlier, he completed four historical dramas that will be popular only in Sweden.   DRAMA

1901   British writer Rudyard Kipling publishes his masterpiece, the novel *Kim*, a tale of India that explores, through the eyes of a military orphan, the clash between British dedication to action and a Tibetan Lama's contemplative quest.   LIT

1901–1903   American novelist Frank Norris writes *The Octopus* (1901) and *The Pit* (1903), two naturalistic, muckraking novels of a projected trilogy about the place of wheat in modern lives. The first explores the conflicts between the railroad trust and the wheat farmer; the second the conflicts between farmers and wheat traders.   LIT

1901   German novelist Thomas Mann publishes the saga of a declining upper-class family, *Buddenbrooks*. Among his later works are *Death in Venice* (1912) and the tale of European decline as seen through the experiences of ailing Hans Castorp, *The Magic Mountain* (1924). Mann will be awarded the 1929 Nobel Prize for literature.   LIT

1901   French poet René Sully-Prudhomme—whose major collections of poetry were published from the 1860s through the 1880s and whose themes included unrequited love, patriotism, and self-sacrifice—becomes the first recipient of the Nobel Prize for literature, to the disappointment of many who expected the honor to go to Russian novelist Leo Tolstoy, author of *War and Peace*, among other works (*see* 1864–1869, LIT).   LIT

1901   Czech composer Antonin Dvořák's opera, the tragic fairy tale *Rusalka*, opens in Prague.   MUSIC

1901   Russian composer Sergey Rachmaninoff presents his Piano Concerto no. 2 in C Minor, reportedly written with the aid of a psychoanalyst who was treating him at the time.   MUSIC

1901   Norwegian painter Edvard Munch completes the painting *Girls on the Bridge*.   PAINT

1901   On December 21 Italian engineer Guglielmo Marconi broadcasts radio waves from England to Newfoundland, marking the invention of radio.   TV&R

1902   *The Lower Depths*, a realistic drama by Russian playwright Maksim Gorky (pen name of Aleksey Peshkov), is staged by the Moscow Art Theatre. The play depicts the sufferings of Moscow's poorer citizens.   DRAMA

1902   British playwright George Bernard Shaw's *Mrs. Warren's Profession*, a play exploring both prostitution and the role of the New Woman, is produced. His *Caesar and Cleopatra* will be performed in both Berlin and New York in 1906.   DRAMA

1902   French filmmaker Georges Méliès, a pioneer of film fantasy and special effects, makes his best-known work, *A Trip to the Moon*.   FILM

1902   American novelist Owen Wister publishes *The Virginian*, which sets the style for future Western novels.   LIT

1902   British novelist Joseph Conrad publishes the novel *Youth* and the short novel *Heart of Darkness*. The latter tells the story of seaman Marlow's encounter with the mad ivory trader Kurtz, whose memorable last words are "The horror! The horror!"   LIT

1902   British novelist Thomas Hardy publishes *Poems of the Past and Present*, which includes "Lausanne" and "The Darkling Thrush."   LIT

1902   British writer Rudyard Kipling publishes the story-and-poem collection *Just So Stories*, illustrated by the author. He will be awarded the 1907 Nobel Prize for literature.   LIT

1902   American novelist Henry James publishes the novel *The Wings of the Dove*. LIT

1902   American novelist Edith Wharton publishes *The Valley of Decision*, a period novel that will become one of her early successes.   LIT

1902   French novelist and thinker André Gide publishes the novel *L'Immoraliste* (*The Immoralist*). Among his later works will be *La Porte étroite* (*Strait Is the Gate*, 1909) and the story *La Symphonie pastorale* (*The Pastoral Symphony*, 1919).   LIT

1902   English composer Edward Elgar composes the first of his five *Pomp and Circumstance* marches for orchestra. No. 5 will be completed in 1930.   MUSIC

1902   American photographer Edward Steichen's work *Rodin with His Sculptures "Victor Hugo" and the "Thinker"* exemplifies the photo-secessionist movement, which opposes realism and develops the idea of art for art's sake. The movement includes Gertrude Kasebier, Clarence White, Alvin Langdon Coburn, Frederick Henry Evans, and Alfred Stieglitz.   PHOTO

1903–1908   In Europe and the United States, American modern dance pioneer Isadora Duncan performs her dances informed by Greek art. They will be marked by stylization, including her appearance in bare feet and her use of scarves. Her work, demeanor, and way of life will influence the development of modern dance.   DANCE

1903–1932   The Wiener Werkstätte (Viennese workshops) are in operation in Vienna, providing space for artists and craftspeople to follow their goals of combining utility with high quality. Products include jewelry and items of home decoration, many reflecting the influence of art nouveau.   DECO

1903   *In the Shadow of the Glen*, a drama by Irish playwright John Millington Synge, is produced. Synge had previously written the play *When the Moon Has Set*—probably in 1901—but it had not been produced.   DRAMA

1903   American filmmaker Edwin S. Porter completes the films *The Life of an American Fireman*, the first known film to use intercutting, and *The Great Train Robbery*, which will influence the genre of film westerns.   FILM

1903   American writer Jack London publishes the novel *The Call of the Wild*.   LIT

1903   Irish poet and dramatist William Butler Yeats publishes *In the Seven Woods*, which includes the poems "The Folly of Being Comforted" and "Adam's Curse."   LIT

1903–1908   British novelist Thomas Hardy publishes the three parts (1903, 1905, 1908) of the epic verse-drama *The Dynasts*.   LIT

1903   A year after his death, British novelist Samuel Butler's masterpiece is published, the satirical, semiautobiographical novel *The Way of All Flesh*.   LIT

1903   American novelist Henry James publishes the short novel *The Beast in the Jungle*. He also publishes the novel *The Ambassadors*, which he will call "frankly, quite the best all round" of his works.   LIT

1903   American scholar and teacher W. E. B. Du Bois publishes *The Souls of Black Folk: Essays and Sketches*, a collection of profiles of African-Americans along with discussions of African-American history, politics, and culture.   LIT

1903   English composer Frederick Delius composes his masterpiece *Sea Drift*.   MUSIC

1903   German composer Anton Bruckner's unfinished Symphony no. 9 in D Minor premieres posthumously in Vienna.   MUSIC

1903   French sculptor Camille Claudel exhibits her piece, *Maturity*, an allegory of her break with French sculptor Auguste Rodin, in the Salon of French artists.   SCULP

1904   The Abbey Theatre, dedicated to presenting Irish drama, opens in Dublin. Its directors include Irish playwrights Lady Gregory and William Butler Yeats. Yeats's *On Baile's Strand* is the first play performed there.   DRAMA

1904   *The Cherry Orchard*, a drama by Russian playwright Anton Chekhov, is produced.   DRAMA

1904   Scottish novelist and playwright James Barrie's children's play *Peter Pan* premieres. Barrie adapted the play from his novel *The Little White Bird*. His comedy *The Admirable Crichton* was produced in 1902.   DRAMA

1904   *The King's Threshold*, a poetic play by Irish playwrights William Butler Yeats and Lady Gregory, is produced. The two will also collaborate on *The Unicorn from the Stars* (1908). Yeats also has written and will write a number of plays alone—some of them in verse, some in prose, including *The Hour-Glass* (1914) and *The Words upon the Window Pane* (1934).   DRAMA

1904   *Riders to the Sea*, a one-act tragedy by Irish playwright John Millington Synge, is produced at the Abbey Theatre in Dublin. Synge's comedy *The Well of the Saints* will be produced in 1905.   DRAMA

1904   The Royal Academy of Dramatic Art is founded in London.   DRAMA

1904–1907   Ten plays by Irish-born British playwright George Bernard Shaw are performed in repertory over three seasons at the Royal Court Theatre in London. They are *Candida, John Bull's Other Island, How He Lied to Her Husband, You Never Can*

Tell (which premiered in 1900), *Man and Superman* (without Act III, which is produced separately as *Don Juan in Hell* in 1907), *Major Barbara, The Doctor's Dilemma, Captain Brassbound's Conversion, The Philanderer* (which was previously performed in a private theater club production), and the one-act *The Man of Destiny*. This huge undertaking establishes Shaw as a highly respected playwright.   DRAMA

1904   Uruguayan playwright Florencio Sánchez's drama *La gringa* (*The Foreign Girl*) is produced. His *Barranca abajo* (*Down the Gully*) will be produced in 1905. These works will be regarded as Sánchez's masterpieces, and he will be seen as one of South America's greatest playwrights.   DRAMA

1904   The first formal movie theater is opened near Pittsburgh, Pennsylvania. Among its first films is a French version of *Potemkin*.   FILM

1904   British novelist Joseph Conrad publishes *Nostromo*, a tale of revolution and moral decay set in the fictitious South American republic of Costaguana.   LIT

1904   Greek poet Constantine Cavafy (pen name of Konstantinos Kaváfis) publishes the pamphlet *Poems*, which will be revised in 1910. His works, including "Ithaca" and "Waiting for the Barbarians," will gain the respect of such writers as American-born British poet T. S. Eliot and British-born American poet W. H. Auden.   LIT

1904   American novelist Henry James publishes the novel *The Golden Bowl*.   LIT

1904   American journalist Lincoln Steffens publishes *The Shame of the Cities*, a collection of his muckraking studies of the corruption of American cities. The articles first appeared in *McClure's* magazine.   LIT

1904   Italian composer Giacomo Puccini's opera *Madame Butterfly*, set near Nagasaki, Japan, opens in Milan.   MUSIC

1904   The London Symphony Orchestra gives its initial concert.   MUSIC

1904   Czech composer Leoš Janáček's opera *Jenůfa* opens in Brno. It will bring him renown when it comes to Prague and Vienna in 1916.   MUSIC

1904   The first of American composer George M. Cohan's major works, *Little Johnny Jones*, debuts on Broadway. It generates a number of song standards, including "Give My Regards to Broadway" and "Yankee Doodle Boy." Although most of Cohan's best-known songs will be written for the stage, one of his most famous will not: "Over There," the patriotic World War I song.   MUSIC

1904	Having settled in Paris, Spanish painter Pablo Picasso is in his rose period, when pink and gray tones are dominant and his favorite subjects are acrobats, dancers, and harlequins. He also begins sculpting in this period. PAINT

1904–1905   French painter Henri Matisse completes *Luxe, calme et volupté*, a painting influenced by the neo-impressionist movement. It is shown at the Salon des Indépendents in 1905.   PAINT

1904   American photographer Edward Steichen takes the photograph "The Flatiron." This view of the new three-sided New York building is taken during daylight hours but later will be printed so as to appear a nighttime composition.   PHOTO

1905–1907   Spanish architect Antoni Gaudí designs the Casa Mila in Barcelona. Its fluid appearance embodies art nouveau principles.   ARCH

1905   American actress Ethel Barrymore appears as Nora and her brother John as Dr. Rank in Norwegian playwright Henrik Ibsen's *A Doll's House*. For the next several decades, Ethel will perform in both classical and modern roles, doing some of her best work—such as her 1940 portrayal of Miss Moffat in Emlyn Williams's *The Corn Is Green*—late in life. John will have a similarly distinguished career, with his 1922 Hamlet being perhaps his greatest theatrical performance. But he will leave the stage in 1926 to work primarily in film. Ethel and John's brother Lionel will also gain success as a stage actor, often appearing with John, but like John, will leave the theater to work in film. John's granddaughter Drew Barrymore will enter the family profession early in life, experiencing fame at the age of seven for her role in Steven Spielberg's *E.T., The Extra-Terrestrial* (1982).   DRAMA

1905   Pioneering American cartoonist Winsor McCay develops the early comic strip "Little Nemo in Slumberland." It is the first of several comic strips he will create over the next several years.   GRAPH

1905   Irish writer Oscar Wilde's extended prison letter *De Profundis* is published posthumously.   LIT

1905   The group of writers, artists, and thinkers known as the Bloomsbury group begins to meet in Bloomsbury, London. The group, which includes Virginia and Leonard Woolf, Vanessa and Clive Bell, Lytton Strachey, and E. M. Forster, will continue to meet until Virginia Woolf's suicide in 1941.   LIT

1905   British novelist E. M. Forster publishes his first novel, *Where Angels Fear to Tread*.   LIT

1905   American novelist Edith Wharton publishes *The House of Mirth*, a social satire
                of marriage in the upper levels of New York society that centers on the efforts
                of an outsider to acquire a society husband.   LIT

1905   German poet Rainer Maria Rilke publishes the collection *Das Stunden-Buch*
                (*The Book of Hours*). Later works include the series *Duineser Elegien* (*Duino
                Elegies*, 1923) and the cycle *Die Sonette an Orpheus* (*The Sonnets to Orpheus*,
                1923).   LIT

1905   French composer Claude Debussy's symphonic poem *La Mer* premieres in Paris,
                representing the culmination of impressionist pictorialism and technique. MUSIC

1905   German composer Richard Strauss's intensely emotional opera *Salomé*, based
                on the play by Irish writer Oscar Wilde (*see* 1896, DRAMA) and including the
                popular "Dance of the Seven Veils," opens in Dresden.   MUSIC

1905   In France the Salon d'Automne exhibits the work of the fauves (French for
                "wild beasts"), a group of artists led by Henri Matisse who employ bright,
                pure, nonnaturalistic colors disconnected from traditional representation.
                Other fauvists include André Derain, Raoul Dufy, Georges Braque, Albert
                Marquet, Georges Rouault, and Maurice de Vlaminck.   PAINT

1905–1906   French painter Henri Matisse paints *The Joy of Life*, an archetypal fauvist work. PAINT

1905   French painter Georges Rouault paints the violently expressive *Head of Christ*. PAINT

1905   In Dresden, Ernst Ludwig Kirchner, Emil Nolde, and other artists found the
                German expressionist group Die Brücke (the Bridge), which will last until 1913.
                The German expressionists use color and shape primarily to express intense emo-
                tion and tortured psychological states rather than to represent nature.   PAINT

1906   American architect Frank Lloyd Wright designs Oak Park Unity Temple near
                Chicago.   ARCH

1906   The novel *Sister Carrie* by American novelist Theodore Dreiser is published in
                the United States after six years of controversy over its alleged immorality. LIT

1906   The American writer Upton Sinclair publishes the searing novel *The Jungle*, a
                grim look at the life of an immigrant who becomes brutalized by working in
                the Chicago stockyards. This exposé of the meat-packing industry will be
                championed by generations of animal-rights activists and vegetarians.   LIT

1906   American short-story writer William Sydney Porter, known as O. Henry, pub-
                lishes the collection *The Four Million*, titled to show how large is the popula-

tion of New York in contrast to the few who belong to "high society." The collection contains the story "The Gift of the Magi."   LIT

1906   French painter André Derain paints *London Bridge*.   PAINT

1906–1909   Now in his Negro period, Spanish painter Pablo Picasso creates increasingly abstract forms. A characteristic work is *Les Demoiselles d'Avignon* (1907), influenced by French painter Paul Cézanne's post-impressionist paintings and by African masks.   PAINT

1906   American painter John Sloan, who will be a member of the ashcan school (*see* 1908, PAINT), paints *Dust Storm, Fifth Avenue*.   PAINT

1907   *Une Puce à l'oreille* (*A Flea in Her Ear*), a farcical comedy by French playwright Georges Feydeau, premieres. Feydeau will eventually write more than 60 farces.   DRAMA

1907   *The Playboy of the Western World*, a comedy that is widely seen as the greatest play by Irish playwright John Millington Synge, is produced at the Abbey Theatre in Dublin. It leads to rioting in the theater. Synge's comedy *The Tinker's Wedding*, also a controversial work, will be produced in 1909 in London.   DRAMA

1907   The first daily comic strip, "Mr. Mutt," appears in the *San Francisco Chronicle*. Created by Bud Fisher, it will later be renamed "Mutt and Jeff."   GRAPH

1907   British novelist Joseph Conrad publishes *The Secret Agent*.   LIT

1907   Irish writer James Joyce publishes *Chamber Music*, a collection of poetry.   LIT

1907   In England the Fabian Arts Group, with financial help from Irish-born British playwright George Bernard Shaw, begins publication of the modernist journal *The New Age*, which will publish work by Ezra Pound, Edwin Muir, T. E. Hulme, and Katherine Mansfield.   LIT

1907   The cowboy hero Hopalong Cassidy makes his first appearance in the novel *Bar 20* by American writer Clarence E. Mulford. Several Hopalong Cassidy books will followed, as will more than 60 Cassidy movies, beginning in 1935 and starring William Boyd.   LIT

1907   Russian writer Maksim Gorky publishes the novel *Mother*. Among his other works will be the autobiographical trilogy *Childhood* (1913–1914), *My Apprenticeship* (1916), and *My Universities* (1923).   LIT

1907   German composer Gustav Mahler's Symphony no. 8 in E-flat Major (*The Symphony of a Thousand*) is presented.   MUSIC

1907   Hungarian composer Franz Lehár's operetta *The Merry Widow* opens in New York to great success.   MUSIC

1907–1908   Austrian painter Gustav Klimt paints *The Kiss*.   PAINT

1907   The first exhibition of cubist works is held in Paris. Spearheaded by Spanish painter Pablo Picasso and French painter Georges Braque, the movement uses abstract geometric shapes to represent subjects. Other cubist painters will include Juan Gris, Fernand Léger, Roger de La Fresnaye, and Robert Delaunay. The cubist movement will end with World War I.   PAINT

1907   American painter and illustrator Rockwell Kent paints *Winter, Monhegan Island*. PAINT

1907   American photographer Alfred Stieglitz demonstrates his "straight," modern approach in the photograph *The Steerage*, from a trip to Europe. He will also

---

The First Movie Star

The first American movie star to be known to the public by name is today hardly remembered. Florence Lawrence (1886–1938) of Ontario, Canada, became a popular favorite in U.S. films by D. W. Griffith and others produced by the Biograph Company. But despite lead roles in such features as *Salomé, The Zulu's Heart, The Viking's Daughter, An Awful Moment,* and *Antony and Cleopatra* (all 1908), she was known to audiences only as the Biograph Girl. Movie studios of that era declined to identify actors by name lest they demand higher wages.

In 1910 upstart movie producer Carl Laemmle, who later founded Universal Pictures, lured Lawrence from Biograph to his own studio, IMP (Independent Motion Picture Company of America). In a publicity stunt, Laemmle circulated rumors that the Biograph Girl was dead, then debunked the story himself, stating in an advertisement that "enemies" of IMP were responsible for the tale. The ad reported that Florence Lawrence, formerly the Biograph Girl, was not only alive but was now the "Imp Girl," soon to star in her first IMP picture, *The Broken Oath*.

With one actress having been given a name, there was no going back. It became common practice for movie performers to be known by name, and silent film stars such as Mary Pickford, Douglas Fairbanks, and Charlie Chaplin were soon commanding enormous salaries, just as the studios had feared.

As for Florence Lawrence, her star faded when she was seriously hurt in a movie stunt in 1914 and forced to withdraw from movies for several years. A comeback attempt in the early 1920s failed, and by the 1930s she was working only as an extra. She committed suicide at age 52.

become known for his hundreds of photographs of his wife, American painter Georgia O'Keeffe. PHOTO

1908   The plastic Bakelite is developed by American L. H. Baekeland. First commercially manufactured in 1909, it will become a popular base for jewelry over the next several years. DECO

1908   British novelist Ford Madox Ford founds the journal *The English Review*, which publishes work by Thomas Hardy, Henry James, D. H. Lawrence, Wyndham Lewis, and H. G. Wells. LIT

1908   British novelist E. M. Forster publishes *A Room with a View*. LIT

1908   American novelist Henry James publishes the novel *The Princess Casamassima*. LIT

1908–1923   American essayist and journalist H. L. Mencken coedits the national periodical *The Smart Set* and establishes a journalistic reputation throughout the United States. LIT

1908   The ashcan school of artistic realism is founded in Philadelphia by American artist Robert Henri, with colleagues George Bellows, William Glackens, George Luks, Everett Shinn, and John Sloan. It will be popular until World War I. PAINT

1908   The building of the Musée Royal de l'Afrique Centrale is completed in Tervueren, Belgium, just outside of Brussels. It will contain the greatest collection of Congolese artifacts for artists to study. SCULP

1908   In India, an art object called the Reliquary of Kanishka is discovered. In the way it incorporates a number of artistic styles, it represents the cosmopolitan sensibility of the Kushan empire (78–144). SCULP

1909   The opera-ballet *The Golden Cockerel*, by Russian composer Nikolay Rimsky-Korsakov, is posthumously produced in Moscow. DANCE

1909   Russia's Sergey Diaghilev premieres his Ballet Russe in Paris, introducing the Russian tradition to the United States and Europe, and ushering in modern ballet. DANCE

1909   Swedish playwright August Strindberg writes the autobiographical drama *Stora Landsvägen* (*The Great Highway*), his last play. DRAMA

1909–1915   American composer Charles Ives writes Piano Sonata no. 2, *Concord, Mass. 1840–1860*. Key and time signatures and bar lines are omitted in parts of the piece, which includes four movements named for New England authors, "Emerson," "Hawthorne," "The Alcotts," and "Thoreau." MUSIC

1909	The opera *Elektra*, by German composer Richard Strauss, a story of hate and murder set to brutal and violent music, opens in Dresden. MUSIC
1909	Austrian-born American composer Arnold Schoenberg composes his atonal Three Piano Pieces, Op. 11. MUSIC
c. 1909–1910	Austrian painter Oskar Kokoschka paints "psychological" portraits that reflect the subject's inner being while also producing highly original lithographs and posters. PAINT
1909	Italian writer Filippo Thommaso Marinetti publishes the *Futurist Manifesto*, in which he advocates a new kind of Italian art celebrating modern mechanization, dynamism, and speed. Painters associated with futurism will include Umberto Boccioni, Carlo Carrà, Giacomo Balla, Luigi Russolo, and Gino Severini. A futurist exhibition will be held in Paris in 1912. PAINT
1909–1914	French painter Maurice Utrillo is in his white period, characterized by light tones in his paintings and considered by many his most fertile period. PAINT
1909	Spanish artist Pablo Picasso leaves the Bateau-Lavoir and settles in a studio on the Boulevard de Clichy. There he will make his first cubist sculptures, including a bronze portrait of his companion Fernande Olivier. SCULP
1909–1910	Romanian sculptor Constantin Brancusi and Italian sculptor Amedeo Modigliani work together in Paris. Influenced by African and Asian carving styles, dedicated to simple, almost abstract form, Brancusi will influence later artists, not least by reviving the physical art of carving. SCULP
1910s	In the United States and Europe, the South American dance called the tango gains popularity. DANCE
1910s	Tin Pan Alley, the New York base for popular songwriting and publishing, begins to thrive. Its denizens, including Irving Berlin, Sammy Cahn, and Jerome Kern, will dominate American popular music for half a century. MUSIC
1910s	German sculptor Wilhelm Lehmbruck combines elements of Gothic elongation with Rodin's expressive energy for a series of looming monumental figures. SCULP
1910	Russian composer Igor Stravinsky's ballet *The Firebird* meets with enthusiastic response when it premieres in Paris. DANCE
1910	*Chantecler*, the last produced play by French playwright Edmond Rostand, is produced. Some critics regard it as his finest work. DRAMA

1910   *Justice*, a drama critical of England's prison system by British novelist and play-wright John Galsworthy, premieres. *Loyalties*, a Galsworthy play exploring anti-Semitism, will be produced in 1922.   DRAMA

1910   *The Guardsman*, a play by Hungarian playwright Ferenc Molnár, premieres. It will be revived frequently in the years to come. Molnár's *Lilies* had been pro-duced in 1909; it will serve as the basis for the American musical *Carousel* (1945).   DRAMA

1910   American cartoonist John Randolph Bray patents the cel process for film ani-mation.   FILM

1910   Irish poet and dramatist William Butler Yeats publishes the collection *The Green Helmet and Other Poems*, which includes "No Second Troy," "The Fascination of What's Difficult," and "The Coming of Wisdom with Time."   LIT

1910   British novelist E. M. Forster publishes *Howards End*, memorable for its epi-graph, "Only connect . . ."   LIT

c. 1910–   Expressionist music, written in a deeply subjective and introspective style, reach-
1929   es its height in the works of such Austrian composers as Arnold Schoenberg and Alban Berg.   MUSIC

1910   British composer Ralph Vaughan Williams presents the orchestral work *Fantasia on a Theme by Thomas Tallis* for strings, and the choral work *A Sea Symphony*.
                                                                                            MUSIC

1910   Operas of the year include Italian composer Giacomo Puccini's *The Girl of the Golden West* and French composer Jules Massenet's *Don Quichotte*.   MUSIC

1910   American composer Victor Herbert writes his best-known score, for the Broadway show *Naughty Marietta*. Many of its songs, including "Tramp, Tramp, Tramp," and "Ah, Sweet Mystery of Life" will become musical standards.   MUSIC

1910   French painter Henri Rousseau paints *The Dream*.   PAINT

1910–1913   Russian painter Wassily Kandinsky completes the first entirely abstract, or nonrepresentational, paintings: *Compositions*, *Improvisations*, and *Impressions*. Abstract art will become a major force in 20th-century painting.   PAINT

1910–1912   British critic and painter Roger Fry introduces Britain to the works of promi-nent modern painters Paul Cézanne, Henri Matisse, and Vincent van Gogh, among others, at post-impressionist exhibitions in British galleries.   PAINT

1910   German ethnographer Leo Frobenuis discovers a number of lifelike terra-cotta sculptures in the Yoruban center of Ife in Nigeria.   SCULP

1911   American architect Frank Lloyd Wright designs his home, Taliesin, in Spring Green, Wisconsin. It will be rebuilt twice.   ARCH

1911   Russian composer Igor Stravinsky's ballet *Pétrouchka* opens in Paris. Its novel rhythm and harmony, vivid colors, and subtle characterization contribute to its impact.   DANCE

1911   British dancer Vernon Castle marries American dancer Irene Foot, thus entering into a dance partnership that will spawn several popular dances, including the Castle walk and the hesitation waltz.   DANCE

1911   Irish-born British playwright George Bernard Shaw's satire *Fanny's First Play* is produced. A send-up of several contemporary British drama critics, it is Shaw's first significant commercial success. *Androcles and the Lion* will follow in 1913.

DRAMA

1911   British novelist Joseph Conrad publishes *Under Western Eyes*.   LIT

1911   American novelist Theodore Dreiser publishes the controversial novel *Jennie Gerhardt,* about the conflicts faced by a young German immigrant woman who becomes pregnant out of wedlock.   LIT

1911   American novelist Edith Wharton publishes *Ethan Frome,* the tragedy of the married couple Ethan and Zenobia Frome and Zenobia's cousin Mattie.   LIT

1911–1913   German composer Anton Webern, a follower of Austrian-born American composer Arnold Schoenberg, composes his strictly atonal *Five Orchestral Pieces,* Op. 10, with the longest piece lasting a minute and the shortest being fewer than seven measures. Webern's works become the basis for later serial music.   MUSIC

1911   German composer Gustav Mahler's *Das Lied von der Erde* (*The Song of the Earth*) is presented posthumously in Munich.   MUSIC

1911   German composer Richard Strauss's comic opera *Der Rosenkavalier* (*The Knight of the Rose*) opens in Dresden.   MUSIC

1911   Prolific American composer Irving Berlin (born Israel Baline) writes his first international song success, "Alexander's Ragtime Band." His first published song was "Marie from Sunny Italy" in 1907.   MUSIC

1911	The German expressionist group Der Blaue Reiter ("The Blue Horseman") is founded in Munich by Wassily Kandinsky, Franz Marc, Paul Klee, and August Macke; it will be dissolved by 1914. PAINT
1911	French painter Georges Braque paints the cubist work *The Portuguese,* the first painting to incorporate stenciled lettering. PAINT
1911	French painter Henri Matisse paints *The Red Studio.* PAINT
1911–1912	Dutch painter Piet Mondrian completes *Flowering Apple Tree,* a series of paintings in which the subject becomes less representational, reflecting the artist's interest in abstract art and cubism. PAINT
1911	German sculptor Ernst Barlach travels to Russia and studies the simple forms of the preindustrial age. He decides not to carve his *Man Drawing a Sword* completely free from a massive block of wood. SCULP
1912	Gerhart Hauptmann, considered the preeminent playwright of German naturalism, is awarded the Nobel Prize for literature. His dramas include *Vor Sonnenaufgang* (*Before Dawn,* 1889) and *Die Weber* (*The Weavers,* 1892). DRAMA
1912	In the United States film attendance reaches 5 million patrons daily. FILM
1912	African-American poet and novelist James Weldon Johnson publishes the novel *The Autobiography of an Ex-Coloured Man,* about a light-skinned African-American who passes for Caucasian. The book is originally published anonymously. LIT
1912	American publisher Harriet Monroe founds the literary magazine *Poetry* in Chicago. It will grow to have wide influence in the literary community. LIT
1912	American poet Robinson Jeffers publishes his first collection of poems *Flagons and Apples.* Later collections will include *Dear Judas* (1929), *Such Counsels You Gave to Me* (1937), and *Be Angry at the Sun* (1941). LIT
1912	Indian writer Rabindranath Tagore publishes the poetry collection *Gitanjali.* The prolific author's works include poetry, philosophy, fiction, drama, and essays. LIT
1912	Austrian-born American composer Arnold Schoenberg's melodramatic song cycle *Pierrot Lunaire* for singing narrator and chamber orchestra, is presented in Berlin. MUSIC

1912–1938	British-born conductor Leopold Stokowski becomes chief conductor of the Philadelphia Symphony Orchestra. During his final two seasons, he will share his position with Eugene Ormandy. MUSIC
1912	Synthetic cubism supersedes the earlier phase of cubism, known as analytic cubism. Unlike the earlier phase, which concentrated on geometric form rather than color, the new phase, typified by Spanish painter Juan Gris (pseudonym of José González), makes use of color, decorative shapes, and collage. PAINT
1913	Designed by American architect Cass Gilbert, the Woolworth Building in New York City is constructed. The 792-foot building celebrates the five-and-ten cent store empire of Frank W. Woolworth. ARCH
1913	Russian composer Igor Stravinsky's ballet *Le Sacre du printemps* (*The Rite of Spring*) is produced in Paris. With its harsh sound and wild rhythms, it causes a storm of indignation at its first performance. DANCE
1913	Indian writer Rabindranath Tagore is awarded the Nobel Prize for Literature, the same year that his play *Dakaghan* (*The Post Office*) is produced. Tagore's *Visarjana* (*Sacrifice*) was produced in 1890. DRAMA
1913	British novelist Joseph Conrad publishes *Chance*. LIT
1913	British novelist D. H. Lawrence publishes the autobiographical novel *Sons and Lovers*. LIT
1913	In London British social reformers Sidney and Beatrice Webb found the political periodical *The New Statesman*, which will become highly influential in the coming decades. LIT
1913	American novelist Willa Cather publishes the novel *O Pioneers!* about Swedish settlers, primarily Alexandra Bergson, and their experiences in the new land of Nebraska. LIT
1913	American poet Joyce Kilmer publishes the poem "Trees" in *Poetry* magazine. The poem gains wide popularity; it is the center of his collection *Trees and Other Poems* (1914). LIT
1913	American novelist Henry James publishes the historical essay *Mont-Saint-Michel and Chartres*, a study of the unity of the medieval world as seen through Chartres cathedral and the Abbey Church at Mont-Saint-Michel. The book was printed privately in 1904. LIT
1913–1920	American poet Vachel Lindsay establishes himself through the publication of several collections during the decade: *General William Booth Enters into Heaven*

and Other Poems (1913); The Congo and Other Poems (1914); The Chinese Nightingale and Other Poems (1917); and The Golden Whales of California and Other Rhymes (1920). 									LIT

1913–1927 	French novelist Marcel Proust publishes the novel À la recherche du temps perdu (Remembrance of Things Past) about the nature of time and memory. 		LIT

1913 	Spanish philosopher and writer Miguel de Unamuno y Jugo publishes the meditative treatise Del sentimiento trágico de la vida en los hombres y los pueblos (The Tragic Sense of Life). Among his novels is Niebla (Mist, A Tragicomic Novel, 1914). 									LIT

1913 	French painter Georges Braque invents papier collé, a variety of collage in which pieces of decorative paper are incorporated into a painting. 		PAINT

1913 	Italian futurist painter and sculptor Umberto Boccioni paints Dynamism of a Cyclist. 									PAINT

1913 	French painter Marcel Duchamp completes his second version of Nude Descending a Staircase, combining elements of cubism and futurism. 		PAINT

1913 	The Armory Show in New York City introduces post-impressionist and cubist works to the American audience. 							PAINT

1913 	Italian futurist painter and sculptor Umberto Boccioni attempts to represent the motion of the human form and not the figure itself in his bronze sculpture Unique Forms of Continuity in Space. 						SCULP

1914–1917 	The Lincoln Memorial is designed by American architect Henry Bacon and built in Washington, D.C. It houses a massive statue of President Lincoln designed by American sculptor Daniel Chester French. 			ARCH

1914 	Irish-born British playwright George Bernard Shaw's play Pygmalion is produced. It will form the basis for the popular American musical My Fair Lady (see 1956, DRAMA). Shaw's Heartbreak House will be produced in 1920. He will be awarded the 1925 Nobel Prize for literature. 			DRAMA

1914 	Irish poet and dramatist William Butler Yeats publishes the collection Responsibilities, which includes the poems "The Grey Rock," "The Hour Before Dawn," "The Magi," "The Dolls," and "A Coat." 				LIT

1914 	British novelist Thomas Hardy publishes Satires of Circumstance, Lyrics and Reveries, which includes the elegiac "Poems of 1912–1913" written in memory of his wife Emma. 							LIT

1914	Irish writer James Joyce publishes *Dubliners*, an evocative collection of short stories about life in and around his native Dublin. LIT
1914	American poet Robert Frost publishes the collection *North of Boston*, which contains such well-known poems as "Mending Wall," "Home Burial," and "Death of the Hired Man." LIT
1914	In *Poetry* magazine American poet Carl Sandburg publishes what will come to be his most famous poem, *Chicago*, ode to the "Hog Butcher for the World." LIT
1914	Chilean poet Gabriela Mistral (pen name of Lucila Godoy Alcayaga) publishes the collection *Sonetos de la muerte*. Her later works will include *Ternura* (1924) and *Tala* (1938). LIT
1914	American writer Edgar Rice Burroughs publishes the first of his approximately 30 Tarzan books, *Tarzan of the Apes*. *See also* 1932, FILM. LIT
1914	British composer Ralph Vaughan Williams composes *A London Symphony* (Symphony no. 2), which combines the extroverted energy of Edward Elgar with poetic contemplation. MUSIC
1914	The American Society of Composers, Authors and Publishers (ASCAP) is founded by American composer Victor Herbert for the purpose of protecting copyright and performing rights. MUSIC
1914–1917	Popular World War I songs include George M. Cohan's "Over There," Ivor Novello's "Keep the Home Fires Burning," and Jack Judge's "Tipperary." MUSIC
1914	American composer W. C. Handy publishes his song "The St. Louis Blues," which helps to define the blues as a musical genre. MUSIC
1914	Spanish painter Juan Gris, a pioneer of synthetic cubism, uses papier collé in *The Sunblind*. PAINT
1914	Italian painter Giorgio de Chirico, inventor of metaphysical painting, which emphasizes dream imagery and irrationality, paints *The Mystery and Melancholy of a Street*. PAINT
1914	Following a trip to Tunisia, Swiss painter Paul Klee decides to abandon most of his work in black and white and pursue work in color. PAINT
1915	American architect Frank Lloyd Wright designs the Imperial Hotel in Tokyo. ARCH
1915	The Cleveland Play House, which in the 1920s will become America's first nonprofit professional regional theater, opens in Cleveland, Ohio. DRAMA

1915	D. W. Griffith's Civil War epic *The Birth of a Nation*, based on the Thomas Dixon work *The Clansman* and starring Lillian Gish, helps to establish filmmaking as a serious art. Its exaltation of the Ku Klux Klan make it perenially controversial. FILM
1915	American silent film actress Theda Bara, who will create the image of the vamp, has her first starring role, in *A Fool There Was*. FILM
1915	British novelist Joseph Conrad publishes *Victory*. LIT
1915	British novelist D. H. Lawrence publishes *The Rainbow*, which is banned for indecency. LIT
1915	British poet Rupert Brooke's five war sonnets, including "The Soldier," are published. LIT
1915	British novelist Ford Madox Ford publishes the novel *The Good Soldier*. LIT
1915	British novelist Virginia Woolf publishes her first novel, *The Voyage Out*. LIT
1915	American poet Edgar Lee Masters publishes *Spoon River Anthology*. LIT
1915–1916	American poet Robert Frost publishes the poem "The Road Not Taken," which ends, "I took the one less traveled by / And that has made all the difference." LIT
1915–1923	American poet Wallace Stevens writes the poem "Sunday Morning." The sensual and complex poem about a woman at breakfast on Sunday morning will become one of Stevens's most praised works. LIT
1915	Austrian novelist and short-story writer Franz Kafka writes the story "The Metamorphosis," about a man, Gregor Samsa, who awakens to find himself transformed into a cockroach. Among his later works will be the novels *The Castle* (1922) and *The Trial* (1925). LIT
1915	English novelist and short-story writer Somerset Maugham publishes the novel *Of Human Bondage*. Among his later novels will be *The Moon and Sixpence* (1919), *Cakes and Ale* (1930), and *The Razor's Edge* (1944). His short story "Miss Thompson" (1921) will introduce the character of "loose" woman Sadie Thompson. LIT
1915	The neoclassical German composer Max Reger composes *Mozart Variations*. MUSIC
1915	A vorticist exhibition is held in Britain. The avant-garde British arts movement, influenced by Italian futurism, has writer Wyndham Lewis as its principal spokesperson. Painters associated with it include C. R. W. Nevinson and William Roberts. PAINT

1915 French painter Marc Chagall paints *The Birthday*. PAINT

1915 The Dadaist movement is founded in Zurich and New York by a group of disillusioned American and European artists, including Romanian poet Tristan Tzara and French painters Hans Arp and Marcel Duchamp. Rooted in the cynicism of the First World War, Dada is devoted to the pursuit of antiart and illogic. The word *Dada* is French for hobby horse. PAINT

1915 Romanian sculptor Constantin Brancusi sculpts *Le Nouveau-Né*. SCULP

1916 *Theatre Arts*, a periodical which will run serious articles on a variety of theater-related topics, is founded in Detroit. It will merge with *The Stage* in 1948 and the resulting publication will be in business until 1964. DRAMA

1916 Notable films include D. W. Griffith's *Intolerance*, Charlie Chaplin's *The Pawn Shop*, and Thomas Ince's *Civilization* (all U.S.). FILM

1916 Irish writer James Joyce publishes the autobiographical novel *A Portrait of the Artist as a Young Man*. It was first published in American poet Ezra Pound's journal *The Egoist* in 1914 and 1915. LIT

1916 A year before his death in combat during World War I, British critic, biographer, and nature writer Edward Thomas publishes his first book of poetry. Like his posthumous volumes published in 1917 and 1918, it is admired for its subtlety and intensity. LIT

1916–1951 American poet Carl Sandburg publishes a number of collections of expressive, inclusive American poetry: *Chicago Poems* (1916); *Cornhuskers* (1918); *Smoke and Steel* (1920); *Slabs of the Sunburnt West* (1922); *Good Morning, America* (1928); *The People, Yes* (1936); and *Collected Poems* (1951). LIT

1916 Spanish novelist Vicente Blasco Ibáñez publishes *The Four Horsemen of the Apocalypse*. LIT

1916 Spanish composer Manuel de Falla debuts his symphonic impressions, *Noches en los jardines de España* (*Nights in the Gardens of Spain*) in Madrid. MUSIC

1916 British composer Gustav Holst composes the programmatic suite *The Planets* for orchestra, organ, and women's chorus. MUSIC

1916–1937 French painter Georges Rouault paints *The Old King*, the color shapes and black outlines of which reflect his early training in making stained glass. PAINT

1916 Russian sculptors and brothers Naum (Pevsner) Gabo and Antoine Pevsner breathe new life into constructivism, a movement founded by Vladimir Tatlin

c. 1913, when they create architectonic works that betray the influences of technology, cubism, and futurism.   SCULP

1917   Spanish painter Pablo Picasso and French designer Jean Cocteau design costumes and scenery for the Russian art critic and impresario Sergey Diaghilev's ballet *Parade*, one of several Diaghilev works to which they will contribute.

DANCE

c.1917   Dutch architect Gerrit Thomas Rietveld designs a chair that appears light and dematerialized.   DECO

1917–1921   German-born artist George Grosz completes a series of satirical drawings, *The Face of the Ruling Class*.   GRAPH

1917   American-born British poet T. S. Eliot publishes "The Love Song of J. Alfred Prufrock," a meditation on, among other subjects, the futility of existence in modern times.   LIT

1917   American poet Edna St. Vincent Millay publishes what will become one of her most noteworthy poetry collections, *Renascence*.   LIT

1917–1948   American poet Ezra Pound publishes the first three *Cantos*, a series of poems that he will continue to write and publish through the 1960s. *A Draft of XXX Cantos* will be published in 1933, *Eleven New Cantos* in 1934, and *Pisan Cantos, LXXI to LXXXV* in 1948.   LIT

1917   French symbolist poet Paul Valéry publishes the work *La Jeune Parque*. Among his later works will be the monologues "Le Cimetière Marin" and "Fragments du Narcisse," collected in the book *Charmes* (1922).   LIT

1917   German composer Hans Pfitzner's opera *Palestrina* is produced in Munich.   MUSIC

1917   Russian composer Sergey Prokofiev composes *Classical Symphony* no. 1 in D.   MUSIC

1917   French composers Georges Auric, Louis Durey, Arthur Honegger, Darius Milhaud, Francis Poulenc, and Germaine Tailleferre form the group eventually known as Les Six. Reacting against the vagueness of impressionism, they endorse the simplicity and clarity of the neoclassical movement.   MUSIC

1917   Dutch painters Piet Mondrian and Theo van Doesburg cofound the arts magazine and movement *De Stijl*. Mondrian begins to paint his works in geometric shapes and a mix of primary colors, black, white, and gray. He names the artistic theory behind his compositions neo-plasticism.   PAINT

1917   French artist Marcel Duchamp sends a urinal listed as "an enameled pottery piece called *Fountain*" to the first exhibit of the Society of Independents in New York. The jury will reject Duchamp's submission. He will continue to exhibit manufactured objects, or "ready-mades," as an intellectual challenge to traditional concepts of painting and sculpture. Such actions will help define the "antiart" character of the Dada movement.   SCULP

1917   In the United States, amplitude modulation (AM) radio is pioneered through the development of a superheterodyne circuit by Army Signal Corps officer Edwin Armstrong.   TV&R

1918   American architect Frank Lloyd Wright designs the Robie house in Chicago, a classic example of his prairie style, conceived in terms of low horizontal lines and abstract blocks.   ARCH

1918   In Germany architect Walter Gropius founds the Bauhaus, a school that seeks to unify the arts within the world of architecture in the service of the mass-production needs of the modern age. He will leave the Bauhaus in 1928.   ARCH

1918   The Yiddish Art Theatre opens in New York City. Through the late 1930s, it will present high-quality Jewish theater.   DRAMA

1918   Notable films include Abel Gance's *The Tenth Symphony* (France), Charlie Chaplin's *A Dog's Life* (U.S.), and Ernst Lubitsch's *Carmen* (Germany).   FILM

1918   American cartoonist Winsor McCay creates what may be the first feature-length animated film, *The Sinking of the Lusitania*. Notable McCay shorts of the time include *Gertie the Dinosaur* (1914) and *Little Nemo* (1911).   FILM

1918   British poet and editor Robert Bridges publishes a collection of his late friend British poet Gerard Manley Hopkins's work. Unpublished in Hopkins's lifetime, the poems, which include "Pied Beauty," "God's Grandeur," "The Windhover," and "That Nature Is a Heraclitean Fire," gain praise from modernist critics and poets and come to exercise a wide influence.   LIT

1918   American novelist Willa Cather publishes *My Antonia*, a novel about Czech settlers in Nebraska, particularly a woman named Antonia Shimerda.   LIT

1918   American historian Henry Adams publishes *The Education of Henry Adams*. Written in the third person, it is as much a search for a unified vision of the age as an ironic examination of his life. The chapter "The Dynamo and the Virgin" will become accepted as a standard for the comparison of the unity of the past and the incomprehensible disarray of the modern age. The book was privately printed in 1907.   LIT

1918	Hungarian composer Béla Bartók's one-act opera *Bluebeard's Castle,* opens in Budapest. MUSIC
1918	French composer Erik Satie writes his serious symphonic drama *Socrate.* MUSIC
1918	In the final year of World War I, the New York Philharmonic Society bans compositions by living German composers. The German conductor of the Boston Symphony Orchestra, Karl Muck, is arrested as an enemy alien. MUSIC
1918	Russian painter Kasimir Malevich's *White on White,* a white square on a white background, is an exemplar of suprematism, a Russian abstract-art movement that he founded in 1913. Related to constructivism (*see* 1916, SCULP), suprematism intends to free art from the burden of representationalism altogether. PAINT
1918	Swiss architect Charles-Édouard Jeanneret, known as Le Corbusier, and French painter Amédée Ozenfant publish *Après le cubisme,* a treatise decrying the deterioration of synthetic cubism. The work is tied to the founding by the two men of the artistic movement known as purism. PAINT
1919	*Le Bourgmestre de Stilmonde,* which will be regarded as perhaps the finest drama by Belgian poet and playwright Maurice Maeterlinck, is produced. Maeterlinck won the Nobel Prize for literature in 1911. DRAMA
1919	The German horror film *Das Cabinett des Dr. Caligari* (*The Cabinet of Dr. Caligari*) opens. Directed by Robert Wiene, it draws from the German expressionist movement to define the aesthetic world of the horror film for decades to come. FILM
1919	Irish poet and dramatist William Butler Yeats publishes the collection *The Wild Swans at Coole,* which includes the title poem along with such works as "An Irish Airman Foresees His Death," "Upon a Dying Lady," "Ego Dominus Tuus," and "The Double Vision of Michael Robartes." LIT
1919	British novelist Virginia Woolf publishes the influential essay "Modern Fiction." LIT
1919–1948	American journalist and essayist H. L. Mencken publishes *The American Language,* a pioneering reference work and study of the differences between the English and American tongues. The work will see supplements in 1945 and 1948. LIT
1919	American novelist Sherwood Anderson publishes *Winesburg, Ohio,* a novel of linked tales about the repressed inhabitants of the eponymous town. LIT
1919	The Los Angeles Orchestra offers its first concert. MUSIC

1919	American jazz music becomes popular in Europe, with tours by jazz musicians like Paul Whiteman and Jelly Roll Morton and long-term engagements by Duke Ellington to follow in the coming decade. **MUSIC**
c.1919	Italian painter Amedeo Modigliani paints *Reclining Nude*. **PAINT**
1919	French painter Fernand Léger paints *The City*, a work influenced by synthetic cubism. **PAINT**
1919	French Dadaist painter Marcel Duchamp creates *L.H.O.O.Q.*, a reproduction of Italian artist Leonardo da Vinci's *Mona Lisa* with a mustache and goatee. **PAINT**
1919	More than 300 works of Swiss painter Paul Klee are exhibited in Germany by Munich art dealer Goltz. The exhibition establishes Klee as a painter of international importance. **PAINT**
1919	American painter George Bellows completes the portrait *Mrs. Chester Dale*. **PAINT**
1919	Romanian sculptor Constantin Brancusi strives to visualize abstract form in the bronze *Bird in Space*. **SCULP**
1920s	The Cotton Club becomes a popular night spot in Harlem, New York City. Featuring top black musical talent, it is open only to whites. **DANCE**
1920s	The Lindy hop, a fast-moving social dance named for American aviator Charles Lindbergh, becomes popular in the United States. **DANCE**
1920s	Latin American theater becomes more experimental and technically sophisticated. Though it still follows European trends, it focuses increasingly on themes and styles developed internally. **DRAMA**
1920s	American journalist and essayist H. L. Mencken edits the *American Mercury*, one of the most respected and influential periodicals of its day. **LIT**
1920s	Little magazines such as *Poetry*, *Story*, and *transition* are popular methods of introducing and nurturing new literary talent, and gain a wide readership. **LIT**
1920s	Several students at Vanderbilt University, including John Crowe Ransom, Allen Tate, Cleanth Brooks, and Robert Penn Warren, comprise an influential American literary circle that will become known as the fugitives, agrarians, or Nashville group. **LIT**
c. 1920s	The neoclassical movement in music fosters a return to aesthetic ideals and formal methods of the 17th and 18th centuries, recast in modern idioms. It is

represented by the works of such composers as Igor Stravinsky, Béla Bartók, and Paul Hindemith. MUSIC

1920s   Popular songs of the day include "Tea for Two," "Barney Google," "Bye, Bye Blackbird," "I Found a Million-Dollar Baby in the Five-and-Ten Cent Store," "Yes, We Have No Bananas," "Show Me the Way to Go Home," "Blue Skies," "Ol' Man River," "Makin' Whoopee," "Star Dust," and "Singin' in the Rain." MUSIC

1920s   French painter Raoul Dufy is active in popularizing modern art for larger audiences. PAINT

1920s   Beginning in this decade, American photographer Edward Steichen gains wide exposure as a portrait photographer for mass-market periodicals. Among his more well-known portraits will be *Greta Garbo* (1928), taken for *Vanity Fair*, which captures her elusive appeal. PHOTO

1920s   American photographer James Van Der Zee becomes a leading artist of the Harlem Renaissance with his telling, stately portraits of African-Americans. PHOTO

1920s   Hungarian-born constructivist painter and photographer László Moholy-Nagy experiments with expressions of time, space, and imagination through the creation of photograms, which involves removing the camera lens before exposing the photographic paper to light. PHOTO

1920s   American artist Man Ray creates the Rayogram, a collage of objects placed onto photographic paper and exposed to light. PHOTO

1920s   Blackfoot artist Hart Merriam Schultz, working under the name Lone Wolf, is one of the first 20th-centuryNative American artists to produce sculpture. SCULP

1920   French composer Maurice Ravel completes the dance poem for orchestra *La Valse*, which uses the waltz form to portray the transition from pre-World War I social elegance to postwar decline. DANCE

1920   Russian composer Igor Stravinsky's ballets *Pulcinella* and *Le Chant du rossignol* (*The Song of the Nightingale*) are produced at the Paris Opera. DANCE

1920   In Los Angeles American dancer Ruth St. Denis and her husband, dancer Ted Shawn, form the influential Denishawn school of dance. DANCE

1920   *El maleficio de la mariposa* (*The Butterfly's Curse*), the first full-length play by Spanish poet and playwright Federico García Lorca, is produced. Lorca's historical drama *Mariana Pineda* will be produced in 1927. His comedy *La zapatera prodigiosa* (*The Shoemaker's Amazing Wife*) will be produced in 1930. DRAMA

1920   *Beyond the Horizon*, the first full-length play by American playwright Eugene
                O'Neill, is produced on Broadway. It will win the Pulitzer Prize. O'Neill's *The
                Emperor Jones*, a drama featuring a black protagonist, is also produced this year.
                                                                                    DRAMA

1920   Notable films include Paul Wegener and Carl Boese's *The Golem* (Germany)
                and Paul Powell's *Pollyanna* (U.S.), starring Mary Pickford.   FILM

1920   British novelist D. H. Lawrence publishes *Women in Love*. Like *The Rainbow*
                (1915), it explores human relationships with great psychological and poetic
                power.   LIT

1920   A collection of British poet Wilfrid Owen's poems is published posthumous-
                ly, following his death in combat during World War I.   LIT

1920   American poet Ezra Pound publishes the influential poem about war and art,
                "Hugh Selwyn Mauberley."   LIT

1920   American novelist Sinclair Lewis publishes his satire of middle-class midwest-
                ern existence, *Main Street*.   LIT

1920   American novelist F. Scott Fitzgerald publishes his first novel, *This Side of
                Paradise,* and first collection of short stories, *Flappers and Philosophers.* This year
                he marries Southern beauty Zelda Sayre. The two will become one of the most
                talked-about literary couples of the 20th century.   LIT

1920   American novelist Edith Wharton publishes *The Age of Innocence*, a novel of
                manners set in upper-class New York in the 1870s that tells of the unfulfilled
                love between Newland Archer and Countess Ellen Olenska. The book will win
                the Pulitzer Prize.   LIT

1920–1922   Norwegian novelist Sigrid Undset, who will be awarded the 1928 Nobel Prize
                for literature, publishes the saga *Kristin Lavransdatter*. Her later works will include
                The Snake Pit.   LIT

c.1920   The German word *kitsch*, meaning "vulgar trash," gains use to denote inau-
                thentic or highly commercial artistic creations from souvenirs to paintings.   PAINT

1920   In Canada the association of painters known as the Group of Seven is formed.
                The members, who will develop Canada's first distinctive national movement
                in painting, include Franklin Carmichael, Lawren Harris, A. Y. Jackson, Frank
                Johnston, Arthur Lismer, J. E. H. Macdonald, and Frederick Varley. Their work
                is heavily influenced by the expressionist movement.   PAINT

1920–1970   Hungarian-born photographer André Kertész practices photography. His work, such as *Blind Musician* (1921), will be highly informed by the work of French photographer Eugène Atget.   PHOTO

1920   Soviet painter and sculptor Vladimir Tatlin completes his model for a monument to the Third International that is meant to have a height of more than 1,300 feet. Though the monument is never built, Tatlin's ambitious model, combining painting, sculpture, architecture, and technology, represents the high point of the constructivist movement that he founded in 1913.   SCULP

1920   On November 2 KDKA in Pittsburgh, Pennsylvania, becomes the first radio broadcasting station in the world. Developed by Westinghouse engineer Frank Conrad, its first broadcasts are the result of the 1920 U.S. presidential election, in which Warren G. Harding is elected.   TV&R

1921   *Shuffle Along*, the first all-black Broadway musical, opens to critical acclaim. The show helps to usher in the period of African-American artistic flowering known as the Harlem Renaissance.   DANCE

1921   *Sei personaggi in cerca d'autore (Six Characters in Search of an Author)*, by Italian playwright Luigi Pirandello, is produced in Rome. It will become his most famous play.   DRAMA

1921   *The Circle*, perhaps the best play by British novelist and playwright Somerset Maugham, premieres. Other notable plays of his will include *The Constant Wife* (produced in 1926), *The Sacred Flame* (1928), *The Breadwinner* (1930), and *For Service Rendered* (1932).   DRAMA

1921   Sir John Gielgud, who will be considered one of the greatest British actors of the 20th century, makes his debut at the Old Vic. The grandnephew of actress Ellen Terry (*see* 1856, DRAMA), he will be best known for his Shakespearean roles—especially Hamlet, probably his best role of all—and for his performances as Trigorin in Chekhov's *The Seagull* (1956), as Raskolnikoff in an adaptation of Dostoyevsky's *Crime and Punishment* (1946), and in Harold Pinter's *No Man's Land* (1975). He will also be a director and a repertory company manager, and appear memorably as a character player in films.   DRAMA

1921   *Anna Christie*, a feminist drama by American playwright Eugene O'Neill, is produced. The story of a prostitute and a crude sailor transformed by their love for one another, it will earn O'Neill his second Pulitzer Prize.   DRAMA

1921   Notable films include Charlie Chaplin's *The Kid*, D. W. Griffith's *Dream Street*, and Rex Ingram's *Four Horsemen of the Apocalypse* (all U.S.).   FILM

1921   Irish poet and dramatist William Butler Yeats, who will be awarded the 1923 Nobel Prize for literature, publishes the collection *Michael Robartes and the Dancer*, which includes the title poem along with such works as "Easter, 1916," "A Prayer for My Daughter," and "A Meditation in Time of War." Also included is the poem "The Second Coming," from which come the lines, "Things fall apart; the centre cannot hold" and "And what rough beast, its hour come round at last, / Slouches toward Bethlehem to be born?"   LIT

1921   British novelist D. H. Lawrence publishes the nonfiction work *Psychoanalysis and the Unconscious.*   LIT

1921   American novelist Willa Cather publishes *One of Ours,* a Pulitzer Prize-winning novel of a family death in World War I.   LIT

1921–1961   American poet Marianne Moore publishes her first collection of poetry, *Poems.* Subsequent collections will include *Observations* (1924), *What Are Years?* (1941), and *Collected Poems* (1951), for which she will win the Pulitzer Prize.   LIT

1921   Austrian playwright, novelist, and poet Franz Werfel completes the play *Bocksgesang* (*Goat Song*). His later works will include the play *Juarez* (1924) and the novel *The Song of Bernadette* (1941), which will be the basis of a film.   LIT

1921   Russian composer Sergey Prokofiev's farcical opera *The Love for Three Oranges,* produced in Chicago, is his first great operatic success.   MUSIC

1921   Italian conductor Arturo Toscanini opens the remodeled Teatro alla Scala, Milan.   MUSIC

1921   Italian tenor Enrico Caruso dies on August 2 in Naples, where he was born in 1873. His career as an opera singer began in 1894 and took off in 1898, when he sang lead tenor in Giordano's *Fedora* at Teatro Lirico in Milan; he made his La Scala debut in 1900 in *La Bohème,* his London debut in *Rigoletto* at Covent Garden in 1902 and his American debut in *Rigoletto* at the Metropolitan Opera in 1903. Although his work, which extended to some French operas but rarely to German ones, was highly acclaimed in Europe and Latin America, he was most successful performing in Italian operas for American audiences.   MUSIC

1921   Spanish painter Pablo Picasso paints the synthetic cubist work *Three Musicians.*   PAINT

1921   French cubist painter Georges Braque completes *Still Life with Guitar.* One of his many still-life paintings, it is an early example of his post–World War I aesthetic variance from friend and colleague Spanish painter Pablo Picasso, with whom he founded cubism.   PAINT

1921–1924   German painter Max Ernst paints *The Elephant Célébes*, a work that will be regarded as surrealist after the founding of that movement in 1924.   PAINT

1921   American photographer Lewis Hine takes the photograph *Steamfitter*, one of his many photos of children and adults at work.   PHOTO

1922   American playwright Anne Nichols's comedy *Abie's Irish Rose*, about an interfaith (Jewish-Christian) marriage, begins its long run (2,327 performances).   DRAMA

1922   *Trommeln in der Nacht* (*Drums in the Night*), a drama by German playwright Bertolt Brecht, is produced. Brecht's *Im Dickicht der Städte* (*The Jungle of the Cities*) and *Mann ist Mann* (*A Man's a Man*) will be produced in 1923 and 1926, respectively.   DRAMA

1922   Italian playwright Luigi Pirandello's tragedy *Enrico IV* (*Henry IV*) is produced.   DRAMA

1922   *Back to Methuselah*, considered by Irish-born British playwright George Bernard Shaw to be his finest work, is produced.   DRAMA

1922   American playwright Eugene O'Neill's *The Hairy Ape*, an expressionistic drama exploring class conflict, is produced.   DRAMA

1922   Notable films include F. W. Murnau's *Nosferatu* (Germany); D. W. Griffith's *Orphans of the Storm* (U.S.); and Robert Flaherty's landmark documentary *Nanook of the North* (U.S.), which sets a standard for the genre.   FILM

1922   Banned as obscene in England and America, Irish writer James Joyce's *Ulysses* is published in Paris. The most prominent example of stream-of-consciousness technique, the novel details the adventures of Leopold Bloom and Stephen Dedalus in Dublin on a single day, June 16, 1904 (which will become known as "Bloomsday"). It alludes throughout to Greek poet Homer's epic poem *The Odyssey* (eighth century B.C.), the central character of which, Odysseus, is known in Latin as Ulysses.   LIT

1922   British novelist D. H. Lawrence publishes the novel *Aaron's Rod* and the short-story collection *England, My England*.   LIT

1922   British novelist and playwright John Galsworthy completes the sequence of novels known as *The Forsyte Saga*, which began in 1906 with *A Man of Property*.   LIT

1922   British novelist Virginia Woolf publishes *Jacob's Room*, her first experimental novel employing stream of consciousness and the first to be published by Hogarth Press, founded with her husband, Leonard Woolf.   LIT

1922	American-born British poet T. S. Eliot publishes *The Waste Land*. The complex epic poem will be considered by many his most accomplished work. LIT
1922	American novelist Sinclair Lewis publishes the novel *Babbitt*, a satiric indictment of the middle-class American businessman. Following publication of the novel the word "Babbitt" will come to be part of the American lexicon. LIT
1922–1928	American poet Edwin Arlington Robinson is awarded the Pulitzer Prize three times during the 1920s: for *Collected Poems* (1922), *The Man Who Died Twice* (1925), and *Tristram* (1928). LIT
1922	Under the guidance of American editors DeWitt and Lila Acheson Wallace, the *Reader's Digest* begins publication. It is meant to serve as a portable collection of articles from prominent periodicals. LIT
1922	English novelist Rebecca West publishes *The Judge*. Her later works will include *The Thinking Reed* (1936), *The Fountain Overflows* (1956), and the nonfiction work *Black Lamb and Grey Falcon* (1942), an examination of Yugoslavia. LIT
1922	German poet and novelist Hermann Hesse publishes the novel *Siddhartha*. Among his later works will be *Steppenwolf* (1929) and *Magister Ludi* (1943). He will be awarded the 1946 Nobel Prize for literature. LIT
1922	The International Society for Contemporary Music (I.S.C.M.) forms at Salzburg. Its headquarters will be established in London in 1923. MUSIC
1922	American jazz trumpeter and singer Louis Armstrong joins King Oliver's Creole Jazz Band in Chicago. He will join the Fletcher Henderson orchestra in 1924 and will make his first record, "Everybody Loves My Baby." MUSIC
1922	Swiss artist Paul Klee paints *Twittering Machine*. PAINT
1922	An international Dadaist exhibition is held in Paris, bringing together many European and American Dada artists. PAINT
1923	The Chicago Tribune Building is designed by architect Raymond Hood. ARCH
1923	*L'Uomo del fiore in bocca* (*The Man with a Flower in His Mouth*), a one-act drama about a cancer patient by Italian playwright Luigi Pirandello, is produced. His *Come tu mi vuoi* (*As You Desire Me*) and *Quando si è qualcuno* (*When One Is Somebody*) will be produced in 1930 and 1933, respectively. Pirandello will be awarded the 1934 Nobel Prize for literature. DRAMA
1923	*The Shadow of a Gunman*, the first play by Irish playwright Sean O'Casey, is produced at the Abbey Theatre in Dublin. DRAMA

1923   *Saint Joan*, a historical play by Irish-born British playwright George Bernard Shaw, is produced. Some critics will view this treatment of the legend of Joan of Arc as Shaw's finest play.   DRAMA

1923   American actors Alfred Lunt and Lynn Fontanne, married since 1922, appear together for the first time in American playwright Paul Kester's *Sweet Nell of Old Drury*. Later joint performances will include Ferenc Molnár's *The Guardsman* (1924) and Noel Coward's *Design for Living* (1933).   DRAMA

1923   *The Adding Machine*, an expressionistic fantasy play by American playwright Elmer Rice, is produced. His *Street Scene*, a realistic depiction of poverty, will be produced in 1929 and will win the Pulitzer Prize.   DRAMA

1923   Notable films include Harold Lloyd's *Why Worry*, Cecil B. De Mille's *The Ten Commandments*, and Allan Dwan's *Robin Hood*, starring Douglas Fairbanks (all U.S.).   FILM

1923   The Eastman Kodak Company introduces 16-millimeter film for amateur use. It will become the favorite medium for student, industrial, and educational films.   FILM

1923   Syrian writer Kahlil Gibran publishes *The Prophet*, an often translated and reprinted work of inspiration.   LIT

1923   American publisher Frank Gannett founds the Gannett Company, which unites four upstate New York newspapers and over the years will come to encompass many dozens more.   LIT

1923   American writer of the Harlem Renaissance Jean Toomer publishes *Cane*, a multigenre exploration of modern African-American life.   LIT

1923   American poet Robert Frost publishes the poem "Stopping by Woods on a Snowy Evening," about a traveler who has stopped to view the snow while remembering that he has "miles to go before I sleep."   LIT

1923   American poet Wallace Stevens publishes the poem "The Anecdote of the Jar," about a jar left on a hill in Tennessee. Employed for most of his life at a Connecticut insurance company, Stevens will publish a vast number of collections: *Harmonium* (1923); *Ideas of Order* (1935); *Owl's Clover* (1936); *The Man with a Blue Guitar and Other Poems* (1937); *Parts of a World* (1942); *Notes Toward a Supreme Fiction* (1942), and others.   LIT

1923   American poet William Carlos Williams publishes the four-stanza 16-word poem "The Red Wheelbarrow." It will become one of his best-known works.   LIT

1923   American poet e. e. cummings publishes his first collection of poetry, *Tulips and Chimneys*. Subsequent volumes will include *XLI Poems* (1925), *5* (1926), and *No thanks* (1935).   LIT

1923   The weekly newsmagazine *Time* is published for the first time on March 3 by American reporters Henry Luce and Briton Hadden. It will form the basis for a publishing empire and will set a standard for weekly news periodicals.   LIT

1923   Austrian-born American composer Arnold Schoenberg demonstrates his 12-tone technique in *Five Piano Pieces*, Op. 23, and the *Serenade for Seven Instruments and Bass Voice*, Op. 24.   MUSIC

1923   French composer Arthur Honegger debuts his symphonic poem *Pacific 231*, inspired by the movement of a locomotive.   MUSIC

1923   German composer Paul Hindemith composes the song cycle *Das Marienleben* (*The Life of Mary*) for piano and soprano.   MUSIC

1923   American jazz pianist, bandleader, and composer Duke Ellington moves from his native Washington, D.C., to New York City, where he organizes the first big-band jazz orchestra, comprising ten members by 1927, when he will begin headlining at the Cotton Club in Harlem. He will earn international recognition for his *Mood Indigo* in 1930.   MUSIC

1923   Spanish artist Pablo Picasso completes the paintings *Lady with a Blue Veil*, *Melancholy*, and *Women*.   PAINT

1924   Dutch architect Gerrit Thomas Rietveld designs Schroeder house in Utrecht. Its rectangular shapes and primary colors are characteristic of the De Stijl movement. *See* 1917, PAINT.   ARCH

1924   American historian and critic Lewis Mumford completes *Sticks and Bones*, a history of architecture.   ARCH

1924   The realistic tragedy *Juno and the Paycock*, the first major work by Irish playwright Sean O'Casey, is produced in Dublin.   DRAMA

1924   A department of drama is established at Yale University, with George Pierce Baker as its head. It will become a separate graduate school in 1955, which many will come to view as America's best theater training center.   DRAMA

1924   *All God's Chillun Got Wings* and *Desire Under the Elms*, two controversial dramas by American playwright Eugene O'Neill, are produced.   DRAMA

1924   German-born American actress Katharine Cornell, who will be respected as much
            for her character as for her acting ability, stars in the title role of Irish-born British
            playwright George Bernard Shaw's *Candida*. Later she will portray the English poet
            Elizabeth Barrett in Rudolf Besier's *The Barretts of Wimpole Street* (1931).   DRAMA

1924   Notable films include John Ford's *The Iron Horse* and Raoul Walsh's *The Thief
            of Baghdad* (both U.S.); F. W. Murnau's *The Last Laugh* (Germany); and Jean
            Renoir's *Nana* (France).   FILM

1924   British novelist E. M. Forster publishes *A Passage to India*, his last and greatest
            novel.   LIT

1924–1933   With drama critc and editor George Jean Nathan, American journalist and essay-
            ist H. L. Mencken founds and edits the influential periodical *American Mercury.*
                                                                                                 LIT

1924   American writer Ernest Hemingway debuts with the story collection *In Our
            Time.* The stories are based on Hemingway's early life in Michigan.   LIT

1924   American novelist Herman Melville's short novel *Billy Budd, Sailor*, is pub-
            lished posthumously. This tale of Budd and master-at-arms Claggart, written
            late in Melville's life, sets forth the author's position on the confrontation
            between good and evil.   LIT

1924   Chilean poet Pablo Neruda (born Neftalí Ricardo Reyes Basualto) publishes
            the collection *Veinte poemas de amor y una canción desesperada*. Later collections
            will include *Residencia en la tierra* (1932–1935) and *The Selected Poems of Pablo
            Neruda* (1970).   LIT

c. 1924   Russian scientist Leo Theremin invents the earliest electronic musical instru-
            ment, the theremin.   MUSIC

1924   Russian-American conductor Serge Koussevitzky becomes the conductor of the
            Boston Symphony Orchestra, a position he will hold until 1949. He will be
            known for his support of modern music.   MUSIC

1924   Spanish painter Juan Gris paints *Violin and Fruit Dish*.   PAINT

1924   In France André Breton publishes the *Surrealist Manifesto*, heralding the found-
            ing this year of surrealism, which works with dream and fantasy imagery and
            the irrational. Salvador Dalí, René Magritte, Max Ernst, André Masson, and
            Joan Miró are among the best-known surrealist painters. The movement will
            last until World War II.   PAINT

1924   Spanish painter Joan Miró completes the surrealistic work *Catalan Landscape*.   PAINT

1924   American painter George Bellows paints *The Dempsey-Firpo Fight*, which shows
            fighter Jack Dempsey being knocked through the ropes in a 1923 bout with
            Luis Firpo. Dempsey came back to win the fight.   PAINT

1924   The first successful 35-millimeter camera, the Leica, is developed in Germany.
            It will become a standard for both professional and amateur photographers.
                                                                                     PHOTO

1924   Romanian sculptor Constantin Brancusi sculpts *Le Commencement du monde*.   SCULP

1924   There are 2.5 million radios in American households, signaling the immense
            popularity of the new form of communication.   TV&R

1925   The Charleston, a fast-paced social dance, sweeps American and European
            dance halls and clubs.   DANCE

1925   American jazz singer and dancer Josephine Baker, who will become a natural-
            ized French citizen in 1937, performs in Paris in *La Revue Nègre*.   DANCE

1925   *Hay Fever*, a comedy by British actor and playwright Noel Coward, is produced
            in New York and London. *Private Lives* and *Design for Living*, both sophisticat-
            ed comedies, will be produced in 1930 and 1933, respectively.   DRAMA

1925   Notable films include Harold Lloyd's *The Freshman*, Charlie Chaplin's *The Gold
            Rush*, and King Vidor's *The Big Parade* (all U.S.).   FILM

1925   Russian director Sergei Eisenstein's film about the 1905 Russian revolution,
            The Battleship Potemkin, which will become known for its treatment of the
            attack on the Odessa steps, is exhibited.   FILM

1925   British novelist Virginia Woolf publishes *Mrs. Dalloway*, as well as the collection
            of essays *The Common Reader*, which will be followed in 1932 by *The Second
            Common Reader*.   LIT

1925   American novelist Theodore Dreiser publishes *An American Tragedy*, a novel
            inspired by the murder case of Chester Gilette and his victim, Grace Brown.
            The book is an immediate success.   LIT

1925   African-American poet Countee Cullen establishes himself as a literary force
            with his first collection, *Color*. Among his later collections will be *Copper Sun*
            (1927) and *Brown Girl* (1928).   LIT

1925   American novelist Sinclair Lewis publishes *Arrowsmith*, his satire of the med-
            ical profession as seen through the experiences of Dr. Martin Arrowsmith. LIT

1925   American novelist F. Scott Fitzgerald publishes *The Great Gatsby*, about the promises of the 1920s as seen through the misplaced dreams of the title character. The book will become known as Fitzgerald's finest work.   LIT

1925–1929   American poet Marianne Moore serves as editor of the literary magazine *The Dial*.   LIT

1925   Irish novelist and short-story writer Liam O'Flaherty publishes the novel *The Informer*, which will be made into an Academy Award–winning film. Other works will be collected in *The Stories of Liam O'Flaherty* (1956).   LIT

1925   African-American actor and bass singer Paul Robeson makes his first concert appearance, in New York City. He will become known for his rendition of "Ol' Man River" in Jerome Kern's play *Show Boat* (1928), which will be made into a movie in 1936. He will also distinguish himself in Eugene O'Neill's *Emperor Jones* (play, 1925; film, 1933), among other plays. His winning of the International Stalin Peace Prize in 1952, at the height of the McCarthy era of anti-Communist hysteria, will result in career difficulties for him in the United States; perhaps as a consequence he will live and tour exclusively abroad from 1958 to 1963.   MISC

1925   Austrian composer Alban Berg's atonal opera *Wozzeck* is produced in Berlin.   MUSIC

1925   Russian composer Dmitry Shostakovich's Symphony no. 1, composed as a 19-year-old graduate student at the Leningrad Conservatoire, debuts to critical acclaim.   MUSIC

c. 1925   American painter George Luks paints *Boy with Baseball*.   PAINT

1925   On March 3 the U.S. Congress authorizes Gutzon Borglum to carve a colossal memorial of the busts of Washington, Jefferson, Lincoln, and Theodore Roosevelt on the face of Mount Rushmore in the Black Hills of South Dakota. The project will be finished in 1941 by Borglum's son Lincoln.   SCULP

1926   The buildings of the Bauhaus at Dessau, designed by German architect Walter Gropius, are prominent early examples of the international style, which takes a formalistic, simplified approach emphasizing austere skeletons and large areas of glass. Other proponents of the style in the 1920s include Le Corbusier and Mies van der Rohe. The style will become dominant in the building of skyscrapers in the 1950s and 1960s.   ARCH

1926   Hungarian composer Béla Bartók's expressionist ballet *The Miraculous Mandarin* is produced in Cologne. The ballet is widely banned for its erotic and violent subject.   DANCE

1926   The Civic Repertory Company is founded in New York City by American actress
               and director Eva Le Gallienne. The company will provide serious theater at inex-
               pensive ticket prices for the next seven years.   DRAMA

1926   *Exiles*, the only play by Irish writer James Joyce, premieres in London. It will be
               revived in 1970 and 1971 by British playwright Harold Pinter .   DRAMA

1926   Irish playwright Sean O'Casey's drama *The Plough and the Stars* is produced at
               Dublin's Abbey Theatre. This play about the Easter Rising of 1916 leads to a riot.
                                                                                  DRAMA

1926   *The Great God Brown*, a complex drama by American playwright Eugene O'Neill,
               is produced. The play's actors wear elaborate masks at certain times.   DRAMA

1926   Notable films include Fritz Lang's *Metropolis* and F. W. Murnau's *Faust* (both
               Germany) and Alan Crosland's *Don Juan* (U.S.), the first film to be shown with
               Vitaphone music and sound effects.   FILM

1926   Italian-born American actor and international film heartthrob Rudolph Valentino
               dies (*b.* 1895) following completion of the movie *Son of the Sheik*.   FILM

1926   American short-story writer and critic Dorothy Parker, a sardonically witty member
               of the Algonquin Roundtable, publishes *Enough Rope*, her first book of verse.   LIT

The Origin of "Star Dust"

"Star Dust," one of the most widely recorded romantic ballads of the 20th century, was
written not by a weepy writer locked in a garret but by an eager law student noodling
on a piano in a law school lounge. In 1927 Indiana University law student Hoagy
Carmichael was taking a break from his studies at a meeting place called the Book
Nook when he conjured up a haunting tune on the lounge's old upright piano. The
melody lacked a name until his friend Stuart Gorrell called it "Star Dust" because it
played like "dust from stars drifting down through the summer sky."

Though Carmichael was already a working composer, with "Riverboat Shuffle" to
his credit, it would take a decade and several musical incarnations to establish "Star
Dust" as a standard. Originally recorded in 1927 as an up-tempo number, it was
reborn as a ballad in 1930 by Isham Jones and his orchestra. In this form it became
the basis for two definitive big-band recordings in 1936—one by Tommy Dorsey, one
by Benny Goodman. They, along with the 1940 rendition by Artie Shaw and his
orchestra, made it one of the signature romantic ballads of the swing era.

1926	American poet Carl Sandburg publishes the first part of his biography of Abraham Lincoln in two volumes entitled *Abraham Lincoln: The Prairie Years*. The second part, in four volumes entitled *Abraham Lincoln: The War Years*, will be published in 1939 and will win a Pulitzer Prize. LIT
1926	American writer Ernest Hemingway publishes *The Sun Also Rises*, about the aimless post–World War I existence of American Jake Barnes and his love affair with Lady Brett Ashley. LIT
1926	African-American poet Langston Hughes publishes his first collection of poems, *The Weary Blues*. Later volumes will include *The Dream-Keeper* (1932) and *Montage of a Dream Deferred* (1951). LIT
1926	British playwright A. A. Milne publishes the children's book about the bear with "very little brain," *Winnie-the-Pooh*. Milne will later write a companion volume, *The House at Pooh Corner* (1928). LIT
1926	Argentinian poet and novelist Ricardo Güiraldes publishes his best-known work, *Don Segundo Sombra*, an homage to the gaucho, or cowboy. LIT
1926	Italian composer Giacomo Puccini's opera in three acts *Turandot* is produced posthumously at La Scala in Milan. MUSIC
1926	British composer William Walton's Suite no. 1, *Façade*, with its music-hall influences, is an immediate success. MUSIC
1926	Belgian surrealist painter René Magritte paints *The Menaced Assassin*. PAINT
1926–1934	British painter Stanley Spencer paints a series of oil murals for the Sandham Memorial Chapel at Burghclere in England, which, by depicting the life of a soldier who died in Macedonia, serves to honor all soldiers. PAINT
1926	American painter Georgia O'Keeffe completes one of her trademark works, *Black Iris*, an enlarged, sensuous view of a flower. PAINT
1926	Spanish painter Joan Miró paints *Dog Barking at the Moon* and *Person Throwing a Stone at a Bird*. PAINT
1926	American radio entrepreneur David Sarnoff founds NBC, the National Broadcasting Company, a network of nine radio stations. TV&R
1927	In Europe and the United States the slow and simple foxtrot becomes a fashionable social dance. DANCE
1927	*The Royal Family*, by American playwright George S. Kaufman and American

playwright and novelist Edna Ferber, is produced. Kaufman and Ferber will later write the plays *Dinner at Eight* (1932) and *Stage Door* (1936), each of which will be made into a popular movie.   DRAMA

1927   Notable films include Clarence Brown's *Flesh and the Devil* and Cecil B. De Mille's *King of Kings* (both U.S.).   FILM

1927   American actress Clara Bow becomes known as the "It" girl after starring in the silent film *It*.   FILM

1927   The first feature film with extended sound sequences, Alan Crosland's *The Jazz Singer*, premieres. The musical drama of family travail about the career decisions of a cantor's son (Al Jolson) ushers in the end of the silent era and the beginning of sound films.   FILM

1927   The zany American comedy team Laurel and Hardy, comprising the slim, English-born Stan Laurel and the rotund Oliver Hardy, begin their long-lived collaboration. Their best-known films will include *The Music Box* and *Fra Diavolo* (both 1933) and *Way Out West* (1937).   FILM

1927   American writer Ernest Hemingway publishes *Men Without Women*, a collection of 14 short stories, which contains the classic "The Killers," concerning the fatalistic resignation of ex-boxer Ole Andreson to his impending execution by gangsters.   LIT

1927   British novelist Virginia Woolf publishes the novel *To the Lighthouse*.   LIT

1927   American journalist Don Marquis publishes *archy and mehitabel*, a prose collection about a cat and a cockroach who live in the New York *Sun* newspaper building where Marquis works. The amusing characters will spark many sequels.   LIT

1927   American novelist Willa Cather publishes the novel *Death Comes to the Archbishop*, about two Catholic clergymen in New Mexico. It will become one of her most highly regarded novels.   LIT

1927   Irish novelist Elizabeth Bowen publishes *The Hotel*. Among her later works will be *The House in Paris* (1935) and *The Heat of the Day* (1949).   LIT

1927   French novelist François Mauriac publishes his novel of sin and marriage, *Thérèse Desqueyroux*.   LIT

1927   French composer Maurice Ravel composes the sinuous orchestral piece *Boléro*, which will become his best-known work.   MUSIC

1927   American jazz musician Bix Beiderbecke joins the Paul Whiteman orchestra. An influential songwriter and performer, his compositions and music will help shape American jazz.   MUSIC

1927   American modernist painter Edward Hopper completes *Manhattan Bridge.*   PAINT

1927   American painter John Sloan paints *The Lafayette.*   PAINT

1927   Television is demonstrated for the first time in the United States by American Telephone & Telegraph executive Walter Gifford, who broadcasts images of Secretary of Commerce Herbert Hoover from Washington, D.C., to an audience in New York City.   TV&R

1928   British architect Elisabeth Scott designs the Shakespeare Memorial Theatre at Stratford-upon-Avon.   ARCH

1928   German playwright Bertolt Brecht achieves his first great success when *Die Dreigroschenoper* (*The Threepenny Opera*), his adaptation of English playwright John Gay's *The Beggar's Opera*, is produced in Berlin. The show includes music by German-born American composer Kurt Weill, and Brecht and Weill will collaborate on several operas, including *Happy End* (1929).   DRAMA

1928   *Strange Interlude*, a nine-act drama by American playwright Eugene O'Neill, is produced. This unusually long play features asides in which the actors address the audience directly. It will net O'Neill his third Pulitzer Prize. O'Neill's *Lazarus Laughed*, a play about the resurrection of Lazarus, is also produced this year.
                                                                        DRAMA

1928   Notable films include René Clair's *The Italian Straw Hat* and Carl Dreyer's *The Passion of Joan of Arc* (both France); G. W. Pabst's *Pandora's Box* (Germany); and Sergei Eisenstein's *October* (U.S.S.R.).   FILM

1928   American animated filmmaker Walt Disney's first Mickey Mouse cartoons, "Plane Crazy," "Gallopin' Gaucho," and "Steamboat Willie," are shown. The third marks the first Mickey Mouse cartoon to include sound sequences.   FILM

1928   The first color motion pictures are shown in Rochester, New York, by American inventor George Eastman.   FILM

1928   Irish poet and dramatist William Butler Yeats publishes the collection *The Tower*, which includes the title poem along with such works as "Sailing to Byzantium," "Leda and the Swan," "Among School Children," "A Man Young and Old," and "All Souls' Night."   LIT

1928	British novelist Dorothy L. Sayers publishes *The Unpleasantness at the Bellona Club*, one of her many detective novels featuring Lord Peter Wimsey. LIT
1928	British novelist Thomas Hardy's posthumous poetry collection *Winter Words in Various Moods and Metres* is published. LIT
1928	British novelist D. H. Lawrence publishes a two-volume collection of his poetry and his last novel, the notorious *Lady Chatterley's Lover*. LIT
1928	British novelist Virginia Woolf publishes her most commercially successful work, the fantastic novel *Orlando*, the story of an androgynous person who lives through four centuries. A year later Woolf will publish the feminist classic *A Room of One's Own*. LIT
1928	American poet and playwright Steven Vincent Benét publishes the epic poem that spans much of the Civil War, *John Brown's Body*. The poem will win the Pulitzer Prize. LIT
1928	American poet Archibald MacLeish publishes the poem *The Hamlet of A. MacLeish*, about the despair of the modern age. LIT
1928–1940	Russian novelist Mikhail Sholokhov publishes *Tikhiy Don* (*And Quiet Flows the Don*, English translation, 1934), the first half of his four-volume novel *The Quiet Don*. The second half, *The Don Flows Home to the Sea*, will be published in 1940. The novel, concerning the impact of the Bolshevik revolution on life in Russia's Don Cossack region, is considered the greatest work of early Soviet literature. He will be awarded the 1965 Nobel Prize for literature. LIT
1928	Spanish poet Federico García Lorca publishes the collection *Romancero Gitano*. Among his later works will be *Poeta en Nueva York* (1929, published 1940) and *Llanto por Ignacio Sánchez Mejías* (1935). LIT
1928	Italian conductor Arturo Toscanini leaves his position as musical director at La Scala in Milan and becomes principal conductor of the New York Philharmonic-Symphony Orchestra. He will remain there until 1936, when he will depart to conduct the NBC Symphony (1937–1954). MUSIC
1928	Self-taught Spanish classical guitarist and teacher Andrés Segovia, who has been playing since 1909, when he was 16, makes his debut in the United States at New York's Town Hall. He will transcribe for the guitar one of Bach's *Chaconne* from the Partita no. 2 for violin, among other guitar transcriptions that he will make throughout his long and influential career. In 1981 his work will be commemorated by the founding of the Segovia International Guitar Competition, and King Juan Carlos of Spain will make him marquis of Salobreia. MUSIC

1928	American painter Charles Demuth paints *The Figure 5 in Gold*. **PAINT**
1928	Station WGY in Schenectady, New York, makes the first scheduled television broadcasts in history. **TV&R**
1929–1930	Swiss architect Le Corbusier designs Villa Savoye at Poissy, France. His 1923 book *Towards a New Architecture* has already established him as a spokesperson for modern architecture. **ARCH**
1929–1931	On the former site of the Waldorf-Astoria Hotel in New York City, the Empire State Building is constructed. At 1,250 feet and 102 stories, it will be the tallest building in the world for decades. *See* 1972 and 1973, ARCH. **ARCH**
1929–1933	The Palace of the League of Nations in Geneva, Switzerland, is constructed. **ARCH**
1929	American dancer Martha Graham founds her own dance troupe. Over the next several decades it will be a seminal force in modern dance, with productions that include American composer Aaron Copland's *Appalachian Spring* (1944). **DANCE**
1929	Irish-born British playwright George Bernard Shaw's play *The Apple Cart* is produced. *Too True to Be Good* (1932), *Geneva* (1938), and *In Good King Charles' Golden Days* (1939) will follow. **DRAMA**
1929	*The Silver Tassie*, a pacifist drama about World War I by Irish playwright Sean O'Casey, is produced in London and New York. O'Casey's *Within the Gates*, *The Star Turns Red*, and *Red Roses for Me* will premiere in 1934, 1940, and 1943, respectively. **DRAMA**
1929	The Academy of Motion Picture Arts and Sciences, founded two years earlier, presents its Academy Awards, which will become known as Oscars, for the first time. In a ceremony at the Hollywood Roosevelt Hotel, best-picture honors go to *Wings*, with best actor to Emil Jannings for *The Last Command* and *The Way of All Flesh*. The best-actress award goes to Janet Gaynor and the best-director award to Frank Borzage, both for *Seventh Heaven*. Gaynor's best-actress award also reflects her work in *Street Angel* and *Sunrise*. **FILM**
1929	Notable films include Ernst Lubitsch's *The Love Parade* and Harry Beaumont's *Broadway Melody* (both U.S.). **FILM**
1929	American mystery writers and cousins Frederic Dannay and Manfred Lee, who share the pseudonym Ellery Queen, publish *The Roman Hat Mystery*, the first of the series of novels starring the detective Ellery Queen. They will also write about detective Drury Lane under the pen name Barnaby Ross **LIT**

1929   American mystery novelist and former private detective Dashiell Hammett
            publishes his first novel, *Red Harvest*. The innovative "hard-boiled" style exhib-
            ited in this and future detective novels, including *The Maltese Falcon* (1930)
            and *The Thin Man* (1934), will prove highly influential.   LIT

1929   British poet, novelist, and critic Robert Graves publishes the memoir *Goodbye
            to All That*.   LIT

1929   American writer Ernest Hemingway publishes the novel *A Farewell to Arms*,
            about the disillusionment caused by World War I as seen through the experi-
            ences of American ambulance driver Frederic Henry.   LIT

1929   American novelist Sinclair Lewis publishes *Dodsworth*, a critique of the spoiled,
            self-involved American woman as embodied by Fran Dodsworth.   LIT

1929   American novelist William Faulkner publishes *The Sound and the Fury*, a com-
            plex work about the decaying aristocratic Compson family in Mississippi. He
            also publishes the novel *As I Lay Dying*.   LIT

1929   American humorist James Thurber and American essayist E. B. White cowrite
            a parody of modern sexual psychology, *Is Sex Necessary?*   LIT

1929   German novelist Erich Maria Remarque publishes the World War I novel *All
            Quiet on the Western Front*. Among his later works will be the novel *A Time to
            Love and a Time to Die* (1954).   LIT

1929   British novelist and playwright J. B. Priestley publishes the novel *The Good
            Companions*. Among his later works will be the play *An Inspector Calls*, a domes-
            tic comedy, and the novel *The Image Men* (1968).   LIT

1929   Experimental French writer and filmmaker Jean Cocteau publishes the novel *Les
            Enfants terribles*. Later works will include the plays *La voix humaine* (*The Human
            Voice*, 1930) and *La machine infernale* (*The Infernal Machine*, 1934).   LIT

1929–1930   Austrian painter Oskar Kokoschka paints *Jerusalem*, one of his many land-
            scapes of towns as seen from high above.   PAINT

1929   The Museum of Modern Art opens in New York, with an exhibition of works
            by French painters Paul Cézanne, Paul Gauguin, and Georges Seurat and
            Dutch painter Vincent van Gogh. In 1939 the museum will move to its new
            site on 53rd Street.   PAINT

1929   Spanish painter Salvador Dalí joins the surrealist movement. Through his
            works, which embody a hallucinogenic sense of reality, he becomes one of sur-
            realism's most famous artists.   PAINT

1929   American painter Edward Hopper paints *The Lighthouse at Two Lights*.   PAINT

1929   German photographer August Sander publishes his collection of portraits of Germans, *Face of Our Time*. The work is both a model of the new objectivity movement and a commentary on the rise of Nazism.   PHOTO

1930s   Faced with competition from film and radio, vaudeville declines and soon vanishes. *See* 1881, DRAMA.   DRAMA

1930s   This decade produces a great many of the finest film actors of all time; some began acting earlier, and many will continue their careers in subsequent decades. Among those whose performances are most memorable are Laurence Olivier, Vivien Leigh, Katharine Hepburn, Bette Davis, James Stewart, Charlie Chaplin, Marlene Dietrich, Greta Garbo, James Cagney, Mae West, Hedy Lamarr, Edward G. Robinson, Jean Harlow, Claudette Colbert, the Marx Brothers, Mickey Rooney, Peter Lorre, Boris Karloff, Bela Lugosi, Claude Rains, Joan Crawford, Merle Oberon, Gary Cooper, Helen Hayes, Douglas Fairbanks, Shirley Temple, Errol Flynn, Olivia de Havilland, Fredric March, Henry Fonda, Carole Lombard, Clark Gable, Humphrey Bogart, Greer Garson, Myrna Loy, and Cary Grant.   FILM

1930s   Silkscreen, originally developed earlier this century for commercial textile printing, becomes a medium for fine artists.   GRAPH

1930s   Popular songs of the day include "Body and Soul," "I Got Rhythm," "Georgia on My Mind," "Minnie the Moocher," "Goodnight, Sweetheart," "Brother, Can You Spare a Dime," "Night and Day," "Boulevard of Broken Dreams," "Stormy Weather," "Easter Parade," "Blue Moon," "The Continental," "Begin the Beguine," "Just One of Those Things," "I Can't Get Started," "Pennies from Heaven," "Bei mir bist Du schön," "The Lady Is a Tramp," "A Foggy Day in London Town," "Jeepers Creepers," "Falling in Love with Love," "Over the Rainbow," "Beer Barrel Polka," and "I'll Never Smile Again."   MUSIC

1930s   Much American popular music is generated by Broadway shows, particularly those of Richard Rodgers and Lorenz Hart, Cole Porter, and Irving Berlin.   MUSIC

1930s   Beginning with her first recordings in 1935, American jazz singer Billie Holiday establishes herself as a defining presence in jazz music. Among her best-known works are "Strange Fruit" and "Gloomy Sunday."   MUSIC

1930s   Using the newly developed hand-held cameras, photojournalists record world events large and small for popular magazines like *Life* and *Time*. Among the first successful photojournalists are Erich Salomon, Felix Man, Brassaï, and Henri Cartier-Bresson. Dorothy Lang, who chronicles the Great Depression for the Farm Security Administration, generates widespread compassion for the suffering, notably through her photos of migrant workers in California.   PHOTO

1930s	Spanish sculptor Julio González establishes wrought iron as an important medium for sculpture while working in Paris. His pieces will influence artists in the 1960s and 1970s in creating violently expressive sculpture in wrought iron and welded steel. SCULP
1930s	During this decade and next, radio comedies enjoy great success on the airwaves. Among the most popular are *The Jack Benny Show*, *Fibber McGee and Molly*, and *The Edgar Bergen–Charlie McCarthy Show*. TV&R
1930	Designed by Raymond Hood and John Mead Howells, the 36-story Daily News Building is constructed in New York City. It houses the staff of the tabloid with the highest circulation in the United States. ARCH
1930	Notable films include Lewis Milestone's *All Quiet on the Western Front* and Clarence Brown's *Anna Christie* (both U.S.) and Josef von Sternberg's *The Blue Angel* (Germany). FILM
1930	Approximately 250 million people around the world attend movies once a week, with 115 million of them Americans. FILM
1930	In an attempt to counteract negative views of the American film industry, the Motion Picture Production Code is developed by the Motion Picture Producers and Distributors of America (MPPDA). The rules regulating onscreen morality will become known as the Hays Code, after Will Hays, head of MPPDA. FILM
1930	British-born American poet W. H. Auden publishes *Poems*, including "This Lunar Beauty" and "Petition." LIT
1930–1932	German-born American classics scholar Edith Hamilton becomes known as a popularizer of ancient history with the publication of *The Greek Way* (1930) and *The Roman Way* (1932). Her *Mythology* (1942) will become an enduringly popular work in its field. LIT
1930	American-born British poet T. S. Eliot publishes the poem *Ash-Wednesday*, an exploration of faith and religion in current times. LIT
1930	In accepting the Nobel Prize for literature, American novelist Sinclair Lewis makes a speech titled "The American Fear of Literature," critical of conservative antagonism toward contemporary writing. LIT
1930	American poet Hart Crane publishes the multipart poem *The Bridge*. Both a celebration of the Brooklyn Bridge and an exploration of what Crane calls "the Myth of America," it will become his best-known work. LIT

1930–1935   American writer Katherine Anne Porter publishes two collections of stories under the title *Flowering Judas*. Later short-story and short-novel collections will include *The Leaning Tower and Other Stories* (1944) and *Pale Horse, Pale Rider* (1939).   LIT

1930–1936   American novelist John Dos Passos publishes the *U.S.A.* trilogy: *The 42nd Parallel* (1930), *1919* (1932), and *The Big Money* (1936). The books will become known for their blend of journalism, prose poetry, and sketches of important personages of the day and everyday people.   LIT

1930   African-Cuban poet Nicolás Guillén publishes *Motivos de Son*, his first book of poetry. One of Latin America's greatest poets, he will be known for inventing the *son*, a literary form based on popular Afro-Cuban music, and for his dedication to revolution.   LIT

1930   Sir Adrian Boult becomes musical director of the newly formed BBC Symphony Orchestra.   MUSIC

1930   Russian composer Igor Stravinsky composes *Symphony of Psalms*.   MUSIC

1930   Dutch painter Piet Mondrian paints *Composition in Red, Yellow and Blue*.   PAINT

1930   Dutch painter Christian Küpper, known as Theo van Doesburg, publishes *Art Concret*, a treatise outlining the nonfigurative abstract art that will be known as concrete art. The work is written in opposition to the constructivist exhibition group known as the Cercle et Carré (Circle and Square).   PAINT

1930   American painter Grant Wood completes *American Gothic*. At an exhibition at the Art Institute of Chicago, it will win a bronze medal.   PAINT

1930–1931   American painter Thomas Hart Benton completes a number of murals of American life for the New School of Social Research in New York City. His stylized depiction of Americans will become prototypical.   PAINT

1930–1980   By capturing the "decisive moment" of an experience, French photographer Henri Cartier-Bresson becomes one of the most important photojournalists of the 20th century. His work combines influences of several of the major artistic movements of the century, including surrealism and abstract art. Collections of his works will be found in *The Europeans* (1955) and *Man and Machine* (1969), among others.   PHOTO

1930–1950   American photographer Edward Weston establishes himself as a creator of sensuous but unadorned photographic images, such as his studies of female nudes.   PHOTO

1930–1950	American combat photographer Robert Capa illustrates the immediacy of war in his photos of the Spanish Civil War, notably the 1936 photo *Death of a Loyalist Soldier*, and of the D-Day invasion of World War II. He will be killed by a mine in Vietnam in 1954. PHOTO
1931–1947	The Rockefeller Center complex is constructed in New York City. ARCH
1931	The New Negro Art Theatre Dance Group, the first professional black dance group, is founded in New York by American dancer Helmsley Winfield. DANCE
1931	Irish-born English choreographer Dame Ninette De Valois founds the Sadler's Wells Ballet School. She will direct the Sadler's Wells Ballet, which will eventually become the Royal Ballet. DANCE
1931	The Group Theatre, a production company dedicated to presenting serious contemporary drama, is formed in New York City by Harold Clurman, Cheryl Crawford, and Lee Strasberg. It will present premieres of several works by American playwright Clifford Odets, including *Awake and Sing!* (1935), *Waiting for Lefty* (1935) and *Golden Boy* (1937) before closing in 1941. DRAMA
1931	*Mourning Becomes Electra*, a 13-act trilogy by American playwright Eugene O'Neill, is produced. *Ah, Wilderness!*, an O'Neill comedy, will be produced in 1933. He will be awarded the 1936 Nobel Prize for literature. DRAMA
1931	Notable films include Charlie Chaplin's *City Lights*, James Whale's *Frankenstein*, and Lewis Milestone's *The Front Page* (all U.S.). FILM
1931	British novelist Virginia Woolf publishes the novel *The Waves*. LIT
1931	Russian-born American anarchist Emma Goldman publishes her autobiography *Living My Life*. LIT
1931	American novelist and critic Edmund Wilson publishes a book of literary essays, *Axel's Castle*. Among his subjects are James Joyce, Gertrude Stein, and William Butler Yeats. LIT
1931	American historian and journalist Frederick Lewis Allen publishes an informal chronicle of the 1920s, *Only Yesterday*. The book will become a best-seller and will be followed by a sequel chronicling later years, *Since Yesterday*. LIT
1931	American humorist James Thurber publishes his first collection of humorous essays, *The Owl and the Attic*. Later volumes will include *My Life and Hard Times* (1933) and *The Beast in Me and Other Animals* (1948). From the 1920s much of his work appeared in the *New Yorker*. LIT

1931	Spanish painter Salvador Dalí paints *Persistence of Memory*.	PAINT
1931	French painter Henri Matisse completes *The Dance*, a series of murals at the Barnes Foundation in Merion, Pennsylvania.	PAINT
1931–1932	American painter Ben Shahn gains prominence through his gouaches of the Sacco and Vanzetti trials. He had earlier created similar gouaches to illustrate the Dreyfus case.	PAINT
1932	Notable films include Mervyn LeRoy's *I Am a Fugitive from a Chain Gang* and Edmund Goulding's *Grand Hotel* (both U.S.); Fritz Lang's *M* (Germany); and René Clair's *À Nous la Liberté* (France).	FILM
1932	*Tarzan, the Ape Man* is the first Tarzan film to star American actor and Olympic swimming champion Johnny Weissmuller. Several Tarzan sequels featuring Weissmuller will follow.	FILM
1932	British-born American poet W. H. Auden publishes the poetry collection *The Orators*.	LIT
1932–1962	American novelist William Faulkner publishes some of his best-known works, including *Light in August* (1932), *Absalom, Absalom!* (1936), *Intruder in the Dust* (1948), and *A Fable* (1954), for which he will win the Pulitzer Prize. His final work is *The Reivers* (1962). In 1949 he is awarded the Nobel Prize for literature.	LIT

The Make-Believe Ballroom

In New York City during the Great Depression, people who wanted to dance to the latest swing music didn't have to visit pricey ballrooms or settle for dime-a-dance joints. Instead an announcer named Martin Block on radio station WNEW-AM guided dancers onto the floor of *The Make-Believe Ballroom*. Starting in the depths of the Depression in 1934, the program played only the hottest dance music of its day. As music changed over the decades, the show came to include swing, big band, and jazz sounds. Like its latter-day compatriot, *American Bandstand*, *The Make-Believe Ballroom* served as a launching pad for many a musician's career; a personal appearance on the show signaled an artist's success.

Despite the birth of rock-'n'-roll in the 1950s, *The Make-Believe Ballroom* remained true to its origins in 20th-century American ballroom dance music. The "Ballroom" remained open until WNEW-AM went off the air in December 1992. For nearly 60 years it remained an archetypal example of radio's capacity for kindling imagination through sound.

1932   American novelist Pearl S. Buck publishes her novel of Chinese life *The Good Earth*, for which she will win the Pulitzer Prize. In 1938 she will be awarded the Nobel Prize for literature.   LIT

1932   Italian poet Salvatore Quasimodo publishes the collection *Oboe sommerso*. His later works will include *Poesie nuove* (1942) and *La terra impareggiable* (1958).   LIT

1932   Irish novelist and short-story writer Sean O'Faolain publishes his first story collection, *Midsummer Night Madness*. Later works will include *A Nest of Simple Folk* (1933) and the story collections *The Man Who Invented Sin* (1947) and *The Talking Trees* (1979).   LIT

1932   British novelist Aldous Huxley publishes the futuristic satire *Brave New World*. His earlier works include *Crome Yellow* (1921) and *Point Counter Point* (1928).   LIT

1932   Indian poet and philosopher Sir Muhammad Iqbal publishes *Jāvīd-nāmeh*, or *The Song of Eternity*, a Persian, Muslim version of Italian poet Dante's *Divine Comedy* (*see* 1307–1321, LIT).   LIT

1932   The London Philharmonic Orchestra is founded by Sir Thomas Beecham.   MUSIC

1932–1933   Mexican painter Diego Rivera paints the fresco series *Detroit Industry* in the Detroit Institute of Arts. With other Mexican painters such as José Clemente Orozco and David Alfaro Siqueiros, Rivera has led a revival of the fresco as a medium of public art.   PAINT

1932   Polaroid film, the first synthetic light-polarizing film, is developed by American inventor Edwin Herbert Land.   PHOTO

1932   American artist Alexander Calder creates a new form of sculpture of carefully balanced metal plates, rods, and wires which can be moved either by air currents or mechanical means. French painter Marcel Duchamp will visit Calder's studio in Paris and name the constructions "mobile."   SCULP

1932–1950   George Burns and Gracie Allen perform their one-of-a-kind comedy on radio; they will continue the show for eight years thereafter on television.   TV&R

1933   The highly influential Bauhaus school of architecture, which moved to Berlin from Dessau in 1932, is closed by the Third Reich.   ARCH

1933   Revolutionary Russian choreographer George Balanchine comes to the United States and, with Lincoln Kirstein, founds the School of American Ballet. In 1948 its dance company will become the New York City Ballet, with Kirstein its director.   DANCE

1933   American stage-trained dancer Fred Astaire (born Frederick Austerlitz) appears in his first film with American actress Ginger Rogers, *Flying Down to Rio*. The two will be paired in several films, including *Top Hat* (1935) and *Swing Time* (1936), through which they will revolutionize the use of dance in films, making it a medium to further plot development and embody romance.   DANCE

1933   Adolf Hitler comes to power, and German playwright Bertolt Brecht and his family go into exile, moving to Switzerland, then to Denmark, then to Finland, and finally to the United States in 1941. Brecht will write much of his major work abroad, including *The Caucasian Chalk Circle* in 1945, a drama set in war-torn Soviet Georgia.   DRAMA

1933   Helen Hayes, among the preeminent actresses of 20th-century American theater, takes on one of her most-admired roles, as Mary Queen of Scots in Maxwell Anderson's *Mary of Scotland*. Her other notable roles include the title character in Laurence Housman's *Victoria Reigns* (1935), and Viola in Shakespeare's *Twelfth Night* (1940).   DRAMA

1933   Thingspiel, a type of pageant play staged outdoors, begins to flourish in Germany. The form promotes German nationalism—particularly its Nazi manifestation.   DRAMA

1933   *Bodas de sangre* (*Blood Wedding*), the first play in a tragic trilogy by the Spanish poet Federico García Lorca, is produced. *Yerma*, the second play, will be produced in 1934. *La casa de Bernarda Alba* (*The House of Bernarda Alba*) will be produced in 1945. This group of plays will be seen as Lorca's greatest work. *Blood Wedding* and *Bernarda Alba* will continue to be revived frequently.   DRAMA

1933   Notable films include George Cukor's *Dinner at Eight*, Frank Lloyd's *Calvacade*, and Merian C. Cooper and Ernest B. Schoedsack's *King Kong* (all U.S.); and Fritz Lang's *The Testament of Dr. Mabuse* (Germany).   FILM

1933   Irish poet and dramatist William Butler Yeats publishes the collection *The Winding Stair and Other Poems*, which includes "For Anne Gregory," "Byzantium," and "A Woman Young and Old." Many of the poems in a collection published the previous year, *Words for Music Perhaps and Other Poems*, are incorporated into later editions of this collection.   LIT

1933   British poet Stephen Spender publishes his first important collection, *Poems*.   LIT

1933   American novelist Nathaniel West publishes the tragic novel about an advice-to-the-lovelorn columnist, *Miss Lonely-Hearts*. He also will be known for his dark 1939 novel *The Day of the Locust*.   LIT

1933	French novelist André Malraux publishes the novel *La Condition humaine* (*Man's Fate*). Among his later works will be the novel *L'Espoir* (*Man's Hope*, 1938) and *Le Temps du mépris* (*Days of Wrath*, 1935). **LIT**
1933	American experimental writer Gertrude Stein publishes her autobiography (titled as though it were that of her secretary and lifelong companion), *The Autobiography of Alice B. Toklas*, which describes the community of expatriates in Paris. **LIT**
1933–1939	About 60,000 writers, artists, and musicians emigrate from Germany beginning with the rise of Adolf Hitler and continuing up until the outbreak of World War II. Many of those who remain will be counted among the victims of the Holocaust, which claims the lives of at least six million Jews and five million others between 1933 and 1945. **MISC**
1933	French-American composer Edgard Varèse, pioneer of electronic music, composes *Ionization* for 13 percussionists. Other important works of his will include *Density 21.5* for solo flute (1936), *Equatorial* (1934, revised 1961), and *Déserts* (1950–1954). **MUSIC**
1933–1950	German expressionist painter Max Beckmann begins the nearly two-decade-long project of painting the nine triptychs known as *Departure*. Begun in the year he was removed by the Nazis from his teaching position in Frankfurt, *Departure* reflects his views on life, society, and the human tendency toward evil. **PAINT**
1933	Mexican painter Diego Rivera paints the fresco *Man at the Crossroads* for Rockefeller Center in New York City. Because the mural includes a portrait of founder of the Soviet Union, Vladimir Lenin, it will eventually be replaced by a mural created by British painter Sir Frank Brangwyn. **PAINT**
1933	Transylvanian-born French photographer Brassaï (born Gyula Halász) publishes the collection *Paris de nuit* (*The Secret Paris of the 30s*). His eye for capturing the dark haunts of the city will make him known as "the Eye of Paris." **PHOTO**
1933	American Edwin H. Armstrong develops frequency modulation (FM), which reduces static and increases sound fidelity in radio transmission. The same year the all-metal radio tube is developed by the Marconiphone Company. **TV&R**
1933–1945	Throughout his 12 years in office, United States president Franklin Delano Roosevelt employs radio to transmit regular broadcasts known as "fireside chats." They are early examples of the political power of a mass medium. **TV&R**
1934	African-American painter Aaron Douglas produces murals celebrating his community's African heritage for the Harlem branch of the New York Public Library. **ARCH**

1934   *The Children's Hour*, the first play by American playwright Lillian Hellman, is produced. The story of two teachers whose lives are destroyed by a student's false accusations of lesbianism, this drama will be a success on Broadway.   DRAMA

1934   The American musical *Anything Goes*—with book by Guy Bolton, P. G. Wodehouse, Howard Lindsay, and Russel Crouse, and lyrics and music by Cole Porter—premieres on November 21.   DRAMA

1934   Notable films include W. S. Van Dyke's *The Thin Man* and John Ford's *The Lost Patrol* (both U.S.) and Alexander Korda's *The Private Life of Henry VIII* (U.K.).   FILM

1934   Frank Capra's *It Happened One Night* becomes the first film to capture all four major Academy Awards—for best picture, actor, actress, and director. The comic love story about a runaway heiress (Claudette Colbert) and a newspaper reporter (Clark Gable) spurs the development of the new genre of screwball comedy.   FILM

1934   American novelist James M. Cain publishes the popular mystery novel *The Postman Always Rings Twice*. It will be the basis for films in 1946 and 1988.   LIT

1934   British novelist, poet, and critic Robert Graves publishes his most popular works, *I, Claudius* and *Claudius the God*, two historical novels narrated by the Roman emperor Claudius.   LIT

1934   Welsh poet Dylan Thomas publishes his first collection, *Eighteen Poems*, noted for their violent imagery and suggestive language.   LIT

1934   American critic Malcolm Cowley publishes *Exile's Return*, a memoir of the American writers of the "lost generation" who went to Europe in the post–World War I years, including Ernest Hemingway, F. Scott Fitzgerald, John Dos Passos, and Hart Crane.   LIT

1934   American novelist F. Scott Fitzgerald publishes the novel *Tender Is the Night*.   LIT

1934   Danish short-story writer Isak Dinesen (pen name of Baroness Karen Blixen) publishes the collection *Seven Gothic Tales*. Her later work, *Out of Africa*, will be the basis of an Academy Award–winning film.   LIT

1934   Ecuadorian novelist Jorge Icaza publishes the social realist novel *Huasipungo*, which exposes the inhuman treatment of Indians in his country.   LIT

1934   American writer Henry Miller publishes *Tropic of Cancer* in Paris, which is banned in the U.S. until 1961 on the grounds of obscenity. It will be followed in 1939 by *Tropic of Capcricorn*.   LIT

1934   German composer Paul Hindemith composes the opera and symphony *Mathis der Maler* (*Mathis the Painter*).   MUSIC

1935   Dance impresario Lincoln Kirstein's book *Dance* is the first important history of the art form by an American.   DANCE

1935   The Latin American rumba becomes a popular social dance in the United States and Europe.   DANCE

1935   *Night Must Fall*, a drama which Welsh actor and playwright Emlyn Williams both wrote and acted in, premieres.   DRAMA

1935   *Murder in the Cathedral*, a drama by American-born British poet T. S. Eliot about the murder of Thomas à Becket, premieres in England.   DRAMA

1935   English actors John Gielgud and Laurence Olivier (*see* 1937, DRAMA), who will come to be regarded as two of the finest actors of the century, take turns portraying Mercutio and Romeo in Gielgud's production of English dramatist William Shakespeare's *Romeo and Juliet*, which Gielgud also directs.   DRAMA

1935   The American musical *Porgy and Bess*—with book and lyrics by Dubose Heyward and Ira Gershwin and music by George Gershwin—premieres on October 10. It is considered a revolutionary blend of folk music and Broadway force. George Gershwin, who will die of a brain cyst at the age of 38 in 1937, will be regarded as one of the foremost American composers of his day, and Ira Gershwin, who will live until 1983, as one of the most important lyricists.   DRAMA

1935   Notable films include Alfred Hitchcock's *The 39 Steps*, John Ford's *The Informer*, Frank Lloyd's *Mutiny on the Bounty*, and Rouben Mamoulian's *Becky Sharp*, the first three-color Technicolor feature film (all U.S.).   FILM

1935   Irish poet and dramatist William Butler Yeats publishes the collection *A Full Moon in March*. Many of its poems will later be gathered under the title *Parnell's Funeral and Other Poems* in his collected *Poems*. These include 12 "Supernatural Songs," such as "Ribh in Ecstasy," "The Four Ages of Man," "Meru," and "What Magic Drum?"   LIT

1935   British officer T. E. Lawrence's *The Seven Pillars of Wisdom* is published. The account of his role in the Arab revolt against the Ottoman Empire was previously published in abbreviated form as *The Revolt in the Desert*, 1927. His account will be the basis for David Lean's film *Lawrence of Arabia* (1962).   LIT

1935   American novelist John O'Hara publishes *Butterfield 8*, introducing woman-about-town Gloria Wandrous.   LIT

1935   American memoirist Clarence Shepard Day Jr. publishes the hugely successful nostalgic reminiscence *Life with Father*. A sequel, *Life with Mother*, is published in 1937, after Day's death.   LIT

1935–1967   American philosopher and scholar Will Durant and his wife Ariel Durant publish the ten volumes of *The Story of Civilization* series, which presents philosophy to a wide audience. They include *Our Oriental Heritage* (1935), *The Life of Greece* (1939), *Caesar and Christ* (1944), *The Age of Faith* (1950), *The Renaissance* (1953), *The Reformation* (1957), *The Age of Reason Begins* (1961), *The Age of Louis XIV* (1963), *The Age of Voltaire* (1965), and *Rousseau and Revolution* (1967).   LIT

1935   American novelist Thomas Wolfe publishes *Of Time and the River*.   LIT

1935   American poet Wallace Stevens publishes the poem "The Idea of Order at Key West."   LIT

1935   Highly secretive novelist B. Traven, of undisclosed origin, publishes the dark novel *The Treasure of Sierra Madre*. It will be the basis for an Academy Award–winning motion picture.   LIT

Portraits in the Subway

One of the earliest and most long-lived purposes for photography was the personal portrait. Although by the mid-1800s the photographic process had become inexpensive enough for even the average working person to afford a portrait, cumbersome equipment prohibited anything but a stationary, often self-conscious pose.

By the 1930s the hand-held single-lens camera allowed for more spontaneous views of events and people. Along with revolutionizing the recording of history through photojournalism in magazines like *Time* and *Life*, it made possible what American photographer Walker Evans called the "unposed portrait." He explored the possibilities of this type of portraiture on the trains of the New York City subway.

Using a concealed camera, Evans photographed portraits of dozens upon dozens of what he called "unselfconscious captive sitters" during the late 1930s and early 1940s. Although he considered the subway a "dream 'location' for any portrait photographer weary of the studio and the parade of vanity," he also felt the artistic conflict of capturing the image of an unwitting subject. In a draft of a text to accompany his book of subway photos, he called his clandestine approach a "rude and imprudent invasion" and himself a "penitent spy and an apologetic voyeur."

The photographs were collected in the 1966 book *Many Are Chosen*, published two decades after Evans's original "invasion."

1935   Swing music, a style of jazz, becomes popular in the United States and Europe,
              having begun to evolve as early as 1930. Primarily a rhythmic change, it is
              characterized by an equal weight being given to four beats of the bar and by
              extended improvisational solos by instrumentalists, of whom the most promi-
              nent are Coleman Hawkins, Lester Young, and Roy Eldridge, among others.
              Drummers and guitarists are given solo roles for the first time, and big dance
              bands predominate, especially those led by Benny Goodman, Artie Shaw,
              Count Basie, Fletcher Henderson, and Duke Ellington. A corresponding phase
              of popular music is also known as swing; its defining practitioners include
              trombonist and dance-band leader Glenn Miller; Jimmy Dorsey, a clarinetist,
              saxophonist, and dance-band leader; and his brother Tommy Dorsey, a trom-
              bonist and dance-band leader.   MUSIC

1935   American jazz singer Ella Fitzgerald is "discovered" in Harlem by drummer
              and bandleader Chick Webb, who invites her to join his band. Upon his death
              in 1939, Fitzgerald will take over as bandleader until 1942, when she will
              begin appearing with all the major jazz ensembles. Highly regarded for her
              scat singing and improvisational facility, she will be awarded the National
              Medal of Arts in 1987.   MUSIC

1935   New York City's Village Vanguard, which will become the world's longest-run-
              ning continuous jazz club, is founded.   MUSIC

1935   Belgian surrealist painter René Magritte paints *Les Promenades d'Euclid*. PAINT

1935–1943   The Federal Arts Project is instituted under the auspices of the Works Progress
              Administration of the U.S. government, creating public art for the nation and
              providing jobs for thousands of unemployed artists and craftspeople during
              the Great Depression. Departments of the project include the Federal Art
              Project, the Federal Music Project, Federal Theatre Project, and the Federal
              Writers Project.   PAINT

1935–1939   British art historian Kenneth Clark completes a catalogue of Italian artist
              Leonardo da Vinci's drawings at Windsor Castle, Britain, and follows four years
              later with a monograph on the artist. These, along with other critical works,
              will establish him as a champion of art understanding.   PAINT

1935   British painter Ben Nicholson creates a series of cubist- and Mondrian-influ-
              enced reliefs that will put him at the forefront of British abstract artists. Between
              1932 and 1951 he is married to British artist Barbara Hepworth.   PAINT

1935   Having already established himself as a leading abstract artist and contributor
              to art magazines, English painter and graphic artist John Piper becomes art edi-
              tor of the avant-garde quarterly *Axis*.   PAINT

1936–1937	American architect Frank Lloyd Wright designs the Kaufmann house, "Falling Water," in Bear Run, Pennsylvania. The house is cantilevered over a waterfall. ARCH
1936	The Moiseyev Dance Company is founded in Moscow by Russian dance impressario Igor Moiseyev. It will become known for its interpretations of Russian folk dances. DANCE
1936	*An Actor Prepares*, the first of several books on acting by Russian actor and director Konstantin Stanislavsky, is published in English. In this work, which will be particularly influential in America (*see* 1949, DRAMA), Stanislavsky sets out the approach to acting that he and his students have taken over the years at the Moscow Art Theater (*see* 1898, DRAMA). He encourages actors to draw on inner feelings and personal experiences to create realistic, full-bodied characters. DRAMA
1936	*You Can't Take It with You*, a comedy by American playwrights Moss Hart and George S. Kaufman, premieres. It will receive the Pulitzer Prize. Hart and Kaufman will later write *The Man Who Came to Dinner* (1939). DRAMA
1936	Notable films include Frank Capra's *Mr. Deeds Goes to Town*, Charlie Chaplin's *Modern Times*, and Robert Z. Leonard's *The Great Ziegfeld* (all U.S.); and Fritz Lang's *Fury* (Germany). FILM
1936	American novelist William Faulkner publishes the novel *Absalom, Absalom!*, which continues the story of the Compson family begun in *The Sound and the Fury* (1929). LIT
1936	American novelist Margaret Mitchell publishes *Gone with the Wind*. The saga of Scarlett O'Hara, Rhett Butler, and the ravages experienced by the South during the Civil War will be a perennial best-seller. *See also* 1939, FILM. LIT
1936	American broadcaster and lecturer Dale Carnegie publishes *How to Win Friends and Influence People*, which will be one of the world's most successful how-to manifestos for building confidence. LIT
1936	American writer James Agee and photographer Walker Evans publish *Let Us Now Praise Famous Men*, an account of the poverty and quiet dignity of three sharecropping families in the South. The work had originally been commissioned by *Fortune* magazine. LIT
1936	On November 23 *Life* magazine begins publication in the United States under American businessman Henry Luce. It will become one of the most widely read weekly general-interest magazines in history. LIT

1936   American composer Samuel Barber composes his best-known work, *Adagio for Strings*.   MUSIC

1936   American photographer Margaret Bourke-White takes the cover photo for the first issue of *Life*, of Fort Peck Dam in Montana. Her eye for drama and the sculptural qualities in photography will make her one of the most popular photojournalists of the 20th century.   PHOTO

1936   The British Broadcasting Company (BBC) sets up the world's first electronic television system.   TV&R

1937   The Mordkin Ballet, the company that will become the American Ballet Theater, is founded. It will operate under the name of Mordkin Ballet until 1940, when it will be known as Ballet Theater. From 1956 it will be the American Ballet Theater.   DANCE

1937   Hungarian-born designer and architect Marcel Breuer establishes himself in the United States after more than a decade of designing furniture at the Bauhaus in Germany (1914–1928). His furniture designs using wood and steel tubing will have a lasting effect in modern design.   DECO

1937   *Le Voyageur sans bagages* (*Traveler without Luggage*), the first pièce noire—melancholy play—by French playwright Jean Anouilh, is produced. *La Sauvage* (*The Restless Heart*), another pièce noire, will be produced in 1938.   DRAMA

1937   British actor Laurence Olivier joins the Old Vic theater company, where, over the next two seasons and under the direction of Tyrone Guthrie (*see* 1963, DRAMA), he will play Hamlet, Macbeth, Henry V, Iago, Coriolanus, and Sir Toby Belch (in *Twelfth Night*), establishing himself as an actor of great distinction. Over the following decades, he will pursue a very successful career as a stage and film actor and director.   DRAMA

1937   Notable films include Jean Renoir's *La Grande Illusion* (France) and George Cukor's *Camille* and Walt Disney's *Snow White and the Seven Dwarfs* (both U.S.); *Snow White* is the first feature-length color animated Disney cartoon.   FILM

1937   British novelist C. S. Forester begins his popular series of novels about naval hero Horatio Hornblower with *The Happy Return*.   LIT

1937   British novelist J. R. R. Tolkien publishes the fantasy novel *The Hobbit*, introducing the intrepid hobbit Bilbo Baggins and the wizard Gandalf. *See also* 1954–1955, LIT.   LIT

1937 · British-born American poet W. H. Auden publishes the poetry collection *On This Island* and the poem "Spain," concerning the Spanish Civil War, in which he served as an ambulance driver for the Republicans. · LIT

1937 · American novelist and journalist John Phillips Marquand publishes the popular saga *The Late George Apley*, which will win the Pulitzer Prize. · LIT

1937 · African-American novelist Zora Neale Hurston publishes the feminist novel *Their Eyes Were Watching God*. · LIT

1937 · American novelist John Steinbeck publishes *Of Mice and Men*. · LIT

1937 · British novelist Evelyn Waugh publishes *A Handful of Dust*. Later novels will include the comic novel *The Loved One* (1948) and *Brideshead Revisited*, which becomes the basis for a BBC-TV mini-series. · LIT

1937–1954 · Italian conductor Arturo Toscanini is director of the National Broadcasting Company Symphony Orchestra, formed especially for him by NBC. · MUSIC

1937 · German composer Carl Orff composes his scenic oratorio *Carmina Burana* based on 25 Latin poems written by students in the 13th century at a Bavarian monastery. · MUSIC

1937 · Russian composer Dmitry Shostakovich's masterpiece, Symphony no. 5, Op. 47, is performed during a celebration in honor of the 20th anniversary of the Russian Revolution. · MUSIC

1937 · The Count Basie Orchestra, led by American jazz pianist and bandleader Count Basie, becomes one of the primary big bands of the swing era and showcases the talent of tenor saxophonist Lester Young, whose playing will exert an important influence on the development of "cool" jazz in the late 1940s and early 1950s. · MUSIC

1937 · As part of its repression of modern art, the Third Reich presents an exhibition of *Entartete Kunst*, or degenerate art, in Munich. Among the artists condemned because their work does not adhere to Reich ideology are Dutch painter Vincent van Gogh, French painter Henri Matisse, and Spanish painter Pablo Picasso. Thousands of works of modern art—many of which will be destroyed—are removed from galleries across Germany by the Nazis. · PAINT

1937 · Spanish painter Pablo Picasso completes the painting *Guernica*, which captures the horror brought to the town of Guernica during the Spanish Civil War. · PAINT

1937   Romanian sculptor Constantin Brancusi creates his monumental ensemble for his hometown of Targu-Jiu, including the *Gate of the Kiss*, the *Table of Silence*, and *Endless Column*, which is nearly 100 feet high.   SCULP

1938   The Lambeth walk becomes a popular social dance in the United States and Europe.   DANCE

1938   *Le Bal des Voleurs* (*Thieves' Carnival*), the first pièce rose—romantic play—by French playwright Jean Anouilh, is produced. *Léocadia* (*Time Remembered*), another pièce rose, will be produced in 1940.   DRAMA

1938   *The Corn Is Green*, an autobiographical play by Welsh playwright and actor Emlyn Williams, is produced. The author also acts in the play, which will be generally regarded as his best.   DRAMA

1938   *Our Town*, a play depicting small-town life by American playwright Thornton Wilder, premieres. Following a successful professional run, it will become a perennial high school drama club favorite.   DRAMA

1938   Notable films include Frank Capra's *You Can't Take It with You* and Alfred Hitchcock's *The Lady Vanishes* (both U.S.) and Sergei Eisenstein's *Alexander Nevsky* (U.S.S.R.).   FILM

1938   In June *Action Comics* No. 1 introduces Superman, the caped hero with amazing superpowers, created by Jerry Siegel and Joe Shuster. Batman, created by Bob Kane, will be introduced in the May 1939 *Detective Comics*. In the coming decades, a horde of superheroes, most with special powers and secret identities, will flourish in American comic books.   GRAPH

1938   Irish poet and dramatist William Butler Yeats publishes the collection *New Poems*, which includes "Lapis Lazuli," "Beautiful Lofty Things," "The Curse of Cromwell," "Parnell," and "The Municipal Gallery Re-visited."   LIT

1938   British novelist Daphne Du Maurier publishes *Rebecca*, which will be filmed by Alfred Hitchcock in 1940.   LIT

1938   British novelist, poet, and critic Robert Graves publishes the first edition of his *Collected Poems*.   LIT

1938   Poems published this year by Irish poet Louis MacNeice include "The Sunlight on the Garden," "Bagpipe Music," and "Good Dream."   LIT

1938   British novelist Graham Greene publishes *Brighton Rock*, his first novel explicitly exploring Catholic themes. Other Greene novels of this type will include

The Power and the Glory (1940), *The Heart of the Matter* (1948), *The End of the Affair* (1951), and *The Quiet American* (1955).   LIT

1938   American novelist and journalist Marjorie Kinnan Rawlings publishes the novel *The Yearling*, about a boy's attachment to a deer.   LIT

1938   German composer Werner Egk's opera *Peer Gynt* is produced in Berlin.   MUSIC

1938   American jazz musician Benny Goodman and his orchestra hold the first swing concert in Carnegie Hall, New York City. Members of his band include Harry James, Ziggy Elman, Gene Krupa, and Lionel Hampton.   MUSIC

1938   The Cloisters, a museum of medieval art, is built in upper Manhattan as a separate extension of the Metropolitan Museum of Art.   PAINT

1938   American naive painter Anna Mary "Grandma" Moses has the first exhibition of her work in a drugstore in Hoosick Falls, New York.   PAINT

1938   American photographer Walker Evans has his first showing at the Museum of Modern Art, providing the basis for his book *American Photographs*. Among his other works will be *Photographs* (1938) and *First and Last* (1978).   PHOTO

1938   American radio and theater impresario Orson Welles and his Mercury Players stage a radio drama based on the H. G. Wells novel *The War of the Worlds* on October 30. So realistic is the broadcast that many listeners fear the country is being invaded by aliens.   TV&R

1939   American composer Aaron Copland's ballet *Billy the Kid* is produced in New York, and has a consciously created "American sound."   DANCE

1939   *My Heart's in the Highlands* and *The Time of Your Life*, plays by American playwright William Saroyan, premieres. *Time* will win the Pulitzer Prize, but Saroyan will decline it.   DRAMA

1939   *Ondine*, which will be generally regarded as the best play by French novelist and playwright Jean Giraudoux, is produced.   DRAMA

1939   *The Little Foxes*, a drama by American playwright Lillian Hellman, is produced. A tale of greed and social climbing in a turn-of-the-century Southern family, this play will become Hellman's most famous work.   DRAMA

1939   In what will be considered the peak year of the Hollywood studio system, 400 movies are released, of which the biggest box-office success is David O. Selznick's MGM production of *Gone with the Wind*, directed by Victor Fleming. The adaptation of American novelist Margaret Mitchell's 1936 novel of the Civil War and

Reconstruction stars Vivien Leigh as Scarlett O'Hara and Clark Gable as Rhett Butler. Made for $3.9 million, it will, by the 1990s, have earned more than $79 million.   FILM

1939   Other notable films include Victor Fleming's *The Wizard of Oz*, Frank Capra's *Mr. Smith Goes to Washington*, John Ford's *Stagecoach* and *Drums Along the Mohawk*, George Stevens's *Gunga Din*, Howard Hawks's *Only Angels Have Wings*, George Cukor's *The Women*, William Wyler's *Wuthering Heights*, and Edmund Goulding's *Dark Victory* (all U.S.); Jean Renoir's *La Règle du jeu* (*The Rules of the Game*) and Marcel Carné's *Le Jour se lève* (*Daybreak*) (both France); and Zoltan Korda's *The Four Feathers* and Carol Reed's *The Stars Look Down* (both U.K.).   FILM

1939   After years of languishing in low-budget westerns, American actor John Wayne (born Marion Morrison) establishes himself as a prototypical Hollywood star through his performance as the Ringo Kid in John Ford's *Stagecoach*.   FILM

1939   Irish poet and dramatist William Butler Yeats dies (*b.* 1865). His last collection, *Last Poems and Two Plays*, is published posthumously this year. It includes "The Black Tower," "Cuchulain Comforted," "Long-legged Fly," "The Circus Animals' Desertion," and "Politics." Also included is "Under Ben Bulben," which gives the epitaph on Yeats's tombstone in Drumcliff churchyard under the mountain Ben Bulben in County Sligo, Ireland: "Cast a cold eye / On life, on death. / Horseman, pass by!"   LIT

1939   American mystery novelist Raymond Chandler publishes his first novel, *The Big Sleep*, introducing hard-boiled private detective Philip Marlowe, who returns in a series of novels that also include *Farewell, My Lovely* (1940) and *The Lady in the Lake* (1943). The books will spawn a number of films.   LIT

1939   Irish writer James Joyce's novel *Finnegans Wake* is published in complete form. Previously published in parts as *Work in Progress* from 1928 to 1937, the experimental work is rich in verbal play and mythological, historical, and literary allusion. It centers on the dreams of Dublin tavern-keeper Humphrey Chimpden Earwicker and his family as they sleep through a single night.   LIT

1939   The *Collected Poems* of British poet A. E. Housman is published posthumously.
                                                                                                  LIT

1939   British writer Christopher Isherwood publishes *Goodbye to Berlin*, a semiautobiographical fiction collection that includes the sketch "Sally Bowles," which will serve as the basis for John Van Druten's play *I Am a Camera* (1951), which in turn will provide the basis for the Broadway musical *Cabaret* (1968) and its Academy Award–winning film adaptation (1972).   LIT

1939	Welsh writer Richard Llewellyn publishes his novel of memory and Welsh mining life, *How Green Was My Valley*. The book will become a best-seller in the United States and will be made into an Academy Award–winning film by John Ford in 1941. LIT
1939–1945	Well-known World War II correspondents include William Shirer, Ernie Pyle, A. J. Liebling, and radio commentator Edward R. Murrow, whose war reports, which begin with the words, "This is London," become famous. LIT
1939	American novelist John Steinbeck publishes *The Grapes of Wrath*, an indictment of the treatment of those attempting to escape the ravages of the Dust Bowl and the Great Depression. The book will win the Pulitzer Prize and inspire an Academy Award–winning film. LIT
1939	American novelist and short-story writer Eudora Welty publishes the short story "Petrified Man." LIT
1939–1940	Shortly after his death, two works by American novelist Thomas Wolfe are published: *The Web and the Rock* (1939) and *You Can't Go Home Again*. Both works concern the character George "Monk" Webber. LIT
1939	Australian novelist Patrick White publishes his first novel *Happy Valley*. Later works will include *The Tree of Man* (1955) and *Voss* (1957). LIT
1939	Following the Spanish Civil War, cellist Pablo Casals leaves Spain in protest against the policies of dictator Francisco Franco. MUSIC
1939–1945	Popular World War II songs include "Roll Out the Barrel," "The White Cliffs of Dover," "I'll Be Seeing You," "Praise the Lord and Pass the Ammunition," "Hang Out the Washing on the Siegfried Line," and "Lili Marlene," sung memorably by German-born American film star Marlene Dietrich. MUSIC
1939	American composer Irving Berlin's "God Bless America" is popularized by singer Kate Smith, among others, and becomes an informal anthem of the country. It also becomes one of Smith's signature songs. American folk composer Woody Guthrie will later respond to the song with his own socially inclusive brand of patriotism in "This Land Is Your Land." MUSIC
1939	American jazz tenor saxophonist Coleman Hawkins, who played with Fletcher Henderson's band in New York from 1923 to 1934, releases what will become known as his most influential recording, *Body and Soul*. MUSIC
1939–1941	Spanish painter Joan Miró paints the *Constellation* series of 23 paintings in gouache and oil on paper; these will be considered among his finest works. PAINT

1939–1958	American photographer Berenice Abbott, a former student of American photographer Man Ray, compiles a series of highly stylized photos that illustrate the laws of physics. PHOTO
1939	American artist Joseph Cornell shows a series of surrealist "collage sculptures" and "constructions" in a solo exhibition at the Julien Levy Gallery in New York, consisting of hand-made boxes containing several manufactured items. Cornell's boxes will foreshadow Robert Rauschenberg's "combines" of the 1950s. SCULP
1939	FM radios are first sold commercially. TV&R
1940s	The jitterbug, a fast dance developed for the 4/4 syncopation of swing music, dominates the dance floor in the United States and Europe. DANCE
1940s	Canada encourages the development of contemporary art by Eskimo craft workers practicing traditional styles. The works produced include carved figures in whalebone, ivory, and soapstone and lithographs printed with stone. The art of the Eskimo (or Inuit) peoples of the Bering Sea and Canada dates back at least 2,000 years. DECO
1940s	Among the actors who deliver memorable performances during these years are Ingrid Bergman, Joan Fontaine, singing partners Jeannette MacDonald and Nelson Eddy, the comedy team Bud Abbott and Lou Costello, W. C. Fields, Joseph Cotten, Deborah Kerr, Ralph Richardson, Judy Garland, John Wayne, Ethel Waters, Lena Horne, Cab Calloway, Lauren Bacall, Betty Grable, Gregory Peck, Barbara Stanwyck, John Huston, Lana Turner, Alec Guinness, Tyrone Power, Rosalind Russell, William Powell, Spencer Tracy, Irene Dunne, Rex Harrison, Gene Tierney, Jane Wyman, Jennifer Jones, and Charles Boyer. *See also* 1930s and 1950s, FILM. FILM
1940s	Popular songs of the decade include "South of the Border," "How High the Moon," "Oh, Johnny (How You Can Love)," "Blueberry Hill," "I Got It Bad and That Ain't Good," "Bewitched, Bothered, and Bewildered," "Chattanooga Choo-Choo," "That Old Black Magic," "Paper Doll," "Mairzy Doats," "People Will Say We're in Love," "Sentimental Journey," "Rum and Coca-Cola," "Come Rain or Come Shine," "Almost Like Being in Love," "Buttons and Bows," "Some Enchanted Evening," and "Bali Ha'i." MUSIC
1940s	Bebop, or bop, an improvisational form of jazz, is developed by alto saxophonist Charlie "Bird" Parker, trumpeter and composer Dizzy Gillespie, and pianist Thelonious Monk, among others. MUSIC
1940s	African-American painter Jacob Lawrence begins to produce primitivistic, highly decorative works on ghetto life and other social themes. PAINT

1940s	French painter Georges Rouault, who developed his own form of expressionism, turns to creating religious art. PAINT
1940	The Katherine Dunham Dance Company debuts off-Broadway. Named for the African-American dancer and anthropologist, it will be followed in 1944 by the New York–based Katharine Dunham School of Dance, which will teach both dance and cultural studies. DANCE
1940	Walt Disney Productions releases the animated features *Pinocchio* and *Fantasia.* Other notable films include Alfred Hitchcock's *Rebecca*, John Ford's *The Grapes of Wrath*, Charlie Chaplin's *The Great Dictator*, Sam Wood's *Our Town*, and the first of the Bing Crosby–Bob Hope–Dorothy Lamour "Road" movies from Paramount, Victor Schertzinger's *Road to Singapore* (all U.S.). FILM
1940	British-born American poet W. H. Auden publishes the poetry collection *Another Time*, which includes "Lay Your Sleeping Head, My Love" and "In Memory of W. B. Yeats." LIT
1940	Welsh poet Dylan Thomas publishes the story collection *Portrait of the Artist as a Young Dog.* LIT
1940	American writer Ernest Hemingway publishes *For Whom the Bell Tolls*, about Robert Jordan, an American volunteer for the Loyalists during the Spanish Civil War, and his love for a young Spanish woman, Maria. LIT
1940	African-American novelist Richard Wright publishes *Native Son.* LIT

The Constellations of World War II

Just as Pablo Picasso had been prompted by the Spanish Civil War to create one of his most intense works, *Guernica*, Spanish surrealist painter Joan Miró responded to the horrors of World War II by creating the 23 paintings that some would consider his finest works, the *Constellation* series. In 1940, when he started the series of mainly gouache and oil studies, he had settled near Normandy, hoping to escape the path of World War II. However, when Hitler's troops bombed the region in May 1940 and France went under Vichy rule, Miró was forced to abandon his home. Back in Spain Miró saw the war escalate, yet was able to complete the paintings by the fall of 1941. Including such influential works as *The Passage of the Divine Bird* and *The Beautiful Bird Revealing the Unknown to a Pair of Lovers*, the *Constellation* paintings radiate a delicacy, precision, and simultaneous wildness and serenity. They stand as a deliberate artistic response to the chaos of war.

1940   American poet e. e. cummings publishes his poem about the span of human existence, *Anyone Lived in a Pretty How Town*. It will become one of his best-known works.   LIT

1940   American novelist John O'Hara publishes the story collection *Pal Joey*. The title story, about a small-time heel, will be adapted by Richard Rodgers and Lorenz Hart into a Broadway musical.   LIT

1940   American painter Anna Mary "Grandma" Moses has her first major one-person show in New York City, after being championed by collector Louis Calder.   PAINT

1940   French painter Pierre Bonnard, known for his luxurious use of color and great popularity with audiences and collectors, is elected a member of the Royal Academy.   PAINT

1940   In the United States, 30 million homes have radios.   TV&R

1941   German playwright Bertolt Brecht's play *Mutter Courage und ihre Kinder* (*Mother Courage and Her Children*) is produced. Brecht's *Leben des Galilei* (*The Life of Galileo*) and *Der gute Mensch von Sezuan* (*The Good Person of Szechuan*) will be produced in 1943.   DRAMA

1941   *Blithe Spirit*, a comedy by British actor and playwright Noel Coward, is produced in New York and London. It will run in London for 1,997 performances.   DRAMA

1941   *Watch on the Rhine*, a political drama by American playwright Lillian Hellman, premieres. It will be followed by *The Searching Wind* (1944), a play also on political themes, and *Another Part of the Forest* (1946).   DRAMA

1941   RKO releases the film *Citizen Kane*, a fictionalized biography of publishing tycoon William Randolph Hearst. Produced, directed, and coscripted (with Herman J. Mankiewicz) by 25-year-old Orson Welles, *Citizen Kane* is hailed by critics as a rich, innovative masterpiece of filmmaking.   FILM

1941   Other notable films include Howard Hawks's *Sergeant York*, Michael Curtiz's *Dive Bomber*, George Cukor's *The Philadelphia Story*, Victor Fleming's *Dr. Jekyll and Mr. Hyde*, John Ford's *How Green Was My Valley*, John Huston's *The Maltese Falcon*, Preston Sturges's *The Lady Eve*, George Waggner's *The Wolf Man*, and Walt Disney Productions' *Dumbo* (all U.S.).   FILM

1941–1945   American illustrator Norman Rockwell, known for his covers of the *Saturday Evening Post*, executes a poster series on the Four Freedoms that circulates widely during American involvement in World War II.   GRAPH

1941   British novelist Virginia Woolf's last novel, *Between the Acts*, is published posthumously.   LIT

1941   The final, unfinished novel of American novelist F. Scott Fitzgerald, *The Last Tycoon*, is published posthumously.   LIT

1941   Hungarian-born British novelist Arthur Koestler publishes *Darkness at Noon*, about the terrors of totalitarianism. His later works will include the novel *The Ghost in the Machine* (1967) and *Janus: A Summing Up*. He will die by his own hand in 1983.   LIT

The Ending That Almost Wasn't: *Meet John Doe*

In his 1971 autobiography, *The Name Above the Title*, director Frank Capra writes that *Meet John Doe*, his first independent feature made by Frank Capra Productions and not by Columbia, had five different endings. His chapter on the movie is called, "Five Endings in Search of an Audience."

In this 1941 movie, Capra planned to probe "the agony of disillusionment and the wild, dark passions of mobs." In so doing, he hoped to convince critics that the Academy Award–winning director of *It Happened One Night* and *Mr. Smith Goes to Washington* could produce more than "Capra-corn."

In the film, a drifter (Gary Cooper) is tempted by money and glory to become John Doe, a radio celebrity and leader of a populist social movement. When Doe defies the politician who is manipulating him (Edward Arnold), he engineers Doe's downfall, and the American public turns against him. "But now," says Capra, "what happens to John Doe?"

The film opened for two weeks in six major cities, with four different endings. The endings varied on whether Doe jumped from a skyscraper (as he announced he would do) and on who or what led him to his decision. Although the press received the movie well, Capra was displeased with all of the endings. Not until he received a letter from a man who called himself "John Doe" did he realize what the ending should be. The letter said in part, "The only thing that can keep John Doe from jumping to death is the John Does themselves . . . if they ask him."

Capra called his cast together and filmed Doe being saved at midnight by the reporter (Barbara Stanwyck) who is in love with him, her editor (James Gleason), and a group of ordinary people who have been helped by John Doe. Still, Capra felt that this ending was "the best of a sorry lot." He felt he had created a movie with no answers for an audience that needed them.

1941   Endowed by American businessman Paul Mellon in 1937, the National
        Gallery of Art opens in Washington, D.C.   PAINT

1941   American realist painter Edward Hopper completes *Nighthawks*, which epitomizes
        his ability to convey the alienation of urban life.   PAINT

1941   Several artists focus their works on the activity and effects of World War II,
        including Henry Moore (drawings of refugees in London), Paul Nash (*Bombers
        Over Berlin*), and Feliks Topolski (drawings of British armies). PAINT

1941   American photographer Ansel Adams composes *Moonrise, Hernandez, New
        Mexico*, one of the dozens of his photographs that use composition and tonal
        variety to establish him as a foremost 20th-century landscape photographer.
                                                                        PHOTO

1942   *Rodeo*, choreographed by American dancer Agnes De Mille, premieres. In 1943
        De Mille will bring ballet to the Broadway musical through her choreography
        of Rodgers's and Hammerstein's *Oklahoma!*   DANCE

1942   *The Skin of Our Teeth*, a play by American playwright Thornton Wilder, pre-
        mieres.   DRAMA

1942   American actors Hume Cronyn and Jessica Tandy marry. In the years to come,
        they will appear together on stage many times. Notable joint performances will
        include Anton Chekhov's *Three Sisters* and Arthur Miller's *Death of a Salesman*
        during the first season of the Guthrie Theatre in Minneapolis (1963–1964), and
        in New York, Edward Albee's *A Delicate Balance* (1966) and Samuel Beckett's
        Happy Days (1972).   DRAMA

1942   Warner Bros. releases Michael Curtiz's *Casablanca*, starring Humphrey Bogart
        and Ingrid Bergman. The World War II romantic drama will become one of the
        most popular films of all time. Though released in a limited run this year, it
        will not be nominated for an Oscar until the 1943 awards, when it will win
        Oscars for best picture, director, and screenplay.   FILM

1942   Other notable films include Walt Disney Productions' *Bambi*, William Wyler's
        Mrs. Miniver, Michael Curtiz's *Yankee Doodle Dandy*, Mervyn LeRoy's *Random
        Harvest*, Irving Rapper's *Now, Voyager*, David Butler's *Road to Morocco*, and Sam
        Wood's *The Pride of the Yankees* (all U.S.).   FILM

1942   American political cartoonist Herblock (Herbert Block) wins his first Pulitzer
        Prize for his work. He will win a second Pulitzer Prize in 1954. GRAPH

1942   American novelist Cornelia Otis Skinner and American periodical editor Emily
        Kimbrough publish the sprightly novel *Our Hearts Were Young and Gay*. It will
        generate a film adaptation in 1944.   LIT

1942   Algerian-born French writer Albert Camus publishes the existentialist novel
        The Stranger. He also publishes the philosophical essay *The Myth of Sisyphus*
        (1942). Among his later works will be the novel *The Plague* (1947). He will be
        awarded the Nobel Prize for literature in 1957.   LIT

1942   British scholar and writer C. S. Lewis publishes his epistolary work on evil, *The
        Screwtape Letters*. Among his later works will be the series of children's books,
        The Chronicles of Narnia.   LIT

1942   Magnetic recording tape, which will revolutionize the recording industry, is
        invented.   MUSIC

1942   In the movie *Holiday Inn* singer Bing Crosby introduces Irving Berlin's "White
        Christmas," which almost immediately becomes a holiday song standard and
        one of the most widely recorded songs in history.   MUSIC

1942   American jazz singer and pianist Sarah Vaughan joins the Earl Hines band (as
        both singer and pianist) after winning an amateur singing contest at the
        Apollo Theater in Harlem, New York City. She will later play with the bands of
        Billy Eckstine and John Kirby before embarking on a solo career that will also
        take her into the realms of pop and classical music.   MUSIC

1942   German-born American painter Hans Hofmann paints *The Wind*, in which he
        experiments with drip techniques later applied on a larger scale by Jackson
        Pollock. *See* 1947, PAINT.   PAINT

1942   German sculptor Arno Breker opens an exhibition of monumental figurative
        sculpture illustrating the ideologies of Germany's Third Reich at the Musée de
        l'Orangerie.   SCULP

1943   Construction on the Pentagon, the largest office building in the world at 6.5
        million square feet, is completed in Alrington, Virginia. It will house the
        Department of Defense, which will be created in 1949.   ARCH

1943   *Les Mouches (The Flies)*, the first play by French philosopher and writer Jean-
        Paul Sartre, is produced.   DRAMA

1943   Mexican playwright Rodolfo Usigli's historical drama *Corona del sombra (Crown
        of Shadow)* is produced. He will also write the play *El Gesticulador (The Imposter)*.
        Both will be seen as classics of Latin American theater.   DRAMA

1943   The American musical *Oklahoma!*—with book and lyrics by Oscar Hammerstein II, music by Richard Rodgers, and choreography by Agnes De Mille—premieres on March 31. This landmark work is revolutionary in having songs and dances that advance the story.   DRAMA

1943   Notable films include Sam Wood's *For Whom the Bell Tolls*, Howard Hughes's *The Outlaw*, Frank Borzage's *Stage Door Canteen*, and Vincente Minnelli's *Cabin in the Sky* (all U.S.); and Sergei Eisenstein's *Ivan the Terrible* (U.S.S.R.).   FILM

1943   Russian-born American novelist Ayn Rand publishes *The Fountainhead*, the story of the rise of a talented though self-involved architect. The book, which becomes a best-seller, typifies the way Rand interweaves her objectivist philosophy into her works.   LIT

1943   American-born British poet T. S. Eliot publishes the poem *Four Quartets.*   LIT

1943   French philosopher and writer Jean-Paul Sartre publishes the treatise *Being and Nothingness*, which provides the basis for existentialism. His later works include the play *No Exit.*   LIT

1943   French novelist, essayist, and aviator Antoine de Saint-Exupéry publishes the fable *Le Petit Prince* (*The Little Prince*), about the search for what is important in life. An earlier collection of stories and meditations is *Wind, Sand, and Stars* (1939).   LIT

1943   American singer and pianist Nat King Cole (Nathaniel Adams Coles) releases the first of his 86 Top-40 singles and 17 Top-40 albums to hit the charts between now and 1964. Grounded in gospel, Cole will record everything from jazz instrumentals and sentimental ballads to Christmas carols. Among his hits will be recordings of "Get Your Kicks on Route 66," "Sweet Lorraine," "Mona Lisa," "Nature Boy," and "Unforgettable." His daughter, Natalie Cole, will debut as a singer in 1975 and will earn fame in her own right as a vocalist in blues, pop, rock, soul, and gospel.   MUSIC

1943   Now living in New York, Dutch painter Piet Mondrian completes *Broadway Boogie Woogie*, which will become one of his best-known works.   PAINT

1943   American abstract expressionist painter Jackson Pollock gains his first solo exhibition.   PAINT

1943   American painter Thomas Hart Benton paints *July Hay*.   PAINT

1943   British sculptor Barbara Hepworth initiates an individual sculptural style in a series of hollow wood pieces that combine painting and sculpture, surrealist biomorphisim, and organic abstraction.   SCULP

1944   American composer Aaron Copland's evocative ballet *Appalachian Spring*, is
            danced by Martha Graham in Washington, D.C.. **DANCE**

1944   French playwright Jean Anouilh's drama *Antigone*, based on Sophocles' classic
            (*see* 442 B.C., DRAMA), is produced in Paris during the German Occupation. It
            will become Anouilh's best-known play outside of France. **DRAMA**

1944   *Huisclos* (*No Exit*), a drama by French philosopher and writer Jean-Paul Sartre,
            is produced. It will generally be viewed as Sartre's greatest theatrical work. **DRAMA**

1944   Notable films include Leo McCarey's *Going My Way*, Vincente Minnelli's *Meet
            Me in St. Louis*, Mervyn LeRoy's *30 Seconds Over Tokyo*, George Cukor's *Gaslight*,
            Frank Capra's *Arsenic and Old Lace*, Howard Hawks's *To Have and Have Not*,
            and Clarence Brown's *National Velvet* (all U.S.); and Laurence Olivier's *Henry V*
            (U.K.). **FILM**

c. 1944   Dutch artist M. C. Escher designs surrealist prints fraught with optical illusion,
            memorably of staircases leading in several directions at once. **GRAPH**

1944   Canadian-born American writer Saul Bellow publishes his first novel, *Dangling
            Man*. **LIT**

1944   Stationed in the South Pacific with the Army during World War II, American
            poet Karl Shapiro publishes the collection *V-Letter and Other Poems*, about the
            experience and effects of war. It will win the Pulitzer Prize. **LIT**

1944   British writer Eric Arthur Blair, known as George Orwell, publishes the politi-
            cal fable *Animal Farm*. His later novels include the antitotalitarian work *1984*.
            Much of his nonfiction work will be published in *Collected Essays, Journalism
            and Letters* (1968). **LIT**

1944   Argentinian short-story writer and poet Jorge Luis Borges publishes the col-
            lection *Ficciones*. His poetry will be collected in *Selected Poems: 1923–1967*
            (1972). **LIT**

1944   American composer William Schuman's *Secular Cantata No. 2*, "A Free Song,"
            wins the first Pulitzer Prize for music. **MUSIC**

1944   English composer Ralph Vaughan Williams composes his masterpiece
            Symphony no. 5 in D. **MUSIC**

1944   Thirty thousand fans riot at New York's Paramount Theater where Frank "the
            Voice" Sinatra is to appear. Sinatra also appeared at the Paramount in 1942,
            when his popularity was beginning to crest; by 1944 he is at peak popularity.
            Among the songs he will be best known for recording are "Strangers in the

Night," "Under My Skin," "It Was a Very Good Year," "New York, New York," and "My Way." *See also* 1966, MUSIC.   MUSIC

1944   American painter Arshile Gorky paints *The Liver Is the Cock's Comb*.   PAINT

1945–1958   American architect Frank Lloyd Wright designs the Guggenheim Museum, New York City.   ARCH

1945   After temporarily immigrating to the United States from occupied France in 1941, Russian-born designer and painter Marc Chagall designs costumes and sets for Russian composer Igor Stravinsky's ballet *Firebird*.   DANCE

1945   *La Folle de Chaillot* (*The Madwoman of Chaillot*), a play by French novelist and playwright Jean Giraudoux, premieres in Paris. It will be revived many times, enjoying popularity both in France and abroad.   DRAMA

1945   *The Glass Menagerie*, the first critically and commercially successful play by American playwright Tennessee Williams, premieres. It tells the story of Laura, a young disabled woman living in a fantasy world, her disaffected brother Tom, and their domineering mother Amanda.   DRAMA

1945   Notable films include Leo McCarey's *The Bells of St. Mary's*, Alfred Hitchcock's *Spellbound*, George Sidney's *Anchors Aweigh*, Billy Wilder's *The Lost Weekend*, Michael Curtiz's *Mildred Pierce*, and Elia Kazan's *A Tree Grows in Brooklyn* (all U.S.).   FILM

1945   Political cartoonist Bill Mauldin wins the Pulitzer Prize for his works. He gained fame for his World War II cartoons and will win a second Pulitzer Prize in 1959.   GRAPH

1945   American novelist Kathleen Winsor publishes *Forever Amber*.   LIT

1945   Chinese writer Lao She's *Rickshaw Boy* is translated into English. His work is known for its satirical humor.   LIT

1945   African-American novelist Richard Wright publishes the autobiographical *Black Boy*.   LIT

1945   British composer Benjamin Britten's opera *Peter Grimes* opens in London. It is hailed as marking a new era in English opera and establishes his reputation worldwide.   MUSIC

1945   Jazz trumpeter and bandleader Miles Davis, who will be considered among the greatest jazz musicians of all time, begins recording, with saxophonist Herbie Fields. A veteran of Billy Eckstine's band and Charlie Parker's quintet, the 19-

year-old Davis will be credited with several jazz breakthroughs during his career. With arranger Gil Evans, he will evolve what will come to be known as "cool" jazz in the early 1950s; in subsequent years he will pioneer new areas of fusion jazz and create controversial new forms of jazz influenced by rock and funk.   MUSIC

1945   Spanish painter Pablo Picasso paints *The Charnel House*.   PAINT

1945   Following the end of World War II this year, the center of the art world shifts from Paris to New York, where abstract expressionism will be the dominant movement in painting into the 1960s. Abstract expressionist works are typically large, bold, nonrepresentational works in revolt against traditional styles. Painters associated with the movement, which will also be referred to as the New York school, include Jackson Pollock, Arshile Gorky, Hans Hofmann, Franz Kline, Willem de Kooning, Lee Krasner, Barnett Newman, Mark Rothko, and Adolph Gottlieb. *See also* 1947 and c. 1950, PAINT.   PAINT

1945   Five thousand American homes now have television sets. Three years later, the number will be 1 million homes. By 1968 Americans will own 78 million television sets.   TV&R

1946   American architect R. Buckminster Fuller designs Dymaxion House.   ARCH

1946   The new Bodleian Library opens at Oxford University, England.   ARCH

1946   What will become the New York City Ballet is founded as the Ballet Society by Russian-born choreographer George Balanchine and American dance impresario Lincoln Kirstein.   DANCE

1946   French actor and mime Marcel Marceau introduces his character Bip, a white-faced clown at the Théâtre de Poche in Paris. He will portray this character throughout the world for years to come.   DRAMA

1946   *The Iceman Cometh*, a drama by American playwright Eugene O'Neill, premieres. O'Neill's *A Moon for the Misbegotten* will be produced in 1947.   DRAMA

1946   Notable films include William Wyler's *The Best Years of Our Lives*, Frank Capra's *It's a Wonderful Life*, Walt Disney Productions' *Song of the South*, Howard Hawks's *The Big Sleep*, Charles Vidor's *Gilda*, King Vidor's *Duel in the Sun*, Alfred Hitchcock's *Notorious*, Tay Garnett's *The Postman Always Rings Twice*, Clarence Brown's *The Yearling*, Alfred E. Green's *The Jolson Story*, and Robert Siodmak's *The Killers* (all U.S.); David Lean's *Brief Encounter* and *Great Expectations* (both U.K.); and Roberto Rossellini's *Open City* (Italy).   FILM

1946   American journalist John Hersey publishes *Hiroshima*, an account of the effects of the atomic bombing of that Japanese city by the United States.   LIT

1946   American poet and novelist Robert Penn Warren publishes his Pulitzer Prize–winning novel *All the King's Men*, inspired by the career of Louisiana politician Huey Long.   LIT

1946   American novelist Carson McCullers publishes *The Member of the Wedding*, the story of how a young girl, Frankie, views her brother's upcoming wedding. LIT

1946   American poet Robert Lowell publishes the collection *Lord Weary's Castle*, which will win the Pulitzer Prize. Other collections will include *Life Studies* (1959) and *For the Union Dead* (1964).   LIT

1946–1963 American poet William Carlos Williams publishes the first four books of his poem *Paterson* (for Paterson, N.J.) in 1946. Book V will be published in 1958; he will be working on Book VI at the time of his death in 1963.   LIT

1946   Greek novelist Nikos Kazantzakis publishes the novel *Zorba the Greek*. Both it and his later novel, *The Last Temptation of Christ*, will be made into films. LIT

1946   French artist Jean Dubuffet gains his first exhibition. Employing common materials and an unrefined spontaneity, his work embodies the movement known as art brut.   PAINT

1946   Australian painter Sir Sidney Nolan, who will become one of his country's foremost artists, begins a series of paintings centered on national folk hero Ned Kelly.   PAINT

1947   *L'Invitation au château* (*Ring Round the Moon*), a play by French playwright Jean Anouilh, is produced. Anouilh's *La Répétition, ou l'Amour puni* (*The Rehearsal*) will be produced in 1950, *La Valse des toréadors* (*The Waltz of the Toreadors*) in 1952, and *Pauvre Bitos, ou le Dîner des têtes* (*Poor Bitos*) in 1956.   DRAMA

1947   *Les Bonnes* (*The Maids*), the first drama by French writer Jean Genet, is staged in Paris by French director Louis Jouvet. It is based on the true story of two sisters, maids in a provincial French home, who kill their abusive employers.   DRAMA

1947   *A Streetcar Named Desire*, a drama by American playwright Tennessee Williams, premieres. Character Blanche DuBois speaks a line—"I have always depended on the kindness of strangers"—which will become a famous camp phrase. In 1951 *Streetcar* will be filmed by Elia Kazan, the director of the original play.   DRAMA

1947   *All My Sons*, which will become the first successful play by American playwright Arthur Miller, premieres.   DRAMA

1947   Notable films include Elia Kazan's *Gentleman's Agreement*, George Seaton's *Miracle on 34th Street*, Michael Curtiz's *Life with Father*, and Charlie Chaplin's *Monsieur Verdoux* (all U.S.); and Michael Powell and Emeric Pressburger's *Black Narcissus* (U.K.).   FILM

1947   American novelist James Michener publishes his first book, the short-story collection *Tales of the South Pacific*, which wins the Pulitzer Prize and becomes the basis for the musical *South Pacific* (1949). He will later become the author of a series of long, popular, semidocumentary novels, including *Hawaii* (1959), *The Source* (1965), and *Centennial* (1974).   LIT

1947   American novelist John Steinbeck publishes the parablelike short novel *The Pearl*, about the disastrous consequences of finding a precious gem.   LIT

1947   British novelist Malcolm Lowry publishes *Under the Volcano*.   LIT

1947   German-born poet and playwright Nelly Sachs publishes the poetry collection *Dwellings of Death*, about the Holocaust. Later collections will include *And No One Knows Where to Go* (1957).   LIT

1947   French writer André Gide is awarded the Nobel Prize for literature. His works include the collection of prose poems *Fruits of the Earth* (1897), which did not become popular until the 1920s, when it influenced the existentialist writers Albert Camus and Jean-Paul Sartre, among others; *The Counterfeiters* (1926), a complex novel involving multiple plots; and *The Journals of André Gide, 1889–1949* (1950). In 1909 he launched the influential literary periodical *Nouvelle Revue Française*.   LIT

1947   American composer Charles Ives wins the Pulitzer Prize for his Symphony no. 3, written in 1911.   MUSIC

1947   American singer Mahalia Jackson releases her album *Move On Up a Little Higher*, for which she becomes known as the "Gospel Queen." She will sing at the inauguration of President John F. Kennedy in 1961 and at the civil rights march on Washington, D.C., in 1963.   MUSIC

1947   American painter Jackson Pollock begins painting in a "drip and splash" style, abandoning the traditional brush and easel for more chaotic methods of applying paint. The style, known as action painting, is one form of abstract expressionism. Pollock's *Composition No. 1* is a characteristic work.   PAINT

1947   The one-step Polaroid camera is developed by American inventor Edwin Herbert Land.   PHOTO

1947   Swiss sculptor Max Bill erects *Continuity* in Zurich, a monument that is based on the principle of the Möbius strip or band, which possesses only a single surface and a single edge.   SCULP

1948   The Ballets de Paris de Roland Petit is founded by French dancer Roland Petit. DANCE

1948   Russian-born choreographer George Balanchine becomes artistic director and choreographer of the New York City Ballet.   DANCE

1948   *Les Mains sales* (*Dirty Hands*), a drama by French philosopher and writer Jean-Paul Sartre, is produced. Sartre's *Le Diable et le bon dieu* (*The Devil and the Good Lord*) will be staged in 1951. These plays and Sartre's earlier dramas reflect his existential philosophy. He will be awarded the 1964 Nobel Prize for literature.   DRAMA

1948   *Summer and Smoke*, a drama by American playwright Tennessee Williams, premieres. It will be followed by *The Rose Tattoo* (1951) and *Camino Real* (1953).   DRAMA

1948   Notable films include Howard Hawks's *Red River*, Norman Z. McLeod's *The Paleface*, Jules Dassin's *The Naked City*, Jean Negulesco's *Johnny Belinda*, John Huston's *The Treasure of the Sierra Madre* and *Key Largo*, and Anatole Litvak's *The Snake Pit* (all U.S.); Michael Powell and Emeric Pressburger's *The Red Shoes*, Laurence Olivier's *Hamlet*, and Carol Reed's *The Fallen Idol* (all U.K.); and Vittorio De Sica's *The Bicycle Thief* (Italy).   FILM

1948   British poet, novelist, and critic Robert Graves publishes *The White Goddess*, a study of mythology in relation to poetic inspiration.   LIT

1948   American novelist and short-story writer Truman Capote publishes *Other Voices, Other Rooms*. Later celebrated works will include the short novel about New York–original Holly Golightly, *Breakfast at Tiffany's* (1958), and the non-fiction-based novel *In Cold Blood* (1965).   LIT

1948   American novelist Norman Mailer publishes the World War II novel *The Naked and the Dead*.   LIT

1948   South African novelist Alan Paton publishes the novel *Cry, the Beloved Country*. LIT

1948   German composer Richard Strauss composes his *Vier letzte Lieder* (*Four Last Lieder*) for soprano and orchestra.   MUSIC

1948   French musician Pierre Schaeffer inaugurates "musique concrète" at a Paris radio studio. It works by replacing the traditional material of music (instrumental and vocal sounds) with recorded sounds such as noises and percussion.   MUSIC

1948   The long-playing vinyl phonograph record is developed by CBS engineer Peter Goldmark. The record runs at a speed of 33⅓ revolutions per minute and plays for about 45 minutes. It will change the creation and marketing of popular music.   MUSIC

1948   American blues guitarist John Lee Hooker's composition and recording "Boogie Chillun" is his first hit, selling a million copies over the next five years. His 1949 hit, "Crawlin' King Snake," will be covered frequently in the late 1960s by such blues-based rock bands as the Doors.   MUSIC

1948   American painter Robert Motherwell begins the series of works *Elegy to the Spanish Republic*, which will eventually encompass more than 100 paintings.   PAINT

1948   American painter Andrew Wyeth comes to international prominence with his painting *Christina's World*.   PAINT

1948   American painter and member of the New York school Barnett Newman establishes himself as an abstract expressionist by the end of the 1940s, particularly with his monochromatic 1948 painting *Onement I*.   PAINT

1948   Swiss sculptor Alberto Giacometti displays very thin, frail, almost sticklike bronze figures at an exhibition in New York.   SCULP

1948   The transistor, which will greatly reduce the size of radios and televisions, is developed for Bell Laboratories by American physicists William Shockley, John Bardeen, and Walter Brattain.   TV&R

1948   *The Toast of the Town*, which will later be known as *The Ed Sullivan Show*, debuts on TV. The variety show featuring acts ranging from top Broadway talent to vaudevillian exotica will run until 1971. It will be noted for memorable appearances by Elvis Presley and the Beatles.   TV&R

1949   The samba, a Latin American dance, becomes popular in the United States and Europe.   DANCE

1949   *The Cocktail Party*, a drawing-room comedy by the American-born British poet T. S. Eliot, is performed at the Edinburgh Festival. *The Confidential Clerk* and *The Elder Statesman*, both comedies by Eliot, will be performed at the festival in 1953 and 1958, respectively. T. S. Eliot was awarded the 1948 Nobel Prize for literature.   DRAMA

1949   *Haute surveillance* (*Deathwatch*), a drama by French writer Jean Genet, opens in a production that Genet helps direct.   DRAMA

1949   American director and teacher of acting Lee Strasberg becomes artistic director
                of the Actors Studio, a New York City workshop devoted to the Method, an
                inner-directed approach to acting derived from the ideas of Konstantin
                Stanislavsky (*see* 1936, DRAMA). Workshop members will include the American
                actors Marlon Brando, James Dean, Montgomery Clift, Geraldine Page, Shelley
                Winters, Dustin Hoffman, Robert De Niro, Al Pacino, and Ellen Burstyn.   DRAMA

1949   *Death of a Salesman*, a drama written by American playwright Arthur Miller and
                directed by Elia Kazan, premieres. This tale of traveling salesman Willy Loman
                and his family will win the Pulitzer Prize and will be considered by some to
                be Miller's best play and an example of modern tragedy.   DRAMA

1949   The American musical *South Pacific*—with book by Oscar Hammerstein II and
                Joshua Logan, lyrics by Hammerstein, and music by Richard Rogers—pre-
                mieres on April 7. It stars Mary Martin and Ezio Pinza.   DRAMA

1949   Notable films include George Cukor's *Adam's Rib*, William A. Wellman's
                Battleground, Allan Dwan's *The Sands of Iwo Jima*, and Henry King's *Twelve O'Clock
                High* (all U.S.); Carol Reed's *The Third Man* (U.K.); Roberto Rossellini's *Stromboli*
                (Italy); and Jean-Pierre Melville's *Les Enfants terribles* (France).   FILM

1949   African-American poet Gwendolyn Brooks publishes the collection *Annie Allen*.
                The Chicago-based poems will win the Pulitzer Prize.   LIT

1949   British author Nancy Mitford publishes the novel of English society, *Love in a
                Cold Climate*. Later works will include *The Blessing* (1951).   LIT

1949   French novelist and philosopher Simone de Beauvoir publishes the philo-
                sophical treatise *The Second Sex*, which will become one of the foundational clas-
                sics of the "second wave" of feminism. The English translation will be published in
                1953. Among her later works will be the novel *The Mandarins* (1954; 1957) and her
                study of aging, *The Coming of Age* (1970; 1972).   LIT

1949   American short-story writer Shirley Jackson publishes the tale of small-town
                cruelty, "The Lottery."   LIT

1949   *Mode de valeurs et d'intensités* for piano, by French composer Olivier Messiaen,
                will greatly influence experimentalist composers Pierre Boulez and Karlheinz
                Stockhausen.   MUSIC

1949–1951   In thanks to the nuns who nursed him following operations for cancer, French
                painter Henri Matisse designs and creates artwork for the Chapel of the Rosary of
                Vence. The artwork includes murals on tile and stained-glass windows.   PAINT

1949   Austrian expressionist painter Oskar Kokoschka is given an exhibition at the
            Museum of Modern Art, New York City. During a decades-long career he has
            become known for his telling portraits of people and towns, as well as his
            work with the Wiener Werkstätte.   PAINT

1950s   The international style of architecture, originating in the work of such archi-
            tects as Walter Gropius, Ludwig Mies van der Rohe, and Le Corbusier in the
            1920s, becomes the preferred mode for building skyscrapers. *See* 1926, ARCH.   ARCH

1950s   The Royal Ballet is founded in London. Among the choreographers for this
            classically oriented ballet are Anthony Tudor and Sir Frederick Ashton.   DANCE

1950s–1960s Calligraphy and wood-block printing are two areas that distinguish Japanese
            artists such as Shunsho Machi, Fumio Kitaoka, and Okiie Hashimoto.   DECO

1950s   Off-Broadway theater flourishes in New York City, gaining the attention of crit-
            ics and increasingly presenting artistically and commercially successful shows. DRAMA

1950s   Among the actors who deliver memorable performances during this decade are
            Gloria Swanson, William Holden, Montgomery Clift, Frank Sinatra, Joan
            Bennett, Kim Novak, Elizabeth Taylor, Marlon Brando, Shelly Winters, Gene
            Kelly, Sidney Poitier, Debbie Reynolds, Susan Hayward, Harry Belafonte, Ava
            Gardner, Burt Lancaster, Kirk Douglas, Donna Reed, Leslie Caron, David Niven,
            Grace Kelly, Marilyn Monroe, Hope Lange, Louis Armstrong, Tony Curtis, Jack
            Lemmon, José Ferrer, James Mason, Simone Signoret, Dorothy Dandridge, Pearl
            Bailey, Anthony Quinn, Audrey Hepburn, James Dean, Joanne Woodward, Yves
            Montand, Maurice Chevalier, Sammy Davis Jr., Rita Hayworth, Paul Newman,
            Natalie Wood, Ernest Borgnine, Peter Ustinov, Robert Mitchum, Lee Remick,
            George C. Scott, Eva Marie Saint, Doris Day, Rock Hudson, Yul Brynner, Brigitte
            Bardot, and Sophia Loren. *See also* 1940s and 1960s, FILM.   FILM

1950s   Spanish painter Joan Miró experiments with etchings, lithographs, and illus-
            tration of books, including *Ubu Roi*.   GRAPH

1950s   Popular songs of the decade include "Mona Lisa," "Goodnight Irene," "In the
            Cool, Cool, Cool of the Evening," "Hello, Young Lovers," "Jambalaya," "I Love
            Paris," "(How Much Is That) Doggie in the Window," "Stranger in Paradise,"
            "Mister Sandman," "Young at Heart," "Three Coins in the Fountain," "Love Is
            a Many-Splendored Thing," "Rock Around the Clock," "Hound Dog," "Blue
            Suede Shoes," "Que Sera Sera," "Young Love," "Maria," "Volare," "Mack the
            Knife," "Personality," "Tom Dooley," "High Hopes."   MUSIC

1950s   American painter Willem de Kooning paints the highly abstracted, energeti-
            cally painted *Woman* series.   PAINT

1950s   American abstract painter and art critic Ad Reinhardt, who works within many artistic styles, including abstract expressionism, turns to monochromatic painting during the decade.   PAINT

1950s   American photographers Irving Penn and Richard Avedon become known for their expressive work in advertising and fashion photography for mass-market periodicals like *Life* and *Vogue*. In 1957 Avedon will serve as inspiration for the main character in the film *Funny Face* and will also act as its visual consultant.   PHOTO

1950s   Russian-born American sculptor Louise Nevelson begins to construct images of found pieces of wood. Her objects will take on the form of large wall units in the 1960s, decorated with motifs inspired by sculpture on Mayan ruins.   SCULP

1950s   Late in this decade, American sculptor John Chamberlain produces works known as "junk sculpture" made of fragments of old machinery.   SCULP

1950s   Sid Caesar, Imogene Coca, Carl Reiner, and Howard Morris star in the comedy series *Your Show of Shows* (1950–1954) and *Caesar's Hour* (1954–1957).   TV&R

1950   The United Nations Building is completed in New York City.   ARCH

1950   The one-act *La Cantatrice chauve* (*The Bald Soprano*), the first play by French absurdist playwright Eugène Ionesco, is produced. It will be followed by *La Leçon* (*The Lesson*, 1951), *Les Chaises* (*The Chairs*, 1952), *Victimes du devoir* (*Victims of Duty*, 1953), *Jacques, ou la Soumission* (*Jacques, or the Submission*, 1955), and several other short works.   DRAMA

1950   *Come Back Little Sheba*, the first and perhaps best drama by American playwright William Inge, is produced. The show stars actress Shirley Booth, who will also perform in the 1952 film version.   DRAMA

1950   The American musical *Guys and Dolls*—with book by Jo Swerling and Abe Burrows and music and lyrics by Frank Loesser—premieres on November 24. It is based on stories by American yarn spinner Damon Runyon.   DRAMA

1950   Notable films include Joseph L. Mankiewicz's *All About Eve*, John Huston's *The Asphalt Jungle*, Billy Wilder's *Sunset Boulevard*, George Cukor's *Born Yesterday*, Henry Koster's *Harvey*, Walt Disney Productions' *Cinderella*, and Vincente Minnelli's *Father of the Bride* (all U.S.); Akira Kurosawa's *Rashomon* (Japan); and Max Ophuls's *La Ronde* and Jean Cocteau's *Orphée* (both France).   FILM

1950   American science-fiction writer and founder of the Church of Scientology Layfette Ronald (L. Ron) Hubbard publishes *Dianetics: The Modern Science of Mental Health*. The book will become a best-seller and will be the basis for the Scientology movement.   LIT

1950   English philosopher, mathematician, and writer Bertrand Russell wins the Nobel
              Prize for literature for being, in the words of Anders Österling of the Swedish
              Academy, "one of our time's brilliant spokesmen of rationality and humanity, as
              a fearless champion of free speech and free thought in the West."   LIT

1950   American blues singer and guitarist B. B. King records his first hit, *3 O'Clock
              Blues*. His fame will grow throughout the 1950s and 1960s, when it will spread
              to Europe, which he will tour for the first time in 1968. In 1981 he will win a
              Grammy Award for his album *There Must Be a Better World Somewhere*.   MUSIC

c. 1950   Color field painting is developed in the late 1940s and early 1950s by such
              artists as Barnett Newman, Mark Rothko, and Helen Frankenthaler. The paint-
              ings make use of large areas of single colors. The movement will sometimes be
              considered a variety of abstract expressionism, sometimes a separate entity. It
              is related to post-painterly abstraction. *See* 1960s, PAINT.   PAINT

1950   Austrian painter Oskar Kokoschka paints the *Prometheus* ceiling for Count
              Seilern's house, Princes Gate, London.   PAINT

1950   American painter Jackson Pollock paints *Autumn Rhythm* and *One*.   PAINT

1950   American painter Mark Rothko paints *No. 10*.   PAINT

1950–1958   Spanish painter Joan Miró designs *Mur du Soleil* and *Mur de la Lune*, ceramic
              murals for the UNESCO Building, New York City. The works are examples of
              his experimentation in forms that will continue for the rest of his life. PAINT

1950   American painter Franz Kline, who will become known for his idiosyncratic
              expressive form of abstract expressionism, has his first one-man show in New
              York City.   PAINT

1950–1970   American photojournalist W. Eugene Smith is active, creating works of "rea-
              soned passion" such as *Tokomo in Her Bath* (1971), which conveys the sorrow
              of a mother whose son has died of mercury poisoning.   PHOTO

1950–1980   French photographer Robert Doisneau uses wit to capture incidences of human
              pleasure and shortcoming, in such photos as *The Kiss* and *Side Glance* (1953).
                                                                                        PHOTO

1950   American photographer Paul Strand, who combines in his work humanism
              and principles of modern art, publishes the collection *Time in New England*.
              His later collections will include *Un Paese* (1955) and *Living Egypt* (1969). PHOTO

1950–1951   The highest-rated TV program of the season is *Texaco Star Theater* (NBC). Other top-rated programs are *Your Show of Shows* (NBC) and *The Lone Ranger* (ABC).   TV&R

1951   The National Ballet of Canada is founded in Toronto by Celia Franca.   DANCE

1951   *The Autumn Garden*, a drama by American playwright Lillian Hellman, premieres. It will be followed by her stage adaptation of Voltaire's *Candide* (1956) and her play *Toys in the Attic* (1960).   DRAMA

1951   *Requiem for a Nun*, the only play by American novelist William Faulkner, is published. It is a sequel to his novel *Sanctuary*.   DRAMA

1951   Notable films include John Huston's *The African Queen*, Vincente Minnelli's *An American in Paris*, Robert Wise's *The Day the Earth Stood Still*, George Stevens's *A Place in the Sun*, Elia Kazan's *A Streetcar Named Desire*, and Walt Disney Productions' *Alice in Wonderland* (all U.S.).   FILM

1951   British-born American poet W. H. Auden publishes the poetry collection *Nones*, which includes the poem "Their Lonely Betters."   LIT

1951   Two years before his death, Welsh poet Dylan Thomas publishes the poem "Do Not Go Gentle into That Good Night" (revised 1952). His *Collected Poems* will be published in 1953.   LIT

1951   Irish playwright and novelist Samuel Beckett, writing in French, publishes *Molloy* and *Malone meurt* (*Malone Dies*), the first two novels of a trilogy that concludes with *L'Innommable* (*The Unnamable*, 1953).   LIT

1951   American novelist James Jones publishes *From Here to Eternity*, a best-seller about U.S. Army life in Hawaii before the 1941 Japanese attack on Pearl Harbor.   LIT

1951   American author J. D. Salinger publishes the novel *The Catcher in the Rye*. Main character Holden Caulfield, who spends much of his energy striving to avoid phonies, will become a prototypical postwar young hero. Salinger's later works will include *Nine Stories* (1953), *Franny and Zooey* (1961), *Raise High the Roof-Beam, Carpenters* (1963) and *Seymour: An Introduction* (1963).   LIT

1951   American poet Langston Hughes publishes the poem "Harlem," which begins, "What happens to a dream deferred?" In its day it becomes a representative work for African-Americans, and it will become one of Hughes's signature works.   LIT

1951–1953   Russian-born American writer Isaac Asimov publishes the science-fiction novels known as *The Foundation* trilogy (*Foundation, Foundation and Empire, Second Foundation*), which originally appeared as individual stories in pulp magazines.   LIT

1951   British composer Benjamin Britten's somber opera *Billy Budd* opens in London.

MUSIC

1951   Ralph Vaughan Williams's opera *The Pilgrim's Progress* opens in London. MUSIC

1951   American soprano Maria Callas, who will be regarded as one of the greatest dramatic opera singers of the century, joins La Scala in Milan, where she will remain until 1958; she will return to La Scala from 1960 to 1962.   MUSIC

1951   American composer John Cage writes *Imaginary Landscape No. 4* for 12 radios, 24 musicians, and a conductor. Each performance is unique because as the piece progresses, each radio is tuned to a different station and the volume is changed.   MUSIC

1951   American rhythm-and-blues and soul singer, songwriter, arranger, and pianist Ray Charles records his first hit, "Baby Let Me Hold Your Hand." Among his best-known recordings will be his "What'd I Say" (1959), his version of the popular standard "Georgia on My Mind" (1960), his cover of Percy Mayfield's rhythm-and-blues number "Hit the Road, Jack" (1961) and his rendition of Don Gibson's ballad "I Can't Stop Loving You" (1962), previously popularized by country singer Hank Williams.   MUSIC

1951   American photographer Aaron Siskind creates the photo *New York 2*, an example of the trend toward abstraction in post–World War II photography.   PHOTO

1951–1952   The highest-rated TV program of the season is *Arthur Godfrey's Talent Scouts* (CBS). Other top-rated programs are *I Love Lucy* (CBS) and *Your Show of Shows* (NBC).   TV&R

1952   Finnish-American architect Eero Saarinen designs the General Motors Technical Center in Warren, Michigan. It is to be one of his many influential designs in the United States; another will be Dulles International Airport in Virginia.   ARCH

1952   The ballet Folklórico de México is founded in Mexico City by Amalia Hernández of the National Institute of Fine Arts. Originally conceived to create works for television, it will evolve into Mexico's national company.   DANCE

1952   American dancer and actor Gene Kelly establishes himself as a foremost dancer and choreographer with his starring role in the Stanley Donen film *Singin' in the Rain*. His supple, athletic approach contrasts with the cool, light style of American actor and dancer Fred Astaire. Kelly's dance with umbrella in hand on a rain-drenched street will become a landmark film sequence that will be parodied by Malcolm MacDowell in Stanley Kubrick's *A Clockwork Orange* (1971).   DANCE

1952   *The Mousetrap* by Agatha Christie begins its run on the British stage. Still running more than four decades later, it will become the longest-running play in theater history.   DRAMA

1952   Circle-in-the-Square, a theater which will present acclaimed productions of work by Tennessee Williams, Eugene O'Neill, Dylan Thomas, and many others, opens in New York City on February 2.   DRAMA

1952   The Cinerama widescreen process, developed by Fred Waller, is unveiled in the feature-length travelogue *This Is Cinerama*, narrated by Lowell Thomas and memorable for its realistic roller-coaster sequence.   FILM

1952   Notable films include Gene Kelly and Stanley Donen's *Singin' in the Rain*, Fred Zinnemann's *High Noon*, John Ford's *The Quiet Man*, Cecil B. De Mille's *The Greatest Show on Earth*, and Charlie Chaplin's *Limelight* (all U.S.); and Vittorio De Sica's *Umberto D* (Italy).   FILM

1952   American novelist John Steinbeck publishes the family saga and study of brotherly conflict, *East of Eden*. He will be awarded the 1962 Nobel Prize for literature.   LIT

Brooklyn Writers

While many American writers have aspired to making their name in the bright lights of Manhattan, a large number have plied their craft just over the river in the unheralded borough of Brooklyn.

For some, like Neil Simon or Alfred Kazin, Brooklyn was a birthplace and a source of memory. For others, like Truman Capote, it was a destination. As he put it in his essay, "A House on the Heights" (1959), "I live in Brooklyn. By choice."

Among those who have passed through Brooklyn long enough to immortalize the borough in their works and be counted as native sons or daughters are:

Truman Capote—lived for part of his adulthood in Brooklyn Heights. Reimagined Brooklyn in the essays "Brooklyn" (1946) and "A House on the Heights" (1959).

Alfred Kazin—born and raised in Brownsville, Brooklyn. Recalled in memoir *A Walker in the City* (1951).

Marianne Moore—lived for part of her later adult life in Brooklyn. Immortalized Brooklyn Bridge in poem "Granite and Steel" (1966).

Neil Simon—born and raised in Brooklyn. Remembered Brooklyn in autobiographical play *Brighton Beach Memoirs* (1983).

Walt Whitman—attended grade school in Brooklyn, edited the Brooklyn *Times* and Brooklyn *Daily Eagle*, had his self-published *Leaves of Grass* printed there in 1855. Remembered Brooklyn in "Crossing Brooklyn Ferry" (1856).

Thomas Wolfe—lived there for three years writing the novel *October Fair*, parts of which were incorporated into *Of Time and the River* (1935). Recalled South Brooklyn in short story "Only the Dead Know Brooklyn."

1952	American novelist Ralph Ellison publishes *Invisible Man*, an archetypal view of the African-American experience. It will win the National Book Award. LIT
1952	American novelist Bernard Malamud publishes the baseball novel *The Natural*, about the gifted but doomed player Roy Hobbes. LIT
1952	American writer Ernest Hemingway publishes his short novel, *The Old Man and the Sea*, about the struggle of a Cuban fisherman to snare a marlin. Hemingway will be awarded the Nobel Prize for literature in 1954. LIT
1952	American essayist E. B. White publishes *Charlotte's Web*, the story of a talented spider named Charlotte and a pig named Wilbur. It will become a classic children's novel. LIT
1952	American poet Frank O'Hara publishes his first collection, *A City Winter*. Among his later collections will be *Oranges* (1953), *Meditations in an Emergency* (1957), and *Lunch Poems* (1964). LIT
1952	German composer Hans Werner Henze's first opera *Boulevard Solitude* opens in Hanover. MUSIC
1952	Welsh poet Dylan Thomas writes the radio play *Under Milk Wood*. TV&R
1952	Hand-held transistor radios are first marketed in the United States by the Japanese company Sony. TV&R
1952–1953	The highest-rated TV program of the season is *I Love Lucy* (CBS). Other top-rated programs include *Arthur Godfrey's Talent Scouts* (CBS) and *Dragnet* (NBC). TV&R
1953	French playwright Jean Anouilh's *L'Alouette* (*The Lark*), a historical play about Joan of Arc, is produced. Anouilh's *Becket, ou l'Honneur de Dieu*, a historical play about Thomas à Becket, is produced. DRAMA
1953	Irish playwright and novelist Samuel Beckett's play *En Attendant Godot* (*Waiting for Godot*) is produced. It will be very popular in France and abroad, and it will be regarded by many as Beckett's greatest work. DRAMA
1953	*The Crucible*, a drama by American playwright Arthur Miller, premieres. The story of the witchcraft trials in 17th-century Salem, Massachusetts, it is Miller's response to the witch-hunts of Senator Joseph McCarthy and the House Un-American Activities Committee. DRAMA
1953	Notable films include Fred Zinnemann's *From Here to Eternity*, George Stevens's *Shane*, William Wyler's *Roman Holiday*, Billy Wilder's *Stalag 17*, Walt

Disney Productions' *Peter Pan*, Byron Haskin's *War of the Worlds*, and John Ford's *Mogambo* (all U.S.); and Federico Fellini's *I Vitelloni* (Italy), which will be considered by some his masterpiece.   FILM

1953   Henry Koster's biblical epic *The Robe*, released by 20th Century-Fox and starring Richard Burton and Jean Simmons, is the first movie filmed in the widescreen process CinemaScope.   FILM

1953   Arch Oboler's *Bwana Devil* is the first 3-D, or three-dimensional, film to be shown commercially. The 3-D effect requires the audience to wear special glasses.   FILM

1953   African-American novelist and essayist James Baldwin publishes the novel *Go Tell It on the Mountain*, based in part on his life experiences in Harlem.   LIT

1953   American poet Theodore Roethke publishes *The Waking: Poems 1933–1953*, which will win the Pulitzer Prize. Other collections include *Words for the Wind* (1959) and *The Far Field* (1964).   LIT

1953   English science-fiction writer Arthur C. Clarke publishes the novel *Childhood's End*.   LIT

1953   British prime minister Winston Churchill (1940–1945 and 1951–1955) wins the Nobel Prize for literature. His works include memoirs, speeches, biographies, and histories.   LIT

1953   American country-music singer, songwriter, and guitarist Hank Williams dies at the age of 29 of a heart condition complicated by drugs and alcohol. He leaves a legacy of immensely popular songs—among them, "Your Cheatin' Heart" and "Move It On Over"—that will be frequently covered by other artists. His son, Hank Williams Jr., will become a popular country-music performer in his own right.   MUSIC

1953   American abstract expressionist painter Larry Rivers completes *Washington Crossing the Delaware*, inspired by German-born American painter Emanuel Leutze's painting of the same name. *See* 1851, PAINT.   PAINT

1953   German sculptor Mathias Golritz establishes an experimental museum in Mexico City called the Echo to display massive geometric steel structures. His compositions will influence artists of the 1960s, who will emphasize the duplicability of their works by leaving the execution to others.   SCULP

1953–1954   The highest-rated TV program of the season is *I Love Lucy*. Other top-rated programs are *You Bet Your Life* (NBC) and *The Milton Berle Show* (NBC).   TV&R

1954   American dancer Robert Joffrey founds the Joffrey Ballet in New York. It will feature works by American choreographers Twyla Tharp and Alvin Ailey, among others.   DANCE

1954   French ballet impresario Maurice Béjart becomes director of the Ballets de l'Étoile.   DANCE

1954   American playwright Thornton Wilder's *The Matchmaker*, a rewrite of his earlier work *The Merchant of Yonkers*, premieres. It will be the basis for the highly successful musical *Hello, Dolly! See* 1964, DRAMA.   DRAMA

1954   Notable films include Elia Kazan's *On the Waterfront*, Alfred Hitchcock's *Rear Window*, Edward Dmytryk's *The Caine Mutiny*, Michael Curtiz's *White Christmas*, George Cukor's *A Star Is Born*, William A. Wellman's *The High and the Mighty*, and Jean Negulesco's *Three Coins in the Fountain* (all U.S.); Akira Kurosawa's *The Seven Samurai* (Japan); Federico Fellini's *La Strada* (Italy); and Henri-Georges Clouzot's *Diabolique* (France).   FILM

1954–1955   British novelist J. R. R. Tolkien publishes the fantasy trilogy *The Lord of the Rings*, consisting of the novels *The Fellowship of the Rings*, *The Two Towers*, and *The Return of the King. See also* 1937, LIT.   LIT

1954   British poet Cecil Day-Lewis publishes his *Collected Poems*. He began publishing poetry in the 1920s, when he was a member of the left-wing group of poets centering on W. H. Auden.   LIT

1954   American novelist and short-story writer Eudora Welty publishes *The Ponder Heart*, a short novel. Other works include *The Robber Bridegroom* (1942) and several story collections, including *Delta Wedding* (1946).   LIT

1954   Already a published poet, British novelist Kingsley Amis publishes the comic work *Lucky Jim*, his first novel. Later works will include *That Uncertain Feeling* (1955) and *Jake's Thing* (1978). He will win the Booker Prize for the novel *The Old Devils* (1986). His son Martin Amis will become a celebrated novelist in his own right. *See* 1986, LIT.   LIT

1954   British composer Benjamin Britten's eerie opera *The Turn of the Screw* opens in Venice.   MUSIC

1954   Italian-born composer Gian Carlo Menotti's opera *The Saint of Bleecker Street* opens in New York. It wins the Pulitzer Prize in 1955.   MUSIC

1954   Austrian-born composer Arnold Schoenberg's unfinished opera *Moses and Aron* opens posthumously in Hamburg.   MUSIC

1954   The Newport Jazz Festival in Newport, Rhode Island, is held for the first time. The annual event will feature some of the most important jazz musicians in the business.   MUSIC

1954   American tenor saxophonist Sonny Rollins, in a recording session with jazz trumpeter and bandleader Miles Davis (*see* 1945, MUSIC), introduces three of his compositions, which will eventually become jazz standards: "Airegin," "Doxy," and "Oleo."   MUSIC

1954   Blending elements of rhythm-and-blues and rockabilly in his singing style, Memphis truck driver Elvis Aaron Presley, born in 1935 in Tupelo, Mississippi, records his first commercially successful record, "That's All Right, Mama" and "Blue Moon of Kentucky." (Other exponents of this new style, known as rock-abilly, will be Carl Perkins, whose "Blue Suede Shoes" will be a hit for both Perkins and Presley in 1956, and Presley's high-school classmate Johnny Burnette.) A subsequent contract with RCA, several gold records ("Hound Dog" and "Don't Be Cruel," among others), a history-making appearance on *The Ed Sullivan Show*, and a film career beginning with *Love Me Tender* will make Elvis Presley the most influential rock musician of the decade, despite the fact that most of the songs he will make famous were written by others. *See also* 1968, MUSIC.   MUSIC

1954   American rock group Bill Haley and His Comets release a cover of Joe Turner's "Shake, Rattle and Roll" to great success. In 1955 they will re-release their cover of Sunny Dae's "Rock Around the Clock" (when originally released by Haley this year just prior to "Shake, Rattle and Roll," it has little impact) and it will become a number-one hit. Haley will be displaced from his status as best-known rock musician by Elvis Presley in1956.   MUSIC

1954   British painter Francis Bacon reworks Spanish painter Velázquez's portrait of Pope Leo X in *Head Surrounded by Sides of Beef*.   PAINT

1954   British painter Graham Sutherland completes his *Portrait of Churchill*, which is disliked by the British prime minister (1940–1945 and 1951–1955) and which will eventually be destroyed by his family.   PAINT

1954   RCA markets the first color television set.   TV&R

1954–1955   The highest-rated TV program of the season is *I Love Lucy* (CBS). Other top-rated programs include *The Jackie Gleason Show* (CBS) and *The Toast of the Town* (CBS).   TV&R

1954   Televisions are found in 29 million American homes.   TV&R

1954   In an early example of the power of TV to affect national events, American jour-
            nalist Edward R. Murrow mounts an influential attack on Communist-hunting
            Wisconsin senator Joseph McCarthy on the program *See It Now*.   TV&R

1955   Architect Frederick Gibberd designs the London Airport.   ARCH

1955   *Bus Stop*, a drama by the American playwright Willian Inge, is produced. His
            other works include *Picnic* in 1953 and *The Dark at the Top of the Stairs*, which
            will be produced in 1957.   DRAMA

1955   *A View from the Bridge* and *A Memory of Two Mondays*, one-act plays by
            American playwright Arthur Miller, premiere. (*A View from the Bridge* will be
            expanded to three acts in 1956). This year Miller also marries actress Marilyn
            Monroe. *After the Fall*, a Miller drama which will open in 1964, will be seen by
            many as a depiction of the playwright's relationship with Monroe.   DRAMA

1955   *Cat on a Hot Tin Roof*, a drama by American playwright Tennessee Williams,
            premieres. Set on a Mississippi Delta plantation, it tells of the conflicts within
            a family following the father's diagnosis with cancer. A highly bowdlerized ver-
            sion of *Cat* will be made into a popular 1958 film starring Elizabeth Taylor,
            Paul Newman, and Burl Ives.   DRAMA

1955   Notable films include Delbert Mann's *Marty*, Alfred Hitchcock's *To Catch a
            Thief*, Joshua Logan's *Picnic*, John Ford and Mervyn LeRoy's *Mister Roberts*, and
            Walt Disney Productions' *Lady and the Tramp* (all U.S.); Ingmar Bergman's
            Smiles of a Summer Night (Sweden); Jules Dassin's *Rififi* (France); and Laurence
            Olivier's *Richard III* (U.K.).   FILM

1955   On September 30, 24-year-old American actor James Dean (*b.* February 8,
            1931) dies in a car crash after rocketing to stardom earlier this year with his
            intense performances in Nicholas Ray's *Rebel Without a Cause* and Elia Kazan's
            East of Eden. His third and last starring film, George Stevens's *Giant*, will be
            released next year. His status as a pop icon of troubled youth will only grow
            after his death.   FILM

1955   British poet Philip Larkin publishes the collection *The Less Deceived*.   LIT

1955   American essayist and novelist Anne Morrow Lindbergh, wife of aviator
            Charles Lindbergh, publishes the memoiristic *Gift from the Sea*. For decades
            the philosophical book will remain a favorite among female readers.   LIT

1955–1963   African-American novelist and essayist James Baldwin publishes three collec-
            tions of essays on race and society: *Notes of a Native Son* (1955); *Nobody Knows
            My Name* (1961); and *The Fire Next Time* (1963).   LIT

1955   Russian-born American novelist Vladimir Nabokov publishes *Lolita,* a novel about
                a nymphet named Lolita Haze and a pedophile named Humbert Humbert, who
                falls in love with her. Originally published in France, it stirs controversy in the
                United States, where it will not be published until 1958.   LIT

1955   American poet Elizabeth Bishop publishes *Poems,* a collection of two volumes
                of poetry, *North & South* and *A Cold Spring.* She will be awarded the Pulitzer
                Prize in the same year for her work.   LIT

1955   British novelist William Golding publishes the novel *Lord of the Flies.*   LIT

1955   American Southern writer Flannery O'Connor publishes her short-story collec-
                tion *A Good Man Is Hard to Find.*   LIT

1955   British composer Michael Tippett's visionary first opera *The Midsummer Marriage*
                opens in London.   MUSIC

1955   Chuck Berry, who will be considered the first important American rock musician
                who wrote most of his own songs, records his first number-one song, "Maybellene";
                other hits will include "Johnny B. Goode" and "Roll Over Beethoven."   MUSIC

1955   The American rock musician Little Richard (Richard Wayne Penniman)
                launches his two-year recording career, releasing such classics as "Tutti Frutti,"
                "Long Tall Sally," and "Good Golly, Miss Molly" before renouncing the life of
                a rock star for the ministry.   MUSIC

c. 1955   In California American artist Richard Diebenkorn and other figurative expres-
                sionists break away from abstract expressionism, applying brushwork inspired
                by the latter movement to studies of figures.   PAINT

1955   American painter Robert Rauschenberg creates the combine painting *Bed.* Like
                such other works of his as *Canyon* (1959), it incorporates collage, assorted
                objects, and energetic brushwork.   PAINT

1955   Spanish painter Salvador Dalí completes *The Lord's Supper,* a late example of
                the religiously oriented works he had been working on since the 1940s. Other
                such works include *The Crucifixion of St. John of the Cross* (1951).   PAINT

1955   Spanish painter Pablo Picasso's works are exhibited widely in Europe, notably
                in Munich, Hamburg, and Paris.   PAINT

1955   The humanistic international photography exhibit "The Family of Man"
                begins its run at the Museum of Modern Art, New York. Organized by pho-
                tography department director Edward Steichen, it becomes one of the most
                popular exhibitions of its day.   PHOTO

1955	Japanese-American sculptor Isamu Noguchi erects his Fountain of Peace for the UNESCO House in Paris. He will explore the Japanese tradition of garden-making and lay the foundation for the land art movement in the United States during the 1970s. The Isamu Noguchi Garden Museum will open in 1985 in Long Island City, New York. SCULP
1955–1956	The highest-rated TV program of the season is *The $64,000 Question* (CBS). Other top-rated programs are *I Love Lucy* (CBS) and *The Ed Sullivan Show* (CBS). TV&R
1955–1956	The 39 half-hour episodes of the TV comedy *The Honeymooners* air on CBS. Starring comedians Jackie Gleason, Art Carney, Audrey Meadows, and Joyce Randolph as the protoptypical Brooklyn couples the Kramdens and Nortons, the series will gain a reputation as one of the most inspired comedies in TV history. It will gain cult status as new generations come to know it through reruns. TV&R
1956–1958	German-born architect Ludwig Mies van der Rohe and American architect Philip Johnson design the Seagram Building in New York City, a classic work of the international style. ARCH
1956	British playwright John Osborne's *Look Back in Anger* premieres in London. A forceful look at British working-class life, the play will be seen as a landmark work, the first of many "kitchen sink" dramas. Osborne's play *The Entertainer* will be produced in 1957, and his *Inadmissible Evidence* will premiere in 1964. DRAMA
1956	*My Fair Lady*, an American musical based on Irish-born British playwright George Bernard Shaw's *Pygmalion*, opens on Broadway. With a score by Alan Jay Lerner and Frederick Loewe, this show, directed by Moss Hart and starring Rex Harrison and Julie Andrews, will be enormously popular. *See also* 1914, DRAMA. DRAMA
1956	*Long Day's Journey into Night*, a realistic, autobiographical drama written by American playwright Eugene O'Neill in 1941, is produced for the first time in New York. Winning O'Neill a Pulitzer posthumously, *Long Day's Journey* will be the playwright's most popular and, in the minds of many, best work. DRAMA
1956	Notable films include Cecil B. De Mille's *The Ten Commandments*, Michael Anderson's *Around the World in Eighty Days*, Walter Lang's *The King and I*, George Stevens's *Giant*, and William Wyler's *Friendly Persuasion* (all U.S.); Jean Renoir's *Paris Does Strange Things* and Alain Resnais's *Night and Fog* (both France); and Ingmar Bergman's *The Seventh Seal* (Sweden). FILM
1956	American novelist Grace Metalious publishes *Peyton Place*, a critical melodrama of small-town life. LIT

1956   American Beat poet Allen Ginsberg publishes the epic, personal poem "Howl," which incurs obscenity charges that are eventually dismissed.   LIT

1956   American novelist Saul Bellow publishes *Seize the Day*, a collection of three short stories, a play, and a short novel.   LIT

1956   American poet Richard Wilbur publishes his third collection of poems, *Things of This World*, which will win the Pulitzer Prize and National Book Award. Other collections include *Ceremony* (1950) and *The Beautiful Changes* (1947).   LIT

1956   American country-music singer and songwriter Johnny Cash records what will become perhaps hist best-known song, "I Walk the Line." Two years ago he recorded another signature tune, "Folsom Prison Blues." Among his many hits will be a 1963 recording of "Ring of Fire," cowritten by Merle Haggard and June Carter (Cash's future wife), and a 1964 cover of Bob Dylan's "It Ain't Me Babe." In the course of his career he will collaborate with Carl Perkins, Jerry Lee Lewis, and Waylon Jennings, among others. His daughter, Rosanne Cash, will become a popular singer in her own right.   MUSIC

1956   British painter Richard Hamilton paints the collage *Just What Is It That Makes Today's Home So Different, So Appealing?*, which anticipates the popular culture concerns of pop art. *See* 1960s, PAINT.   PAINT

1956   American painter Ellsworth Kelly creates *Atlantic*, an example of hard edge painting, which emphasizes sharp edges around color areas.   PAINT

1956–1957   The highest-rated TV program of the season is *I Love Lucy* (CBS). Other top-rated programs are *The Ed Sullivan Show* (CBS) and *The Jack Benny Show* (CBS). TV&R

1957   Russian composer Igor Stravinsky's ballet *Agon*, a prominent example of his final period of 12-tone serial music, opens in Paris.   DANCE

1957   Irish playwright Samuel Beckett's play *Fin de partie* (*Endgame*) is produced in London. Beckett's monologue *Krapp's Last Tape* will be produced in 1958.   DRAMA

1957   *Le Balcon* (*The Balcony*), a drama by French writer Jean Genet, is produced in London. Set in an elite brothel during a revolution, it is both ritualistic and realistic.   DRAMA

1957   The dramatic musical *West Side Story* opens on Broadway. Inspired by Shakespeare's *Romeo and Juliet*, it is choreographed by Jerome Robbins, with music by Leonard Bernstein and lyrics by Stephen Sondheim. The musical, which explores cultural hatreds through the conflicts between young Puerto Ricans and more established immigrants in New York City, heralds a turn toward musicals with darker themes.   DRAMA

1957   Notable films include Frank Borzage's *A Farewell to Arms*, Stanley Donen's *Funny Face*, Sidney Lumet's *12 Angry Men*, Billy Wilder's *Witness for the Prosecution*, Nunnally Johnson's *The Three Faces of Eve*, and Mark Robson's *Peyton Place* (all U.S.); and David Lean's *Bridge on the River Kwai* and Charlie Chaplin's *A King in New York* (both U.K.).   FILM

1957   American Beat writer Jack Kerouac publishes *On the Road*, a novel with commentary about a trip across the United States. The book becomes known as a signature work of the Beat Generation.   LIT

1957   American writer James Agee publishes the novel *A Death in the Family*, based on his father's death. It will win a Pulitzer Prize.   LIT

1957   Russian-born American novelist Vladimir Nabokov publishes the novel *Pnin*. LIT

1957   American writer Mary McCarthy publishes a memoir of her difficult childhood, *Memories of a Catholic Girlhood*.   LIT

The West Side of *West Side Story*

In 1949 producer Jerome Robbins conceived the idea for a Broadway musical based on *Romeo and Juliet*. According to composer Leonard Bernstein, the musical would tell "a tragic story in musical-comedy terms, using only musical-comedy techniques," and would be set amid the current conflicts of the day. In the 1949 plans for the play, that meant the differences between Catholics and Jews.

But by 1955 one of the major conflicts of the day had become the gang wars between newly immigrated Puerto Ricans and established ethnic groups on New York's near West Side. "[W]e . . . have come up with what I think is going to be it," wrote Bernstein, "two teen-age gangs, one the warring Puerto Ricans, the other self-styled 'Americans.' Suddenly it all springs to life. I hear rhythms and pulses, and—most of all—I can sort of feel the form." *Romeo and Juliet* was becoming *West Side Story*.

West Side Story made its Broadway debut on September 26, 1957. It won two Tony awards and was hailed for its groundbreaking integration of music, dance, and social commentary.

More than 40 years after its debut, *West Side Story* remains fresh in part because the conflicts that spurred its plot still fuel urban life. However, the West Side that gave title to the play has disappeared. In 1962 the depressed New York neighborhood was cleared to make room for the glittering theater complex known as Lincoln Center. The razing of the buildings that made way for Lincoln Center erased the West Side of *West Side Story*.

1957   American novelist and short-story writer John Cheever publishes the novel *The Wapshot Chronicle*.   LIT

1957   British poet Ted Hughes publishes his first collection, *The Hawk in the Rain*, to great success. Later volumes will include *Crow* (1970) and *Selected Poems: 1957–1967* (1972). The husband of American poet Sylvia Plath, he will edit her *Selected Poems* (1985).   LIT

1957   Russian novelist Boris Pasternak publishes the novel *Doctor Zhivago*, for which he will be awarded the Nobel Prize for literature in 1958. Under pressure from the Communist Party (he is called a traitor in the press and expelled from the Soviet Writers' Union), he will reject the prize, just days after he will have expressed his gratitude for the award to the Swedish Academy.   LIT

1957–1958   French tapestry artist and sculptor Henri-Georges Adam completes the monument *Beacon of the Dead*, for display at the Nazi World War II death camp Auschwitz.   SCULP

1957–1958   The highest-rated TV program of the season is *Gunsmoke* (CBS). Other top-rated programs are *Have Gun Will Travel* (CBS) and *General Electric Theater* (CBS).   TV&R

1957   Stereo (or stereophonic) records, which allow for the projection of sound from two sources, become popular in the United States and Europe.   TV&R

1957   American radio personality Dick Clark moves his pop music and dance program *American Bandstand* to television, where it will become an influential pop music forum. In subsequent decades he will become a familiar face to television audiences tuning in to watch his annual New Year's Eve celebration and countdown in Times Square, New York City.   TV&R

1958   The cha-cha, a Latin-inspired dance, becomes popular in the United States and Europe.   DANCE

1958   American dancer Alvin Ailey founds the Alvin Ailey American Dance Theatre. Among its best-known works will be the American spirituals-inspired "Revelations," which will premiere in 1960. Among its most celebrated dancers will be Judith Jamison, who will become director of the troupe following Ailey's death in 1989.   DANCE

1958   German playwright Bertolt Brecht's *Der Aufhaltsame Aufstieg des Arturo Ui* (*The Resistible Rise of Arturo Ui*) is produced. Brecht's *Die Heilige Johanna der Schlachthöfe* (*St. Joan of the Stockyards*), which transposes the legend of Joan of Arc to 20th-century Chicago, will be staged in 1959.   DRAMA

1958	*The Birthday Party*, the first full-length play by British playwright Harold Pinter, premieres in London. DRAMA
1958	*Suddenly Last Summer*, a drama by American playwright Tennessee Williams, opens. It will be made into a popular 1959 movie starring Katharine Hepburn, Elizabeth Taylor, and Montgomery Clift. DRAMA
1958	Notable films include Alfred Hitchcock's *Vertigo*, Richard Brooks's *Cat on a Hot Tin Roof*, and Vincente Minnelli's *Gigi* (all U.S.); Jacques Tati's *Mon Oncle* (France); and Andrej Wajda's *Ashes and Diamonds* (Poland). FILM
1958	British novelist T. H. White concludes the tetralogy *The Once and Future King*, consisting of four novels based on Arthurian legend, beginning with *The Sword in the Stone* (1939). LIT
1958–1972	American science-fiction novelist Ursula K. Le Guin publishes her *Earthsea* trilogy, about the Wizard Ged on the islands of Earthsea. LIT
1958	American poet Ezra Pound is released from a U.S. federal insane asylum after being placed there instead of facing trial for treason during World War II. LIT
1958	Nigerian writer Chinua Achebe publishes his novel of colonial rule, *Things Fall Apart*. Among his later works will be the story collection *Girls at War* (1972) and the novel *Arrow of God* (1964). LIT
1958	The Tchaikovsky piano competition in Moscow is won by American Van Cliburn. MUSIC
1958	American composer Samuel Barber's opera *Vanessa*, with a libretto by Italian-born composer Gian Carlo Menotti, wins the Pulitzer Prize. MUSIC
1958–1969	American composer Leonard Bernstein serves as musical director of the New York Philharmonic Orchestra, helping it achieve increased prestige and boosting concert attendance. MUSIC
1958	American popular singer Bobby Darin (Walden Robert Cassatto) records his first hit, "Splish Splash," which will be followed in 1959 by "Dream Lover," "Queen of the Hop," and a memorable pop version of "Mack the Knife," from the Kurt Weill–Bertolt Brecht collaboration *The Threepenny Opera* (*see* 1928, DRAMA). MUSIC
1958	In New York American artist Jasper Johns has his first one-man show. Among his best-known works will be the series *Targets, Flags,* and *Numbers*, heavily textured encaustic paintings of everyday two-dimensional objects. PAINT

1958–1959   American New York school painter Mark Rothko completes his *Black on Maroon* and *Red on Maroon* paintings, a group of nine creations that will be considered among his masterworks. The works were originally created for a New York City restaurant.   PAINT

1958   American photographer Minor White takes the photograph *Ritual Branch*, an example of the influence of abstract expressionism on his work.   PHOTO

1958–1959   The highest-rated TV program of the season is *Gunsmoke* (CBS). Other top-rated programs are *Wagon Train* (NBC) and *I've Got a Secret* (CBS).   TV&R

1959–1970   Russian ballerina Natalia Makarova dances with the Kirov Ballet, becoming known as one of the most inspired interpreters of dance in the twentieth century. Among her roles are Giselle in *Giselle* and Odette/Odile in *Swan Lake*.   DANCE

1959   *Tueur sans gages* (*The Killer*), a full-length drama by French absurdist playwright Eugène Ionesco, is produced. Elie Berenger, the play's central character, will reappear in Ionesco's *Rhinocéros* (produced in 1960) and *Le Roi se meurt* (*Exit the King*, 1962).   DRAMA

1959   *Les Nègres* (*The Blacks*), a play by French writer Jean Genet, opens. It will have a long off-Broadway run in 1961.   DRAMA

1959   *The Zoo Story*, a one-act drama that is the first play by American playwright Edward Albee, premieres in Berlin. Albee's *The Death of Bessie Smith* and *The American Dream*, both one-act plays, will premiere in 1960 and 1961, respectively.   DRAMA

1959   African-American playwright Lorraine Hansberry's drama *A Raisin in the Sun*, starring Sidney Poitier and Claudia McNeil, is produced. It is the first play written by a black woman to be staged on Broadway, and it will enjoy great critical and commercial success. With this play she becomes the youngest American playwright to win the best play award from the New York Drama Critics' Circle.   DRAMA

1959   *Sweet Bird of Youth*, a drama by American playwright Tennessee Williams, premieres. *The Night of the Iguana* will open in 1961.   DRAMA

1959   The American musical *Gypsy*—starring Ethel Merman, with book by Arthur Laurentes, lyrics by Stephen Sondheim and music by Jule Styne—premieres on May 21. It will be revived on Broadway in the 1990s, with Tyne Daly in the starring role.   DRAMA

1959   Notable films include William Wyler's *Ben Hur*, Otto Preminger's *Anatomy of a Murder*, Alfred Hitchcock's *North by Northwest*, Billy Wilder's *Some Like It Hot*, George Stevens's *The Diary of Anne Frank*, Michael Gordon's *Pillow Talk*, and

Howard Hawks's *Rio Bravo* (all U.S.); Federico Fellini's *La Dolce Vita* (Italy); Carol Reed's *Our Man in Havana* (U.K.); and Alain Resnais's *Hiroshima, Mon Amour* (France).   FILM

1959   American science-fiction writer Walter M. Miller Jr. publishes *A Canticle for Liebowitz*, concerning the monastic preservation of civilization after a nuclear holocaust.   LIT

1959   American short-story writer Grace Paley publishes her first collection *The Little Disturbances of Man*. Her later collections will include *Enormous Changes at the Last Minute* (1974) and *Later the Same Day* (1985).   LIT

1959   American novelist William S. Burroughs publishes *Naked Lunch*.   LIT

1959   German novelist Günter Grass publishes *The Tin Drum*, about the rise of Nazism in the town of Danzig. It will become part of the Danzig Trilogy, the other novels of which will be *Cat and Mouse* (1963) and *Dog Years* (1965). LIT

1959   American rock musician Buddy Holly (Charles Harden Holley) dies at the age of 22 in a plane crash in Clear Lake, Iowa, on February 2. His first album, recorded with his band, the Crickets, just two years earlier, yielded the hit songs "That'll Be the Day," "Peggy Sue" and "Oh Boy," among others. A film version of his life will be released in 1978.   MUSIC

1959   American photographer and filmmaker Robert Frank publishes the controversial book of photographs *The Americans*, which provides pointed, ironic commentary on the emptiness of modern American existence.   PHOTO

1959–1960   The highest-rated TV program of the season is *Gunsmoke* (CBS). Other top-rated programs are *Father Knows Best* (CBS) and *Perry Mason* (CBS).   TV&R

1960s   The Stuttgart Ballet, the first important German ballet troupe, is founded. Housed in the Württemberg Staatstheater, it is directed by John Cranko.   DANCE

1960s   Among the actors who deliver memorable performances during this decade are Albert Finney, Dean Stockwell, Michael Caine, Geraldine Page, Robert Redford, Jane Fonda, Janet Leigh, Anthony Perkins, Robert Mitchum, Shirley MacLaine, Jeanne Moreau, Catherine Deneuve, Jean-Paul Belmondo, Jean-Paul Trintignant, Jean Seberg, Anouk Aimée, Dustin Hoffman, Faye Dunaway, Warren Beatty, Martin Sheen, Steve McQueen, Robert Wagner, Lee Marvin, Anne Bancroft, Jon Voight, Collen Dewhurst, Vanessa Redgrave, Lynn Redgrave, Rod Steiger, Julie Christie, Omar Sharif, Barbra Streisand, Sean Connery, Anne Bancroft, Ann-Margret, Maureen Stapleton, Peter Sellers, Robert Duvall, Walter Matthau, Charlton Heston, and Peter O'Toole. *See also* 1950s and 1970s, FILM.   FILM

1960s	Popular songs of the decade include "The Twist," "Where the Boys Are," "Moon River," "(Theme from) Exodus," "Days of Wine and Roses," "Blowin' in the Wind," "Those Lazy, Hazy, Crazy Days of Summer," "I Want to Hold Your Hand," "Like a Rolling Stone," "Hello, Dolly!," "Satisfaction," "Baby Love," "My Girl," "King of the Road," "Downtown," "A Hard Day's Night," "Eleanor Rigby," "Born Free," "Ballad of the Green Berets," "Hey Jude," "Mrs. Robinson," "Aquarius/Let the Sun Shine," and "A Boy Named Sue." MUSIC
1960s	In the middle to later part of this decade, psychedelic rock flourishes briefly, generating such one-hit wonders as "In-a-Gadda-Da-Vida" by Iron Butterfly, "I Had Too Much to Dream Last Night" by the Electric Prunes, "Incense and Peppermints" by the Strawberry Alarm Clock, "Psychotic Reaction" by the Count Five, and "Pushin' Too Hard" by the Seeds. MUSIC
1960s	Pop art, influenced by popular culture and commercial art, comes into fashion. The movement is linked most memorably with American artist Andy Warhol, whose works include repeated rows of images of such products and celebrities as Campbell's Soup, Coca-Cola bottles, Marilyn Monroe, and Elvis Presley, achieved through silkscreen printing. PAINT
1960s	Post-painterly abstraction, a movement that rejects the textured surfaces of abstract expressionism for large areas of unmodulated color, is practiced by such artists as Helen Frankenthaler, Morris Louis, Kenneth Noland, Frank Stella, and Ellsworth Kelly. PAINT
1960s	American pop artist Tom Wesselmann paints the series *The Great American Nude*. PAINT
1960s	After having his works exhibited in the Family of Man exhibit at the Museum of Modern Art in 1955, American photographer Garry Winogrand becomes known for his lively "street" photography. PHOTO
1960s	American artist George Segal creates life-sized white plaster figures cast from life to be placed among everyday elements of the real environment. SCULP
1960s	American artist Dan Flavin appropriates the fluorescent light tube as his sculptural medium for pieces he calls "Icons." SCULP
1960s	Swedish-born American artist Claes Oldenburg reflects the pop art agenda by looking to popular urban culture for sources and material for a series of soft sculptures of commonplace, vastly enlarged objects. SCULP
1960s	Conceptual art, an artistic approach in which the idea behind the work, rather than its aesthetically pleasing execution, is of greatest value. Often everyday

objects are presented in these artworks, as in American artist Joseph Kosuth's *One and Three Chairs*.   SCULP

1960   Swiss architect Le Corbusier designs the Monastery La Tourette at Eveux, near Lyons, France.   ARCH

1960   Philadelphia-born singer Chubby Checker spurs a dance craze with his recording of the Hank Ballard song "The Twist." The song reaches number one on pop music charts and spurs the development of discotheques.   DANCE

1960   British playwright Harold Pinter's drama *The Caretaker* is produced. Pinter's *The Homecoming* will be produced in 1965.   DRAMA

1960   *Oh Dad, Poor Dad, Mamma's Hung You in the Closet and I'm Feelin' So Sad*, a black comedy by American playwright Arthur Kopit, is produced.   DRAMA

1960   The musical *The Fantasticks* by Tom Jones and Harvey Schmidt premieres in New York in May. It will continue its uninterrupted run for decades.   DRAMA

1960–1961   *An Evening with Mike Nichols and Elaine May*, a selection of comedy skits directed by Arthur Penn, is performed on Broadway, where it runs for nine months.   DRAMA

1960   Notable films include Billy Wilder's *The Apartment*, Stanley Kubrick's *Spartacus*, Alfred Hitchcock's *Psycho*, John Sturges's *The Magnificent Seven* (a remake of Kurosawa's *The Seven Samurai*), Otto Preminger's *Exodus*, Richard Brooks's *Elmer Gantry* (all U.S.); Luchino Visconti's *Rocco and His Brothers* (Italy); Karel Reisz's *Saturday Night and Sunday Morning* (U.K.); and Jules Dassin's *Never on Sunday* (Greece).   FILM

1960   American novelist John Barth publishes *The Sot-Weed Factor*, a novel based on the life of satirist Ebenezer Cook, author of the 1708 work *The Sot-Weed Factor; or A Voyage to Maryland*. The book will be revised in 1966.   LIT

1960   American writer John Updike publishes the novel *Rabbit, Run*, the first of several novels about suburbanite Harry Angstrom. Later *Rabbit* novels will include *Rabbit Redux* (1971), *Rabbit Is Rich* (1981), and *Rabbit at Rest* (1990).   LIT

1960   American novelist Harper Lee publishes *To Kill a Mockingbird*, a haunting tale of childhood and racial injustice. Her first novel will win the Pulitzer Prize.   LIT

1960   American composer Elliott Carter's String Quartet no. 2 wins the Pulitzer Prize.   MUSIC

1960   American tenor and soprano saxophonist, bandleader, and composer John Coltrane debuts with his own group at New York's Jazz Gallery in May, after having played in Miles Davis's quintet (1955–1957), Thelonious Monk's quartet (1957), and in various other arrangements with Cannonball Adderley, Bill Evans, and others. With McCoy Tyner, Elvin Jones, and Jimmy Garrison, Coltrane's quartet will be renowned internationally until the mid-1960s, when he will begin switching personnel frequently in an effort to explore new sounds. His best-known albums include *Blue Train* (1957), *Giant Steps* (1959), and *A Love Supreme* (1964); he is also noted for his playing on Miles Davis's *Kind of Blue* (1959).   MUSIC

1960   American singer Roy Orbison, possessed of a wide-ranging tenor voice unmatched among his contemporaries in rock, writes and records his first hit, "Only the Lonely." More hits will follow throughout the decade, among them "Cryin'" and "Oh, Pretty Woman." After a long fallow period in the 1970s and early 1980s, his career will be revived in 1986 when David Lynch includes Orbison's 1963 ballad "In Dreams" in his film *Blue Velvet*. Orbison will die of a heart attack in 1988 after having just recorded *The Traveling Wilburys* with ex-Beatle George Harrison, Bob Dylan, Tom Petty, and Jeff Lynne.   MUSIC

1960   Leading postwar Dutch abstract artist Karel Appel, known for the strong expressiveness of his work, wins the Guggenheim Award for abstract painting for his work, *Woman with Ostrich*.   PAINT

1960–1961   The highest-rated TV program of the season is *Gunsmoke* (CBS). Other top-rated programs are *The Andy Griffith Show* (CBS) and *The Untouchables* (ABC).   TV&R

1960   Approximately 100 million television sets are in homes in the United States and Europe, with 85 million of them in the United States.   TV&R

1960   Presidential candidates Vice-President Richard Nixon and Senator John Kennedy appear in a televised presidential debate. The TV camera favors the youthful-looking Kennedy over the perspiring Nixon.   TV&R

1961   Irish playwright Samuel Beckett's monologue *Oh! Les Beaux Jours* (*Happy Days*) is produced. Beckett's plays *Comédie* (*Play*) and *Va et Vient* (*Come and Go*) will be produced in 1963 and 1966, respectively.   DRAMA

1961   The Shakepeare Memorial Theatre Company becomes the Royal Shakespeare Company. Under the guidance of British director Peter Hall, the company will present a variety of classical and modern plays at Aldwych Theatre in London, while performing mostly Shakespeare at Stratford-upon-Avon.   DRAMA

1961   Cafe La Mama, which will be called La Mama Experimental Theater Club, is founded by Ellen Stewart in New York City. This avant-garde theater group will provide a venue for new and experimental plays.   DRAMA

1961   Notable films include Blake Edwards's *Breakfast at Tiffany's*, Robert Wise and Jerome Robbins's *West Side Story*, Anthony Mann's *El Cid*, and Stanley Kramer's *Judgment at Nuremburg* (all U.S.); François Truffaut's *Jules and Jim* and Alain

Resnais's *Last Year at Marienbad* (both France); and Luis Buñuel's *Viridiana* (Spain).   FILM

1961   John Huston's *The Misfits* is the last film of actors Clark Gable and Marilyn Monroe. Gable died in 1960; Monroe will die on August 5, 1962.   FILM

1961   American journalist Theodore H. White publishes the Pulitzer Prize–winning *The Making of the President: 1960*, an influential account of the 1960 presidential campaign.   LIT

1961   American novelist Walker Percy publishes his first novel, *The Moviegoer*, the story of inveterate moviegoer Binx Bolling, who finds himself on a spiritual and philosophical quest.   LIT

1961   Under his birth name LeRoi (LeRoy) Jones, African-American poet and playwright Amiri Baraka publishes his first collection of poetry, *Preface to a Twenty-Volume Suicide Note*. Jones will assume the name Amiri Baraka ("blessed prince") in 1967.   LIT

1961   American novelist Joseph Heller publishes his satire of World War II, *Catch-22*, the title phrase of which will become part of the American lexicon.   LIT

1961   West Indian novelist and essayist V. S. Naipaul publishes the novel *A House for Mr. Biswas*. Among his later novels is *The Mimic Men* (1967). His nonfiction works will include *Among the Believers: An Islamic Journey* (1981) and *Finding the Center: Two Narratives* (1985).   LIT

1961   British novelist Iris Murdoch publishes the novel *A Severed Head*. Her later works will include *The Book and the Brotherhood* (1987).   LIT

1961   British novelist Muriel Spark publishes the novel *The Prime of Miss Jean Brodie*, about an idiosyncratic teacher and her pupils.   LIT

1961   American composer Walter Piston's Symphony no. 7 wins the Pulitzer Prize. MUSIC

1961   American folk singer Bob Dylan (born Robert Allan Zimmerman) makes his first concert appearance at Gerde's Folk City in Greenwich Village, New York City, opening for blues guitarist John Lee Hooker (*see* 1948, MUSIC). By the end of the decade, Dylan's songs of cultural commentary and disaffection will become anthems of his age. Among the best known will be "Blowin' in the Wind," "Like a Rolling Stone," "The Times They Are a-Changin'," "Subterranean Homesick Blues," and "Rainy Day Women." The Turtles will cover his "It Ain't Me Babe" and the Byrds his "Mr. Tambourine Man."   MUSIC

1961   German-born painter Hans Hofmann paints *The Golden Wall*.   PAINT

1961   The Museum of the Chinese Revolution opens in Beijing, China.   PAINT

1961   British painter Allen Jones establishes himself as a pop artist in the "Young
            Contemporaries" pop art exhibition in London.   PAINT

1961–1962   The highest-rated TV program of the season is *Wagon Train* (NBC). Other top-
            rated programs are *Bonanza* (NBC) and *Hazel* (NBC).   TV&R

1962   British ballerina Margot Fonteyn and Russian dancer Rudolf Nureyev begin
            their lengthy partnership in London's Royal Ballet.   DANCE

1962   The New York Shakepeare Festival, which had been founded in 1954 by
            American director Joseph Papp, moves to the Delacorte Theater, an open-air
            facility built for it in New York City's Central Park. The company presents
            Shakespeare plays, and later it will stage other classical and contemporary
            works as well. Admission will always be free. The festival will continue to oper-
            ate thereafter.   DRAMA

1962   *The Milk Train Doesn't Stop Here Anymore*, a drama by American playwright
            Tennessee Williams, premieres. It will be followed by *In the Bar of a Tokyo Hotel*
            (1969), *Small Craft Warnings* (1972), *Vieux Carré* (1977), *Clothes for a Summer
            Hotel* (1980), and several other plays that generally will be seen as minor
            works.   DRAMA

1962   *Who's Afraid of Virginia Woolf?*, the first full-length play by American play-
            wright Edward Albee, premieres in New York City. The tale of an evening of
            drinking and "games" in the home of a New England college professor, this
            powerful, popular drama will be seen by many as Albee's best work and a great
            modern play. It will be filmed in 1966 by director Mike Nichols, with
            Elizabeth Taylor and Richard Burton playing the leading roles.   DRAMA

1962   David Lean's *Lawrence of Arabia*, released by Columbia, introduces Peter
            O'Toole as British officer T. E. Lawrence and Egyptian actor Omar Sharif as
            Bedouin leader Sherif Ali. With a screenplay by playwright Robert Bolt, the
            epic film draws on Lawrence's classic account of his adventures in Arabia, *The
            Seven Pillars of Wisdom* (1935).   FILM

1962   John Ford's *The Man Who Shot Liberty Valance* is the first film to team American
            stars James Stewart and John Wayne.   FILM

1962   Terence Young's *Dr. No* makes a star of Scottish actor Sean Connery as super-
            spy James Bond, also known as 007, from the series of thrillers by English nov-
            elist Ian Fleming. The film is the first in a long series of films that will succes-
            sively star Connery, George Lazenby, Roger Moore, Timothy Dalton, and Pierce
            Brosnan as Bond.   FILM

1962   Notable films include *How the West Was Won* (U.S.), by John Ford, George Marshall, and Henry Hathaway; *The Longest Day* (U.S.), by Andrew Marton, Ken Annakin, and Bernhard Wicki; Blake Edwards's *The Days of Wine and Roses*, Robert Mulligan's *To Kill a Mockingbird*, and John Frankenheimer's *The Manchurian Candidate* (all U.S.); Jean-Luc Godard's *My Life to Live* (France); and Vittorio De Sica's *The Condemned of Altona* (Italy).   FILM

1962   American short-story writer and novelist Katherine Anne Porter publishes the novel *Ship of Fools*.   LIT

1962   American novelist Ken Kesey publishes the novel *One Flew Over the Cuckoo's Nest*, about life inside a psychiatric ward. The book, which will be made into an Academy Award–winning film in 1975, is based on Kesey's earlier experiences and work in an asylum.   LIT

1962   Russian-born American novelist Vladimir Nabokov publishes *Pale Fire*, a novel consisting of a poem written by professor John Shade and the lengthy commentary of editor Charles Kinbote.   LIT

1962   English novelist Doris Lessing publishes the feminist novel about a woman's search for self-definition *The Golden Notebook*. She has also written the short-story collection *The Habit of Loving*.   LIT

1962   Russian novelist Aleksandr Solzhenitsyn publishes his first novel, *One Day in the Life of Ivan Denisovich*, about a 24-hour span in a Stalinist prison camp. He will win the Nobel Prize for literature in 1970 for his works, which will by then have included *Cancer Ward* (part I, 1968; part II, 1969) and *The First Circle* (1968). *See also* 1973–1975, LIT.   LIT

1962   English novelist and critic Anthony Burgess publishes his futuristic novel of an "ultraviolent" society, *A Clockwork Orange*. Among his other works will be the novel *The Long Day Wanes* (1964).   LIT

1962   Conductor Leopold Stokowski founds the American Symphony Orchestra in New York City.   MUSIC

1962   British composer Michael Tippett's opera *King Priam*, with its sparse and abrasive style, opens.   MUSIC

1962   To mark the opening of Britain's Coventry cathedral, British composer Benjamin Britten composes *War Requiem*, which interweaves music with verse by war poets.   MUSIC

1962   American composer Robert Ward's opera *The Crucible*, produced in New York in 1961, wins the Pulitzer Prize.   MUSIC

1962   American folk-singing group Peter, Paul, and Mary (Peter Yarrow, Paul Stookey, and Mary Travers) spark a new generation's interest in folk music through their renditions of protest songs like Pete Seeger's "If I Had a Hammer" and, in the next year, Bob Dylan's "Blowin' in the Wind."   MUSIC

1962   Soul music begins to attain mainstream popularity with the success of performers like Sam Cooke, whose 1962 dance tune "Twistin' the Night Away" and earlier love ballad "Wonderful World" (1960) place him on the charts. *See also* 1963, MUSIC.   MUSIC

1962–1963   The highest-rated TV program of the season is *The Beverly Hillbillies* (CBS). Other top-rated programs are *The Red Skelton Show* (CBS) and *Ben Casey* (ABC).   TV&R

1962   American first lady Jacqueline Kennedy conducts a nationally televised tour of the White House, which receives critical acclaim and high ratings.   TV&R

1963   The musical comedy *A Funny Thing Happened on the Way to the Forum*, with book by Burt Shevelove and Larry Gelbart and music and lyrics by Stephen Sondheim, premieres on Broadway. Starring Zero Mostel as Pseudolus, the musical is based on the work of Roman playwright Plautus (*see* 254 B.C., DRAMA). It will be filmed in 1966.   DRAMA

1963   American playwright Neil Simon's *Barefoot in the Park* is produced. It will be followed by *The Odd Couple* (1965), *Plaza Suite* (1968), *The Last of the Red Hot Lovers* (1969), *The Prisoner of Second Avenue* (1971), *Chapter Two* (1977), *Brighton Beach Memoirs* (1983), and *Biloxi Blues* (1984); as well as by Simon books for several musicals, including *Sweet Charity* (1966) and *Promises, Promises* (1968). Nearly all of Simon's plays will be enormous commercial successes.   DRAMA

1963   Notable films include Alfred Hitchcock's *The Birds*, Stanley Kramer's *It's a Mad Mad Mad Mad World*, Billy Wilder's *Irma La Douce*, John Sturges's *The Great Escape*, Martin Ritt's *Hud*, Ralph Nelson's *Lilies of the Field*, and Jerry Lewis's *The Nutty Professor* (all U.S.); Tony Richardson's *Tom Jones* and Terence Young's *From Russia with Love* (both U.K.); Robert Bresson's *Pickpocket* (France); Federico Fellini's $8^1/2$ (Italy); Luchino Visconti's *The Leopard* (France/Italy); Ingmar Bergman's *The Silence* (Sweden); and Orson Welles's *The Trial* (France/Italy/West Germany).   FILM

1963   The most notorious screen couple of the day is American actress Elizabeth Taylor and British actor Richard Burton, who met while filming Joseph L. Mankiewicz's expensive flop *Cleopatra*, released this year. Taylor and Burton divorce their spouses and go on to marry and divorce each other twice, while costarring together in a number of films, including Mike Nichols's *Who's Afraid of Virginia Woolf?* (1966).   FILM

1963   British novelist John le Carré (pen name of David Cornwell) publishes the
            international best-seller *The Spy Who Came in from the Cold*, marked by his dis-
            tinct blend of moral analysis and espionage adventure. Le Carré will become
            known particularly for the shrewd, aging secret agent George Smiley, hero of a
            series of novels including *Tinker, Tailor, Soldier, Spy* (1974).   LIT

1963   American writer Mary McCarthy publishes the novel *The Group*, a biting, comic
            look at the lives of several graduates of a prominent women's college.   LIT

1963   Japanese novelist Mishima Yukio (born Kimitake Hiraoka) publishes *The
            Sailor Who Fell from Grace with the Sea*. Among his other works is *Confessions of
            Mask* (1949).   LIT

1963   American singer James Brown, blending elements of gospel and rhythm-and-
            blues, releases his album *Live at the Apollo* (recorded in October 1962), which
            charts at number two in the United States. He will become known as the
            "Godfather of Soul" for hits like "Papa's Got a Brand New Bag" and "I Got You (I
            Feel Good)" (both 1965) and "Get Up, I Feel Like Being a Sex Machine" (1970).
                                                                                          MUSIC

Competition for the Singing Nun

On December 26, 1963, the number-one pop hit in America was "Dominique" by
Belgian religious singer Soeur Sourire, known as the Singing Nun. American musical
tastes were about to be altered radically, for this was also the day that the Beatles
released their single "I Want to Hold Your Hand."

Already a sensation in England and continental Europe, the Liverpool-based band,
with their mop-top haircuts and lapelless jackets, now became extraordinarily popular
in America as well. Aided by their appearance on *The Ed Sullivan Show* in February
1964, the Beatles—John Lennon, Paul McCartney, George Harrison, and Ringo Starr—
occupied the top five places in the charts by March. By the end of 1964 they had
released 29 singles, including such original hits as "She Loves You," "Can't Buy Me
Love," "Please Please Me," "I Saw Her Standing There," "From Me to You," "All My
Loving," "Do You Want to Know a Secret," and "A Hard Day's Night," and covers of
other artists' songs such as "Twist and Shout" and "Roll Over Beethoven."

As proof of the eclecticism of American popular culture, the Singing Nun was not
completely overwhelmed. In 1966, the same year that John Lennon declared in an
interview that the Beatles were more popular than Jesus, the MGM musical biography
The Singing Nun, starring Debbie Reynolds and Ricardo Montalban, was a big box-
office success. Its most memorable song was "Dominique."

1963	The Beach Boys' pop paeans to the surfing way of life, "Surfin' Safari" and "Surfin' USA," showcasing the vocal harmonies of all five band members, mark the beginning of a rock subgenre called the California sound. Anthems to the automobile like "Little Deuce Coupe" will add to the mystique of the Beach Boys as the most important California troubadours. MUSIC
1963	The Liverpool-based rock group the Beatles sweeps England with the rhythm-and-blues-influenced hits "Love Me Do," "Please Please Me," "From Me to You," and "She Loves You." Over the decade the group, consisting of John Lennon, Paul McCartney, George Harrison, and Ringo Starr (Richard Starkey), will become an international cultural force and change the face of 20th-century popular music. MUSIC
1963	English guitarist Eric Clapton joins the English blues band the Yardbirds, which launches his career as well as those of two other English guitarists: Jeff Beck, who will replace Clapton (who will go on to form Cream; *see* 1966, MUSIC) after the Yardbirds have a hit with "For Your Love" in 1965, and Jimmy Page, who will go on to form the bluesy heavy-metal rock band Led Zeppelin with Robert Plant (*see* 1968, MUSIC). MUSIC
1963	American country-music singer Patsy Cline (Virginia Patterson Hensley) dies at the age of 30 in a plane crash in Camden, Tennessee, on March 5. Considered one of the greatest female country-music singers of all time, she recorded her first hit, "Walkin' After Midnight," in 1957. MUSIC
1963	American pop artist Roy Lichtenstein paints *Wham!*, one of his many works that blow up comic book images, faithfully reproducing the dots and primary colors. PAINT
1963	The Guggenheim Museum in New York City holds an exhibition of pop art, including works by Andy Warhol and Robert Rauschenberg. PAINT
1963–1964	The highest-rated TV program of the season is *The Beverly Hillbillies* (CBS). Other top-rated programs are *The Dick Van Dyke Show* (CBS) and *Petticoat Junction* (CBS). TV&R
1963	The four-day television coverage of the assassination and burial of President John F. Kennedy will redefine the medium as a unifying public force. TV&R
1964	A spate of frenetic go-go dances, including the monkey, the watusi, and the frug become popular in American and European discotheques and go-go clubs. DANCE
1964	*Entertaining Mr. Sloane*, the first play by British playwright Joe Orton, is produced. His other black comedies *Loot* and *What the Butler Saw* will be produced in 1966 and 1969, respectively. DRAMA

1964   *Incident at Vichy*, a historical drama by American playwright Arthur Miller, premieres. In 1968 Miller's drama *The Price* will open.   DRAMA

1964   American playwright Edward Albee's *Tiny Alice* is produced in New York City. The difficult, dense work puzzles many critics and theatergoers.   DRAMA

1964   The American musical *Hello, Dolly!*, starring Carol Channing, with book by Michael Stewart and lyrics and music by Jerry Herman, premieres on January 16. It is based on American playwright Thornton Wilder's *The Matchmaker*.   DRAMA

1964   The American musical *Fiddler on the Roof* premieres on September 22. Starring Zero Mostel and Bea Arthur, with book by Joseph Stein, lyrics by Sheldon Harnick and music by Jerry Bock, the play about tradition and change in a Russian Jewish family will be revived often after its initial run.   DRAMA

1964   China's communist government restricts performances of classical Peking opera, limiting it largely to festival occasions. Western-style musical theater will become more prominent in China.   DRAMA

1964   Notable films include Robert Stevenson's *Mary Poppins*, George Cukor's *My Fair Lady*, Anthony Mann's *The Fall of the Roman Empire*, George Pal's *The Seven Faces of Dr. Lao*, and Blake Edwards's *The Pink Panther* (all U.S.); Vittorio De Sica's *Marriage Italian-Style* and *Yesterday, Today, and Tomorrow* (both Italy); Masaki Kobayashi's *Kwaidan* (Japan); and Guy Hamilton's *Goldfinger*, Richard Lester's *A Hard Day's Night*, and Peter Glenville's *Becket* (all U.K.).   FILM

1964   Sidney Lumet's drama *Fail-Safe* and Stanley Kubrick's black comedy *Dr. Strangelove or How I Learned to Stop Worrying and Love the Bomb* both depict the accidental triggering of nuclear war.   FILM

1964   Sergio Leone's *A Fistful of Dollars*, the first of his "spaghetti westerns," makes a star of American actor Clint Eastwood as the laconic "Man with No Name."   FILM

1964   American mystery writer John D. MacDonald publishes the novels *The Deep Blue Good-By* and *Nightmare in Pink*, part of the long-running series featuring the detective Travis McGee and having a color in the title.   LIT

1964   *A Moveable Feast*, the autobiographical recounting of the post–World War I European life of American writer Ernest Hemingway is published posthumously, following his self-inflicted death.   LIT

1964   Welsh-born British writer Roald Dahl, author of the children's book *James and the Giant Peach* (1961), publishes the children's book *Charlie and the Chocolate Factory*.   LIT

1964   American novelist Hubert Selby Jr. publishes the controversial novel *Last Exit to Brooklyn*, which becomes the subject of an obscenity trial in England as a result of its realistic depiction of prostitution, homosexuality, and urban violence.   LIT

1964   The Museum of African Art is founded in Washington, D.C. It will later be incorporated into the Smithsonian Institution (1979) and renamed the National Museum of African Art (1981).   MISC

1964   American composer Roger Sessions composes the opera *Montezuma*.   MUSIC

1964   Beatlemania sweeps the United States, as the British rock band the Beatles releases six number-one hits during the year, more than any other new act in rock history. They win this year's Grammy Award for Best New Artist, star in Richard Lester's film *A Hard Day's Night*, and make a famous appearance on television's *The Ed Sullivan Show*. The Beatles will continue to be the decade's most popular band until their breakup in 1970. *See* 1963, MUSIC.   MUSIC

1964   The British rock band the Rolling Stones, led by singer Mick Jagger, release their first album, *The Rolling Stones: England's Newest Hitmakers*. Their angry, energetic sound will help define 1960s youth rebellion, through songs such as "Satisfaction," "Get Off My Cloud," and "Paint It Black." They will become one of the most popular and long-lasting rock bands, continuing to tour in their fourth decade.   MUSIC

1964   The "British invasion" of the American rock music scene is perpetuated with the success of "You Really Got Me," the first hit released by the Kinks, featuring brothers Ray Davies and Dave Davies (both on vocals and guitar).   MUSIC

1964   American painter Helen Frankenthaler paints *Interior Landscape*.   PAINT

1964   American painter Ellsworth Kelly paints *Red/Blue*.   PAINT

1964   The nonrepresentational artistic style known as op art, which relies on optical illusions that often imply movement, comes into fashion in the fine and popular arts.   PAINT

1964   American sculptor David Smith erects his stainless steel *Cubi* series outside his farm at Bolton Landing, New York. The pieces will eventually be placed in major museums.   SCULP

1964–1965   The highest-rated TV program of the season is *Bonanza* (NBC). Other top-rated programs are *Bewitched* (ABC) and *The Fugitive* (ABC).   TV&R

1965   Robert Wise's *The Sound of Music*, based on the Rodgers and Hammerstein stage musical and starring Julie Andrews and Christopher Plummer, is released by 20th Century-Fox. It will unseat *Gone with the Wind* (1939) to become the top-grossing film of all time. *See also* 1972, FILM.   FILM

1965   Other notable films include David Lean's *Doctor Zhivago*, Carol Reed's *The Agony and the Ecstasy*, George Stevens's *The Greatest Story Ever Told*, Blake Edwards's *The Great Race*, and Fred Coe's *A Thousand Clowns* (all U.S.); Richard Lester's *Help!*, John Schlesinger's *Darling*, and Roman Polanski's *Repulsion* (all U.K.); Jean-Luc Godard's *Alphaville* (France); Michelangelo Antonioni's *Red Desert* (France/Italy); and Federico Fellini's *Juliet of the Spirits* (Italy).   FILM

1965   American director James Ivory, working in India, gains international notice with the drama *Shakespeare Wallah*, coscripted with Polish-born Ruth Prawer Jhabvala and produced by Indian Ismail Merchant. The Merchant-Ivory-Jhabvala team will become known in the 1980s and 1990s for their British-made, beautifully mounted, emotionally nuanced literary adaptations, including *A Room with a View* (1985) and *Howards End* (1992).   FILM

1965   American novelist Frank Herbert publishes the science-fiction classic *Dune*, first in a series of novels about the desert planet Arrakis that will also include *Dune Messiah* (1969) and *Children of Dune* (1976).   LIT

1965   American poet Randall Jarrell publishes a collection of autobiographical poems, *The Lost World*.   LIT

1965   Based on a number of interviews with the African-American leader, American writer Alex Haley writes *The Autobiography of Malcolm X*. The book is published near the time of Malcolm X's assassination in 1965.   LIT

1965   American journalist Tom Wolfe ushers in the age of new journalism with the publication of *The Kandy-Kolored Tangerine-Flake Streamline Baby*. He will follow it in 1968 with *The Electric Kool-Aid Acid Test*, based on the experiences of American novelist Ken Kesey.   LIT

1965   British novelist John Fowles publishes *The Magus*. Among his later works is *The French Lieutenant's Woman* (1969).   LIT

1965   Italian novelist Italo Calvino publishes the short-story collection *Cosmicomics*. He will be known for his fantastic, ironic writing in this and other works, including *Mr. Palomar* (1985).   LIT

1965   Playing songs like Bob Dylan's "Mr. Tambourine Man," the Byrds become early experimenters with electronically amplified folk music, creating a subgenre of popular music called "folk rock."   MUSIC

1965   Epitomizing what will become known as the San Francisco sound, which blends folk and psychedelic elements, the group Jefferson Airplane is formed in that city by vocalist Marty Balin and guitarist Paul Kantner. In 1966 vocalist Grace Slick leaves the band the Great Society to join Jefferson Airplane, which will become best known for the songs "White Rabbit," written by Slick, and "Somebody to Love," written by Slick's brother-in-law, Darby Slick; both songs were previously performed with the Great Society.   MUSIC.

1965   The all-female group the Supremes exemplifies the Detroit-based Motown sound with the hits "Stop! In the Name of Love," "Back in My Arms Again," and "I Hear a Symphony." Led by Diana Ross, the Supremes will become the most popular female singing group of the decade. Other important Motown acts are (or will include) the Temptations, Martha and the Vandellas, Gladys Knight and the Pips, the Four Tops, the Jackson Five, and the Miracles, featuring singer and songwriter Smokey Robinson, who will produce songs by Marvin Gaye, among others.   MUSIC

1965   American rhythm-and-blues singer Wilson Pickett releases "In the Midnight Hour," which will become a soul classic. His much-covered "Mustang Sally," written by Mack Rice, formerly of the Falcons (for whom Pickett sang in the early 1960s), will chart in 1966.   MUSIC

1965   American artist Frank Stella paints *Empress of India*.   PAINT

1965   His work gaining newfound interest since the 1950s, an exhibition of Swiss sculptor Alberto Giacometti's work is held in London.   SCULP

1965–1966   The highest-rated TV program of the season is *Bonanza* (NBC). Other top-rated programs are *Gomer Pyle, U.S.M.C.* (CBS) and *Batman* (ABC).   TV&R

1966   American architect Robert Venturi publishes *Complexities and Contradictions in Modern Architecture*. He becomes a leading figure in postmodernist architecture, which advocates an eclectic style that makes use of popular culture, historical associations, and humor.   ARCH

1966   American playwright Edward Albee's drama *A Delicate Balance* is produced in New York City. It will be awarded the Pulitzer Prize.   DRAMA

1966   *Les Paravents* (*The Screens*), a drama by French writer Jean Genet, opens in Paris.   DRAMA

1966   Notable films include Mike Nichols's *Who's Afraid of Virginia Woolf?*, John Ford's *7 Women*, Billy Wilder's *The Fortune Cookie*, and Norman Jewison's *The Russians Are Coming, the Russians Are Coming* (all U.S.); Michelangelo Antonioni's *Blowup* (U.K./Italy); Roman Polanski's *Cul-de-Sac* and Fred Zinnemann's *A Man for All*

Seasons (both U.K.); Ingmar Bergman's *Persona* (Sweden); Claude Lelouch's *A Man and a Woman* (France); Pier Paolo Pasolini's *The Gospel According to St. Matthew* (Italy/France); and Sergio Leone's *The Good, the Bad, and the Ugly* (Italy/Spain). FILM

1966   Chinese writer Lao She (*b.* 1899) dies during the Cultural Revolution, reportedly killed for writing works opposed by the state. LIT

1966   American novelist Bernard Malamud publishes *The Fixer*. The story of anti-Semitism in Russia in the early 20th century will win the Pulitzer Prize. LIT

1966   American writer Susan Sontag publishes the essay collection, *Against Interpretation*, which establishes her as a critic of culture and the arts. LIT

1966   American novelist John Barth publishes *Giles-Goat Boy*. LIT

1966   Irish poet Seamus (Justin) Heaney publishes the collection *Death of a Naturalist*. Later collections include *Door into the Dark* (1969). He will also publish a prose collection, *Preoccupations: Selected Prose 1968–1978*. LIT

1966–1983   French-born American diarist Anaïs Nin (*d.* 1977) publishes the multivolume *Diary of Anaïs Nin*, part of it posthumously. LIT

1966   American poet Anne Sexton publishes her Pulitzer Prize–winning volume of verse, *Live or Die*. LIT

1966   American composer Samuel Barber's opera *Antony and Cleopatra* opens the Metropolitan Opera Company's first season at Lincoln Center in New York. MUSIC

1966   After an absence of several years from the pop charts, American singer and actor Frank Sinatra returns with *Strangers in the Night*, which will win the Grammy Award for record of the year. His next massive success will be the 1993 album of pairings with contemporary artists, *Duets*. *See also* 1944, MUSIC. MUSIC

1966   Cream, the British "supergroup" famed for its lengthy, improvisational live performances, is formed by drummer Ginger Baker, basssist Jack Bruce, and guitarist Eric Clapton, a veteran of the Yardbirds (*see* 1963, MUSIC). Their album *Disraeli Gears* (1967) generates the hit "Sunshine of Your Love." Two years after their breakup in 1968, Clapton will form Derek and the Dominoes, who will have a hit with "Layla," among other songs. MUSIC

1966   Scottish folk singer Donovan (born Donovan Phillips Leitch) has an American hit with his "Mellow Yellow"; his "Sunshine Superman" will chart in Britain the following year, along with "Mellow Yellow." In 1972 he will write the score for Franco Zefferelli's film about 13th-century Italian saint Francis of Assisi, *Brother Sun, Sister Moon.*   MUSIC

1966   The Jewish Museum of New York opens an exhibition of minimal sculpture called "Primary Structures," featuring such artists as Donald Judd, Sol LeWitt, and Carl André.   SCULP

1966–1967   The highest-rated TV program of the season is *Bonanza* (NBC). Other top-rated programs are *The Lucy Show* (CBS) and *Green Acres* (CBS).   TV&R

1967   The John Hancock Center opens in Chicago. More than 1,100 feet in height, it is, at its completion, the second tallest building in the world, but will fall to fifth place by 1973.   ARCH

1967   *Rosencrantz and Guildenstern Are Dead*, a drama by Czech-born British playwright Tom Stoppard, is produced. His later plays will include *After Magritte* (produced in 1970), *Travesties* (1974), and *The Real Thing* (1982).   DRAMA

1967   *Relatively Speaking*, a comedy by British playwright Alan Ayckbourn, premieres. His comedies *Absurd Person Singular* and *Bedroom Farce* will be produced in 1973 and 1977, respectively.   DRAMA

1967   One of the first rock musicals, *Hair* opens in New York on October 29, with book and lyrics by Gerome Ragni and James Rado and music by Galt MacDermott. Billed as an "American tribal love-rock musical," it will become a cultural marker of its time.   DRAMA

1967   American on- and offscreen couple Spencer Tracy and Katharine Hepburn star in their last of nine films they made together, Stanley Kramer's *Guess Who's Coming to Dinner.* Tracy, who wins an Academy Award for his performance, dies this year. Their other films include *Adam's Rib* (1949) and *Pat and Mike* (1952).   FILM

1967   Notable films include Arthur Penn's *Bonnie and Clyde*, Mike Nichols's *The Graduate*, Norman Jewison's *In the Heat of the Night*, and Don Chaffey's *Fantastic Voyage* (all U.S.); Joseph Strick's *Ulysses* (U.K.); Luis Buñuel's *Belle de Jour* (France/Italy); Jacques Tati's *Playtime* (France); Philippe de Broca's *King of Hearts* (France/U.K.); and Bo Widerberg's *Elvira Madigan* (Sweden).   FILM

1967   American novelist Ira Levin publishes *Rosemary's Baby*, about a New York woman who carries the devil's child. The book becomes a best-seller and the basis for a successful film by Roman Polanski (1968).   LIT

1967   American essayist and journalist Norman Podhoretz publishes a memoir of his young adult life in New York, *Making It.*   LIT

1967   American novelist Richard Brautigan publishes *Trout Fishing in America*, which will become a cult favorite in the 1960s.   LIT

1967   Colombian novelist and short-story writer Gabriel García Márquez publishes the saga of magical realism, *One Hundred Years of Solitude*. It establishes him as an important modern talent. Later works will include *Chronicle of a Death Foretold* (1982) and *Love in the Time of Cholera* (1988).   LIT

1967   Aretha Franklin establishes herself as the "Queen of Soul" with her rendition of Otis Redding's "Respect."   MUSIC

1967   The Monterey Pop Festival in Monterey, California, makes stars of blues singer Janis Joplin, guitarist Jimi Hendrix, and singer/songwriter Otis Redding. All three will be dead within three years. Redding dies this year, on December 10, in a plane crash. His posthumously released ballad "(Sittin' on) the Dock of the Bay" is a number-one hit. Joplin and Hendrix will die in 1970.   MUSIC

1967   The first "Human Be-In" is held, at Golden Gate Park in San Francisco, featuring the music of the Quicksilver Messenger Service, Jefferson Airplane, and the Grateful Dead. Under the leadership of Jerry Garcia (lead guitar) and Bob Weir (rhythm guitar) the Grateful Dead will soon acquire a cult following of core fans who will follow the band on their national tours, year after year, decade and decade. Drummer Mickey Hart will be added in 1968.   MUSIC

1967   Brooklyn-born singer Barbra Streisand presents a highly touted concert in Central Park, New York City. It is attended by approximately 135,000 fans.   MUSIC

1967   American painter Richard Diebenkorn begins painting the *Ocean Park* series, which he will continue for decades.   PAINT

1967   American painter Romare Bearden creates the collage *Three Folk Musicians*. Over the decades of his work, Bearden's paintings and collages, influenced by cubism and African sculpture, build a penetrating view of African-American experience.   PAINT

1967–1968   The highest-rated TV program of the season is *The Andy Griffith Show* (CBS). Other top-rated programs are *Family Affair* (CBS) and *The Dean Martin Show* (NBC). The comedy-variety program *The Carol Burnett Show* begins its 11-year run on CBS.   TV&R

1968   The columns of the Parthenon in Athens, Greece, face serious problems of erosion and are in danger of crumbling.   ARCH

1968   Designed by architect Eero Saarinen, the Gateway Arch in St. Louis, Missouri, is completed and dedicated.   ARCH

1968   The foundations of the Temple of Herod are discovered by Benjamin Masar of Jerusalem University. The temple was destroyed in A.D. 70.   ARCH

1968   Polish director Jerzy Grotowski publishes *Towards a Poor Theatre*, a book in which he presents his concept of actor-based theater, theater which is derived from the mental and physical resources of its actors.   DRAMA

1968   *The Increased Difficulty of Concentration*, an abstract drama by Czech playwright Vaclav Havel, is produced. In 1989, Havel will become president of Czechoslovakia (from 1993, the Czech Republic).   DRAMA

1968   The Theatres Act is passed, abolishing government censorship of theater in England. Previously, the Lord Chamberlain's Office had had the power to prevent the public performance of plays it deemed morally offensive.   DRAMA

1968   American actor James Earl Jones, widely considered to be the greatest black actor of his generation, opens on Broadway in *The Great White Hope*, a play by Howard Slacker about boxer Jack Johnson. Jones will appear in many classical and contemporary stage, film, and television roles, including Othello and Macbeth for Joseph Papp's New York Shakespeare Festival.   DRAMA

1968   Notable films include Peter Yates's *Bullitt*, William Wyler's *Funny Girl*, John Wayne's *The Green Berets*, Gene Saks's *The Odd Couple*, Franklin J. Schaffner's *Planet of the Apes*, Mel Brooks's *The Producers*, Roman Polanski's *Rosemary's Baby*, and George A. Romero's *Night of the Living Dead* (all U.S.); Stanley Kubrick's *2001: A Space Odyssey*, Carol Reed's *Oliver!*, and George Dunning's animated Beatles film *Yellow Submarine* (all U.K.); Franco Zeffirelli's *Romeo and Juliet* and Roger Vadim's *Barbarella* (U.K./Italy); Andrej Wajda's *Gates to Paradise* (U.K./West Germany); François Truffaut's *The Bride Wore Black* (France); Jean-Luc Godard's *Weekend* (France/Italy); Ingmar Bergman's *Shame* (Sweden); and Sergei Bondarchuk's *War and Peace* (U.S.S.R.).   FILM

1968   While in prison African-American political activist Eldridge Cleaver writes *Soul on Ice*, a personal treatise on anger and violence.   LIT

1968   American novelist and essayist Joan Didion publishes the essay collection *Slouching Toward Bethlehem*. Like her 1979 collection *The White Album*, it examines the decay of modern culture, often seen through the California experience.   LIT

1968   American avant-garde composer Philip Glass presents his *Pieces in the Shape of a Square* in New York.   MUSIC

1968   German electronic music pioneer Karlheinz Stockhausen composes the experimental work *Spiral* for a soloist with short-wave radio receiver.   MUSIC

1968   German composer Hans Werner Henze's oratorio *The Raft of Medusa*, a musi-
            cal protest against inhumanity, is performed.   MUSIC

1968   American country singer Tammy Wynette releases her hit "Stand by Your
            Man."   MUSIC

1968   The British blues-based rock band Led Zeppelin is formed by Jimmy Page, for-
            merly the guitarist for the Yardbirds (*see* 1963, MUSIC), vocalist Robert Plant, bassist
            John Paul Jones, and drummer John Bonham. Although they will contribute
            many memorable songs throughout their prolific career, they will perhaps be best
            remembered for "Stairway to Heaven" (1971), one of the first heavy-metal rock
            ballads (the other being Aerosmith's "Dream On," released in 1973).   MUSIC

1968   Santana, an American band that combines Latin sounds with blues, debuts at
            the Fillmore West in San Francisco. Led by the Mexican-born guitarist and
            vocalist Carlos Santana, the band will become known for its long improvisa-
            tional solos. Its first album will generate the hit "Evil Ways" in 1970. Santana's
            biggest hit single, a cover of Fleetwood Mac's "Black Magic Woman," will chart
            in January 1971; it will be followed closely by their cover of Tito Puente's "Oye
            Como Va."   MUSIC

1968   American folk singer, songwriter, and guitarist Judy Collins releases the album
            that will become her all-time best-seller, *Wildflowers,* containing her own com-
            positions as well as versions of songs by Jacques Brel, Bertolt Brecht and Kurt
            Weill. It also includes her rendition of Joni Mitchell's "Both Sides Now," which
            wins a Grammy Award for best folk performance of 1968.   MUSIC

1968   American rock musician Elvis Presley makes his "comeback special," which airs
            on NBC on December 3, pulling in the largest viewing audience of the year for
            a musical special. Clad in black leather and sporting sideburns, the still-slender
            Presley sings "Trouble," "Guitar Man," and "If I Can Dream" and reestablishes
            his reputation as a charismatic live performer.   MUSIC

1968   The British rock band the Moody Blues release their concept album *Days of
            Future Passed,* which features passages by the London Festival Orchestra and
            generates the hits "Nights in White Satin" and "Tuesday Afternoon."   MUSIC

1968   The California-based band Steppenwolf releases its self-titled debut album, which
            spawns two million-selling singles, "Born to Be Wild" and "Magic Carpet Ride."
                                                                                   MUSIC

1968   American photorealist Chuck Close paints *Self-Portrait.* Photorealists (also
            called superrealists or hyperrealists) paint with the precise, exhaustive detail
            found in photographs, and they often work from photographs. Other photo-
            realists include Don Eddy, Richard Estes, and Audrey Flack.   PAINT

1968–1969   The highest-rated TV program of the season is *Rowan & Martin's Laugh-In* (NBC). Other top-rated programs are *Mayberry R.F.D.* (CBS) and *Julia* (NBC).   TV&R

1969   The Dance Theater of Harlem is founded by American dancer Arthur Mitchell. The first black principal dancer for the American Ballet Theater and member of the New York City Ballet, Mitchell is said to have been prompted to develop an American dance company upon hearing of the assassination of civil rights leader Martin Luther King Jr. in 1968.   DANCE

1969   The Body Politic, a nonprofit theater, is founded in Chicago. Its emergence marks the beginning of the city's Off-Loop theater movement. Victory Gardens Theater, Steppenwolf Theatre Company, Wisdom Bridge Theatre, and others will soon be established, providing Midwesterners with high quality, affordable plays.   DRAMA

1969   Notable films include Paul Mazursky's *Bob and Carol and Ted and Alice*, George Roy Hill's *Butch Cassidy and the Sundance Kid*, Arthur Penn's *Alice's Restaurant*, Dennis Hopper's *Easy Rider*, John Schlesinger's *Midnight Cowboy*, Henry Hathaway's *True Grit*, Sydney Pollack's *They Shoot Horses, Don't They?*, and Sam Peckinpah's *The Wild Bunch* (all U.S.); Charles Jarrott's *Anne of the Thousand Days*, Karel Reisz's *Isadora*, and Richard Attenborough's *Oh! What a Lovely War* (all U.K.); Ingmar Bergman's *The Passion of Anna* (Sweden); Eric Rohmer's *My Night at Maud's*, François Truffaut's *The Wild Child*, and Constantin Costa-Gavras's *Z* (all France); and Federico Fellini's *Fellini Satyricon* (Italy).   FILM

1969   American novelist Mario Puzo publishes *The Godfather*. The saga of the Corleone crime family will become a best-seller and will generate three films.   LIT

1969   American poet John Berryman publishes the complete collection of his 385 poems in *The Dream Songs*. In process since 1955, it will win the National Book Award and Bollingen Prize.   LIT

1969   American novelist Kurt Vonnegut publishes his antiwar novel *Slaughterhouse-Five*, which ranges through time and into outer space as the author struggles to come to terms with the American firebombing of Dresden during World War II.   LIT

1969   American novelist Philip Roth publishes the novel *Portnoy's Complaint*, in which he explores contemporary Jewish male identity.   LIT

1969–1971   Avant-garde French composer Pierre Boulez becomes director of the New York Philharmonic.   MUSIC

1969   The Woodstock Music and Art Fair, near Bethel, New York, attracts more than 400,000 enthusiasts for three days of "peace, love and music." Dozens of musicians perform, including the Who, Jimi Hendrix, Janis Joplin, the Grateful Dead, Sly & the Family Stone, Joe Cocker, Santana, and Joan Baez. A defining moment for the baby-boomer generation, it will be commemorated in 1994 by a cross-generational Woodstock concert near the original site.   MUSIC

1969   *Tommy*, the world's first rock opera, by Peter Townshend of the Who, is performed in New York City. It will be made into a Ken Russell film in 1975 and adapted into a Tony-winning Broadway musical in 1993.   MUSIC

1969   The British rock band King Crimson is formed by guitarist Robert Fripp and bassist and vocalist Greg Lake, among others. In the following year the band releases *In the Court of the Crimson King*, whose title track will be among their most memorable songs, even though it only charts at number 80 in the United States. Greg Lake will leave in 1970 to form Emerson, Lake, and Palmer (ELP), whose experiments in fusing rock with classical music will result in a unique arrangement and recording of 19th-century Russian composer Modest Mussorgsky's "Pictures at an Exhibition" in 1971.   MUSIC

1969   Canadian singer and songwriter Joni Mitchell (Roberta Joan Anderson) releases her album *Clouds*, containing her own version of her composition "Both Sides Now," which was a success for Judy Collins last year. Mitchell's jazz-influenced album *Hejira* (1976) will chart at number 13 in the United States. She will move further into jazz in 1979, when she will record with guitarist Pat Metheny, saxophonist Michael Brecker, bassist Jaco Pastorius, drummer Don Alias, and keyboardist Lyle Mays for her forthcoming double-live album *Shadows and Light* (1980).   MUSIC

1969   The northern Californian band Creedence Clearwater Revival releases "Proud Mary," written by lead singer and guitarist John Fogerty. It will sell a million copies and be covered successfully by Ike & Tina Turner and Elvis Presley, among others.   MUSIC

1969–1970   The highest-rated TV program of the season is *Rowan & Martin's Laugh-In* (NBC). Other top-rated programs are *Gunsmoke* (CBS) and *Family Affair* (CBS). TV&R

1970s   Among the actors who deliver memorable performances during this decade are Jack Nicholson, Al Pacino, Robert De Niro, Harvey Keitel, Clint Eastwood, Donald Sutherland, Gene Hackman, Malcolm MacDowell, Alan Arkin, Diane Keaton, Woody Allen, James Caan, Liv Ullman, Richard Dreyfuss, Ellen Burstyn, Sam Waterston, Cicely Tyson, Jodie Foster, Sissy Spacek, Christohper Reeve, Sylvester Stallone, John Travolta, Sally Field, Alan Bates, Diahaan Carroll, Peter Finch, Christopher Walken, Kris Kristofferson, Gerard Depardieu, Glenda Jackson, Oliver Reed, Liza Minelli, and Isabelle Adjani. *See also* 1960s and 1980s, FILM.   FILM

1970s   Popular songs of the decade include "Bridge Over Troubled Water," "Your Song," "Stairway to Heaven," "It's Too Late," "Imagine," "(Theme from) Shaft," "American Pie," "Aqualung," "Killing Me Softly (with His Song)," "Superstition," "The Way

We Were," "Born to Run," "Taxi," "(You're) Havin' My Baby," "Feelings," "The Hustle," "(Don't Stop) Thinkin' About Tomorrow," "Stayin' Alive," "Hotel California," "Piano Man," "Maggie May," "ABC," and "Bad Girls."   MUSIC

1970s   American feminist artist Miriam Shapiro becomes well known for her decorative mixed-media works on fabric, associated with the pattern and decoration movement.   PAINT

1970s   German-born British photographer Bill Brandt and American photographer Jerry Uelsmann represent two photographers practicing the movement toward the fantastic in photography. The movement effects a troubled representation of reality through the use of photographic manipulation.   PHOTO

1970s   American artist Duane Hanson creates strikingly realistic figures from models using painted polyester and fiberglass.   SCULP

1970   Notable films include Bob Rafelson's *Five Easy Pieces*, George Seaton's *Airport*, Arthur Hiller's *Love Story*, Robert Altman's *M*A*S*H* and *Brewster McCloud*, Mike Nichols's *Catch-22*, Arthur Penn's *Little Big Man*, and Franklin J. Schaffner's *Patton* (all U.S.); Ken Russell's *The Music Lovers* and Billy Wilder's *The Private Life of Sherlock Holmes* (both U.K.); *Tora! Tora! Tora!* by Richard Fleischer, Toshio Masuda, and Kinji Fukasuku (U.S./Japan); François Truffaut's *Bed and Board* (France); Elio Petri's *Investigation of a Citizen Above Suspicion* (Italy); Akira Kurosawa's *Dodeskaden* (Japan); and Luis Buñuel's *Tristana* (France/Spain).   FILM

1970   With their song "Bridge Over Troubled Water," taken from the album of the same name, American singing duo Paul Simon and Art Garfunkel become one of the few musical acts in history to top the American and British singles and album charts simultaneously. They will sweep the Grammy Awards the following year, winning six in all. Simon & Garfunkel first came to prominence in 1965 with "The Sound of Silence," which was followed by "Homeward Bound," "I Am a Rock," "Scarborough Fair/Canticle" and, from the soundtrack to Mike Nichols's film *The Graduate*, "Mrs. Robinson."   MUSIC

1970   The American band Crosby, Stills, Nash & Young releases its debut album, *Deja Vu*. Comprising four members, each of whom does triple duty on guitar, vocals, and songwriting, CSNY is David Crosby, formerly of the Byrds; Stephen Stills and Neil Young, both formerly of Buffalo Springfield; and Graham Nash, formerly of the Hollies. Among CSNY's best-known hits will be Young's "Ohio" and Stills's "Love the One You're With." Prior to the addition of Young, who will go on to have a successful solo career, Crosby, Stills & Nash released Nash's "Marrakesh Express" and Stills's "Suite: Judy Blue Eyes" (written for singer Judy Collins), both from their 1969 self-titled debut album.   MUSIC

1970	British heavy-metal band Black Sabbath, featuring lead singer Ozzy Osbourne, releases its second album, *Paranoid*, which generates three of what will become the band's best-known songs: the title track, "War Pigs," and "Iron Man." MUSIC
1970	Canadian rock band Guess Who releases its best-selling criticism of American superficiality, "American Woman." MUSIC
1970	Two of the Woodstock generation's best talents, both of them blues-based musicians, are found dead of drug-related causes this year at the age of 27: singer Janis Joplin, known for "Piece of My Heart" and her rendition of Kris Kristofferson's "Me and Bobby McGee," among other songs; and electric guitarist and singer Jimi Hendrix (born James Marshall), who found fame with "Purple Haze," "Foxy Lady," "Crosstown Traffic," and Bob Dylan's "All Along the Watchtower," among other songs. MUSIC
1970	American artist Philip Pearlstein creates paintings of nude figures, often in domestic surroundings, that are minutely realistic and unidealized. His work is related to photorealism, though more emotional in tone and based on live models rather than photographs. *See also* 1968, PAINT. PAINT
1970	American photographer and physician Eliot Porter publishes the collection of wildlife photos *Appalachian Wilderness*. Among his later collections will be *Birds of North America—A Personal Selection* (1972) and *Eliot Porter's Southwest* (1985). PHOTO
1970	American artist Robert Smithson completes his major earthwork piece, *Spiral Jetty*, a mud and rock coil in the Great Salt Lake. The work is not intended to endure as Smithson allows for the process of erosion to take place. The project will survive only in photographs. SCULP
1970–1971	The highest-rated TV program of the season is *Marcus Welby, M.D.* (ABC). Other top-rated programs are *Here's Lucy* (CBS) and *Ironside* (NBC). TV&R
1971	The Standard Oil of Indiana Building opens in Chicago, outstripping the John Hancock Center in height. *See* 1967, ARCH. ARCH
1971	The witty and idiosyncratic dance troupe the Pilobolus Dance Theater is founded by Americans Robb Pendleton and Jonathan Wolken. DANCE
1971	*The Basic Training of Pavlo Hummel* and *Sticks and Bones*, two dramas by American playwright David Rabe, are produced in New York City. The first is about an American soldier in Vietnam. The second is about a Vietnam veteran who has just returned to America. DRAMA

1971   Notable films include William Friedkin's *The French Connection*, Peter
            Bogdanovich's *The Last Picture Show*, Robert Mulligan's *Summer of '42*, Norman
            Jewison's *Fiddler on the Roof*, T. C. Frank's *Billy Jack*, Don Siegel's *Dirty Harry*,
            Alan J. Pakula's *Klute*, Robert Altman's *McCabe and Mrs. Miller*, Clint Eastwood's
            Play Misty for Me, and Gordon Parks's *Shaft* (all U.S.); Ken Russell's *The Devils*,
            Sam Peckinpah's *Straw Dogs*, John Schlesinger's *Sunday Bloody Sunday*, and
            Stanley Kubrick's *A Clockwork Orange* (all U.K.); Louis Malle's *Murmur of the
            Heart* and Eric Rohmer's *Claire's Knee* (both France); Nicolas Roeg's *Walkabout*
            (Australia); Ingmar Bergman's *The Touch* (Sweden); and Bernardo Bertolucci's
            The Conformist (France/Italy/West Germany).   FILM

1971   A year after his death, British novelist E. M. Forster's novel *Maurice*, concerning
            a homosexual relationship, is published for the first time since it was written
            around 1912.   LIT

1971   Filmmaker, writer, and comedian Woody Allen publishes his first collection of
            essays, *Getting Even*. His other books will include *Without Feathers* (1975), *Side
            Effects* (1980), and *The Floating Light Bulb* (1982).   LIT

1971   American artist Chris Burden has himself shot in the left arm by a friend for
            the artwork called *Shoot*.   MISC

1971   American songwriter Carole King wins the Grammy Award for best female con-
            temporary vocal performer, and her album *Tapestry* wins for album of the year.
            The album will sell more than 15 million copies and help to usher in an era of
            singer-songwriters, including Carly Simon and Jackson Browne. Previously, King
            had been part of a phenomenally successful 1960s songwriting team with Gerry
            Goffin; their work included "Up on the Roof" and "Locomotion."   MUSIC

1971   American singer and songwriter Jim Morrison, the leader of the psychedel-
            ic/blues-based California rock band the Doors, is found dead in Paris. The
            charismatic singer led the Doors—featuring keyboardist Ray Manzarek, gui-
            tarist Robby Krieger, and drummer John Densmore—to fame with such hits as
            "Light My Fire," "Break on Through," and "L.A. Woman." Interest in the band
            will be rekindled at least twice: in 1979, when Morrison's "The End" is fea-
            tured on the soundtrack to Francis Ford Coppola's anti-Vietnam War film
            Apocalypse Now, and in 1991, with the release of Oliver Stone's hagiographic
            film *The Doors*, starring Val Kilmer as Morrison.   MUSIC

1971   Progressive rock, featuring such groups as Jethro Tull and Pink Floyd (*see* 1973,
            MUSIC), becomes popular. The Philly sound develops in Philadelphia as a soul
            music rival to Detroit's Motown, with groups like the Stylistics and the
            Spinners.   MUSIC

1971   The British rock group Ten Years After's song "I'd Love to Change the World,"
            whose refrain continues with the lines "but I don't know what to do, so I'll
            leave it up to you," reflects a common sentiment as 1960s-style activism grad-
            ually gives way to the political apathy that will characterize certain segments
            of the "me generation" of the 1970s.   MUSIC

1971   British rock singer Rod Stewart, formerly of the Jeff Beck Group and the Small
            Faces, releases "Maggie May," which tops the British and American charts in
            the same week as does its parent album, *Every Picture Tells a Story.*   MUSIC

1971   American painter Willem de Kooning paints *Amityville.*   PAINT

1971   Norman Lear's situation comedy *All in the Family* begins its eight-year run on
            CBS. Starring Carroll O'Connor as the bigoted Archie Bunker, Jean Stapleton
            as his devoted, cockeyed wife Edith, Rob Reiner as liberal son-in-law
            "Meathead," and Sally Struthers as awakening feminist daughter Gloria, it will
            poke fun at contemporary attitudes—both liberal and conservative—with a
            groundbreaking openness. It will be the highest-rated TV program of the
            1971–1972 season alongside other top-rated programs such as *The Flip Wilson
            Show* (NBC) and *Gunsmoke* (CBS).   TV&R

1971   Television advertisements for cigarettes are banned in the United States. Print
            advertisements remain legal.   TV&R

1971   American public television begins broadcasting *Masterpiece Theatre,* the long-
            running anthology series showcasing British dramatic programs, usually
            broadcast in several parts and often based on literary works. In years to come,
            PBS will offer many programs first seen in Britain, including Alistair Cooke's
            America (BBC, 1972) and *Monty Python's Flying Circus* (BBC, 1969–1974). TV&R

1972   The World Trade Center, designed by American architect Minoru Yamasaki,
            opens in New York City. With its twin 110-story towers rising 1,377 feet, it is
            briefly the tallest building in the world before being displaced the next year by
            the Sears Tower. Both are taller than the previous record-holder, the Empire
            State Building. *See also* 1929–1931 and 1973, ARCH.   ARCH

1972   San Francisco's skyline is redefined by the pyramidal Transamerica Building,
            designed by William L. Pereira Associates and opening this year.   ARCH

1972   The campy musical *Grease,* set in the 1950s, opens on Broadway and a nostal-
            gia craze sweeps the United States. Randal Kleiser will direct a film version of
            the musical, starring John Travolta, in 1978. The play will be revived on
            Broadway in 1994.   DRAMA

1972   *The Tooth of Crime,* a drama by American playwright Sam Shepard, premieres. Shepard's *The Curse of the Starving Class* will be produced in 1977.   DRAMA

1972   American performance artist Laurie Anderson—who will become known for multimedia performance pieces mixing photography, film, drawings, animation, the spoken word, and music—presents *Story Show,* one of her first works.   DRAMA

1972   Paramount releases Francis Ford Coppola's *The Godfather,* starring Marlon Brando, Al Pacino, Robert Duvall, and James Caan. The epic saga of the Corleone crime family is based on the 1969 novel by Mario Puzo, with a screenplay by Puzo and Coppola. The film sets a new record for all-time box office sales. It will win three Oscars, including a best actor Oscar refused by Marlon Brando, and will lead to two sequels. *See* 1974 and 1990, FILM.   FILM

1972   Notable films include Bob Fosse's *Cabaret,* John Boorman's *Deliverance,* Michael Ritchie's *The Candidate,* Ronald Neame's *The Poseidon Adventure,* Peter Bogdanovich's *What's Up, Doc?,* and Gordon Parks Jr.'s *Superfly* (all U.S.); Ken Russell's *The Boy Friend* and Peter Medak's *The Ruling Class* (both U.K.); Luis Buñuel's *The Discreet Charm of the Bourgeoisie,* Eric Rohmer's *Chloe in the Afternoon,* and Robert Bresson's *Four Nights of a Dreamer* (all France); Werner Herzog's *Aguirre, the Wrath of God* (West Germany); Federico Fellini's *Roma* (Italy); and Ingmar Bergman's *Cries and Whispers* (Sweden).   FILM

1972   British novelist Margaret Drabble publishes *The Needle's Eye.* Her other novels include *A Summer Bird-Cage* (1963) and *The Garrick Year* (1964).   LIT

1972   American composer Leonard Bernstein presents his Mass for the opening of the John F. Kennedy Center for the Performing Arts in Washington, D.C.   MUSIC

1972   American singer Helen Reddy makes the feminist anthem "I Am Woman" the pop rallying cry of the women's liberation movement.   MUSIC

1972   The American rock band the Eagles release their self-titled debut album, which contains the hits "Take It Easy" and "Witchy Woman." Future hits will include "One of These Nights," "Lyin' Eyes," "Hotel California," and "Life in the Fast Lane."   MUSIC

1972   American artist Andy Warhol paints *Mao,* executed with silkscreen and paint on canvas.   PAINT

1972   In Italy Michelangelo's sculpture *Pietà* is mutilated with a hammer by a vandal.   SCULP

1972–1973	The highest-rated TV program of the season is *All in the Family* (CBS). Other top-rated programs are *Sanford and Son* (NBC) and *Maude* (CBS). **TV&R**
1973	The Sears Tower, designed by Skidmore, Owings & Merrill, opens in Chicago. At 110 stories and 1,454 feet, it is the tallest building in the world. *See also* 1972, ARCH. **ARCH**
1973	American playwright Lanford Wilson's *The Hot l Baltimore* is produced. It will run off-Broadway for 1,166 performances. Wilson's *Balm in Gilead* had been produced in 1965. His *5th of July* and *Talley's Folly* will be produced in 1978 and 1979, respectively. **DRAMA**
1973	British playwright Peter Shaffer's drama *Equus* is produced. His historical play *Amadeus* will be produced in 1979. Both will be great successes; *Amadeus* will be made into an Academy Award–winning movie in 1984. **DRAMA**
1973	Notable films include George Roy Hill's *The Sting*, George Lucas's *American Graffiti*, William Friedkin's *The Exorcist*, Sidney Lumet's *Serpico*, Sydney Pollack's *The Way We Were*, Martin Scorsese's *Mean Streets*, John Waters's *Pink Flamingos*, and Mel Brooks's *Blazing Saddles* (all U.S.); Lindsay Anderson's *O Lucky Man!* (U.K.); Fred Zinnemann's *The Day of the Jackal* (U.K./France); François Truffaut's *Day for Night* and Jean-Luc Godard's *Tout Va Bien* (both France); Cheng Chang Ho's *Five Fingers of Death* (China); Bernardo Bertolucci's *Last Tango in Paris* (France/Italy); Djibril Diop Mambety's *Touki-Bouki* (Senegal); and Ingmar Bergman's *Scenes from a Marriage* (Sweden). **FILM**
1973	The erotic film *Deep Throat* is ruled "indisputably and irredeemably obscene" by a New York Criminal Court judge. The film, one of many sexploitation entries during the 1960s and 1970s, creates an uproar across the United States. **FILM**
1973	Bernardo Bertolucci's highly charged *Last Tango in Paris*, starring Marlon Brando and Maria Schneider, generates controversy for its sexual frankness. In its day it marks the limits to which an artistic film can take the presentation of sex on-screen. **FILM**
1973	American novelist Erica Jong publishes *Fear of Flying*, a best-selling novel about a woman, Isadora Wing, who practices sexual freedom. The book will generate controversy and many imitators. **LIT**
1973	American novelist Thomas Pynchon publishes *Gravity's Rainbow*, his darkly comic, phantasmagoric novel of German missile development during World War II. **LIT**

1973–1975   Russian novelist Aleksandr Solzhenitsyn writes the novel *The Gulag Archipeligo*.
               It will bring about his exile to the West in 1974. Twenty years later, in 1994,
               following the fall of the Soviet Union, he will return to Russia.   LIT

1973   American poet Adrienne Rich publishes the collection *Diving into the Wreck*,
               which, like her collections over the previous decade, takes a feminist approach
               to women's experiences. Her 1976 prose collection *Of Woman Born* will con-
               centrate on the experience and public perception of motherhood.   LIT

1973   British science-fiction writer Arthur C. Clarke publishes the novel *Rendezvous
               with Rama*.   LIT

1973   British composer Benjamin Britten's *Death in Venice* premieres.   MUSIC

1973   From Honolulu American rock musician Elvis Presley presents a globally tele-
               vised concert to benefit the battleship *Arizona*.   MUSIC

1973   Southern rock, or rock influenced by country-western music, reaches main-
               stream American audiences through groups such as the Allman Brothers Band,
               ZZ Top, Lynyrd Skynyrd, and the Marshall Tucker Band. (Lynyrd Skynyrd's
               "Free Bird," released in 1975, will become one of the genre's most popular
               songs of the decade.) The sound will be revived in the early 1990s by the Black
               Crowes, among others.   MUSIC

1973   The British band Pink Floyd releases its concept album about madness, *Dark
               Side of the Moon*.   MUSIC

1973   The British rock band Deep Purple releases "Smoke on the Water," from their
               1972 album *Machine Head*.   MUSIC

1973   Among the songs that rise to the top of the American popular music charts this
               year are Roberta Flack's "Killing Me Softly (with His Song)," Elton John's
               "Crocodile Rock," and Stevie Wonder's "You Are the Sunshine of My Life" and
               "Superstition"; former Velvet Underground member Lou Reed's "Walk on the
               Wild Side" reaches number 16.   MUSIC

1973–1974   The highest-rated TV program of the season is *All in the Family* (CBS). Other
               top-rated programs are *The Sonny and Cher Comedy Hour* (CBS) and *The Mary
               Tyler Moore Show* (CBS).   TV&R

1974   Citing personal and artistic reasons, Russian ballet dancer Mikhail Baryshnikov,
               of the Kirov Ballet, defects to the West while touring with the Bolshoi Ballet in
               Toronto.   DANCE

1974   Notable American dance works include George Balanchine's *Coppelia*, Jerome Robbins's *Four Bagatelles* and *Dybbuk Variations*, and Eliot Feld's *Sephardic Songs*.   DANCE

1974   Notable films include Francis Ford Coppola's *The Godfather Part II* and *The Conversation*, Mel Brooks's *Young Frankenstein*, Roman Polanski's *Chinatown*, Martin Scorsese's *Alice Doesn't Live Here Anymore*, Terrence Malick's *Badlands*, and Tobe Hooper's *The Texas Chainsaw Massacre* (all U.S.); Ted Kotcheff's *The Apprenticeship of Duddy Kravitz* (Canada); Louis Malle's *Lacombe, Lucien* (France); Alain Resnais's *Stavisky* (France/Italy); Rainer Werner Fassbinder's *Effi Briest* (West Germany); Federico Fellini's *Amarcord* (Italy); and Ingmar Bergman's *The Magic Flute* (Sweden).   FILM

1974   British poet Philip Larkin publishes his final book of poems, *High Windows*, including the poems "The Old Fools" and "The Building."   LIT

1974   American essayist Annie Dillard publishes the collection of nature essays, *Pilgrim at Tinker Creek*, which will win the Pulitzer Prize.   LIT

1974   American publishing phenomenon Stephen King publishes his first novel, *Carrie*, the story of a lonely girl with telekinetic powers. King's brand of horror in such works as *The Shining* (1977), *Misery* (1987), and *Needful Things* (1991) will dominate the fiction best-seller list for decades; many of them will be made into movies.   LIT

1974   Notable musical works include German composer Hans Werner Henze's opera *Rachel, la cubana*, German composer Mauricio Kagel's String Quartet and *Mirum fur Tuba*, and British composer Elisabeth Luytens's *The Winter of the World* and *Plenum III*.   MUSIC

1974   Among the songs that make it into the Top 40 of the American popular music charts this year are Bachman-Turner Overdrive's "You Ain't Seen Nothing Yet" and "Takin' Care of Business," Bad Company's "Can't Get Enough," Steely Dan's "Rikki, Don't Lose That Number," and Billy Joel's "Piano Man."   MUSIC

1974   American artist Jasper Johns creates the oil, encaustic, and collage on canvas work *Corpse and Mirror*.   PAINT

1974–1975   The highest-rated TV program of the season is *All in the Family* (CBS). Other top-rated programs are *M*A*S*H* (CBS) and *The Waltons* (CBS).   TV&R

1975   Notable dance works include American choreographer Merce Cunningham's *Rebus* and *Changing Steps/Loops*, Russian-born choreographer George Balanchine's *Sheherezade*, and Soviet choreographer Yuri Grigorivich's *Ivan the Terrible*.   DANCE

1975   British playwright Harold Pinter's *No Man's Land* is produced. His drama *Betrayal* will be produced in 1978.   DRAMA

1975   American playwright Edward Albee's *Seascape* premieres in a production directed by the author. It will win the Pulitzer Prize.   DRAMA

1975   The American musical *A Chorus Line*—with book by James Kirkwood and Nicholas Dante, lyrics by Edward Kleban, and music by Marvin Hamlisch—premieres on April 15. The high-concept, behind-the-scenes musical will become Broadway's all-time longest-running show.   DRAMA

1975   Steven Spielberg's *Jaws* becomes the all-time box office champion, unseating *The Godfather* (1972). Starring Roy Scheider, Robert Shaw, and Richard Dreyfuss, the shark thriller is based on the best-selling novel by Peter Benchley. The film establishes Spielberg as a major director and helps to establish the summer blockbuster as a driving force in the way Hollywood studios plan their annual schedule of films.   FILM

1975   Other notable films include Robert Altman's *Nashville*, Milos Forman's *One Flew Over the Cuckoo's Nest*, Sidney Lumet's *Dog Day Afternoon*, and Hal Ashby's *Shampoo* (all U.S.); Stanley Kubrick's *Barry Lyndon*, Terry Gilliam's *Monty Python and the Holy Grail*, and Ken Russell's *Tommy* (all U.K.); Akira Kurosawa's *Dersu Uzala* (Japan); Peter Weir's *Picnic at Hanging Rock* (Australia); François Truffaut's *The Story of Adele H.* (France); Werner Herzog's *Every Man for Himself and God Against All* (West Germany); and Michelangelo Antonioni's *The Passenger* (Italy).   FILM

1975   British painter David Hockney creates stage sets for a production of Stravinsky's 1951 opera *The Rake's Progress*, inspired by the engravings by William Hogarth (*see* 1735, PAINT).   MUSIC

1975   American opera singer Beverly Sills makes her Metropolitan Opera debut in Rossini's *The Siege of Corinth*.   MUSIC

1975   Notable musical works include Finnish composer Aulis Sallinen's opera *Ratsumies*, American composer Charles Wuorinen's opera *The W. of Babylon*, American composer Carmen Moore's *Wildfires and Field Songs* and *Museum Piece*, American composer Virgil Thomson's *Family Portrait*, Swiss composer Heinz Holliger's Quartet for Strings, and British composer Benjamin Britten's *Sacred and Profane* for five unaccompanied voices.   MUSIC

1975   New Jersey-born rock musician Bruce Springsteen records the album *Born to Run*, which plumbs traditional American longings for love, freedom, and the open road. The album immediately makes him a rock icon; the title song becomes a rock anthem. *See also* 1984, MUSIC.   MUSIC

1975	American producer-songwriter Van McCoy's instrumental hit "The Hustle" ushers in the most popular dance craze since the twist. MUSIC
1975	The Top 40 American popular music songs include American singer Linda Ronstadt's cover of the Everly Brothers' "When Will I Be Loved," English country singer Olivia Newton-John's "Have You Never Been Mellow," the theatrically made-up band Kiss's "Rock 'n' Roll All Nite," and American country singer Willie Nelson's "Blue Eyes Crying in the Rain." American singer Dolly Parton is voted female vocalist of the year by the Country Music Association, and the Canadian band Rush is named most promising group in the Juno awards. MUSIC
1975	American painter Jasper Johns creates several encaustic crosshatched works, including *Weeping Women* and *The Barber's Tree*. PAINT
1975	American painter Willem de Kooning paints *Whose Name Was Writ in Water*. PAINT
1975	American artist Roy Lichtenstein paints *Cubist Still Life with Lemons*. PAINT
1975	The Japanese company Sony introduces the Betamax, the first home videocassette recorder (VCR). A competing format, VHS, made by JVC, will become the dominant system in American homes during the 1980s. TV&R
1975–1976	The highest-rated TV program of the season is *All in the Family* (CBS). Other top-rated programs are *Laverne & Shirley* (ABC) and *Rhoda* (CBS). TV&R
1976	*For Colored Girls Who Have Considered Suicide When the Rainbow Is Enuf*, a drama by African-American playwright Ntozake Shange, is produced. It will be very successful critically and commercially. DRAMA
1976	Mexican playwright Oscar Villegas's *Atlantida* (*Atlantis*) is produced. DRAMA
1976	Notable films include Sidney Lumet's *Network*, Martin Scorsese's *Taxi Driver*, Alan J. Pakula's *All the President's Men*, John Avildsen's *Rocky*, and Brian De Palma's *Carrie* (all U.S.); François Truffaut's *Small Change* and Eric Rohmer's *The Marquise of O* (both France); Wim Wenders's *Kings of the Road* (West Germany); Alain Tanner's *Jonah Who Will Be 25 in the Year 2000* (Switzerland); and Richard Lester's *Robin and Marian* (U.K.). FILM
1976	Chinese-American writer Maxine Hong Kingston publishes *The Woman Warrior: Memoirs of a Girlhood Among Ghosts*, about the women in her Chinese family. LIT
1976	American short-story writer Raymond Carver publishes the collection, *Will You Please Be Quiet, Please*, which establishes him as an important modern talent.

Later collections will include *What We Talk About When We Talk About Love* (1981), *Cathedral* (1983), and *Where I'm Calling From* (1988). LIT

1976   American conductor and opera director Sarah Caldwell is the first woman to conduct New York's Metropolitan Opera, with a performance of *La Traviata*. MUSIC

1976   The opera *Einstein on the Beach* by American composers Philip Glass and Robert Wilson premieres at the Avignon Festival in France to immediate acclaim. MUSIC

1976   Musical works commissioned to celebrate the U.S. bicentennial include John Cage's *Renga* with *Apartment House 1776*, Morton Subotnick's *Before the Butterfly*, and Gian Carlo Menotti's Symphony no. 1. MUSIC

1976   Punk rock bands, including the Ramones and Blondie, perform at such New York clubs as Max's Kansas City and CBGB. In England, the Sex Pistols release their first single, "Anarchy in the U.K.," and in the following year, their banned anti-monarchy song "God Save the Queen" reaches number one on the British pop charts. MUSIC

1976   Disco becomes the dominant pop music form, making stars of artists such as Donna Summer, Gloria Gaynor, the Andrea True Connection, and K.C. & the Sunshine Band. MUSIC

1976   Despite the competition from punk and disco at opposite ends of the popular music spectrum, mainstream rock acts continue to chart. Among them are Peter Frampton (formerly of Humble Pie), whose double album *Frampton Comes Alive!* featuring "Show Me the Way" becomes the most successful live album in rock history, selling more than 10 million copies; the Steve Miller Band, whose album *Fly Like an Eagle* goes platinum; and sisters Ann and Nancy Wilson's band Heart, whose album *Dreamboat Annie* generates the hits "Magic Man" and "Crazy on You." MUSIC

1976   American painter Andrew Wyeth depicts Andy Warhol in *Portrait of Andy*. PAINT

1976   American painter Elizabeth Murray paints *Beginner*. PAINT

1976   American painter Alfred Leslie paints *Our Family in 1976*. PAINT

1976   American photographer Richard Avedon publishes the collection *Portraits*, which contains his seemingly unadorned yet compelling, sometimes disturbing views of people. PHOTO

1976   In April Bulgarian-born artist Christo works with 65 workers to install his *Running Fence*, a nylon ribbon 25 miles long strung through the California countryside between the Pacific coast and the town of Petaluma. The project will begin to be dismantled in October.   SCULP

1976–1977   The highest-rated TV program of the season is *Happy Days* (ABC). Other top-rated programs are *M*A*S*H* (CBS) and *The Six Million Dollar Man* (ABC).   TV&R

1977   British architect Richard Rogers and Italian architect Renzo Piano design the Pompidou Center, an art museum and performing arts center in Paris.   ARCH

1977   The modern aluminum-faced Citicorp Center opens in New York City. Designed by Hugh Stubbins & Associates, it marks the city skyline with its sharply diagonal roof. The firm also designs the Federal Reserve Bank Building, which opens in Boston this year.   ARCH

1977   Notable dance works include American choreographer Twyla Tharp's *Simon Medley* and *MUD*.   DANCE

1977   *American Buffalo*, a drama by American playwright David Mamet, premieres, providing Mamet with his Broadway debut.   DRAMA

1977   The American musical *Annie*, based on the comic strip *Little Orphan Annie*, premieres on April 21. Its book is by Thomas Meehan, lyrics by Martin Charnin, and music by Charles Strouse.   DRAMA

1977   Woody Allen and his film *Annie Hall* win Oscars for best picture, director, and original screenplay, setting a new, more serious direction for the filmmaker, whose earlier films were purely comic.   FILM

1977   George Lucas's *Star Wars*, released by 20th Century-Fox, sets a new all-time box office record, establishes Lucas as an independent entertainment mogul, and opens the way for a flood of big-budget science-fiction blockbusters. Two sequels will follow, *The Empire Strikes Back* (1980) and *The Return of the Jedi* (1983). A restored and enhanced version of *Star Wars* will be released in 1997.   FILM

1977   Notable films include Steven Spielberg's *Close Encounters of the Third Kind*, Fred Zinnemann's *Julia*, Herbert Ross's *The Turning Point*, and John Badham's *Saturday Night Fever* (all U.S.); Luis Buñuel's *That Obscure Object of Desire* (Spain/France); Moshe Mizrahi's *Madame Rosa* (France); Bruce Beresford's *The Getting of Wisdom* (Australia); Paolo and Vittori Taviani's *Padre Padrone* (Italy); and Bernardo Bertolucci's *1900* (Italy/France/West Germany).   FILM

1977   British novelist Barbara Pym publishes the novel *Quartet in Autumn*, her first major success since her novels of the 1950s, including *Excellent Women* (1952).   LIT

1977   Notable American musical works include Leon Kirchner's opera *Lily*, Ned
             Rorem's organ suite *A Quaker Reader*, Elliott Carter's *A Symphony of Three
             Orchestras*, George Crumb's large-scale orchestral work *Star-Child*, Roque
             Cordero's *Soliloquies No. 3* for solo clarinet, Leonard Bernstein's *Songfest*, and
             Roger Sessions's *Five Pieces for Piano*.   MUSIC

1977   British singer and songwriter Elvis Costello (born Declan MacManus) makes
             his name as an idiosyncratic musician and commentator on the human condi-
             tion with his album *My Aim Is True*.   MUSIC

1977   American rock musician Elvis Presley dies at Graceland, his Memphis home,
             on August 16. So intense is the loyalty of his fans that decades after his death
             pilgrimages will be made to his home and grave, making Presley the foremost
             celebrity icon of American pop culture.   MUSIC

1977   The British-American band Fleetwood Mac releases the album *Rumours*, which
             will eventually sell more than 15 million copies on the strength of such hits as
             "Go Your Own Way," "You Make Loving Fun," and "Don't Stop."   MUSIC

1977   The British rock group Queen releases the anthemic "We Are the Champions,"
             which will become a staple at sports stadiums across the United States from
             now on.   MUSIC

1977   The American rock group Boston experiences its peak popularity, with four Top 40
             hits: "More Than a Feeling," "Peace of Mind," "Long Time," and "Don't Look Back."
                                                                                            MUSIC

1977   British painter David Hockney paints *Looking at Pictures on a Screen* and *My
             Parents*.   PAINT

1977   American painter Robert Moskowitz paints *The Swimmer*.   PAINT

1977   French painter Balthus (Count Balthasaiklossowski) paints *Nude in Profile*.   PAINT

1977   American artist Cindy Sherman creates the photographic series *Untitled Film
             Stills*.   PHOTO

1977–1988   The highest-rated TV program of the season is *Laverne & Shirley* (ABC). Other
             top-rated programs are *60 Minutes* (CBS) and *Charlie's Angels* (ABC).   TV&R

1977   For eight consecutive nights the TV mini-series *Roots* (ABC), about a black fam-
             ily's history through slavery and freedom in the United States, is broadcast to
             record-breaking ratings.   TV&R

1978   Chinese-American architect I. M. Pei designs the east wing of the National
            Gallery of Art in Washington, D.C.   ARCH

1978   Notable dance works include Belgian choreographer Maurice Béjart's *Gaité
            Parisienne* and American choreographer Martha Graham's *The Owl and the
            Pussycat, Ecuatorial*, and *The Flute of Pan*.   DANCE

1978   *Buried Child*, a drama by American playwright Sam Shepard, premieres. It will
            win the Pulitzer Prize. Shepard's *True West* and *A Lie of the Mind* will be pro-
            duced in 1980 and 1985, respectively.   DRAMA

1978   Notable films include Michael Cimino's *The Deer Hunter*, John Carpenter's
            Halloween, and Hal Ashby's *Coming Home* (all U.S.); Bertrand Blier's *Get Out
            Your Handkerchiefs* (France/Belgium); Rainer Werner Fassbinder's *The Marriage
            of Maria Braun* (West Germany); and Claude Chabrol's *Violette* (France).   FILM

1978   British novelist Graham Greene publishes *The Human Factor*, a spy thriller with
            the moral concerns typical of his work. *See also* 1938, LIT.   LIT

1978   American novelist John Irving publishes the tragicomic best-selling novel *The World
            According to Garp*. Later works will include *A Prayer for Owen Meany* (1989).   LIT

1978   Polish-born Yiddish writer Isaac Bashevis Singer, an American immigrant, wins the
            Nobel Prize for literature. His works include the novel *The Family Moskat* (1950). LIT

1978   The Metropolitan Opera transmits its first live telecast from New York, *La Bohème*
            with Renata Scotto and Luciano Pavarotti.   MUSIC

1978   György Ligeti's opera *Le Grand Macabre* premieres in Sweden; Krzysztof Penderecki's
            opera *Paradise Lost* and Concerto for Violin premiere in the United States.   MUSIC

1978   Notable American musical works include Samuel Barber's *Third Essay for
            Orchestra*, Charles Wuorinen's *Percussion Symphony* and *Two-Part Symphony*,
            Morton Subotnick's *Dance! Cloudless Sulphur* for tape and dancers, and Elie
            Siegmeister's *A Set of Houses* and *City Songs*. French composer Pierre Boulez
            premieres an orchestral version of his *Notations*; German composer Isang Yun
            premieres *Muak* (*Fantasy for Orchestra*).   MUSIC

1978   Reflecting the diversity of popular music, hard rock acts like Foreigner, Styx, and
            Kansas, share the airwaves with disco superstars the Bee Gees, seven of whose
            songs are featured on the soundtrack to John Badham's *Saturday Night Fever*, star-
            ring John Travolta. Meanwhile, a new style of alternative rock is pioneered by the
            American band Talking Heads, featuring singer and songwriter David Byrne, which
            releases the song "Psycho Killer," and the British band the Cure, which debuts with
            "Killing an Arab," inspired by Albert Camus's *The Stranger* (*see* 1942, LIT).   MUSIC

1978	American painter Elizabeth Murray paints *Children Meeting*.	PAINT

1978   In New York the "Bad Painters" and "New Imagists" exhibitions launch a new form of representational art called neo-expressionism, which uses expressive color and brushwork and intentionally primitive styles. Artists associated with the movement include American painter Joan Brown and German painter Anselm Kiefer.   PAINT

1978–1979   The highest-rated TV program of the season is *Laverne & Shirley* (ABC). Other top-rated programs are *Mork & Mindy* (ABC) and *All in the Family* (CBS).   TV&R

1979   Russian ballet dancers Alexander Godunov and Leonid and Valentina Kozlov defect to the United States during a tour of the Bolshoi Ballet, in which they were principal dancers.   DANCE

1979   The works of 19th-century Danish choreographer Auguste Bournonville are introduced to the United States in a national tour by the Royal Danish Ballet.   DANCE

1979   British composers Andrew Lloyd Webber and Tim Rice, known for their 1971 rock opera *Jesus Christ Superstar*, see the premiere of their rock opera musical *Evita* on Broadway, which heralds the beginning of a near-dominance of Lloyd Webber musicals—including *Cats* (1981), *Phantom of the Opera* (1986), and *Sunset Boulevard* (1993)—in American theater over the coming two decades.   DRAMA

1979   British playwright Caryl Churchill's *Cloud Nine*, a comedy about sex roles and imperialism, is produced. She had previously written *Vinegar Tom* (produced in 1976). Churchill's *Top Girls* will be produced in 1982, *Serious Money* in 1987.   DRAMA

1979   American actor and playwright Spalding Gray begins to write and perform a series of autobiographical monologues, which will include *Sex and Death to the Age of 14*, *Booze, Cars and College Girls*, *India and After*, *Interviewing the Audience*, and *Swimming to Cambodia*. He will be at the forefront of the new field of performance art.   DRAMA

1979   Notable films include Blake Edwards's *10*, Robert Benton's *Kramer vs. Kramer*, Woody Allen's *Manhattan*, James Bridges's *The China Syndrome*, Francis Ford Coppola's *Apocalypse Now*, and Martin Ritt's *Norma Rae* (all U.S.); Bruce Beresford's *Breaker Morant* and George Miller's *Mad Max* (both Australia); Luchino Visconti's *The Innocent* (Italy); and Rainer Werner Fassbinder's *Despair* (West Germany).   FILM

1979   American journalist Tom Wolfe publishes *The Right Stuff*, an iconoclastic study of the seven Mercury astronauts. It will be the basis of a 1983 film.   LIT

1979   British poet Thom Gunn publishes *Selected Poems: 1950–1975*. Later works include *The Passages of Joy* (1982) and *The Occasions of Poetry* (1982).   LIT

1979   South African novelist Nadine Gordimer publishes the political novel *Burger's Daughter*. Among her other works are the novel *The Conservationist* (1974) and the story collection *Something Out There* (1984).   LIT

1979   Other notable literary works include American Norman Mailer's *The Executioner's Song*, a novel about real-life killer Gary Gilmore; West Indian V. S. Naipaul's *A Bend in the River*; American William Styron's *Sophie's Choice*; American Geoffrey Wolff's study of his father, *The Duke of Deception*; American Joan Didion's *The White Album*; and American Robert Penn Warren's collection *Now and Then: Poems 1976–1978*.   LIT

1979   The world's oldest orchestra, founded in 1548, Dresden State Orchestra, gives its first New York performance at Lincoln Center, featuring the music of Beethoven, Mozart, and Brahms.   MUSIC

1979   American opera singer Beverly Sills retires as a singer and becomes the music director of the New York City Opera.   MUSIC

1979   British recording artist Joe Jackson releases new-wave albums *Look Sharp!* and *I'm the Man*. His later albums will run the gamut from jazz to classical, showcasing his talents as a composer and pianist.   MUSIC

1979   The American rock band Cheap Trick's live album *Cheap Trick at Budokan*, recorded in Japan, where the group's following is huge, will remain on American charts for one year.   MUSIC

1979   American new-wave act the B-52's, whose most prominent members will be vocalist and organist Kate Pierson and vocalist and keyboardist Fred Schneider, release their quirky self-titled album, which contains the track "Rock Lobster." Their popularity will peak in 1980, then fade until 1989, when their "Love Shack" is voted best single of the year by the editors of *Rolling Stone*.   MUSIC

1979   American painter Philip Johnson executes *Paintsplats*; American artist Claes Oldenburg creates *Model* and *Crusoe Umbrella*.   PAINT

1979   Mexican artist Rufino Tamayo gains his first major United States retrospective at New York's Whitney Museum of American Art.   PAINT

1979   The growing popularity of minimalist art is suggested in U.S. exhibitions of artists such as Joseph Beuys and Richard Artschwager.   PAINT

1979   American artist Judy Chicago organizes a team of female artists for the collab-
              orative feminist project *The Dinner Party*. The place settings at the large trian-
              gular table represent 39 women from history. The suggestion of vaginal shapes
              in the abstract designs of some of the plates causes controversy.   SCULP

1979   A retrospective of the works of sculptor George Segal is held at the Walker Art
              Center in Minneapolis.   SCULP

1979–1980   The highest-rated TV program of the season is *60 Minutes* (CBS). Other top-
              rated programs are *Three's Company* (ABC) and *That's Incredible* (ABC).   TV&R

1980s   Break dancing, based on urban street dancing, becomes popular in the United
              States.   DANCE

1980s   Among the actors who deliver memorable performances during this decade are
              Meryl Streep, Harrison Ford, Kevin Costner, Willem Dafoe, Dennis Hopper,
              Isabella Rossellini, Kyle MacLachlan, Susan Sarandon, Melanie Griffith, Meg
              Ryan, Michelle Pfeiffer, Tom Cruise, Mel Gibson, Kevin Kline, Richard Gere,
              Robin Williams, Daniel Day-Lewis, Holly Hunter, William Hurt, John Hurt,
              Jessica Lange, Sigourney Weaver, Shirley MacLaine, Glenn Close, Michael
              Douglas, Helena Bonham Carter, Bette Midler, Lily Tomlin, Anjelica Huston,
              Dianne Wiest, John Malkovich, Ray Liotta, Morgan Freeman, Annette Bening,
              Emma Thompson, Kenneth Branagh, Billy Crystal, Kathleen Turner, Kurt
              Russell, Debra Winger, Nicolas Cage, Cher, Danny Aiello, Olympia Dukakis,
              Mia Farrow, Michael Keaton, Whoopi Goldberg, Charlie Sheen, Marlee Matlin,
              Michael J. Fox, Tim Robbins, Mary Tyler Moore, Timothy Hutton, Dudley
              Moore, Ben Kingsley, Jessica Tandy, and *Saturday Night Live* veterans Steve
              Martin, Bill Murray, and Eddie Murphy. *See also* 1970s and 1990s, FILM.   FILM

1980s   American artist Keith Haring becomes famous for his white chalk-line draw-
              ings on black backgrounds in empty advertising signboards in New York City
              subway stations.   GRAPH

1980s   Popular songs of the decade include "Sailing," "Bette Davis Eyes," "Up Where We
              Belong," "Ebony and Ivory," "Every Breath You Take," "Born in the U.S.A.," "Material
              Girl," "Thriller," "Beat It," "Karma Chameleon," "What's Love Got to Do with It,"
              "Purple Rain," "We Are the World," "Graceland," "That's What Friends Are For,"
              "Somewhere Out There," "Don't Worry, Be Happy," "Sweet Child O' Mine," "So
              Emotional," "Forever Your Girl," "Girl You Know It's True," and "Straight Up." MUSIC

1980   American architects Philip Johnson and John Burgee design the Crystal
              Cathedral in Garden Grove, California.   ARCH

1980   The U.S. architectural firm Gruzen & Partners designs New York City's Grand
              Hyatt Hotel, with an atrium four stories high.   ARCH

1980   American avant-garde choreographer Laura Dean's first ballet, *Night*, pre-
        mieres with the Joffrey Ballet.   DANCE

1980   Notable films include Jim Abrahams's *Airplane!*, Martin Scorsese's *Raging Bull*,
        James Bridges's *Urban Cowboy*, Robert Redford's *Ordinary People*, and Stanley
        Kubrick's *The Shining* (all U.S.); Gillian Armstrong's *My Brilliant Career*
        (Australia); François Truffaut's *The Last Metro* (France); Akira Kurosawa's
        Kagemusha (Japan); Vladimir Menshov's *Moscow Does Not Believe in Tears*
        (U.S.S.R.); and Jamie Uys's *The Gods Must Be Crazy* (Botswana).   FILM

1980   South African novelist J. M. Coetzee, known for his fictional explorations of
        imperialism and apartheid, publishes *Waiting for the Barbarians*.   LIT

1980   Italian semiotician and essayist Umberto Eco publishes his first novel, *The
        Name of the Rose*. The cerebral tale of murder in a Benedictine monastery
        becomes a surprise international best-seller.   LIT

1980   Other notable literary works include the posthumously published novel by
        American John Kennedy Toole, *A Confederacy of Dunces*; South African Andre
        Brink's *A Dry White Season*; Italian Italo Calvino's collection, *Italian Folktales*;
        American Walker Percy's *The Second Coming*; Briton P. D. James's *Innocent
        Blood*; American Donald R. Justice's collection, *Selected Poems*; and American
        Philip Levine's two collections, *Ashes* and *7 Years from Somewhere*.   LIT

1980   In celebration of the bicentennial of Los Angeles, the opera *The Sinking of the
        Titanic* by West German William Dieter Siebert has its United States premiere
        at the University of California, Los Angeles. The opera requires the perfor-
        mance area to become a ship that must be deserted by its audience.   MUSIC

1980   The Pulitzer Prize–winning symphony *In Memory of a Summer Day* by David
        Del Tredici premieres in St. Louis.   MUSIC

1980   On December 8, John Lennon, formerly of the Beatles, is shot and killed out-
        side his apartment building in New York City by deranged fan Mark Chapman.
        Lennon's album with wife Yoko Ono *Double Fantasy*, released earlier in the year,
        will reach number one on the pop music charts.   MUSIC

1980   Notable popular music debuts include the album *Boy* by the Irish new-wave
        band U2, which will be widely regarded as one of the most innovative and tal-
        ented rock bands of the 1980s and 1990s; the self-titled album by the
        Pretenders, led by Ohio-born Chrissie Hynde; and classically trained singer Pat
        Benatar's first rock album. This is also a big year for heavy-metal/punk band
        AC/DC, whose *Back in Black* is a big seller; singer/songwriter Tom Petty, who
        will go on to collaborate with some of the best talents of the next two decades
        after earning his first platinum album with *Damn the Torpedoes*; British band

the Clash, whose double album *London Calling* spawns their first American chart single; and British new-wave synthesized electronic dance band Depeche Mode, which forms this year.   MUSIC

1980   American jazz trumpeter Wynton Marsalis joins Art Blakey's Jazz Messengers. In 1981 he will tour with Herbie Hancock, Ron Carter, and Tony Williams, and in 1982 he will form a quintet with his brother Branford Marsalis, a tenor and soprano saxophonist. (Their father, Ellis Marsalis, is a jazz pianist.) In 1984 Wynton Marsalis will become the first musician to win Grammy Awards for both a jazz recording—his album *Think of One* (1982)—and a classical recording—his recording of trumpet concertos.   MUSIC

1980   German painter Anselm Kiefer executes *To the Unknown Painter*.   PAINT

1980   A few months before his death this year, the Metropolitan Museum of Art presents an exhibit of American artist Clyfford Still's abstract paintings, the museum's largest-ever one-man exhibition by a living artist.   PAINT

1980   A major retrospective of Spanish painter Pablo Picasso draws record crowds at the Museum of Modern Art, New York City.   PAINT

1980   American photographer Irving Penn publishes the collection *Flowers*, which contains many of his arresting recent works.   PHOTO

1980   American artist Jeff Koons begins a sculptural program called "The New" consisting of a series of vacuum cleaners encased in Plexiglas with fluorescent lights, displayed next to advertising posters.   SCULP

1980   American entrepreneur Ted Turner founds the Cable News Network (CNN). Over the next few years, cable television stations of many kinds will proliferate. TV&R

1980–1981   The highest-rated TV program of the season is *Dallas* (CBS). Other top-rated programs are *The Love Boat* (ABC) and *Little House on the Prairie* (NBC).   TV&R

1981   Several experimental dance festivals are held across the United States, including the American Dance Festival in Durham, North Carolina, and a "Next Wave" program at the Brooklyn Academy of Music. Dancers include Americans Laura Dean and Trisha Brown.   DANCE

1981   Notable films include Steven Spielberg's *Raiders of the Lost Ark*, Louis Malle's *Atlantic City*, Warren Beatty's *Reds*, and Mark Rydell's *On Golden Pond* (all U.S.); Hugh Hudson's *Chariots of Fire* and Karel Reisz's *The French Lieutenant's Woman* (both U.K.); Peter Weir's *Gallipoli* (Australia); Rainer Werner Fassbinder's *Lili Marleen* (West Germany); and Bill Forsyth's *Gregory's Girl* (Scotland).   FILM

1981   Notable literary works include American Toni Morrison's *Tar Baby*; Briton D.
            M. Thomas's *The White Hotel*; American John Updike's third "Rabbit" novel
            Rabbit Is Rich; American Donald Barthelme's *Sixty Stories*; Argentinian Jorge
            Luis Borges's *Borges: A Reader*; and American Lisel Mueller's *The Morning of the
            Poem*.   LIT

1981   The first exhibition of pre-Columbian art exhibited outside Central America,
            called "Between Continents; Between Seas: Pre-Columbian Art of Costa Rica,"
            is shown at the National Gallery of Art, Washington, D.C.   MISC

1981   American composer Roger Sessions's Concerto for Orchestra is premiered in
            Boston; American composer Ned Rorem's Double Concerto for Cello and
            Piano is debuted in Cincinnati.   MUSIC

1981   American composer Philip Glass premieres two operas: *The Panther* at the
            Houston Opera and *Satyagraha* at the Brooklyn Academy of Music.   MUSIC

1981   A triple bill of works by Russian composer Igor Stravinsky, with designs by British
            painter David Hockney, is staged at the Metropolitan Opera House.   MUSIC

1981   Symphony in F Major, a newly discovered work by Wolfgang Amadeus Mozart,
            is premiered near Munich, West Germany. The piece was written when Mozart
            was nine years old.   MUSIC

1981   After an 11-year separation (*see* 1970, MUSIC), American folk duo Paul Simon
            and Art Garfunkel reunite for a widely attended concert in New York's Central
            Park. They will reunite again for a sellout concert series in 1993.   MUSIC

1981   On August 1 the music television cable station MTV takes to the air with its
            first video, "Video Killed the Radio Star" by the Buggles. The use of videos will
            revolutionize the way rock music is presented to its audience, making it as much
            a visual as an aural medium.   MUSIC

1981   Among the notable rock debuts this year are those of the American band
            R.E.M., led by Michael Stipe, whose first single, "Radio Free Europe," is voted
            best independent single of the year by the editors of the *Village Voice*; American
            Joan Jett, formerly of the Runaways, who releases her first album with the
            Blackhearts, *Bad Reputation*; and British punk rocker Billy Idol, formerly of the
            band Generation X, who moves to New York City and releases a solo version
            of the Gen X song "Dancing with Myself."   MUSIC

1981   Jamaican vocalist and guitarist Bob Marley, who did much to popularize reg-
            gae in the 1960s and 1970s with the Rastafarian band the Wailers, dies of lung
            cancer and a brain tumor at the age of 36, one month after receiving Jamaica's
            Order of Merit for his body of work.   MUSIC

1981	American artist Robert Ryman paints *Paramount*.	PAINT
1981	American artist Romare Bearden creates the collage *Artist with Painting and Model*.	PAINT
1981	American painter Alice Neel executes *Self-Portrait*.	PAINT
1981	American artist Robert Moskowitz creates the pastel on paper work *Red Mill*.	PAINT
1981	American pop sculptor Claes Oldenburg creates the 38-foot *Flashlight* for the University of Nevada at Reno.	SCULP
1981–1982	The highest-rated program of the season is *Dallas* (CBS). Other top-rated programs are *60 Minutes* (CBS) and *The Dukes of Hazzard* (CBS).	TV&R
1982	Chinese-American architect I. M. Pei designs the Fragrant Hills Hotel in Beijing, China, and the Texas Commerce Tower in Houston, Texas.	ARCH
1982	American architect Michael Graves designs the Humana Building in Louisville, Kentucky, an important work of postmodern architecture.	ARCH
1982	The Vietnam Veterans Memorial, designed by American architect Maya Lin, is completed in Washington, D.C. The stark wall of names of those killed in the war stirs great controversy.	ARCH
1982	*Master Harold . . . and the Boys*, a drama about apartheid by South African playwright Athol Fugard, premieres. In 1984 his *The Road to Mecca* will be produced.	DRAMA
1982	American playwright Christopher Durang's comedy *Sister Mary Ignatius Explains It All for You* premieres. Durang's *Beyond Therapy* and *The Marriage of Bette and Boo* will be produced in 1982 and 1985, respectively.	DRAMA
1982	Notable films include Steven Spielberg's *E.T., The Extra-Terrestrial*, Sydney Pollack's *Tootsie*, Taylor Hackford's *An Officer and a Gentleman*, Tobe Hooper's *Poltergeist*, Wayne Wang's *Chan Is Missing*, and Blake Edwards's *Victor/Victoria* (all U.S.); Jean-Jacques Beineix's *Diva* and Daniel Vigne's *The Return of Martin Guerre* (both France); Richard Attenborough's *Gandhi* (U.K./India); and Rainer Werner Fassbinder's *Lola* (West Germany).	FILM
1982	American novelist Anne Tyler publishes *Dinner at the Homesick Restaurant*, the story of a troubled family. The book is instrumental in establishing Tyler's themes and her popularity.	LIT

1982   American novelist and poet Alice Walker publishes the epistolary novel *The Color Purple*, about the struggles of African-American women in the South. LIT

1982   Australian novelist Thomas Keneally publishes *Schindler's Ark*, a novelistic account of European businessman's Oskar Schindler's moves to save Jews from death during the Holocaust. In the United States the novel will be known as *Schindler's List*. LIT

1982   Other notable literary works include American Saul Bellow's *The Dean's December*; American Paul Theroux's *The Mosquito Coast*; and Briton Graham Greene's *Monsignor Quixote*. LIT

1982   American singer Michael Jackson, late of the Motown group the Jackson Five, becomes a recording superstar with his album *Thriller*. Six of the nine album cuts become major hits, most notably "Beat It" and "Billie Jean." Jackson's fashion preferences (a gloved hand) and his stylized expressive dance steps exert a powerful influence on early 1980s culture. MUSIC

1982   British musician Peter Gabriel, the lead singer of Genesis until 1975, when he was replaced as vocalist by the band's drummer, Phil Collins, inaugurates the annual World of Music Art and Dance (WOMAD) festival in Somerset, anticipating the popularity of what will become known as "world music." Gabriel's lyrics combine social awareness with self-parody, as in such songs as "Games Without Frontiers," "Shock the Monkey," "Sledgehammer," and "Big Time." MUSIC

1982   The artsy electronic British group Roxy Music, featuring vocalist Bryan Ferry and keyboardist Brian Eno, releases its last studio album, *Avalon*, which generates the hits "More Than This" and the title track. MUSIC

1982   American painter Joseph Beuys executes *Monuments to the Stag*. PAINT

1982   American painter Elizabeth Murray paints *Keyhole*. PAINT

1982–1983   The highest-rated TV program of the season is *60 Minutes* (CBS). Other top-rated programs are *M*A*S*H* (CBS) and *Magnum, P.I.* (CBS). TV&R

1983   Two new buildings by leading architects are erected on Madison Avenue in New York City: Philip Johnson's AT&T building at 56th Street and Edward Larrabee Barnes's IBM building at 57th Street. ARCH

1983   American architect Frank Gehry designs the Norton house in Venice, California. ARCH

1983   Rudolf Nureyev, a former Russian ballet dancer who defected to the West, becomes director of the Paris Opera Ballet. DANCE

1983	American choreographer Paul Taylor's *Sunset* is premiered. DANCE
1983	*Glengarry Glen Ross*, a drama by American playwright David Mamet, is produced. It will win the Pulitzer Prize. DRAMA
1983	Notable films include James L. Brooks's *Terms of Endearment*, Lawrence Kasdan's *The Big Chill*, Adrian Lyne's *Flashdance*, Paul Brickman's *Risky Business*, and Woody Allen's *Zelig* (all U.S.); Peter Weir's *The Year of Living Dangerously* (Australia/U.S.); Ingmar Bergman's *Fanny and Alexander* (Sweden); Federico Fellini's *And the Ship Sails On* (Italy); and Ettore Scola's *La Nuit de Varennes* (Italy/France). FILM
1983	American novelist and short-story writer Mark Helprin publishes *Winter's Tale*, a complex and fanciful epic of New York City. LIT
1983	American writer John Updike publishes the essay collection *Hugging the Shore*, which will win the Pulitzer Prize. LIT
1983	British novelist Fay Weldon publishes *The Life and Loves of a She-Devil*. Her earlier works include *The Fat Woman's Joke* (1967). LIT
1983	Other notable literary works include Briton John le Carré's *The Little Drummer Girl*; Pulitzer Prize–winning American Galway Kinnell's *Selected Poems*; Colombian Gabriel García Márquez's *Chronicle of a Death Foretold*; American Lewis Thomas's essay collection, *Late Night Thoughts on Listening to Mahler's Ninth Symphony*; and American Raymond Carver's *Cathedral*. LIT
1983	American composer William Mayer's opera *A Death in the Family*, based on the James Agee novel, is premiered at the Minnesota Opera. MUSIC
1983	The Nashville Network premieres on cable television, highlighting the growing mainstream interest in country-and-western music. MUSIC
1983	The British rock group the Police gain wide success with their album *Synchronicity*. The group's bleak, intellectual outlook is highlighted in hit songs such as their paean to possessive love, "Every Breath You Take." Lead singer, songwriter, and bass player Sting will leave the group to pursue a successful solo career in 1984. MUSIC
1983	Led by Scottish-born singer Annie Lennox, the British group Eurythmics, whose popularity will be fueled by innovative music videos, has a million-selling single with "Sweet Dreams (Are Made of This)," from the album of the same name. Lennox will have a successful solo career in the 1990s. MUSIC
1983	American artist Jasper Johns paints *Racing Thoughts*. PAINT

| 1983 | American painter Brice Marden paints *Elements IV*. | PAINT |

1983   In photos like *Gregory Watching the Snow Fall*, British painter David Hockney creates collages influenced by the painting movements of the 20th century.   **PHOTO**

1983   American sculptor Richard Serra erects *Clara-Clara* in the Jardin des Tuileries in Paris, France. The huge steel creation will be a part of his "Prop" series on exhibition at the Georges Pompidou Center in France.   **SCULP**

1983–1984   The highest-rated TV program of the season is *Dallas* (CBS). Other top-rated programs are *Dynasty* (ABC) and *Falcon Crest* (CBS).   **TV&R**

1984   The Martha Graham dance troupe presents its first interpretation of the Russian composer Stravinsky's ballet *The Rite of Spring*.   **DANCE**

1984   African-American playwright August Wilson's play *Ma Rainey's Black Bottom* premieres. It will be followed by *Joe Turner's Come and Gone* (produced in 1986), *Fences* (1987), and *The Piano Lesson* (1988).   **DRAMA**

1984   Notable films include Milos Forman's *Amadeus*, Sergio Leone's *Once Upon a Time in America*, Ron Howard's *Splash*, Martin Brest's *Beverly Hills Cop*, and Jim Jarmusch's *Stranger Than Paradise* (all U.S.); Roland Joffe's *The Killing Fields*, David Lean's *A Passage to India*, and Neil Jordan's *The Company of Wolves* (all U.K.); and Andrei Tarkovsky's *Nostalghia* (U.S.S.R./Italy).   **FILM**

1984   American novelist and short-story writer Louise Erdrich publishes her novel *Love Medicine*, an exploration of three generations of Turtle Mountain Chippewas in the Great Plains.   **LIT**

1984   A collection of the works of American poet Richard Hugo, *Making Certain It Goes On: The Collected Poems*, is published posthumously.   **LIT**

1984   British novelist Julian Barnes publishes *Flaubert's Parrot*, a fictional blend of biography and fantasy.   **LIT**

1984   Czech novelist and short-story writer Milan Kundera, known for writing on political and erotic themes, publishes his best-known novel, *The Unbearable Lightness of Being*.   **LIT**

1984   American novelist Jay McInerney publishes *Bright Lights, Big City*, the story of a rootless young professional in New York City.   **LIT**

1984   Other notable literary works include American Eudora Welty's writing memoir *One Writer's Beginnings*; Briton Angela Carter's *Nights at the Circus*; American

Philip Levine's *Selected Poems*; Briton J. G. Ballard's *Empire of the Sun*; and American Joan Didion's novel *Democracy*.   LIT

1984   Two exhibitions from the People's Republic of China tour the United States: Contemporary Chinese Painting and an exhibition on loan from the Shanghai Museum of artifacts from the Neolithic era.   MISC

1984   The success of American singer-songwriter Bruce Springsteen's *Born in the USA* album and tour establishes him as a rock superstar. *See also* 1975, MUSIC.   MUSIC

1984   American new-wave rock singer Cyndi Lauper makes a splash with "Girls Just Want to Have Fun" and "She Bop" from her debut album, *She's So Unusual*. The video for the first single is voted best female video at the second annual American Video Awards.   MUSIC

1984   American recording artist Prince (born Prince Rogers Nelson), who will become known as "the artist formerly known as Prince" after he adopts a symbol for his name, releases the movie and album *Purple Rain*.   MUSIC

1984   American painters Andy Warhol, Jean-Michel Basquiat, and Francesco Clemente paint *Polestar*.   PAINT

1985   New works by American choreographer Paul Taylor include *Last Look* and *Roses*; new works by Russian-born choreographer George Balanchine include *Native Green*.   DANCE

1985   Notable films include Robert Zemeckis's *Back to the Future*, Sydney Pollack's *Out of Africa*, and Peter Weir's *Witness* (all U.S.); Agnès Varda's *Vagabond* (France); Jean-Luc Godard's *Hail Mary* (France/Switzerland); Dorris Dorrie's *Men* (West Germany); Akira Kurosawa's *Ran* (Japan); and Terry Gilliam's *Brazil* and Stephen Frears's *My Beautiful Laundrette* (both U.K.).   FILM

1985   American novelist Anne Tyler publishes the novel *The Accidental Tourist*, a family drama about a disaffected travel writer and a dog trainer who find love. LIT

1985   Other notable literary works include American Larry McMurtry's *Lonesome Dove*; Italian Italo Calvino's *Mr. Palomar*; Mexican Carlos Fuentes's *The Old Gringo*; and Chilean Isabel Allende's *The House of the Spirits*.   LIT

1985   American composer Stephen Albert's Pulitzer Prize–winning work *Symphony, RiverRun*, premieres in Washington, D.C.   MUSIC

1985   To provide aid to Africa, American composer Quincy Jones arranges the recording of the Michael Jackson–Lionel Richie anthem of global solidarity, "We Are the World." It is recorded in January by more than 30 top vocal artists, including Michael Jackson, Bruce Springsteen, Billy Joel, Cyndi Lauper, Lionel Richie, Kenny Rogers, and Stevie Wonder.   MUSIC

1985   In July Irish rock musician Bob Geldof organizes Live Aid, benefit concerts held in London and Philadelphia that feature more than 50 pop stars and groups, including Bob Dylan, Tina Turner, David Bowie, Dire Straits, and Neil Young.   MUSIC

1985   American singer Madonna (Madonna Louise Veronica Ciccone) cements her place as a 1980s pop icon with the success of her 1984 album *Like a Virgin*, her steamy music videos, and a starring role in Susan Seidelman's quirky comedy *Desperately Seeking Susan* this year. Madonna's outrageous attitude and chameleonlike changes of image will contribute as much as her music to her success.   MUSIC

1985   In Canada, the Vancouver Jazz Festival is founded.   MUSIC

1985   Canadian-American painter Dorothea Rockburne paints *Interior Perspective (Discordant Harmony)*.   PAINT

1985   "Red Grooms: Retrospective, 1956–1984," a collection of the works of the modern American artist, is held at the Pennsylvania Academy of Fine Arts.   PAINT

1985   American artist Cindy Sherman completes the photographic series *Grotesques*.   PHOTO

1985   Bulgarian-born artist Christo wraps the Pont Neuf Bridge in Paris with 47,680 square yards of tan nylon.   SCULP

1985   A collection of works by American sculptor Mark di Suvero is exhibited at the Storm King Art Center in Mountainville, New York, in celebration of the center's 25th anniversary.   SCULP

1985   American sculptor Louise Bourgeois has her first large-scale exhibition at the Museum of Modern Art.   SCULP

1985–1986   The highest-rated TV program of the season is *Dynasty* (ABC). Other top-rated programs are *The Cosby Show* (NBC), *Dallas* (CBS), and *Family Ties* (NBC).   TV&R

1986   Notable films include Woody Allen's *Hannah and Her Sisters*, Oliver Stone's *Platoon*, David Lynch's *Blue Velvet*, Francis Ford Coppola's *Peggy Sue Got Married*, James Cameron's *Aliens*, and Tony Scott's *Top Gun* (all U.S.); James Ivory's *A Room with a View*, Alex Cox's *Sid and Nancy*, and Neil Jordan's *Mona Lisa* (all U.K.); Jovan Acin's *Hey Babu Riba* (Yugoslavia); Chen Kaige's *Yellow Earth* (China); Claude Berri's *Manon of the Spring* and Alain Cavalier's *Therese* (both France); and Bertrand Tavernier's *Round Midnight* (U.S./France).   FILM

1986–1991   American writer and artist Art Spiegelman redefines the graphic novel with *Maus: A Survivor's Tale*, about his father's experiences in a concentration camp during World War II and his life afterward. The book, published in two parts, will win the Pulitzer Prize.   GRAPH

1986   Canadian novelist and poet Margaret Atwood publishes the speculative gender work *The Handmaid's Tale*. Earlier novels include *Surfacing* (1972) and *Bodily Harm* (1983). Her collections of poetry include *The Animals in That Country* (1968) and *Selected Poems* (1976).   LIT

1986   British writer Martin Amis, son of novelist Kingsley Amis (*see* 1954, LIT), publishes the short-story collection *Einstein's Monsters*, centered on the theme of nuclear war.   LIT

1986   Other notable literary works include Italian Primo Levi's *The Monkey's Wrench*; Briton Iris Murdoch's *The Good Apprentice*; American Oliver Sacks's study of his patients, *The Man Who Mistook His Wife for a Hat*; American Louise Erdrich's *The Beet Queen*; West Indian-born Derek Walcott's *Collected Poems 1948–1984*; American Robert Coles's examination, *The Moral Life of Children*; and American Robert Stone's *Children of Light*.   LIT

1986   Russian-born pianist Vladimir Horowitz holds his first concert in Moscow since his departure in 1925. The widely attended concert is not acknowledged by the Soviet government.   MUSIC

1986   American composer Anthony Davis's opera *X* (*The Life and Times of Malcolm X*), has its formal premiere at the New York City Opera.   MUSIC

1986   Rap music, which began in the mid-1970s among black and Hispanic youth in New York City's outer boroughs, becomes increasingly popular. The Queens-based Run-DMC's album *Raisin' Hell* is the first of the genre to go platinum. Among the many successful rap artists and acts will be Ice Cube, Ice-T, Public Enemy, and Queen Latifah.   MUSIC

1986   American artist Roy Lichtenstein paints *Mural with Blue Brushstroke* for the lobby of New York's Equitable Life Assurance Center.   PAINT

1986   "Diego Rivera: A Retrospective," the first retrospective exhibition of the Mexican painter of murals, opens at the Detroit Institute of Arts and travels internationally during the next year.   PAINT

1986   A newly developing artistic movement, neo-geo, which combines abstract painting and representational sculpture, is featured in several shows in American galleries and museums.   PAINT

| 1986–1987 | The highest-rated TV program of the season is *The Cosby Show* (NBC). Other top-rated programs are *Murder, She Wrote* (CBS), *Cheers* (NBC), and *Miami Vice* (NBC).   TV&R |

1987 | Japanese architect Kenzo Tange wins the Pritzker Architecture Prize. In England community architect Ralph Erskine wins the Royal Gold Medal for Architecture.   ARCH

1987 | Belgian choreographer Maurice Béjart permanently moves his Ballet of the Twentieth Century from Brussels, Belgium, to Lausanne, Switzerland.   DANCE

1987 | Notable films include James L. Brooks's *Broadcast News*, Adrian Lyne's *Fatal Attraction*, Norman Jewison's *Moonstruck*, and Brian De Palma's *The Untouchables* (all U.S.); Louis Malle's *Au Revoir Les Enfants* (France); Gabriel Axel's *Babette's Feast* (Denmark); John Boorman's *Hope and Glory* (U.K.); Juzo Itami's *A Taxing Woman* (Japan); and Bernardo Bertolucci's *The Last Emperor* (Italy/U.K./China).   FILM

1987 | American journalist Tom Wolfe publishes the novel *The Bonfire of the Vanities*, a satire of greed, race relations, and criminal justice.   LIT

1987 | Other notable American literary works include Toni Morrison's *Beloved*, T. Coraghessan Boyle's *World's End*, Joyce Carol Oates's *You Must Remember This*, and Annie Dillard's memoir, *An American Childhood*. In England Irish-born Brian Moore publishes *The Colour of Blood* and Nigerian-born Amos Tutuola publishes *Pauper, Brawler, and Slanderer*. In West Germany the Swiss dramatist and novelist Friedrich Dürrenmatt publishes the novel *Der Auftrag*.   LIT

1987 | New musical works include American composer Steven Paulus's *Construction Symphony*, French composer Olivier Messiaen's *Bird Sketches* for piano, and British composer Robert Saxton's choral work *I Will Awake the Dawn*.   MUSIC

1987 | American painter Brice Marden executes *Diptych*; American painter Robert Ryman paints *Constant*.   PAINT

1987 | The first retrospective of German neoexpressionist artist Anselm Kiefer begins at the Art Institute of Chicago and travels to Philadelphia, Los Angeles, and New York in 1988.   PAINT

1987–1988 | The highest-rated TV program of the season is *The Cosby Show* (NBC). Other top-rated programs are *Cheers* (NBC), *Night Court* (NBC), and *Moonlighting* (ABC).   TV&R

1988   As part of a national architecture project called Grands Projets, France's Louvre Museum is remodeled by Chinese-American architect I. M. Pei. One element is a modern 65-foot glass pyramid.   ARCH

1988   Several activities between United States and Soviet ballets and dance troupes mark improving relations between the countries, including the exchange of guest artists between the New York City and Bolshoi Ballets.   DANCE

1988   American playwright Wendy Wasserstein's drama about womanhood and feminism, *The Heidi Chronicles*, is produced. It will win the Pulitzer Prize and a Tony award. Her play *The Sisters Rosensweig* will be produced in 1993.   DRAMA

1988   Notable films include Stephen Frears's *Dangerous Liaisons*, Penny Marshall's *Big*, Jonathan Demme's *Married to the Mob*, Barry Levinson's *Rain Man*, and Robert Zemeckis's *Who Framed Roger Rabbit?* (all U.S.); David Cronenberg's *Dead Ringers* (Canada); Zhang Yimou's *Red Sorghum* (China); Giuseppe Tornatore's *Cinema Paradiso* (Italy/France); Bertrand Tavernier's *Beatrice* (France); and Wim Wenders's *Wings of Desire* (West Germany/France).   FILM

1988   American novelist Don De Lillo publishes the novel *Libra*, which uses the Lee Harvey Oswald assassination of President John F. Kennedy to explore larger meanings in modern America.   LIT

1988   Other notable literary works include Briton Fay Weldon's *The Hearts and Lives of Men*; Colombian Gabriel García Márquez's *Love in the Time of Cholera*; American Raymond Carver's collection, *Where I'm Calling From*; and Nigerian Chinua Achebe's *Anthills of the Savannah*.   LIT

1988   Poetic works include U.S. poet laureate Richard Wilbur's *New and Collected Poems*; Polish poet Czeslaw Milosz's *The Collected Poems: 1931–1987*; Nigerian poet Wole Soyinka's *Mandela's Earth and Other Poems*; Russian-American poet Joseph Brodsky's *To Urania*; and American poet John Hollander's *Harp Lake*.   LIT

1988   The Shaping of Daimyo Culture 1185–1868, the most wide-ranging exhibition of works from the Japanese feudal age, begins at the National Gallery of Art, Washington, D.C.   MISC

1988   Notable American compositions include Elliott Carter's Oboe Concerto, which receives its American debut with the San Francisco Symphony Orchestra, and John Cage's first operas, *Europeras 1 & 2*, which are premiered in Purchase, New York.   MUSIC

1988   American singer Whitney Houston becomes the first person to release seven consecutive chart-topping songs in the United States, breaking the previous record of six, held by the Beatles and the Bee Gees.   MUSIC

| 1988 | Heavy-metal groups like Guns N' Roses, Def Leppard, Van Halen, Metallica, and the Scorpions gain popularity, countering a resurgence of classic rock from the 1960s and 1970s. **MUSIC** |

1988–1989   The highest-rated TV program of the season is *The Cosby Show* (NBC). Other top-rated programs are *Roseanne* (ABC), *A Different World* (NBC), and *Cheers* (NBC). **TV&R**

1989   Chinese-American architect I. M. Pei designs the Bank of China building in Hong Kong. **ARCH**

1989   Architect Pierre Fakhoury designs the Basilica of Our Lady of Peace in Yamoussoukro, Ivory Coast, the tallest church in Christendom, with a dome 525 feet high. **ARCH**

1989   Conflicts with the board of trustees lead Russian dancer Mikhail Baryshnikov to resign as artistic director of the American Ballet Theater, a post he held since 1980. **DANCE**

1989   Notable films include Tim Burton's *Batman*, Bruce Beresford's *Driving Miss Daisy*, Gus Van Sant's *Drugstore Cowboy*, Kenneth Branagh's *Henry V*, and Steven Soderbergh's *sex, lies and videotape* (all U.S.); Jane Campion's *Sweetie* (Australia); Peter Greenaway's *The Cook, the Thief, His Wife and Her Lover* (France/Netherlands); Wayne Wang's *Life Is Cheap . . . But Toilet Paper Is Expensive* (Hong Kong); Percy Adlon's *Rosalie Goes Shopping* (West Germany); Patrice Leconte's *Monsieur Hire* (France); and Jim Sheridan's *My Left Foot* (Ireland). **FILM**

1989   The first films designated for inclusion in the U.S. National Film Registry, part of the 1988 National Film Preservation Act that honors works that are "culturally, historically, or esthetically significant," are *The Best Years of Our Lives* (1946); *Casablanca* (1942); *Citizen Kane* (1941); *The Crowd* (1928); *Dr. Strangelove, or, How I Learned to Stop Worrying and Love the Bomb* (1964); *The General* (1927); *Gone with the Wind* (1939); *The Grapes of Wrath* (1940); *High Noon* (1952); *Intolerance* (1916); *The Learning Tree* (1969); *The Maltese Falcon* (1941); *Mr. Smith Goes to Washington* (1939); *Modern Times* (1936); *Nanook of the North* (1922); *On the Waterfront* (1954); *The Searchers* (1956); *Singin' in the Rain* (1952); *Snow White and the Seven Dwarfs* (1937); *Some Like It Hot* (1959); *Star Wars* (1977); *Sunrise* (1927); *Sunset Boulevard* (1950); *Vertigo* (1958); and *The Wizard of Oz* (1939). **FILM**

1989   Indian-born British writer Salman Rushdie publishes the novel *The Satanic Verses*, resulting in a death sentence from the government of Iran, which accuses him of blasphemy against Islam. Rushdie is forced to go into hiding. His other works include *Midnight's Children* (1981). **LIT**

1989   Other notable literary works include American E. L. Doctorow's *Billy Bathgate*;
               American Allan Gurganus's *Oldest Living Confederate Widow Tells All*; American
               Amy Tan's first work, *The Joy Luck Club*; and American John Berryman's
               Collected Poems, 1937–1971, published posthumously.   LIT

1989   In October a bill is passed in the U.S. Congress that prohibits the National
               Endowment for the Arts (NEA) from funding artworks deemed obscene as
               defined in a 1973 ruling by the U.S. Supreme Court. It will prompt NEA chair-
               man John Frohnmayer to ask artists to sign antiobscenity loyalty oaths, which
               will in turn result in the refusal of some artists and organizations to accept
               NEA grants.   MISC

c. 1989   Vinyl records are phased out of music stores, replaced by the cleaner-sound-
               ing, smaller, and more expensive compact discs.   MUSIC

1989   American recording artist Janet Jackson, younger sister of superstar Michael
               Jackson, has a number-one hit with "Miss You Much," from her number-one
               album *Janet Jackson's Rhythm Nation 1814*, which will remain on the charts into
               1991. In 1990 she will win eight awards, including top rhythm-and-blues artist,
               at the *Billboard* Music Awards Show in Santa Monica, California.   MUSIC

1989   A retrospective of the works of modern American painter Helen Frankenthaler
               opens at the Museum of Modern Art in New York City and travels across the
               United States.   PAINT

1989–1990   The highest-rated TV program of the season is *Roseanne* (ABC). Other top-rated
               programs are *LA Law* (NBC), *The Wonder Years* (ABC), and *60 Minutes* (CBS).
                                                                                               TV&R

1990s   Among the actors who deliver memorable performances are Sean Penn,
               Anthony Hopkins, Ralph Fiennes, John Cusack, John Travolta, Danny DeVito,
               Sam Jackson, Geena Davis, Jim Carrey, Uma Thurman, Gary Oldman, Sharon
               Stone, Arnold Schwarzenegger, Aidan Quinn, Brad Pitt, Joe Pesci, Juliette
               Lewis, Bruce Willis, Demi Moore, Wynona Ryder, Johnny Depp, Leonardo
               DiCaprio, Matt Dillon, Bridget Fonda, Danny Glover, Mary-Louise Parker,
               Sarah Jessica Parker, Mary Stuart Masterson, Larry Fishburne, Sam Neill, Liam
               Neeson, Laura Dern, Wesley Snipes, Elizabeth Shue, Kathy Bates, Pierce
               Brosnan, Goldie Hawn, Val Kilmer, Tom Hanks, Jeremy Irons, Hugh Grant,
               Rupert Everett, Natasha Richardson, Miranda Richardson, Helen Mirren, Joan
               Cusack, Angela Bassett, Nicole Kidman, Julia Roberts, Patrick Stewart, Denzel
               Washington, Jennifer Jason-Leigh, Alec Baldwin, Matthew Broderick, Macaulay
               Culkin, Antonio Banderas, and Kyra Sedgwick. *See also* 1980s, FILM.   FILM

1990   Japanese architect Kenzo Tange designs the twin tower City Hall in Tokyo.   ARCH

1990   The renovated main building at Ellis Island in New York harbor is opened to the public in September. Once the initial processing center for millions of immigrants to the United States, it is now a museum of immigration. Architects include Beyer Blinder Belle of New York City and Notter Finegold & Alexander of Boston.   ARCH

1990   American dancer and choreographer Martha Graham premieres her first work accompanied by popular music: *Maple Leaf Rag*, set to the music of American ragtime composer Scott Joplin.   DANCE

1990   The largest gathering of American dance companies ever held takes place at the 1990 Dance Biennial in France.   DANCE

1990   Notable films include Kevin Costner's *Dances with Wolves*, Andrew Bergman's *The Freshman*, Martin Scorsese's *GoodFellas*, Chris Columbus's *Home Alone*, Paul Verhoven's *Total Recall*, and Francis Ford Coppola's *The Godfather Part III* (all U.S.); Pedro Almodóvar's *Tie Me Up! Tie Me Down!* (Spain); Jim Sheridan's *The Field* (Ireland); and Akira Kurosawa's *Akira Kurosawa's Dreams* (Japan).   FILM

1990   American artist Jenny Holzer, known for her electronic signs of pointed social and political statement, is awarded the grand prize at the Venice Biennale in Italy.   GRAPH

1990   Notable literary works include American John Updike's final novel about Rabbit Angstrom, *Rabbit at Rest*; South African J. M. Coetzee's *Age of Iron*; Irish Edna O'Brien's collection, *Lantern Slides*; Briton A. S. Byatt's *Possession*; and American Thomas Pynchon's *Vineland*, his first work in 17 years.   LIT

1990   American poetic works include Anthony E. Hecht's *The Transparent Man* and U.S. poet laureate Mark Strand's *The Continuous Life*.   LIT

1990   The National Endowment for the Arts revokes grants to four American performance artists whose work is deemed sexually controversial: Karen Finley, John Fleck, Holly Hughes, and Tim Miller. In a similar move, the NEA revokes grants to the University of Pennsylvania's Institute of Contemporary Art, the sponsor of a photographic exhibition of erotic works by American photographer Robert Mapplethorpe. *See also* 1990, PHOTO.   MISC

1990   American composer Mel Powell's concerto *Duplicates*, winner of the Pulitzer Prize for Music, premieres at the Los Angeles Philharmonic.   MUSIC

1990   In October American composer Leonard Bernstein announces his retirement as musical director of the New York Philharmonic, five days before his death from a heart attack. Among his compositions are the ballet *Fancy Free* (1944) and the musical *West Side Story* (1957).   MUSIC

1990   Notable popular recording artists include the Irish singer Sinead O'Connor, whose cover of Prince's ballad "Nothing Compares 2 U," from her second album, *I Do Not Want What I Haven't Got*, becomes one of the fastest-selling singles of all time; American rap artist MC Hammer (born Stanley Kirk Burrell), whose video for the dance hit "U Can't Touch This" becomes the most heavily rotated MTV video of the year, thanks in part to its sampling of Rick James's "Super Freak"; and California crooner Chris Isaak, whose third album, *Heart-Shaped World*, performs poorly until its extracted single "Wicked Game" takes off on the coattails of David Lynch's film *Wild at Heart*, the soundtrack to which includes an instrumental version of the song.   MUSIC

1990   American guitarist and vocalist Bonnie Raitt, whose range encompasses blues, country, rhythm-and-blues, and rock, sweeps the Grammy Awards, winning four awards in all, including album of the year for *Nick of Time* and best traditional blues recording for her version of John Lee Hooker's "I'm in the Mood."   MUSIC

1990   American blues guitarist Stevie Ray Vaughan dies at the age of 35 in a helicopter crash, six months after winning best contemporary blues recording, for *In Step*, at this year's Grammy Awards.   MUSIC

1990   In March a decade-long project to clean and restore paintings by Michelangelo in Rome's Sistine Chapel is completed.   PAINT

1990   An exhibition of sexually suggestive photographs by American photographer Robert Mapplethorpe at the Contemporary Arts Center in Cincinnati, Ohio, prompts public protests and a lawsuit against the Center's director Dennis Barrie. He will be acquitted of obscenity charges by the Ohio municipal court. *See also* 1990, MISC.   PHOTO

1990–1991   The highest-rated TV show of the season is *Cheers* (NBC). Other top-rated TV shows include *Roseanne* (ABC), *60 Minutes* (CBS), and *Murphy Brown* (CBS).   TV&R

1991   American choreographer Merce Cunningham creates the performance *Trackers*.   DANCE

1991   Notable films include Jonathan Demme's *Silence of the Lambs*, Barry Levinson's *Bugsy*, John Singleton's *Boyz N the Hood*, Ridley Scott's *Thelma & Louise*, Oliver Stone's *JFK*, and Terry Gilliam's *The Fisher King* (all U.S.); Claude Chabrol's *Madame Bovary* (France); Carlos Saura's *Ay, Carmela!* (Spain); Zhang Yimou's *Raise the Red Lantern* (China/Taiwan/Hong Kong); Gabriele Salvatores's *Mediterraneo* (Italy); and Sven Nykvist's *The Ox* (Sweden).   FILM

1991   *Beauty and the Beast*, a Disney studios animated film featuring the voice of Angela Lansbury and the music of Howard Ashman and Alan Menken, becomes the first animated movie to be nominated for an Oscar for best picture.   FILM

1991   Notable literary works include American Diane Wood Middlebrook's biography *Anne Sexton*, which will raise questions about its gathering of sources; South African Nadine Gordimer's collection *Jump and Other Stories*; American Amy Tan's *The Kitchen God's Wife*; and Canadian Douglas Coupland's *Generation X: Tales for an Accelerated Culture*.   LIT

1991   American poetic works include John Ashbery's *Flow Chart*, Philip Levine's *What Work Is*, and William Bronk's collections, *Death Is the Place*, *Life Supports*, and *Living Instead*.   LIT

1991   The exhibition "Degenerate Art: The Fate of the Avant-Garde in Nazi Germany," which features works repressed by Hitler during his rule, begins its tour in Los Angeles. By the end of next year it will have traveled internationally and will have completed its tour in Berlin.   MISC

1991   The controversial opera *The Death of Klinghoffer*, by composer John Adams and librettist Alice Goodman, premieres at the Brooklyn Academy of Music. It is based on the experiences of American tourist Leon Klinghoffer, who died at the hands of pro-Palestinian terrorists on the cruise ship the *Achille Lauro*.   MUSIC

1991   The first annual American cross-country musical tour Lollapalooza begins its run at Irvine Meadows Amphitheater, near Los Angeles. The tour, arranged by musician Perry Farrell of the group Jane's Addiction, features such alternative rock groups as Siouxsie and the Banshees, Living Colour, Nine Inch Nails, and the Butthole Surfers.   MUSIC

1991–1995   "Alternative" rock becomes mainstream with the phenomenal success—initially through word of mouth—of guitar-oriented "grunge" groups like Nirvana, Pearl Jam, Stone Temple Pilots, Soundgarden, Alice in Chains, Hole, L7, Screaming Trees, and Tool; pop music is also challenged by "gangsta rappers" like Snoop Doggy Dogg and Ice-T, whose lyrics are filled with images of street violence.   MUSIC

1991   Interest in the work of Mexican painter Frida Kahlo is heightened by the publication of at least two biographies this year and the pop star Madonna's publicly expressed admiration of the artist's work; 55 of Kahlo's 143 paintings were highly symbolic self-portraits.   PAINT

1991   Bulgarian-born artist Christo sets up his umbrella project, in which 1,340 blue umbrellas are positioned in Japan and 1,760 yellow umbrellas are put up in California. The project is dismantled after two people are injured.   SCULP

1991–1992   The highest-rated TV show of the season is *60 Minutes* (CBS). Other top-rated TV shows include *Cheers* (NBC), *Murphy Brown* (CBS), and *Roseanne* (ABC).

TV&R

1992   The centennial of Russian composer Tchaikovsky's Christmas ballet *The Nutcracker* is celebrated with myriad presentations worldwide, including an idiosyncratic adaptation called *The Hard Nut* at the Brooklyn Academy of Music.

DANCE

1992   Notable films include Clint Eastwood's *Unforgiven*, Spike Lee's *Malcolm X*, Robert Altman's *The Player*, Martin Brest's *Scent of a Woman*, and Francis Ford Coppola's *Bram Stoker's "Dracula"* (all U.S.); Régis Wargnier's *Indochine* (France); Neil Jordan's *The Crying Game* and James Ivory's *Howards End* (both U.K.); and Alfonso Arau's *Like Water for Chocolate* (Mexico).

FILM

1992   Notable literary works include Briton Peter Ackroyd's *English Music*; Nigerian Ben Okri's *The Famished Road*; American Terry McMillan's *Waiting to Exhale*; and American Cormac McCarthy's *All the Pretty Horses*.

LIT

1992   American poetic works include Tess Gallagher's collection *Moon Crossing Bridge*, William Bronk's *Some Words*, John Ashbery's *Hotel Lautréamont*, and David Ferry's *Gilgamesh*.

LIT

1992   The opera *The Voyage* by American composer Philip Glass, which celebrates the 500th anniversary of explorer Christopher Columbus's first voyage to the New World, premieres at New York's Metropolitan Opera.

MUSIC

1992   Country music continues to rise in popularity, with performers like Garth Brooks, Reba McEntire, Vince Gill, Clint Black, and Wynonna and Naomi Judd.

MUSIC

1992–1993   The highest-rated TV show of the season is *60 Minutes* (CBS). Other top-rated TV shows include *Roseanne* (ABC), *Northern Exposure* (CBS), and *Seinfeld* (NBC).

TV&R

1992   In May, after nearly three decades of dominating the late-night TV talk show forum, Nebraska-born comedian Johnny Carson retires as host of *The Tonight Show* (NBC). He is replaced by comedian Jay Leno.

TV&R

1993   American inventor and engineer Chuck Hoberman completes *Iris Dome* and *Expanding Geodesic Sphere*, examples of his large-scale work combining architecture, robotics, and sculpture.

ARCH

1993   Honoring the memories of the six million Jews and five million others systematically killed during the Nazi Holocaust (1933–1945), the United States

Holocaust Memorial Museum opens in Washington, D.C. It is designed by architect James I. Freed of the firm Pei Cobb Freed & Partners.   ARCH

1993   To spark interest from younger audiences, the Joffrey Ballet premieres a new ballet, *Billboards*, which features the music of American rock musician Prince.   DANCE

1993   American dancer and choreographer Twyla Tharp teams with Russian dancer Mikhail Baryshnikov in a national tour called *Cutting Up*.   DANCE

1993   American playwright Terrence McNally's *A Perfect Ganesh* is produced. Previous works had included *Frankie and Johnny in the Clair de Lune* (produced in 1988), *The Lisbon Traviata* (1989), and *Lips Together, Teeth Apart* (1991).   DRAMA

1993   American playwright Tony Kushner's *Angels in America: A Gay Fantasia on National Themes, Part I: Millennium Approaches* opens on Broadway at the Walter Kerr Theater. It will win the Pulitzer Prize and several Tony awards. *Part II: Perestroika*, also a Tony winner, will be produced later in the year.   DRAMA

1993   Notable films include Steven Spielberg's *Jurassic Park*, Jonathan Demme's *Philadelphia*, Martin Scorsese's *The Age of Innocence*, and Andrew Davis's *The Fugitive* (all U.S.); Chen Kaige's *Farewell My Concubine* (China); Fernando Trueba's *Belle Epoque* (Spain); Ang Lee's *The Wedding Banquet* (U.S./Taiwan); Mike Leigh's *Naked* and James Ivory's *The Remains of the Day* (both U.K.); and Jane Campion's *The Piano* (Australia/France).   FILM

1993   Notable literary works include Irish Roddy Doyle's *Paddy Clarke Ha Ha Ha*, which will win the Booker Prize; Indian Vikram Seth's *A Suitable Boy*; American E. Annie Proulx's *The Shipping News*, which will win the National Book Award; and Japanese Banana Yoshimoto's *Kitchen*.   LIT

1993   American novelist Alan Lightman's *Einstein's Dreams* interweaves narrative with a discussion of the properties of physics.   LIT

1993   American poet Maya Angelou composes the poem "On the Pulse of Morning" for the inauguration of President Bill Clinton. Other original works of poetry this year include A. R. Ammons's *Garbage* and Donald Hall's *The Museum of Clear Ideas*.   LIT

1993   American poet Rita Dove is named U.S. poet laureate. In 1986 she was awarded the Pulitzer Prize for *Thomas and Beulah*.   LIT

1993   The Biennial Exhibition at the Whitney Museum of American Art in New York sparks criticism for its choice of politically driven works and objects that were not artistic in origin.   MISC

1993   The 45th annual Venice Biennale begins in Venice, Italy, on June 13. The
             American representative for this international exhibition is sculptor Louise
             Bourgeois, who will be the subject of a retrospective show the following year
             at the Brooklyn Museum.   MISC

1993   The Vienna Festival premieres two new operas: *Homage to Zhivago* by Russian
             composer Alfred Schnittke and *The Cave* by American composer Steve Reich.   MUSIC

1993   American abstract painter Robert Ryman receives his first comprehensive ret-
             rospective at the Museum of Modern Art. He is known for his studies of the
             sensual, tactile elements of the medium, notably in his "white paintings."   PAINT

1993   Japanese sculptor Osami Tamaka creates constructions drawn from Asian and
             minimalist sources consisting of weathered wood beams and blocks of white
             paraffin wax.   SCULP

1993–1994   The highest-rated TV show of the season is *Home Improvement* (ABC). Other
             top-rated shows include *Seinfeld* (NBC), and *Frasier* (NBC).   TV&R

1994   French architect Christian de Portzamparc wins the Pritzker Prize. He is best
             known for the City of Music center in Paris.   ARCH

1994   Among new choreographic works premiered worldwide are two creations by
             American choreographer Jerome Robbins, *A Suite of Dances* for Mikhail
             Baryshnikov and dances for the School of the American Ballet, and American
             choreographer Mark Morris's *The Office*, about the war in Bosnia-Herzegovina.
             Revivals include *The Sleeping Beauty* from England's Royal Ballet and a 100th
             birthday retrospective of the works of Martha Graham by the Martha Graham
             Dance Company.   DANCE

1994   A $150 grant from the Minneapolis, Minnesota, Walker Art Center to a per-
             formance artist who performs ritual skin carving to heighten AIDS awareness
             prompts stern congressional debate and a 5 percent cut in the National
             Endowment for the Arts budget for 1994–1995.   DRAMA

1994   *Three Tall Women*, by American playwright Edward Albee, premieres. It will win
             the Pulitzer Prize for drama.   DRAMA

1994   Dominating the Broadway stage this year are musical revivals, including those
             of *Damn Yankees* (1955), with music and lyrics by Richard Adler and Jerry Ross;
             Grease (1972), with music and lyrics by Jim Jacobs and book by Warren Casey;
             and *Carousel* (1945), with music by Richard Rodgers and lyrics by Oscar
             Hammerstein. They are spurred by the recent successful revivals of *Gypsy*
             (1959), with music by Jule Styne and lyrics by Stephen Sondheim, and *Guys
             and Dolls* (1950), with music and lyrics by Frank Loesser.   DRAMA

1994   After nearly two decades of directing some of the top money-making movie suc-
        cesses in history (*Jaws; E.T., The Extra-Terrestrial; Raiders of the Lost Ark*),
        American director Steven Spielberg wins artistic accolades and the best picture
        and best director Academy Award for the Holocaust-inspired drama *Schindler's
        List.*   FILM

1994   Notable films include Jan de Bont's *Speed*, the Walt Disney Company's *The
        Lion King*, Robert Redford's *Quiz Show*, Robert Zemeckis's *Forrest Gump*,
        Quentin Tarantino's *Pulp Fiction*, and Steve James's documentary *Hoop Dreams*
        (all U.S.); Mike Newell's *Four Weddings and a Funeral* (U.K.); Atom Egoyan's
        Exotica (Canada); P. J. Hogan's *Muriel's Wedding* (Australia); Gianni Amelio's
        Lamerica (Italy); Yury Mamin's *Window to Paris* (Russia); Abbas Kiarostami's
        Through the Olive Trees (Iran); Zhang Yimou's *To Live* (China); Ang Lee's *Eat
        Drink Man Woman* (Taiwan); and Cheik Boukouré's *Le Ballon d'or* (Guinea).
                                                                                    FILM

1994   Rubberfaced Canadian comedian Jim Carrey gains stardom with the success of
        broadly comic films *Ace Ventura, Pet Detective; The Mask;* and *Dumb and
        Dumber.*   FILM

1994   West Indian writer V. S. Naipaul publishes the autobiographically influenced
        series of linked stories, *A Way in the World.*   LIT

1994   American novelist E. L. Doctorow publishes *The Waterworks*, which, like other
        Doctorow novels such as *Ragtime* (1976) and *Billy Bathgate* (1989), is set in
        New York City in the past.   LIT

1994   Notable works about the African-American experience include *The Rage of the
        Privileged Class*, by Ellis Close; *Colored People: A Memoir*, by Henry Louis Gates
        Jr.; and *Parallel Time: Growing Up in Black and White*, by Brent Staples. LIT

1994   Notable fiction includes *The Crossing*, by American Cormac McCarthy; *Collected
        Stories*, by American Grace Paley; *The Stone Diaries*, by American-Canadian
        Carol Shields; *None to Accompany Me*, by South African Nadine Gordimer.   LIT

1994   Notable nonfiction includes *No Ordinary Time*, about Franklin and Eleanor
        Roosevelt, by American Doris Kearns Goodwin; *How We Die*, by American
        Sherwin Nuland; *Winchell*, about the columnist Walter Winchell, by American
        Neal Gabler; *Red Azalea*, a memoir by Chinese writer Anchee Min; and *Zlata's
        Diary*, by Bosnian teenager Zlata Filipovic of war-torn Sarajevo.   LIT

1994   Some museum openings worldwide include the George Gustav Heye center of
        the Smithsonian Institution's National Museum of the American Indian (U.S.)
        and the Museum of Modern and Contemporary Art (Switzerland).   MISC

1994   American composer Morton Gould's *Stringmusic*, which will win a Pulitzer
            Prize, premieres.   MUSIC

1994   A concert to celebrate the World Cup soccer finals features tenors José Carreras,
            Placido Domingo, and Luciano Pavarotti. It is broadcast worldwide.   MUSIC

1994   New York City's Metropolitan Opera dismisses soprano Kathleen Battle for
            "unprofessional actions" during rehearsals.   MUSIC

1994   After a decades-long absence from the concert stage, American singer Barbra
            Streisand mounts an international concert tour. Despite costly tickets, the tour
            plays to sellout audiences.   MUSIC

1994   American ballad singer Tony Bennett, who first attained fame in the 1950s and
            1960s with such hits as "Rags to Riches," "Stranger in Paradise," and "I Left My
            Heart in San Francisco," is embraced by a younger generation with the release of
            the soundtrack to his MTV special *Tony Bennett Unplugged*.   MUSIC

1994   In April, American singer/songwriter Kurt Cobain, leader of the alternative rock
            group Nirvana, commits suicide at the age of 27. He is survived by his wife,
            singer/songwriter Courtney Love, and their daughter, Frances Bean Cobain.   MUSIC

1994   At the Woodstock 25th anniversary concert in Saugerties, New York, perfor-
            mances are given by Nine Inch Nails, the Red Hot Chili Peppers, Cypress Hill,
            Green Day, Bob Dylan, and Crosby, Stills & Nash, among others.   MUSIC

1994   The Bastille Opera of Paris dismisses its music director, South Korean-born
            Myung-Whun Chung, despite a term marked by international acclaim.   MUSIC

1994   Contemporary artists exhibited in New York's galleries this year include painter
            Pat Adams, nouveau surréaliste sculptor Robert Gober, Jenny Holzer, Ann Agee,
            Donald Lipski, Julian Schnabel, John Baldessari, and Richard Serra.   PAINT

1994   Two multimedia installations by the late American composer John Cage are
            exhibited in New York: "Rolywholyover A Circus" and "The First Meeting of
            the Satie Society."   PAINT

1994   The Andy Warhol Museum opens in a converted warehouse in the artist's
            hometown of Pittsburgh, Pennsylvania.   PAINT

1994   At the Vatican, the cleaning and restoration of Michelangelo's frescoes is com-
            pleted with the unveiling of *The Last Judgment* in April.   PAINT

1994   Exhibits by painters Willem de Kooning and multimedia artist Bruce Nauman
            survey decades of work.   PAINT

1994   The work of American photographer Lee Friedlander is exhibited at the Museum of Modern Art. Beginning in 1979, his extended series of photographic studies has explored the nature of human communication.   PHOTO

1994   With blanket coverage of the slow-speed chase of athlete/actor O. J. Simpson along a California highway, American TV broadcasting begins a multiyear preoccupation with the investigation into the murder of Nicole Brown Simpson and Ronald Goldman and with O. J. Simpson's criminal and civil trials.   TV&R

1994–1995   The highest-rated TV show this season is *Seinfeld* (NBC). Other top-rated shows include *Roseanne* (ABC) and *Home Improvement* (ABC).   TV&R

1995   In a *New Yorker* article on dance aesthetics, "Discussing the Undiscussable," American dance critic Arlene Croce derides the manipulative emotions aroused in what she calls "victim art," exemplified in the work "Still/Here" by American dancer Bill T. Jones.   DANCE

1995   At Russia's Bolshoi Ballet, Yury Grigorovich, longtime artistic director of the Bolshoi Ballet, resigns; he is replaced by Vladimir Vasilyev.   DANCE

1995   Royal Danish Ballet artistic director Peter Schaufuss leaves the company following a management dispute. Later he agrees to return to stage selected dances.   DANCE

1995   Using music by Rossini, American choreographer Twyla Tharp creates her first work for Britain's Royal Ballet.   DANCE

1995   Michael Flatley, an American-born dancer of Irish ancestry, stars in and choreographs *Riverdance—The Show*, an Irish step-dancing extravaganza. Next year he will create the even more popular show *Lord of the Dance*.   DANCE

1995   At Britain's Royal Court Theatre Upstairs, Sarah Kane's graphically violent play *Blasted* generates critical conflict.   DRAMA

1995   American playwright Terrence McNally's *Love! Valour! Compassion!* wins the Tony for best play. Horton Foote's *The Young Man from Atlanta* wins the Pulitzer Prize for drama.   DRAMA

1995   British plays remain popular in the United States, with new openings including Tom Stoppard's *Arcadia*, David Hare's *Racing Demon*, and Harold Pinter's *Moonlight*.   DRAMA

1995   French-Canadian experimental director Robert Lepage debuts *The Seven Streams of the River Ota*, a five-hour project on Hiroshima that links the nuclear bombing with two other modern tragedies, the Holocaust and the AIDS epidemic.   DRAMA

1995   Exiled Nigerian writer and Nobel laureate Wole Soyinka's controversial play *The Beatification of Area Boy* premieres at Britain's West Yorkshire Playhouse. The play is banned in Nigeria.   DRAMA

1995   To celebrate the origins of cinema, several international filmmakers present original films using an original 1896 Lumière camera. Among filmmakers participating are Chinese director Zhang Yimou and American director Spike Lee.   FILM

1995   Notable films include Mel Gibson's *Braveheart* and Mike Figgis's *Leaving Las Vegas* (both U.S.); Chris Noonan's *Babe* (Australia); Claude Sautet's *Nelly et Monsieur Arnaud* (France); Joseph Vilsmaier's *Brother of Sleep* (Germany); Pedro Almodóvar's *The Flower of My Secret* (Spain); Savva Kulish's *The Iron Curtain* (Russia); Martin Sulik's *The Garden* (Slovakia); Jafar Panahi's *The White Balloon* (Iran); Yun Ichikawa's *Tokyo Koydai* (Japan); Zhang Yimou's *Shanghai Triad* (China); Idrissa Ouedraogo's *Africa, My Africa* (Burkina Faso); and Tran Anh Hung's *Cyclo* (Vietnam).   FILM

1995   Notable fiction includes American Richard Ford's *Independence Day* (winner of the Pulitzer Prize); Briton Pat Barker's *The Ghost Road* (winner of the Booker Prize); Australian Tim Winton's *The Riders*; German Günter Grass's *Ein Weiter Feld*; French writer Nathalie Serraute's *Ici*; Italian Antonio Tabucchi's *Sostiene Pereira*; Russian Mikhail Kurayev's *Blokada*; Egyptian Babā' Tāhir's *Love in Exile*; and the "Cloth Tiger" series in China.   LIT

1995   Notable nonfiction includes American Mary Karr's *The Liars' Club*; American Simon Schama's *Landscape and Memory*; Briton Ian McKillop's *F. R. Leavis: A Life in Criticism*; German Victor Klemperer's *Ich will Zeugnis ablegen bis zum letzten*; French writer André Compte-Sponville's *Petit Traité des grandes vergus*; Polish writer Jerzy Giedroyé's *Autobiography for Four Hands*; Brazilian Hermo Vianna's *O mistério do samba*; and Japanese writer Eisuke Nakazono's *Life of Toni Ryūzō-den*.   LIT

1995   Notable works of poetry include American William Matthews's *Time & Music*; Australian David Malouf's *Selected Poems 1959–1989*; Canadian Robert Bringhurst's *The Calling: Selected Poems 1970–1995*; Japanese poet Sachiko Yoshihara's *Hakkō*; and Portuguese writer Nuno Júdice's *Meditação sobre ruínas*.   LIT

1995   In Germany, the Reichstag is wrapped in silver fabric by artist Christo and his wife.   MISC

1995   CD-ROM and other varieties of computer technology expand the possibilities for accessing and appreciating artwork in museums in the U.S., England, and elsewhere. The Vatican library, for example, makes 20,000 images from rare documents available to scholars on the Internet.   MISC

1995   In the United States, the 16-million image Bettman Archive is purchased by
            American entrepreneur Bill Gates, founder of Microsoft, who also gains elec-
            tronic rights to one-half million images, including artworks of major muse-
            ums such as the National Gallery of London.   MISC

1995   New operas include *Harvey Milk* by Stewart Wallace and Michael Korie (U.S.),
            Modern Painters by David Lang and Manuela Hoelterhoff (U.S.), and *Freispruch
            für Medea* by Rolf Liebermann (Germany).   MUSIC

1995   Orchestral works include Joseph Schwantner's *Evening Land*, Christopher Rouse's
            Second Symphony, Toru Takemitsu's *Family Tree*, Karlheinz Stockhausen's *Helicopter
            Quartet*, and Frank Martin's *Die Weise von Liebe und Tod des Cornets*.   MUSIC

1995   The San Francisco Jazz Festival, an increasingly important international event,
            features fusions of jazz with other musical forms, including rock and rap, in
            styles known as hip-bop or acid jazz. Bands at the festival include T. J. Kirk,
            Glenn Spearman's big band, and Jon Jang's Pan-Asian Arkestra.   MUSIC

1995   "Britpop" sweeps the popular music scene, spearheaded by such new guitar-
            based British bands as Bush, Oasis, Blur, Pulp, Suede, and Supergrass. Other
            popular performers include Hootie and the Blowfish, Alanis Morissette,
            Elastica, and Courtney Love's band Hole.   MUSIC

1995   The first volume of the "Beatles Anthology," a collection of previously unre-
            leased tracks by the British band, is released. It includes "Free As a Bird," a
            recording by the late John Lennon newly augmented by the surviving ex-
            Beatles' accompaniment.   MUSIC

1995   On March 31, Tejano singer Selena (Selena Quintanilla Perez) is murdered by
            a disgruntled employee.   MUSIC

1995   The Grateful Dead announces its disbanding following the death on August 9
            of lead member Jerry Garcia.   MUSIC

1995   The exhibit "Hidden Treasures Revealed" at the Hermitage in St. Petersburg,
            Russia, features 74 paintings that include several Impressionist works hidden
            in the Soviet Union during World War II. Among artists featured are Matisse,
            Degas, and Monet.   PAINT

1995   The Art Institute of Chicago holds a well-attended retrospective of the works
            of French Impressionist painter Claude Monet, which offers the largest collec-
            tion of his works ever exhibited together.   PAINT

1995	American photographer Duane Michals creates "Dr. Duane's Famous Magic Act Starring Duane Michals and John Painter." Other works will include 1997's "Salute, Walt Whitman." **PHOTO**
1995	British artist Damien Hirst wins the Turner Prize. The young artist's works include a dead cow and her calf preserved in glass tanks. **SCULP**
1995–1996	The highest-rated TV program of the season is *ER* (NBC). Other top-rated programs include *Seinfeld* (NBC) and *Friends* (NBC). **TV&R**
1996	Spanish architect Jose Rafael Moneo is the first Spaniard to win the Pritzker Architecture Prize. His works include the National Museum of Roman Art in Merida and the San Pablo Airport in Seville. **ARCH**
1996	In China, the new building of the Shanghai Museum opens. Its postmodern design recalls the shape of a Chinese ceremonial bronze. **ARCH**
1996	Husband and wife dancers Eiko and Koma Otake win a MacArthur Fellowship. **DANCE**
1996	The musical *Rent* wins the Pulitzer Prize for drama and the Tony for best musical in the same year that its young author, Jonathan Larson, dies. **DRAMA**
1996	Terrence McNally's *Master Class* wins the Tony for best play, while George C. Wolfe wins the Tony for best director of a musical for *Bring in 'Da Noise, Bring in 'Da Funk*. **DRAMA**
1996	Plays opening in Britain include Harold Pinter's *Ashes to Ashes*, Stephen Poliakoff's *Blinded by the Sun*, and Jez Butterworth's *Mojo*. Plays opening in New York include Christopher Durang's *Sex and Longing*, Cynthia Ozick's *The Shawl*, David Hare's *Skylight*, and Ronald Harwood's *Taking Sides*. **DRAMA**
1996	Notable films include Roland Emmerich's top-grossing *Independence Day*, Anthony Minghella's Oscar-winning *The English Patient*, Cameron Crowe's *Jerry Maguire*, Milos Forman's *The People vs. Larry Flynt*, and Billy Bob Thornton's *Sling Blade* (all U.S.); Danny Boyle's *Trainspotting* (U.K.); Scott Hicks's *Shine* (Australia); Jan Sverák's *Kolya* (Czech Republic); and Lars von Trier's *Breaking the Waves* (Denmark/Netherlands/Sweden/France). **FILM**
1996	Canadian director David Cronenberg's *Crash* is honored at the Cannes Film Festival and becomes an international success. However, the film's lurid content—about people with a sexual fetish for car crashes—also inspires controversy and delays its release in the United States. **FILM**

1996   Notable books include American David Foster Wallace's novel *Infinite Jest*;
            American Frank McCourt's memoir *Angela's Ashes*; American Jonathan Harr's
            nonfiction account *A Civil Action*; American Andrea Barrett's *Ship Fever and
            Other Stories*; Irish writer Seamus Deane's novel *Reading in the Dark*; Briton
            Graham Smith's novel *Last Orders*; and Briton Beryl Bainbridge's novel *Every
            Man for Himself*.   LIT

1996   Polish poet Wislawa Szymborska is honored with the Nobel Prize for litera-
            ture. The Pulitzer Prize for poetry this year goes to Jorie Graham for *The Dream
            of the Unified Field*; the National Book Award for poetry to Hayden Carruth for
            Scrambled Eggs & Whiskey: Poems 1991–1995.   LIT

1996   In Vienna, Austria, 8,000 pieces of art stolen by the Nazis from Jews who died
            in the Holocaust are auctioned, with the proceeds to go to Holocaust sur-
            vivors. The sale earns $14.5 million. The art had been hoarded by the Austrian
            government since the end of World War II.   MISC

1996   Works by Chinese sculptor Cai Guo Qiang and Japanese photo artist Yasumasa
            Morimura are exhibited at the Guggenheim SoHo in New York. Other Asian
            artists rising in international prominence include Marikuo Mori, Hiroshi
            Sugimoto, Chen Yifei, and Yayoi Kusama.   MISC

1996   Best-selling pop music albums include No Doubt's *Tragic Kingdom*, Celine
            Dion's *Falling into You*, Bush's *Razorblade Suitcase*, Mariah Carey's *Daydream*,
            and the Fugees' *The Score*.   MUSIC

1996   On September 13, rap artist Tupac Shakur dies of wounds sustained six days
            earlier in a drive-by shooting in Las Vegas, Nevada. He was known as a leading
            performer of "gangsta rap," a genre often criticized for glorifying violence. On
            March 9, 1997, rival rapper the Notorious B.I.G. (Christopher G. Wallace) will
            also be shot to death.   MUSIC

1996   South African-born Dutch artist Marlene Dumas paints *Pink Puff*. Like many of
            her works, including *Black Drawings* (1991–1992) and *Group Show* (1993), it is
            laced with erotic and racial tension.   PAINT

1996   American artist Carol Diehl paints *The Green Painting* and *Summer 1996*.   PAINT

1996   American minimalist Ellsworth Kelly creates an installation composed of
            seven four-sided panels, each painted a different color.   PAINT

1996   The US$1.6 million sale of *View of Geelong*, a painting by 19th-century
            Australian artist Eugene von Guerard, sets a record for the amount paid for an
            Australian work of art.   PAINT

1996–1997	The highest-rated TV program of the season is *ER* (NBC). Other top-rated programs include *Seinfeld, Friends, Suddenly Susan, The Naked Truth,* and *Fired Up* (all NBC). TV&R
1996	The U.S. Congress requires television manufacturers to equip new sets with "v-chips," hardware that allows parents to block out violent programming. TV&R
1997	In Seattle, the Henry Art Gallery, an important forum for the city's contemporary art, moves into a new space designed by Charles Gwathmey. ARCH
1997	Dance companies performing in New York include the Lisbon-based dance company Ballet Gulbenkian and the London-based Shobana Jeyasingh Dance Company, and Batoto Yetu, an African-American troupe that performs African dances. DANCE
1997	New musicals include *Titanic, The Life, Steel Pier,* and *Jekyll & Hyde*; musical revivals include *Chicago*. DRAMA
1997	New American plays include William Luce's *Barrymore* and Wendy Wasserstein's *An American Daughter*. DRAMA
1997	American experimental playwright and director Lee Breuer stages a musical puppet version of *Peter Pan* called *Peter and Wendy*. Breuer is known for such avant-garde works as *Shaggy Dog Animation* and *The Saint and the Football Players*. DRAMA
1997	In Berlin, the Berliner Ensemble produces the play *Eva—Hitler's Beloved* by Stefan Kolditz. DRAMA
1997	Notable films include Steven Spielberg's *The Lost World: Jurassic Park,* Mike Newell's *Donnie Brasco,* Quentin Tarantino's *Jackie Brown,* James Cameron's *Titanic,* Curtis Hanson's *L.A. Confidential,* Paul Thomas Anderson's *Boogie Nights,* Clint Eastwood's *Midnight in the Garden of Good and Evil,* and Gus Van Sant Jr.'s *Good Will Hunting* (all U.S.); and Peter Cattaneo's *The Full Monty* (U.K.). Also premiering in the United States this year are Ryad Chaia's *Al Leja* (Syria), Chang Tso-Chi's *Ah-Chung* (Taiwan), and Helke Misselwitz's *Little Angel* (Germany). FILM
1997	Notable books include American Thomas Pynchon's novel *Mason & Dixon*; American Kirsten Bakis's novel *Lives of the Monster Dogs*; American Kathryn Harrison's memoir of father-daughter incest, *The Kiss*; Indian writer Arundhati Roy's novel *The God of Small Things*; Martinican Patrick Chamoiseau's novel *Texaco* and memoir *School Days*; and German W. G. Sebald's novel *The Emigrants*. LIT

1997   The Asia Society, in New York City, presents "Contemporary Art in Asia: Traditions/Tensions," featuring works by 27 artists, including Bali's I Wayan Bendi, Korea's Soo-Ja Kim, Thailand's Chatchai Puipia, Indonesia's Heri Dono, and India's Ravinder G. Reddy.   MISC

1997   The line between vandalism and performance art grows fuzzier as Russian artist Alexander Brener sprays a dollar sign on Kazimir Malevich's *White Cross on Gray* in Amsterdam. Similar incidents have occurred at other exhibitions within the past year.   MISC

1997   The rap album *Life After Death* by the Notorious B.I.G., who is shot to death this year (*see also* 1996, MUSIC), rises to the top of the charts. Other best-selling albums include the Spice Girls' *Spice*, Mary J. Blige's *Share My World*, and George Strait's *Carrying Your Love with Me*.   MUSIC

1997   The Afropop band Zap Mama, led by Zairian-Belgian Marie Daulne, receives international attention for its album *7*.   MUSIC

1997   The Cuban government sponsors the Cuban Record Fair, a trade show to spotlight artists such as NG la Banda and Lucretia, who are growing in international popularity.   MUSIC

1997   In the United States, celebrations are held to honor the 80th birthday of composer Lou Harrison, who premieres several works this year, including "Rhymes with Silver," commissioned by the Mark Morris Dance Group.   MUSIC

1997   American folk singer and songwriter John Denver dies (*b.* 1943). Voted entertainer of the year by the Country Music Association in 1976, he recorded his first hit single, "Take Me Home, Country Roads," written by Fat City members Bill Danoff and Taffy Nivert, in 1971. Denver is also remembered for his "Leaving on a Jet Plane," which was a hit for Peter, Paul, and Mary in 1969, and his 1973 single "Rocky Mountain High," extracted from the 1972 album of the same name.   MUSIC

1997   German artist Sigmar Polke, creator of such works as the painting *Laterna Magica*, is honored with a retrospective in Berlin.   PAINT

1997   Colombian artists Maria Tereza Hincapié, Natalia Granada, and Oscar Muñoz exhibit new works at Bogotá's Garcés Velásquez Gallery.   PAINT

1997   American artist Kara Walker's graphic vignettes of African-American history are shown at the Institute of Contemporary Art in Boston and elsewhere.   PAINT

1997   At the Hirshhorn Museum, in Washington, D.C., a retrospective of the works of Canadian photographer Jeff Wall showcases his talent for combining documentary realism with staged movement by actors. Other photographers cur-rently blending the real and imagined include Tina Barney, Philip-Lorca diCorcia, Nancy Burson, and Thomas Demand.   PHOTO

1997   The Franklin D. Roosevelt Memorial opens in Washington, D.C. Designed by Lawrence Halprin and incorporating sculptures by George Segal and Neil Estrin, the memorial has engendered controversy over its placement and its nondepiction of Roosevelt's disability.   SCULP

1997   American artist Michael Ashkin, whose work incorporates model buildings and vehicles, exhibits the sculpture No. 49 at the Whitney Biennial.   SCULP

1997   American artist Lita Albuquerque wins a prize at the International Cairo Biennial for her large-scale, ephemeral, cosmology-inspired artwork displayed at the pyramids of Giza. The work raises controversy when some Egyptians perceive that it contains Stars of David.   SCULP

1997   In an episode of the comedy *Ellen*, Ellen Morgan, portrayed by former stand-up comedian Ellen DeGeneres, becomes the first leading character in a prime-time television series to "come out" as a gay person. Herself a lesbian, DeGeneres had carefully guarded her privacy until this year, when she comes out publicly just before the airing of the *Ellen* episode.   TV&R

Appendix:
Birth and Death Dates

Adam, Robert	1728–1792	Bach, Johann Sebastian	1685–1750
Adams, Ansel	1902–1984	Bacon, Francis (essayist)	1561–1626
Adams, Henry	1838–1918	Bacon, Francis (painter)	1910–1992
Addison, Joseph	1672–1719	Baez, Joan	1941–
Aeschylus	c. 525–c. 456 B.C.	Baker, Josephine	1906–1975
Ailey, Alvin	1931–1989	Balanchine, George	1904–1983
Albee, Edward	1928–	Baldwin, James	1924–1987
Alberti, Leon Battista	1404–1472	Ball, Lucille	1911–1989
Alcott, Louisa May	1832–1888	Balzac, Honoré de	1799–1850
Alger, Horatio, Jr.	1832–1899	Bancroft, Anne	1931–
Allen, Gracie	1902–1964	Bara, Theda	1885–1955
Allen, Woody	1935–	Baraka, Amiri (LeRoi Jones)	1934–
Altman, Robert	1925–	Barber, Samuel	1910–1981
Andersen, Hans Christian	1805–1875	Barlach, Ernst	1870–1938
Anderson, Laurie	1947–	Barrie, James	1860–1937
Anderson, Sherwood	1876–1941	Barrymore, Ethel	1879–1959
André, Carl	1935–	Barrymore, John	1882–1942
Andrews, Julie	1935–	Barrymore, Lionel	1878–1954
Angelico, Fra	c. 1400–1455	Barth, John	1930–
Angelou, Maya	1928–	Barthelme, Donald	1931–1989
Anouilh, Jean	1910–1987	Bartholdi, Frédéric Auguste	1834–1904
Antelami, Benedetto	fl. 12th cent.	Bartók, Béla	1881–1945
Antonioni, Michelangelo	1912–	Baryshnikov, Mikhail	1948–
Aristophanes	c. 448–c.380 B.C.	Bashō	1644–1694
Aristotle	384–322 B.C.	Battle, Kathleen	1948–
Armstrong, Louis	1900–1971	Baudelaire, Charles	1821–1867
Arnold, Matthew	1822–1888	Baum, L. Frank	1856–1919
Arp, Hans	1887–1966	Beardsley, Aubrey	1872–1898
Ashbery, John	1927–	Beatty, Warren	1937–
Ashton, Frederick	1906–1988	Beaumont, Francis	1584–1616
Asimov, Isaac	1920–1992	Beckett, Samuel	1906–1990
Astaire, Fred	1899–1986	Beethoven, Ludwig van	1770–1827
Atget, Eugène	1857–1927	Behn, Aphra	1640–1989
Attenborough, Richard	1923–	Béjart, Maurice	1928–
Atwood, Margaret	1939–	Bellini, Gentile	1429–1507
Auden, W. H.	1907–1973	Bellini, Giovanni	c. 1430–1516
Austen, Jane	1775–1817	Bellow, Saul	1915–
Bacall, Lauren	1924–	Benét, Stephen Vincent	1898–1943

369

Bennett, Tony	1926–		Brecht, Bertolt	1898–1956
Benny, Jack	1894–1974		Britten, Benjamin	1913–1976
Berg, Alban	1885–1935		Brontë, Charlotte	1816–1855
Bergen, Edgar	1903–1978		Brontë, Emily	1818–1848
Bergman, Ingmar	1918–		Brown, James	1933–
Bergman, Ingrid	1915–1982		Browne, Thomas	1605–1682
Berle, Milton	1908–		Browning, Elizabeth Barrett	1806–1861
Berlin, Irving	1888–1989		Browning, Robert	1812–1889
Berlioz, Hector	1803–1869		Bruckner, Anton	1824–1896
Bernhardt, Sarah	1844–1923		Bruegel, Pieter, the Elder	c. 1525–1569
Bernini, Gian Lorenzo	1598–1680		Brunelleschi, Filippo	1377–1446
Bernstein, Leonard	1918–1990		Bryant, William Cullen	1794–1878
Berruguette, Alonso	c. 1489–1561		Brynner, Yul	1915–1985
Berry, Chuck	1926–		Buck, Pearl S.	1892–1973
Berryman, John	1914–1972		Buckminster Fuller, R.	1895–1983
Bertolucci, Bernardo	1940–		Bulwer-Lytton, Edward	1803–1873
Bierce, Ambrose	1842–1914?		Buñuel, Luis	1900–1983
Bill, Max	1908–1994		Bunyan, John	1628–1688
Bizet, Georges	1838–1875		Burbage, Richard	c. 1567–1619
Blake, William	1757–1827		Burke, Edmund	1729–1797
Boccioni, Umberto	1882–1916		Burne-Jones, Edward	1833–1898
Bogart, Humphrey	1899–1957		Burnett, Carol	1933–
Bogdanovich, Peter	1939–		Burney, Fanny	1752–1840
Bonnard, Pierre	1867–1947		Burns, George	1896–1996
Booth, Edwin Thomas	1833–1893		Burns, Robert	1759–1796
Booth, John Wilkes	1839–1865		Burroughs, Edgar Rice	1875–1950
Booth, Junius Brutus, Jr.	1821–1883		Burroughs, William S.	1914–1997
Booth, Junius Brutus, Sr.	1796–1852		Burton, Richard	1925–1984
Borges, Jorge Luis	1899–1987		Bustelli, Franz Anton	1723–1763
Borglum, Gutzon	1867–1941		Butler, Samuel	1835–1902
Borodin, Aleksandr	1833–1887		Buxtehude, Dietrich	1637–1707
Borzage, Frank	1893–1962		Byrd, William	1543–1623
Bosch, Hieronymus	c. 1450–1516		Byron, Lord	
Boswell, James	1740–1795		(George Gordon)	1788–1824
Botticelli, Sandro	c. 1444–1510		Caccini, Giulio	c. 1545–1618
Bouchardon, Edme	1698–1762		Caesar, Sid	1922–
Boulez, Pierre	1925–		Caffiéri, Jean Jacques	1725–1792
Bourke-White, Margaret	1904–1971		Cage, John	1912–1992
Bournonville, Auguste	1805–1879		Cagney, James	1899–1986
Brady, Mathew	1823–1896		Caine, Michael	1933–
Brahms, Johannes	1833–1897		Calder, Alexander	1898–1976
Bramante, Donato	1444–1514		Calderón de la Barca, Pedro	1600–1681
Branagh, Kenneth	1960–		Callas, Maria	1923–1977
Brancusi, Constantin	1876–1957		Calvino, Italo	1923–1985
Brando, Marlon	1924–		Cameron, Julia Margaret	1815–1879
Braque, Georges	1882–1963		Campion, Jane	1955–

Camus, Albert	1913–1960
Canova, Antonio	1757–1822
Cantor, Eddie	1892–1964
Capa, Robert	1913–1954
Capote, Truman	1924–1984
Capra, Frank	1897–1991
Caravaggio, Michelangelo	c. 1565–1609
Carlyle, Thomas	1795–1881
Carmichael, Hoagy	1899–1981
Carmona, Luis Salvador	1709–1767
Carney, Art	1918–
Carpeaux, Jean-Baptiste	1827–1875
Carreras, José	1946–
Carroll, Lewis	
(Charles Dodgson)	1832–1898
Carson, Johnny	1925–
Carter, Elliott	1908–
Cartier-Bresson, Henri	1906–
Caruso, Enrico	1873–1921
Cash, Johnny	1932–
Castle, Vernon	1887–1918
Castro, Felipe de	1711–1775
Cather, Willa	1873–1947
Catullus	c. 84–54 B.C.
Cellini, Benvenuto	1500–1571
Cervantes, Miguel de	1547–1616
Cézanne, Paul	1839–1906
Chagall, Marc	1889–1985
Chamberlain, John	1927–
Chandler, Raymond	1888–1959
Chaplin, Charlie	1889–1979
Chardin,	
Jean-Baptiste-Siméon	1699–1779
Charles, Ray	1930–
Chaucer, Geoffrey	c. 1340–1400
Cheever, John	1912–1982
Chekhov, Anton	1860–1904
Chen Kaige	1952–
Cher	1946–
Chevalier, Maurice	1888–1972
Chirico, Giorgio de	1888–1978
Chopin, Frédéric	1810–1849
Chopin, Kate	1851–1904
Chrétien de Troyes	fl. 1165–1190
Christie, Agatha	1891–1976
Christo (Christo Javacheff)	1935–

Churchill, Caryl	1938–
Cicero, Marcus Tullius	106–43 B.C
Cimabue	
(Bencivieni di Pepo)	c. 1240–1302
Clapton, Eric	1945–
Clark, Dick	1929–
Cline, Patsy	1932–1963
Clodion (Claude Michel)	1738–1814
Close, Glenn	1947–
Coetzee, J. M.	1940–
Cohan, George M.	1878–1942
Colbert, Claudette	1905–1996
Cole, Nat King	1919–1965
Coleridge, Samuel Taylor	1772–1834
Colette, Sidonie-Gabrielle	1873–1954
Collot, Marie-Anne	1748–1821
Confucius	c. 551–479 B.C.
Congreve, William	1670–1729
Connery, Sean	1930–
Conrad, Joseph	1857–1924
Constable, John	1776–1837
Cooke, Sam	1931–1964
Cooper, Gary	1901–1961
Cooper, James Fenimore	1789–1851
Copland, Aaron	1900–1990
Coppola, Francis Ford	1939–
Corneille, Pierre	1606–1684
Cornell, Katharine	1893–1974
Corot,	
Jean-Baptiste-Camille	1796–1875
Corradini, Antonio	1668–1752
Correggio	
(Antonio Allegri)	c. 1494–1534
Cosby, Bill	1937–
Costner, Kevin	1955–
Courbet, Gustave	1819–1877
Coward, Noel	1899–1973
Coysevox, Antoine	1640–1720
Cranach, Lucas, the Elder	1472–1553
Crane, Hart	1899–1932
Crane, Stephen	1871–1900
Crawford, Joan	1904–1977
Cronyn, Hume	1911–
Crosby, Bing	1903–1977
Cruise, Tom	1962–
Cruz, Juana Inés de la	1651–1695

Cukor, George	1899–1983	Disney, Walt	1901–1966
cummings, e. e.		Doctorow, E. L.	1931–
(Edward Estlin)	1894–1962	Domenico Veneziano	?–1461
Cunningham, Merce	1922–	Domingo, Placido	1941–
Curtis, Tony	1925–	Donatello	1386–1466
Curtiz, Michael	1888–1962	Donen, Stanley	1924–
Daguerre,		Donne, John	1572–1631
Louis-Jacques-Mandé	1789–1851	Dorsey, Jimmy	1904–1957
Dalí, Salvador	1904–1989	Dorsey, Tommy	1905–1956
Dante Alighieri	1265–1321	Dos Passos, John	1896–1970
Darin, Bobby	1936–1973	Dostoyevsky, Fyodor	1821–1881
Daumier, Honoré	1808–1879	Douglas, Kirk	1916–
David, Jacques-Louis	1748–1825	Dowland, John	c. 1563–1626
Davis, Bette	1908–1989	Doyle, Arthur Conan	1858–1930
Davis, Geena	1957–	Dreiser, Theodore	1871–1945
Davis, Miles	1926–1992	Dreyfuss, Richard	1947–
Davis, Sammy, Jr.	1925–1990	Dryden, John	1631–1700
Day, Doris	1924–	Dubuffet, Jean	1901–1985
Day-Lewis, Daniel	1957–	Duchamp, Marcel	1887–1968
de Havilland, Olivia	1916–	Dufay, Guillaume	c. 1400–1474
de Kooning, Willem	1904–1997	Dufy, Raoul	1887–1953
De Niro, Robert	1943–	Dumas, Alexandre, père	1802–1870
De Palma, Brian	1940–	Duncan, Isadora	1878–1927
De Sica, Vittorio	1902–1974	Dunstable, John	c. 1380–1453
Dean, James	1931–1955	Durang, Christopher	1949–
Debussy, Claude	1862–1918	Dürer, Albrecht	1471–1528
Defoe, Daniel	c. 1600–1731	Dvořák, Antonín	1841–1904
Degas, Edgar	1834–1917	Dylan, Bob	1941–
Delacroix, Eugène	1798–1863	Eakins, Thomas	1844–1916
Delius, Frederick	1862–1934	Eastwood, Clint	1930–
Della Robbia, Luca	c. 1400–1482	Edison, Thomas Alva	1847–1931
De Mille, Agnes	1905–1993	Edwards, Blake	1922–
De Mille, Cecil B.	1881–1959	Eisenstein, Sergei	1898–1948
Demme, Jonathan	1944–	Elgar, Edward	1857–1934
Demuth, Charles	1883–1935	Eliot, George	
Desprez, Josquin	c. 1440–1521	(Mary Ann Evans)	1819–1880
Diaghilev, Sergey	1872–1929	Eliot, T. S.	1888–1965
Dickens, Charles	1812–1870	Ellington, Duke	1899–1974
Dickinson, Emily	1830–1886	Ellison, Ralph	1914–1994
Dickson, W. K. L.	1860–1935	Elssler, Fanny	1810–1884
Diderot, Denis	1713–1784	Emerson, Ralph Waldo	1803–1882
Didion, Joan	1934–	Ernst, Max	1891–1976
Diebenkorn, Richard	1922–	Euripides	c. 480–406 b.c.
Dietrich, Marlene	1901–1992	Evans, Walker	1903–1975
Dillard, Annie	1945–	Fairbanks, Douglas	1883–1939
Dinesen, Isak (Karen Blixen)	1885–1962	Falconet, Étienne	1716–1791

Falla, Manuel de	1876–1946	Gaskell, Elizabeth	1810–1865
Farquhar, George	1678–1707	Gay, John	1685–1732
Farrow, Mia	1945–	Genet, Jean	1910–1986
Faulkner, William	1897–1962	Gershwin, George	1898–1937
Fellini, Federico	1920–1993	Gershwin, Ira	1896–1983
Feydeau, Georges	1862–1921	Ghiberti, Lorenzo	c. 1381–1455
Field, Sally	1946–	Giacometti, Alberto	1901–1966
Fielding, Henry	1707–1754	Giambologna	1529–1608
Fitzgerald, F. Scott	1896–1940	Gibbons, Orlando	1585–1625
Fitzgerald, Ella	1918–1996	Gide, André	1869–1951
Flaubert, Gustave	1821–1880	Gielgud, John	1904–
Flaxman, John	1755–1826	Gillespie, Dizzy	1917–1993
Fleming, Victor	1883–1949	Ginsberg, Allen	1926–1997
Fletcher, John	1579–1625	Giorgione	c. 1476–1510
Fonda, Henry	1905–1982	Giotto di Bondone	c. 1267–1337
Fonda, Jane	1937–	Girardon, François	1628–1565
Fonteyn, Margot	1919–1991	Giraudoux, Jean	1882–1944
Ford, Ford Madox	1873–1939	Gish, Lillian	1896–1993
Ford, Harrison	1942–	Glass, Philip	1937–
Ford, John	1895–1973	Gleason, Jackie	1916–1987
Forman, Milos	1932–	Glinka, Mikhail	1804–1857
Forster, E. M.	1879–1970	Gluck, Christoph Willibald	1714–1787
Fosse, Bob	1927–1987	Godard, Jean–Luc	1930–
Foster, Jodie	1962–	Goethe,	
Foster, Stephen	1826–1864	Johann Wolfgang von	1749–1832
Frank, Robert	1924–	Gogh, Vincent van	1853–1890
Frankenheimer, John	1930–	Gogol, Nikolai	1809–1852
Frankenthaler, Helen	1928–	Goldberg, Whoopi	1949–
Franklin, Aretha	1942–	Golding, William	1911–1993
Franklin, Benjamin	1706–1790	Goldoni, Carlo	1707–1793
Frescobaldi, Girolamo	1583–1643	Goldsmith, Oliver	1728–1774
Friedkin, William	1939–	González, Julio	1872–1942
Frost, Robert	1874–1963	Gorky, Arshile	1904–1948
Fuentes, Carlos	1929–	Gorky, Maksim	1868–1936
Fugard, Athol	1932–	Goujon, Jean	c. 1510–1565
Gable, Clark	1901–1960	Gounod, Charles	1818–1893
Gabo, Naum (Pevsner)	1890–1977	Goya, Francisco de	1746–1828
Gainsborough, Thomas	1727–1788	Grable, Betty	1916–1973
Galsworthy, John	1867–1933	Graham, Martha	1895–1991
Gance, Abel	1889–1981	Grant, Cary	1904–1986
Garbo, Greta	1905–1990	Grass, Günter	1927–
García Márquez, Gabriel	1928–	Gray, Spalding	1941–
Gardner, Alexander	1821–1882	Greco, El (Doménikos	
Garfunkel, Art	1942–	Theotokópoulos)	c.1541–1614
Garland, Judy	1922–1969	Greenough, Horatio	1805–1852
Garrick, David	1717–1779	Grieg, Edvard	1843–1907

Griffith, D. W.	1875–1948	Hepworth, Barbara	1903–1975
Grimm, Jakob	1785–1863	Herbert, George	1593–1633
Grimm, Wilhelm	1786–1859	Heredia, José María	1803–1839
Gris, Juan	1887–1972	Herrick, Robert	1591–1674
Gropius, Walter	1883–1969	Hesse, Hermann	1877–1962
Grosz, George	1893–1959	Heston, Charlton	1923–
Grotowski, Jerzy	1933–	Hildebrandt,	
Grünewald, Matthias	c. 1475–1528	Johann Lukas von	1668–1745
Guinness, Alec	1914–	Hindemith, Paul	1895–1963
Guthrie, Woody	1912–1967	Hitchcock, Alfred	1899–1980
Hackman, Gene	1931–	Hockney, David	1937–
Haley, Bill	1925–1981	Hoffman, Dustin	1937–
Hammerstein, Oscar	1895–1960	Hofmann, Hans	1880–1966
Hammett, Dashiell	1894–1961	Hogarth, William	1697–1764
Hamsun, Knut	1859–1952	Holbein, Hans,	
Handel, George Frideric	1685–1759	the Younger	c. 1497–1543
Handy, W. C.	1873–1958	Holden, William	1918–1981
Hanks, Tom	1956–	Holiday, Billie	1915–1959
Hansberry, Lorraine	1930–1965	Holly, Buddy	1936–1959
Hanson, Duane	1925–1996	Holst, Gustav	1874–1934
Hardy, Oliver	1892–1957	Homer	c. 9th cent. B.C.
Hardy, Thomas	1840–1928	Homer, Winslow	1836–1910
Harlow, Jean	1911–1937	Honegger, Arthur	1892–1955
Harrison, George	1943–	Hope, Bob	1903–
Harrison, Rex	1908–1990	Hopkins, Anthony	1937–
Hart, Moss	1904–1961	Hopper, Edward	1882–1967
Hart, Lorenz	1895–1943	Horace	65–8 B.C.
Harte, Bret	1836–1902	Houdon, Jean-Antoine	1741–1828
Hauptmann, Gerhart	1862–1946	Housman, A. E.	1859–1936
Havel, Vaclav	1936–	Houston, Whitney	1963–
Hawks, Howard	1896–1977	Howells, William Dean	1837–1920
Hawthorne, Nathaniel	1804–1864	Hughes, Langston	1902–1967
Haydn, Franz Joseph	1732–1809	Hugo, Victor	1802–1885
Hayes, Helen	1900–1993	Hunter, Holly	1958–
Hayworth, Rita	1918–1987	Hurston, Zora Neale	1901–1960
Hazlitt, William	1778–1830	Hurt, William	1950–
Heine, Heinrich	1797–1856	Huston, John	1906–1987
Heller, Joseph	1923–	Ibsen, Henrik	1828–1906
Hellman, Lillian	1905–1984	Inge, William	1913–1973
Hemingway, Ernest	1899–1961	Ingemann, Bernard Severin	1789–1862
Hendrix, Jimi	1942–1970	Ingram, Rex	1895–1969
Henri, Robert	1865–1929	Ingres,	
Henry, O.		Jean-Auguste-Dominique	1780–1867
(William S. Porter)	1862–1910	Ionesco, Eugène	1912–1994
Hepburn, Katharine	1907–	Irving, Henry	1838–1905
Hepburn, Audrey	1929–1993	Irving, Washington	1783–1859

Isherwood, Christopher	1904–1986
Ivanov, Lev	1834–1905
Ives, Charles	1874–1954
Jackson, Michael	1958–
Jackson, Shirley	1919–1965
Jagger, Mick	1943–
James, Harry	1916–1983
James, Henry	1843–1916
Janáček, Leoš	1854–1928
Jenney, William Le Baron	1832–1907
Joffrey, Robert	1930–1988
Johns, Jasper	1930–
Johnson, Philip	1906–
Johnson, Samuel	1709–1784
Jolson, Al	1886–1953
Jones, Inigo	1573–1652
Jones, James Earl	1931–
Jonson, Ben	1572–1637
Joplin, Scott	1868–1917
Joplin, Janis	1943–1970
Joyce, James	1882–1941
Judd, Donald	1928–1994
Juvenal	60–140
Kafka, Franz	1883–1924
Kahlo, Frida	1907–1954
Kandinsky, Wassily	1866–1944
Karloff, Boris	1887–1969
Kaufman, George S.	1889–1961
Kazan, Elia	1909–
Kazantzakis, Nikos	1883–1957
Kean, Edmund	1789–1833
Keaton, Diane	1946–
Keats, John	1795–1821
Kelly, Gene	1912–1996
Kelly, Grace	1928–1982
Kemble, Fanny	1809–1893
Kemble, John Philip	1757–1823
Kemble, Charles	1775–1854
Kent, Rockwell	1882–1971
Kern, Jerome	1885–1945
Kerouac, Jack	1922–1969
Kertész, André	1894–1985
Kesey, Ken	1935–1995
King, Carole	1942–
Kipling, Rudyard	1865–1936
Kirstein, Lincoln	1907–1996

Klee, Paul	1879–1940
Klimt, Gustav	1862–1918
Kline, Franz	1910–1962
Kokoschka, Oskar	1886–1980
Kollwitz, Käthe	1867–1945
Koons, Jeff	1955–
Korda, Alexander	1893–1956
Kubrick, Stanley	1928–
Kurosawa, Akira	1910–
Kyd, Thomas	1558–1594
Lagerlöf, Selma	1858–1940
Lamb, Charles	1775–1834
Lancaster, Burt	1913–1994
Lao-tzu	c. 6th cent. B.C.
Lasso, Orlando di	1532–1594
Latrobe, Benjamin Henry	1766–1820
Laurel, Stan	1890–1965
Lawrence, D. H.	1885–1930
Le Brun, Charles	1619–1690
Le Corbusier (Charles Jeanneret)	1887–1965
Le Gallienne, Eva	1899–1991
Le Gros, Pierre	1666–1719
Le Lorrain, Robert	1666–1743
Lean, David	1908–1991
Lear, Edward	1812–1888
Lear, Norman	1922–
Lee, Spike	1957–
Lehmbruck, Wilhelm	1881–1919
Leigh, Vivien	1913–1967
Lemmon, Jack	1925–
Lemoyne, Jean-Baptiste	1704–1778
Lennon, John	1940–1980
Leonardo da Vinci	1452–1519
Lermontov, Mikhail	1814–1841
Lerner, Alan Jay	1918–1986
Lessing, Doris	1919–
Levinson, Barry	1942–
Lewes, George Henry	1817–1878
Lewis, Jerry Lee	1935–
Lewis, Sinclair	1885–1951
LeWitt, Sol	1928–
Li Po	701–762
Lichtenstein, Roy	1932–
Ligeti, György	1923–
Lind, Jenny	1820–1887

Lippi, Fra Filippo	c. 1406–1469	Mann, Thomas	1875–1955
Liszt, Franz	1811–1886	Mantegna, Andrea	1431–1506
Little Richard	1932–	Marceau, Marcel	1923–
Lloyd, Harold	1893–1971	March, Fredric	1897–1975
Lloyd Webber, Andrew	1948–	Marivaux, Pierre Carlet de	1688–1763
Loesser, Frank	1910–1969	Marlowe, Christopher	1564–1593
Lombard, Carole	1908–1942	Martí, José	1853–1895
Lombardo, Tullio	c. 1455–1532	Marvell, Andrew	1621–1678
London, Jack	1876–1916	Marx, Chico (Leonard)	1886–1961
Longfellow,		Marx, Groucho (Julius)	1890–1977
Henry Wadsworth	1807–1882	Marx, Harpo (Arthur)	1888–1964
Lorca, Federico García	1898–1936	Masaccio (Tommaso	
Loren, Sophia	1934–	di Simone Guidi)	1401–1428
Lorenzi, Battista	1527–1594	Massenet, Jules	1842–1912
Lorrain, Claude	1600–1682	Matisse, Henri	1869–1954
Louis, Morris	1912–1962	Maugham, Somerset	1874–1965
Lowell, Robert	1917–1977	Maupassant, Guy de	1850–1893
Lowry, Malcolm	1909–1957	Mauriac, François	1885–1970
Loy, Myrna	1905–1993	McCarey, Leo	1898–1969
Lubitsch, Ernst	1892–1947	McCarthy, Mary	1912–1989
Lucas, George	1944–	McCartney, Paul	1942–
Lugosi, Bela	1882–1956	McIntire, Samuel	1757–1811
Lully, Jean-Baptiste	1632–1687	McNally, Terence	1939–
Lumet, Sidney	1924–	Meadows, Audrey	1924–1996
Lumière, Auguste	1862–1954	Méliès, Georges	1861–1938
Lumière, Louis	1864–1948	Melville, Herman	1819–1891
Lunt, Alfred	1892–1977	Menander	c. 324–293 B.C.
Macaulay,		Mencken, H. L.	1880–1956
Thomas Babington	1800–1859	Mendelssohn, Felix	1809–1847
MacDowell, Edward	1860–1908	Menotti, Gian Carlo	1911–
Machado de Assis,		Meredith, George	1828–1909
Joaquim Maria	1839–1908	Mérimée, Prosper	1803–1870
Machiavelli, Niccolò	1469–1527	Messiaen, Olivier	1908–1993
MacLaine, Shirley	1934–	Michelangelo Buonarroti	1475–1564
Maeterlinck, Maurice	1862–1949	Midler, Bette	1945–
Magritte, René	1898–1967	Mies van der Rohe, Ludwig	1886–1969
Mahler, Gustav	1860–1911	Millay, Edna St. Vincent	1892–1950
Mailer, Norman	1923–	Miller, Arthur	1915–
Makarova, Natalia	1940–	Miller, Glenn	1904–1994
Mallarmé, Stephane	1842–1898	Miller, Henry	1891–1980
Malory, Thomas	?–1471	Millet, Jean-François	1814–1875
Malraux, André	1901–1976	Milton, John	1608–1674
Mamet, David	1947–	Minnelli, Liza	1946–
Manet, Édouard	1832–1883	Minnelli, Vincente	1903–1986
Mankiewicz, Joseph L.	1909–1993	Miró, Joan	1893–1983
Mann, Anthony	1906–1967	Mistral, Frédéric	1830–1914

Mitchell, Arthur	1934–
Mitchell, Margaret	1900–1949
Modigliani, Amedeo	1884–1920
Moiseyev, Igor	1906–
Molière, Jean-Baptiste	1622–1673
Molnár, Ferenc	1878–1952
Mondrian, Piet	1872–1944
Monet, Claude	1840–1926
Monk, Thelonious	1917–1982
Monroe, Marilyn	1926–1962
Montaigne, Michel de	1533–1592
Montañes, Juan Martinez	1568–1649
Monteverdi, Claudio	1567–1643
Moore, Henry	1898–1986
Moore, Marianne	1887–1972
Moore, Mary Tyler	1937–
Morisot, Berthe	1841–1895
Morley, Thomas	1557–1602
Morris, William	1834–1896
Morrison, Toni (Chloe Wofford)	1931–
Moses, "Grandma" Anna	1860–1961
Motherwell, Robert	1915–1991
Mozart, Wolfgang Amadeus	1756–1791
Munch, Edvard	1863–1944
Murasaki, Shikibu	c. 978–1026
Murrow, Edward R.	1908–1965
Musset, Alfred de	1810–1857
Mussorgsky, Modest	1839–1881
Muybridge, Eadweard	1830–1904
Myron	c. 480–440 B.C.
Nabokov, Vladimir	1899–1977
Naipaul, V. S.	1932–
Neruda, Pablo	1904–1973
Neumann, Johann Balthasar	1687–1753
Nevelson, Louise	1900–1988
Newman, Barnett	1905–1971
Newman, Paul	1925–
Nichols, Mike	1931–
Nicholson, Jack	1937–
Niepce, Joseph Nicéphore	1765–1833
Niven, David	1909–1983
Noguchi, Isamu	1904–1988
Norris, Frank	1870–1902

Nureyev, Rudolf	1938–1993
Oates, Joyce Carol	1938–
O'Casey, Sean	1880–1964
O'Connor, Carroll	1924–
O'Connor, Flannery	1925–1964
O'Keeffe, Georgia	1887–1987
Oldenburg, Claes	1929–
Olivier, Laurence	1907–1989
O'Neill, Eugene	1888–1953
Orff, Carl	1895–1982
Orozco, José Clemente	1883–1949
Orton, Joe	1933–1967
Orwell, George (Eric Blair)	1903–1950
Osborne, John	1929–1994
O'Toole, Peter	1932–
Ouedraogo, Idrissa	1952–
Ovid	43 B.C.–A.D. 17
Pacino, Al	1940–
Paine, Thomas	1737–1809
Palladio, Andrea	1508–1580
Palmer, Erastus Dow	1817–1904
Papp, Joseph	1921–1991
Parker, Charlie	1920–1955
Parks, Gordon	1912–
Pasternak, Boris	1890–1960
Pavarotti, Luciano	1935–
Paxton, Joseph	1801–1865
Peck, Gregory	1916–
Pei, I. M.	1917–
Pepys, Samuel	1633–1703
Percy, Walker	1916–1990
Peri, Jacopo	1561–1633
Permoser, Balthasar	1651–1732
Petipa, Marius	1822–1910
Petit, Roland	1924–
Petrarch	1304–1374
Pfeiffer, Michelle	1957–
Piaf, Edith	1915–1963
Picasso, Pablo	1881–1973
Pickford, Mary	1893–1979
Pigalle, Jean-Baptiste	1714–1785
Pilon, Germain	c. 1535–1590
Pindar	c. 522–439 B.C.
Pinero, Arthur Wing	1855–1934
Pinter, Harold	1930–
Pirandello, Luigi	1867–1936

Pisano, Giovanni	c. 1245–1314	Redgrave, Vanessa	1937–
Pisano, Nicola	c. 1220–c. 1284	Reed, Carol	1906–1976
Pissarro, Camille	1830–1903	Rembrandt van Rijn	1606–1669
Piston, Walter	1894–1976	Renoir, Jean	1894–1979
Plath, Sylvia	1932–1963	Renoir, Pierre-Auguste	1841–1919
Plato	c. 428–347 B.C.	Resnais, Alain	1922–
Plautus	c. 254–184 B.C.	Reynolds, Joshua	1723–1792
Plutarch	c. 48–122	Ribera, José de	1591–1652
Poe, Edgar Allan	1809–1849	Ribera, Pedro de	1681–1742
Poitier, Sidney	1924–	Richardson, Henry Hobson	1838–1886
Polanski, Roman	1933–	Richardson, Ralph	1902–1983
Pollaiuolo, Antonio del	1431–1498	Riis, Jacob	1849–1914
Pollock, Jackson	1912–1956	Rilke, Rainer Maria	1875–1926
Pope, Alexander	1688–1744	Rimbaud, Arthur	1854–1891
Porter, Cole	1891–1964	Rimsky-Korsakov, Nicolay	1844–1908
Porter, Edwin S.	1869–1941	Rivera, Diego	1886–1957
Porter, Katherine Anne	1890–1980	Rivers, Larry	1923–
Pound, Ezra	1885–1972	Robards, Jason, Jr.	1922–
Poussin, Nicolas	1594–1665	Robbins, Jerome	1918–
Power, Tyrone	1913–1958	Robeson, Paul	1898–1976
Praxiteles	c. 370–333 B.C.	Robinson, Edward G.	1893–1973
Préault, Antoine-Auguste	1809–1879	Robinson, Henry Peach	1830–1901
Preminger, Otto	1905–1986	Rockwell, Norman	1894–1978
Presley, Elvis	1935–1977	Rodgers, Richard	1902–1979
Primaticcio, Francesco	1504–1570	Rogers, Ginger	1911–1995
Prokofiev, Sergey	1891–1953	Roseanne	1952–
Proust, Marcel	1871–1922	Ross, Diana	1944–
Puccini, Giacomo	1858–1924	Rossellini, Roberto	1906–1977
Puget, Pierre	1620–1694	Rossellino, Bernardo	1409–1464
Pugin, Augustus	1812–1852	Rossetti, Christina	1830–1894
Purcell, Henry	1659–1695	Rossetti, Dante Gabriel	1828–1882
Pushkin, Aleksandr	1799–1837	Rossini, Gioacchino	1792–1868
Pynchon, Thomas	1937–	Rostand, Edmond	1868–1918
Queirolo, Francesco	1704–1762	Roth, Philip	1933–
Rabe, David	1940–	Rothko, Mark	1903–1970
Rabelais, François	c. 1494–1553	Rouault, Georges	1871–1958
Rachel (Élisa Félix)	1820–1858	Roubillac, Louis-François	c. 1700–1762
Rachmaninoff, Sergey	1873–1943	Rousseau, Henri	1844–1910
Racine, Jean	1639–1699	Rubens, Peter Paul	1577–1640
Rameau, Jean-Philippe	1683–1764	Rubinstein,	
Raphael (Raffaello Sanzio)	1483–1520	Anton Gregoryevich	1829–1894
Rauschenberg, Robert	1925–	Rude, François	1784–1855
Ravel, Maurice	1875–1937	Rushdie, Salman	1947–
Ray, Man	1890–1977	Saarinen, Eero	1910–1961
Redding, Otis	1941–1967	Saint-Saëns, Camille	1835–1921
Redford, Robert	1937–	Salinger, J. D.	1919–

Salvi, Nicola	1697–1751	Siddons, Sarah	1755–1831
Sánchez, Florencio	1875–1910	Sidney, Philip	1554–1586
Sand, George		Sills, Beverly	1929–
(Amandine Dudevant)	1804–1876	Simon, Neil	1927–
Sandburg, Carl	1878–1967	Simon, Paul	1942–
Sander, August	1876–1964	Sinatra, Frank	1915–
Sappho	7th cent. B.C.	Sinclair, Upton	1878–1968
Sarandon, Susan	1946–	Singer, Isaac Bashevis	1904–1991
Sargent, John Singer	1856–1925	Sluter, Claus	?–1405
Saroyan, William	1908–1981	Smith, David	1906–1965
Sartre, Jean-Paul	1905–1980	Smith, W. Eugene	1918–1978
Satie, Erik	1866–1925	Smithson, Robert	1938–1973
Scarlatti, Alessandro	1660–1725	Solzhenitsyn, Aleksandr	1918–
Schlesinger, John	1926–	Sondheim, Stephen	1930–
Schlüter, Andreas	1664–1714	Sophocles	c. 496–c.406 B.C.
Schoenberg, Arnold	1874–1951	Southey, Robert	1774–1843
Schubert, Franz	1797–1828	Soyinka, Wole	1934–
Schultz, Hart Merriam		Spacek, Sissy	1949–
(Lone Wolf)	1882–1970	Spenser, Edmund	c. 1552–1599
Schumann, Robert	1810–1856	Spielberg, Steven	1947–
Schütz, Heinrich	1585–1672	Springsteen, Bruce	1949–
Schwarzenegger, Arnold	1947–	St. Denis, Ruth	1877–1968
Scopas	fl. 4th–cent. B.C.	Stallone, Sylvester	1946–
Scorsese, Martin	1942–	Stanwyck, Barbara	1907–1990
Scott, George C.	1926–	Stapleton, Jean	1923–
Scott, Walter	1771–1832	Starr, Ringo	1940–
Seeger, Pete	1919–	Steele, Richard	1672–1729
Segal, George	1924–	Steichen, Edward	1879–1973
Selznick, David O.	1902–1965	Stein, Gertrude	1874–1946
Seneca, Lucius Annaeus	c. 4 B.C.–A.D. 65	Steinbeck, John	1902–1968
Serra, Richard	1939–	Stella, Frank	1936–
Sessions, Roger	1896–1985	Sterne, Laurence	1713–1768
Seurat, Georges	1859–1891	Stevens, George	1904–1975
Sexton, Anne	1928–1974	Stevens, Wallace	1879–1955
Shaffer, Peter	1926–	Stevenson, Robert Louis	1850–1894
Shahn, Ben	1898–1969	Stewart, James	1908–1997
Shakespeare, William	1564–1616	Stieglitz, Alfred	1864–1946
Shange, Ntozake	1948–	Stoker, Bram	1847–1912
Shaw, Artie	1910–	Stone, Oliver	1946–
Shaw, George Bernard	1856–1950	Stoppard, Tom	1937–
Shelley, Mary Wollstonecraft	1797–1851	Stowe, Harriet Beecher	1811–1896
Shelley, Percy Bysshe	1792–1822	Strauss, Johann	1825–1899
Shepard, Sam	1943–	Strauss, Richard	1864–1949
Sheridan, Richard Brinsley	1751–1816	Stravinsky, Igor	1882–1971
Shostakovich, Dmitry	1906–1975	Streep, Meryl	1951–
Sibelius, Jean	1865–1957	Streisand, Barbra	1942–

Strindberg, August	1849–1912		Twain, Mark	
Styron, William	1925–		(Samuel L. Clemens)	1835–1910
Sullivan, Louis Henry	1856–1924		Tyler, Anne	1941–
Swift, Jonathan	1667–1745		Uccello, Paolo	c. 1396–1475
Swinburne, Algernon Charles	1837–1909		Uelsmann, Jerry	1934–
Synge, John Millington	1871–1909		Updike, John	1932–
Tagore, Rabindranath	1861–1941		Usigli, Rodolfo	1905–1979
Talbot, William Henry Fox	1800–1877		Valentino, Rudolph	1895–1926
Tallis, Thomas	c. 1505–1583		Van Der Zee, James	1886–1983
Tamaka, Osami	1952–		Van Eyck, Jan	c. 1370–c. 1440
Tamayo, Rufino	1899–1991		Varda, Agnès	1928–
Tandy, Jessica	1909–1994		Varèse, Edgard	1883–1965
Tanner, Henry O.	1859–1937		Vasari, Giorgio	1511–1574
Tatlin, Vladimir	1885–1953		Vaughan, Sarah	1924–1990
Taylor, Elizabeth	1932–		Velásquez, Diego	1599–1660
Taylor, Paul	1930–		Verdi, Giuseppi	1813–1901
Tchaikovsky, Pyotr Ilich	1840–1893		Vergara, Ignacio de	1715–1776
Telemann, Georg Philipp	1681–1767		Verlaine, Paul	1844–1896
Tennyson, Alfred (Lord)	1809–1892		Vermeer, Jan	1632–1675
Terry, Ellen	1847–1928		Verne, Jules	1828–1905
Thackeray,			Veronese, Paolo	1528–1588
William Makepeace	1811–1863		Verrocchio, Andrea del	1435–1488
Tharp, Twyla	1941–		Vidor, King	1894–1982
Thomas, Dylan	1914–1953		Virgil	70–19 B.C.
Thompson, Emma	1959–		Vivaldi, Antonio	1678–1741
Thomson, Virgil	1896–1989		Voltaire	1694–1778
Thoreau, Henry David	1817–1862		Vonnegut, Kurt	1922–
Tiffany, Louis Comfort	1848–1933		Vuillard, Édouard	1868–1940
Tintoretto	1518–1594		Wagner, Richard	1813–1883
Tippett, Michael	1905–		Walker, Alice	1944–
Titian (Tiziano Vecelli)	c. 1490–1576		Walton, William	1902–1983
Tolstoy, Leo	1828–1910		Ward, John Quincy Adams	1830–1910
Tomé, Narciso	1690–1742		Warhol, Andy	1930–1987
Tomlin, Lily	1939–		Warren, Robert Penn	1905–1989
Toulouse-Lautrec, Henri de	1864–1901		Washington, Denzel	1954–
Townshend, Peter	1945–		Wasserstein, Wendy	1950–
Tracy, Spencer	1900–1967		Waters, John	1946–
Trollope, Anthony	1815–1882		Wayne, John	1907–1979
Truffaut, François	1932–1984		Weber, Carl Maria von	1786–1826
Tudor, Anthony	1909–		Webern, Anton	1883–1945
Turgenev, Ivan	1818–1883		Webster, John	c. 1580–1634
Turner, Joseph M. W.	1775–1851		Wedekind, Frank	1864–1918
Turner, Ted	1938–		Weill, Kurt	1900–1950
Turner, Tina	1938–		Welles, Orson	1915–1985
			Wells, H. G.	1866–1946

Welty, Eudora	1909–	Wilton, Joseph	1722–1803
West, Benjamin	1738–1820	Wise, Robert	1914–
Weston, Edward	1886–1958	Wodehouse, P. G.	1881–1975
Weyden, Rogier van der	c. 1400–1464	Wolfe, Thomas	1900–1938
Wharton, Edith	1862–1937	Wolfe, Tom	1931–
Whistler,		Wonder, Stevie	1950–
James Abbott McNeill	1834–1903	Wood, Grant	1891–1942
White, E. B.	1899–1985	Woodward, Joanne	1930–
Whitman, Walt	1819–1892	Woolf, Virginia	1882–1941
Whittier, John Greenleaf	1807–1892	Wordsworth, William	1770–1850
Wilde, Oscar	1854–1900	Wren, Christopher	1632–1723
Wilder, Billy	1906–	Wright, Frank Lloyd	1869–1959
Wilder, Thornton	1897–1975	Wright, Joseph	1756–1793
Willaert, Adriaan	1490–1562	Wright, Patience Lovell	1725–1786
Williams, Emlyn	1905–1987	Wright, Richard	1908–1960
Williams, Hank	1923–1953	Wycherley, William	1640–1716
Williams, Ralph Vaughan	1872–1958	Wyeth, Andrew	1917–
Williams, Tennessee	1911–1983	Wyler, William	1902–1981
Williams, William Carlos	1883–1963	Wynette, Tammy	1942–
Wilson, August	1945–	Yeats, William Butler	1865–1939
Wilson, Edmund	1895–1972	Zimmerman, Johann Baptist	1680–1758
Wilson, Lanford	1937–	Zinnemann, Fred	1907–1997

Bibliography

Abrams, M. H., ed. *The Norton Anthology of English Literature*, rev. ed. New York: W. W. Norton & Co., 1968.

Adepegba, C. O. *Yoruba Metal Sculpture*. Ibaadan: Ibaadan University Press, 1991.

Amiet, Pierre. *Art of the Ancient Near East*. New York: Harry N. Abrams, 1980.

Ammer, Christine. *Harper's Dictionary of Music*. New York: Harper & Row, 1972.

Ancient Treasures in Terracotta of Mali and Ghana. New York: African-American Institute, 1981.

Apel, Willi. *Harvard Dictionary of Music*, 2nd ed. Cambridge, MA: The Belknap Press, Harvard University Press, 1972.

Appiah, Kwame Anthony, and Henry Louis Gates, Jr., eds. *The Dictionary of Global Culture*. New York: Alfred A. Knopf, 1997.

Art of the Congo. Minneapolis, MN: Walker Art Center, 1967.

Austin, William A. *Music in the 20th Century: From Debussy Through Stravinsky*. New York: W. W. Norton & Co., 1966.

Balanchine, George, and Francis Mason. *101 Stories of the Great Ballets*. New York: Anchor/Doubleday, 1989.

Banham, Martin, ed. *The Cambridge Guide to World Theatre*. Cambridge, UK: Cambridge University Press, 1988.

Barnett, R. D. *Assyrian Sculpture in the British Museum*. London: McClelland and Stewart, 1975.

Bauer, Marion, Ethel Peyser, and Elizabeth E. Rogers. *Music Through the Ages*, 3rd ed. New York: G. P. Putnam's Sons, 1967.

Bishop, Robert. *American Folk Sculpture*. New York: E. P. Dutton and Co., 1974.

Blom, Eric. *Grove's Dictionary of Music and Musicians*, 5th ed. New York: St. Martin's Press, 1962.

Bordman, Gerald. *The Oxford Companion to American Theatre*. Oxford, UK: Oxford University Press, 1984.

Britannica Online.

Brooks, Tim. *The Complete Directory to Prime Time TV Stars: 1946–Present*. New York: Ballantine, 1987.

Brooks, Tim, and Earle Marsh. *The Complete Directory to Prime Time Network TV Shows: 1946-Present*. New York: Ballantine, 1985.

Brose, David S. *Ancient Art of the American Woodland Indians*. New York: Harry N. Abrams, 1985.

Brownstone, David M., and Irene M. Franck. *Timelines of the Arts and Literature*. New York: HarperCollins, 1994.

Burbank, Richard. *Twentieth-Century Music: Orchestral, Chamber, Operatic, & Dance Music 1900–1980*. New York: Facts on File, 1984.

Cheney, Sheldon. *Sculpture of the World*. New York: Viking Press, 1968.

Chilvers, Ian, Harold Osborne, and Dennis Farr. *The Oxford Dictionary of Art*. Oxford, UK: Oxford University Press, 1988.

Corey, Melinda, and George Ochoa. *A Cast of Thousands: A Compendium of Who Played What in Film*. New York: Facts on File, 1992.

Craven, Roy C. *A Concise History of Indian Art*. New York: Praeger Publishers, 1976.

Craven, Wayne. *Sculpture in America*. New York: Thomas Y. Crowell Co., 1968.

Current Biography 1940–Present (electronic). New York: H. W. Wilson.

Easby, Elizabeth Kennedy, and John F. Scott. *Before Cortés: Sculpture of Middle America*. New York: Metropolitan Museum of Art, 1970.

Editions d'Art Albert Skira. *Sculpture: Fifteenth to Eighteenth Century*. New York: Rizzoli International Publications, 1987.

Ewen, David. *American Composers: A Biographical Dictionary*. New York: G. P. Putnam's Sons, 1982.

Eyo, Ekpo. *Two Thousand Years of Nigerian Art*. Lagos, Nigeria: Federal Dept. of Antiquities, 1977.

Facts on File Weekly World News Digest. New York: Facts on File News Services.

Ferrier, Jean-Louis. *Art of Our Century*. New York: Prentice Hall, 1988.

Gammond, Peter. *Classical Music: An Illustrated Guide to Composers*. New York: Acorn Publishing, 1980.

Godine, David R. *200 Years of American Sculpture*. New York: Whitney Museum of American Art, 1976.

Goulding, Phil G. *Classical Music: The 50 Greatest Composers and Their 1,000 Greatest Works*. New York: Fawcett Columbine, 1992.

Gray, Anne. *The Popular Guide to Classical Music*. New York: Carol Publishing Group, 1993.

Grout, Donald Jay, and Claude V. Palisca. *A History of Western Music*, 4th ed. New York: W. W. Norton & Co., 1980.

Grun, Bernard. *The Timetables of History*, 3rd ed. New York: Simon & Schuster, 1975.

Hafner, German. *Art of Crete, Mycenae, and Greece*. New York: Harry N. Abrams, 1968.

Hardy, Phil, and Dave Laing. *The Faber Companion to 20th-Century Popular Music*. London: Faber and Faber, 1990.

Hartnoll, Phyllis, ed. *The Oxford Companion to the Theatre*, 4th ed. Oxford, UK: Oxford University Press, 1983.

Haskins, James. *Black Dance in America*. New York: HarperCollins, 1990.

Higgins, Reynold. *Minoan and Mycenaen Art*. London: Thames and Hudson, 1967.

Highwater, Jamake. *Arts of the Indian Americas*. New York: Harper & Row, 1983.

Hochman, Stanley. *McGraw-Hill Encyclopedia of World Drama*. New York: McGraw-Hill, 1984.

Janson, H. W., and Anthony F. Janson. *History of Art*, 4th ed. New York: Harry N. Abrams, 1991.

Jasen, David A. *Tin Pan Alley*. New York: Donald I. Fine, 1988.

Jones, Arthur F. *HarperCollins College Outline: Introduction to Art*. New York: HarperPerennial, 1992.

Katz, Ephraim. *The Film Encyclopedia*, 2nd ed. New York: HarperPerennial, 1994.

Kernfeld, Barry, ed. *The New Grove Dictionary of Jazz*. New York: St. Martin's Press, 1988, 1994.

Kirkpatrick, John, et al. *The New Grove Twentieth-Century American Masters*. New York: W. W. Norton & Co., 1987.

Lapiner, Alan. *Pre-Columbian Art of South America*. New York: Harry N. Abrams, 1976.

Leroi-Gourhan, André. *Treasures of Prehistoric Art*. New York: Harry N. Abrams, 1968.

Levy, Judith S., and Agnes Greenhall. *The Concise Columbia Encyclopedia*. New York: Avon, 1983.

Lucie-Smith, Edward. *The Thames and Hudson Dictionary of Art Terms*. London: Thames and Hudson Ltd., 1988.

The Metropolitan Museum of Art Guide. New York: The Metropolitan Museum of Art, 1983.

Michalowski, Kazimierz. *Great Sculpture of Ancient Egypt*. New York: William Morrow and Co., 1978.

Minott, Charles. *HarperCollins College Outline: History of Art*. New York: HarperPerennial, 1992.

Murphy, Bruce, ed. *Benét's Reader's Encyclopedia*, 4th ed. New York: HarperCollins, 1996.

Murray, Margaret Alice. *Egyptian Sculpture*. London: Duckworth, 1930.

Nite, Norm N. *Rock On Almanac, The First Four Decades of Rock 'n' Roll: A Chronology.* New York: Harper & Row, 1989.

Nobel Prize Winners. New York: H. W. Wilson, 1987.

Nobel Prize Winners: 1989–1991 Supplement. New York: H. W. Wilson, 1992.

Nobel Prize Winners: 1992–1996 Supplement. New York: H. W. Wilson, 1997.

O'Neil, Thomas. *The Grammys: For the Record.* New York: Penguin Books, 1993.

Osborne, Harold, ed. *An Illustrated Companion to the Decorative Arts.* London: Wordsworth Editions, 1989.

Ousby, Ian, ed. *The Cambridge Guide to Literature in English.* Cambridge, UK: Cambridge University Press, 1988.

Pericot-Garcia, Luis. *Prehistoric and Primitive Art.* New York: Harry N. Abrams, 1967.

Perkins, George, Barbara Perkins, and Phillip Leininger. *Benét's Reader's Encyclopedia of American Literature.* New York: HarperCollins, 1991.

Pollitt, J. J. *Art and Experience in Classical Greece.* New York: Cambridge University Press, 1988.

Post, Chandler. *A History of European and American Sculpture,* Cambridge, MA: Harvard University Press, 1921.

Read, Herbert, ed. *The Thames and Hudson Dictionary of Art.* London: Thames and Hudson, 1985.

Rees, Dafydd, and Luke Crampton, eds. *Rock Movers & Shakers.* Santa Barbara, Calif.: ABC-CLIO, 1991.

Rosenblum, Robert, and H. W. Janson. *19th-Century Art.* Englewood Cliffs, NJ: Prentice-Hall, and New York: Harry N. Abrams, 1984.

Rothschild, Lincoln. *Sculpture Through the Ages.* New York: McGraw-Hill, 1942.

Sackett, Susan. *The Hollywood Reporter Book of Box Office Hits.* New York: Billboard Books, 1990.

Sandars, N. K. *Prehistoric Art in Europe.* Baltimore, MD: Penguin Books, 1968.

Scarre, Chris. *Smithsonian Timelines of the Ancient World.* London: Dorling Kindersley, 1993.

Sculpture Since the Sixties. New York: Whitney Museum of American Art, 1988.

Shaw, Arnold. *Dictionary of American Pop/Rock.* New York: Schirmer Books, 1982.

Slonimsky, Nicolas. *The Concise Baker's Biographical Dictionary of Musicians.* New York: Schirmer Books, 1988.

Stern, Jane, and Michael Stern. *Jane & Michael Stern's Encyclopedia of Pop Culture.* New York: HarperPerennial, 1992.

Strong, Donald. *Roman Art and Architecture.* Middlesex, England: Penguin Books, 1988.

Swann, Peter C. *Art of China, Korea, and Japan.* New York: Frederick A. Praeger, 1963.

Trager, James. *The People's Chronology.* New York: Henry Holt & Co., 1992.

Westrup, Sir Jack, F. L. L. Harrison, and Conrad Wilson. *Collins Dictionary of Music,* 3rd ed. London: Collins, 1988.

Wetterau, Bruce. *The New York Public Library Book of Chronologies.* New York: Prentice-Hall, 1990.

Wheeler, Mortimer. *Roman Art and Architecture.* London: Thames and Hudson, 1979.

Wilson Biographies (electronic). New York: H. W. Wilson.

Index

All names mentioned in the chronology have been given main entries in the index. Principle works have also been given main entries, but lesser-known works have been indexed under the names of the artists who produced them.

A

a cappella vocal style, 81
Abbey of St. Denis (near Paris), 47
Abbey of St. Martial (Limoges) music school, polyphony and, 46
Abbey Theatre (Dublin), 211
Abbott, Berenice
  Eugène Atget and, 203
  series of photographs, 268
Abbott, Bud, 268
Abelam people (New Guinea), ceremonial houses, 206
Abelard, Peter, Héloïse and, 46
Abie's Irish Rose (Nichols), 235
Abrahams, Jim, *Airplane!*, 339
Absalom, Absalom! (Faulkner), 253, 261
absolute pitch, tuning fork, 117
abstract expressionism, 277
  action painting, 279
absurd, theater of the, precursor, 193
Académie Royale de Danse (France), 106
Académie Royale des Operas (France), 109
Academy Awards
  first, 247
  first film to capture four major, 257
Academy of Ancient Music (London), 122
Academy of Motion Picture Arts and Sciences, 247
Academy of San Fernando (Spain), 127
Accademia de' Floridi (Bologna), 95
Accademia del Disegno (Florence), 80
Accademia di Belle Arti (Venice), 144
Accademia di San Luca (Rome), 82
Accidental Tourist, The (Tyler), 346
Accius, Lucius, 25
AC/DC (band), 339
Achaemenid dynasty, carvings, 16
Achebe, Chinua
  Anthills of Savannah, 350
  Things Fall Apart, 299
acid jazz, 363
Acin, Jovan, *Hey Babu Riba*, 347
Ackroyd, Peter, *English Music*, 356
Acropolis
  Erectheum, 17, 20
  Parthenon, 18
  Propylaea, 19

acting
  actor-based theater, 318
  Stanislavsky, Konstantin, 202, 261, 282
  Strasberg, Lee, 282
acting companies, Lord Chamberlain's Men (King's Men), 87
Action Comics, 264
action painting, Pollock, Jackson, 279
actors. *See also names of individual actors and actresses*
  women as, in London, 105
Actors Studio (New York City), Strasberg, Lee, 282
adab tradition, 39
Adam, Henri-Georges, *Beacon of the Dead*, 298
Adam, Nicolas-Sébastien
  Basin of Neptune at Versailles, 123
  marble figurine of Prometheus, 123
Adam, Robert and James, Osterly Park and Syon House, 128
Adams, Ansel, *Moonrise, Hernandez, New Mexico*, 272
Adams, Hannah
  Alphabetical Compendium of the Various Sects . . . from the Beginning of the Christian Era, 136
  A Summary History of New England, 140
Adams, Henry
  Democracy, 188
  The Education of Henry Adams, 228
  History of the United States of America During the Administrations of Thomas Jefferson and James Madison, 194
  Life of Albert Gallatin and *John Randolph*, 186
Adams, John, *The Death of Klinghoffer*, 355
Adams, Pat, 360
Adam's Rib (film), 282
Adamson, Robert, 159
Adderley, Cannonball, 303
Addison, Joseph
  The Spectator, 116
  The Tatler, 116
Adena culture (Ohio River valley)
  houses of, 11
  iconography, 21
  stone pipes depicting male figures, 10
Adjani, Isabelle, 321
Adler, Richard, *Damn Yankees*, 358
Adlon, Percy, *Rosalie Goes Shopping*, 351
Admirable Crichton, The (Barrie), 211